Changing Times

ECONOMIC AND SOCIAL HISTORY OF BRITAIN

General Editor: Martin Daunton

Changing Times

Economics, Policies, and Resource
Allocation in Britain since 1951

MARTIN CHICK

OXFORD
UNIVERSITY PRESS

OXFORD

UNIVERSITY PRESS

Great Clarendon Street, Oxford, OX2 6DP,
United Kingdom

Oxford University Press is a department of the University of Oxford.
It furthers the University's objective of excellence in research, scholarship,
and education by publishing worldwide. Oxford is a registered trade mark of
Oxford University Press in the UK and in certain other countries

First Edition published in 2020

Impression: 1

Published in the United States of America by Oxford University Press
198 Madison Avenue, New York, NY 10016, United States of America

British Library Cataloguing in Publication Data

Data available

Library of Congress Control Number: 2019941466

ISBN 978–0–19–955278–8 (hbk.)
ISBN 978–0–19–955277–1 (pbk.)

Printed and bound in Great Britain by
Clays Ltd, Elcograf S.p.A.

To Mary, Margaret and Ken
Some of your yesterdays
And to Bruno
For all of your tomorrows

Acknowledgements

Time and money for some of the research and writing of this book were provided by the Leverhulme Trust, the British Academy, and the AHRC as part of its Caring for the Future project based at the University of Edinburgh. I am very grateful to the funding bodies for their help and to my research project colleagues for their tolerance and good humour. Once a month my physiotherapist Carly Cowell has stoically sought to reverse some of the worst consequences of my daily scribblings, while Rosemary Wiseman, Jim, Maggie, and Lavinia Cellan-Jones have provided a happy home from home during my research trips to London. Many academics have discussed the ideas in this book with me, but two deserve a special mention. In Edinburgh, my office next-door neighbour, Trevor Griffiths, has long had to listen to my latest ramblings and speculative ravings, and I am extremely appreciative of his patience and perception. In Cambridge, Martin Daunton has unflinchingly replied to my intermittent spasms of emails, and both he and Claire Daunton have been extremely generous and kind whenever I have visited them. Martin has been the ideal general editor, encouraging me to pursue some of my stranger lines of research but also gently reminding me that someone other than myself might wish to read this book. I am very grateful to him for all of his comments on the various drafts and also for the informed and constructive comments offered by OUP's anonymous reader of the submitted manuscript.

As ever, none of this would have happened without Hatty. This is the third book that she has had to live through, and I can only thank her again for her kindness, patience, and love. I have no idea if she will read this book, but if she does then she will discover what some of my long silences staring out of the window were about. The book is dedicated to my sisters and brother with whom I grew up in Bishop's Stortford in the sixties and seventies, and who will remember the economic difficulties of those days. It is also dedicated to my grandson Bruno who has brought such joy, and who will, for better and for worse, know an economy different from that discussed in this book. Perhaps if he ever reads this book he will understand some of why that is so.

Contents

List of Tables

1

Change Over Time

Changing Times, the title of this book, refers both to the changes which occurred in Britain from 1951, and also to the interest in the concepts of time (and space) which give shape to this book. The book is predominantly concerned with the economic development of Britain since 1951, with an attendant interest in how the benefits of economic growth were distributed. Specific aspects of that economic development are identified and assigned individual chapters. These run as follows: public expenditure and the role of the state (chapter 2); labour markets and industrial policy (chapter 3); poverty and inequality (chapter 4); health and education (chapter 5); the privatization of nationalized industries and public housing (chapter 6); environmental policy (chapter 7); trade and exchange rates (chapter 8); and the financial crash of 2008 (chapter 9). As well as its interest in economic growth and distribution in Britain since 1951, this book is also concerned with how and why government economic policy changed from 1951. To provide a general context in which the analysis can be set, the book begins with a brief narrative of the main phases in the development of the British economy since 1951.

An Economic Narrative

In the general election of Thursday 25 October 1951, the Labour Party received more votes but won fewer seats than the Conservative Party. Since its landslide election victory in July 1945, the Labour government with Clement Attlee as its prime minister had nationalized major industries such as electricity, gas and coal, established the National Health Service, introduced many of the recommendations of the 1942 Beveridge Report on the social security system, launched a large public housing construction programme, and accepted the wartime government's commitment to maintaining a low rate of unemployment. Even though the Conservative Party was elected to government in 1951 with the seventy-six-year-old Winston Churchill as prime minister, and was to remain in government until the general election of 15 October 1964, much of the Attlee governments' legislative achievement remained intact. What did change was the growing concern with Britain's rate of economic growth compared to that of other developed economies.[1] A failure to undertake adequate investment was often adduced as a cause of low growth and with the aim of encouraging more investment, the Labour government elected on 16 October 1964 with Harold Wilson as prime minister introduced a *National Plan* in 1965 with a growth target of 3.5–4.0%. That Plan was abandoned in 1967 amidst economic difficulties which saw the pound devalued against the dollar and the subsequent decision of the Labour Chancellor of the Exchequer Roy Jenkins to impose the hitherto largest reduction of demand on the post-war economy.[2] Increasingly, there was a willingness to question whether fundamental changes were required in the aims and mechanisms of government economic policies. The Conservative government elected on 18 June 1970 with Edward Heath as prime minister sought further reductions in the role of the government in the economy, but its intentions were overtaken by events. Unemployment began to rise and, surprisingly, so too did inflation. By 1973, the post-war period known as the Golden Age (1945–1973) had come to an end.

That Golden Age was characterized by low unemployment and low inflation accompanied by continuous economic growth. Between 1951 and 1973, the annual growth rate of U.K. GDP averaged 2.4% which was historically high for the U.K. but lower in the Golden Age than that of other developed economies. Sweden (3.0%), France (4.4%), Germany (4.8%), Italy (5.5%), and Japan (7.9%) all enjoyed higher rates of growth.[3] In terms of GDP per head, economies like France and West Germany caught up and then overtook the U.K. between 1950 and 1973.[4] That there was a high rate of economic growth after the war surprised many economic commentators and advisors, who generally feared that the post-war world would return to its more familiar pattern of unemployment and uneven growth. Indeed, looking backwards from the current century, the Golden Age still stands out as untypical. In historic terms its low rate of unemployment was striking. Between 1945 and 1973 the unemployment rate averaged 2.1% compared with 5.5% in 1871–1891, 6.2% in 1892–913, 10.9% in 1921–1938, and 10.1% in 1974–1999.[5] European growth rates of 4–5% per annum and Japanese growth of around 8% now seem

---

[1] Clarke and Trebilcock (eds.), *Understanding Decline*.
[2] Cairncross and Eichengreen, *Sterling in Decline*.
[3] Matthews, Feinstein, and Odling-Smee, *British Economic Growth*, Table 2.5.
[4] Crafts, *Forging Ahead*, p. 80, Table 5.1.
[5] Hatton and Boyer, 'Unemployment and the U.K. labour market', *European Review of Economic History*, p. 38, Table 1. The unemployment rate is the number unemployed divided by the labour force. The labour force is the unemployed plus employed wage and salary earners.

enviable. If the Golden Age is regarded as being unusual, then more usual conditions began to reappear from 1968. In both 1971 and 1972, the level of unemployment rose above 1 million, fell slightly in 1973 and 1974, but returned to above the politically sensitive level of 1 million in 1975. Unemployment was never to fall below 1 million again. Inflation also rose, peaking at 26.9% in August 1975.[6] That inflation and unemployment rose at the same time was unexpected, and pointed to the breakdown of the Phillips Curve, an economic observation which noted an inverse relationship between a (say, downward) movement in the level of unemployment and an (upward) movement in the rate of increase of wages; and vice versa. To the breakdown of familiar assumptions such as the Phillips Curve could be added the collapse of familiar institutions of the Golden Age, notably the Bretton Woods system of fixed, but adjustable, exchange rates which had been agreed in 1944. By March 1973 the Bretton Woods system had ceased to exist, adding both to economic uncertainty and to the sense of change. When between October 1973 and the end of 1974, real oil prices rose threefold from $1.89 to $6.15 per barrel as the Organization of the Petroleum Exporting Countries (OPEC) began to restrict supply in an effort to punish the U.K., the United States and the Netherlands for supplying oil to Israel in the Yom Kippur war (6–25 October 1973), this gave a further boost to inflation.[7] Oil prices almost doubled again between 1978 and 1979.[8] Without the Bretton Woods system, the U.K. briefly joined the European Economic Community's (EEC) managed currency 'snake', not least in an effort to show goodwill to the EEC to which the U.K. acceded on 1 January 1973. The U.K.'s two previous applications to join in 1963 and 1967 had been vetoed by Charles de Gaulle, the president of France. After a brief dalliance with the European snake whose EEC member countries' currencies moved against each other within a tunnel of 2.25% either side of a central rate, the U.K. left the snake and allowed the pound to float. When in 1976 floating resembled drowning, assistance was sought from the International Monetary Fund. In exchange, the U.K. government had to sign a 'letter of intent' in December 1976 in which it agreed, grudgingly, to reduce planned public expenditure and to adopt a more monetarist approach to economic management.[9] While the government had already publicly announced a monetary target for the first time in July 1976, in exchange for the International

---

[6] Britton, *Macroeconomic Policy in Britain*, p. 27.
[7] Griffin and Steele, *Energy, Economics and Policy*, p. 18.
[8] *BP Statistical Review of World Energy*, June 2013.
[9] Brittan, *Against the Flow*, p. 121; Roberts, *When Britain Went Bust*. Harold Lever described the attitude of the Labour Chancellor Denis Healey and his Permanent Secretary Douglas Wass as one of 'unbelieving monetarism'.

Monetary Fund (IMF) line of credit, the government had to undertake to restrict monetary growth and contain the rate of increase of domestic credit.[10] In this sense, monetarism and the targeting of inflation rather than unemployment as the main focus of economic policy preceded the election of the Conservative government on 3 May 1979 with Margaret Thatcher as prime minister. Similarly, the sale of council houses and the sale of publicly owned industries were undertaken prior to May 1979, often by the Labour governments (1974–1979) of Harold Wilson (1974–1976) and James Callaghan (1976–1979). What was different about the Thatcher government was the determined conviction with which programmes of privatization and monetarism were promoted and implemented.

As with the Attlee governments of 1945–1951, what characterized the Conservative Party under Margaret Thatcher both in opposition (1975–1979) and then in government was the extent to which dissatisfaction with the existing way of doing things encouraged new ideas and fresh approaches to economic policy. With inflation and unemployment rising, with the collapse of Bretton Woods, with the accession to the EEC in 1973, and with oil price hikes enhancing the value of the North Sea oil which flowed from 1975, fresh thinking to address old and new problems was encouraged. The general context for such deliberations was a long-standing dissatisfaction with the U.K.'s comparative economic growth rate, an increasingly political focus on public expenditure and the public sector borrowing requirement, and a concern that the initiative and entrepreneurship required to rekindle growth were being suppressed by an onerous system of taxation.

The added enthusiasm for monetarism and the reduction of public expenditure were evident in the early years of the Thatcher government, although the effects of their implementation allied to a rising exchange rate earned the government much unpopularity. Unemployment, which had roughly stabilized at 1.4 million in 1976, began rising again in 1980 (1.8 million) and 1981 (2.6 million), before reaching a post–World War II peak of 3.2 million in 1984. The post-war unemployment rate also peaked at 11.77% in 1984.[11] An accompanying rise in inflation in the early years of the first Thatcher government and a fall in GDP in 1980 and 1981 earned the pejorative sobriquet of 'stagflation'.[12] In the context of rising unemployment, both the government's publication of the Medium Term Financial Strategy (MTFS) in March 1980 which sought to

[10]   Burk and Cairncross, 'Goodbye, Great Britain', p. xiii.
[11]   A Millennium of Macroeconomic Data for the U.K.. The Bank of England's Collection of Historical Macroeconomic and Financial Statistics, version 3.1, October 2017, A.50.
National Statistics, Economic Trends: Annual Supplement, 2000, Table 3.4.
[12]   Meade, Stagflation, vol. 1.
Vines, Maciejowski and Meade, Stagflation, vol. 2.

reduce the growth in money supply and government borrowing, and the government's willingness to allow the dollar: sterling exchange rate to rise rapidly from $1.92 in 1978 to $2.33 in 1980 at a cost to U.K. export competitiveness, were highly controversial. As unemployment rose, the share of those employed in manufacturing industry fell. The pace and extent of the fall in employment in manufacturing was striking. As a share of total employees in Britain, those in manufacturing fell from 32.3% in 1977, to 30.3% in 1980, 27.5% in 1982, 24.3% in 1986 and 22.7% in 1990.[13] Had it not been for the rise in the government's popularity during and after the Falklands War in April 1982, it is unclear that the Thatcher Conservative government would have been re-elected.[14] Thereafter, both the political and economic fortunes of the government improved. By 1986, oil prices were almost one-quarter of their 1980 level, the inflation rate was down to below 3.5%, and economic growth had resumed. Unemployment remained above 3 million, although changes were made both to the definition of who was unemployed and to the calculation of the unemployment rate.[15] Margaret Thatcher remained as prime minister until 22 November 1990, and with her successor John Major winning the 9 April 1992 general election, it was not until 1 May 1997 that the Labour Party returned to government under the premiership of Tony Blair. He remained as prime minister until 27 June 2007 when Gordon Brown took over as leader of the Labour Party, and thereby became prime minister. During that long sub-period from 1979 until 2008, there was an improvement in the relative growth performance of the U.K. economy (See Table 1.1). In terms of real GDP per person, because U.K. growth slowed less than that of France and West Germany, the U.K. moved ahead of France by 2007, and closed the gap with West Germany.[16]

Although not necessarily related to the improved relative growth performance, during the sub-period 1979–2008 there was also a significant change in

[13] *Annual Abstract of Statistics*, 1982, Table 6.2; 1988, Table 6.2; 1992, Table 6.1.

[14] Hacche and Taylor, *Inside the Bank of* England, p. 197.

[15] Bartholomew, Moore, Smith, and Allen, 'The measurement of unemployment', JRSS, p. 165.

Until 1982, unemployed people registered both to seek jobs and/or to receive benefits. The unemployment data was for jobseekers registered as looking for work at Job Centres, irrespective of whether they were also claiming benefits. From October 1982, the system changed, and adult claimants were no longer required to register at a Job Centre as well as at a benefit office. The measure of unemployment switched to being a 'claimant count', i.e. of those claiming unemployment benefits, and therefore excluded those seeking work but not benefits.

Changes were also made in 1986 to what constituted the unemployment rate. Prior to 1986 the unemployment rate referred to the percentage of the labour force who were registered as unemployed. Thereafter the unemployment rate referred to the percentage of the working population who were unemployed. As the working population included not only the labour force but also the armed services and the self-employed, it made for a larger denominator, thereby reducing the unemployment rate by about 2% in 1986.

[16] Crafts, *Forging Ahead*, p. 104.

Table 1.1. GDP annual growth rates: France, Germany, Japan, U.K., and U.S.A., 1980–2016 (%)

	France	Germany	Japan	U.K.	U.S.A.
1980	1.6	1.4	2.8	-2.0	-0.2
1981	1.1	0.5	4.2	-0.8	2.6
1982	2.5	-0.4	3.4	2.0	-1.9
1983	1.3	1.6	3.1	4.2	4.6
1984	1.5	2.8	4.5	2.3	7.3
1985	1.6	2.3	6.3	4.2	4.2
1986	2.4	2.3	2.8	3.1	3.5
1987	2.6	1.4	4.1	5.3	3.5
1988	4.7	3.7	7.1	5.7	4.2
1989	4.4	3.9	5.4	2.6	3.7
1990	2.9	5.2	5.6	0.7	1.9
1991	1.0	5.1	3.3	0.7	-0.1
1992	1.6	1.9	0.8	0.4	3.6
1993	-0.6	-1.0	0.2	2.5	2.7
1994	2.3	2.5	0.9	3.9	4.0
1995	2.1	1.7	2.7	2.5	2.7
1996	1.4	0.8	3.1	2.5	3.8
1997	2.3	1.8	1.1	4.0	4.5
1998	3.6	2.0	-1.1	3.1	4.4
1999	3.4	2.0	-0.3	3.2	4.7
2000	3.9	3.0	2.8	3.7	4.1
2001	2.0	1.7	0.4	2.5	1.0
2002	1.1	0.0	0.1	2.5	1.8
2003	0.8	-0.7	1.5	3.3	2.8
2004	2.8	1.2	2.2	2.4	3.8
2005	1.6	0.7	1.7	3.1	3.3
2006	2.4	3.7	1.4	2.5	2.7
2007	2.4	3.3	1.7	2.4	1.8
2008	0.2	1.1	-1.1	-0.5	-0.3
2009	-2.9	-5.6	-5.4	-4.2	-2.8
2010	2.0	4.1	4.2	1.7	2.5
2011	2.1	3.7	-0.1	1.5	1.6
2012	0.2	0.5	1.5	1.5	2.2
2013	0.6	0.5	2.0	2.1	1.7
2014	0.9	1.9	0.3	3.1	2.6
2015	1.1	1.7	1.1	2.3	2.9
2016	1.2	1.9	1.0	1.8	1.5

Source: OECD. Stat., *National Account Statistics.*

the role of government. The privatization of telecommunications (1984), gas (1986), electricity (1990) and other industries wholly or partly owned by the government marked a *volte face* on the question of the public ownership of utilities, as did Tony Blair's successful fight in 1995 to remove the commitment to common ownership contained in clause IV of the constitution of the Labour

Party. The sale of council houses and the introduction of the Right To Buy in 1980 similarly marked a significant reduction in the state provision and financing of public housing. More generally, the share of national income spent on net public investment fell from 7.6% in 1967–1968 to almost zero in 2000. This change in the economic and social role of the state was also reflected in its industrial policy, where it moved from backing particular companies to a more supply-side approach in which it concentrated on creating the systemic conditions which would allow growth to flourish. More emphasis was placed on improving the skills of the workforce, although the Labour government also introduced university fees in 1998. While as a return on higher education fees, high and rising salaries in the growing financial sector might have been attractive, this route was not available to, or sought by, every graduate. The financial sector, notably in London, had benefited from the removal of restrictions which in due course followed the collapse of Bretton Woods. The restrictions on exchange controls were ended in October 1979 allowing U.K. residents freely to invest their money overseas for the first time since World War II. One consequence was an increase in overseas portfolio holdings from a total of £12 billion in 1979 to around £100 billion by the end of 1985.[17] Further deregulation in the U.K. followed, culminating in 1986 in the 'Big Bang' removal of trading restrictions and barriers to competition. Investment banks steadily bought out the traditional brokers. In the same year, 1986, the Single European Act (SEA) committed the European Community to create a single market in goods, services, capital, and labour. This suited the U.K. economy, which was increasingly strong in financial and business services and as such was more likely to benefit from the SEA than had manufacturing from the EEC customs union. As manufacturing's share of GDP and employment fell, while that of the financial sector and the salaries of CEOs rose, so a growing gap emerged between the 'haves', the 'have nots', and the 'have lots'. Both poverty and wealth clustered in separate households to a greater extent than in the past. While regional unemployment rates fell and were narrower than in the 1930s, differences in household incomes were significant, and from 1979 income inequality widened for the first time since World War II.[18] Statistically, if not politically, the rise in income inequality was overshadowed by the increase in wealth inequality, although tax reforms which reduced income tax rates while treating wealth transfers more leniently evinced little immediate political interest in reversing such changes in inequality.

---

[17] Bond, Davis, and Devereux, *Capital Controls*, p. 5.
[18] Gazeley and Newell, 'Unemployment', Table 10.3.

Economic growth came to an abrupt halt in 2008 and GDP was 4.9% lower in 2009 as a direct result of the financial crisis commonly identified with the collapse of the investment bank Lehman Brothers in the United States in September 2008.[19] An immediate and medium-term response to the financial crash was Quantitative Easing (QE), the purchase of bonds by the Bank of England with created money. By August 2016 the Bank of England had purchased £435 billion of government bonds. With interest rates having been cut in the wake of the crash from 5% to 0.5% in late 2008, the scope for reducing rates further was restricted. QE, by raising the price of bonds, reduced their yield, thereby making more money available at a low rate of interest. Controversially, as with the MTFS of 1980, the government decided in an 'emergency' budget in June 2010 to introduce an austerity programme designed to reduce the budget deficit and the national debt, even though many argued that financial probity was being pursued at the expense of economic growth. Again, the Chancellor was Conservative (Howe in 1980, Osborne in 2010) although it was formally a Conservative–Liberal Democratic government in power between May 2010 and May 2015. Again, this time wages and unemployment moved together, although not upwards as in 1979–1981, but downwards. While the unemployment rate did rise from 5.33% in 2007 to 8.11% in 2011, after that it fell consistently to reach 4.9% in 2016. The level of unemployment fell from 2.6 million in 2011 to 1.6 million in 2016. By then, total employment was at a post-1945 high of 31.7 million (23.6 million in 1951).[20] Yet with these movements in the rate and level of unemployment, the wage rate did not pick up. Again, the Phillips Curve had gone missing.[21]

While unemployment fell, and employment rose, real earnings fell. In June 2018 real average weekly earnings remained 6.5% below their level of February 2008. Previously in the Golden Age, real earnings had grown at an average annual rate of 2.72% in 1951–1973 and by 1.58% in 1973–2001.[22] At the same time, as real earnings fell for many households, QE and low interest rates had the effect of increasing asset prices, to which the U.K. government added in the case of housing by introducing 'Help To Buy' and other schemes designed to encourage home ownership. In this context, voters were asked in a referendum on 23 June 2016, 'Should the U.K. remain a member of the

---

[19] Kirby, with Barrell and Whitworth, 'Prospects for the U.K. economy', Table A3.
[20] *A Millennium of Macroeconomic Data for the U.K.. The Bank of England's Collection of Historical Macroeconomic and Financial Statistics*, version 3.1, October 217, A.50.
National Statistics, *Economic Trends: Annual Supplement*, 2000, Table 3.4.
[21] Bell and Blanchflower, 'The lack of wage growth'; Farmer, *Prosperity For All: How To Prevent Financial Crises*, ch. 4.
[22] Gazeley, 'Income and living standards, 1870–2010', p. 153.

European Union or leave the European Union?'. Of the 72.2% of the electorate who voted, 51.9% (17.4 million) voted to leave and 48.1% (16.1 million) to remain. The majority of those voting in Wales (52.5%) and England (53.4%), but outside London, voted to leave the European Union; a majority in Scotland (62.0%) and Northern Ireland (55.8%) voted to remain.[23]

At the time of writing it is not clear on what terms the U.K. will leave the European Union, let alone what the effects of leaving might be. Two effects were immediately apparent after the Brexit vote. The exchange rate fell from its pre-referendum level, as too did foreign direct investment into the U.K. in the face of the uncertainty surrounding the U.K.'s future economic relationship with the members of the European Union. Estimates of the likely cost of Brexit vary and are contentious, but annual economic growth looks likely to persist at just under 2%. In a broad sense, with setbacks in 1979–1981 and 2008–2009, the story of almost continuous economic growth since World War II will continue. Over the entire period 1948–2013 the compound annual rate of real GDP growth was 2.6%.[24] At that rate national income doubled every twenty-eight years. While other economies, notably China and India, came to enjoy much higher rates of economic growth and closed the gap between them and the U.K. in per capita terms, this does not detract from the substantial improvement in both global and U.K. living standards in the seventy years since 1945.[25] (See Table 1.2) Across time and space, the extent of the improvements in global living standards provided by over seventy years of

Table 1.2. National GDP per capita (1990, US $), selected economies

	France	Germany	U.K.	U.S.A.	Japan	China	India
1951	5,461	4,206	7,123	10,116	2,126	596	623
1961	7,718	7,952	8,857	11,402	4,426	548	758
1971	11,845	11,077	10,941	15,304	10,040	907	856
1981	14,840	14,149	12,747	18,856	13,754	1,231	977
1991	17,724	16,606	16,196	22,876	19,358	1,935	1,305
2001	20,931	18,985	20,702	28,782	20,998	3,528	1,957
2011	22,303	21,380	22,375	31,163	22,228	8,039	3,583
2016	22,567	22,122	23,887	33,259	23,808	9,885	4,602

Source: Maddison Project.

[23] O'Rourke, *Short History*, ch. 8; Wren-Lewis, *The Lies We Were Told*.
[24] Gross domestic product is the total of all goods and services produced in a certain time period, usually a year. How well such a measure captures the value of all the output in a modern economy is a matter of current debate. Coyle, *GDP: A Brief But Affectionate History*.
Office for National Statistics National Archives, National Archives, release 23 August 2013.
[25] In 1951, U.K. GDP per capita was twelve times that of China and eleven times that of India. By 2016, the U.K. GDP per capita was 2.4 times that of China and 5.2 that of India.

economic growth since 1945 is commonly remarked on.[26] This is seen in a range of indicators, be it the fall in infant mortality, the rise in life expectancy, or the availability of consumer durables.

Population

As a result of this economic growth, national income per member of the U.K. population trebled in real terms between 1951 and 2016. The population of Britain which enjoyed this economic growth itself grew in size, from 49.8 million in 1951 to 60.8m in 2011, mainly as a result of increased longevity. It was not until the 1970s that migration made a net contribution to the size of the population of Britain. Net emigration was over one-third of a million in 1971–1980, but immigration then exceeded emigration by 74,300 in 1981–1990 and by 575,100 in 1991–2000.[27] Often immigrants came to Britain in response to political upheavals and/or economic difficulties in their countries. In response to the partition of India in August 1947, when 17.5 million people crossed the border, some of those living in the most affected areas of the Indian and Pakistani Punjab and Pakistani-administered Kashmir decided to emigrate to Britain. The Mirpur District of Pakistani-administered Kashmir and the nearby Chhach area of Campbellpur District might have accounted for 80% of the British Pakistani population.[28] In 1948 the British Nationality Act allowed persons with Imperial or Commonwealth citizenship to settle in Britain.[29] In the 1950s early migrants came from the West Indies, where economic and living conditions were significantly lower than those in Britain. Greater numbers arrived from the Caribbean in the 1960s.[30] When in 1971, West Pakistan and East Pakistan split to become Pakistan and Bangladesh, again residents of Pakistan and Bangladesh migrated to Britain.[31] In the 1990s there was an influx of East European Muslims fleeing from the warzones in Bosnia and Kosovo as well as refugees from Afghanistan, Somalia, Turkey, and Iraq.[32] Immigrants tended to settle in the larger towns and cities, and they could choose to live in close communities. The Sylheti Bangladeshis were an extreme case of this, with nearly one-quarter of the British Bangladeshi population living in the single London Borough of Tower Hamlets.[33]

---

[26] Rosling, Rosling, and Rosling Rönnlund, *Factfulness*.
[27] Hatton, 'Explaining trends in UK immigration', *Journal of Population Economics*, Table 2.
[28] Ballard, *Desh Pardesh*.   [29] Panayi, 'Immigration, multiculturalism and racism'.
[30] Haskey, 'Demographic issues'.   [31] Peach, 'South Asian migration', p. 133.
[32] Peach, 'Muslims in the 2001 census'.   [33] Peach, 'Does Britain have ghettos?'.

Early immigrants were often single men, but after the passing of the 1962 Commonwealth Immigration Act wives were able to join their husbands.[34] They often took on jobs which others did not wish to do. As economic growth picked up in Britain, so too were there stronger financial incentives for migrants to move to Britain to work and fewer incentives for U.K. citizens to emigrate. In the 1990s the net immigration of 'skilled' workers was more than double the net flow of 'unskilled' workers with the rise in net immigration coming from the relatively developed Organization for Economic Cooperation and Development (OECD) countries.[35]

Over the entire post-war period, the dominant factor causing the population to increase was the falling death rate. A falling death rate ran ahead of a falling birth rate with the result that the population grew in size and aged. That there were two post-war baby booms, the first in 1945–1954, with its peak in 1947, and the other in1961–1965, with its peak in 1964, did not prevent the birth rate falling over the second half of the twentieth century.[36] In England and Wales, the fall was greatest among women aged between twenty and twenty-four, with a smaller decrease among women aged between twenty-five and twenty-nine. While in 1976, 69% of live births were to women in their twenties, by 1998 this proportion had fallen to 48%. The mean age at child-bearing rose from 26.4 in 1976 to 28.9 in 1998.[37] The birth rate fell as the incentives for, and means of, postponing births improved. The oral contraceptive pill became available in the mid-1960s and its use increased in the early 1970s. Sterilization gained in popularity with both men and women in the 1980s, when it became more common as a method of contraception than the pill among women over thirty. In 1998, 12% of men and 11% of women were sterilized for contraceptive purposes. Use of the oral contraceptive pill was highest, at 28%, in the mid-1970s and early 1980s, but usage then fell and has never attained its previous level. Abortion became legal in 1967 and in 1974 family planning services were brought into the National Health Service.

A falling birth rate interspersed with peaks in the first two post-war decades allied to a falling death rate created an ageing demographic structure. In 1951, there were 5.7 million people aged sixty-five and over in the U.K.; by 2010, there were 10.5 million.[38] In 1951, of those aged over sixty-five, two-thirds were aged between sixty-five and seventy-four with only 4% of them being

---

[34] Ballard, 'Migration and kinship', p. 223.
[35] Hatton, 'Explaining trends in UK immigration', pp. 721, 725, 736.
[36] Leach, Phillipson, Biggs, and Money, 'Sociological perspectives', p. 1.
[37] Botting and Dunnell, 'Trends in fertility and contraception', p. 35.
[38] Calculated from Rutherford, 'Population ageing'.

over eighty-five years in age. In 2012, 51% of those aged over sixty-five were between sixty-five and seventy-four, but 14% were aged over eighty-five.[39] The extent to which those over sixty-five formed an influential 'grey power' group is debated, but it is agreed that this group was more likely to vote in general elections than younger cohorts.[40] Certainly the introduction of a 'triple lock' on the new state pension in 2016 whereby pensions were uprated in line with the highest one of inflation, earnings, or simply by 2.5% p.a., reflects a political mindfulness on this issue of common concern to pensioners.[41] While turnout in general elections fell from around 80% of British voters in the 1950s to around 60% in the 2000s, the old continued to be more likely to vote. (Table 1.3) As such, politicians were likely to be responsive, not only to the increasing claims made by the older age groups on the health and social security programmes, but also to where and how they voted. As electoral turnout fell, so too did traditional political affiliations diminish. While in the 1960s around 45% of British Election Study (BES) respondents identified very strongly with a political party, only 11% on average did so in the 2000s. In the 1960s, 'class' was an important predictor of political affiliation. Half of manual workers voted Labour, while only about 16% of the middle classes did so. In 1964, around two-thirds of BES respondents in the main middle-class groups voted Conservative, while only 20–25% of voters in the manual working-class groups did so. In 1951, 65% of the working population were in working-class jobs: by 1991, just 38% were. As notions of class and the old industrial bases declined, so from the 1970s were voters more willing to choose between parties and to judge governments on their performance. In the 1979 election, it was skilled manual workers in South East England who supported Mrs Thatcher, having lost faith in the 1974–1979 Labour (and Lib–Lab) governments. For Labour, the decline of the traditional working class prompted the party to broaden its appeal to particular groups, such as young women, and in so doing reverse the traditional gender gap in British voting behaviour.[42] Increasingly, parties emphasized their competence to be in government, and voters seemed increasingly willing to punish governments for incompetence. The Conservatives lost the 1997 election in conditions of economic growth because of their perceived mismanagement of the 1992 Exchange Rate Mechanism (ERM) crisis. The Labour government won two further periods in government after its election in 1997 because of its perceived competence. In Scotland, that the

[39] Rutherford, 'Population ageing'.   [40] Walker, 'Ageing and generational politics'.
[41] Hood and Himaz, A Century of Fiscal Squeeze, p. 187.
[42] Norris, 'Gender: A gender-generation gap?'.

Table 1.3. Parliamentary general election results since 1945

| | England and Wales | Scotland | Number of U.K. Members of Parliament elected | | | | | | |
	Number of votes cast as % of electorate	Number of votes cast as % of electorate	Conservative	Labour	Liberal/ Liberal Democrat*	Social Democratic Party	Scottish National Party	Plaid Cymru	Others**
5 July 1945	75.5	75.1	212	393	12	–	–	–	23
23 Feb 1950	84.4	80.9	297	315	9	–	–	–	4
25 Oct 1951	82.8	81.2	320	295	6	–	–	–	4
26 May 1955	77.0	75.1	344	277	6	–	–	–	3
8 Oct 1959	79.1	78.1	364	258	6	–	–	–	2
15 Oct 1964	77.1	77.6	303	317	9	–	–	–	1
31 March 1966	76.1	76.0	253	363	12	–	–	–	2
18 June 1970	71.2	73.5	330	287	6	–	1	–	6
28 Feb 1974	78.1	77.9	296	301	14	–	7	2	15
10 Oct 1974	72.5	74.5	276	319	13	–	11	3	13
3 May 1979	75.2	76.0	339	268	11	–	2	2	13
9 June 1983	71.8	71.8	396	209	17	6	2	2	18
11 June 1987	74.8	74.3	375	229	17	5	3	3	18
9 April 1992	77.5	74.2	336	271	20	–	3	4	17
1 May 1997	71.5	71.3	165	418	46	–	6	4	20
7 June 2001	59.3	58.1	166	412	52	–	5	4	20

Continued

Table 1.3. *Continued*

	England and Wales	Scotland	Number of U.K. Members of Parliament elected						
	Number of votes cast as % of electorate	Number of votes cast as % of electorate	Conservative	Labour	Liberal/ Liberal Democrat*	Social Democratic Party	Scottish National Party	Plaid Cymru	Others**
5 May 2005	61.4	60.8	198	355	62		6	3	22
6 May 2010	65.4	63.8	306	258	57		6	3	20
7 May 2015	66.0(E) 65.7(W)	71.0	331	232	8		56	3	20
8 June 2017	69.1(E) 68.6(W)	66.4	317	262	12		35	4	20

* Liberals before 1992

** Others includes the Speaker

Source: The number of M.P.s elected to the House of Commons was: 640 (1945); 625 (1950, 1951); 630 (1955, 1959, 1964, 1966, 1970, 1974, 1979); 650 (1983, 1987); 651 (1992); 659 (1997, 2001); 646 (2005); 650 (2010, 2015, 2017).
The Representation of the Peoples Act 1969 lowered the minimum voting age from twenty-one to eighteen years with effect from 16 February 1970.

Sources: 1945–2010: Annual Abstract of Statistics, various.
2015: The Electoral Commission, *U.K. General Election Results*, electoralcommission.org.uk
2017: House of Commons, *General Election, 2017: Results and Analysis,* second edition, Briefing Paper Number CBP7979, updated 3 April 2018.

Scottish National Party (SNP) won a substantial increase in those voting for it in the 2007 Scottish Parliament election and became by a small margin the largest party in Holyrood was in part due to the perceived diminishing competence of the Labour-controlled Scottish Executive.[43] The formation of a SNP minority government in Scotland in 2007 also highlighted the decline of the political fortunes of the Conservative Party in Scotland. In 1955 the Conservative and Unionist Party had secured half of the Scottish vote. By the twenty-first century it won little more than a quarter. As the socio-economic characteristics of Scotland and England became more similar, so their voting behaviour became more different. The revival of the SNP preceded the exploitation of oil in the North Sea, just as the decline of the Conservative Party's fortunes in Scotland predated Margaret Thatcher's becoming prime minister.[44] Both oil and Margaret Thatcher may have hastened political change in Scotland, but a sharp decline of the Conservative vote in Scotland did not occur until 1987.[45] The process and pace of deindustrialization was striking in the traditional industrial areas of Scotland and it weakened traditional union links as well as a sense of common cause and purpose with workers in disappearing manufacturing industries elsewhere in Britain. Ironically the one-time Conservative and Unionist Party which promoted devolution gained least from it in Scotland. From 1998, Scotland has its own parliament and executive. Wales gained its own assembly and, from 2006, a Welsh Assembly Government. London gained a new strategic authority (the Greater London Authority) and a mayor from 2000. Andy Burnham became the first Mayor of Greater Manchester on 4 May 2017. Otherwise, the extent of devolved and regional arrangements in Britain was limited. The North-East region of England voted heavily against having an elected regional assembly in a referendum in 2004.[46]

Political power in Britain remained concentrated in the main two political parties. This was in contrast to the declining interest in politics at Westminster. While in the 1970s, the two parties won some 60% of the available electoral vote, in the 1980s this share fell to less than 55%, to 43% in 2001 and to 42% in 2005.[47] As governments were elected by a diminishing share of the electorate, so too did attention also move away from the floor of the House of Commons. Newspaper coverage of the debates in the House of Commons shrank, even if there was a new ability to keep abreast of proceedings on the parliamentary

[43] Pattie and Johnston, 'Voting and identity', pp. 468, 471, 478.
[44] Seawright and Curtice, 'The decline of the Scottish conservative and unionist party'.
[45] Finlay, 'Thatcherism, unionism and nationalism', p. 167.
[46] Tomkins, 'Constitutionalism', p. 250.
[47] Pattie and Johnston, 'Voting and identity', pp. 461–83, p. 465.

website. While in in early 1930s, the daily coverage of Parliament in *The Times* varied between 450 and 1,050 lines, and that *in The Guardian* averaged between 300 and 700 lines, by 1992 neither paper carried more than one hundred lines per day.[48, 49] Newspaper sales themselves fell, and the emergence of the internet deprived newspapers of a steady revenue from classified advertising. The pace of the drop in newspaper sales was eye-catching. The best-selling newspaper, *The Sun*, saw its (January) monthly circulation fall from 3 million in 2010 to a little over 1.5 million in 2018, a figure tellingly almost attained by the *Metro* free paper. In 1987 *The Sun* had a monthly circulation of just over 4 million. Among broadsheets, the monthly circulation of *The Times* fell from over 821,000 in 1997 to 440,558 in 2018.[50] As newspaper circulation declined and T.V. stations increased, thereby splitting the viewing figures for all channels, so the public space for discussion of matters of interest to the population fractured.[51] Yet throughout all this, the grip on government of the traditional two parties remained very strong. The short-lived renaissance of the Liberal Party in the 1970s, the formation of the Social Democratic Party (SDP) in 1981, and their alliance in the 1983 and 1987 general elections testified to the ability of a new party or grouping to attract votes, but insufficiently so as to overcome the two-party system in terms of winning parliamentary seats. Governments, albeit elected by a diminishing share of the electorate, could implement programmes of a strong political flavour. In contrast to the Attlee governments' (1945–1951) programme of public housing, nationalization, and commitment to low unemployment, the Thatcher governments (1979–1990) pursued the privatization of nationalized industries, the sale of council houses, and the adoption of the control of inflation, rather than low unemployment, as the principal aim of macro-economic policy. As such, the often dull and pragmatic politics of Britain has been interspersed with politically motivated, distinctive programmes whose example, as with privatization, has been copied internationally. Over the whole period since 1951, there was a shift to and then away from what might be crudely characterized as collective, provisionist, often monopolistic, non-market-based approaches by governments to the financing, sourcing, and distribution of health, housing, education, electricity, and other services. The trend was towards an approach which made greater use of competitive markets, in which government played a reduced role in ownership and fixed capital investment, and in which greater

---

[48] Riddell, 'Political Journalism', pp. 172–86, p. 180. This data is from sample days in a survey organized by Jack Straw in 1992, when he was a member of Labour's Shadow Cabinet.
[49] Peter Riddell, 'Political Journalism', pp. 172–86, p. 180.
[50] Audit Bureau of Circulation.
[51] Davis, *The Mediation of Power*, p. 2. Habermas, *The Structural Transformation of the Public Sphere*.

emphasis was placed on individual choice and responsibility. Frequently, this is characterized as a neo-liberal programme, with the term neo-liberal alluding to an increased willingness to use market mechanisms as a preferred allocative mechanism, and a concern to preserve and encourage the accumulation of capital assets.[52] A complementary approach to analysing such changes is to think of them in terms of time (and space). This is a less typical approach, but it does draw attention to the different and changing uses made of time in the public and private allocation of resources. In examining the development of the British economy since 1951, this book is concerned with changes in the sources of growth and also the distribution of its benefits as seen through the optic of time (and space). In a light sense, the concerns of the book are with the political economy of growth, similar to those of the economist David Ricardo. As Ricardo noted in the preface to his 1871 book *On the Principles of Political Economy and Taxation*, 'the produce of the earth' was divided between the landowners, owners of capital, and labourers, and that 'to determine the laws which regulate this distribution is the principal problem in Political Economy'.[53]

Time and Change

In analysing these changes and questions, this book adopts what was referred to at the start of this chapter as a temporal approach. Many of the cited policy changes reflected a shift in the proportionate emphasis on different forms of time, between the present and the future, as well as a shift in the apportionment of benefits between the public and private, and the collective and the individual. Part of the theoretical role of the state is to overcome inefficiencies in the market's accommodation of time, although the size and mechanisms of the state itself were also contested. Some like Keynes and Beveridge had a politically liberal view of what the size and role of the state might be. Neither wanted a large state. Some of this can be seen in the mechanisms chosen. Beveridge's advocacy of a social insurance basis for the social security system encouraged the idea that contributors were paying contributions so as to insure themselves against risks being realized in the future. Your pension was yours, because you had previously contributed into a fund so as finance it. In time, the Beveridge social insurance scheme mutated into a more explicitly

---

[52] Mirowski, 'Defining neoliberalism', pp. 417–55; Mirowski, *Never Let A Serious Crisis Go To Waste*; Harvey, *The Enigma of Capital*.
[53] Ricardo, *On the Principles of Political Economy and Taxation*.

tax-financed scheme with different temporal expectations. Now, you received your pension because current taxpayers were willing to finance it. They in turn expected their retirement to be funded by the next generation of tax-payers. This overlapping generations (OLG) model was an implicit contract between generations, between taxpayers (mainly of working age) and usually non-working older claimants in a different generation.[54] It was developed theoretically by the French economist Maurice Allais in France and popular-ized by American economists, notably Paul Samuelson.[55] It was applied to a range of practical issues and shaped thinking on the economics of such policy concerns as the national debt as well as the financing of social security.[56] It tended to assume that economic growth would continue and that the ratio between taxpayers and recipients of tax-financed payments (the dependency ratio) would not get out of kilter.[57]

The assumption that economic growth would continue; that the economy would have higher income and wealth in the future underpinned much of the thinking on how the present should treat the future. The compounding power of economic growth over time was emphasized in a paper, 'Economic Possibilities for our Grandchildren', written by the Cambridge economist John Maynard Keynes in 1928 and read to a student society at Winchester School. This was the *alma mater* of Keynes's younger friend and fellow aca-demic Frank Ramsey.[58] For his part, in 1928 in his article on 'A mathematical theory of saving'[59] in *The Economic Journal*, of which J.M. Keynes was editor, Ramsey considered the temporal issue of what proportion of its income a society should save for the purposes of investment. This formed an important contribution to discussions of how the present should value the future in terms of the present. One question which immediately arose was whether benefits in the future should be regarded as having the same value as those in the present. If a future society had a higher income than the present, then how much of its consumption should the present sacrifice in the form of investment (postponed consumption) for the benefit of the future. Should

[54] Emmerson, Heald, and Hood, *The Changing Face of Retirement*, p. 6.

[55] The work by Allais on the OLG appeared in an appendix of *Économie et Intérêt* (1947). The cal-culations in *Économie et Intérêt* (1947) were checked by the younger French economist Gerard Debreu before he took up a Rockefeller grant to travel to the United States, where he eventually gained a research position at Cowles in Chicago. Quite whether Samuelson and Debreu discussed Allais' work together is unclear.

Allais, *Économie et Intérêt*, Annexe 2; Düppe and Weintraub, p. x; Solow, 'Overlapping generations', p. 39; Geanakoplos, 'Overlapping generations model of general equilibrium'; Samuelson, 'An exact consumption loan model of interest'.

[56] Diamond, 'Social Security'; Solow, 'Overlapping generations', p. 39; Kotlikoff, 'Paul Samuelson's amazing intergenerational transfer'.

[57] Samuelson, 'An exact consumption-loan model of interest'; Weil, 'Overlapping generations'.

[58] Keynes, 'Economic possibilities'.   [59] Ramsey, 'A mathematical theory of saving'.

one in short 'discount' the future, by reducing the value of its future benefits at an annual rate so as to be better able to compare the mooted future benefits at their 'present value'? In a sense, whereas discounting looks from the future back to the present, compound growth gains power as it moves from the present to the future. For both Keynes and Ramsey, the object of striking the right balance between consumption in the present and investment for the future was to attain a position of 'Bliss'. Philosophically, Ramsey was reluctant to 'discount later enjoyments in comparison with earlier ones, a practice which is ethically indefensible and arises merely from the weakness of the imagination'. However, Ramsey did accept that given expectations of economic growth, trade-offs between present and future would be made, and discounting would occur.[60]

The context in which this economic and philosophic work on time emerged was one in which the understanding of time itself was being overturned. The publication by Albert Einstein (1879–1955) of his Special Theory of Relativity in 1905 and his General Theory in 1915 marked a fundamental development in the prevailing view of time, and its related concept of space.[61] Not only did Einstein challenge Sir Isaac Newton's view of Space and Time as absolute measures, but in doing so Einstein made use of non-Euclidean approaches to mathematics which thereby challenged its traditional axiomatic basis.[62, 63] This altered approach to time and space sent shockwaves through mathematics and physics and then on to philosophy and economics. In one response the mathematician Alfred Whitehead and the philosopher Bertrand Russell wrote their three-volume *Principia Mathematica* in 1910, 1912, and 1913 which sought to re-establish mathematics on an axiomatic basis.[64] Critical of Russell's use of logic in the *Principia* was his young student Ludwig Wittgenstein, whose *Tractatus* was translated into English by Frank Ramsey in 1922. Keynes's own early academic work arose from his interest in mathematics and philosophy, and his work on probability, risk, and uncertainty suffused *The General Theory* of 1936. In chapter 2 of *The General Theory*,

[60] Ramsey, 'A mathematical theory of saving', p. 541.

[61] See Schlick, *Space and Time in Contemporary Physics*; Feynman, *Six-Not-So-Easy Pieces*, 1997, chapters 4–6.

[62] Friedman, 'Space, time and geometry', pp. 409–10. Einstein's development of the concept of space-time built on developments in non-Euclidean geometry initially in 1826 by the Russian mathematician Lobačevskiĭ, the Hungarian mathematician Janos Bolyai, the German mathematician, Bernhard Riemann, and Hermann von Helmoltz, whose ideas were used in turn by Einstein in moving to the fourth dimension using Riemann manifolds. These 'n-fold extended manifolds' gave a new, broader, and special meaning to the term 'space'. This altered approach to space challenged Euclid's fifth postulate concerning parallel lines, and undermined the axiomatic foundations of mathematics.

[63] Friedman, 'Space, time and geometry', p. 407.
Aleksandrov, Kolmogorov and Lavrent'ev, *Mathematics*, pp. 56–7.

[64] Russell and Whitehead, *Principia Mathematica*, 3. volumes.

Keynes drew unflattering comparisons between classical economists and the practitioners of Euclidean geometry, with the 'classical theorists' resembling 'Euclidean geometers in a non-Euclidean world who, discovering that in experience straight lines apparently parallel often meet, rebuke the lines for not keeping straight'. Instead, Keynes argued that there was 'no remedy except to throw over the axiom of parallels and to work out a non-Euclidean geometry'.[65] Whether *The General Theory* was an effort to do for economics what Einstein had done for physics is unclear.[66] Arthur Pigou, the Professor of Political Economy at Cambridge, specifically observed that: 'Einstein actually did for Physics what Mr Keynes believes himself to have done for Economics. He developed a far-reaching generalization under which Newton's results can be subsumed as a special case.'[67]

This interest in time, in the relationship between the present and the future was, unsurprisingly, to continue into the post–World War II period. One sense of the legacy of the interwar discussions of the role of time is evident in chapter 2 on 'Economics, ethics and climate change' of the 2007 *The Economics of Climate Change: The Stern Review*.[68] Not only is Ramsey's work used but of the thirty-seven bibliographical references to the chapter, seven (by Pigou, Keynes, Knight, Ramsey, and Hotelling) were written between 1921 and 1931. The valuation of the future in terms of the present was increasingly used in private industrial companies from the 1950s. From the 1960s the practice of discounting was promoted by the Treasury within the U.K. government.[69] In the Treasury, this interest in discounting was not born primarily of any intellectual conversion to the merits of discounting but rather because it offered a means of exerting greater influence over the amount and type of fixed capital investment undertaken in nationalized industries, the national health service, and the public housing programme. In the immediate post–World War II period, government made play of the fact that it could borrow more cheaply than could private companies, and was therefore better placed than them to finance the construction of public housing, schools, hospitals, and investment in the nationalized industries. Prices and rents were set so as to cover the total costs of such investment. As public expenditure rose, and especially as from the 1970s the share of public expenditure devoted to social security and health increased, so too were techniques required which could limit or constrain this and other public expenditure. Investment in particular was targeted.

[65] Keynes, *The General Theory*, p. 16. [66] Togati, 'Keynes as Einstein', p. 118.
[67] Togati, 'Keynes as Einstein', p. 118. [68] Stern, *The Economics of Climate Change*, pp. 25–45.
[69] Chick, *Electricity*.

Increasingly, dissatisfaction was expressed with the post-war practice in nationalized industries and public housing of charging prices to cover average costs. Pricing looked backwards, to cover the *ex post* costs of the assets. Discounting looked forward and asked not only to what extent future discounted revenues covered the present, *ex ante*, costs of proposed new investment, but also, what were the opportunity costs of such public investment. How might the public funds be used better, if indeed they need be used at all? Moreover, in thinking about the additional costs of each new investment, the analysis moved away from its former average perspective to one that was marginal. What were the marginal costs of building, or not building, one more coal pit?

Once proposed projects were appraised in terms of their marginal present costs and discounted benefits, the question arose as to who those beneficiaries might be. In higher education, amidst the expansion of the sector in the 1960s, the Treasury increasingly asked what the benefits of higher education were, and if they existed, to what extent did they mainly go to the individual rather than to society as a whole. If the benefits were increasingly private rather than public, then why should not individuals pay for what was increasingly termed as an investment in human capital from which individuals were to enjoy discounted benefits. A similar move to assessing the future benefits accruing to individuals became popular in assessing the merits of individuals receiving elective treatments in hospitals or benefiting from road improvements which would reduce the risk of road accidents occurring. From the 1970s, the combination of growing political concern with public expenditure, the reduction in the share of the labour force employed in large, national, unionized manufacturing industries, the shift towards thinking of public investment in terms of its discounted benefits, and the increasing emphasis placed on the private rather than public benefits of that investment encouraged a general move towards a more individualistic approach to public investment. This greater individualization accorded with the political language of improving choice, but it also carried with it a transfer of risk from the state to the individual. It is this shift away from what might crudely be dubbed a collectivist, provisionist, average-cost-based pricing state which is a running concern in this book, with the underpinning argument being that these changes were underpinned by and reflected in the changing use made by the state of the concept of time. Such changes were important as they coincided, from the 1970s, with the withdrawal of the state from much investment activity. They also coincided with the breakdown of a largely fixed set of international exchange rates in a system in which the movement of financial capital was restricted. As access to financial capital was increased, as the administrative rationing of capital in the U.K. was reduced, then the holders of capital enjoyed a flexibility and mobility of their wealth which was much less available to labour, even if it was now dubbed as human capital. Finance was attracted to assets which rose in price, placing them further beyond the reach of those whose incomes were not increasing at the same rate. For the fortunate, the state might transfer assets to them, be they council houses or shares in privatized former nationalized industries. These acts of privatization themselves reflected changed attitudes concerning the obligations of the present to the future. The acquisition of capital was promoted from the 1970s as an important incentive for entrepreneurship, effort, and growth. That relied on assets being attainable. One consequence of the liberalization of financial and capital markets, of the state reduction in the provision of assets like housing, and the ease and low cost of raising financial capital which even preceded the quantitative easing response to the financial crisis of 2008 was the creation of fissures in society between those who could and could not afford to buy assets. This in part is the answer to the conundrum of why after seventy years of economic growth, many of the issues which concerned the Attlee governments of 1945–1951, be it housing, public services, inequality, or the casualization of labour, still resonate strongly today.

Bibliography

Aleksandrov, A.D., A.N. Kolmogorov, and M.A. Lavrent'ev, *Mathematics: Its Content, Methods and Meaning*, 1999, New York: Dover Publications. First published M.I.T. Press, Cambridge, Mass., 1963.

Allais, Maurice, *Économie et Intérét*, 1998, Paris: Clément Juglar.

Ballard, R., *Desh Pardesh: The South Asian Presence in Britain*, 1994, London: Hurst and Company.

Ballard, Roger, 'Migration and kinship: the differential effect of marriage rules on the processes of Punjabi migration to Britain', in Colin Clarke, Ceri Peach, and Steven Vertovec, (eds.), *South Asians Overseas: Migration and Ethnicity*, 1990, Cambridge and New York: Cambridge University Press, pp. 219–49.

Bartholomew, David, Peter Moore, Fred Smith, and Paul Allen, 'The measurement of unemployment in the U.K.', *Journal of the Royal Statistical Society*, Series A, Vol. 158, No. 3, 1995, pp. 363–417.

Bell, David N.F., and David G. Blanchflower, 'The lack of wage growth and the falling NAIRU', *National Institute Economic Review*, No. 245, August 2018, R40–R55.

Bolt, Jutta, and Jan Luiten van Zenden, *The First Update of the Maddison Project Re-estimating Growth Before* 1820, consulted on 31 August 2017.

Bond, Stephen, Evan Davis, and Michael Devereux, *Capital Controls: The Implications of Restricting Overseas Portfolio Capital*, 1987, London: The Institute for Fiscal Studies.

Botting, Bev, and Karen Dunnell, 'Trends in fertility and contraception in the last quarter of the twentieth century', *Population Trends*, 100, Summer 2000, pp. 32–9.

British Petroleum, *BP Statistical Review of World Energy*, June 2013, London: British Petroleum.

Brittan, Samuel, *Against the Flow: Reflections of an Individualist*, 2005, London: Atlantic Books.

Britton, A.J.C., *Macroeconomic Policy in Britain, 1974–1987*, 1991, Cambridge: National Institute of Economic and Social Research, Cambridge University Press.

Burk, Kathleen, and Alec Cairncross, *'Goodbye, Great Britain'*, 1992, New Haven and London: Yale University Press.

Cairncross, Alec, and Barry Eichengreen, *Sterling in Decline: The Devaluations of 1931, 1949 and 1967*, 1983, Oxford: Basil Blackwell.

Chick, Martin, *Electricity and Energy Policy in Britain, France and the United States since 1945*, 2007, Cheltenham: Edward Elgar.

Clarke, P., and C. Trebilcock (eds.), *Understanding Decline: Perceptions and Realities of British Economic Performance*, 1997, Cambridge: Cambridge University Press.

Coyle, Diane, *GDP: A Brief but Affectionate History*, 2014, Princeton: Princeton University Press.

Crafts, Nicholas, 'UK real national income, 1950–1998: Some grounds for optimism', *National Institute Economic Review*, vol. 181, no. 1, July 2002, pp. 87–95.

Crafts, Nicholas, *Forging Ahead, Falling Behind and Fighting Back: British Economic Growth from the Industrial Revolution to the Financial Crisis*, 2018, Cambridge: Cambridge University Press.

Davis, Aeron, *The Mediation of Power: A Critical Introduction*, 2007, London and New York: Routledge, p. 2.

Diamond, Peter, 'Social security, the great budget, and national savings', in Michael Szenberg, Lall Ramrattanm, and Aron A. Gottesman (eds.), *Samuelson Economics and the Twenty-First Century*, 2006, Oxford: Oxford University Press, pp. 42–53.

Düppe, Till and E. Roy Weintraub, *Finding Equilibrium: Arrow, Debreu, McKenzie and the Problem of Scientific Credit*, 2014, Princeton: Princeton University Press.

Emmerson, Carl, Katherine Heald, and Andrew Hood, *The Changing Face of Retirement: Future Patterns of Work, Health, Care and Income among the Older Population*, IFS Report, R95, 2014, London: Institute for Fiscal Studies.

Farmer, Roger E.A., *Prosperity For All: How To Prevent Financial Crises*, 2017, New York: Oxford University Press.

Feynman, Richard, *Six-Not-So-Easy Pieces: Einstein's Relativity, Symmetry, and Space-Time*, 1997, Reading, Mass.: Harlow: Addison-Wesley.

Finlay, Richard, 'Thatcherism, unionism and nationalism: a comparative study of Scotland and Wales', in Ben Jackson and Robert Saunders, *Making Thatcher's Britain*, 2012, Cambridge: Cambridge University Press, pp. 165–79.

Friedman, Michael, 'Space, time and geometry', in Michael Janssen and Christoph Lehner (eds.), *The Cambridge Companion to Einstein*, 2014, New York: Cambridge University Press, pp. 398–420.

Gazeley, Ian, 'Income and living standards, 1870–2010', in R. Floud, J. Humphries, and P. Johnson(eds.), *The Cambridge Economic History of Modern Britain: Vol. I. 1870 to the Present*, 2014, Cambridge: Cambridge University Press, pp. 151–80.

Gazeley, Ian, and Andrew Newell, 'Unemployment', in Nicholas Crafts, Ian Gazeley, and Andrew Newell, *Work and Pay in 20th Century Britain*, 2007, Oxford: Oxford University Press, pp. 225–63.

Geanakoplos, John, 'Overlapping generations model of general equilibrium' in John Eatwell, Murray Milgate and Peter Newman, *The New Palgrave: A Dictionary of Economics*, 1987, London and Basingstoke: Macmillan, pp. 767–779.

Griffin, James M., and Henry B. Steele, *Energy, Economics and Policy*, 1980, New York: Academic Press.

Habermas, Jürgen (translated by Thomas Burger with the assistance of Frederick Lawrence), *The Structural Transformation of the Public Sphere: An Inquiry into a Category of Bourgeois Society*, 1989 (first published 1962), Cambridge: Polity.

Hacche, Graham, and Christopher Taylor, *Inside the Bank of England: Memoirs of Christopher Dow, Chief Economist 1973-84*, 2013, Houndmills: Palgrave Macmillan.

Harvey, David, *The Enigma of Capital and the Crises of Capitalism*, 2010, London: Profile Books.

Haskey, J., 'Demographic issues in 1975 and 2000', *Population Trends*, 100, Summer 2000, pp. 20–31.

Hatton, Timothy J., 'Explaining trends in UK immigration', *Journal of Population Economics*, vol. 18, no. 4, Dec., 2005, pp. 719–40.

Hatton, Timothy J., and George R. Boyer, 'Unemployment and the U.K. labour market before, during and after the Golden Age', *European Review of Economic History*, 9, 2005, pp. 35–60.

Hood, C., and R. Himaz, *A Century of Fiscal Squeeze: 100 Years of Austerity, Politics and Bureaucracy in Britain*, 2017, Oxford: Oxford University Press.

Keynes, J.M., 'Economic possibilities for our grandchildren', in *Essays in Persuasion*, 1963, New York: W.W. Norton, pp. 358–73.

Keynes, John Maynard, Moggridge, Donald (ed.), *The General Theory of Employment, Interest and Money*, First edition 1936, paperback edition 1974, London: The Royal Economic Society and Macmillan.

Kirby, Simon, with Ray Barrell and Rachel Whitworth, 'Prospects for the U.K. economy', *National Institute Economic Review*, No. 216, April 2011, pp. F39–61,

Knight, Frank. H., *Risk, Uncertainty and Profit*, 1921: New York: Houghton Mifflin Co.

Kotlikoff, Laurence J., 'Paul Samuelson's amazing intergenerational transfer', in Michael Szenberg, Lall Ramrattan, and Aron A. Gottesman (eds.), *Samuelsonian Economics and the Twenty-First Century*, 2006, Oxford: Oxford University Press, pp. 42–53.

Leach, R., C. Phillipson C, S. Biggs, and A. Money, 'Sociological perspectives on the baby boomers: An exploration of social change', *Quality in Ageing and Older Adults*, vol. 9, no. 4, 2008, pp. 19–26.

Matthews, R.C.O., C.H. Feinstein, and J.C. Odling-Smee, *British Economic Growth, 1956–1973*, 1982, Oxford: Clarendon Press.

Meade, James, *Stagflation, vol. 1: Wage-Fixing*, 1982, London: George Allen & Unwin.

Mirowski, Philip, 'Defining neoliberalism', in Philip Mirowski and Dieter Plehwe, *The Road From Mont Pèlerin: The Making of the Neoliberal Thought Collective*, 2009, Cambridge, Mass.: London: Harvard University Press, pp. 417–55.

Mirowski, Philip, *Never Let a Serious Crisis Go To Waste: How Neoliberalism Survived the Financial Meltdown*, 2013, London: Verso.

National Statistics, *Economic Trends: Annual* Supplement, 2000, London: The Stationery Office.

Norris, Pippa, 'Gender: A gender-generation gap?', in Geoffrey Evans and Pippa Norris, *Critical Elections: British Parties and Voters in Long-Term Perspective*, 1999, London: Sage.

O'Rourke, Kevin. *A Short History of Brexit: From Brentry to Backstop*, 2019, London: Pelican.

Office for National Statistics, *Annual Abstract of Statistics*, London: ONS, 2011, No. 147.

Panayi, Panikos, 'Immigration, multiculturalism and racism', in Francesca Carnevali and Julie-Marie Strange (eds.), *20th Century Britain: Economic, Cultural and Social Change*, 2007, second edition, Harlow: Pearson Education, pp. 247–61.

Pattie, Charles, and Ron Johnston, 'Voting and identity', in Matthew Flinders, Andrew Gamble, Colin Hay, and Michael Kenny (eds.), *The Oxford Handbook of British Politics*, 2009, Oxford: Oxford University Press, pp. 461–83.

Peach, Ceri, 'Does Britain have ghettos?', *Transactions of the Institute of British Geographers*, vol. 22, no. 1, 1996, pp. 216–35.

Peach, Ceri, 'South Asian migration and settlement in Great Britain, 1951–2001', *Contemporary South Asia*, vol. 15, no. 2, 2006a, pp. 133–46.

Peach, Ceri, 'Muslims in the 2001 census of England and Wales: Gender and economic disadvantage', *Ethnic and Racial Studies*, vol. 29, No. 4, 2006b, pp. 629–55.

Ramsey, F.P., 'A mathematical theory of saving', *The Economic Journal*, vol. 38, no. 152, Dec. 1928, pp. 543–59.

Ricardo, David, *On the Principles of Political Economy and* Taxation, volume 1, edited by Piero Sraffa with the collaboration of M.H. Dobb, 2004, Indianapolis: Liberty Fund.

Riddell, Peter, 'Political Journalism', in Matthew Flinders, Andrew Gamble, Colin Hay, and Michael Kenny (eds.), *The Oxford Handbook of British Politics*, 2009, Oxford: Oxford University Press, pp. 172–86.

Roberts, Richard, *When Britain Went Bust: The 1976 IMF Crisis*, 2017, London: OMFIF.

Rosling, Hans, Ola Rosling, and Anna Rosling Rönnlund, *Factfulness*, 2018, London: Sceptre.

Russell, B., and A.N. Whitehead, *Principia Mathematica*, 3. volumes, 1910–13, Cambridge: Cambridge University Press.

Rutherford, Tom, 'Population ageing: statistics', House of Commons Library, SN/SG/3228, Last updated 10 February 2012.

Samuelson, Paul, *Foundations of Economic Analysis*, 1947, Cambridge MA: Harvard University Press.

Samuelson, Paul A., 'An exact consumption loan model of interest, with or without the social contrivance of money', *Journal of Political Economy*, vol. 66, no. 6, 1958, pp. 467–82.

Schlick, Moritz, *Space and Time in Contemporary Physics: An Introduction to the Theory of Relativity and Gravitation*, 1920, Oxford: Clarendon Press.

Seawright, David, and John Curtice, 'The decline of the Scottish conservative and unionist party 1950–92: Religion, ideology or economics?', *Contemporary British History*, vol. 9, no. 2, 1995, pp. 319–42.

Solow, Robert, 'Overlapping generations', in Michael Szenberg, Lall Ramrattan, and Aron A. Gottesman (eds.), *Samuelsonian Economics and the Twenty-First Century*, 2006, Oxford: Oxford University Press, pp. 35–41.

Stern, Nicholas, *The Economics of Climate Change: The Stern Review*, 2007, Cambridge: Cambridge University Press.

Stiglitz, Joseph E., 'In praise of Frank Ramsey's contribution to the theory of taxation', *The Economic Journal*, vol. 125, no. 583, March 2015, pp. 235–68.

Togati, Teodoro Dario, 'Keynes as the Einstein of economic theory', *History of Political Economy*, vol. 33, no. 1, 2001, pp. 117–38.

Tomkins, Adam., 'Constitutionalism', in Matthew Flinders, Andrew Gamble, Colin Hay, and Michael Kenny, *The Oxford Handbook of British Politics*, 2009, Oxford: Oxford University Press, pp. 239–61.

Vines, David, Jan Maciejowski, and James Meade, *Stagflation, vol. 2: Demand Management*, 1983, London: George Allen & Unwin.

Walker, Alan, 'Ageing and generational politics', in Matthew Flinders, Andrew Gamble, Colin Hay, and Michael Kenny, *The Oxford Handbook of British Politics*, 2009, Oxford: Oxford University Press, pp. 664–83.

Weil, Philippe, 'Overlapping generations: The first jubilee', *Journal of Economic Perspectives*, Vol. 22, No. 4, Fall 2008, pp. 115–34.

Wren-Lewis, Simon, *The Lies We Were Told: Politics, Economics, Austerity and Brexit*, 2018, Bristol: Bristol University Press.

2

Time, Capital Investment, and the State

If the Government is to take responsibility for guaranteeing employment and improving the standard of life, it must decide for itself the rate of capital investment, the manner in which the investment is carried out, and the priorities which are assigned to the various schemes of capital expenditure.

Nicholas E. H. Davenport, *Vested Interests or Common Pool?*, 1943, p. 164[1]

A hallmark of the early post–World War II period was the heavy involvement of the state in fixed capital investment, namely investment in buildings, plants and machinery, and infrastructure. The launch of a large programme of financing and providing public housing, the nationalization of industries and the identification by governments of fixed capital investment as an important causal factor in economic growth all reflected the important role assigned to and assumed for fixed capital investment. That it should be the state undertaking a large share of total fixed capital investment activity was contended, and had formed an important strand of the intellectual arguments between Keynes and Hayek in the 1930s. In part this expanded programme of public investment was a component of the increased public expenditure which followed World War II. Having been around 15% of GDP before World War I, and around 30% in the interwar years, after World War II public expenditure was persistently a little under 40% of GDP for much of the 1950s and 1960s, and from the late 1960s and thereafter mainly above 40%. (See Table 2.1) In part this was due to the displacement effect of World War II when wartime welfare needs and the government's ability to raise revenue both increased. Both the enhanced ability to collect taxation and the perceived greater need and demand for services funded from public expenditure persisted beyond the end of the war.[2] Public expenditure was also subject to a Relative Price Effect, in which the price of what was bought by government rose almost twice as much as the prices involved in spending as a whole. In current

[1] Davenport, *Vested Interests*, p. 164.
[2] Peacock and Wiseman, *The Growth of Public Expenditure*.
Middleton, *Government Versus The Market*.

Table 2.1. Components of public sector expenditure (economic categories) % of GDP

	Total managed expenditure	Current spending	Public sector net investment	Depreciation
1949–1950	38.4	33.2	1.7	3.6
1954–1955	38.5	30.9	4.1	3.5
1959–1960	36.7	29.8	3.4	3.4
1964–1965	38.0	28.8	5.5	3.7
1969–1970	41.4	31.3	6.2	3.9
1974–1975	47.0	36.6	5.8	4.6
1979–1980	43.7	36.5	2.9	4.6
1984–1985	46.3	40.0	2.1	4.2
1989–1990	37.5	33.0	1.5	2.9
1994–1995	40.5	36.8	1.6	2.1
1999–2000	36.0	33.3	0.7	2.0
2004–2005	40.1	36.4	1.8	1.9
2009–2010	45.7	40.4	3.3	2.0
2014–2015	40.6	37.0	1.7	2.0

Source: Institute for Fiscal Studies, LR Gov Spending Data. Accessed 18 May 2017.

prices, while from 1948 to 1985, GNP in money terms increased about twenty-nine-fold, government current expenditure on goods and services increased over forty-fold. In constant prices, from 1948 while GNP had grown 2.5-fold by 1990, government spending had increased only two-fold.[3] In general, while as a share of GDP, total public sector expenditure fluctuated during the post-war period, across the entire period it changed little, being 38.4% in 1949–1950 and 40.6% in 2014–2015.

As the public finances tightened, so too did public investment become subject to closer scrutiny. Not only did the privatization of nationalized industries and some public housing move responsibility for continuing fixed capital investment in these areas to private owners, but there was more generally a reduction in public investment. Net public investment peaked at 7.6% of GDP in 1967–1968 and by 2000 was close to zero. In altering its approach towards public investment, governments also made a changing use of time in their consideration of potential investment. Rather than emphasizing the benefits of the lower-cost state financing of public projects, there was a move towards emphasizing and scrutinizing the future benefits of the proposed projects. One effect of this was to identify the particular beneficiaries of projects and to calculate the public and private benefits to them of the proposed expenditure. In addition, concerned to keep government fixed capital investment off its

---

[3] Hatton and Chrystal, 'The Budget and fiscal policy', p. 55.

budget sheet, governments also moved towards effectively renting major investment projects, such as schools and hospitals, from the private sector. In short, across the seventy years following 1945, there were significant and telling changes in the state's role in public investment, which both reflected changing times and were enabled by a changing use of time in the consideration of such investment.

Keynes and Hayek

The role of the state in relation to fixed capital investment had formed an important element of the arguments between John Maynard Keynes and Friedrich von Hayek in the 1930s. Lionel Robbins at the London School of Economics, then the youngest professor of economics in Britain, invited Hayek to the LSE to give four lectures on Prices and Production in February 1931. Robbins had already argued in 1930 with Keynes on the Committee of Economists of the larger Economic Advisory Council.[4] In 1932, Hayek was appointed to the Tooke Chair of Economic Science and Statistics at the LSE.[5] At the LSE Hayek's colleagues included the economists John Hicks and Nicholas Kaldor.[6] Hicks developed an early and, at the time, controversial form of what became the IS/LM interpretation of Keynes's *The General Theory*, while the Hungarian economist Kaldor was to become economic adviser to the Wilson Labour governments. Hayek was to remain at the LSE until 1950, when he moved to the Committee on Social Thought at the University of Chicago.

While at the LSE, for much of the 1930s Hayek became engaged in a fundamental disagreement with Keynes (and also the economist Piero Sraffa) over the role which might be played by capital investment, the rate of interest and time in stimulating an economic recovery.[7] For Hayek, the rate of interest reflected a community's time preference between consumption in the present and in the future, and as such this then influenced choices between capital

---

[4] Howson, *Lionel Robbins*.
[5] Leijonhufvud, 'Hicks on time and money', p. 27.
[6] Other LSE colleagues included R.G.D. Allen, Marian Bowley, Ursula Webb-Hicks, Abba Lerner, Vera Smith-Lutz, Richard Sayers, and G.L.S. Shackle.
[7] This influence and distinction can be seen in Keynes's 1930 book, *A Treatise on Money* and in Hayek's *Prices and Production* (1931) and *Monetary Theory and the Trade Cycle* (1933). Caldwell, 'Hayek and the Austrian tradition', p. 22. Both Hayek and Keynes seemed to accept Knut Wicksell's development, notably in *Interest and Prices*, of the dichotomy between a natural and a market rate of interest. Wicksell, *Interest and Prices*.

(postponed consumption) and consumption goods.[8] When the rate of interest was low, indicating a low time preference of present over future, so too were more capital-intensive forms of investment favoured. For Hayek these more capital-intensive forms of investment took longer to bring to fruition, but because they embodied an accumulated series of production stages, they offered improved productivity so long as the capital project was completed.[9] In effect, the capital stock was an accumulation over time of stages of production mediated through the rate of interest. However, these capital projects might not be completed when increasing credit by banks drove a market rate of interest below what was regarded as the natural rate of interest.[10] In an economy in which resources were all being used, this lower market rate would divert resources into capital investment projects, imposing 'forced savings' on consumers. It was a paper (in German) later translated as 'The "Paradox" of Savings' by Hayek which had originally caught Robbins's attention.[11] However, as the effects of the divergence of the market and natural rate of interest became apparent and projections of future demand were viewed as overly sanguine, then longer-term capital investment projects could be abandoned before their completion. Such cancellations could contribute to a downturn in the trade cycle, but for Hayek all that could then be done was to wait for the market rate to return to alignment with the natural rate of interest. Injecting money into the economy would only keep the market rate lower artificially, and exacerbate the initial misleading of investors by having a market rate of interest which was not the natural rate of interest.[12]

For the Keynes of *The General Theory* (1936), the dominant influence on capital investment formation was the expected rate of return, what was termed the expected marginal efficiency of investment. Interest rates became a reflection in part of liquidity preference, the rates that were required to hold differing non-money financial investments. In *The General Theory*, the central chapter was chapter 11 on the marginal efficiency of investment, although it was entitled the marginal efficiency of capital.[13] In that chapter Keynes argued that it was the prospective, not the existing, rate of return on additional, marginal fixed capital investment which was the strongest influence on

---

[8] Laidler, 'Hayek on Neutral Money and the Cycle'; Laidler, *Fabricating The Keynesian Revolution*.

[9] Caldwell, *Contra Keynes and Cambridge*, p. 15.

[10] Caldwell, *Contra Keynes and Cambridge*, pp. 15–16, footnote 55.

The expansion of credit could be due to a spontaneous action. See Hayek, *Monetary Theory and the Trade Cycle*, chap 4; *Prices and Production*, lecture 4.

[11] Howson, *Lionel Robbins*, p. 178.

[12] Caldwell, *Contra Keynes and Cambridge*, p. 17.

[13] Kahn, *The Making of Keynes' General Theory*, p. 142.

whether individuals and firms undertook new fixed capital investment.[14] The differing stance of Keynes and Hayek regarding capital investment and capital stock had implications for their respective approaches to the scope for influencing capital investment so as to affect the progress of the trade cycle. For Hayek, the stance of waiting for the market rate of interest to realign itself with the natural rate provided some of the basis for his wider positive, nomocratic view of the role for the state in economic management. Since Keynes prioritized the marginal efficiency of investment and argued sequentially that it preceded an ability to influence liquidity preference and the multiplier effects of the consumption function (and need not require that there be a *unique* rate of interest, since as liquidity preference changes, so too could interest rates), then he was drawn towards a more active approach to economic management. For Keynes, the state could play a role in influencing the marginal efficiency of investment, not least in mitigating the 'uncontrollable and disobedient psychology of the business world' and in assisting, the 'return of confidence' needed to revive the marginal efficiency of capital which was 'so insusceptible to control in an economy of individualistic capitalism'.[15] Keynes wrote of a socialization of investment, which was different from State socialism:

> The State will have to exercise a guiding influence on the propensity to consume partly through its scheme of taxation, partly by fixing the rate of interest, and partly, perhaps, in other ways. Furthermore, it seems unlikely that the influence of banking policy on the rate of interest will be sufficient by itself to determine an optimum rate of investment. I conceive, therefore, that a somewhat comprehensive socialisation of investment will prove the only means of securing an approximation to full employment; though this need not exclude all manner of compromises and of devices by which the public authority will co-operate with private initiative. But beyond this no obvious case is made out for a system of State Socialism which would embrace most of the economic life of the community. It is not the ownership of the

---

[14] Keynes defined the 'marginal efficiency of capital as being equal to that rate of discount which would make the present value of the series of annuities given by the returns expected from the capital-asset during its life just equal to its supply price'.
Keynes, *The General Theory*, pp. 135. Moreover, Keynes emphasized that his discussions of a return on capital was on the *prospective* yield of capital and not on its *current* yield.
Kahn, *The Making of Keynes*, p. 146.

[15] Harcourt, *On Skidelsky's Keynes*. Keynes, *The General Theory*, p. 317. 'For my own part I am now somewhat sceptical of the success of a merely monetary policy directed towards influencing the rate of interest. I expect to see the State, which is in a position to calculate the marginal efficiency of capital-goods on long views and on the basis of the general social advantage, taking an ever greater responsibility for directly organising investment; since it seems likely that the fluctuations in the market estimation of the marginal efficiency of different types of capital, calculated on the principles I have described above, will be too great to be offset by any practicable changes in the rate of interest.'
Keynes, *The General Theory*, p. 164.

instruments of production which it is important for the State to assume. If the State is able to determine the aggregate amount of resources devoted to augmenting the instruments and the basic rate of reward to those who own them, it will have accomplished all that is necessary. Moreover, the necessary measures of socialisation can be introduced gradually and without a break in the general traditions of society.[16]

Keynes did not advocate the socialization (nationalization) of industries and while he favoured government action to influence expectations of the marginal efficiency of investment, like Hayek, he was wary of large organizational units and large government.[17] For all of his economic arguments with Hayek during the 1930s, he welcomed Hayek's political 'grand book', *The Road To Serfdom*, when it was published in 1944. As Keynes wrote to Hayek: 'Morally and philosophically I find myself in agreement with virtually the whole of it; and not only in agreement, but in deeply moved agreement.'[18]

Keynes died on 21 April 1946 and Hayek was never to write substantial economic theory again after the effort of completing his book *The Pure Theory of Capital* in 1941.[19] With Keynes dead and Hayek awaiting rediscovery, one of the main legacies of World War II was what both men viewed as being undesirable, namely an expansion in the size of government and of the share of resources devoted to public expenditure. In the post-war Golden Age, the relationship between the state and large areas of capital investment was significantly different from that argued for by Keynes in *The General Theory*. Beginning with the Attlee governments (1945–1951), not only did the state both nationalize major industries but it also financed a major construction programme of public housing. Of the large house-building programme launched by the Attlee governments, 90% was allocated to tenants by the state.[20] By 1954, of all fixed capital investment, 21.9% was accounted for by public corporations, 7.2% by central government and 22.5% by local authorities, with the private sector accounting for the remaining 49.2%.[21]

While Keynes had argued for a 'comprehensive socialisation of investment' as 'the only means of securing an approximation to full employment' but not 'for a system of State Socialism' and not for 'the ownership of the instruments of production', the state control over capital which was established in the early

---

[16] Keynes, *General Theory*, p. 378; Davidson, *John Maynard Keynes*, p. 67.
[17] Keynes, 'The end of Laissez-Faire (1926)', p. 313.
[18] Keynes, *Activities, 1940–1946*: vol. 27, pp. 385–8. Keynes to Hayek, 28 June 1944, in Skidelsky 'Hayek versus Keynes', p. 83. Kresge, in 'Editorial Foreword', in Caldwell, *Contra Keynes and Cambridge*, p. x.
[19] F.A. Hayek, *The Pure Theory*.   [20] Chick, *Industrial Policy in Britain*, p. 30.
[21] Feinstein, *Statistical Tables*, Table 39.

post–World War II period bore heavy elements of both what Keynes did and did not want. This changed role for the state in relation to fixed capital investment was remarked upon in a paper by Dennis Robertson, Keynes's one-time friend and colleague at King's College, Cambridge. Addressing the Liverpool Statistical Society on 11 January 1952, Robertson observed:

> It seems to me that the most significant economic difference between the England of 1950 and the England of 1910 in which I began to study economics does not lie in the vast extension of social services, nor in the fact that certain branches of industrial activity have been nationalized, nor even in the greater preoccupation with high employment as the supreme objective of policy, though it is not unconnected with any of these things. It lies rather in the fact that the State has claimed the right and assumed the duty of making and implementing on behalf of the community one of the most fundamental of economic choices, namely the distribution of productive resources between present and future uses. In other words it has taken upon itself the responsibility for determining the rate of growth of the community's real capital.[22]

Investment

As a factor in economic growth, fixed capital investment as a share of GNP was to increase for much of the Golden Age, peaking towards the end of the 1960s and subsequently trending downwards (see Table 2.2).[23] Some of this investment may have represented a response to the underinvestment during the preceding decades of the twentieth century. In the U.K., in the forty years preceding 1948 the domestic stock of fixed capital is estimated to have risen at a rate of scarcely more than 1% per annum.[24] That gross capital formation as a share of GDP almost doubled in the Golden Age did not assuage concerns that the U.K.'s lower rate of economic growth compared with its international competitor economies arose from an insufficiency of investment.[25] While different post-war governments chose differing economic approaches (France, economic planning; West Germany, a social market economy; Japan, Ministry of International Trade and Industry (MITI) and picking winners), all of these policies focussed on fixed capital investment. The Wilson Labour governments of 1964–1966 sought to increase investment by improving people's 'Keynesian'

---

[22] Robertson, 'British national investment policy', p. 116.
[23] The rise in gross capital formation to 20.1% of GDP in 1990 reflects the fall in GDP that year.
[24] Matthews, 'Why has Britain had full employment?', p. 561; Marglin and Schor, *The Golden Age of Capitalism*, p. 47.
[25] Hill, 'Growth and investment'.
Denison, *Why Growth Rates Differ*.

Table 2.2. Gross capital formation
as percentage of GDP

1950	12.0
1955	17.1
1960	19.0
1965	20.3
1970	20.2
1975	19.4
1980	17.6
1985	18.4
1990	20.1
1995	17.0
2000	17.5
2005	17.1
2010	15.6
2015	16.9

Note: Gross Capital Formation comprises
Gross Fixed Capital Formation, changes in
inventories and acquisitions less disposal
of valuables.

(2010–2015) ONS website, *UK National
Accounts: The Blue Book*, release date
29 July 2016

Sources: (1950–2005) National Statistics,
Economic Trends Annual Supplement, 2006
edition, Palgrave Macmillan, Table 2.1A.

expectations of what the returns on capital investment would be.[26] The Labour
government established the Department of Economic Affairs (DEA) in 1964
and published *The National Plan* in 1965.[27] The Plan was a manifestation of
Prime Minister Harold Wilson's view that 'steady industrial expansion and a
strong currency in world markets can be achieved only by the introduction
of purposive economic planning', planning in this instance seeming to mean
indicative planning intended to raise expectations sufficiently so as to bring forth
more fixed capital investment and thereby improve economic performance.[28]
A growth rate of 4% was posited for the economy. The DEA was in part designed
as a counterweight to the Treasury which, because of its concerns with inflation
and the balance of payments, was seen as unduly timorous in encouraging
investment and growth. In the interdepartmental struggle which ensued between
1964 and 1967, the Treasury emerged the victor albeit amidst the debris of the
1967 devaluation of sterling and the subsequent largest deflationary public
expenditure cuts since the war.[29]

[26] Albin, 'Uncertainty'; Malinvaud, 'Decentralized procedures'; Kornai and Liptak, 'Two-level
planning'; Meade, *Theory of Indicative Planning*.
[27] TNA T342/429, 'Industrial Policy', Pliatzky, June 1975, para. 5.
[28] Opie, 'Economic planning and growth', p. 149; Meade, *The Theory of Indicative Planning*.
[29] Cairncross and Eichengreen, *Sterling in Decline*, p. 195.

That gross capital formation as a share of GDP was proportionately lower than that of major competitors did not necessarily indicate that low investment was a cause of low economic growth. The direction of causation might run in the opposite direction, from low growth to low investment, rather than vice versa. Of relevance here is not so much the internationally comparative low investment/GDP ratio, but the comparatively lower returns on capital in sectors like manufacturing for that already lower quantity of fixed capital investment which had been undertaken. In manufacturing the investment: output ratio rose (i.e. less output per unit of investment) from 11.8 in 1951–1955 to 13.8 by 1968–1973. In commerce, the investment: output ratio rose from 5.7 to 13.0 over the same years. The profit rate in manufacturing also fell, from 10.7% in 1951–1955 to 5.7% in 1968–1973. In commerce, the fall in the profit rate was from 19.1% to 14.5% over the same period.[30] Changing an investment:output ratio for one of output:capital, unsurprisingly, does not change the general story, as evidenced in comparisons for British and German manufacturing.[31] In comparison with West Germany, U.K. returns on capital both measured in terms of output and profit were commonly lower, often by between one-third to one-half. If anything, it was surprising that as much capital investment was undertaken in the U.K., although inducements to invest were introduced and tax arrangements did become more favourable from the early 1950s to the 1960s.[32] By 1975–1976 the gross profit share in the U.K. stood at substantially less than half the levels of the United States, France, or Germany, and not much more than a quarter of that in Japan.[33] This all added to the surprise that capital investment remained as stable as it did in the U.K.[34]

Just as gross capital formation as a share of GDP levelled off in the mid-1960s and then began a trend decline as a share of GDP, so too did public sector investment, one of its main components. What was surprising was the extent and rate of its proportionate fall. Public sector net investment peaked at 7.6% of GDP in 1967–1968 and then began to fall from 1968–1969 (when it was 6.7% of GDP). It fluctuated steadily downwards during the 1970s reaching 1.5% in 1981/2, before it virtually ground to a halt in 1999–2000. This fall in investment was complemented by a shift within public expenditure in the ratio of current: investment spending from 10:1 in 1958–1959 to 118:1 in

---

[30] Matthews, Feinstein, and Odling-Smee, *British Economic Growth*, Table 13.1, p. 399.
[31] Crafts, 'Economic Growth', Table 9.10, p. 278; Crafts, *Forging Ahead*, pp. 83–4.
[32] Matthews, Feinstein, Odling-Smee, *British Economic Growth*, pp. 365–6.
[33] Brown, 'Inflation', pp. 1–12, p. 7; OECD, *Towards Full Employment*, pp. 303–8.
[34] Marglin and Schor, *The Golden Age of Capitalism*, p. 7; King, 'The U.K. profits crisis'.

1988–1989, before it fell back to 70:1 in 2000–2001 and 19:1 in 2007–2008.[35] While public sector net investment/GDP did pick up proportionately in the middle of the first decade of the twentieth-first century, the higher percentage share in 2009–2010 reflects the slump in GDP (see Table 2.1). Accompanying the fall in public sector net investment was a reduction in the stock of public assets, a consequence for example of the transfer of public assets into private ownership in the privatization programme and the sale of council houses. The net worth of the public sector is estimated to have risen from 41.7% of GDP in 1970–1971 to 77.1% of GDP in 1980–1981 before falling to 62.8% in 1990–1991 and to 15.6% in 1999–2000.[36]

However, the transfer of nationalized industries and housing from public to private ownership, did not necessarily mean that the flow of fixed capital investment into these industries and housing need fall; indeed, given the public finance constraints from the mid-1970s, investment might well have been higher in private than in public ownership. Apart from the size of any flow of investment, what private ownership could also do was alter its character. This happened in housing. While the annual share of investment in housing remained broadly unchanged, less was invested in the construction of rented accommodation for low-income groups.[37] Between 1950 and 1994 there was a switch round both in the source and the direction of investment in housing. Whereas in 1950, investment in private dwellings was 3.4% and investment in public housing was 16.3% of total gross domestic fixed capital formation in housing, by 1994 these contributions had been reversed, with 18.2% private and 2.7% public (Table 2.3).[38] While total investment in dwellings remained fairly constant at around 20% of GDFCF, the number of completed houses fell (Table 2.4). Fewer, more expensive houses were built. While the activity of housing associations did increase significantly towards the end of the twentieth century, it did not compensate for the collapse in house construction activity by local authorities, new towns and government departments, which fell from 147,600 in 1975 to 1,900 in 1994.

What then explains this reduction in investment by the state? To a small extent, it may reflect the slight fall and levelling off of GDFCF/GDP within the economy as a whole, but the extent of the decline in public net investment is much greater than this general fall. While the reduction in investment changed the nature of the state, it also arose from an increased questioning as

[35] Crawford, Emmerson, and Tetlow, *A Survey of Public Spending*, p. 16.
[36] Florio, *The Great Divestiture*, Table 8.3, p. 279.
[37] Florio, *The Great Divestiture*, p. 276.
[38] Central Statistical Office, *Economic Trends, Annual Supplement* 1996, Table 1.8.

Table 2.3. Gross domestic fixed capital formation, by sector and by dwellings

	Analysed by sector as percentage of total GDFCF			Dwellings as percentage of total GDFCF		
	Private sector	General government	Public corporations	Private	Public	Total
1950	52.3	30.9	16.6	3.4	16.3	19.7
1955	54.4	25.9	19.6	10.1	12.8	22.9
1960	61.1	20.3	18.6	11.6	6.4	18.0
1965	58.0	22.5	19.5	12.5	8.4	20.1
1970	57.7	25.1	17.2	11.0	8.2	19.2
1975	57.6	23.7	18.6	13.0	9.3	22.3
1980	70.0	13.6	16.4	14.7	6.2	20.9
1985	78.9	11.3	9.8	15.9	4.2	20.1
1990	83.6	11.8	4.6	16.0	3.9	19.9
1994	82.6	12.6	4.8	18.2	2.7	20.9

Source: Economic Trends, Annual Supplement 1996, Table 1.8.

Table 2.4. Housing completions (Great Britain, thousands)

	Private enterprise	Housing associations	Local authorities, new towns and government departments	Total
1950	27.4	1.6	169.2	198.2
1955	113.5	4.6	199.4	317.5
1960	168.6	1.8	127.4	297.8
1965	213.8	4.0	164.5	382.3
1970	170.3	8.5	171.6	350.4
1975	150.8	14.7	147.6	313.1
1980	128.4	21.1	86.0	235.5
1985	156.5	13.1	27.2	196.8
1990	160.7	17.0	16.6	194.3
1994	146.0	34.3	1.9	182.2

Source: Economic Trends, 1996, p. 191.

to the role of the state. The inflation of the 1970s, especially in the U.K. where it was significantly higher than in its main competitor economies, contributed to weakening public confidence in the economic competence of government. The rate of inflation reached 16% in 1974 and over 24% in 1975, to peak in August 1975 at 26.9% (Table 2.5).[39] There was also some slowing of growth in 1974 and 1975 (and again in 1980 and 1981). Established economic relationships were seen to falter. With both inflation and unemployment rising at the same time, the observed inverse relationship (the Phillips Curve) between the

[39]   Britton, *Macroeconomic Policy*, p. 264.

Table 2.5. Gross domestic product and retail prices, 1971–1990

	GDP at factor cost (£M, 1990 prices)*	GDP at factor cost** (volume 1990 prices, 1990=100)	Index of retail prices*** (all items, 1985=100)
1971	312,855	65.3	21.4
1972	321,555	67.1	23.0
1973	345,816	72.2	25.1
1974	340,683	71.1	29.1
1975	338,138	70.6	36.1
1976	347,129	72.5	42.1
1977	356,101	74.4	48.8
1978	365,920	76.4	52.8
1979	375,974	78.5	59.9
1980	368,216	76.9	70.7
1981	364,055	76.0	79.1
1982	370,493	77.4	85.9
1983	384,351	80.3	89.8
1984	392,067	81.9	94.3
1985	407,844	85.2	100.0
1986	424,214	88.6	103.4
1987	443,817	92.7	107.7
1988	465,746	97.3	113.0
1989	476,228	99.4	121.8
1990	478,886	100.0	133.3

* Source: Economic Trends, Annual Supplement 1996, p. 12, Table 1.2.
** Source: Economic Trends, Annual Supplement 1996, p. 8, Table 8.
*** Source: Economic Trends, Annual Supplement, 1996, Table 2.1, p. 149.

two variables (the real variable of unemployment and the nominal variable of inflation) appeared to have broken down.[40] The Phillips Curve was always an observation rather than a theory, and it had little, if nothing, to do with J.M. Keynes himself, although it had been commonly adduced by some Keynesians. Nonetheless, its demise provided a fillip for neoclassical economists critical of the causal claims of Keynesians. Keynesianism did not appear to have a certain solution for rising inflation, and the Keynesian economist John Hicks gave three lectures on 24–26 April 1973 on 'The Crisis in Keynesian Economics'.[41] Keynesians admitted that Keynes's *The General Theory* had not addressed the problem of inflation, but mainly because that had not been the problem he had intended to address in that particular book.[42]

---

[40] Phillips, 'The relation between unemployment'.
Forder, *Macroeconomics and the Phillips Curve Myth*, 2014, ch.1.
Lipsey, 'The relation between unemployment'; Lipsey, 'The place of the Phillips Curve'.
[41] Hicks, *The Crisis*.
[42] That Keynes himself had been extremely aware of the danger of inflation was evident in his work in everything from *The Royal Commission on Indian Finance and Currency 1913-1914* to his

The increased questioning of the competence and role of government fed into a longer running discussion as to why U.K. economic growth was lower than that of its main competitor economies. An increasingly popular strand of the argument concerned incentives. The argument that high marginal rates of taxation penalized entrepreneurship and initiative was attractive in an economy whose base of taxpayers had grown significantly since 1939. The wartime ratchet effect on taxpaying had been higher than its effect on public expenditure, and government revenue had risen from 23.4% of GDP in 1939 to 37.6% in 1945. This compared with 9.0% in 1900 and 40.2% in 2000.[43] On the eve of World War II the standard rate of income tax was 29%, and most people in manual or service sector employment earned too little to pay income tax. This changed after the war. PAYE was introduced in 1944 and more earners fell into the tax net as the tax exemption rate fell to half of average income.[44]

By the 1970s, perceptions of public resistance to further increases in taxation were being discussed in the Treasury. The view taken was that further rises in direct taxation were not possible and that the limits of this form of taxation had been reached.[45] If tax revenue could not be increased, then attention turned to what public expenditure could be cut. Political store came to be set in the Public Sector Borrowing Requirement (PSBR) and concern with it grew in the 1970s. Formally the Public Sector Borrowing Requirement was the difference between total (central, local, and public enterprise) government receipts and expenditure. Politically it came to be viewed as an indicator both of the government's intentions and performance. While the PSBR had not been a major concern to policymakers in the 1950s and 1960s, a mixture of inflation and recession produced in 1975 a PSBR of over £10 billion, just under 10% of GDP and from that the fear that the public sector finances were getting out of control.[46] Public sector net borrowing also peaked in 1975/6 at 6.4% of GDP (Table 2.6).

In part, targeting the PSBR was seen as being as an indicator of the government's resolve to reduce inflation and to promote economic growth, even if

publication in 1940 of *How To Pay for the War*; Johnson, *Collected Writings of John Maynard Keynes*, vol. XV, ch. 2; Keynes, *How To Pay for the War*.

---

[43] Clark and Dilnot, *Long-Term Trends*, p. 4. While fewer than 4 million families were paying income tax in 1938, in 1948–1949 that number was 14.5 million and 21.4 million by 1978–1979. It was only a little higher at 21.5 million in 1988–1989.

[44] Gazeley, 'Income and living standards, 1870–2010', p. 173.

[45] TNA T326/1063, Smethurst, note, 'The case for easy money', January 1970. 'The view has got about that further rises in direct taxation are impossible (some taxable capacity has been reached), and further rises in indirect taxation are unlikely from this Government, at least as they run up to an election. So, if further fiscal manoeuvre is impossible, turn to monetary policy—at least the academics seem to think there may be something in it, and it's over a decade since it was an important weapon.'

[46] Britton, *Macroeconomic Policy*, p. 25.

Table 2.6. Public sector net borrowing, 1970/1–1988/9% of GDP

1970/1	1971/2	1972/3	1973/4	1974/5	1975/6	1976/7	1977/8	1978/9	1979/80
−0.6	1.0	2.6	4.1	5.7	6.4	5.0	3.9	4.5	3.7

1980/1	1981/2	1982/3	1983/4	1984/5	1985/6	1986/7	1987/8	1988/9
4.3	2.0	2.6	3.3	3.3	2.1	1.9	0.9	−1.1

Office for National Statistics and Office for Budget Responsibility.

Source: House of Commons Library, 'Government borrowing, debt and debt interest: historical statistics and forecasts', Briefing paper, Number 05745, 2 May 2017.

necessary in the face of rising unemployment, a fall in the exchange rate, and bankruptcies.[47] In part it was also seen as providing a bulwark against the disdained fine-tuning associated with Harold Wilson's economic planning.[48] Early signs of the concern with the PSBR can be discerned in the aftermath of the 1967 devaluation of sterling, when the IMF had strongly encouraged the use of a measure of Domestic Credit Expansion (DCE) to provide some sense of the stance of monetary policy in an open economy with a fixed exchange rate.[49] The implementation of the targets agreed with the IMF led to a sharp fiscal contraction, with the PSBR moving from 4.55% of GDP in 1967 to a surplus of 1.14% in 1969. Yet while these DCE targets introduced in 1969–1970 and 1970–1971 were the first examples of the use of monetary aggregates as measures and partial instruments of policy, they did not establish a rigorous relationship between the PSBR and the growth rate of the money supply.[50] At much the same time as the devaluation of sterling on 18 November 1967, interest in the growth of the money supply and the use of monetary targets was beginning to be discussed more publicly, notably by Samuel Brittan in the *Financial Times* and by Peter Jay in *The Times*. Jay had joined *The Times* as an economics correspondent in 1967.[51] Under the editorship of William Rees-Mogg, *The Times* first began to publish monetary statistics on 24 September 1968 as well as publishing leaders on the benefits of understanding the role of the money surplus.[52] From April 1974, in the Conservative Party, Sir Keith Joseph became a leading political advocate of monetarism, attracted both by

---

[47] Notes of a meeting in Chancellor of the Exchequer's office, 5 October 1979, para. 5.

[48] Notes of a meeting in Chancellor of the Exchequer's office, 5 October 1979.

[49] Artis and Nobay, 'Two aspects'; Oliver, *Whatever Happened to Monetarism?*, p. 29.

[50] TNA T378/89, Middleton, paper, 'The exchange rate and monetary policy', September 1977, para. 18.

[51] Jackson, 'The think-tank archipelago', p. 54.

[52] Oliver, *Whatever Happened to Monetarism?*, p. 53; 'Understanding the role of money supply', *The Times*, leader, 15 October 1968.

monetarism's potential for combating inflation and also by the liberal outlook of monetarists like Milton Friedman.

Expressed very simply, the quantity theory of money claimed that the value of money varied in inverse proportion to its quantity, with that relationship depending on the demand to hold wealth in the form of money expressed as a proportion of income.[53] While the 1958 Radcliffe Report had regarded the demand for money function as essentially non-existent, the view that variations in the quantity of money mattered for prices, if not for real income, gained supporters.[54] Strong dissenters still existed. Amongst the earliest of Keynes's followers, James Meade wrote of the 'mumbo-jumbo' of monetarism and the economist and (Wilson) Labour government economic advisor Nicholas Kaldor was scathing in his attacks on monetarism and its use.[55] Within government, the virtues or otherwise of monetarism had been discussed with renewed interest since shortly after the devaluation of sterling in 1967. A Monetary Policy Group was hosted by the Treasury, and papers on monetary theory fed into it by economists like Andrew Britton, Michael Beenstock, and Charles Goodhart (Bank of England). In January 1970 Goodhart sought to lay out the essential differences between the Keynesians and monetarists. One such concerned how changes in the quantity of money influenced expenditure decisions (the transmission mechanism). Keynesians thought monetary policy affected expenditure decisions by changing the returns (interest rate) on financial assets, Keynes in *The General Theory* having compared the marginal efficiency of capital investment with returns on alternative assets with varying states of liquidity. However, if monetary policy influenced expenditure through the mechanism of interest rates, then this raised the question of why not act on interest rates directly, rather than via the conduit of money supply. In contrast, a monetarist view was that money was a close substitute, not just for a small range of paper financial assets, but more generally for all assets, physical and financial. As such changes in money balances affected expenditure without reliance on a change of interest rates in a small set of financial markets.[56]

While within government and amongst some macroeconomists there was a growing interest in monetary policy, there remained a gap between its

[53] Kaldor, *The Scourge of Monetarism*, p. 19.

[54] Laidler, 'Monetarism: An interpretation'; Laidler and Parkin, 'Inflation: A Survey'.

[55] Meade asked why, if the aim of some monetarists was to control the stock of money(M) so as to influence the velocity of money(MV) in such a way that this control of prices and transactions (PT) would restrict movements in prices (P), they did not simply concentrate on the flow of MV (and thereby on PT as MV=PT) rather than on M. Meade, *Full Employment Regained?*; Meade, 'Comment', p. 52; Kaldor, *The Scourge of Monetarism*, p. 32.

[56] TNA T326/1065, Goodhart, paper, 'The importance of money: summary', January 1970, paras. 2, 17.

theoretical exposition and its practical implementation.[57] As the monetary economist David Laidler remarked when commenting on a 1979 Treasury paper on monetary policy, to have suggested five years previously that a paper on 'achieving monetary targets, originating in the Treasury (would be) discussed by a dyed-in-the-wool Monetarist, with authors and discussant finding much to agree about' would have seemed very unlikely.[58] Yet Laidler also emphasized the experimental quality of what was being considered. While in theory he could manipulate the IS/LM model such as to keep the money supply on target since 'we *do* know enough about its structure, and about the value of its exogenous variables to perform the necessary calculations,...we certainly *do not* know enough about the British Economy to be able to put any of the lessons that we might learn from the model to use in trying to achieve similar targets there.'[59] The future Chancellor, Nigel Lawson, was also to refer to the 'experimental' quality of the use of monetary policy,[60] as too did the American economist James Tobin in comments to the Treasury and Civil Service Committee in 1981.[61]

There was also concern with how monetary policy might translate between economies. The recent best-known work on monetarism had been undertaken in the United States and was most identified with the economist Milton Friedman of the University of Chicago. Friedman's work showed long-run evidence of an association between changes in money stock and in money incomes, but there were serious differences of opinion among economists as to whether he was observing correlation or causation, and whether, if causation, its direction ran from money stock to money income as Friedman asserted.[62] The applicability to the U.K. of Friedman's historical work based on U.S. data and conditions was questioned by U.K. government economists. That ideas could be transplanted from the U.S. where labour unions were weaker and where central fiscal change was more difficult was uncertain.[63] As with the collapse of the Phillips Curve, a difficulty of operating monetary policies in the 1970s and 1980s was that econometric relationships established in the 1950s and 1960s concerning the supply of, and demand for, money related to a period of comparative stability compared with the 1970s.

[57] Laidler, 'Monetary policy in Britain'; Cobham, 'Convergence'.
[58] TNA ES 140/01, Laidler, comments on 'Monetary targets and the Public Sector Borrowing Requirement', July 1979.
[59] TNA ES 140/01, Laidler, comments on 'Monetary targets and the Public Sector Borrowing Requirement', July 1979.
[60] Lawson, 'The British Experiment'.
[61] Oliver, *Whatever Happened to Monetarism?*, p. 38.
[62] Hammond, *Theory and Measurement*.
[63] TNA T378/89, Couzens, paper, 'Policy and the monetary aggregates', June 1976, para. 4.

The Medium Term Financial Strategy (MTFS)

While there were continuing arguments about the priority given to monetary policy within macroeconomic policy, much more controversial was the political use made of monetary arguments to attempt to reduce public expenditure. With the election of the first Thatcher government in May 1979, there was increased discussion of the targeting of money supply, with much of the tenor of the economic-political ambitions being captured in the MTFS which was launched in Geoffrey Howe's Budget speech of 26 March 1980. In that speech Howe specifically remarked that the strategy was not to be confused with a national plan, 'for it is concerned with only those things—very few of them—that the Government actually have within their power to control'.[64] This resembled Milton Friedman's earlier complaint against central banks being charged with maintaining 'a stable price level'. While, like Hayek, Friedman favoured the use of rules, in this case price stability was the wrong kind of rule because 'it is in terms of objectives that the monetary authorities do not have the clear and direct power to achieve by their own actions'.[65] The fear was that lacking adequate powers for the task of price control, the central bank would seek to acquire more.

That a medium-term strategy should be published was seen as important as both lending credibility to the government's counter-inflation policy and for allowing time for growing awareness of this new credibility to act on people's expectations of future price movements. Somewhat ironically, the University of Chicago economist Robert Lucas's work on rational expectations had shown how the unpredictability of monetary policy could interfere with the information-revealing function of prices.[66] While Friedman had emphasized the theoretical neutrality of money, 'the unimportance of money' as he called it, in his Presidential Address to the American Economic Association, he was sufficiently pragmatic to recognize that there would be real effects as the economy adjusted to monetary shocks.[67] To avoid real effects, one must avoid monetary shocks, that is, unforeseen changes in the money stock.[68] In a sense, that was what the MTFS attempted to do, while also respecting its perceived neutrality of money and not disturbing the structure of relative prices.

Sitting alongside the MTFS in Howe's Budget was that other acronym, the PSBR. In his March 1980 Budget, Howe not only announced planned

[64]   1980 Budget, 26 March 1980, Hansard HC [981/1439–91].
[65]   Milton Friedman with the assistance of Rose D. Friedman, *Capitalism and Freedom*, chapter 3, 'The control of money', p. 53.
[66]   Lucas and Rapping, 'Real wages'; Lucas, 'Expectations'.
[67]   Friedman, 'The role of monetary policy'.   [68]   Hahn, *Money and Inflation*, p. 45.

reductions in the growth rate of money supply, but also in the PSBR/GDP ratio over the next four years[69] with the PSBR being identified as 'a main determinant of money growth'. This was little more than an assertion, and one which attracted the derision of no less than Milton Friedman, who informed a House of Commons committee that 'there is no necessary relation between the size of the PSBR and monetary growth'. In 1984 Friedman seemed unconcerned when the United States' budget deficits rose to almost 4% of GNP.[70] There was also a danger with the MTFS approach that fiscal policy would become partly geared to meeting monetary targets, which, as Milton Friedman told the Treasury and Civil Service Committee on 11 June 1980, was not a sensible way to conduct either fiscal or monetary policy.[71] Certainly, work by the Treasury which was completed in the month before the election of the first Thatcher government seemed to show, if anything, an inverse relationship between the PSBR and the growth of M3 between 1972 and 1978 (see Table 2.7).[72]

Theoretical considerations aside, the economic conditions in which the MTFS was published were tough. The output measure for GDP had fallen by nearly 6% between the fourth quarter of 1979 and 1980; manufacturing output had fallen by 15% over the same period. Stock-building, worth some 1.25% of GDP in 1979 went negative to at least a similar extent in 1980. Unemployment which was 1.3 million at the end of 1979 was over 2.1 million by the end of 1980. Interest rates rose at the end of 1979 although Minimum

Table 2.7. The PSBR and the growth of £M3

	PSBR £BN	% of GDP at market prices	Growth of £M3(%)*
1972–73	2.5	3.8	25.2
1973–74	4.4	6.1	24.0
1974–75	7.9	9.1	8.4
1975–76	10.6	9.8	6.9
1976–77	8.5	6.8	8.4
1977–78	5.5	3.8	14.5

*Growth of seasonally adjusted stock between the ends of successive first quarters

TNA ES140/01, 'Monetary targets and the PSBR' by P E Middleton, C.J. Mowl, J.C. Odling-Smee, and C.J. Riley, 27 April 1979, para. 10.

Source: Financial Statistics, Table 7.1 and 7.3, *Economic Trends*

[69] Congdon, 'The Analytical Foundations'; Congdon, *Reflections*, p. 118; Cmnd.7746, The Government's Expenditure Plan 1980–81; Jackson, 'The public expenditure cuts'.

[70] *Memoranda on Monetary Policy*, 1980, p. 56; Congdon, *Keynes, the Keynesians and Monetarism*, pp. 5–6.

[71] Friedman, 'Memorandum'.

[72] TNA ES140/01, 'Monetary targets and the PSBR' by P E Middleton, C.J. Mowl, J.C. Odling-Smee, and C.J. Riley, 27 April 1979, para. 10.

Lending Rate was cut from 17% to 16% in July 1980. By the fourth quarter of 1980 the exchange rate index was 13% up on a year earlier.[73] Over two years the appreciation was 24%. The views of economists were sought by government, but often those invited to meetings with the Chancellor or, as on 13 July 1980[74] to lunch with Mrs Thatcher at Chequers, were broadly sympathetic to the government's economic ambitions.

More critical economic views abounded, most famously as expressed in March 1981 when 364 economists wrote a letter to *The Times* urging a rejection of monetary policy and stating that there was 'no basis in economic theory or supporting evidence for the Government's belief that by deflating demand they will bring inflation permanently under control and thereby induce an automatic recovery in output and employment'. One concern was that this targeting of both Money Supply and PSBR would intensify downturns in the cycle and would be 'pro' rather than counter-cyclical. However, among those outside advisers who had access to the prime minister and the Chancellor, there was strong support for the MTFS approach with its emphasis on the PSBR. Patrick Minford (Professor of Applied Economics, University of Liverpool), Tim Congdon (L. Messel, stockbrokers), Gordon Pepper (W.Greenwell & Co., gilt-edged brokers) and Brian Griffiths (Professor of Banking and International Finance, City University Business School) met with the Chancellor and all pressed for a substantial reduction in the PSBR.[75] Gordon Pepper appears to have had privileged access to the prime minister, and Margaret Thatcher saw copies of his Monthly Bulletin for W. Greenwell & Co.[76] As its Monthly Bulletin (No. 100) for January 1980 made clear:

> It should also be remembered that inflation is caused by too much money chasing too few goods. The cure has two parts—less money and more goods. The case against shock treatment on the monetary side does not apply to the other half of the cure. Shock tactics should definitely be used to increase the supply of goods, e.g. reductions in marginal rates of total taxation coupled with substantial cuts in public expenditure.[77]

[73] Britton, *Macroeconomic Policy*, pp. 49–50, 53.

[74] TNA PREM 19/197, Lunch at Chequers, Sunday 13 July 1980. Present were: the Prime Minister; the Chancellor of the Exchequer; the Chief Secretary; Sir Douglas Wass; Terry Burns; Robin Matthews; Brian Griffiths; Douglas Hague; Patrick Minford; James Ball; and Christopher Foster. Terry Burns had also suggested inviting Alan Budd (or Jim Ball) and Geoffrey Maynard of Chase Manhattan. On the list of potential invitees, Margaret Thatcher had written in 'And Alan Walters if he is here'.

[75] Notes of a meeting in Chancellor of the Exchequer's office, 5 October 1979, para. 20.

[76] TNA PREM 19/183, meetings, Pepper and Thatcher, 18 May, 4 and 18 July 1979.

[77] TNA PREM 19/183, meeting, Pepper and Thatcher, 18 July 1979.
Monthly Bulletin of W. Greenwell & Co. This included the Monthly Bulletin, No. 100. for January 1980, Appendix.

Such bulletins mattered because they were read inside government. At the meeting on 5 October 1979 to discuss the idea of the MTFS, materials from the June 1979 issue of L. Messel & Co's *Financial Analysis* formed one of the position papers for the meeting.[78]

Public Expenditure: Changes in the Books and Off the Books

Arguably, for all of the attention paid to monetary policy, the MTFS and the PSBR, the greatest change from the mid-1970s was not in the amount of public expenditure but in its composition. In short, there was a shift in the type of public expenditure which the government was prepared to finance, and a change in the financial methods for so doing. For all of the targeting of public expenditure and the highlighting of taxation in elections, neither taxation nor public expenditure changed much in aggregate during the Thatcher (and later) governments. Between 1979 and 1997 the ratio of taxation to GDP increased by two percentage points, while over the same period total public spending fell from 43 to 39% of GDP. What did change was the structure of taxation (see chapter 4) and the composition of public expenditure. Notable from the late 1960s and early seventies was the increased share accounted for by the social security and health programmes (see Table 2.8). Other components of public expenditure, notably defence expenditure, oscillated. High during the Korean War (1950–1953) it fell from the mid-1950s, not least as the U.K.'s world role diminished as reflected in its East of Suez decision to close major military bases in South East Asia and parts of the Middle East from the end of the 1960s. In the 1990s there may have been some 'peace premium' following the ending of the Cold War. That defence expenditure as a share of GDP then rose in this century reflected continuing commitments in Iraq and Afghanistan. Since, unlike health, defence expenditure is not strongly related to national income, economic growth in the later 1980s and the 1990s, and then its fall from 2008, also contributed to reducing and then increasing the share of GDP accounted for by defence. In general, defence spending as a share of total public spending declined from the mid-1980s, from 10.7% in 1985–1986, 6.6% in 1997–1998, and 5.0% by 2014–2015.

---

[78] Congdon, *Reflections*, p. 3. For the text from L. Messel & Co's quarterly forecast of financial flows, *Financial Analysis* (June 1979), see Congdon, *Reflections*, pp. 55–65. Sir Keith Joseph's private papers contain a photocopy on Joseph Sebag & Co headed paper of 'Gilt Edged News Letter, no. 11, October 1975 "Six Pounds"' by A.A. Walters, Cassel Professor of Economics, LSE. Keith Joseph papers, Bodleian Library Oxford, KJ 10/6.

Table 2.8. Components of public sector expenditure(main programmes) % of GDP

	Social security	Health	Education	Defence	Public order and safety	Transport
1949–1950	4.1	3.6	–	–	–	–
1954–1955	4.0	2.9	2.8	8.4	–	–
1959–1960	4.9	3.1	3.5	6.1	–	–
1964–1965	5.2	3.3	4.2	5.6	–	–
1969–1970	6.5	3.5	4.7	4.5	–	–
1974–1975	7.3	4.3	5.5	4.5	–	–
1979–1980	8.5	4.2	5.0	4.4	1.5	1.5
1984–1985	10.5	4.6	4.8	5.0	1.8	1.7
1989–1990	8.5	4.2	4.5	3.6	1.8	1.3
1994–1995	11.1	5.2	4.8	3.1	2.1	1.5
1999–2000	10.1	5.0	4.3	–	2.6	1.9
2004–2005	10.7	6.5	5.1	–	2.3	2.2
2009–2010	12.5	7.8	5.9	–	2.5	2.3
2014–2015	11.8	7.4	4.7	–	2.0	1.65

Source: Institute for Fiscal Studies, LR Gov Spending Data. Accessed 18 May 2017.

What was also notable about the changes in public expenditure from the late 1960s was the decline in public sector net investment (see Table 2.1). Part of this fall in public sector net investment is explained by the reduction in public investment in housing and the nationalized industries. Part again was simply a consequence of fixed capital investment being squeezed out by the rising share of public expenditure accounted for by health and social security. Transfer payments began to displace public investment. Yet, because of sensitivity to increasing the PSBR, new means were also devised for taking necessary investment off the public accounts. The fall in public sector net fixed investment in part reflected a move towards buying services from private providers of built facilities, rather than making upfront public financing available for the capital investment projects. One such approach was the use of the Private Finance Initiative (PFI).

The Private Finance Initiative

In education, health, and prisons, the move to buying a stream of services from a PFI provider rather than putting upfront public financing was announced in Chancellor Norman Lamont's Autumn Statement of 1992. Introduced by a Conservative government, the PFI approach was embraced with most enthusiasm by the Labour governments of Blair and Brown.[79] As a

---

[79] Offer, 'Patient and impatient capital', p. 16.

stream of purchased services, the PFI projects ought not to appear in the PSBR in an income and expenditure flow-based system of national accounts, even though they looked to all intents and purposes like capital infrastructure projects.[80] However, that the state was not providing upfront capital did not necessarily mean that risks had been transferred to the supplier of the service. Traditionally, the Treasury had been concerned by cost and time overruns on public construction projects, but such risks could be accommodated in penalty clause contracts with constructors. Also, a tangible asset was left. As well as the risks of construction, there were also potential risks attached to raising finance, although such risks were familiar and, as with construction, low. The third, and social risk, concerned the length of time for which clients would continue to take services. The political hue of governments could change and governments in Western Europe had walked away from nuclear power. Such risks and the difficulties of specifying service requirements made these incomplete contracts of higher risk than the risks arising from construction or finance, but this particular higher risk was bundled up in the general total risk pricing assessment for the whole project.[81] This third risk tended to be understated in value-for-money (VFM) comparisons.[82] Given the difference in risk of different phases of each project, the application of a 6% VFM, which was estimated to be the social rate of time preference, was inappropriate. In 2003 the Treasury reduced this to 3.5%, which was significantly lower than any discount rate which was used when appraising private sector projects. In the wake of the 2008 crisis this rate remained unchanged, making it twice as high as the rate at which government could borrow.[83]

These and other concerns with the PFI assignment of costs and risks plus, following the 2008 crash, the wider differential between public and private costs of borrowing, removed much of the attraction of the PFI model. Specific academic studies in health expressed concern at the cost of the PFI model, as did House of Commons committees. Not that the impact of PFI should be overstated. Following a slow initial take-up, it was decided in November 1994 that the PFI should become the preferred option for capital projects.[84] During 2000, the inclusion of PFI investments would only have raised gross public investment from 1.7% to 2.1% of GDP, still leaving it at about half its 1985 level. Between 1997 and 2002, over 500 PFI project contracts were signed. The

[80] Helm, oral evidence to the House of Commons Treasury Committee on the Private Finance Initiative, 14 June 2011.

[81] Jackson, 'The Private Finance Initiative', pp. 16–17; Hart, 'Incomplete contracts'.

[82] Grout, 'The economics of the Private Finance Initiative'.

[83] Offer, 'Patient and impatient capital'.

[84] H.M. Treasury, 1996, Treasury Committee, sixth report, The Private Finance Initiative.

total value of these contracts was £22 billion. As such, PFI spending was about 10% of public sector gross capital spending. In terms of its impact on net public sector debt it was even less significant. For example, if PFI expenditure had instead been incurred by the public sector through traditional public sector procurement then net public sector debt as a proportion of GDP would have been only 1% higher in 2001/02, i.e. 37.9% instead of 36.8%.[85] As nominal interest rates fell as part of QE, then so too did PFI contracts look increasingly expensive.

Shifting Times

Couched within the move away from the upfront financing of capital projects was a shift in the time perspective from which potential projects were viewed. In the 1940s and 1950s, the tendency in considering potential investment in the nationalized industries and in public housing was to consider the costs of the upfront financing of the projects and then to compare that with the likely benefits provided by the resulting investment projects. In thinking about the costs of finance, the ability of government to raise money at a lower cost than private operators was emphasized. The benefits of the project, be it in electricity or housing, tended to be viewed as much for what it contributed to increasing total output and how it made that output more available to lower-income groups. Prices and rents were set so as to cover the average costs of supplying all electricity and housing, and the tendency was for houses and electricity to be provided by monopoly organizations in a broadly collectivist manner. As the investment component of public expenditure was squeezed so too was increasing use made of approaches to investment appraisal which emphasized the projected discounted benefits of the project. Once projects came off the public books then this shift forward in time became even more explicit. Further, in thinking about the value of future benefits, the tendency was to think not only about the future discounted value of projects, but also to think of these benefits in terms of their marginal contribution. What was the benefit of investing, or not investing, one more pound in a proposed project? This further moved the approach towards investment away from any collectivist, provisionist sense and more towards an individualistic, marginal approach firmly rooted in the evaluation of future benefits over time. The approach to road construction and improvement provides a neat illustration of this.

---

[85]   Peter Jackson, 'The Private Finance Initiative', p. 5.

Roads, Vehicles, and Time

Over the post-war period there was a substantial increase in car ownership and the use of roads. The total number of vehicles registered for the first time increased from about 414,000 p.a. in 1951 to a peak of over 3.2 million vehicles p.a. in early 2000. The proportion of households with access to a car or a van rose from 14% in 1951 to 75% in 2010.[86] Over the entire period from 1950 to 2010, the number of private and light goods vehicle and other vehicles in Britain increased from around 4 million in 1950 to over 34 million in 2010, an average growth rate of 3.7% p.a.[87] This increased demand was often met by building more roads, notably the construction of motorways. The first phase of work was begun on the 73-mile St. Albans-Hertfordshire section of the M1 in March 1958, with the entire motorway being completed in October 1959.[88] As with many public investments, there was no attempt to price access to the roads in terms of time and space, so congestion on the most popular roads intensified. Indeed, initial responses to the problem of congestion in towns were firmly opposed to economic approaches to the problem. The 1963 (Colin) Buchanan report which was concerned with traffic in towns not only viewed the satisfaction of its environmental concerns as a non-negotiable priority, but also preferred the physical division of London into precincts into which only local traffic would be allowed.[89] The resistance to the use of economic mechanisms reflected Buchanan's view of cars as a great agent of personal liberty for people, but it was an approach increasingly and theoretically effectively challenged by economists.[90] Two British economists, Beesley and Foster, applied cost–benefit analysis (CBA), first in a retrospective study of the M1 motorway and then to argue the case for construction of the Victoria tube line in London.[91] In 1964 there was also the Smeed Report on road pricing, from a committee chaired by the director of the Road Research Laboratory. The CBA approach was also applied to the question of where to site new and additional airport capacity. Appropriately, Buchanan wrote a minority report rejecting the CBA approach as used in the Roskill Commission on the Third London Airport.[92]

---

[86] Department of Transport, *Transport Statistics, Great Britain*, 2011.
[87] There was some tailing off in 2008 (0.7%), 2009 (0.1%) and 2010 (0.5%).
[88] Short, Pont, and Huang, 'Safety and reliability of distributed embedded systems'.
[89] Hall, 'The Buchanan Report', pp. 7–8.   [90] Buchanan, *Mixed Blessing*.
[91] Hall, 'The Buchanan Report', p. 7. For a critique of Buchanan's approach, see Beesley and Kain, 'Urban form, car ownership and public policy'; Beesley and Kain, 'Forecasting car ownership and use'; Sunstein, *The Cost-Benefit Revolution*; Self, *Econocrats and the Policy Process*.
[92] Hall, 'The Buchanan Report', p. 7.

Yet, the problem remained that congestion, where time was a function of space, increased. Such congestion worked against some of the initial reasons for building roads, namely to speed up the pace of travel. The potential temporal benefit of roads could be measured both in terms of time as well as over time. Against a background of a long-run improvement in productivity and as a consequence the increasing economic value of working labour and its time, then in as much as net transport investment enabled travel times to be reduced, it represented an uncommon instance of rising marginal efficiency of capital.[93] The time-saving aspect of putative transport projects, both for users of new transport links and for users of existing capacity from which demand had shifted made proposed projects very suitable for cost–benefit analysis, as too did the social costs and benefits of transport. The cost–benefit analysis of the proposed construction of the Victoria underground line in London confirmed that not only were savings in terms of time available on the new underground line itself, but also on the roads from which traffic was diverted.[94] The factoring-in of the value of time and of time-savings became of increasing importance in transport infrastructure projects, although it was vulnerable to a potentially inescapable illogicality. As the value of time rose on the back of rising productivity, so the case for building more roads so as to reduce journey times also seemed to strengthen. Yet such investment by the current generation to benefit future, wealthier generations whose productivity and value of time would consequently increase further had a vicious circling quality to it. As the government economist J L. Carr commented in 1970: it 'seems superficially nonsensical to argue that, the richer we expect our children to be, the more we should deprive ourselves (and the children) of present benefits in order to build more roads so that they can drive everywhere faster in the 1980s than in the 70s, and so on ad infinitum.'[95] One route from the vicious towards a more virtuous circle involved the recognition that as productivity, per capita income, and the value of time rose in the future, then so too would the value set on scarce assets, notably good property in desirable locations and, arguably, amenity (unspoilt countryside). Such developments would increase the opportunity-cost value of new roads and externalities.

---

[93]   TNA T316/85, Carr, paper, 'The value of time through time', January 1970, para. 1.

[94]   Foster and Beesley, 'Estimating the social benefit'; Beesley and Foster, 'The Victoria Line'. On the economic costs and benefits of pricing cars and motorcycles using roads in Central London, see the work commissioned by the Ministry of Transport from J.M. Thomson of the LSE and published in the *Journal of the Royal Statistical Society*, 1967. J.M. Thomson, 'Evaluation of two proposals'. Recommended by the Treasury's K.E. Couzens as providing a good introduction to CBA were the articles by: Feldstein; Peters; and Prest and Turvey.

[95]   TNA T316/85, Carr, note, 'Value of time', January 1970.

Road Accidents and the Economic Value of Life

As the economic value of the working labour force rose, so too did the rate of return on road and transport improvements designed to reduce injuries and prevent fatalities. As with the general approach to public fixed capital investment in the nationalized industries (see chapter 6), the appraisal of the value of prevented fatalities (VPF) shifted from being undertaken on an *ex post* (after the event) to an ex *ante* (before the event) basis. From the interwar period and until the 1960s the main approach used by the Road Research Laboratory was to adopt an *ex* post approach to calculating the monetary cost to society of an 'average' accident.[96] The alternative was an *ex* ante approach, which asked about the benefit to society including the individual concerned, when a death was prevented. In the '*ex post*' approach the individual concerned was excluded from the society being considered. In the '*ex ante*' approach he/she was included. On an '*ex post*' basis when an individual was killed, it was agreed that society lost the present value of his/her future output but at the same time gained to the extent that it no longer had to provide his/her future consumption. The measure of lost output was therefore taken net of consumption. On the *ex ante* basis, which measured the benefit of keeping an individual alive who, but for the introduction of some safety measure, would have been dead, it was agreed that the measure of output should be gross and not net of consumption. On this basis, since the individual was alive and able to enjoy his/her consumption, this consumption was a benefit to him/her and, since he/she was a member of society, a benefit to society. Consumption was therefore not netted out of output.[97]

Moving from an *ex post* to an *ex ante* approach resulted in a sharp increase in the valuation of human life. The *ex ante* treatment of the individual resulted in new valuations of accidents and casualties. In 1970, the valuation of a life saved was almost doubled, with the valuations in 1970 prices being £17,000 for a fatality, £900 for a serious injury and £30 for a slight injury.[98] Expressed in 2004 prices, the VPF of a road fatality rose from £37,500 in 1952 to £1,384,500 in 2004, a thirty-seven-fold increase.[99] As an *ex ante* approach to preventing fatalities was adopted, so it became tempting to distinguish

---

[96] Reynolds, 'The costs of road accidents'.
[97] TNA MT 120/186, Bird, paper, 'The prediction', August 1965, para. 11.
TNA MT 92/404, Jukes, note, 'Accident costs', August 1970, para. 10.
TNA, MT92/481, paper, 'Accident cost valuation', paras. 9, 12.
[98] TNA MT 120/186, Dale, paper, 'Differentiation of road casualty costs', December 1970.
[99] NERA Economic Consulting, *Human Costs of a Nuclear Accident: Final Report*, 3 July 2007. Cols. 1–4: A. Evans, evidence to the House of Lords Economics Affairs Committee Inquiry into the Government's policy on the management of risk, 2006.

between the economic value of the individual lives which were being saved. This value arose from their annual output and the number of expected future years of work. It became possible to differentiate the Value of Prevented Fatalities by age, income, and gender. So, for example, motorcyclists tended to be young men whereas pedestrian casualties were weighted towards old people and children. In economic terms, the young and employed were worth more than the old and retired; the individual motor cyclist or car occupant was worth more than the individual pedestrian.[100] The economic value of the retired was treated as nil since retired people had no present output, and consumed either out of past earnings (savings) or from transfer payments (e.g. old age pensions). However, the fact that the rest of society was prepared to forego some consumption so as to finance pensions to allow non-producers to consume suggested that this provided a minimum estimate of the value of life of these non-producers which was how the £5,000 non-economic (or subjective) cost value was derived. Thus, the consumption stream of retired people was used as a basis for calculating the subjective cost.[101] While the economic approach began to distinguish between the economic value of individuals, there was a political reluctance also to do so. It was recognized that 'ministers see objections to a method of calculation which explicitly values the life of one human being higher than that of another whatever the yardstick used. Differentiation by reference to sex and income seem particularly open to objection.'[102] This political reluctance to differentiate according to earnings therefore had to coexist with a willingness to quantify the value of time savings made by different groups.[103]

What was perhaps surprising given the political sensitivity of the calculation of the (VPF) rate of return on road improvements was that a sharp differential should exist between the VPF on roads and railways. Given the rising VPF on roads, and the lower rate and level of fatalities on railways, it is surprising that the marginal cost of expenditure of VPF on railways was about one hundred times higher than that on roads. While the annual number of road fatalities p.a. on roads peaked at 8,000 in 1966 and by 2000 was down to 3,679 p.a., the disparity in spending on preventing fatalities on roads, compared with on railways, was consistent with a wider unequal allocation of resources between

[100] TNA MT 92/404, Dale, paper, 'Differentiation of road casualty costs', paras. 4, 6.

[101] TNA MT 92/404, Mooney, note, October 1970, para. 4.

[102] TNA MT 92/404, Dale, paper, 'Differentiation of road casualty costs', para. 5.

[103] As the civil servant and economist Gavin Mooney commented: 'While it might appear the case to some that economists are prepared to play God and place a value on human life (a point I do not accept), I do feel it would be a God-playing exercise to differentiate in the values of human life on the basis of age and sex'. TNA MT 92/404, Mooney, paper, 'Accident cost differentiation', August 1970, para. 7.

road and rail. In the present century, railways conveyed only about 7% of the national passenger miles (mainly in London and the South East) and a similar proportion of freight tonne-miles. Most of the rest was on roads. In 1950 cars, vans, and taxis accounted for 27% of all passenger distance travelled; by 2014 that proportion was 83%. Household expenditure on ownership and use of cars was about 12% of all expenditure, putting it on a par with housing and food and drink. Expenditure on transport was 2%. Yet railways received a subsidy of about £5 billion p.a. and were used by a higher-income group. Railways attracted a great deal of attention in public debate and the 2000 *Ten Year Transport Plan* diverted a disproportionate share of public investment towards them.[104] Expenditure on average road schemes produces benefits in excess of four times their cost. Roads raise in terms of Fuel Duty and Vehicle Excise Duty (£40 billion p.a.) sufficient to cover their costs and potential improvements. That roads remain under supplied and irrationally priced, and that they struggle to gain sufficient resources, may reflect a public perception that they are paying general taxation rather than any specific charge for road use. On rail, fares are paid, and both the level of fares and the quality of service provided are issues of political and public contention.

This chapter has outlined the main changes, both in the main categories within public expenditure and in the type of project which was favoured. The move to spend a higher proportion of total public expenditure on health and social security was accompanied by a squeezing of the funds available for pubic fixed capital investment projects. The possibility of increasing the total size of the public expenditure budget was constrained by an electoral and political unwillingness to increase taxation for this purpose. Thus, while public expenditure as a share of total GDP remained reasonably constant, within that expenditure there was a shift from new investment to transfer payments. Often this was accompanied by an altered approach to the discussion of public investment which increased the emphasis on testing and discounting the potential benefits rather than underlining the ability of the government to fund such projects at a lower borrowing cost than the private sector. This shift in time perspective was reflected both in the decline in public sector net investment and also in the increased use of newer economic techniques within government, such as cost–benefit analysis. Most of the early projects, whether applied to roads or London underground lines, specifically sought to measure the economic value of time and of human life. This theme was to recur in discussions elsewhere, notably in health (see chapter 5) and the role

---

[104] Glaister and Smith, 'Roads: a utility', p. 370.

which should be played by market mechanisms in such approaches to the valuation of the future. Before moving on to a discussion of such uses of time, another area in which the state changed both its aims and mechanisms is discussed, namely the labour market and the evolving nature, both in time and space, of industrial policy.

Bibliography

Albin, Peter S., 'Uncertainty, information exchange and the theory of indicative planning', *The Economic Journal*, vol. 81, no. 321, March 1971, pp. 61–90.

Artis, M.J., and A.R. Nobay, 'Two aspects of the monetary debate', *National Institute Economic Review*, vol. 49, no. 1, August 1969, 33–51.

Bateman, Bradley W., 'Keynes and Keynesianism', in Roger E. Backhouse and Bradley W. Bateman, 2006, *The Cambridge Companion to Keynes*, Cambridge, Cambridge University Press, pp. 275–7.

Beesley, M.E., and C.D. Foster, 'The Victoria Line: Social benefits and finance', *Journal of the Royal Statistical Society*, Series A(general), vol. 128, no. 1, 1965, pp. 67–88.

Beesley, M.E., and J.F. Kain, 'Urban form, car ownership and public policy: an appraisal of "Traffic in Towns"', *Urban Studies*, 1, 1964, pp. 174–203.

Beesley, M.E., and J.F. Kain, 'Forecasting car ownership and use', *Urban Studies*, 2, 1965, pp. 163–85.

Britton, A.J.C., *Macroeconomic Policy in Britain, 1974-1987*, 1991, Cambridge: National Institute of Economic and Social Research, Cambridge University Press.

Brown, A.J., 'Inflation and the British sickness', *The Economic Journal*, vol. 89, no. 353, March 1979, pp. 1–12.

Buchanan, Colin, *Mixed Blessing: The Motor in Britain*, 1958, London: Leonard Hill.

Cairncross, Alec, and Barry Eichengreen, *Sterling in Decline: The Devaluations of 1931, 1949 and 1967*, 1983, Oxford: Basil Blackwell.

Caldwell, Bruce, (ed.), *The Collected Works of F.A. Hayek: vol. 9, Contra Keynes and Cambridge*, 1995, London: Routledge.

Caldwell, Bruce, 'Hayek and the Austrian tradition', in Edward Feser (ed.), *The Cambridge Companion to Hayek*, 2006, Cambridge: Cambridge University Press, pp. 13–35.

Central Statistical Office, *Economic Trends, Annual Supplement 1996 Edition*, 1995, London: HMSO.

Chick, Martin, *Industrial Policy in Britain, 1945-1951: Economic Planning, Nationalisation and the Labour Governments*, 1998, Cambridge: Cambridge University Press.

Clark, Tom, and Andrew Dilnot, *Long-Term Trends In British Taxation and Spending*, 2002, Institute for Fiscal Studies, Briefing Note, No. 25.

Clark, Tom, and Andrew Dilnot, *Measuring the UK Fiscal Stance Since The Second World War*, 2002, Institute for Fiscal Studies, Briefing Note No. 26.

Cobham, David, 'Convergence, divergence and realignment in British macroeconomics', *Banca Nazional del Lavoro Quarterly* Review, 149, 1984, pp. 159–76.

Congdon, Tim, 'The analytical foundations of the Medium-Term Financial Strategy', *Fiscal Studies*, vol. 5, no. 2, May 1984, pp. 17–29.

Congdon, Tim, *Reflections On Monetarism: Britain's Vain Search for a Successful Economic Strategy*, 1992, Aldershot: Edward Elgar.

Congdon, Tim, *Keynes, the Keynesians and Monetarism*, 2007, Cheltenham: Edward Elgar.

Crafts, N.F.R., 'Economic Growth', in N.F.R. Crafts and Nicholas Woodward, *The British Economy Since 1945*, 1991, Oxford, Oxford University Press, pp. 261–90.

Crafts, Nicholas, *Forging Ahead, Falling Behind and Fighting Back: British Economic Growth from the Industrial Revolution to the Financial Crisis*, 2018, Cambridge: Cambridge University Press.

Crawford, Rowena, Carl Emmerson, and Gemma Tetlow, *A Survey of Public Spending*, September 2009, IFS Briefing Note, BN 43, p. 16.

Davenport, Nicholas E.H., *Vested Interests or Common Pool?*, 1943, London: Victor Gollancz Ltd., p. 164.

Davidson, Paul, *John Maynard Keynes*, 2007, Basingstoke, Houndmills: Palgrave Macmillan.

Denison, E.F., *Why Growth Rates Differ: Postwar Experience in Western Countries*, 1967, Washington: Brookings Institution.

Feinstein, C.H., *Statistical Tables of National Income, Expenditure and Output of the U.K. 1955–1965*, 1972, Cambridge: Cambridge University Press, Table 39.

Feldstein, Martin S., 'Cost benefit analysis and investment in the public sector', *Public Administration*, vol. 42, no. 4, December 1964, pp. 351–72.

Florio, Massimo, *The Great Divestiture: Evaluating the Welfare Impact of the British Privatizations 1979–1997*, 2004, Cambridge, Mass.: The MIT Press.

Forder, James, *Macroeconomics and the Phillips Curve Myth*, 2014, Oxford: Oxford University Press.

Foster, C.D., and M.E. Beesley, 'Estimating the social benefit of constructing an underground railway in London', *Journal of the Royal Statistical Society*, vol. 126, 1963, pp. 46–58.

Friedman, Milton, with the assistance of Rose D. Friedman, *Capitalism and Freedom*, 2002 (originally published 1962), Chicago and London: The University of Chicago Press.

Friedman, M., 'The role of monetary policy', *American Economic* Review, vol. 58, no. 1, March 1968, pp. 1–17.

Friedman, Milton, 'Memorandum: Response to questionnaire on monetary policy', in Milton Friedman, *Monetarist Economics*, 1991, Oxford: Basil Blackwell, pp. 49–62.

Gazeley, Ian, 'Income and living standards, 1870–2010', in R. Floud, J. Humphries, and P. Johnson (eds.), *The Cambridge Economic History of Modern Britain: Vol. I. 1870 to the Present*, 2014, Cambridge: Cambridge University Press, pp. 151–80.

Glaister, Stephen, and John W. Smith, 'Roads: a utility in need of a strategy', *Oxford Review of Economic Policy*, vol. 25, no. 3, 2009, pp. 368–90.

Grout, P.A., 'The economics of the Private Finance Initiative', *Oxford Review of Economic Policy*, December 1997, vol. 13, issue 4, pp. 53–66.

Hahn, Frank, *Money and Inflation*, 1982, Oxford: Basil Blackwell.

Hall, P., 'The Buchanan Report: Forty years on', *Proceedings of the Institution of Civil Engineers: Transport*, 157, Issue TR1, February 2004, pp. 7–14.

Hammond, J. Daniel, *Theory and Measurement: Causality Issues in Milton Friedman's Monetary Economics*, 1996, Cambridge: Cambridge University Press.

Harcourt, G.C., *On Skidelsky's Keynes and Other Essays*, 2012, Basingstoke: Palgrave Macmillan.

Hart, Oliver D., 'Incomplete contracts and the theory of the firm', *Journal of Law, Economics and Organisation*, vol. 4, no. 1, Spring 1988, pp. 119–39.

Hatton, T.J. and K. Alec Chrystal, 'The Budget and fiscal policy', in N.F.R. Crafts and Nicholas Woodward (eds.), *The British Economy Since 1945*, 1991, Clarendon Press: Oxford, pp. 52–88.

Hayek, F.A., *Prices and Production*, 1931, London: Routledge.

Hayek, F.A., *Monetary Theory and the Trade Cycle*, 1933, London: Jonathan Cape.

Hayek, F.A., *The Pure Theory of Capital*, 1941, London: Macmillan.

Helm, Dieter, oral evidence to the House of Commons Treasury Committee on the Private Finance Initiative, 14 June 2011.

Hicks, John, *The Crisis in Keynesian Economics*, 1974, Oxford: Basil Blackwell.

Hill, T.P., 'Growth and investment according to international comparisons', *The Economic Journal*, vol. 74, no. 294, June 1964, pp. 287–304.

Howson, Susan., *Lionel Robbins*, 2011, Cambridge: Cambridge University Press.

Jackson, Ben., 'The think-tank archipelago: Thatcherism and neo-liberalism', in Ben Jackson and Robert Saunders, *Making Thatcher's Britain*, 2012, Cambridge: Cambridge University Press, pp. 43–61.

Jackson, P.M., 'The public expenditure cuts: rationale and consequences', *Fiscal Studies*, March 1980, vol. 1, issue 2, pp. 66–82.

Jackson, Peter, *The Private Finance Initiative: From The Foundations Up-A Primer*, 2004, Edinburgh: The David Hume Institute.

Johnson, Elizabeth (ed.), *The Collected Writings of John Maynard Keynes, vol. XV, Activities, 1906–1914: India and Cambridge*, 1971, London: The Royal Economic Society, Macmillan.

Kaldor, Nicholas, *The Scourge of Monetarism*, 1982, Oxford: Oxford University Press.

Kahn, Richard F., *The Making of Keynes' General Theory*, 1984, Cambridge: Cambridge University Press.

Keynes, John Maynard, *How To Pay for the War*, 1940, London: Macmillan.

Keynes, John Maynard, *The Means To Prosperity*, 1933, London: Macmillan. This pamphlet is an enlarged version of four articles printed in *The Times* in March 1933.

Keynes, John Maynard., Moggridge, Donald (ed.), *The General Theory of Employment, Interest and Money*, First edition 1936, paperback edition 1974, London: The Royal Economic Society and Macmillan.

Keynes, John Maynard, 'The end of Laissez-Faire (1926)', in *Essays in Persuasion*, 1963, W.W. Norton and Company, New York, pp. 312–22.

Keynes, J.M., *Activities, 1940–1946: Shaping the Post-war World; Employment and Commodities*, vol. 27 of *The Collected Writings of John Maynard Keynes*, 1980, Cambridge: Cambridge University Press for The Royal Economic Society.

Keith Joseph papers, Bodleian Library Oxford, KJ 10/6.

King, M.A., 'The U.K. profits crisis: Myth or reality?', *The Economic Journal*, vol. 85, no. 337, March 1975, pp. 33–54.

Kornai, J. and T. Liptak, 'Two-level planning', *Econometrica*, vol. 33, no. 1, Jan. 1965, pp. 141–69.

Kresge, Stephen, editorial forward to Bruce Caldwell(ed.), *Contra Keynes and Cambridge*, 1995, University of Chicago Press, Liberty Fund, Indianapolis, pp. ix–xi.

Lawson, Nigel, 'The British Experiment', in Forrest H. Capie and Geoffrey E. Wood, (eds.) *Policy Makers in Policy: The Mais Lectures*, 2001, London: Routledge.

Laidler, David, 'Hayek on Neutral Money and the Cycle', 1992, London, ON: Department of Economics, University of Western Ontario.

Laidler, David, *Fabricating the Keynesian Revolution: Studies of the Inter-War Literature on Money, the Cycle and Unemployment*, 1999, Cambridge, Cambridge University Press.

Laidler, D., 'Monetarism: An interpretation and an assessment', *The Economic Journal*, vol. 91, no. 361, March 1981, pp. 1–28.

Laidler, David, 'Monetary policy in Britain: Success and shortcomings', *Oxford Review of Economic Policy*, vol. 1, no. 1, Spring 1985, pp. 35–43.

Laidler, David and Michael Parkin, 'Inflation: A survey', *The Economic Journal*, vol. 85, no. 340, December 1975, pp. 741–809.

Leijonhufvud, Axel, 'Hicks on time and money', in D.A. Collard, D.R. Helm, M.F.G. Scott, and A.K. Sen (eds.), *Economic Theory and Hicksian Themes*, 1984, Oxford: Oxford University Press, pp. 26–46.

Lipsey, Richard, 'The relation between unemployment and the rate of change of money wage rates: a further analysis', *Economica*, N.S. 27, no. 105, Feb. 1960, pp. 1–13.

Lipsey, Richard G., 'The place of the Phillips Curve in macroeconomic models', in A.R. Bergstrom, A.J.L. Catt, M.H. Peston, and B.D.J. Silverston (eds.), *Stability and Inflation: A Volume of Essays to Honour the Memory of A. W.H.Phillips*, 1977, New York: John Wiley and Sons, pp. 49–75.

Lucas, R., 'Expectations and the neutrality of money', *Journal of Economic Theory*, 1972, vol. 4, issue 2, pp. 103–24.

Lucas, R., and L. Rapping, 'Real wages, employment and inflation', *Journal of Political Economy*, vol. 77, issue 5, 1969, pp. 721–54.

Malinvaud, E., 'Decentralized procedures for planning', in E. Malinvaud and Bacharach (eds.), *Activity Analysis in the Theory of Growth and Planning*, 1967, London: Macmillan, pp. 170–208.

Marglin, S.A., and Juliet B. Schor (eds.), *The Golden Age of Capitalism*, Oxford: Clarendon paperbacks, first published 1990, pbk. 1991.

Matthews, R.C.O., 'Why has Britain had full employment since the war?', *The Economic Journal*, vol. 78, no. 311, Sept. 1968, pp. 555–69.

Matthews, R.C.O., C.H. Feinstein, and J.C. Odling-Smee, *British Economic Growth, 1856–1973*, 1982, Oxford: Oxford University Press.

Meade, J.E., *The Theory of Indicative Planning*, 1970, Manchester: Manchester University Press.

Meade, J.E., 'Comment on the papers by Professors Laidler and Tobin', *The Economic Journal*, vol. 91, no. 361, March 1981, pp. 49–55.

Meade, J.E., *Full Employment Regained?* 1995, Cambridge: Cambridge University Press.

Middleton, Roger, *Government Versus The Market: The Growth of the Public Sector, Economic Management and British Economic Performance, c. 1890–1979*, 1996, Cheltenham: Edward Elgar.

OECD, *Towards Full Employment and Price Stability* (McCracken Report), 1977, Paris: OECD.

Offer, Avner, 'Patient and impatient capital: time horizons as market boundaries', Discussion Papers in Economic and Social History, University of Oxford, No. 165, August 2018.

Oliver, Michael J., *Whatever Happened to Monetarism? Economic Policy-Making and Social Learning in the United Kingdom since 1979*, 1997, Aldershot: Ashgate Publishing.

Peacock, Alan, and Jack Wiseman, assisted by Jindrich Veverka, *The Growth of Public Expenditure in the United Kingdom*, 1961, National Bureau of Economic Research, Princeton N.J.: Princeton University Press.

Peters, G.H., 'Cost benefit analysis and public expenditure', Eaton Paper No. 8, Institute of Economic Affairs, 1966.

Phillips, A.W., 'The relation between unemployment and the rate of change of money wage rates in the UK, 1861–1957', *Economica*, November 1958, N.S. 25, no. 100, pp. 283–99.

Prest, A.R., and R. Turvey, 'Cost Benefit Analysis : a Survey', *The Economic Journal*, vol. 75, no. 300, 1965, pp. 683–735.

Reynolds, D.J., 'The cost of road accidents', *Journal of the Royal Statistical Society*, Series A (general), vol. 119, no. 4, 1956, pp. 393–408.

Robertson, D.H., 'British national investment policy', in D.H. Robertson, *Utility And All That*, 1952, London: George Allen & Unwin, pp. 116–31.

Self, Peter, *Econocrats and the Policy Process: The Politics and Philosophy of Cost-Benefit Analysis*, 1975, Boulder, Colorado: Westview Press.

Short, Michael, Michael J. Pont, and Qiang Huang, 'Safety and reliability of distributed embedded systems: Simulation of motorway traffic flows', Technical Report ESL 04–02, 11 October 2004.

Skidelsky, Robert, 'Hayek versus Keynes: The road to reconciliation', in Edward Feser (ed.), *The Cambridge Companion to Hayek*, 2006, Cambridge: Cambridge University Press, pp. 82–110.

Sunstein, Cass R., *The Cost-Benefit Revolution*, 2018, The MIT Press, Cambridge, Mass.: London.

Thomson, J.M., 'Evaluation of two proposals for traffic restraint in Central London', *Journal of the Royal Statistical Society*, A30, vol. 130, part 3, 1967, pp. 327–77.

TNA ES 140/01, David Laidler (Department of Economics, University of Western Ontario, London, Ontario, Canada), Comments on 'Monetary targets and the Public Sector Borrowing Requirement' by P.E. Middleton, C.J, Mowl, J.C. Odling-Smee and C.J.Riley. Comments prepared for City University Conference, London, England, July 1979.

TNA MT 92/404, Note on 'Accident Costs', J Jukes, 19 August 1970.

TNA MT 92/404, Note by Gavin Mooney, 13 October 1970.

TNA MT 92/404, 'Differentiation of road casualty costs', memo, L. E. Dale, 30 December 1970.

TNA MT 92/481, Paper on 'Accident Cost Valuation', no date or signed author.

TNA MT 120/186, 'The Prediction and Evaluation of Road Accidents', paper by R.H. Bird 16 August 1965.

TNA MT 120/186, 'Differentiation of road casualty costs', paper by E Dale, 3rd December 1970.

TNA PREM 19/183, note of meeting on 18 July 1979 between Gordon Pepper and the Prime Minister, note, Tim Lankester, 25 July 1979.

Monthly Bulletin of W. Greenwell & Co. This included the Monthly Bulletin, No. 100. for January 1980, Appendix.

TNA PREM 19/197, Note of a discussion at Chequers, Sunday 13 July 1980.

TNA T316/85, 'Value of time in transport investment appraisals', note, J L Carr, 5 January 1970.

TNA T316/85, 'The value of time through time', paper, J. L. Carr, 12 January 1970.

TNA T326/1063, 'The case for easy money', note, R.G. Smethurst to M.V. Posner, 23 January 1970.

TNA T326/1065, 'The importance of money: summary', paper, Bank of England, C.A.E.G., 30 January 1970.

TNA T371/775, note, 'Public Expenditure Cuts 1979–80', Copy of a paper by Mr Cardone, Conservative Research Department.

TNA T378/89, 'Policy and the monetary aggregates', paper by K E Couzens for Treasury Bank of England Working Group, June 1976.

TNA T378/89, 'The exchange rate and monetary policy', paper by Peter Middleton, 13 September 1977.

TNA T388/196, 'The PSBR and the growth of money in the medium term', Paper by A J C Britton, 8 February 1980.

Wicksell, Knut, Interest and Prices, trans. R.F. Kahn, 1936, London: Macmillan.

Notes of a meeting in Chancellor of the Exchequer's office, 5 October 1979.

Cmnd.7746, The Government's Expenditure Plan 1980–81.

Memoranda on Monetary Policy, 1980, London: HMSO, p. 56.

H.M. Treasury, 1996, Treasury Committee, sixth report, The Private Finance Initiative.

3

Time, Labour Markets,
and Industrial Policy

In chapter 2 the rise and then falling away of fixed capital investment as a share of GDP was noted. Of that total investment, during the Golden Age investment in manufacturing formed just under one-quarter of total investment, with investment in dwellings being of a similar magnitude. Investment in gas, electricity, and water accounted for around 12% of total investment.[1] For much of the Golden Age, manufacturing industry was prioritized by government, not least as it was seen as the most likely source of productivity improvement, arising out of technological progress and economies of scale. This was reflected in the Wilson government's *National Plan* and that government paid particular attention to attempting to restructure and modernize designated sections of manufacturing industry. As the Golden Age ended, so too was there a reappraisal both of the aims of macro-economic policy, and of the aims and mechanisms of industrial policy. Not only did this reflect the mid-1970s concern with inflation, although in a context of rising unemployment, but it also arose from the changing perspective of the role and capabilities of the state. Again, as unemployment in manufacturing rose, so too in part did industrial policy move away from targeting help at manufacturing, and moved instead towards creating a supply-side system designed to encourage the growth of new industries.

The Structure of the Economy

The changes in the industrial structure of the economy were considerable, and are reflected in Table 3.1, which is restricted to manufacturing during the Golden Age, and in Table 3.2, which provides snapshots for 1970 and 2010 for all industries. In broad terms the proportionate contribution of agriculture, metals, mechanical engineering, textiles, and vehicles all fell,

---

[1] Central Statistical Office, *National Income and Expenditure: 1971.*

Table 3.1. Shares of value-added in manufacturing, 1951–1973 (percent)

	1951	1964	1973
Food, drink, tobacco	9.5%	11.0%	10.8%
Chemicals	7.2	8.8	7.6
Iron and steel	7.5	6.6	5.0
Electrical engineering	7.4	9.2	10.0
Mechanical engineering and shipbuilding	15.4	15.8	16.9
Vehicles	8.7	10.8	10.7
Other metal industries	7.6	7.9	8.7
Textiles	12.6	7.2	5.9
Clothing	4.9	3.8	3.5
Bricks, pottery, glass, cement	4.2	4.3	4.4
Timber, furniture	3.4	2.9	3.7
Paper, printing, publishing	7.8	7.8	8.5
Leather and other manufacturing	3.8	4.0	4.3
Total manufacturing	100.0	100.0	100.0

Source: Matthews, Feinstein, and Odling-Smee, *British Economic Growth, 1856–1973*, p. 239, Table 2.6.

while that of the business and service sector as well as hotels, retailing, communications, health, and education rose. Some sectors such as construction and its supply industries, such as brick-making and cement, made a fairly constant proportionate contribution, while the fortunes of others such as coal mining declined, as those of gas and oil improved.

Accompanying these shifts in the structure of the economy, were shifts in the distribution of employment. In general from 1973, as employment in manufacturing fell by 5.5 million between 1973 and 2010, that in banking and services rose by 4.8 million. Employment in education, health, and other services also rose by 4.9 million, such that total employment rose from 22.7 million in 1973 to 30.8 million in 2010.[2] Over a slightly longer period and expressed in terms of comparative sectors, in the UK in 1950 46.5% of labour was employed in industry and 28.5% in 1990. This proportionate decline of labour in industry was less in the US. where industry's sectoral share of employment in 1950 was 32.9%, and 21.8%. Outstanding was Germany where industry's sectoral share of employment was 42.1% in 1950 and still 39.7% in 1990. This contrast was also specifically evident in manufacturing where in Germany the share of employment was 31.4% in both 1950 and 1990 compared with the UK (34.9% in 1950 and 20.1% in 1990) and the US. (25% in 1950 and 15.3% in 1990).[3] The corollary of the industrial

---

[2] Griffiths and Wall, *Applied Economics*, Table 1.4.
[3] Broadberry, *Market* Services, Table 4.3.

Table 3.2. Value added by industry as share of GDP (%) Selected industries, 1970 and 2000

Industry	1970	2010
Agriculture	2.85	1.08
Oil and gas	0.07	2.78
Coal and other mining	1.04	0.3
Chemicals and pharmaceuticals	2.06	1.9
Basic metals and metal goods	3.65	1.99
Mechanical engineering	7.79	1.51
Electrical engineering and electronics	2.52	2.68
Vehicles	3.89	1.91
Food, drink, and tobacco	3.07	2.51
Textiles, clothing, and leather	3.64	0.81
Paper, printing, and publishing	1.89	2.53
Other manufacturing	2.31	2.01
Construction	6.02	5.38
Wholesale, vehicle sales, and repairs	7.8	7.04
Retailing	4.03	5.53
Hotels and catering	2.12	3.45
Communications	2.37	3.2
Finance	5.78	4.99
Business services (excluding housing services)	5.76	17.00
Public administration and defence	6.26	5.01
Education	4.18	6.06
Health and social work	3.31	6.91
Others	17.59	13.42
Whole economy	100.0	100.0

Source: Nicholas Oulton and Sylaja Srinivasan, 'Productivity growth in UK industries, 1970–2000: structural change and the role of ICT', *Bank of England Working Paper*, no. 259, 2005.

employment shares was the sectoral share of employment of services which rose in all three economies, but from and to a lower level in Germany: UK (48.4% in 1950 to 69.5% in 1990); US. (56.1% in 1950 to 75.7% in 1990); and Germany (33.6% in 1950 to 56.9% in 1990).[4]

What was striking about the movement of labour out of manufacturing in the UK was its pace and intensity.[5] Unemployment in manufacturing industries increased by 89% between 1980 and 1981 and by 158% between 1979 and 1982 (see Table 3.3). Between 1980 and 1981 the jumps in unemployment in metal manufacture (104%) dominated by iron and steel and metal goods (121%), mechanical engineering (115%), and vehicles (160%) were eye-catching, while total unemployment increased by just over 70% between

---

[4] Broadberry, *Market* Services, Table 2.3.
[5] Singh, 'UK industry'; Matthews and Sargent, *Contemporary Problems*, p. 1; Blackaby, *Deindustrialisation*; Rowthorn and Wells, *De-Industrialisation*.

Table 3.3. Number unemployed in Great Britain, selected industries at June in each year

	1977	1978	1979	1980	1981	1982
Total, all industries and services (1)	1,285,716	1,324,866	1,238,468	1,441,389	2,456,883	2,856,465
Total manufacturing industries	330,576	333,668	314,036	399,714	754,928	811,401
Agriculture, forestry, fishing	23,738	24,087	21,845	22,722	37,844	43,359
Mining and quarrying	16,595	22,125	23,321	24,835	31,648	37,604
Food, drink and tobacco	40,408	43,971	40,340	47,259	72,504	86,622
Coke and petroleum products	2,274	2,057	2,049	2,259	3,647	5,073
Chemicals and allied industries	16,408	16,457	15,490	19,003	33,602	38,388
Metal manufacture	23,622	27,542	25,433	35,741	72,929	72,741
Mechanical engineering	38,063	36,915	34,877	45,169	97,108	100,916
Electrical engineering	26,830	26,798	25,227	30,762	60,503	65,439
Shipbuilding and marine engineering	9,038	8,970	9,987	13,316	16,170	16,093
Vehicles	20,818	19,577	19,660	23,540	61,258	75,920
Metal goods, not elsewhere specified	33,426	33,364	31,728	38,893	86,064	88,683
Textiles	26,547	27,572	24,991	34,985	59,018	57,953
Paper, printing, and publishing	18,621	17,295	16,264	18,754	38,141	42,135
Construction	204,108	186,480	160,012	189,554	356,862	366,354
Gas, electricity, and water	9,213	8,617	7,687	7,589	10,199	13,451
Transport and communication	59,667	58,419	54,334	63,415	105,733	121,784
Distributive trades	131,740	132,680	122,787	146,723	238,046	285,690
Insurance, banking, finance, and business services	28,828	28,126	27,657	34,252	55,408	64,997
Professional and scientific services	48,313	54,082	53,713	61,074	90,268	110,610
Public administration and defence	68,686	76,181	72,323	77,023	105,475	130,731

Sources: CSO, *Annual Abstract of Statistics*, 1981 edition, London: HMSO, 1981, no. 117, Table 6.7.
1981 data from CSO, *Annual Abstract of Statistics*, 1982, London: HMSO, 1982, no. 118, Table 6.7.
1982 data from CSO, *Annual Abstract of Statistics*, 1983, London: HMSO, 1983, no. 119, Table 6.7.

1980 and 1981.[6] As manufacturers of internationally traded goods, these industries were subject to competition in their export and domestic markets. Not only did the two oil price hikes of 1973/4 and 1979/80 raise their energy costs while reducing aggregate demand as expenditure on oil increased its share of industrial and household budgets, but the UK's accession to the E.E.C. on 1 January 1973 also intensified competition. So too did the appreciation of the exchange rate, moving from $1.80 in 1976 to $2.32 in 1980.[7] Manufacturing output did subsequently partially recover, passing its 1973 peak in 1990, although by 2009 it had trended down again to its 1973 level.[8]

Unemployment and Employment

The rise in unemployment from the 1970s marked a sharp break with the labour market of the Golden Age. That unemployment was so low for over two decades following the end of World War II surprised many politicians and economists. While their immediate concern was to prevent a repetition of the boom and bust conditions which followed World War I, most assumed that the longer-term concern would be with unemployment, with private investment being a source of weakness.[9] In fact, the average rate of unemployment of the civilian working population was 1.9% between 1951 and 1973, compared with 4.4% in 1857–1913, and 10.6% in 1920–1938.[10] The unemployment rate did then peak at 11.8% in 1984, although by 2016 the unemployment rate of 4.9% was almost back down to its 1975 rate of 4.5%. Nonetheless, while between 1951 and 1970 the level of unemployment was never higher than 1 million people, thereafter it was never again to fall below 1 million. That remains so, even when allowance is made for changes in definitions and measures of unemployment.[11] Yet, at the same time as unemployment rose, so too often did the number in employment. The size of the workforce in 1994

---

[6] General iron and steel manufacture, steel tubes and iron castings combined accounted for over three quarters (76.8%) of employment in 'metal manufacture' in 1976.

[7] Broadberry, 'The performance of manufacturing', p. 65; Central Statistical Office, *Economic Trends, Annual Supplement, 1996*, p. 223, Table 5.1.

[8] Griffiths and Wall, *Applied Economics*, p. 4.

[9] Beveridge, 'The government's employment policy'.

[10] Matthews, Feinstein, and Odling-Smee, *British Economic Growth, 1856–1973*, p. 81, Table 3.18.

[11] Estimates of the number unemployed vary depending on the definition of unemployment. The rate of unemployment also varies depending on the definition of unemployment (numerator) and the definition of what constitutes the labour force or working population (denominator). For example, in 1986 two groups were added to the denominator: the self-employed and those on government training schemes. Increasing the denominator reduces the rate of unemployment. Also see footnote 14 of chapter 1 and Gregg, 'Out for the count'.

was over 2.8 million higher than it had been in 1971. Over the 1971–1994 period the number in employment rose by almost 1 million from 24.5 million in 1971 to 25.5 million in 1994.[12]

Part of the increase in the size of the workforce was accounted for by the increased participation of women. Some of this was a response to rising unemployment among men. As the male unemployment rate rose from 2% in the 1950s to 17% in 1985, so other household members looked for paid work to make up some of the lost household income.[13] The number of women in paid work rose from 7 million in 1951 to 9 million in 1971 and 13 million in 2000.[14] Most of this increase in female participation occurred in the second half of the twentieth century and was mainly due to a higher proportion of married women working. The ability of married women to work was enhanced by an increased, if expensive, supply of childcare and also by an ability to limit their fertility by the use of contraception. The fertility rate per thousand women aged fifteen to forty-four in Britain almost halved from 115 in 1900–1902 to 60 in 1997, with a commensurate fall in the average household size from around 4.6 people in 1900, to fewer than 3 people by 1971 and to 2.4 people per household in 2002.[15] Marriage bars, which had required women to stop work in certain occupations on getting married, were removed in the 1940s and 1950s. Partly as a result, the gender composition of the labour force changed, as too did the gender participation rate. In 1901 the participation rate of men aged fifteen and over was 96%; in 2002 it was 71%. The participation rate of women rose from 36% in 1901 to 56% by 2002.[16]

The incentives for married women to undertake paid employment arose in part from the higher opportunity cost of not working.[17] Women in well-paid work were aware of the career penalties that they might pay for extended maternity breaks and were likely to return to work. Married women may also have worked because of the increased probability of marriages ending in divorce. In England and Wales, the Divorce Reform Act in 1971 added separation and unreasonable behaviour to the existing grounds of adultery and

---

[12] CSO, *Economic Trends*, Annual Supplement, 1996 edition, Table 3.2; Labour Force Survey, Office for National Statistics.
[13] Layard and Nickell, 'Unemployment in Britain', p. 121.
[14] Connolly and Gregory, 'Women and work'.
[15] Horrell, 'The household', p. 121.   [16] Horrell, 'The household', p. 117.
[17] Horrell, 'The household', p. 120. Horrell also reminds readers of the importance of the work of Gary Becker and Jacob Mincer on the allocation of time within the household, and between the household and the paid workplace. Becker, 'A theory of the allocation of time'; Becker, *A Treatise on the Family*; Mincer, 'Labour force participation'.

desertion and formed part of a move towards easier, no-fault divorces. This transferred power within the marriage from the spouse least wanting a divorce to the spouse most wanting it. The divorce rate rose to 30% in 1975 and to 53% in 1995.[18] One result of the increase in the female participation rate was a shift in the income composition of households. Whereas single income 'breadwinner' households formed 36.8% of all households in 1975, this had more than halved to 17.6% by 2001. Over the same period, 1975–2001, work-less households rose from 6.5% to 16.6%, and all-worker households rose 56.7 to 65.8% of households.[19] The Equal Pay Act was passed in 1970, resulting in the abolition of separate pay scales for women workers from 1975. Female relative hourly earnings rose sharply between 1970 and 1977, and by 2010 full-time female earnings had risen from about two-thirds of that of men in 1973 to around four-fifths by 2010.[20]

Industrial Policy, 1951–1970

The rapid shedding of labour in manufacturing which characterized dein-dustrialization both reflected the effects of the first Thatcher government's controversial macroeconomic policy, as well as the impact of increased com-petitive pressures on industries with productivity problems. None of this was inevitable. Germany retained a strong manufacturing sector, and yet manu-facturing had been at the core of UK industrial policy since 1951.[21] This par-ticular interest in manufacturing was identified especially with the Hungarian economist Nicholas Kaldor and, to a lesser extent, his countryman Thomas Balogh, both of whom variously acted as economic advisors to the Labour governments between 1964 and 1976.[22] Essentially Kaldor argued that the faster the rate of growth of the manufacturing sector of the economy, then the faster the rate of growth of total output, this arising from induced productivity gains inside and outside manufacturing. For Kaldor, manufacturing was the sector where the major labour-saving advances in technology occurred, and the sector most subject to increasing returns (both static and dynamic).

---

[18] Horrell, 'The household'.   [19] Gazeley and Newell, 'Introduction', p. 4.
[20] Gazeley, 'Income and living standards, 1870–2010', p. 158.
[21] Scott, 'British regional policy, 1945–51', p. 368.
[22] Thirlwall, *Kaldor*, p. 230. Balogh was appointed as Advisor on Economic Affairs to the Cabinet and Kaldor as Special Advisor to the Chancellor, James Callaghan (1964–1967). Kaldor was to per-form a similar role for two other Labour Chancellors, Roy Jenkins (1967–1968) and Denis Healey (1974 to 1976).

In viewing manufacturing as a greater source of static and dynamic economies of scale, Kaldor drew on the earlier teachings of his former LSE economics lecturer Allyn Young and on the observed relationship between productivity growth and output growth in manufacturing industry which became known as Verdoorn's Law after Kaldor's popularization of Verdoorn's 1949 paper.[23] The Selective Employment Tax (SET) which came into effect on 5 September 1966 was one policy outcome of this thinking.[24] This tax on labour was designed to encourage the substitution of capital for labour and, being rebatable in the public sector and transport at a rate of 130%, was effectively a subsidy in manufacturing industry and a tax on services of about 7% of labour costs.[25]

As a favoured source of economies of scale and improvements in productivity, then where the structure of an industry was thought to be inhibiting the achievement of economies of scale, interest was shown in restructuring that industry. Groups like Political and Economic Planning wrote at length on the need to restructure old, sometimes first industrial revolution industries. Industrial restructuring was a constant of productivity reports, and in 1958, Duncan Burn, the industrial correspondent (1940–1962) of *The Times* edited a two-volume study devoted to the structure of British industry.[26] The question was how best to effect the desired restructuring. There was scepticism as to the ability of market mechanisms to rationalize industries, and little political taste for the political and social costs of their doing so. As Raymond Streat, Chairman of the Cotton Board informed Lancashire MPs in September 1944, most official proposals for modernizing the industry favoured price management since they 'can think of no other alternative to jungle warfare, in which both capital and labour would be lost to the industry never to return or to be regained'.[27] This scepticism as to the effectiveness of market mechanisms for the purposes of restructuring industries was to persist in industrial policy for much of the Golden Age. While at a microeconomic level Kaldor was well aware of the importance of prices as signalling devices, neither he nor Balogh had any delusions as to the extent to which markets were perfect and

[23] Thirlwall, *Kaldor*, pp. 184–5, 189; Thirlwall, 'Rowthorn's Interpretation of Verdoorn's Law'; Verdoorn, 'Fattori che regolano'; Sandilands, 'Nicholas Kaldor's notes'; Young, 'Increasing returns'. Allyn Young left Harvard to succeed Edwin Cannan as Professor of Political Economy in the University of London in 1927, but died soon afterwards from pneumonia in 1929 aged fifty-two.

[24] *Selective Employment Tax*, Cmnd. 2986, 1966.

[25] Graham, 'Industrial Policy', p. 188; Whitley and Worswick, 'The productivity effects'; Reddaway, 'The productivity effects'.

[26] Burn, *The Structure of British Industry*, 2 vols., 1958; Political and Economic Planning, 'The Machine Tool Industry'.

[27] Chick, *Industrial Policy*, p. 170.

competitive. One worry they shared was that any process of industrial restructuring would simply be dominated by the large firms in each industry, although the concern with market power ranked below that with industrial structure and was ambivalent. Balogh did 'not think that it is the abuse of monopoly power that we are suffering from in the main so much as the inefficiency of the small firm'.[28] The concern with the abuse of market power was not so much of an aggressive monopolistic restriction of output, but rather that companies would settle back into enjoying a monopolist's 'quiet life'. As Tony Crosland, the President of the Board of Trade (1967–1969) put it:

> The threat from these giant concerns is not usually that they will be too ruthless or too little public spirited; rather for psychological and sociological reasons which I explained in *The Conservative Enemy* this is most unlikely. It is rather that they will become complacent, un-dynamic and un-enterprising with the passage of time (like, for example, ICI).[29]

Industrial Restructuring

Reflecting his scepticism of how markets worked in practice, Balogh opposed an approach to industrial restructuring by means of monopolies and restrictive practices legislation as in the Monopolies Bill, 'as being based on the philosophy of efficiency through greater competition'[30] and he was as sceptical of 'the Monopolies Commission aspect of the situation as the Restrictive Practices Registrar end' as 'both have been conceived...in the pure dogma of perfect competition, which is completely irrelevant'.[31]

One potential approach to restructuring an industry was to nationalize it and restructure it within its new public monopoly form. Such an approach was commonly advanced for the iron and steel industry, and the industry was nationalized in 1951 during the twilight days of the second Attlee government, before being subsequently denationalized in 1953 during Churchill's Conservative government. The weight of past fixed capital investment sat heavily on the iron and steel industry. Essentially the industry had a structure in which too many plants produced too little in too many places. One part of

---

[28] TNA PREM 13/401, Note, Balogh, February 1965.
[29] Tomlinson, *The Labour Governments 1964-1970*, p. 114; TNA BT 258/2658, Crosland, 24 September 1968; TNA PREM 13/2795, McIntosh, 'Industrial policy', April 1969.
[30] TNA PREM 13/401, Balogh, Note, 'Monopolies Bill', 23rd February 1965.
[31] TNA PREM 13/400, Balogh, 'The Reorganisation of Industry', September 1965.

the problem was that old plant could still be operated at a profit. As with other older industries like cotton, it was not clear why owners should invest in a new plant if they were making profits using older plant whose capital costs were fully paid up. In cotton, a working party led by the City financier Sir George Schuster recognized that a mill equipped in 1906 and now with no capital charges might see little advantage in installing a new plant and that 'from the mere profit-earning stand-point it might well *pay* an individual owner best to take advantage of present easy markets, work his machinery till it is worn out, and then go out of business'.[32] In addition, in the interwar steel industry Richard Thomas had almost gone bankrupt taking on debt in order to expand, and when the dynamic Allan MacDiarmid had moved Stewarts & Lloyds' operation from Scotland to Corby to improve its resource-cost base, the industry's federation, the British Iron and Steel Federation (BISF), had sought to reduce Stewarts & Lloyds competitive advantage by devising cost-pooling arrangements. One major concern for steelmen was that if they built new modern blast furnaces enjoying potentially large economies of scale, would they be able to achieve a sufficient level of capacity utilization of their new plant? The persistence of old, smaller but fully paid-up plants owned by their competitors might prevent that. As a response to the threat of nationalization, the BISF had published a First (1946) and then a Second Plan (1952) in which the modernization and rationalization of the industry was to the fore. Yet, the plant and integrated operations of the First Plan took longer to construct than intended and during that time small plants planned for closure made incremental 'patch-and-mend' investment as to compete against the new plant sufficiently to reduce its capacity utilization. By 1965 the structure of the steel industry in Britain was such as to still have forty-one steel plants, thirty-one of which produced less than 1 million tons, and twenty-three less than half a million tons. It was still short on integrated operations, although ironically the technological basis of the industry began to change, notably in a shift towards the basic oxygen steelmaking (BOS) technology as well as using electric mini-arc smelters and 'mini-mills' which allowed the minimum efficient scale of production to fall. By 1965 only 20% of British steel was made using the BOS process, but the BOS process made 300 tons of steel in thirty-five minutes, while the old open-hearth furnaces required twelve hours.[33] It became increasingly difficult for the British steel industry to compete internationally.[34] Using

---

[32] Working Party Reports, *Cotton*, pp. 69, 75, 90.
[33] Pagnamenta and Overy, *Working Lives*, p. 94.
[34] Broadberry, *The Productivity Race*, p. 309.

the mix of new technology, Japan increased its share of the world steel market from 6% in 1960 to 16% by 1983,[35] UK output fell as did its productivity as plant capacity utilization declined. In Germany output per hour was 125% of the British level in 1973, but 263% by 1979.[36] While once it had been possible to combine low productivity and profit-making, that ceased to apply from the mid-1970s.

A milder approach than nationalization towards restructuring industries was attempted in the establishment of the Industrial Reorganisation Corporation (IRC) in January 1966.[37] In 1965, as part of the Labour Wilson's government plan for the modernization and growth of the economy, its main planning department, the DEA, identified industries for restructuring. Those targeted included the machine tool, computer, motor car, aircraft, general engineering, heavy electricity and electronics industries. Increasing concentration in these industries was seen as a necessary prelude to their becoming more competitive with their international, and especially American, competitors.[38] In fact, in its short life, the IRC was to devote much of its attention to the motor vehicle manufacturing industry, supporting the merger of British Motor Holdings (Austin-Morris-MG and Jaguar) and Leyland Motors (Leyland and Standard) and then lending the resulting British Leyland £10 million to help it buy tools.[39]

Accompanying the Wilson government's plans for the industrial restructuring, were those for industrial modernization. In October 1964, a Ministry of Technology (MinTech) was established which showed an early interest in computers, electronics, machine tools, and telecommunications. One strand of MinTech's approach was to try to improve the flow of expertise and information available to industries, such as by establishing 'scientific neddies' staffed by academic and industrial experts in R&D, science, engineering, computing, management, and business organization and methods. These 'scientific neddies' would determine best practice, and then pass on their recommendations to one or more of the 'little Neddies' which were established for sections of industry. In turn the 'Little Neddy' would undertake a strictly economic assessment aided (and supervised) by the representative of the Technological Committee. Once MinTech had established what constituted

---

[35] Lieberman and Johnson, 'Comparative productivity', p. 2.
[36] Broadberry, *The Productivity Race*, p. 15.
[37] TNA PREM 13/400, Balogh, note, 'Technology', February 1965.
[38] TNA PREM 13/401, Balogh, note, 'Monopolies Bill', February 1965; Broadberry, *The Productivity Race*, p. 326.
[39] Kramer, *State Capital*, p. 3; Hague and Wilkinson, *The IRC*.

minimum acceptable and available standards of performance on the basis of testing machines and processes, then tax advantages, government guarantees, and subsidies would only be offered to investments meeting these standards, not least 'so as to ensure longer runs and advantages of large-scale production'.[40] This association between modernization and industrial restructuring typified MinTech's sponsoring of industrial research schemes through the National Research Development Corporation. As well as improving information flows, it encouraged various UK computer manufacturers to merge to form International Computers Limited (ICL) in 1968. The state took a 10% shareholding in the new company and provided £50 million funding for research and development.[41]

In time during the 1964–1970 Labour governments MinTech's area of responsibility broadened to take in engineering, shipbuilding, and, following its amalgamation with the Ministry of Aviation in February 1967, seemingly almost all government research and development as well as large parts of its industrial procurement.[42] As its ambit widened to include industries for which structural issues were central to productivity, so too did the concerns of MinTech overlap those of the IRC. This Venn diagram of responsibility also began to approximate to a similarity of approach as MinTech under its Minister of Technology, Tony Benn began to push for greater powers of industrial intervention which it gained in the Industrial Expansion Act of 1968, enabling it to fund selected projects without recourse back to Parliament.[43] The provisions of the 1968 Industrial Expansion Act were first used by the government in March 1968 to effect a merger between the computer businesses of ICT, English Electric, and Plessey.[44] Neither the Treasury nor the Confederation of British Industry (CBI) liked the 1968 Industrial Expansion Act, the former worried about its potential implications for public expenditure and the latter concerned at further government intervention in industries. However, the Industrial Expansion Act's bark proved worse than its bite. In practice, it did not unleash a new expansion of industrial spending, and no new industrial boards were ever established. Ultimately, in 1968, with the abolition of the Ministry of Power and the DEA, MinTech, almost as the last man standing, was to take in the steel and fuel industries and the IRC.

---

[40] TNA PREM 13/401, Balogh, note to Chancellor of the Exchequer, February 1965.
[41] Kramer, State Capital, p. 3; Hendry, Innovating for Failure.
[42] Tomlinson, Labour Governments 1964–1970, pp. 105–6; TNA PREM 13/1550, Wilson, 'Ministry of Aviation', November 1966; TNA T325/145, 'The Ministry of Technology', November 1967.
[43] Industrial Expansion (Cmnd. 3509, 1968); Graham, 'Industrial Policy', p. 195.
[44] Industrial Investment: The Computers Mergers Project (Cmnd. 3660, 1968).

Rethinking Industrial Policy in the 1970s

With the passing of the Wilson government in 1970 came to an end a period of attempted economic planning and a technocratic-administered restructuring and modernization of industry. The immediate response of the newly elected Conservative Heath government was to abolish the IRC and MinTech, withdraw investment grants, repeal the Industrial Development Act, and create a giant Department of Trade and Industry. In an early whiff of the shape of things to come, it sought to revive industry by encouraging competition and providing tax incentives. However, in fairly short order, these policy reversals were subsumed by economic events as Rolls Royce, bankrupted in 1971 by its ill-fated RB-211 aircraft engine, and a substantial portion of the shipbuilding industry (including Upper Clyde Shipbuilders (UCS) and Harland & Wolff) were effectively nationalized and investment grants (made over as regional development grants) were reintroduced.[45]

Yet, while the Heath government may have suffered setbacks in its attempt to move away from the Wilson governments' approach to industrial policy, the context in which any industrial policy operated, its mechanisms and aims were all to change over the course of the 1970s. In part, it was simply the changed economic circumstances of the 1970s in which unemployment began to rise which altered some of the concerns of industrial policy. Also important in influencing the development of any industrial policy was the general context of the 1970s in which public finances were tightening, in which the role and instruments of government were being reassessed, and in which consideration of the UK's growth performance was coming increasingly to question the priority given to the manufacturing industry. By the middle of the 1970s, the assumptions, aims, and mechanisms of industrial policy were all being fundamentally reassessed, both inside and outside government.

Inside government, Harold Lever, a businessman and Chancellor of the Duchy of Lancaster (1974–1979), began to criticize Kaldor's prioritization of the needs of manufacturing industry. In June 1975 Nicholas Kaldor and Harold Lever each sent papers to the prime minister arguing over the comparative importance of the manufacturing and service sectors of the economy.[46] Lever was supported by Tony Crosland.[47] When Lever questioned

---

[45] TNA T342/429, Pliatzky, paper, 'Industrial Policy', June 1975, para. 8.
[46] TNA PREM 16/363, Robson, note, S A Robson, July 1975; Graham, 'Industrial Policy' p. 210; Hall, 'Are goods and services different?'.
[47] TNA PREM16/503, Crosland, letter, July 1975.

the priority shown to manufacturing industry, Kaldor returned to his export-led growth hypothesis.[48] In Kaldor's view,

> All fast growing advanced countries are characterized by a rate of growth of manufacturing output which is in excess of the rate of growth of the GDP as a whole; and in all such countries the rate of growth of exports of manufactures was considerably in excess of the rate of growth of the total output of manufactures.[49]

Kaldor's work, Verdoorn's Law, and the criticisms made by economist Bob Rowthorn were discussed in the Treasury in the mid-1970s in the light of the economist Stanislaw Gomulka's 1976 work on the importance of technological innovation and diffusion. Essentially this formed part of the Treasury's own re-evaluation of its understanding of the sources of long-run economic growth.[50]

The Treasury had been particularly provoked into action, or reaction, by the appointment of Tony Benn as Secretary of State for Industry(1974–1975). In his 1974 Green Paper on the 'The Regeneration of British Industry', Benn proposed that a National Enterprise Board be established to channel investment into priority sections of manufacturing industry. These priorities were no longer those of industrial restructuring and modernization, but were widened to include other aims such as participation in companies so as to 'create a better social atmosphere in industry', to 'improve management-labour relations', 'to assist regional policy', and 'to increase accountability to society'. As Benn acknowledged, the Green Paper was 'really an argument' which he subsequently decided to 'underplay', but Treasury officials criticized its pervasive 'sense of populism' and its 'lack of any apparent limitation envisaged on the degree of dirigisme'. During his sixteen months as Secretary of State for Industry between March 1974 and June 1975, Tony Benn developed an unerring ability to provoke Treasury officials. In response to Benn's industrial policy, Treasury mandarins such as Pliatzky and Ryrie launched a fundamental reconsideration of the aims, criteria, and mechanisms of industrial policy.[51] One of their discussion papers was entitled simply 'How to deal with Mr Benn'.[52] Amidst public finance difficulties the Treasury increasingly preferred to view projects through the optic of their likely rate of return

---

[48] TNA PREM 16/503, Lever, letter, August 1975.

[49] TNA PREM 16/363, Kaldor, paper, 'The role of manufacturing industry', para. 9; Thirlwall, *Kaldor*, p. 184; Kaldor, 'Productivity and growth'.

[50] C56 PRO 30/87/156, CES WN 447, Hyman, paper, 'Ramifications of Gomulka's refutation', by G. Hyman, January 1977, p. 8.

[51] TNA T342/339, Pliatzky, letter, June 1974.

[52] TNA T342/340, Ryrie, note, 'How to Deal with Mr. Benn', November 1974, paras. 2–4.

on capital. Benn's interest in assisting worker cooperatives found little empathy in the Treasury, which also remained sceptical of Benn's efforts to obtain financial support for the Scottish Daily News, International Property Development (IPD), Meriden and Aston Martin, all of which had previously been refused as being commercially unviable. The Treasury was also very concerned at Benn's willingness to 'use public ownership in the first instance as an ambulance for failed firms'[53] and that a number of 'lame ducks' would drop into the National Enterprise Board's (NEB) lap. The most important of these were British Leyland (BL); Rolls Royce (the plane engine maker), Alfred Herbert, a major machine tool manufacturer, and Ferranti, which like Rolls Royce, did much work for the Ministry of Defence.[54] Indeed, the government did have to step in to bail out BL, first with a £50 million guarantee in December 1974 while Sir Don Ryder, the head of the NEB, prepared a report on the company and then subsequently by nationalizing the company in 1975 and agreeing to inject £1.4 million over eight years as part of a rescue package. In December 1975 the government also had to bail out Chrysler UK and commit to injecting £162.5 million over four years.[55] By that time, Tony Benn had been moved from Industry to Energy in June 1975 after campaigning for a NO vote in the referendum on the UK's continued membership of the EEC.

The arguments over industrial policy inside government found their echoes outside government too, in newspapers, on television, and within the Conservative and Labour parties. In the *Financial Times* contributions were made by opposition politicians like Keith Joseph and journalists like Samuel Brittan. In the Labour Party, tensions between the future SDP politician, Shirley Williams, and the more left-wing Tony Benn emerged in industrial policy. In response to an earlier paper by Tony Benn on 'A Ten-Year Industrial Strategy for Britain', Shirley Williams submitted a differing paper of her own to the Labour Party's Industrial Policy Sub-Committee.[56] Two months later, at a dinner party hosted by Samuel Brittan, Adam Ridley (economic adviser to the shadow cabinet of Margaret Thatcher) met Walter Eltis (economics lecturer at Oxford University), and Ridley subsequently brought Eltis to Margaret Thatcher's notice in a letter of 2 October 1975. Extracts from the book, *Too Few Producers*, co-authored by Eltis and his Oxford colleague R. W. Bacon of Lincoln College) were subsequently published in *The Sunday Times*. Eltis and

---

[53] Benn, *Against the Tide.*

[54] Kramer, *State Capital,* p. 10; Church, *The Rise and Decline*; Redwood, *Going for Broke.*

[55] Broadberry, *The Productivity Race,* p. 324; Adeney, *The Motor Makers,* p. 281; Young and Hood, *Chrysler UK,* p. 287.

[56] TNA PREM 16/363, Kaldor, paper, 'The role of manufacturing', June 1975, para 1; TNA PREM 16/503, Williams, letter, 'Investment and Growth', July 1975.

Bacon prioritized the needs of a 'wealth-producing' section of the economy whose interest rate–elastic private sector could be crowded out by debt-financed public expenditure.[57] That employment in the manufacturing sector had fallen by 1 million between 1966 and 1976 while employment in the public sector had grown by 1 million might be viewed as a growth of the non-market (i.e. mainly public) sector of the economy at the expense of the market (i.e. private) sector, but even if this view was accepted, the gender balance of the labour shed and recruited differed. Much of the growth of public sector employment was amongst part-time married females, while it was mainly males leaving the manufacturing industry. Although Bacon and Eltis's analysis is often criticized for having a Physiocratic flavour in that a distinction seemed to be made between a market-wealth-creating (manufacturing) sector of the economy and a financially dependent non-wealth-creating public sector, what is more striking is their supply price of finance approach. If the private sector was not able to earn returns which allowed it to compete effectively with the public sector for funds, perhaps it should not have been obtaining that finance anyway.

Changing Horses: Unemployment and Inflation

Distinctions between wealth-creating and other economic activities became more common as the seventies progressed. In similar vein, distinctions also began to be drawn between jobs and 'real jobs', not least when Prime Minister Jim Callaghan announced that the pursuit of a low rate of inflation was to be preferred to a low rate of unemployment as the principal aim of government economic policy. In a passage written by his son-in-law Peter Jay, Callaghan informed the Labour Party Conference in Blackpool in 1976 of the government's new thinking:

> we used to think that you could spend your way out of a recession, and increase employment by cutting taxes and boosting government spending. I tell you in all candour that that option no longer exists, and that in so far as it ever did exist, it only worked on each occasion since the war by injecting a bigger dose of inflation into the economy, followed by a higher level of unemployment as the next step. Higher inflation followed by higher unemployment. We have

---

[57] Keith Joseph papers, KJ 10/5, Eltis, letter, September 1975; Keith Joseph papers, KJ 10/5, Ridley, letter, October 1975. Eltis replied to Ridley that he was 'very agreeably surprised to see the depth of Mrs. Thatcher's and Sir Geoffrey Howe's analysis of what had happened to the economy, and what needs to be done'. Kirby, *The Decline*.

just escaped from the highest rate of inflation this country has known; we have not yet escaped from the consequences: high unemployment. This is the history of the last 20 years.[58]

Callaghan's statement was not so far from Milton Friedman's view that 'what recent British governments have tried to do is to keep unemployment below the natural rate, and to do so they have had to accelerate inflation.'[59] As with industrial policy, the overwhelming sense in macroeconomic policy discussions was that the existing way of doing things was no longer working. The prevailing view for policy purposes had been that of A.W. Phillips, he of the eponymous curve, and the Phillips Curve was subsequently supported by work from Richard Lipsey, based, like Phillips, at the LSE. In his article in the journal *Economica* in November 1958 Phillips noted that for the peacetime years 1861–1956 in the UK the rate at which the nominal wage level changed was a decreasing function of the rate of unemployment. A rate of unemployment of 2–3% seemed to hold the rate of inflation at 2–3%; an unemployment rate of 6–8% seemed to take inflation to zero. The Phillips Curve was criticized by some economists, but so long as Golden Age conditions persisted, government was thought to use it as one means of guiding the economy. Once stagflation appeared, then it became difficult to maintain unthinking adherence to the Phillips Curve and the criticisms began to be listened to. These came from different sources but proved complementary. In part, they placed greater emphasis on the microeconomic underpinnings of macroeconomic policy. Some like Edmund Phelps at Columbia University, as in his edited book *Microeconomic Foundations of Employment and Inflation Theory*, emphasized the intertemporal aspect of wage negotiations and the accelerationist implications of trying to hold unemployment down below its equilibrium level.[60] There was also a move towards applying rational expectations, as originally developed by John Muth in 1961, with developments around a very micro model by R. E. Lucas and in an inter-temporal one by T. J. Sargent.[61] The criticism was that governments which sought to trade off price stability against reduced unemployment ultimately encouraged expectations of regularly increasing wages. Such thinking meshed with Milton Friedman's idea of there being a Natural Rate of Unemployment (NRU) which itself referred back to Irving Fisher's 1926 article, 'A statistical relation between

---

[58] Callaghan, presentation of the Parliamentary Labour Party report, 1976.
[59] Friedman, *Price Theory*, p. 227; Friedman, *Unemployment versus Inflation*.
[60] Phelps, 'Money wage dynamics', p. 227; Phelps, 'Phillips Curves'.
[61] Muth, 'Rational expectations'; Sargent, 'Rational expectations'; Lucas, 'Expectations'; Lucas, 'Some international evidence'.

unemployment and price changes'.[62] The NRU was that rate of employment which was consistent with the existing real conditions in the labour market. Friedman was particularly critical of Phillips's presentation of the demand and supply of labour as being functions of nominal wages, instead of real wages. Friedman saw the rate of wage change as being a function of the unemployment rate plus the expected rate of price inflation, the implicit rationale being that the amount of labour supplied was an increasing function of the expected real value of the nominal wage.[63]

A potential danger of the NRU approach was that it would be seen by politicians as absolving them from political responsibility for what was happening to unemployment.[64] That the Natural Rate Hypothesis would convince policymakers that the rate of unemployment was in the long run independent of the demand-side policies of the government. In the short run, downturns might be interpreted as cyclical movements around and below the natural rate, but the critical issue here was the extent to which short-term cyclical unemployment turned in time into long-term structural unemployment. It was in this context that, following the fall in public sector capital formation, the appreciation of the exchange rate, and the sharp increase in unemployment since 1975, that the 1980 MTFS was highly contentious. In seeking to create a creditable economic strategy so as to manage inflationary expectations downwards, it also adopted a pro-cyclical policy during a slump. The extent to which stocks nosedived in 1980, 1981, and 1982 is striking. As the economist John Hicks noted, this run down of stocks may in turn have reduced any scope for relying on the multiplier to increase economic activity (see Table 3.4). The concern was with the extent to which a pro-cyclical policy increased cyclical unemployment which mutated in time into structural unemployment. In the 1980s economies with larger decreases in inflation and longer disinflationary periods experienced larger increases in their natural rates of unemployment.[65]

What became of increasing concern in the 1980s was not simply the level of unemployment but its persistence even as inflation fell. That as inflation

---

[62] Friedman, 'The role of monetary policy'.

[63] The idea that a steady state of unemployment existed within a dynamic general equilibrium system had existed for some time, but it was Friedman who coined the term 'natural rate'. He likened this to Wicksell's natural rate of interest, in that both sought to distinguish between the real and monetary forces. In this sense, the natural rate as developed by Friedman and Phelps did not correspond to any particular rate of inflation because there could be no long-run trade-off between inflation and unemployment; there was no long-run money illusion and the long-run Phillips curve was vertical.

[64] Hahn, 'Theoretical reflections' on the 'natural rate of unemployment', p. 44.

[65] Ball, 'Hysteresis'; Ball, 'Disinflation'; Ball, Mankiw, and Nordhaus, 'Aggregate demand'; Ball and Mankiw, 'The NAIRU'.

Table 3.4. Stock changes £ million, current prices

	Mining and quarrying	Manufacturing	Electricity, gas, and water supply	Wholesale distribution	Retail distribution	Other industries	All industries
1965	-2	322	35	47	23	36	461
1970	-48	314	-18	111	-6	29	382
1971	29	-162	38	154	8	47	114
1972	-10	-169	1	114	18	71	25
1973	-10	718	-22	312	264	267	1,529
1974	-39	1,086	-6	323	-152	-167	1,045
1975	193	-1,063	98	-247	-91	-244	-1,354
1976	-24	396	73	182	271	3	901
1977	26	807	-88	544	51	484	1,824
1978	112	255	10	560	456	411	1,804
1979	-87	359	-73	1,061	481	421	2,162
1980	302	-2,546	135	-392	-429	358	-2,572
1981	-26	-2,115	130	-260	190	-687	-2,768
1982	108	-1,855	441	-68	1	185	-1,188
1983	-101	-3	432	169	-35	1,003	1,465
1984	-41	836	-445	12	465	470	1,296
1985	-314	-493	373	-85	267	1,073	821
1986	-115	-555	-28	237	720	423	682
1987	-34	-335	-93	587	755	348	1,228
1988	24	873	37	971	791	1,637	4,333
1989	214	164	113	775	346	1,065	2,677
1990	-103	-1,913	-129	-552	181	716	-1,800
1991	172	-3,769	177	-648	-401	-458	-4,927
1992	74	-1,544	-136	96	230	-657	-1,937
1993	-71	-1,544	-253	843	411	912	329
1994	-210	1,231	-533	511	953	1,352	3,303

Source: Central Statistical Office, *Economic Trends: Annual Supplement, 1996 edition*, London: HMSO, 1995, Table 4.7.

slowed the NRU settled at 3 million suggested that an effect of any cyclical unemployment had in fact been to add to structural unemployment. Labour which had remained in unemployment had atrophied. Although by the 1980s, marginal tax rates had fallen, union powers had been curtailed, and the benefit:wage replacement ratio had been reduced, still the NRU was higher than it had been in the inflationary 1970s. In the comparatively low inflation Britain of the 1950s and 1960s, there were roughly twice as many vacancies as unemployed; in the 1980s boom, there were twice as many unemployed as vacancies.[66] Some of the grander claims made by Milton Friedman in his 1976 Nobel Lecture that it was only by *reducing* the rate of inflation that unemployment would be reduced in the long run begged questions as to the length of the long run and raised questions as to whether the rate of unemployment, if related on the way down to inflation, was now less natural than it had been.[67] Among economists, the NAIRU (Non-Accelerating Inflation Rate of Unemployment) came to be preferred to the NRU, in designating the equilibrium rate of unemployment.

As the stock of long-term unemployed grew, so the supply of available labour was lower than it would otherwise have been. Inasmuch as this represented an inward shift of the labour supply curve, wages rates rose and exceeded the rate of inflation. While recent increases in unemployment would add to the number of short-term unemployed and would have a moderating influence on wage claims, as in time the previously short-term joined the ranks of the long-term, so wage claims would rise again. As such, the equilibrium rate of unemployment rose.[68] Employers themselves appeared to be biased against employing the long-term unemployed and used unemployment duration as a screening device. In contrast to the rational expectations approach of drawing the future back into the present, this view of the labour market emphasized the influence of the past on the present. Phelps noted this, arguing that inasmuch as the existing stock of unemployed weighed on current wage negotiations then there may have been a hysteresis effect in unemployment.[69] Hysteresis, a term hailing from the world of electro-magnetic fields and referring to a remaining effect after the original disturbance has been removed, recognizes the dependence of a system on both past and current inputs. Accepting the influence of the past on the present also emphasized the

---

[66]   Nickell, 'Unemployment: Questions and Some Answers', pp. 815–16.
[67]   Friedman, 'Inflation and Unemployment'.
[68]   Burgess and Turon, 'Unemployment dynamics in Britain', p. 445.
[69]   Cross, 'Phelps'; Phelps, *Inflation Policy and Unemployment Theory*; Phelps, 'Phillips curves'.

sequential, rather than the static state, nature of economic decision-making and admitted different times into the moment of decision-making.[70]

For the unemployed, over time their work experience faded, their job-specific skills decayed, and in some cases their former places of work no longer existed. Long-term unemployment was such that by April 1986 of all the male unemployed over the age of twenty-five, over one-half had been on the unemployment register for more than a year. Over a third had been unemployed for at least two years, and more than a quarter had been unemployed for over three years. The UK had more long-term unemployed (defined as more than a year out of work) than any other EEC country, and accounted for almost 30% of all EEC long-term unemployed. Among the unemployed, particular groups stood out. One was the young, especially the under twenties who were more than twice as likely to enter unemployment than any of the over twenty-five age groups and had a 25% chance of entering unemployment in any one year.[71] This reflected in part their high degree of job mobility which resulted in turn from their low levels of specific human capital and the relatively low current costs of unemployment. Their age-related duration data also suggested that it was easier for them to find work again. The probability of entering unemployment fell sharply with age, reaching its lowest level in the forty to fifty-four age group before rising again in old age. Expected durations, on the other hand, rose steadily with age, reflecting the increasing difficulty of finding suitable alternative employment as individuals aged. The unmarried had a much higher incidence of unemployment than their married counterparts, and among the married, those with a large number (four or more) of children had very high unemployment rates.[72] This may have been because the considerable discrepancy in the level of state-provided family support between those in work and those out of work caused men with large families to prolong their unemployment spells in the search for relatively highly paid work.[73] Comparing a year group of married and unmarried men, unmarried men aged thirty-nine had more than a 50% higher incidence of unemployment than their married counterparts, the majority of which may be accounted for by the higher duration of the unmarried. Their probability of entry was only 20% greater. This seems to indicate either that unmarried individuals were more likely to extend their unemployment spells, perhaps because there was less pressure on them to take up another job, or that

---

[70] Nickell, 'Unemployment: A Survey'; Cross, 'Hysteresis'; Rod Cross (ed.), *The Natural Rate of Unemployment*; Hicks, *Economic Perspectives*, p. vii.

[71] Nickell, 'A picture of male unemployment', p. 779.

[72] Nickell, 'A Picture of Male Unemployment in Britain', p. 784.

[73] Daniel and Stilgoe, *Where Are They Now?*.

prospective employers preferred married men because they regarded them as more reliable. There was some casual evidence in favour of this latter proposition and unmarried men of that age were known to be more likely to suffer from such illnesses as mental instability and alcoholism than their married counterparts.

Trade Unions

To the increasing contrast between the industrial policy and macro-economic policy of the Golden Age and that which emerged from the mid-1970s could be added a significant change in governments' approaches to industrial relations. In a break with governments' more consensual approach to industrial relations in the Golden Age, the Thatcher governments passed a series of laws designed to place industrial relations on a more contractual and prescribed basis. This contractual approach reflected some long-standing concerns among employers at the inability of unions at times to enforce agreements, and the perceived infringements on personal liberty represented by some aspects of trade union behaviour. Through this optic which emphasized individual and property rights, trade unions could be viewed as instruments of private coercion employing intimidatory tactics such as mass picketing, and irresponsibly exploiting their freedom from torts and their ability to impose costs with impunity.[74]

Steadily, new laws were passed which curtailed unions' scope for action. The 1980 and 1982 Employment Acts required the closed shop to be agreed by 80% of the workforce, narrowed trade immunity for lawful picketing, made ballots compulsory before strike action could be taken, outlawed secondary strike action, and made it possible to sue unions if they were found to be in breach of the legislation.[75] The Trade Union Act 1984 required senior union officials to be elected by secret ballot and made trade unions' legal immunity for organizing industrial action conditional on the holding of secret ballots.[76] It also withdrew the immunities from official industrial action which had not been the subject of a valid vote. The Employment Act of 1988 gave trade union members the right to refuse to be union member and it also prevented unions from disciplining members who did not support industrial action,

---

[74] Hayek, *The Constitution of Liberty.*
[75] Kondylis and Wadsworth, 'Wages and wage inequality'; Metcalf, 'Trade unions'.
[76] Richardson, 'Trade Unions', p. 431.

even if approved by ballot. In 1990 the Employment Act removed the final immunity from all forms of secondary industrial action.[77] This increased emphasis on a legislative and legal approach to trade unions marked a move towards the view of the relationship between law and economics favoured by Hayek. Margaret Thatcher's liking of Hayek was much more for his writings on law, liberty, and economics, than for any of his work on capital and economic theory. For Hayek, freedom was the absence of coercion, in which powerful interests including government, was subject to the impartial rule of law.[78] Importantly though for Hayek, these laws did not arise from a rush of government legislation, but rather reflected a long-standing, preferably pre-existing, general rule of law.[79]

The use of legislation against unions marked a break in the traditional 'voluntary principle' approach to industrial relations which Professor Wedderburn of the LSE saw as an expression of the fact that 'most workers want nothing more of the law than that it should leave them alone.'[80] Wedderburn, a leading figure in the development of labour law in the UK, was sympathetic to collective bargaining and critical of Hayek's approach to labour relations.[81] Such a pragmatic, flexible, and non-legalistic approach was supposed to encourage 'responsibility'.[82] However, precisely because it was non-legal and voluntary it did not favour stronger legal recognition being given to unions and to collective bargaining, which in turn contributed to an environment in which unions could struggle to deliver on negotiated agreements and where shop stewards struck deals at plant level.[83] It also placed unions in a strange legal position in which formally, given the primacy of the law of contract, there was no legal right to strike and nor were employers legally obliged to recognize trade unions. For this reason, the judicial decision in the 1964 *Rookes v Barnard* judgement in which the House of Lords removed the immunity against legal actions for threatening or inducing a breach of employment contracts which union officers had previously been assumed to enjoy in trade disputes, unsurprisingly caused consternation. Since virtually all strikes involved just such a breach, the judgment was construed as a fundamental attack on the freedom of collective bargaining which unions had thought established for the best

[77]   Atkinson, *Inequality: What Can Be Done?*, p. 130.
[78]   Brittan, *Capitalism and the Permissive Society*, p. 91.
[79]   Brittan, *Capitalism and the Permissive Society*, pp. 96–7; Brittan, *Against the Flow*, p. 310–1.
[80]   TNA LAB 28/365, 'Memorandum of evidence', Flanders, November 1966, p. 24; Wedderburn, *The Worker and the Law*, p. 11.
[81]   Wedderburn, 'Freedom of association'.
[82]   TNA LAB 28/365, 'Memorandum of evidence', Flanders, November 1966, p. 25; Flanders, *Industrial Relations*, p. 32.
[83]   TNA LAB 28/365, 'Memorandum of evidence', Flanders, pp. 10, 28.

part of a century, and which was confirmed by the Trades Disputes Act of 1906. The Labour government restored the legal status quo in the 1965 Trade Disputes Act in return for trade union cooperation on incomes policy and their agreement to the establishment of a Royal Commission (the Donovan Commission) to investigate the state of industrial relations.

The Donovan Commission sat as concern with unofficial or wildcat strikes by unions members grew. The question arose as to whether sanctions could be devised for use against unofficial strikers. Among industrialists, there was concern that if agreements were not honoured, that some recompense and/ or penalty should be available. In a meeting between Harold Wilson and representatives of the motor vehicle industry on 3 September 1965, Lord Rootes argued that since in his view most of the strikes in the motor vehicle manufacturing were unofficial, this demonstrated that 'the voluntary principle had proved inadequate (and that) there should be power to impose penalties on employers, unions or employees who did not honour agreements which they had entered into.'[84] Government also had a growing concern that a 'public interest, third-party' component was missing from the conduct of industrial relations. Two notable legislative approaches to addressing the public effects of unofficial strikes were the Labour government's *In Place of Strife* which did not make it to the statute book and the Conservative government's Industrial Relations Act of 1971 which, obviously, did. Both aimed to circumscribe the right to strike by making unofficial strikes unlawful, and in particular sought to force the unions, via statutory imposition, to police their own rank and file. The underlying philosophy of this legislation was less of an attempt to abandon voluntarism than an exercise to ensure that it worked.[85] The main weakness of this legislation was that it did not take account of the extent of the decentralization and radicalization of the trade union movement. The legislation was seen as having an over-attachment to the rule of law and a blatantly antiunion character, an impression enhanced when trade unionists were jailed (for contempt of the Industrial Court) after refusing to obey legal instructions to abandon picketing.[86] With the return of a Labour government in 1974, the Industrial Relations Act 1971 was repealed in the Trade Union and Labour Relations Act of 1974.

---

[84] TNA PREM 13/402, meeting, Prime Minister and motor industry representatives, September 1965.

[85] Hyman, 1980, p. 133.

[86] TNA CAB 184/150, GEN 181(74), memorandum, 'Imprisonment under the Industrial Relations Act', para. 1. 'Imprisonment is not a remedy available to the Industrial Court on a complaint of unfair industrial practice under the Industrial Relations Act. But, like the High Court, the Industrial Court has powers of committal in cases of contempt. It was these powers that led to the imprisonment of the five dockers in 1972.'

Industrial Disputes

The move towards a legislative approach to trade unions came against the background of the 1970s when it was asserted that union power needed to be curbed. As unemployment rose in the 1970s, so too did the incidence of industrial action (see Table 3.5). Not only was there a higher number of days lost because of stoppages, but the dramatic conflicts stand out in the data (mining, metals, engineering, shipbuilding and vehicles). There was also considerable variety in the nature of strikes. Some focused on wages. Beginning with the miners' strikes of 1971/1972 and 1974, these originated as a straightforward effort to raise wages and to improve working conditions. Miners' wages had fallen relatively for much of the 1960s as increasing use of oil and the mechanization of coal cutting and conveying reduced the industry's demand for labour. The number of wage-earners employed at collieries had fallen from over 700,000 in 1950–1957 to below 300,000 by 1970 while over the same period miners' weekly earnings fell from first place to sixth in the ranking of manual workers' wages. Then as world oil prices rose in the 1970s, so too did the new leader of the National Union of Mineworkers (NUM), Joe Gormley, take the chance to push for higher wages even if at the cost of jobs.[87] Overtime bans were followed by national strikes in 1972 and 1974, the first since 1926, with a three-day week being instituted by the government from the start of 1974. Calling a general election for the 28 February 1974, the Heath government lost, and the incoming Labour government settled with the miners.

In 1979 it was the turn of the Labour government's re-election campaign to be damaged by the recent memory of a national industrial dispute. This was the 1978–1979 'winter of discontent' which Prime Minister James Callaghan, a son of Portsmouth, was unable to make 'glorious summer', limping off instead after defeat in the 3 May 1979 general election to join Eden as the second post-war prime minister never to have won a general election. The public sector strikes of 1978/79 marked the end of attempts to enforce an incomes policy. Beginning as a social compact in 1974 designed to obtain zero real wage growth through consensus, it mutated into a social contract and a phased incomes and prices policy from July 1975. Phase 1 imposed flat-rate increases of £6 a week, and an annual upper income limit, of £8,500, beyond which no wage increases were allowed. Phase 2 of the policy, in July 1976, reduced the nominal increase maximum to £4 a week. By 1978, as real wages fell, not least as the exchange rate rose, so the incomes policy

---

[87] Carruth and Oswald, 'Miners' Wages', pp. 1009–10.

Table 3.5. Working days lost each year through all stoppages in progress, 1970–1982 United Kingdom (thousands)

	1970	1971	1972	1973	1974	1975	1976	1977	1978	1979	1980	1981	1982
All industries and services	10,980	13,551	23,909	7,197	14,750	6,012	3,284	10,142	9,405	29,474	11,964	4,266	5,313
Mining & quarrying	1,092	65	10,800	91	5,628	56	78	97	201	128	166	237	374
Metals, engineering shipbuilding, and vehicles	4,540	6,035	6,636	4,800	5,837	3,932	1,977	6,133	5,985	20,390	10,155	1,731	1,457
Textiles	192	58	236	140	236	257	39	208	131	72	36	20	45
Clothing and footwear	192	13	38	53	19	93	26	56	47	38	8	19	21
Construction	242	255	4,188	176	252	247	570	297	416	834	281	86	44
Transport and communications	1,313	6,539	876	331	705	422	132	301	360	1,420	253	359	1,675
All other industries and services	3,409	586	1,135	1,608	2,072	1,006	461	3,050	2,264	6,594	1,065	1,814	1,697

Notes: This data shows the total working days lost within each year as a result of stoppages in progress in that year whether beginning in that or an earlier year. Figures are based on the Standard Industrial Classification 1968.

Sources: 1970–1979, Central Statistical Office, *Annual Abstract of Statistics, 1981 edition*, London: HMSO, 1981, Table 6.15; 1980–1982, Central Statistical Office, *Annual Abstract of Statistics, 1984 edition*, London: HMSO, 1984, Table 6.14.

began to unravel. The Trades Union Congress (TUC) was unable to get its member unions to continue adhering to the policy and a return to free collective bargaining ensued. The Phase 2 government-recommended nominal pay increase norm of 5% was not rescinded, but in the main it was not adhered to.[88]

Governments' industrial disputes with the miners in the first half of the 1970s and with public sector workers towards the end of the decade essentially concerned wages and had considerable effects on the general public whether in electricity blackouts, the three-day week, or the unburied bodies and uncollected rubbish of the discontented winter. As unemployment rose, so strikes came increasingly to concern job security. Some of the most notable instances of industrial action occurred in more newly nationalized companies like the British Steel Corporation (BSC), British Leyland (BL), and Upper Clyde Shipbuilders (UCS). These strikes were highly televisual, whether it was workers gathered in the BL car park at Longbridge or Jimmy Reid leading the UCS work-in in June 1971 designed to show that the shipyards on the Clyde were viable.

The strikes could be hard-fought, with bitter consequences for the strikers. After BSC losses climbed from £309.4m in 1978/9 to £545m in 1979/8, in December 1979 the BSC management informed the steel unions that 60,000 jobs would go within the year, and the union called what became a thirteen-week and ultimately unsuccessful strike in early 1980. In May 1980, Ian MacGregor succeeded Sir Charles Villiers as the BSC's chairman and closures began. The BSC workforce fell from 186,000 in 1979 to 81,100 by 1982/3.[89] Similarly, the miners' strike of 1984/5 called by the new leader of the NUM, Arthur Scargill in the spring of 1984, concerned jobs, was highly televisual and did raise questions as to the economic cost/benefits of the rate of run-down of the coal mining industry.[90] Strikers often faced a new generation of managers with a more aggressive approach to industrial conflict. New social norms were reflected in the more direct, less consensual style of Michael Edwardes (South Africa), who from 1977 took on the task of rationalizing plants and models to bring BL 'Back From The Brink'; John Harvey Jones, who slimmed down and broke up ICI after it reported its first loss in its history in the third quarter of 1980; Graham Day (Canada) at British Shipbuilders; and Ian MacGregor (U.S.) at British Steel and then at

[88] Kondylis and Wadsworth, 'Wages and wage inequality', p. 83.
[89] Abromeit, *British Steel*, pp. 141–2.
[90] Carruth and Oswald, 'Miners' wages'; Glyn, 'The economic case against pit closures'; Glyn and Machin, *Colliery Closures*; Cooper and Hopper, *Debating Coal Closures*.

the National Coal Board where he referred to his own workforce as 'The Enemy Within'.[91]

The strikes in the motor vehicle and newspaper industries increasingly centred on the threat posed to employment from the introduction of new technology. From the early days of Henry Ford's introduction of flow-assembly production in Britain in 1913, the accommodation of time and its implications for the mix of capital and labour had been a central issue in motor vehicle manufacturing. Concerned to control the rate of production in assembly line production, Ford had paid fixed-day wages in place of the usual piece-rate payments. With wages fixed and higher than the piece-rates earned elsewhere, Ford's management had a strong incentive to replace labour with capital, and to run the more-capital intensive production line as hard as possible.[92] In the first year of the transition to flow production, Ford doubled labour productivity.[93] Managers in UK-owned motor vehicle manufacturers were less willing to adopt Fordist techniques fundamentally because they were unconfident of their ability to obtain the requisite rate and level of output from their workforce. Unlike Ford, they often had larger workforces which reflected the firms' origins in an industrial past in which firms engineered their own components. Not only was the workforce larger, but it was organized around many different and often craft-based unions. Also, having much higher levels of external financing than Ford, managers and owners may have been keen to maintain the stronger relationship between output and labour costs embodied in piece-rate wages than in fixed-day rates. Against a background of low unemployment and lacking sufficient control of the workforce, managers continued to be reluctant to raise their fixed capital costs by investing in new fixed capital investment.[94] The outcome was a perception that unions and management were dominated by 'an institutional conservatism that is seriously hampering technological change'.[95] Put formally and theoretically, where binding contracts were absent and the firm was unconfident of the *ex post* returns or concerned that the returns would flow to labour rather than to capital, then new fixed capital investment formation was likely to have been restricted.[96]

[91] Pettigrew, *The Awakening* Giant.

[92] Lewchuk, *American Technology*, pp.2, 56; Piore and Sabel, *The Second Industrial Divide*; Tolliday and Zeitlin, *The Power To Manage?*; Broadberry, *The Productivity Race*.

[93] Lewchuk, *American Technology*, p. 56.

[94] TNA LAB 28/365, 'Memorandum of evidence', Flanders, November 1966, pp. 16, 25.

[95] TNA LAB 28/281, Royal Commission on Trade Unions, 'evidence', Roberts, March 1966, p. 1; Broadberry, 'Why was unemployment in post-war Britain so low?'.

[96] TNA LAB 28/365, 'Memorandum of evidence', Flanders, November 1966, p. 3; Crafts, 'Deindustrialisation and Economic Growth'. Crafts also cites work by Pratten and Atkinson, and by

One consequence of the managerial reluctance to move more quickly to capital-intensive assembly flow production, was that it effectively negotiated output levels through piece-rate negotiations with union representatives. While specific industrial appellations could apply (as will be seen in newspapers), these union representatives were generally known as shop stewards, of whom there were 175,000 in 1968.[97] Elected by their workmates to whom their prime responsibility lay, these shop stewards had detailed knowledge of very local conditions. If they wished to master the arcane, they could develop a specialist knowledge of the established working practices which underpinned job demarcation but whose details were rarely to be found in craft union rule books. In managing its workforce, a fundamental problem for management, and one by no means confined to the motor vehicle industry, was that it proved difficult to secure centrally negotiated and observed pay and conditions agreements. While a union, or even the TUC, might negotiate pay and conditions agreements with managers, there was no guarantee that these would always be adhered to on the shop floor. Practical negotiations often continued to occur on the shop floor between local managers and shop stewards with national agreements almost coming to be seen as providing a base level from which more rewarding local negotiations could begin.[98] That local disputes and stoppages could have a significant impact on production only strengthened the hands of shop stewards. When in June 1966, there was a stoppage over the piece-work rates of sixty machinists at Standard-Triumph's Coventry plant, more than 14,000 of 15,000 workers at five factories in Coventry, Birmingham, and Liverpool became idle.[99] Where the collateral effects were disproportionate to the size of the local dispute, managers were likely to concede on issues so as to keep production going. By doing so they increased the power of the local, well-informed shop stewards whose credibility and that of their local workforce had little to do with the formal trade union structure.[100] When Michael Edwardes took charge of British Leyland in 1977, he was shown a daily list of disputes which often ran to five sheets. He noted that it 'was to be three years before the daily dispute sheets dwindled to the point where I was able to discontinue them'.[101]

Prais suggesting that 'difficulties over manning levels reduced productivity improvements from introducing new technology'. Prais and A.G. Atkinson, 'The use of manpower'; Prais, *Productivity*.

[97] Crafts, *Forging Ahead*, p. 96.   [98] Turner, 'The Donovan Report'.
[99] TNA LAB 28/365, 'Memorandum of evidence',Flanders, November 1966, p. 19. *Financial Times*, 7 June 1966.
[100] TNA LAB 28/365, 'Memorandum of evidence', Flanders, November 1966, p. 15.
[101] Edwardes, *Back from the Brink*, p. 15; Rhys, *The Motor Industry*, p. 445; Broadberry, *The Productivity Race*, p. 322.

As Ford almost doubled its share of UK car production from 15.4% in 1947 to 28.4% in 1967, so a series of panic mergers were effected among increasingly loss-making UK-owned car manufacturers. In addition to the early post-war mergers, notably those between Standard and Triumph in 1945 and then in 1952 between Austin and Morris to form the British Motor Corporation (BMC), in 1966, BMC merged with the Jaguar Group to form British Motor Holdings (BMH). In 1968 BMH in turn merged with the Leyland Motor Corporation to form the British Leyland Motor Corporation (BLMC).[102] Yet by 1965 fixed capital per employee in Ford UK was £2,903, compared with £882 in British Leyland in 1969.[103] Creating ever larger companies which lacked economies of scale, capital-intensive forms of production, and long-run narrow product ranges provided an inadequate base from which to survive in the increasingly competitive motor vehicle market from the 1970s. By 1989 the BMC/BLMC/Rover group accounted for 35% of UK car production compared with Ford's 29.5%, Vauxhall's 16%, and the 8.3% of the Rootes/Chrysler/Peugeot group.

The difficulties of the UK motor vehicle industry had long roots and while the unions attracted the ire of newspaper commentators in the 1970s and 1980s, the question of why shop stewards enjoyed such alleged influence was asked less often. Not that those in the newspaper industry itself should have been throwing stones. For some time, restrictive and the pejoratively termed 'old Spanish customs' had been of concern to owners of the newspapers. Fathers of the chapel (FoC) operating in a closed shop arguably wielded more power than motor vehicle shop stewards. A chapel was a union shop-floor grouping in printing, and closed shops were either of a pre-entry type requiring union membership before starting work, or, more commonly, post-entry where the union was joined shortly after starting work.[104] As with shop stewards in motor vehicles, so too in newspapers, was the closest loyalty to the chapel fathers. Chapels protected entry into the trade and had their historic origins not in trade unions but in 'societies' and 'associations' which could trace their history through successive apprenticeship laws and regulations back as far as the Elizabethan Statute of Artificers. Of the leading unions, the

---

[102] Broadberry and Leunig, *The Impact of Government Policies on UK Manufacturing*, p. 20.
[103] Lewchuk in Elbaum and Lazonick, *Decline*.
[104] R. Richardson, 'Trade unions and industrial relations', in N.F.R. Crafts and Nicholas Woodward (eds.), *The British Economy*, pp. 417–42, p. 424. Richardson notes that the first major study of the closed shop was by McCarthy(1964) who concluded that the closed shop tended to occur where 'it was almost a necessity if trade unionism was to function at all'. W.E.G. McCarthy, *The Closed Shop in Britain*. By the end of the 1970s about 25% of the workforce was employed in closed shops.

National Graphical Association (NGA) was strongest among compositors while most of the paper handlers and publishing and distribution workers belonged to the Society of Graphical and Allied Trades (SOGAT).[105] That the FoCs wielded such power was in part because of the timeous nature of newspaper publishing and because the proprietors let this accretion of power occur rather than risk further disruption to print runs. As Simon Jenkins, the former editor of *The Times* and the *Evening Standard*, commented: 'In Fleet Street, strikes used to be relatively rare: they were seldom required. The threat of a disruptive chapel meeting was usually sufficient to push management to resolve matters at speed.'[106]

By the 1970s, managers appeared to be more willing to confront such longstanding issues and working practices. In the newspaper industry, during the 1970s, falling profits and then losses together with the increasingly attractive prospect of higher returns on new technology if it could be introduced successfully emboldened management to take on the unions. The technological shift was essentially to litho offset printing, common everywhere except in newspapers, with electronic composition, in place of the highly skilled but technologically redundant techniques of compositing slug lines of metal type or even handpicking mono-type and placing it with spacers into screw-tightened frames. Ultimately the stand-off between the management and the unions resulted in the non-appearance in 1978–1979 of *The Times* and *The Sunday Times*, the papers' sale by the Thomson Organisation to Rupert Murdoch's News International, and his move of print technology out of Fleet Street to Wapping in 1986 amidst fierce union opposition. Less successful were the efforts of Eddie Shah to introduce colour print technology in *Today* in 1986. Few of the issues which were fought over were new. In 1971, in a meeting with Lord Rothschild (Central Policy Review Staff, a government think tank) on the long-term viability of the industry, Marmaduke Hussey, chief executive of *The Times* viewed 'most issues as marginal to the stranglehold of the unions on the industry (which) had resulted in gross overmanning and absurdly high wages and could only be changed by a major confrontation with and defeat of the unions in a prolonged strike'.[107]

Yet for all of the attention given to strikes in the steel, shipbuilding, motor vehicle, newspaper, and coal-mining industries, by international standards the British record on strikes and stoppages looked no worse than that of its

---

[105] Jenkins, *Newspapers*, pp. 48–9; Cleverley, *The Fleet Street Disaster*; Sisson, *Industrial Relations in Fleet Street*.

[106] Jenkins, *Newspapers*, p. 54.

[107] TNA CAB 184/77, meeting, Rothschild and Hussey, December 1971.

Table 3.6. Average weeks of work lost per year though holidays, sickness, and industrial disputes, 1913–1973

	Holidays	Sickness	Industrial Disputes	Total
1913	1.4	1.7	0.07	3.2
1924	2.1	2.2	0.08	4.4
1937	2.3	2.1	0.03	4.5
1951	3.1	2.5	0.01	5.6
1955	3.5	2.3	0.02	5.8
1960	3.6	2.3	0.02	5.9
1964	3.5	2.4	0.01	5.9
1968	3.8	2.3	0.03	6.2
1973	4.7	2.3	0.06	7.0

Source: R.C.O. Matthews, C.H. Feinstein, and J.C. Odling-Smee, *British Economic Growth, 1856–1973*, p. 76, Table 3.16.

main competitors. The impact of industrial disputes on weeks of work lost was low, and much less than the impact of days lost to sickness (Table 3.6). During the 1980s, with the outstanding exception of the NUM strike of 1984–1985, there was a fall both in the incidence and level of industrial of stoppages (see Table 3.7). In part this reflected the contraction in size of manufacturing. This in turn affected the size and influence of the trade union movement, unions' density having been greatest in the older industries, the large workplaces, strongly represented in 'declining' areas of manufacturing, and regionally in Scotland and the north of England.[108] Memories of the Golden Age when trade union membership rose from 8 million in 1945 to peak at 13 million in 1979, some 55% of the employed, were just that; memories.[109] By 2001, only 19% of private sector workers belonged to a trade union, with collective bargaining covering only 30% of private sector employees in 1998. While trade unions were recognized in 50% of workplaces in 1980, by 1998 that share was 24%.[110] While the picketing and secondary action by trade unions attracted attention and offended concerns with liberty and freedom of movement, the loss to output from trade union activity was low and no higher than that in many other economies. Where trade union activity may have had an impact was in discouraging management from introducing new technology and capital investment. Concerned at existing low rates of return on capital investment, management may have held off undertaking more. In the Golden Age

[108]   Millward and Stevens, 'Union density'.
[109]   Kondylis and Wadsworth, 'Wages and wage inequality'.
[110]   Crafts, *Forging Ahead*, p. 113.

Table 3.7. Working days lost each year through all stoppages in progress, 1983–1994 United Kingdom (thousands)

	1983	1984	1985	1986	1987	1988	1989	1990	1991	1992	1993	1994
All industries and services	3,753	27,135	6,399	1,923	3,545	3,702	4,128	1,903	761	528	649	278
Coal extraction	484	22,483	4,142	143	217	222	50	59	29	8	27	–
Other energy and water	888	36	57	6	9	16	20	39	4	26	–	–
Metals, minerals, and chemicals	229	185	167	192	60	70	42	42	27	14	6	8
Engineering and vehicles	1,242	1,965	481	744	422	1,409	617	922	160	63	91	36
Other manufacturing industries	302	510	261	135	115	151	91	106	35	16	13	15
Construction	68	334	50	33	22	17	128	14	14	10	1	5
Transport and communication	295	666	197	190	1,705	1,491	624	177	60	13	160	87
Public admin, sanitary services, and education	115	764	957	449	939	254	2,237	175	362	328	339	92
Medical and health services	6	22	33	11	6	36	151	345	1	1	2	1
All other industries and services	124	170	54	20	53	30	167	20	69	50	9	35

Notes: Stoppages have been classified using Standard Industrial Classification 1980.

Sources: 1983–1987, Central Statistical Office, *Annual Abstract of Statistics, 1989 Edition*, London: HMSO, 1989, Table 6.11; 1988–1991, Central Statistical Office, *Annual Abstract of Statistics*, 1993, London: HMSO, 1993, Table 6.11; 1992–1994, Central Statistical Office, *Annual Abstract of Statistics*, 1997, London: HMSO, 1997, Table 6.10.

of rising investment as a share of GDP and with industrial policy focused on demand-side policies aimed at exploiting economies of scale and technological progress, that managerial failure to secure higher returns from capital was of concern. While newspaper and television coverage of the industrial disputes in industries such as motor vehicle and steel enjoyed focusing on the large gathering of workers raising their hands in very public decisions to take industrial action, what was rarely asked was why there were so many workers there in the first place. That failure to shift adequately to more capital-intensive, technologically based forms of production in the Golden Age reflected a managerial failure to secure high returns on capital investment, and it formed a long-run influence on the rate of deindustrialization and its associated industrial disputes from the mid-1970s.

Capital Changes

Discussion of the low rate of return on capital investment came to the fore from the mid-1970s in discussions of how to reshape industrial policy. Prompted into a fundamental rethink on industrial policy both by the economic circumstances and by its dealings with Tony Benn, economic attention within government shifted away from a concern with the level of investment and more towards its quality. Suggestions that the UK's economic woes stemmed from a lack of investment were increasingly countered with the view that the returns on existing investment were already too low, reflecting a failure to exploit economies of scale and continuing problems of industrial structure.[111] As seen, the Treasury became interested in the work of economists like Gomulka on the importance of technological innovation and diffusion. As employment in heavy manufacturing industry declined and that in financial and other service industries rose, so too industrial policy continued to move away from a Kaldor-style temporal concern with the difficulties of restructuring fixed capital investment in manufacturing industries and encouraging modernization, and towards a more spatial policy concerned with encouraging clusters of growth and creating a system in which growth could occur. In part this both responded to and sought to promote changes in industrial structure. Sources of value added changed and the sources of value added came increasingly from intangible investment (drug patents, software, R&D, design, training) rather than old-style heavy fixed capital investment. Spatially, the virtues of

---

[111] TNA T342/429, Horton, note, 'Background', 1975; Brechling, 'A cross section'; Scherer, 'The determinants of industrial plant sizes', Tables 2, 3, and 4.

agglomeration and knowledge spillovers were emphasized and encouraged by government, with the talk no longer of 'picking winners' but of 'choosing races and placing bets'. By the twenty-first century books were appearing with titles like *Capitalism Without Capital*, which pointed up the intangible nature of much of the investment in the modern digital and pharmaceutical companies.[112] Human capital, knowledge, and patents were the moveable assets of the high-growth companies of the twenty-first century, in sharp contrast to the physical, lumpy manufacturing investments of the past.[113]

Technological progress and regulatory changes also provided a boost to the financial and service sectors of the economy. At a simple level, the development of ATMs removed the need to queue in line at banks to receive cash in exchange for uncrossed cheques. Credit cards moved from being exclusive stores of money (credit) on the Diner's Club card model, to become means of managing or postponing payment for consumption.[114] Restrictions on access to financial capital began to be loosened. Deregulation in the form of the Competition and Credit Control (1971) and the abandonment of supplementary special deposits (the 'corset') in the early 1980s removed restrictions on banking activity. Such technological developments as ATMs and credit cards, allied to the loosening of restrictions on lending also made the control of monetary growth more difficult.[115] What caused problems for monetary control created opportunities for financial institutions. The removal of exchange controls in October 1979 increased the attractions for large U.S. banks, such as Citibank and Chase Manhattan, of expanding into wholesale and corporate banking in the UK There was a rapid growth of assets in the first half of the 1980s as British institutional investors, such as pension funds, insurance companies, unit trusts, and investment trusts significantly increased their overseas investment.[116] Six months after abolishing capital controls, pension funds and insurance companies invested £146 million in foreign equities. By the mid-1980s this figure had risen to £663 million. Further, changes were introduced with the deregulation of the UK securities market in 1986 (the so-called 'Big Bang') and the 1987 Banking Act which encouraged structural change in banking. UK retail banks increased their proportionate presence

---

[112] Haskel and Westlake, *Capitalism Without Capital*.
[113] Broadberry, *The Productivity Race*, p. 72; Romer, 'The origins of endogenous growth'; Caballe and Santos, 'On endogenous growth'; Aghion and Howitt, *Endogenous Growth Theory*; Crafts and Hughes, *Industrial Policy*, p. 5; Hughes, 'Choosing Races'.
[114] Stearns, *Electronic Value Exchange*.
[115] Oliver, *Whatever Happened To Monetarism?*, p. 114.
[116] Bowen, Hoggarth, and Pain, 'The recent evolution of the UK banking industry', pp. 251–3; Shabani, Tyson, Toporowski, and McKinley, *The Financial System in the UK*, p. 13; Coakley and Harris, *The City of Capital*.

Table 3.8. Unemployment rate (16+), UK regions and countries, 2007–2016

	2007	2008	2009	2010	2011	2012	2013	2014	2015	2016
North East	6.1	7.4	9.5	9.7	10.4	10.6	9.9	8.5	7.7	6.6
North West	5.6	6.3	8.5	8.0	8.4	8.5	7.9	7.1	5.3	5.2
Yorks and Humber	5.4	6.2	8.5	8.7	9.4	9.3	9.0	7.4	6.0	5.2
East Midlands	5.0	5.8	7.3	7.4	8.1	7.9	7.4	5.6	4.7	4.3
West Midlands	5.9	6.9	9.4	8.8	9.3	8.7	8.5	6.8	5.8	5.5
East	4.3	4.9	6.3	6.6	6.7	6.6	6.1	5.2	4.0	3.8
London	6.9	7.0	9.2	8.9	9.5	9.2	8.7	7.0	6.1	5.7
South East	4.2	4.4	5.9	6.0	5.9	6.0	5.7	4.8	4.2	4.0
South West	3.9	4.1	6.2	5.9	6.0	5.8	5.8	5.1	3.9	4.1
Wales	5.5	6.3	8.2	8.3	8.3	8.3	7.9	6.8	5.9	4.6
Scotland	4.7	4.9	6.9	7.7	8.2	8.0	7.7	6.2	5.8	4.8
Northern Ireland	4.1	3.9	6.6	7.0	7.2	7.3	7.3	6.4	6.0	6.1
UK	5.2	5.7	7.6	7.6	8.0	7.9	7.5	6.2	5.3	4.9

Source: Office for National Statistics, Regional labour market statistics.

from the mid-1980s. In 1985, their assets represented roughly a quarter of the total; in 1996 this share was nearer 40%. The assets of UK investment banks declined as they were acquired and absorbed into their domestic retail and foreign parents.[117]

Financial service employment grew across the economy, but was strongly concentrated in London.[118] The legacy of deindustrialization persisted in the old manufacturing centres of the Midlands, the North, Yorkshire and Humberside, the North West, Wales and Scotland.[119] Regional differences in rates of unemployment were smaller than in the 1930s, although differences in earnings between regions were marked[120] (Tables 3.8 and 3.9). While prior to the financial crisis of 2008, the employment rate had been high at around 72% for a decade, at the same time the number of people on out-of-work benefits remained at historically unprecedented levels. While in 1979, about 2 million were on out-of-work benefits (750,000 people on Invalidity Benefit (IVB), about 300,000 lone parents on Income Support (IS), and 1.1 million on unemployment benefit), in 1994 the total number on these benefits peaked at about 6 million, and in 2008 it was still well above 4 million. Even given the growth in the labour force over this period, this was a remarkable increase.[121] While the unemployment rate was to fall, economic inactivity

---

[117]   Bowen, Hoggarth, and Pain, 'The recent evolution of the UK banking industry', p. 259.
[118]   Williams, Fender, and Drew, 'Output and employment'.
[119]   Griffiths and Wall, *Applied Economics*, p. 22.
[120]   Hatton and Thomas, 'Labour markets in the interwar period', p. 474.
[121]   Portes, 'Welfare and work', p. F4.

Table 3.9. Median weekly earnings, UK regions and countries, 2006–2016 (even numbered years) Percentage variation from UK median weekly earnings

	2006	2008	2010	2012	2014	2016
North East	88.2	88.1	88.9	90.0	91.9	91.2
North West	94.6	94.2	94.4	93.4	93.6	93.1
Yorks and Humber	93.0	92.8	92.9	92.0	92.3	92.0
East Midlands	95.4	94.0	94.3	94.0	93.3	93.1
West Midlands	93.75	94.0	94.1	92.8	92.9	94.2
East	105.0	104.2	105.0	105.1	104.0	105.6
London	121.1	121.5	121.6	121.2	119.1	117.3
South East	109.6	109.6	110.0	109.9	109.4	108.0
South West	94.8	94.4	94.0	94.3	95.6	95.2
Wales	91.1	88.8	91.4	90.0	92.5	92.4
Scotland	96.4	96.7	97.6	98.4	100.0	99.6
Northern Ireland	96.4	87.2	87.9	90.5	88.6	91.8
UK	100.0	100.0	100.0	100.0	100.0	100.0

Note: Calculated from earnings data in Office for National Statistics, *Annual Survey of Hours and Earnings*.

remained of concern. In the mid-1970s while fewer than 8% of men aged sixteen to sixty-four were economically inactive, by 1998 the proportion had grown to 13% (due mainly to sickness and to a lesser extent earlier retirement among older workers).[122]

New Economies of Scale?

In making the case for giving priority to the needs of manufacturing industry, Kaldor had emphasized its potential for technological growth and the exploitation of economies of scale. While the nature of the capital used moved away from the physical towards the intangible, the new dot.com and digital industries exploited precisely the technological developments and economies of scale of which Kaldor had written. In the information technology industries, the ratio between sunk and marginal costs could be very high.[123] There was literally new sunk investment in laying fibre, but once the channels were dug it was as easy to lay 128 strands of fibre as a single strand, with the marginal cost of the 'excess' investment being low. The knowledge and sunk investment behind the production of the first silicon chip could be enormous, but the marginal cost of subsequently producing thousands of silicon chips

---

[122] Gazeley, 'Manual Work and pay, 1900–70', p. 56.
[123] Stigler, 'The economics of information'.

was then tiny. Similarly, in purely handling information, the same relationship between sunk and marginal costs existed.[124] While Amazon may have begun by selling books and CD, it was in its web services that it was to make substantial profits by exploiting the sunk:marginal cost ratio of information handling.

The development and increasing use of the internet benefited from deregulation and technological progress in telecommunications. It also interacted with and posed a challenge for financial markets. Much of the investment was intangible, in ideas, human capital, and software. Judging its commercial possibilities was difficult, and contained a vicious-virtuous spiral around the concept of economies of scale. Given the ratio of sunk:marginal costs, volume mattered. At low volume, sunk costs weighed on a company; at high volume, marginal costs generated wide profit margins. Whether in search engines or in voice recognition systems, the more that the technology was used, the more it learnt and the better it became. Alphabet, the owners of Google, are the outstanding beneficiaries of such a process. Yet, in their early stages, few internet companies made money. Amazon raised £2.1 billion in investor's money before beginning to break even.[125] Investors were therefore required to invest in their expectations of future earnings, and bubbles emerged, notably the 'dot com' boom in 1999–2000.[126] That share trading based on algorithms with 90% of trades being made by machines contributed to its own 'dot.com' bubble was ironic, as was the decreasing need for profitable internet companies to make use of the stock markets at all.

The internet as a means of trading, buying and selling, discovering information, and communication developed quickly, in part because of the rapid 'Moore's Law' growth of computing power, and also because of its ability to combine developments in a range of technologies such as telecommunications, home computing, and mobile phones. As a revolution, it was an oxymoron, being a breakthrough which made progress in small incremental steps building on existing technology. The hardware costs of entry were not high, and the investment of human capital in frequently learning new techniques and possibilities attracted the young. For those who were interested in computing and the internet, then the main investments were in mastering ideas, standards, specifications, protocols, programming languages, and software.[127] For those who simply wanted to use the technology, entrepreneurs like Steve Jobs at Apple focused on making it intuitive and easy to use.

---

[124] Varian, Farrell, and Shapiro, *Economics of Information Technology*, pp. 4, 10.
[125] Galloway, *The Four*, p. 33.
[126] Varian, Farrell, and Shapiro, *The Economics of Information Technology*, p. 1; Perez, *Technological Revolutions*.
[127] Varian, Farrell, and Shapiro, *Economics of Information Technology*, pp. 5, 7.

The new companies and industries which developed around the internet and the developments in data processing were overwhelmingly located in university cities and towns.[128] Human capital was key. London benefited both from the rapid growth of the international financial centre in the City of London, but also from the development of the digital marketing and retailing industry. London's economy grew at an annual real rate of over 4% p.a., between 1997 and 2007. Employment in the financial centre of the City of London more than doubled from 170,000 in the mid-1980s to over 350,000 by 2007. City bonuses also rose, from about £1 billion in 1990 to a peak of £14 billion in 2008, before collapsing to £2 billion in 2011. The number of people receiving multi-million pound bonuses in the City rose from thirty in 2000 to 1,500 in 2007. London property prices also rose by a third between 1983 and 2014. Yet, despite high property prices, new businesses continued to emerge. Economic recession in Europe provided a further flow of skilled migrants for the immigrant-based London economy. In London, four out of every ten employees in London were born outside the UK. Of these, about three-quarters were born outside the European Economic Area (EEA), the remaining quarter from the other European countries in the EEA. Young people migrated from outside the UK and from within the UK into London, living in its relatively cheaper rental areas (see Tables 3.10 and 3.11) The highest proportions of young people (eighteen to twenty-nine year-olds) were found in Finsbury Park, virtually all of Tower Hamlets (especially Millwall, Blackwall, Bow East, Cubitt Town, Whitechapel, and Bethnal Green) and parts of Camden, Hackney, and Harringey. Typically earning £25,000 to £35,000 in 2014, unlike home owners, they made highly efficient use of the housing stock, renting only as such space as they needed.[129]

In the previous chapter on public expenditure, the fall in capital investment as a share of GDP was noted. In this chapter, fixed capital investment has bulked large and not only has its changing share of GDP been noted, but also its changing form. The weight of the past, of lumpy manufacturing investments which proved difficult to restructure so as to exploit economies of scale moved in time towards the modern data-handling economy which is becoming familiar. While new spatial clusters of growth were formed, less tractable have been the older, leftover clusters of investment. There has been less scope for deploying regional policy to mitigate some of the cost of industrial change which fell predominantly on a male, middle-aged cohort. In temporal terms, some of the altered approach to unemployment arose from changing priorities

---

[128] Galloway, *The Four*, p. 241.   [129] McWilliams, *Flat White Economy*, pp. 23–4, 51.

Table 3.10. Geographical distribution of the population (thousands)

	1951	%	1971	%	1991	%	2001	%	2010	%
Population of Great Britain	48,854	100	54,388	100	55,831	100	57,424	100	60,463	100
England, standard regions:	41,159	84.2	46,412	85.3	47,875	85.7	49,450	86.1	52,234	86.4
North	3,009	6.2	3,152	5.8	3,073	5.5	3,028	5.3	3,101	5.1
Yorkshire & Humberside	4,567	9.3	4,902	9.0	4,936	8.8	4,977	8.7	5,301	8.8
East Midlands	3,118	6.4	3,652	6.7	4,011	7.2	4,190	7.3	4,481	7.4
East Anglia	1,381	2.8	1,688	3.1	2,068	3.7	2,181	3.8	2,372	3.9
South East	14,877	30.5	17,125	31.5	17,511	31.4	18,566	32.3	19,809	32.8
South West	3,479	7.1	4,112	7.6	4,688	8.4	4,943	8.6	5,274	8.7
West Midlands	4,423	9.1	5,146	9.5	5,230	9.4	5,281	9.2	5,455	9.0
North West	6,305	12.9	6,634	12.2	6,357	11.4	6,285	10.9	6,441	10.7
Wales	2,599	5.3	2,740	5.0	2,873	5.1	2,910	5.1	3,006	5.0
Scotland	5,096	10.4	5,236	9.6	5,083	9.1	5,064	8.8	5,222	8.6

Note: Population as enumerated in Census.

Source: *Annual Abstract of Statistics, 2011*, edition, No. 147, Office for National Statistics, 2012, Table 15.5, pp. 259–60.

Table 3.11. Distribution of the population between cities, principal metropolitan, and non-metropolitan areas (thousands)

	1951	%	1971	%	1991	%	2001	%	2010	%
Population of Great Britain	48,854	100	54,388	100	55,831	100	57,424	100	60,463	100
Greater London	8,197	16.8	7,529	13.9	6,829	12.2	7,322	12.8	7,825	12.9
Inner London	3,679	7.5	3,060	5.6	2,599	4.7	2,859	5.0	3,083	5.1
Outer London	4,518	9.2	4,470	8.2	4,230	7.6	4,463	7.8	4,742	7.8
Metropolitan areas of England & Wales	11,365	23.3	11,862	21.8	11,085	19.9	10,888	19.0	14,135	23.4
Tyne and Wear	1,201	2.5	1,218	2.2	1,124	2.0	1,087	1.9	1,120	1.9
West Yorkshire	1,985	4.1	2,090	3.8	2,062	3.7	2,083	3.6	2,250	3.7
South Yorkshire	1,253	2.6	1,331	2.4	1,289	2.3	1,266	2.2	1,328	2.2
West Midlands	2,547	5.2	2,811	5.2	2,619	4.7	2,568	4.5	-	
Greater Manchester	2,716	5.6	2,750	5.1	2,554	4.6	2,516	4.4	2,629	4.3
Merseyside	1,663	3.4	1,662	3.1	1,438	2.6	1,368	2.4	1,353	2.2
Principal metropolitan cities and non-metropolitan districts of England & Wales										
Newcastle	292	0.6	312	0.6	275	0.5	266	0.5	292	0.5
Leeds	505	1.0	749	1.4	707	1.3	716	1.2	799	1.3
Sheffield	513	1.1	579	1.1	520	0.9	513	0.9	556	0.9
Birmingham	1,113	2.3	1,107	2.0	1,005	1.8	985	1.7	1,037	1.7
Manchester	703	1.4	554	1.0	433	0.8	423	0.7	499	0.8
Liverpool	789	1.6	610	1.1	476	0.9	442	0.8	445	0.7
Leicester	285	0.6	285	0.5	281	0.5	283	0.5	307	0.5
Nottingham	308	0.6	302	0.6	279	0.5	269	0.5	307	0.5
Bristol	443	0.9	433	0.8	392	0.7	390	0.7	441	0.7
Plymouth	225	0.5	249	0.5	251	0.4	241	0.4	259	0.4
Cardiff	244	0.5	291	0.5	297	0.5	310	0.5	341	0.6
City of Edinburgh local government district	467	1.0	478	0.9	436	0.8	449	0.8	486	0.8
City of Glasgow local government district	1,090	2.2	983	1.8	629	1.1	579	1.0	593	1.0

Note: Population as enumerated in Census.

Source: *Annual Abstract of Statistics, 2011*, edition, No. 147, Office for National Statistics, 2012, Table 15.5, pp. 259–60.

in government which reflected both changing public finance constraints and a willingness to employ a newer theoretical approach which made more of the need to accommodate future expectations of wages and assistance, as well as seeking to reduce political responsibility for unemployment by distinguishing between natural and unnatural, real and unreal. Spatially, while the loss of employment in the manufacturing sector of the economy was offset by an increase in employment in the financial and business services sector of the economy, and more recently in the digital and IT sector, the new opportunities could arise in different areas and towns in Britain. Migrant and younger labour flowed to them in a way which was more difficult for middle-aged, family-based labour. At one and the same time, social capital including housing was left underused in older, often manufacturing centres, which have not seen transitional recovery, while often younger people crowd into housing stock in growth centres like London. In that sense, housing shortages, high property prices, and regional investment are sides of the same coin. The inequality and poverty which came to coexist are the concern of chapter 4, while, following a discussion of health and education, chapter 6 begins to discuss the main developments affecting the availability and cost of housing.

Bibliography

Abromeit, Heidrun, *British Steel*, 1986, Leamington Spa/Heidelberg: Berg.

Adeney, M., *The Motor Makers: The Turbulent History of Britain's Car Industry*, 1989, London: Fontana.

Aghion, Philippe, and Peter Howitt, *Endogenous Growth Theory*, 1998, Cambridge, Mass.: MIT Press.

Atkinson, Anthony B., *Inequality: What Can Be Done?*, 2015, Cambridge, Mass. and London: Harvard University Press,

Brian Arthur, W., *Increasing Returns and Path Dependence in the Economy*, 1994, Ann Arbor: University of Michigan Press.

Ball, Laurence, 'Hysteresis in unemployment: old and new evidence', March 2009, NBER, Working Paper, 14818.

Ball, Laurence, 'Disinflation and the NAIRU', in Christina D. Romer and David H. Romer (eds.) *Reducing Inflation: Motivation and Strategy*, 1997, Chicago: The University of Chicago Press and NBER.

Ball, Laurence, N. Gregory Mankiw, and William D. Nordhaus, 'Aggregate demand and long-run unemployment', *Brookings Papers on Economic Activity*, 1999, no. 2, pp. 189–251.

Ball, Laurence, and N. Gregory Mankiw, 'The NAIRU in theory and practice', *The Journal of Economic Perspectives*, vol. 16, no. 4, Autumn 2002, pp. 115–36.

Becker, G.S., 'A theory of the allocation of time', *Economic Journal*, vol. 75, no. 299, September 1965, pp. 493–517.

Becker, G.S., *A Treatise on the Family*, 1981, Cambridge, Mass.: Harvard University Press.

Benn, Tony, *Against the Tide: Diaries 1973–1976*, 1989, London: Hutchinson.

Beveridge, W.H., 'The government's employment policy', *The Economic Journal*, vol. 54, no. 214, June–September 1944, pp. 161–76.

Blackaby, Frank, *Deindustrialisation*, 1979, London, NIESR: Heinemann.

Bowen, Alex, Glenn Hoggarth, and Darren Pain, 'The recent evolution of the UK banking industry and some implications for financial stability', in BIS, 'The monetary and regulatory implications of changes in the banking industry', March 1999, *BIS Conference* Papers, vol. 7.1999.

Brechling, F.R., Unpublished NIESR paper, 'A cross section of labour productivity'. Preliminary investigations by NEDO.

Brittan, Samuel, *Capitalism and the Permissive Society*, 1973, London: Macmillan.

Brittan, Samuel, *Against the Flow: Reflections of an Individualist*, 2005, London: Atlantic Books.

Broadberry, S.N., *The Productivity Race: British Manufacturing In International Perspective, 1850–1990*, 1997, Cambridge: Cambridge University Press.

Broadberry, Stephen. *Market Services and the Productivity Race 1850–2000: British Performance in International Perspective*, 2006, Cambridge: Cambridge University Press.

Broadberry, S., 'The performance of manufacturing', in Floud and Johnson (eds.), *The Cambridge Economic History of Modern Britain*, vol. 3, 2004, New York: Cambridge University Press, pp. 57–83.

Broadberry, S.N., 'Why was unemployment in post-war Britain so low?', *Bulletin of Economic Research*, vol. 46, no. 3, 1994, pp. 241–61.

Broadberry, Stephen, and Tim Leunig, *The Impact of Government Policies on UK Manufacturing Since 1945*, 2013, London: Foresight, Government Office for Science.

Burgess, Simon, and Helene Turon, 'Unemployment dynamics in Britain', *The Economic Journal*, vol. 115, issue 503, April 2005, pp. 423–48.

Burn, Duncan, *The Structure of British Industry*, 2 vols, 1958, NIESR, Cambridge: Cambridge University Press.

Caballe, Jordi, and Manuel S. Santos, 'On endogenous growth with physical and human capital', *The Journal of Political Economy*, vol. 101, no. 6 (Dec. 1993), pp. 1042–67.

Cairncross, Alec and Barry Eichengreen, *Sterling in Decline: The Devaluations of 1931, 1949 and 1967*, 1983, Oxford: Basil Blackwell.

James Callaghan's presentation of the report of the PLP to the Labour Party Conference in Blackpool in 1976, available at http://www.britishpoliticalspeech. org/speech-archive.htm?speech=174

Carruth, Alan A., and Andrew J. Oswald, 'Miners' Wages in Post-War Britain: An Application of a Model of Trade Union Behaviour', *The Economic Journal*, vol. 95, no. 380 (Dec., 1985), pp. 1003–20.

Central Statistical Office, *National Income and Expenditure: 1971*, 1971, London: HMSO.

Central Statistical Office, *Economic Trends, Annual Supplement, 1996*, 1996, London: HMSO.

Chick, Martin, *Industrial Policy in Britain, 1945–1951: Economic Planning, Nationalisation and the Labour Governments*, 1998, Cambridge: Cambridge University Press.

Church, Roy, *The Rise and Decline of the British Motor Industry*, 1994, London: Macmillan.

Cleverley, Graham, *The Fleet Street Disaster: British National Newspapers as a Case Study in Mismanagement*, 1976, London: Constable.

Coakley, Jerry, and Laurence Harris, *The City of Capital: London's Role As A Financial Centre*, 1983, Oxford: Blackwell.

Crafts, Nicholas, 'Deindustrialisation and Economic Growth', *The Economic Journal*, vol. 106, no. 434, Jan. 1996, pp. 172–83.

Crafts, Nicholas, and Gianni Toniolo, *Economic Growth in Europe since 1945*, 1996, Cambridge: Cambridge University Press.

Crafts, Nicholas, and Alan Hughes, *Industrial Policy for the Medium to Long-Term*, Centre for Business Research, Working Paper 455, December 2013.

Cross, Rod, 'Phelps, hysteresis and the Natural Rate of Unemployment', *Quarterly Journal of Business and Economics*, vol. 25, no. 1, Winter 1986, pp. 56–64.

Cross, R. B., 'Hysteresis and instability in the natural rate of unemployment', in J.C.Wood and R.N. Woods, (eds.), *The Critical Assessments of Milton Friedman*, 1990, London: Routledge, pp. 1–20.

Cross, Rod (ed.), *The Natural Rate of Unemployment: Reflections on 25 Years of the Hypothesis*, 1995, Cambridge: Cambridge University Press.

Connolly, Sara and Mary Gregory, 'Women and work since 1970', in Nicholas Crafts, Ian Gazeley, and Andrew Newall (eds.), *Work and Pay in Twentieth Century Britain*, 2007, Oxford: Oxford University Press, pp. 142–77.

Cooper, David, and Trevor Hopper, *Debating Coal Closures: Economic Calculation in the Coal Dispute, 1984–5*, 1988, Cambridge: Cambridge University Press.

Daniel, W., and E. Stilgoe, *Where Are They Now? A Follow-Up Study of the Unemployed*, PEP No. 572, October 1977.

Edwardes, Michael, *Back from the Brink: An Apocalyptic Experience*, 1983, London: Collins.

Financial Times, 7 June 1966.

Friedman, Milton, 'The role of monetary policy', *The American Economic Review*, vol. 58, no. 1, March 1968, pp. 1–17.

Flanders, A., *Industrial Relations: What is Wrong with the System?*, 1965, London: Faber & Faber.

Friedman, Milton, *Unemployment versus Inflation: An Evaluation of the Phillips Curve*, IEA Occasional Paper 44, 1975, London: Institute of Economic Affairs.

Friedman, Milton, *Price Theory*, 1976, Chicago: Aldine Publishing Company.

Friedman, Milton, 'Inflation and Unemployment', Nobel Memorial Lecture, 13 December 1976, *The Journal of Political Economy*, vol. 85, no. 3, June 1977, pp. 451–72.

Galloway, Scott, *The Four: The Hidden DNA of Amazon, Apple, Facebook and Google*, 2017, New York: Portfolio/Penguin.

Gazeley, Ian, 'Manual Work and pay, 1900–70', in Crafts, Gazeley, and Newall, *Work and Pay in Twentieth Century Britain*, pp. 55–79.

Gazeley, Ian, and Andrew Newell, 'Introduction', in Crafts, Gazeley, and Newall, *Work and Pay in Twentieth Century Britain*, pp. 1–10.

Gazeley, Ian, 'Income and living standards, 1870–2010' in R. Floud, J. Humphries, and P. Johnson(eds.), *The Cambridge Economic History of Modern Britain: Vol. I. 1870 to the Present*, 2014, Cambridge: Cambridge University Press, pp. 151–80.

Glyn, Andrew, 'The economic case against pit closures prepared for the National Union of Mineworkers', Sheffield National Union of Mineworkers, 1985.

Glyn, Andrew, and Stephen Machin, *Colliery Closures and the Decline of the UK Coal Industry*, 1996, Discussion paper No. 7, Labour Market Consequences of Technical and Structural Change, University of Oxford, Centre for Economic Performance.

Graham, Andrew, 'Industrial Policy', in W. Beckerman, *The Labour Government's Economic Record*, 1975, London: Duckworth, pp. 178–217.

Gregg, Paul, 'Out for the count: a social scientist's analysis of unemployment statistics in the UK', *Journal of the Royal Statistical Society*, Series A, vol. 157, no. 2, 1994, pp. 253–270.

Griffiths, Alan, and Stuart Wall(eds.), *Applied Economics*, 12th edition, 2012, Harlow: Pearson Education, p. 4.

Hague, Douglas, and Geoffrey Wilkinson, *The IRC: an Experiment in Industrial Intervention*, 1983, London: Allen and Unwin.

Hahn, Frank, 'Theoretical reflections on the 'natural rate of unemployment', in Rod Cross(ed.), *The Natural Rate of Unemployment: Reflections on 25 Years of the Hypothesis*, 1995, Cambridge: Cambridge University Press.

Hall, M., 'Are goods and services different?', *Westminster Bank Review*, August 1968.

Haskel, Jonathan, and Stian Westlake, *Capitalism Without Capital: The Rise of the Intangible Economy*, 2018, Princeton: Princeton University Press.

Hatton, Timothy J., and Mark Thomas, 'Labour markets in the interwar period and economic recovery in the UK and the USA', *Oxford Review of Economic Policy*, vol. 26, no. 3, 2010, pp. 463–85.

Hayek, F., *The Constitution of Liberty*, 1960, Chicago: University of Chicago Press.

Hendry, J.K., *Innovating for Failure: Government Policy and the Early British Computer Industry*, 1989, London, MIT Press.

Hicks, John, *Economic Perspectives: Further Essays on Money and Growth*, 1977, Oxford: Oxford University Press.

Horrell, Sara, 'The household and the labour market', in Crafts, Gazeley, and Newall, *Work and Pay in Twentieth Century Britain*, pp. 117–41.

Hughes, A. 'Choosing Races and Placing Bets: UK National Innovation Policy and the Globalisation of the Innovation System', in D. Greenaway (ed.), *The UK in a Global World*, 2012, London: CEPR, pp. 37-70.

Hyman, G. Working Note, paper, 'Ramifications of Gomulka's refutation of the Verdoorn-Kaldor laws', C56 PRO 30/87/156, CES WN 447, January 1977.

Industrial Strategy Commission, *The Final Report of the Industrial Strategy Commission*, November 2017.

Jenkins, Simon, *Newspapers: The Power and the Money*, 1979, London: Faber & Faber.

Keith Joseph papers, Bodleian Library Oxford, KJ 10/5, Letter to Mrs Thatcher, from Adam Ridley, 2nd October 1975.

Keith Joseph papers, Bodleian Library Oxford, KJ 10/5, Letter, Walter Eltis to Adam Ridley, 29 September 1975.

Kaldor, Nicholas, 'Productivity and growth in manufacturing industry: a reply', *Economica*, November 1968, N.S. 35, no. 140, pp. 385–91.

Kirby, Maurice, *The Decline of British Economic Power since 1870*, 1981, London: Allen & Unwin.

Kondylis, Florence, and Jonathan Wadsworth, 'Wages and wage inequality', in Crafts, Gazeley, and Newall, *Work and Pay in Twentieth Century Britain*.

Kramer, Daniel, *State Capital and Private Enterprise: the Case of the UK National Enterprise Board*, 1988, London: Routledge.

Layard, R., and S. Nickell, 'Unemployment in Britain', in C. Bean, R. Layard, and S. Nickell (eds.), *The Rise in Unemployment*, 1986, Oxford: Basil Blackwell, pp. 121–69.

Lewchuk, Wayne, *American Technology and the British Vehicle Industry*, 1987, Cambridge: Cambridge University Press.

Lewchuk, Wayne, 'The British Motor Vehicle Industry: The Roots of Decline' in
B. Elbaum and W. Lazonick, *The Decline of the British Economy*, 1986, Oxford:
Oxford University Press, pp. 135–61.

Lieberman, Marvin B., and Douglas R. Johnson, 'Comparative productivity of
Japanese and U.S. steel producers, 1958–1993', *Japan and the World Economy*,
vol. 11, 1999, pp. 1–27.

Lucas, Robert, 'Expectations and the neutrality of money', *Journal of Economic
Theory*, vol. 4, issue 2, 1972, pp. 103–24.

Lucas, Robert, 'Some international evidence on output-inflation tradeoffs', *The
American Economic Review*, vol. 63, no. 3, June 1973, pp. 326–34.

Machin, S., and S. Wadhwani, 'The effects of unions on organisational change,
investment and employment: evidence from WIRS Data', 1989, London School
of Economics, Centre for Labour Economics Discussion paper no. 355.

Maddison, A., 'Growth and slowdown in advanced capitalist economies: Techniques
of quantitative assessment', *Journal of Economic Literature*, vol. 25, no. 2, 1987,
pp. 649–98.

Matthews, R.C.O., C.H. Feinstein, and J.C. Odling-Smee, *British Economic
Growth, 1856–1973*, 1982, Oxford: Clarendon Press.

Matthews, R.C.O., and J.R. Sargent, 'Introduction', in R.C.O. Matthews and
J.R. Sargent(eds.), *Contemporary Problems of Economic Policy*, 1983, London:
Methuen.

McCarthy, W.E.G., *The Closed Shop in Britain*, 1964, Oxford: Blackwell.

McWilliams, Douglas., *The Flat White Economy*, 2015, London: Duckworth.

Meade, James, *The Theory of Indicative Planning*, 1970, Manchester: Manchester
University Press.

Metcalf, David, 'Trade unions', in R. Dickens, P. Gregg and J. Wadsworth (eds.),
The Labour Market under New Labour: The State of Working Britain, 2003,
London: Palgrave Macmillan, pp. 170–90.

Millward, N. and M. Stevens, 'Union density in the regions: evidence from the
1984 WIRS and the British Social Attitudes Survey Series', *Employment Gazette*,
vol. 96, 1988, pp. 286–95.

Mincer, J., 'Labour force participation of married women: A study of labour supply', in *Aspects of Economics*, a report of the National Bureau of Economic
Research, 1962, Princeton: Princeton University Press.

Muth, John, 'Rational expectations and the theory of price movements',
Econometrica, vol. 29, no. 3, July 1961, pp. 315–35.

Nickell, S. J., 'A picture of male unemployment in Britain', *The Economic Journal*,
vol. 90, no. 360, Dec. 1980, pp. 776–94.

Nickell, Stephen, 'Unemployment: A Survey', *The Economic Journal*, vol. 100, no.
401, June 1990, pp. 391–439.

Nickell, Stephen, 'Unemployment: Questions and Some Answers', *The Economic Journal*, vol. 108, no. 448, May 1998, pp. 802–16.

Opie, Roger, 'Economic planning and growth', in W. Beckerman (ed.), *The Labour Government's Economic Record, 1964–1970*, 1972, London: Duckworth, pp. 157–77.

Oulton, N., and M. O'Mahony, *Changing Fortunes: An Industry Study of British and German Productivity Growth Over Three Decades*, 1994, London: NIESR.

Pagnamenta, Peter, and Richard Overy, *All Our Working Lives*, 1984, London: BBC Books.

Perez, Carlota, *Technological Revolutions and Financial Capital: The Dynamics of Bubbles and Golden Ages*, 2002, Cheltenham: Edward Elgar.

Pettigrew, Andrew, *The Awakening Giant*, 1985, Oxford: Basil Blackwell.

Phelps, E.S., 'Phillips Curves, expectations of inflation and optimal unemployment over time', *Economica*, vol. 34, no. 3, August 1967, pp. 254–81.

Phelps, E.S., 'Money wage dynamics and labour market equilibrium', in E.S. Phelps (ed.), *Microeconomic Foundations of Employment and Inflation Theory*, 1970, New York: Norton, pp. 124–66.

Phelps, Edmund S., *Inflation Policy and Unemployment Theory*, 1972, London: Macmillan.

Phillips, A.W., 'The relation between unemployment and the rate of change of money wage rates in the UK, 1861–1957', *Economica*, vol. 25, issue 100, November 1958, pp. 283–399.

Piore, M. J., and C. F. Sabel, *The Second Industrial Divide: Possibilities for Prosperity*, 1984, New York: Basic Books.

Political and Economic Planning, 'The Machine Tool Industry', *Planning*, 1948, vol. 15, no. 292.

Portes, Jonathan, 'Welfare and work: continuity and change', *National Institute Economic Review*, July 2012, no. 221, F4–F9.

Prais, S. J., *Productivity and Industrial Structure*, 1981, Cambridge: Cambridge University Press.

Prais, C. F., and A. G. Atkinson, 'The use of manpower in British industry', *Department of Employment Gazette*, vol. 84, June 1976, pp. 571–6.

Reddaway, W. B., 'The productivity effects of Selective Employment Tax, a reply', *National Institute Economic Review*, vol. 57, August 1971, pp. 62–8.

Redwood, John, *Going for Broke*, 1984, Oxford: Blackwell.

Rhys, D. G., *The Motor Industry: An Economic Survey*, 1972, London: Butterworths.

Richardson, R., 'Trade Unions', in N.F.R. Crafts and N.W.C. Woodward (eds.), *The British Economy since 1945*, 1991, Oxford: Clarendon Press, pp. 417–42.

Romer, Paul, 'The origins of endogenous growth', *The Journal of Economic Perspectives*, vol. 8, no. 1. Winter, 1994, pp. 3–22.

Rowthorn, R. E., and J. R. Wells, *De-Industrialisation and Foreign Trade*, 1987, Cambridge: Cambridge University Press.

Sandilands, Roger J., 'Nicholas Kaldor's notes on Allyn Young's LSE lectures 1927–1929', *Journal of Economic Studies*, 1990, vol. 17, issue 3/4.

Sargent, Thomas J., 'Rational expectations, the real rate of interest and the "natural" rate of unemployment' in *Brookings Papers on Economic Activity*, no. 2, 1973, pp. 429–72.

Scherer, F. M., 'The determinants of industrial plant sizes in six nations', *The Review of Economics and Statistics*, vol. 55, no. 2, May 1973, pp. 135–45.

Scott, Peter, 'British regional policy, 1945–51: A lost opportunity', *Twentieth Century British History*, vol. 8, issue 3, January 1997, pp. 358–82.

Shabani, Mimoza, Judith Tyson, Jan Toporowski, and Terry McKinley, *The Financial System in the UK*, 2015, London: FESSUD Studies in the Financial System, No. 14.

Singh, Ajit, 'UK industry and the world economy: A case of deindustrialisation?', *Cambridge Journal of Economics*, vol. 1, issue 2, June 1977, pp. 113–36.

Sisson, Keith, *Industrial Relations in Fleet Street: A Study in Pay Structure*, 1975, Oxford: Blackwell.

Stearns, David, *Electronic Value Exchange: Origins of the VISA Electronic Payment System*, 2011, London: Springer.

Stigler, George J., 'The economics of information', *Chicago University Journal of Political Economy*, vol. 69, no. 3, June 1961, pp. 215–25.

Thirlwall, Anthony, *Nicholas Kaldor*, 1987, Brighton: Wheatsheaf.

Thirlwall, A. P., 'Rowthorn's interpretation of Verdoorn's Law', *The Economic Journal*, vol. 90, no. 358, June 1980, pp. 386–88.

TNA BT 258/2658, A. Crosland to H. Wilson, 24 September 1968.

TNA CAB 184/77, Note of a meeting between Lord Rothschild and Marmaduke Hussey, Managing Director, Times Newspapers. Messrs Butler and Waldegrave were also present, 21 December 1971.

TNA CAB 184/150, GEN 181(74), 'Imprisonment under the Industrial Relations Act, Memorandum by the Secretary of State for Employment', para 1.

TNA LAB 28/281, Royal Commission on Trade Unions and Employers' Associations, Evidence submitted by Professor B. C. Roberts, Professor of Industrial Relations, LSE ', March 1966, p. 1.

TNA LAB 28/365, 'Memorandum of evidence to the Royal Commission on Trade Unions and Employers' Associations', submitted by Allan Flanders, Fellow of Nuffield College and University Lecturer in Industrial relations, Oxford, November 1966, p. 10.

TNA LAB 28/365, 'Memorandum of evidence to the Royal Commission on Trade Unions and Employers' Associations', submitted by Allan Flanders, Fellow of Nuffield College and University Lecturer in Industrial relations, Oxford, November 1966, p. 15.

TNA PREM 13/400, 'The Reorganisation of Industry', Note from Balogh to Prime Minister, 8th September 1965.

TNA PREM 13/400, 'Technology', note to Prime Minister from Thomas Balogh, 4th February 1965.

TNA PREM 13/401, Note, T. Balogh to Chancellor of the Exchequer, 17th February 1965.

TNA PREM 13/401, Note on 'The Monopolies Bill', by T. Balogh, 23rd February 1965.

TNA PREM 13/1550, H Wilson to D Healey, 'The future of the Ministry of Aviation', 11 November 1966.

TNA PREM 13/2795, R. McIntosh to H. Wilson, 'Industrial policy and the Monopolies Commission', 25 April 1969.

TNA PREM 16/363, Paper, 'The role of manufacturing industry in Britain's economic future', by Nicholas Kaldor, 30 June 1975.

TNA PREM 16/363, Note, S A Robson to F E R Butler, 21 July 1975.

TNA PREM 16/363, Kaldor, 'The role of manufacturing industry', para. 9.

TNA PREM 13/402, Note of a meeting between the Prime Minister and representatives of the motor industry held at 10 Downing Street on Friday 3rd September 1965 at 3.00 p.m.

TNA PREM 16/503, letter, headed 'Investment and Growth', Shirley Williams (Department of Prices and Consumer Protection) to Prime Minister, 31 July 1975.

TNA PREM16/503, letter, Tony Crosland (Department of the Environment) to Prime Minister, 7 July 1975.

TNA PREM 16/503, letter, Harold Lever (Chancellor of the Duchy of Lancaster) to Denis Healey, 8 August 1975.

TNA T325/145, 'The Ministry of Technology', 11 November 1967.

TNA T342/429, 'Industrial Policy', paper by L. Pliatzky, 30 June 1975, para. 8.

TNA T342/339, Letter from L. Pliatzky to Sir Douglas Henley, 17 June 1974.

TNA T342/340, 'How to Deal with Mr. Benn', Note from W S Ryrie to L Pliatzky, 1 November 1974, paras. 2–4.

TNA T342/429, 'Background for a view of the desired industrial structure', notes, G Horton, 1975.

Tolliday, S., and J. Zeitlin(eds.), *The Power To Manage? Employers and Industrial Relations in Comparative Historical Perspective*, 1991, London: Routledge.

Tomlinson, Jim, *The Labour Governments 1964–1970*, 2004, Manchester: Manchester University Press.

Turner, H. A., 'The Donovan Report', *The Economic Journal*, vol. 79, no. 313, Mar. 1969, pp. 1–10.

Varian, Hal R., Joseph Farrell, and Carl Shapiro, *The Economics of Information Technology: An Introduction*, 2004, Cambridge: Cambridge University Press.

Verdoorn, P. J., 'Fattori che regolano lo sviluppo della produttivita del lavoro', *L'Industria*, vol. 1, 1949, pp. 3–10.

Wedderburn, K. W., *The Worker and the Law*, 1965, Harmondsworth: Penguin.

Wedderburn, K. W., 'Freedom of association and philosophies of labour law', *Industrial Law Journal*, vol. 18, issue 1, 1 March 1989, pp. 1–38.

Whitley, J. D., and G. D. N. Worswick, 'The productivity effects of Selective Employment Tax', *National Institute Economic Review*, vol. 56, issue 1, May 1971, pp. 36–40.

Williams, B., V. Fender, and S. Drew, 'Output and employment in the financial sector', *Economic and Labour Market Review*, vol. 3, no. 7, 2009, pp. 18–25.

Young, Allyn A., 'Increasing returns and economic progress', *The Economic Journal*, vol. 38, no. 152, Dec. 1928, 527–42.

Young, S., and N. Hood, *Chrysler UK: A Corporation in Transition*, 1977, New York: Praeger.

Working Party Reports, *Cotton*, London, HMSO, 1946.

Selective Employment Tax (Cmnd. 2986, 1966).

Industrial Expansion (Cmnd. 3509, 1968).

Industrial Investment: The Computers Mergers Project (Cmnd. 3660, 1968).

Department for Transport (2006), *Transport, Wider Economic Benefits and Impacts on GDP*, London.

4

Poverty and Inequality

In this chapter, the main changes in income and wealth inequality are examined, as is the issue of poverty. While there is not necessarily any relationship between inequality and poverty, the issues of absolute and relative poverty are often caught up in discussions of inequality. Early approaches to addressing absolute poverty centred on the principle of social insurance, as set out in 1942 in the *Report on Social Insurance and Allied Services* (Beveridge Report), although in time this social insurance approach gave way to a more tax-based system. While much of this change reflected dissatisfaction with the (in)ability of social insurance to adapt to political pressure to target relative rather than absolute poverty, there was also more general concern with how the interaction of the tax and benefit systems was affecting incentives to work. While the interaction of the two systems affected those at the lower end of the income scale, there also developed interest in the extent to which a high marginal rate of income taxation was reducing incentives to work among those at the opposite end of the income scale. In the 1980s, changes were made both to the rates of marginal income tax and to the weighting between direct and indirect taxes.

While most attention was paid to changes to the taxation of income and consumption, it was the comparative absence of changes to the taxation of wealth which were as noteworthy. The distribution of wealth, always more unequal than that of income, narrowed between 1951 and 1979, but then began to concentrate again. In 2016, the wealthiest 1% of households held about 20% of household wealth, the top 5% held about 40% and the top 10% held over 50%. Across the entire twentieth century wealth redistribution essentially occurred among the top 20% of wealth holders. Wealth is much more concentrated than income and is mainly held by older households. Inheritance perpetuates this pattern, thereby supporting the intergenerational transfer of inequalities of wealth and opportunity.[1] In the 1980s the rise in overall inequality in the UK was much larger than in the US, but after 1992 it

---

[1] The Gini coefficient for wealth in 2016 was 0.64 for wealth and 0.34 for net income. Thomas Crossley and Cormac O'Dea, 'The distribution of household wealth in the U.K.', 19 April 2016. https://www.ifs.org.uk/publications/8239.

remained at a similar level.[2] The changes in the distribution of wealth from 1995 were strongly affected by changes in housing wealth. Efforts, such as those made by the Meade Committee in the late 1970s, to change the system of inheritance taxation were successfully resisted by the incoming Conservative government for whom the ability to acquire and accumulate capital assets formed an important incentive for work and entrepreneurship.

Measuring Inequality

In measuring inequality the measure commonly used is the Gini coefficient, as developed by the Italian statistician Corrado Gini in 1912.[3] Rather than simply measuring the extent to which incomes varied from the mean, Gini measured the distance between every pair of incomes and plotted the results along the recently developed Lorenz Curve (1905) which necessarily hung below a straight line running at 45 degrees north east of the origin. With the percentage of total income on the Y axis and the percentage of population on the X axis, if income was shared equally with 1% of the population having 1% of income, 2% of the population having 2% of total income and so on, then these combinations of values would sit neatly along the 45 degree diagonal. The greater the degree of inequality, the further the curve would lie from the diagonal. The Gini coefficient measures the ratio of the difference between the line of absolute equity (the diagonal) and the Lorenz curve to the triangular area underneath the diagonal.[4] If incomes are distributed equally, the Gini coefficient will be zero; and if one person has all the income, it will be unity, i.e. 1 being complete inequality and 0 being complete equality.

While the Gini coefficient is the most used measure, theoretically a more satisfying measure of inequality was that developed by the economist Tony Atkinson and which addressed the question of what exactly we mean when we say that one distribution is more unequal than another. Any measure of the degree of inequality must be a measure of the increase in total utility that would be effected by redistribution. All measures of inequality, even the

---

[2] Atkinson, *Inequality: What Can Be Done?*, p. 20.

[3] Gini, *Variabilità e Mutabilità*; Sen, *On Economic Inequality*, chapter 2; Atkinson, 'On the measurement of inequality'; Newbery, 'A theorem on the measurement of inequality'; Sheshinski, 'Relation between a Social Welfare Function and the Gini Index of Inequality'; Backhouse, *The Puzzle of Modern Economics*, p. 66.

[4] Sen, *On Economic Inequality*, pp 30–1. Mathematically, the Gini coefficient is exactly one-half of the relative mean difference, which is the defined as the differences between each income and every other, divided by the average income.

purely mathematical (Gini, coefficient of variation, logarithmic), attribute weights (and each differently) to different forms of inequality within the distribution. Atkinson's measure reflects the value we attach to particular distributions and it does implicitly accommodate society's aversion to inequality. However, while the Atkinson index is appealing because greater equality of income entails greater total utility (provided that income remains unchanged), it is the Gini coefficient which is the most commonly used measure of inequality.[5] This may be in part precisely because Atkinson's measure embodies a value judgement, which a positive economist, seeking to compare 'objectively' the equality of income distribution between countries or over time, is loath to employ.

Income Inequality

In broad terms, income inequality narrowed in the period 1951–1979, but then widened again until 2009–2010. The shift in the Gini coefficient of post-tax income from 0.43 in 1938 to 0.35 in 1949 marked an important break with the past, particularly as it affected the highest income recipients. While the share of total pre-tax income of the top 10% was 45.5% in 1867 and still 40.5% in 1938/9, it fell to 28.3% by 1954 with at least half of the relative reduction at the top occurring during the World War II.[6] The proportion of real disposable income received by the top 1% of the population fell from about 12.5% in 1938 to about 6.5% in 1957.[7] Looking at the distribution of all income, its inequality of distribution fell by some ten percentage points from 1938 to the 1970s and then rose by some ten percentage points between 1977 and 1991.[8] The narrowing of income inequality until 1977 was initially characterized by a period from 1949 until 1957, when the increase in the level of wages and the number of wage earners (until 1955) exceeded salaries and the salaried. Over this period, the average wage in manufacturing increased by 73% and the average salary by 54%. Thereafter between 1957 and 1963 average salaries increased 35% and wages by 31%, but the number of wage earners fell while the ranks of the salaried swelled.[9] During the 1960s the income of the poorest rose more quickly than in the middle and top of the income distribution, reflecting in part the continued development of welfare benefits. Between

---

[5] Phelps Brown, *Egalitarianism*, pp. 277–8; Little, *Ethics, Economics and Politics*, p. 70.
[6] Phelps Brown, *Egalitarianism*, p. 316.
[7] Lydall, 'The long-term trend in the size distribution of income.
[8] Atkinson and Brandolini, 'On data'.   [9] Nicholson, 'The distribution of personal income'.

1961 and 1968, there was a very slight fall in income inequality, followed by a rise between 1968 and 1972 and then a fall again until a turning point was reached in 1977. During the 1970s as a whole there was roughly even income growth across the population. However between 1979 and 1993 the Gini coefficient rose from 0.25 to 0.34 which coincided with a rise in relative poverty at the bottom of the income scale.[10] There was also a strong growth of income from employment among the top 20% of income earners while that of the remaining 80% fell.[11] In part, this reflected changes in employment which rewarded the more educated.[12] While taxation had contributed to reducing income inequality between 1938/9 and to 1972/3, direct taxation became less progressive from the 1970s.[13] To some extent this was offset by benefits in kind like health and education, as well as cash benefits, but nonetheless the rise in income inequality in the UK in the 1980s was notable for its sharpness and persistence.[14] This rise in income inequality in the UK was higher than that in the United States, where the Gini coefficient of inequality for household incomes rose by three and a half percentage points between 1968 and 1992, taking it more or less back to its pre-1960 level.

High Incomes

A particular feature of the increase in income inequality in the UK was the disproportionate increase from 1977 in the income share of those at the very top of the income scale. Using income tax data, the share of the top 1% of income taxpayers rose by 5.5 percentage points between 1979 and 1999, accounting for more than half of the increase in the share of the top 10%. Within this, the majority was actually accounted for by the top 0.5%, whose share of the total more than doubled, rising by 4.4 percentage points. The 0.05% at the very top had by 1997 restored their share to what it had been before World War II. As Tony Atkinson summarized this development: 'Since 1979, we have seen a reversal [in the declining share of top incomes], with

---

[10] Goodman, Johnson, and Webb, *Inequality in the UK*, pp. 91, 93; Hills, *Income Inequality in the UK*, p. 51.

[11] At a household income level, the Gini coefficient fell from 0.26 in 1961 to 0.24 in the late 1970s. It then rose sharply from 1979 reaching 0.34 by 1990 and 0.36 in 2009–10. Gazeley, 'Income and living standards, 1870–2010', p. 160; Atkinson, *Inequality: What Can Be Done?*, p. 20.

[12] Gazeley, 'Income and living standards, 1870–2010', p. 153.

[13] Gazeley, 'Income and living standards, 1870–2010', p. 173.

[14] Atkinson, 'Bringing income distribution in from the cold', p. 301; Gazeley, 'Income and living standards, 1870–2010', p. 175.

shares of the top income groups returning to their position of fifty years earlier. The equalization of the post-war period has been lost.'[15]

While at the end of the 1970s, the richest tenth of the population received 21% of total disposable income, their share rose through the 1980s and 1990s to reach 28–29% by 2002–2003, i.e. as much as for the whole of the bottom half of the population.[16] Over the short period from the late 1970s, the reversal in the direction of income distribution was striking. Viewed over a much longer period, it broke with the historical trend in which since 1867, the average income of the top 10% of the population had fallen from being 5.3 times the mean of all incomes, to being twice the mean by 1978/9.[17]

Low Incomes

The changes at the bottom were equally dramatic. At the end of the 1970s, the poorest tenth of people received about 4% of disposable income. By 1990 this share had fallen to below 3% for the first time in thirty years.[18] The increasing gap between the poorest and richest incomes was also accompanied by changes in the clustering of incomes in-between. During the 1980s, the distinct clump in the concentration of people around middle income levels began to break up and polarize towards high and low incomes. By the early 1990s, relative poverty was twice the level it had been in the 1960s, and three times what it had been in the late 1970s.[19] While the real income of the population as a whole increased by 36% between 1979 and 1990, inequality increased to such an extent that the poorest 10% of the population were 13% absolutely worse off in 1993/4 than they had been in 1979, while the real income of the richest decile rose by 60%.[20] By 1985, according to the (Blue Book) national income series, income inequality was greater than at any time since 1949, and the income share of the richest fifth of the population (at 43.1% of the total) was higher than at any time since World War II.

[15] Atkinson, *Top Incomes in the UK*, p. 38; Hills, *Inequality and the State*, p. 28.
[16] Hills, *Inequality and the State*, p. 263.   [17] Phelps Brown, *Egalitarianism*, p. 316.
[18] Goodman, Johnson and Webb, *Inequality*, pp. 92–3.
[19] Hills, *Inequality and the State*, p. 263.
[20] Barr, *The Economics of the Welfare State*, p. 34.
Hills with Gardiner, *The Future of Welfare*, p. 37.

Income and Earnings

In analysing the causes of these changes in income distribution, it needs noting that the composition of income itself changed. As a proportionate component of incomes, earnings fell from forming three-quarters of all income in the early 1960s, to comprising about 60% by the start of the 1990s.[21] While in 1978, wages and salaries (excluding income from self employment) accounted for nearly two-thirds of household market income, by 1996 this had fallen to only 54%. In contrast, income from self-employment rose from 7 to 8% of income during the 1960s to 11% by the end of the 1980s. That the level of self-employment rose faster than the income share of self-employment reflected the very low level of profits made by many of the newest of the self-employed. Over the 1980s the self-employed made up an increasing proportion of the poorest group. This reflected an increasing number of low-skilled unemployed individuals trying to return to the labour market, being unable to find a job, and using self-employment as a way in, at times making use of such government schemes as the Enterprise Allowance Scheme.[22]

Within earnings, from the late 1970s there was a widening dispersion at both the top and bottom of the range which contributed significantly to growing overall inequality.[23] The widening dispersion of earnings from the late 1970s may have been due both to the easing of wage constraints and to the emergence of new specific demands for labour. The operation of incomes policies during the 1960s and 1970s partially restricted the growth of wage differentials especially for those income policies that contained a flat-rate element, since the same cash increase represented a higher percentage increase for the less well paid than for the more highly paid.[24] Wage Councils, which had dealt with the 10% of the population covered by minimum payments were abolished in 1993, although the power to enforce the set minima in such industries as catering and retail effectively diminished over the 1980s.[25] It is also likely that trade unions had an equalizing effect on the distribution of wages and that the fall in the proportion of the workforce belonging to a trade union from 58% to 42% between 1980 and 1990, and to 27.3% by 1997, will also have contributed to rising wage dispersion.[26] In other

[21] Goodman, Johnson, Webb, *Inequality*, p. 139.
[22] Goodman, Johnson, Webb, *Inequality*, p. 107.
[23] Hills, *Inequality and the State*, p. 263.
[24] Goodman, Johnson, Webb, *Inequality*, p. 167.
[25] Goodman, Johnson, Webb, *Inequality*, p. 169.
[26] Goodman, Johnson, Webb, *Inequality*, p. 169.

countries where the importance of unions did not decline as much as in Britain or where centralized wage bargaining was important, wage differentials did not widen so much.[27] In Britain and the United States, social norms appear to have influenced strongly pay relativities up until the late 1970s, but thereafter a change in government and social attitudes tolerated (if not encouraged) the highly paid accelerating away.[28]

Widening wage differentials were associated with, but by no means entirely explained by, increasing returns to skills and educational qualifications. The possession of qualifications was associated with higher wage premiums in the mid-1990s than in the mid-1970s. For instance, men with a degree had weekly earnings 73% greater than those with no qualifications in the earlier period, but 93% higher in the later one. This occurred despite a substantial increase in the supply of workers with degrees over the period.[29] Premiums also increased for men with lower qualifications compared with those with none. For women, the premium on a degree and lower and middle vocational qualifications increased, but not for higher vocational qualifications or A levels by themselves.[30] One explanation of this close(r) association of wage premiums and qualifications was that the economy embarked on a period of 'skilled-biased' technological change, whose effect may have been heightened by a structural shift in employment from manufacturing to services.[31] The changes in demand for skilled and unskilled workers did not just take place between manufacturing and services but were also within manufacturing. Lacking certified skills, unskilled workers not only experienced a fall in their relative wage, but also in their real wage. Particularly vulnerable were younger workers who were recent entrants into the labour force, whilst the premium to wages that skilled workers could command rose.[32] This fall in real wages cannot be explained by an outward shift in supply of unskilled workers, since the number of people continuing in education beyond the ages of sixteen and eighteen in the UK rose, if anything actually reducing the supply of unskilled workers. Rather, there was simply a fall in the demand for unskilled workers.[33] If unskilled workers became or remained unemployed, they were likely to suffer increasing relative poverty. Average incomes among full-time workers were more than three times those of the unemployed and that gap grew over the 1980s while the real incomes (after housing costs) of the unemployed barely changed between 1979 and the early 1990s. Full-time workers saw their

---

[27] Hills, *Inequality and the State*, p. 81.   [28] Hills, *Inequality and the State*, p. 83.
[29] Hills, *Inequality and the State*, p. 79.   [30] Hills, *Inequality and the State*, p. 80.
[31] Machin, 'The changing nature'; Goodman, Johnson, Webb, *Inequality*, p. 164.
[32] Goodman, Johnson, Webb, *Inequality*, p. 165.
[33] Goodman, Johnson, Webb, *Inequality*, p. 166.

incomes rise by virtually a half. In 1980 the 90th percentile hourly wage was two and half times that of the 10th percentile. This differential had increased to 3.2 times by 1990; and this change over one decade followed a century of stable or falling inequality.[34]

The effects of unemployment were heightened by the increased polarization between households with and without work. In the early 1960s, over a third of people lived in single-earner couple families. By the end of the 1970s, this proportion had shrunk to less than a quarter, and by the early 1990s to around 15%.[35] Certainly the old stereotype of the typical family of working husband, non-working mother, and children had faded. From 1979, there was a fall in the number of people living in families with a full-time worker. Excluding the self-employed, 65% of the population were in this position in 1979, as compared to only 51% by the early 1990s. In the mid-1970s more than a third of working-age households contained one adult who worked and one who did not, and only 7% had no adult in work. By 2001, only a sixth of households had a mix of working and non-working adults, and a sixth had no adult in work.[36] Added to this, there was an increase in the non-employed population. In 1979, 8% of the population were in (non-pensioner) families with no worker. This proportion had doubled by 1992/3.[37] There was a polarization within two-adult households between the 'work-rich' where both worked and the 'work-poor', where neither worked, the phenomenon of 'more work in fewer households'.[38] While the male unemployment rate was 10% in both 1981 and 1996, the proportion of (working age) workless households nearly doubled, from 11% to 19%. The fall in the number of workless families in both the late 1980s and the late 1990s was much less marked than those in unemployment. By 2002, although the employment rate—the proportion of working age adults in work—was the highest for the years shown, worklessness was still far higher than in the 1970s. By 1996, three-quarters of workless households were poor, and they accounted for more than half of all non-pensioners in poverty.[39]

Most of the rise in female participation occurred during the 1960s and 1970s, so prior to the main period of rising household inequality.[40] The proportion of working-age women in part-time work rose from one in five in the early 1960s to one in three by the early 1990s. By the early 1990s, about 74% of working-age men were in employment or self-employment, and about

---

[34] Johnson, 'The assessment: inequality', p. 4.   [35] Goodman, Johnson, Webb, *Inequality*, p. 158.
[36] Goodman, Johnson, Webb, *Inequality*, p. 168; Gregg and Wadsworth, 'More work'.
[37] Johnson, 'The assessment', p. 4.   [38] Atkinson, 'What is happening?', table 5.
[39] Hills, *Inequality and the State*, pp. 85–6.   [40] Goodman, Johnson, Webb, *Inequality*, p. 160.

64% of women. By contrast, in the early 1960s, as many as 92% of men were participating in the workforce, compared with 48% of women.[41] Among two-earner households the rise of the two-earner couple had different effects at different times.[42] Up to the 1970s it was the wives of relatively well-paid men whose employment increased most rapidly, tending to increase household income inequality. In the 1980s, however, the wives of less well-paid (but employed) men tended to catch up. This tended to slow inequality growth among couples with work, but contributed to the growing gap between them and other population groups, such as pensioners, lone parents, or the unemployed.[43]

Social Insurance and the Beveridge Report

On 2 December 1942, the *Report on Social Insurance and Allied Services* (the Beveridge Report) was published and some half a million copies were sold.[44] This Report and the subsequent 1944 White Papers on Social Insurance established the early post-war system of social security.[45] The 'social insurance' of the Report's title was a compulsory scheme for income replacement in the event of stated contingencies such as unemployment, industrial injury, and old age occurring. As a social insurance scheme, risks were pooled and with the immediate exception of pensioners, beneficiaries drew from the fund of pooled contributions built up over time. The costs of the scheme were limited by limiting the risks and the benefits. Risk was limited by including as assumptions underpinning the Report a government commitment, as in the 1944 *White Paper on Employment Policy*, to contain the rate of unemployment and to provide healthcare so as to limit the incidence of ill health and injury. The duration of benefits could also be limited. The payment of unconditional unemployment benefit was limited to six months and thereafter it would be 'conditional upon attendance at a work or training centre'. Claimants had to remain available for work and those 'refusing suitable employment, dismissed for misconduct or leaving their work voluntarily without just causes' would be disqualified from receiving unemployment benefit.[46] This

---

[41] Goodman, Johnson, Webb, *Inequality*, p. 155.
[42] Harkness, Machin and Waldfogel, 'Women's pay and family incomes'.
[43] Hills, *Inequality and the State*, p. 87.
[44] *Social Insurance and Allied Services*, November 1942, Cmd. 6404 (Beveridge Report); Arrow, 'Uncertainty'; Akerlof, 'The market for "lemons"'; Pauly, 'Overinsurance'; Rothschild and Stiglitz, 'Equilibrium'.
[45] *Social Insurance Part I*, Cmnd. 6550 and *Social Insurance, Part II*, Cmnd. 6551.
[46] Beveridge Report, para. 326.

reflected both the insurance nature of the contract with a concern for 'moral hazard' (that being insured against becoming unemployed made you less likely to avoid becoming so) and a concern with one of the Five Giants, that of Idleness, since 'complete idleness even on an income demoralises'.[47] The other giants and their related welfare state programmes were Want (social security), Disease (National Health Service), Squalor (housing) and Ignorance (education).[48] The restrictions on social insurance unemployment benefit constituted a two-way contract, implying a responsibility for the unemployed to seek work, and for the government to seek to ensure that jobs were available to a work-fit labour force. As the Beveridge Report stated:

> The insured person should not feel that income for idleness, however, can come from a bottomless purse. The Government should not feel that by paying doles it can avoid the major responsibility of seeing that unemployment and disease are reduced to a minimum. The place for direct expenditure and organisation by the State is in maintaining employment of the labour and other productive resources of the country, and in preventing and in combating disease, not in patching an incomplete scheme of insurance.[49]

The social insurance scheme was financed on a flat-rate basis. As the ultimate objective of the scheme was to keep people out of poverty, then a risk-related premium (as in a simple insurance scheme) by charging higher premiums to the riskier lower-income groups, would, in itself, place them closer to falling into poverty. Similarly, income-based contributions could draw protests from higher-income groups whose perceived need to insure against entering poverty was small. A flat-rate basis for contributions into a scheme in which risk was pooled was complemented by a flat-rate benefit system in which beneficiaries, irrespective of income, received the same level of payment on the occurrence of a contingent risk.

Beveridge targeted an absolute, rather than a relative, measure of poverty. This reflected the initial restricted scope of earlier studies of poverty which were based mainly in towns beginning with Charles Booth in London and Seebohm Rowntree in York in 1899, and continuing with the studies by Bowley and Burnett-Hurst (1915, 1920); Reading, Northampton, Warrington, Stanley, and Bolton),[50] Bowley and Hogg (1923–4),[51] Llewellyn-Smith in

---

[47] Beveridge Report, paras. 327, 440.   [48] Beveridge Report, para 8.
[49] Beveridge Report, para. 22.
[50] Bowley and Burnett-Hurst, *Livelihood and Poverty*; Bowley and Burnett-Hurst, *Economic Conditions of Working-Class Households*.
[51] Bowley and Hogg, *Has Poverty Diminished?*

(1930–35 London),[52] Owen (Sheffield, 1933),[53] Jones(Merseyside, 1934),[54] Ford (Southampton, 1934),[55] Taylor (Plymouth, 1938),[56] and Tout (Bristol, 1938).[57] It was in his first study of poverty in York that Rowntree developed and formalized the concept of the poverty line, and distinguished between 'primary'(living below the poverty line with insufficient income) and 'second-ary' (living below the poverty line despite having sufficient income) poverty, as well as the concept of poverty over the life cycle. Following Rowntree's broad approach, Bowley, a trained statistician at the London School of Economics, pioneered the use of random sampling.[58] It was in using his own concept of absolute poverty that Beveridge intended to lift beneficiaries out of poverty. On the basis of Seebohm Rowntree's third survey of York published in 1951, absolute poverty appeared greatly diminished, with 3% of the population living in poverty compared with 13% in his interwar study and 30% in his original investigation in 1899.[59] Given the incidence of post-war food subsidies in the early post-war years, the estimates of poverty were likely to be tentative, and subsequent research by Hatton and Bailey has halved Rowntree and Laver's estimate of the fall in poverty, with much of that fall the result of food subsidies.[60] Yet, at the time and using a primary poverty line, Rowntree's sample survey seemed to indicate that poverty had been virtually abolished. With this problem almost cleared up, economists and social scientists could turn their attention elsewhere. As Hatton and Bailey remark, 'It is unfortunate that, in the absence of other comparable studies for the 1950s, this produced a somewhat distorted picture of poverty in the early post war period, an impression which it took two decades to counteract.' Or as the economist Tony Atkinson recalled:

> When I first began studying economics in the early 1960s, few economists were interested in the welfare state. Full employment, rising real wages, state pensions, and child benefit were together assumed to have eliminated poverty. In the UK, according to The Times, there had been a 'remarkable improvement—no less than the virtual abolition of the sheerest want'. According to Anthony Crosland (economist, later Foreign Secretary) in The Future of Socialism, 'primary poverty has been largely eliminated' (1956, p. 59).

[52] Llewellyn-Smith, The New Survey.   [53] Owen, A Survey.
[54] Jones, Social Survey of Merseyside.   [55] Ford, Work and Wealth.
[56] Taylor, A Social Survey.   [57] Tout, The Standard of Living.
[58] Glennerster, Hills, Piachaud and Webb, One Hundred Years.
[59] Glennerster, Hills, Piachaud and Webb, One Hundred Years, p. 31; Rowntree and Lavers, Poverty and the Welfare State.
[60] Glennerster, 'Poverty policy', p. 86.

Social security was a technical topic left to those specialising in social policy and it was rare for an article on this subject to appear in *The Economic Journal* or *American Economic Review*.[61]

Poverty

Ultimately, the greatest charge made against the system of social security which developed after World War II was that poverty persisted, even when a member of a household was in employment. While poverty was 'rediscovered' in the 1960s, in contrast to what was to come, the 1960s and 1970s were a period of relative stability, with poverty still in single figures on the standard benefit level measure, and only around 10% on a half mean income measure. Based on a poverty line of 50% of average income, the poverty headcount increased from 4.4 million people in 1979 to 10.4 million ten years later, the latter figure embracing 19% of the population and 22% of children.[62] Overall relative poverty, which had been about 10% of the population in the 1960s dipped to a low point of 6% in 1977, but then grew very rapidly through the 1980s to peak at 21% in the early 1990s. After a dip and then a rise back in the mid-1990s it fell slowly from 1996/97 and into the twenty-first century. Nonetheless, in 2004 it was still three times its level of the mid-1970s.[63] By 2009–2010, 10 million people were living in relative poverty, which was 4 million more than in 1961. Single-parent households were more likely, and couples without children less likely, to be in poverty.[64]

From the 1980s, Britain's poverty record did not compare well with that of other developed economies, with only the US and Ireland having worse relative poverty rates. It was not just that the number in poverty rose from the late 1970s, but also that other characteristics of poverty, such as its persistence, intensified. Even so, while in any four-year period between 1991 and 2000 about one-third of individuals experienced some poverty, only about one in ten was below 60% of median household income for three or more years, and only one in twenty for all four years.[65] Child poverty became of particular concern at the end of the century and in 1999 the Blair government adopted measures designed to end child poverty by 2020. Gordon Brown, as prime minister, enshrined this ambition in law in the Child Poverty Act

---

[61] Atkinson, *The Economic Consequences*, p. 3.
[62] Atkinson, *Incomes and the Welfare State*, p. 292.
[63] Hills, 'The last quarter century', p. 123.
[64] Gazeley, 'Income and living standards, 1870–2010', p. 172.
[65] Barr, *Economics of the Welfare State*, p. 227.

2010.[66] Considerable progress was made with the poverty rate falling as a share of median income from 22% to 16% between 1992 and 2011.[67] Yet in 2014, the poverty rate in the UK still remained above its level in the 1960s and 1970s, and 3% above its rate when the Child Poverty Action Group was founded in 1965.[68] Poverty was often more persistent in the UK and the US than in other comparable countries. OECD comparisons of poverty durations in the early 1990s suggested that of those who were affected by poverty in a six-year period, the average duration was 2.4 years or less in the Netherlands, Sweden, Germany, and Canada, but three years or more in the UK and US.[69] The poorest decile lost not only in relative terms but also absolutely.[70] Using the standard EU definition of poverty as people living in households with less than 60% of the median income, the Joseph Rowntree Foundation found that in 2000, 13.3 million people in the UK were in poverty, and that this figure had remained unchanged throughout the 1990s, though it had almost doubled in the 1980s from just over 7 million in 1979.[71] In 2000, these 13.3 million people comprised just over 23% of the population; in 1979 the comparable share was 9% of the population. Absolute poverty by headcount in the richest countries in the mid-1990s was much the lowest in the Nordic countries, followed by the mainland West European countries. It was highest in Australia, and also high in the US and the UK. The pattern of inequality was very similar.[72]

The fact and persistence of poverty in working households in the 1970s and 1980s was of particular concern. While rising unemployment decreased their proportionate importance, the largest single group of those in poverty was often households with someone in work. Moreover, this group fell the furthest below the poverty line with an income less than half of the current poverty line. The relative severity of poverty in households with one or more in regular work was greater in 2001/02 than 1899.[73] This was not supposed to happen. Poverty amongst those at work was supposed to be a nineteenth-century problem and the Beveridge Report assumed, against a background of 1930s unemployment, that anyone in employment would be able to support themselves and one child. The cost of raising children was recognized, but the

---

[66] Atkinson, *Inequality: What Can Be Done?*, pp. 23–4.
[67] Atkinson, *Inequality: What Can Be Done?*, p. 24.
[68] Atkinson, *Inequality: What Can Be Done?*, p. 24; Nickell 2004.
[69] Hills, 'Policy challenges and dilemmas', pp. 135, 144; Antolin, Dang, and Oxley, *Poverty Dynamics in Four OECD Countries.*
[70] Barr, *Economics of the Welfare State*, p. 133.
Hills with Gardiner, *The Future of Welfare*, p. 37.
[71] Johnson, 'The welfare state, income and living standards', p. 229.
[72] Barr, *Economics of the Welfare State*, p. 134; Burtless and Smeeding, 'US poverty in a cross-sectional context' in S. Danziger and R. Haveman (eds.) *Understanding Poverty*, Table 1.
[73] Glennerster, Hills, Piachaud, and Webb, *One Hundred Years*, p. 49, Table 3.

provision of family allowances was supposed to remove child-raising as a cause of poverty.

In the negotiations preceding the passing of the social insurance legislation Beveridge had had to concede on grounds of cost that a family allowance should not be paid for the eldest child and that the whole family allowance benefit should be financed by taxation, rather than by social insurance contributions.[74] Hence its rather anomalous move to outside of the social insurance scheme to join government undertakings on health and employment as one of the three 'assumptions'. Yet for Beveridge family allowances were important both specifically for cauterizing a source of poverty but also as a universal benefit for promoting the bearing and raising of children.[75] As was made clear in paragraph 117 of the Beveridge Report, the allowances were

part of social security, and a form of expenditure whose advantage will be felt by married women more than by any class in the community. In the next thirty years housewives as mothers have vital work to do in ensuring the adequate continuance of the British race and of British ideals in the world.[76]

Beveridge, like Keynes, was a member of the Eugenics Society and while the Nazi abominations had seriously compromised the eugenics approach, it is salutary to remember that it was a popular and respectable view amongst Western European intelligentsia before World War II. The Beveridge Report stated clearly that it put 'a premium on marriage, in place of penalizing it' and it was argued that a woman, who on getting married commonly gave up paid work, did on becoming married gain a

legal right to maintenance by her husband as a first line of defence against risks which fall directly on the solitary woman; she undertakes at the same time to perform vital unpaid service and becomes exposed to new risks, including the risk that her married life may be ended prematurely by widowhood or separation.[77]

Priority was given to the needs of the family as the most appropriate unit for the conceiving, bearing, and raising of children. While tax benefits for married men with children had been removed during the war in the interests of improving the equity and efficiency of wartime taxation, a common view, as expressed by Keynes, was that 'the strengthening of the economic

[74] Abel-Smith, 'The Beveridge Report', p. 17.
[75] Thane, 'The debate on the declining birth-rate in Britain'.
[76] Beveridge Report, para. 117.   [77] Beveridge Report, para. 108.

position of the family unit should be a main purpose of social policy now and after the war.'[78]

Social Insurance or Taxation

The flat-in, flat-out basis of the Beveridge scheme limited its ability to finance other than on an absolute level of poverty relief. The alternative was to move towards a tax-funded scheme, with its likely implications for graduated benefits as well as contributions, as has always been recognized in wartime discussions of what became the Beveridge Report. From first principles, the Treasury objected to Beveridge's social insurance contributions as a form of hypothecation, whereby particular revenues were raised for and assigned to particular designated expenditure. Quite apart from its objections to hypothecation per se, the Treasury also objected to the asymmetry wherein 'experience indicated that if such a fund showed a balance, there was a demand for increased benefits; but if it showed a deficit the Treasury was asked to provide a subsidy.'[79] Keynes objected 'to the peculiar method of a poll tax and to the inevitable inadequacy of the contribution so long as it is a poll tax'[80] while his fellow economist James Meade thought that 'the continuation of the principle of social security financed by compulsory *insurance* premiums is probably due to conservatism rather than to any logically more cogent reason.'[81] Yet both Keynes and Meade recognized that given the importance to Beveridge of social insurance, its familiarity to workers and the existence of a mechanism for collecting contributions, it was pragmatic to go with Beveridge's ideas for the moment, although in time Keynes thought that the two systems could be merged. For Keynes the flat-rate contribution was a short-term administrative expedient. For Beveridge it was a matter of principle which helped to define a relationship between its members and the state, different from that between taxpayers and the state.[82] As each member of the scheme made an equal contribution into a fund, then this provided the basis for their equal entitlement to benefit. This was in contrast to the PAYG basis of taxation and

[78] TNA T 171/360, notes on the budget, J.M. Keynes, 3 November 1941. Quoted in Daunton, *Just Taxes*, p. 181.
[79] TNA CAB 87/76: SIC(41), minutes of 4th meeting. Quoted in H. Glennerster and M. Evans, 'Beveridge and his assumptive worlds', p. 59.
[80] TNA T 161/1164/5484971/2, Keynes, letter to Sir R. Hopkins in Glennerster and Evans in Hills, Ditch, and Glennerster, *Beveridge and Social Security*, p. 60.
[81] TNA T230/101, SIC(41)20.
[82] See, for example, his discussions with Keynes in September 1942, TNA T161/1164/S484971/2. Glennerster and Evans, p. 60.

its means-tested payment of social assistance. As a view of citizenship, it was one in which entitlements derived from membership of such a community. As such, the entitlements are not at the whim of the state or of any test, of means or otherwise, which it might construct to determine desert.[83] This is the Beveridge Report commenting on 'the strength of popular objection to any kind of means test':

> This objection springs not so much from a desire to get everything for nothing, as from resentment at a provision which appears to penalise what people have come to regard as the duty and pleasure of thrift, of putting pennies away for a rainy day. Management of one's income is an essential element of a citizen's freedom. Payment of a substantial part of the cost of benefit as a contribution irrespective of the means of the contribution is the firm basis of a claim to benefit irrespective of means.[84]

Social Insurance and Poverty

In his attachment to a subsistence minimum and flat-rate contributions and benefits, Beveridge appears to have been particularly influenced by Rowntree's 1936 study of York, published in 1941 as *Poverty and Progress*[85] which Beveridge took as indicating that the causes of poverty had shifted towards those which were amenable to solution and/or removal through insurance benefits. Unemployment and old age, rather than low wages, were now the main causes of insecurity and poverty. Beveridge believed that means-tested poverty relief would wither away as the entire population was incorporated in the National Insurance scheme. In fact the adequacy of national insurance benefits to keep claimants above the defined poverty line steadily declined. In general, the proportion of the British population receiving means-tested benefits rose from just over 4% in 1948 to 8% in 1974, 16% in 1986 and over 20% in 1994.[86] The number claiming means-tested benefits had doubled from 1 to 2 million between 1948 and 1966, and it was to reach over 4 million by the early 1980s.[87] Means-tested benefits accounted for 42% of total spending on cash benefits in 1948, a figure that fell to 26% by 1965 but then subsequently rose back to 42% of total benefit spending in 1998.[88]

---

[83] Plant, 'Citizenship and social security', p. 155.   [84] Beveridge Report, para. 21.
[85] Glennerster and Evans, 'Beveridge and his assumptive worlds', p. 61.
[86] Evans, 'Social security', p. 302.
[87] Johnson, 'The welfare state', p. 229.   [88] Johnson, 'The welfare state', p. 221.

A persistent contribution to the rise of those receiving means-tested benefits was the problem of rent. Rent was not only the single largest (and non-discretionary) item in the low-income budget, but it was also the cost which varied most geographically. This had clearly concerned Beveridge in his *Report*, and it was only with great reluctance that he had come down in favour of including an average amount for rent in his levels of benefit. In 1948 the main national insurance benefits were paid to a married couple at a rate of £2.10 per week. However, national assistance offered £2 plus rent. It followed that any national insurance beneficiary with a rent of more than 10p per week, and without other resources, was entitled to national assistance. This was certainly not the relationship between national assistance and social insurance intended by Beveridge.[89]

The Rediscovery of Poverty

With the introduction of the Family Expenditure Survey (FES) in 1953/4, initially on a one-off basis but then continuously from 1957, it became possible to use the annual samples of 7,000 households to estimate income, expenditure, and poverty on a national, rather than a local, basis. While the primary purpose of the FES was to gather data on expenditure patterns so as to enable the Retail Price Index to be constructed, it also collected information about household incomes.[90] Using FES data for 1953/4 and 1960, Peter Townsend and Dorothy Wedderburn at the London School of Economics presented preliminary results of their analysis in 1962, with the final results appearing in 1965 in a pamphlet by Abel-Smith and Townsend, *The Poor and the Poorest*.[91] Further analyses along similar lines using FES data in the 1960s and 1970s included those by Atkinson; Fiegehen, Lansley, and Smith; and Beckerman and Clark.[92] Whereas earlier studies, notably those of Rowntree, began from budget standards built up by specifying minimum consumption needs and costing them, Abel-Smith and Townsend's *The Poor and the Poorest* used income poverty lines based on social security rates payable under the means-tested National Assistance scheme.[93] One outcome was the

[89] Dilnot, Kay and Morris, *The Reform of Social Security*, pp. 19–20.

[90] Glennerster, Hills, Piachaud and Webb, *One Hundred Years of Poverty and Policy*, p. 32.

[91] Abel-Smith and Townsend, *The Poor and the Poorest*.

[92] Atkinson, *Poverty in Britain*; Fiegehen, Lansley, and Smith, *Poverty and Progress*; Beckerman and Clark, *Poverty and Social Security*.

[93] Veit-Wilson has emphasized that Rowntree's conception of poverty was broader than a pure minimum subsistence one; in defining poverty at least, though, a subsistence standard was employed. Veit-Wilson, 'Paradigms of poverty'.

'rediscovery' of poverty in 1960s, with Abel-Smith and Townsend estimating an increase in the number of people in poverty from about 4 million in 1953/4 to 7.5 million in 1960.[94] This was surprising given economic growth and low unemployment since the war, and it partly reflected the use of a higher poverty line 140% of the basic 'scale rate' of benefit (on the basis that this allowed for other 'extras' people on National Assistance could get on top of scale rates), which produced a poverty rate of 14.2%.[95] As Abel-Smith and Townsend showed, even so, relative poverty, which affected less than 4% of the population, was at very low levels by modern standards if the standard benefit level was used as the poverty line. Measured in absolute terms, the absolute poverty rate clearly fell between 1953–1954 and 1961.

A response to relative poverty which concentrated on raising benefits threatened the viability of Beveridge's scheme for social insurance. Essentially the scheme was designed to target an absolute level of poverty, but there was political pressure to use it to target a relative measure of poverty. Paradoxically, it was the early financial health of the scheme which encouraged politicians to raise benefit levels so as to reduce the extent of relative deprivation as economic growth and rising living standards made benefits based on absolute poverty measures seem increasingly miserly.[96] It was economic growth which produced a surplus in the National Insurance Fund in its early years, as the rate of post-war unemployment was lower than the rate of 8.5% which had been included in the actuarial calculations. While pensions cost 50% more than expected, this was offset by savings on the anticipated cost of unemployment benefit and family allowances such that by 1955 the total level of benefit expenditure was broadly in line with Beveridge's projections.[97] However by the time of the 1958 public expenditure crisis and tightening public finances, political thoughts were turning away from increasing benefits to increasing contributions. This struck at the flat-in, flat-out basis of the social insurance scheme since increased contributions could only realistically be raised from those whose incomes meant that they were at less risk of poverty than the lower-income groups. In 1961, graduated contributions were introduced and in the 1975 Social Security Act the weekly stamp was replaced with an earnings-related contribution for all employed persons. By 1975, national insurance contributions were entirely earnings-related. In the 1978 Finance Act the government imposed a national insurance surcharge on the employer's

[94] Gazeley, Gutierrez, Newall, Reynolds, and Searle, *The Poor and the Poorest*, p. 3.
[95] Piachaud and Webb, 'Changes in Poverty', p. 47.
[96] Runciman, *Relative Deprivation*.
[97] Dilnot, Kay, and Morris, *Reform of Social Security*, p. 17.

contribution simply to raise more general revenue rather than to balance the notional National Insurance Pound. In 1981 and 1983 employees and their contributions were surcharged for similar general finance reasons. Whereas in 1949, national insurance contributions were 5.5% of the total wage and salary bill, by 1982 this figure was 16.3%.[98] At the same time, the relationship between contributions and benefits eroded, with the entitlement to the basic National Insurance benefits continuing to rely on the number of contributions made but not on their level. In 1948, weekly contributions were 35% of the weekly value of the pension, regardless of earnings. In 1985, at the lower earnings limit, total national insurance contributions formed 19% of the pension. At the upper earnings limit, total contributions formed 144% of the pension.[99]

Lone-Parent Families

As well as targeting relative poverty in general, particular groups also both pointed to difficulties in operating the social security system and to inequity in its operation. Two groups might be taken to illustrate this point: lone parent families, and pensioners. Whatever the arguments over the extent to which poverty was rediscovered by Abel-Smith and Townsend, what was pointed up in their work was that particular groups were vulnerable to poverty. One such was single-parent families, headed predominantly by women. Single-parent families found a social security system essentially structured around households less than suited or sensitive to their needs. As the number of lone-parent families increased, so too did this problem demand attention. Pressure on government to do more for such lone-parent families was stepped up by the establishment of the Child Poverty Action Group in 1965, following Abel-Smith and Townsend's publication of *The Poor and the Poorest* which drew attention to the problem.[100]

The growth in the number of lone-parent families was striking and the Finer Committee which reported in 1974 reflected official recognition of the issue.[101] At 570,000 in 1971, the number of lone-parent families rose to 750,000 in 1976, 940,000 in 1984, and 970,000 in 1985. In 1986 the figure was 1.01 million, 35% higher than a decade before. According to the 1988

[98] Dilnot, Kay, Morris, *Reform of Social Security*, pp. 18–19.
[99] Dilnot and Webb, 'Reforming national insurance contributions', p. 39.
[100] Field, 'A pressure group for the poor'; Abel-Smith and Townsend, *The Poor and the Poorest*; Thane and Davidson, *The Child Poverty Action Group*.
[101] *Report of the Committee on One-Parent Families*, Cmnd. 5629, London, HMSO (1974).

General Household Survey, lone-parent families formed about 16% of all families with dependent children. The growth in numbers was accompanied by an increase in the proportion of lone parents receiving social security benefits and reliant on them for their principal source of income. In 1980, three-quarters of a million lone parents received social security benefits, 44% of whom received supplementary benefit. By 1987 the total number in receipt had increased by 40% to over a million, of whom 60% received supplementary benefit. The adverse economic circumstances of lone parents were further illustrated by DHSS estimates that, in 1982, 41% of lone parents were in the bottom quintile of equivalent gross income, but only 18% of working-age couples with children. Most lone parents were (and are) women: there were nine times as many lone mothers as lone fathers.[102] Lone parents were to remain an important group among the poor. Between 1979 and 1989, not only did the number of lone parents rise sharply from 0.8 million to 1.1 million, but the proportion of those families dependent on Supplementary Benefit (SB)/Income Support (IS) also rose from 38% to 66%. The combination of these two effects pushed the number receiving SB/IS up from 0.3 million to 0.75 million.[103] This was an important driver of child poverty. At the turn of the twenty-first century there was a high rate of lone parenthood—only New Zealand and the US exceeded the UK's 22% rate—and a low proportion of lone parents who were employed.[104] Although family income supplement was not exclusively directed at one-parent families, a high proportion of recipients did fall into this category. A number of specific provisions were also intro-duced; a premium on child benefit, an enhanced tax allowance, and a specially favourable basis for supplementary benefit entitlement.[105]

Long-Term Care

Before considering the financing of pensions, one casualty of the way in which Beveridge's social insurance scheme developed was the diminution in credibility of the concept of social insurance. As the name of the social/national insurance scheme was retained while its insurance principles were undermined as the scheme mutated into a tax, so the political and, frankly,

---

[102] Jenkins, Ermisch and Wright, '"Adverse selection" features', p. 76; Haskey, 'One parent families'; Haskey, 'One parent families and their children'; DHSS (1985), *Reform of Social Security: Background Papers*, vol. 3, Cmnd 9519, London: HMSO.

[103] Giles and Webb, 'A guide to poverty statistics', p. 87.

[104] Hills, 'Policy challenges and dilemmas', p. 139.

[105] Dilnot, Kay, Morris, *Reform of Social Security*, p. 25.

legal credibility of social insurance eroded. Many recognized it to be a tax, and those who did not, did not have their delusions corrected by governments. Similarly, no government sought to correct the misapprehension of some that national insurance contributions provided the bulk of funding for the NHS. This was unfortunate since the later emergence of the problem of financing the cost of long-term care and the random and costly nature of long-term care makes it an attractive subject for social insurance. As yet, few individuals buy such long-term care insurance. This may reflect an insufficiency of attractive private insurance contracts, but it is one area in which the state could compel everyone to take out some regulated form of insurance.[106] Green and White Papers have sought to address a future in which, as the 2006 King's Fund Wanless Review, *Securing Good Care for Older People*, predicted, by 2026, one in five people in England would be over sixty-five, with the number of people over eighty-five growing by two-thirds.[107] The Care and Support Commission led by Andrew Dilnot proposed in its report in July 2011 that the lifetime contribution from an individual's personal wealth should be capped at between £25,000 and £50,000, with £35,000 being considered an appropriate and fair figure. This has the benefit of removing the fear and uncertainty of the current system, but with continuing hotel costs to pay. The point here though, is not to debate the actual costs of the care, but to point up that in a situation in which there is a known, potentially high-cost risk but with a probability of considerably less than one, that a form of compulsory Beveridge-style insurance is one approach to this problem of financing long-term care.

Pensions and Pensioners

Over time, the principal recipients of social security payments were no longer the targeted poor, but the elderly. Pensions and other social security payments to the elderly came to account for half of all social security expenditure by the 1990s. From 1948/9 until 1981/2, expenditure on the basic state pension rose from 1.5% to 4.5% of national income. In 1948, 13% of the population were state pensioners, compared with 19% in 2010. Increases in the state

---

[106] Brown and Finkelstein, 'The interaction of public and private insurance'; Brown and Finkelstein, 'Insuring long-term costs'; Drèze, Pestieau, and Schokkaert, 'Arrow's theorem', p. 104.

[107] Department of Health, *Independence, Well-being and Choice*, Cm 6499, March 2005; Department of Health, *Our Health: our care, our say: a new direction for community services*, CM 6737, January 2006; The King's Fund, *Securing Good Care For Older People*, 2006; Gheera and Long, 'Social care reform'.

pension age were designed to restrict this increase to 21% by 2050, although the option of indexing the retirement age to life expectancy proved unacceptable to politicians.[108] With the effective abandonment of the Beveridge social insurance model, the financing of the state pension was on an Over-Lapping Generations model as developed initially by Allais and Samuelson.[109] There were very respectable arguments for financing state pension schemes on an intergenerational basis and it is as well to recall Keynes's advice to Beveridge not to bother too much about the distant actuarial future: 'The future can well be left to look after itself... It will have far more resources for doing so than the immediate present.'[110] Continued economic growth was assumed, although the dependency ratio between taxpaying workers (the denominator) and pensioners (the numerator) had to remain viable.[111] In the 1990s, there were 10.3 million men and women over state pensionable age and 34.3 million working-age individuals, producing a dependency ratio of 3.3. This dependency ratio was expected to change significantly from 2010, such that by 2030 there will be 33.7 million people of working age and 14 million over pensionable age, a ratio of 2.4 to 1.[112]

Quite what the basis and form of the state pension scheme should be was discussed from very soon after the launch of the post-war social security system. The roots of what became the State Earnings-Related Pension Scheme (SERPS) can be traced right back to the 1950s, and the growing concern with both the adequacy of pensions for those on low incomes and with the perceived inequity of a two-track pensions system in which long-time members of occupational pension schemes enjoyed tax relief in line with income and, as in employment so in retirement, went on to enjoy higher retirement incomes.[113] The form of tax benefits of occupational schemes were that full tax relief was offered on both employers' and employees' contributions into the scheme, and investment income earned by the fund was also untaxed. Income tax only became payable as pensioners drew their pension. Such tax benefits were appealing, especially to those on higher marginal rates of taxation. While before the war around 8% of workers were in private-sector occupational pension schemes, with a further 5% in public-sector schemes, by 1956 the proportion of workers in occupational schemes had leapt up to

[108] Brittan, *Against the Flow*, p. 79; Bozio, Crawford, and Tetlow, *The History of State Pensions*, pp. 64, 66.
[109] Samuelson, 'An exact consumption-loans model'; Aaron, 'The social insurance paradox'.
[110] Harris, 'The Roots of Public Pensions Provision', p. 35.
[111] Pemberton, 'Economic policy', in Wadsworth and Bynner, *Companion to Life Course*, Table 5.3.
[112] Dilnot and Johnson, 'What pension should the state provide?', pp. 5–6.
[113] Pemberton, 'The failure of "nationalisation by attraction"'.

33%, most of this growth having occurred since the end of the war, and with the figure rising by 2.3% a year.[114] From the mid-1960s, occupational pensions contributions were made by just over half of the working population.[115] While the growth of occupational pension schemes removed some of the political pressure to improve the state pension, this did not reduce the need to devise a state pension scheme for those not in occupational pension schemes which was other than the flat-rate scheme originally introduced by Beveridge (and initially funded from general taxation).

In the Labour Party in 1956, Richard Crossman, the pension spokesman for the Party National Executive Committee used the expertise of Richard Titmuss, Brian Abel-Smith, Peter Townsend, and Tony Lynes at the LSE to devise a post-Beveridge answer. The result was *National Superannuation*.[116] This policy document essentially adopted the US model, as the Swedes and the Germans did at about the same time.[117] The Labour Party took Crossman's extensive scheme of 'national superannuation' to the electorate in the 1959 general election, which it lost, and it was not until he was in power as Secretary of State for Health and Social Security in 1968 that Crossman could move towards legislating for a scheme of 'national superannuation'.[118] Although controversial, Crossman's proposals gained parliamentary approval and, but for Labour's defeat in the 1970 general election, would have come into effect.[119] The intention was to extend the benefits of earnings-related pension benefits to all, with the proposed scheme paying a pension equal to approximately 50% of income at retirement. To finance this, higher contributions would be required. These would be invested by the state in stocks and shares in order to build up a large fund out of which the considerably improved pension would be paid.[120] Just as electoral defeat in 1970 had prevented Crossman's scheme coming into effect, so too did defeat in 1974 stymie the Conservative's variant on the theme, albeit one in which the government gave the dominant role in the extension of pension provision to the private sector and supplemented it with a 'state reserve scheme'.[121] This political hokey cokey with the future of the state pension scheme was

---

[114] Hannah, *Inventing Retirement*, p. 40; Pemberton, 'Politics and pensions', p. 47.

[115] Dilnot and Johnson, 'What pension should the state provide?', p. 4.

[116] Labour Party, *National Superannuation*.   [117] Glennerster, 'Why so different?', p. 69.

[118] Labour Party, 'National Superannuation'.

[119] Ogus, 'Great Britain'. The White Paper was *National Superannuation and Social Insurance* (Cmnd. 3883, London, HMSO, 1969) the main provisions of which became the National Insurance and Superannuation Bill 1969.

[120] Pemberton, 'Politics and pensions', p. 49.

[121] The White Paper was *Strategy for Pensions* (Cmnd. 4715, London, HMSO, 1971) which was to become the Social Security Act 1973.

recognized as being unacceptable and attention moved to finding a set of proposals which could command bipartisan support.

The eventual outcome, SERPS, was steered by Barbara Castle into legislative form as the 1975 Social Security Pensions Act and began operation in 1978.[122] Under it, retirement pensioners would receive an earnings-related pension in addition to their basic state pension. The pension was based on the best twenty years of qualifying earnings, these being revalued to the date of retirement in line with national average earnings, and the earnings-related pension being one-quarter of the resulting average. Since it was only earnings after April 1978 that could be considered as qualifying earnings, this scheme would not approach maturity until after 1998 and the scheme was essentially financed on an OLG basis, meaning that its costs would rise over time as the scheme became mature. As such it was affected by future demographic structure, which strongly influenced the ratio between the working population and those claiming SERPS, in addition to the basic pension. Given the twenty-year qualifying period, a pensioner need not have worked a full, say, forty-year working life in order to claim the full benefits of the SERPS. Given that the qualifying twenty years were always the 'best' twenty years, these would almost certainly be higher than his/her average income whilst in paid work. Given that a widow inherited her husband's SERPS if she was over fifty when he died, the usually larger pension was payable until both married partners died. The widow would also continue to receive her own pension, having qualified for that at the earlier pension age of sixty (rather than sixty-five for men). Those whose occupational pension schemes met stated standards were allowed to contract out of SERPS and pay a lower rate of national insurance. Further, from 1988, as concern with the financial costs of SERPS grew, individuals were also able to contract out into defined contribution Personal Pension Plans (PPP) and by April 1990 about 4 million (often younger men) were in such schemes.[123] The effects of allowing such contracting out of SERPS were difficult to predict. In a sense, the state was foregoing funds in the present in the hope of benefiting in the future. Given that the state would still remain responsible for providing the major part of the earnings-related benefits, this was a risky strategy to adopt and if it proved mistaken, relied on the willingness of a subsequent generation to fund the gap. When fully operative, SERPS was expected to cost an additional £10–15 billion at 1982 prices, thus increasing the overall social security budget by around one-third,

---

[122] Maynard in Cooper (ed.) *Social Policy*, pp. 188–9; Social Security Pensions Act 1975. This was followed by a White Paper, *Better Pensions*, (Cmnd. 5713, London, HMSO, 1974).

[123] Dilnot and Johnson, 'What pension should the state provide?', p. 4.

equivalent to approximately ten points on the basic rate of income tax or to an addition of about the same figure to the standard national insurance contribution rate. This was a large price to pay for an improved state pension and the opportunity costs were potentially high. An alternative use of the same money might have been a 60% increase in national insurance benefits, a reduction in the basic rate of income tax to 20%, or a 75% increase in tax thresholds.[124]

With the growth of private pensions, not everyone receiving a state pension was poor. In 2000–2001, 42% of pensioner couples were in the top half of the income distribution.[125] Yet, for those not in such schemes, and especially women who often had fewer contributory years, the ability to finance SERPS adequately remained very important.[126] In the immediate term some fiscal headroom to pay for the growing costs of SERPS over the 1980s and 1990s was created by breaking the link between pensions and earnings. Having roughly doubled between 1948 and the late 1970s, and having increased significantly in real terms between 1971 and 1983, thereafter the proportion of national income spent per pensioner was broadly flat from the early 1980s as the real value of the basic pension stayed much the same until the end of the 1990s. However, its real relative value fell from 26% of average earnings in 1983 to 18% by 1990, and to 16% by 2002. By contrast, the real value of Income Support for pensioners increased steadily from 1976, including through the 1980s, but with particularly large increases from 1998. As a result, the value of the means-tested minimum for a single pensioner was almost as great in relation to average earnings in 2002 as it had been in 1971.[127] By the early twenty-first century, the costs and failings of SERPS led to SERPS accrual being ended on 5 April 2002 when it was replaced by the State Second Pension (S2P) which was introduced in the 2000 Child Support, Pensions and Social Security Act. S2P was designed to serve low and non-earners, as well as helping moderate earners to build up a better second pension. Nonetheless, the payment of pensions remains reliant on the willingness of the government and taxpayers to continue to fund the older generation in this way. The system of providing income for the old remains complex, with the old potentially receiving income from four sources, namely: the basic state

---

[124] Dilnot, Kay, and Morris, *Reform of Social Security*, pp. 26, 60; Hemming and Kay, 'The costs of the State Earnings Related Pension Scheme'; Hemming and Kay, 'Contracting out of the State Earnings Related Pension Scheme'.

[125] Brewer, Clark, and Wakefield, 'Social Security', p. 514.

[126] Pemberton, 'The failure of "nationalisation by attraction"'.

[127] Hills, 'The last quarter century', p. 107.

pension; earnings-related benefits; flat-rate non-contributory benefits, and means-tested benefits.[128]

What in part SERPS did respond to was the problem of poverty amongst female pensioners. Beveridge had originally intended to build into the state social insurance system provision for the needs of women who were not in continuous paid employment. These were rejected by the Treasury and the Attlee government.[129] It is nonetheless surprising given Beveridge's high regard for homemaking and motherhood that no attempt was made in his report to treat these activities as insurable work.[130] Women lost out in almost every which way. The expansion of occupational pension schemes benefited men disproportionately and married women were excluded by prevailing attitudes from most forms of employment in which pensions were available, i.e. white collar jobs in the public sector, banks etc. When the state pension was introduced in 1948, 683,000 people (mainly female) over the age sixty also had to have recourse to means-tested National Assistance. The number rose to almost 1 million in 1951. Older single and widowed women were especially vulnerable to poverty, as Townsend and Wedderburn found from a survey in 1959. Even in 2005, 1.3 million out of 1.9 million recipients of the means-tested Pension Credit were female.[131]

Basic Income and a Negative Income Tax

As the social security system moved away from its original intended basis in social insurance and towards a tax-based approach, then not only did the impact on incentives of the interaction between the systems of social security and taxation become of concern, but also the suitability of the essentially utilitarian basis of taxation for social security was questioned. As economic growth continued, not only did the emergence of relative poverty pose problems for a flat-rate social insurance scheme, but it also raised the question as to whether it would be simpler and more effective simply to provide a guaranteed basic income for everyone living in the economy. Two main complementary approaches were suggested. One was for a payment to be made to each individual; the other was for a negative income tax. In the basic income approach, a threshold is set above which tax is payable. In a negative

[128] Bozio, Crawford and Tetlow, *The History of State Pensions*, p. 4.
[129] Pemberton, Thane, and Whiteside, 'Introduction', p. 5.
[130] Harris, 'The Roots of Public Pensions Provision', p. 36.
[131] Thane, 'The "Scandal" of women's pensions in Britain'.

income tax, those below the threshold receive payments. In the United States, in 1968 the economists J.K. Galbraith, Harold Watts, James Tobin, Paul Samuelson, and Robert Lampman wrote an open letter to Congress asking that 'everyone in the nation is assured an income no less than the officially recognized definition of poverty'.[132] Tobin led in pressing Democratic politicians to introduce a basic income scheme. Milton Friedman, a long-standing supporter of a negative income tax, pressed the case with the Republican Party. In the UK the economist James Meade argued for a social dividend (basic income). All these schemes encountered political opposition because of their effects on taxpayers. The higher the proportion of median income formed by basic income, then the higher the rate of tax required. So, Meade's proposal to set the social dividend equal to the current supplementary benefit, while abolishing national insurance, removing all progression in income taxation, and eliminating the differentiation between the taxation of earned and unearned income, was estimated to require the standard rate of tax to rise to be at least 50%.[133] Modifications to the scheme could then be introduced, such as to the high standard rate of income tax, but these then might include continuing with graduated national insurance contributions, some progressive tax rates on higher incomes, additional wealth taxes, and the extension of the tax base by abolishing reliefs, existing exemptions, and remissions of taxation.[134] In addition, or alternatively, some contingent elements of a social insurance scheme could be introduced, reflecting for example varying regional housing costs, although these risked distorting incentives to work. The tax credit approach was proposed in the UK by Arthur Cockfield with these ideas being developed further by Gordon Brown, Labour Chancellor of the Exchequer, after 1997. Yet, because basic income and negative income tax approaches both raised tax rates for taxpayers, the political obstacles to their introduction remained considerable. As Milton Friedman noted, the only limitation on this sort of levelling up assistance was the wealth and generosity of the electorate.[135]

Related to discussions of basic income and negative income tax and the political resistance to paying higher rates of tax, were the discussions centring on the American philosopher John Rawls's distinction between justice and fairness. For Rawls, utilitarianism which sought to redistribute income so as to maximize total welfare did not have an eye to the fairness of the

[132] Bregman, *Utopia for Realists.*   [133] Meade, *Intelligent Radical's Guide,* p. 89.
[134] Meade, *Intelligent Radical's Guide,* p. 90.
[135] Brittan, *Capitalism and the Permissive Society,* pp. 135, 274. See Friedman, *Capitalism and Freedom,* p. 4.

consequent distribution of that income. Justice could not be derived from the maximization of satisfaction and fairness was better accommodated by the introduction of a form of social contract. Rawls's development of a social contract approach challenged that of utilitarianism, the main difference being that the principles of justice should be established first before any subsequent redistribution of resources were made. To ensure that the initial principles and distribution did not reflect individuals' interests, Rawls advocated applying a veil of ignorance to the starting original position behind which the initial principles were established without knowledge of an individual's particular talents and preferences.[136] Importantly, decisions on the form of the social contract were made collectively, and did not simply arise out of the choices of individuals.[137] Rawls's approach had much in common with the discourse ethics of another philosopher, Jürgen Habermas, and even with the 'judicious spectator' of David Hume who observed without reflecting on his or her own interests.[138] It is also akin to Hayek's approach in as much as Hayek regarded the best safeguard of liberty as not being the market economy but the rule of law. By the 'rule of law' Hayek did not mean constitutionally enacted legislation but rather pre-exiting (behind the veil) general rules which were then applied neutrally by judges.[139] As Hayek concluded chapter nine on ' "Social" Or Distributive Justice' of volume 2 of his book *Law Legislation and Liberty*:

Not only as the basis of the legal rules of just conduct is the justice which the courts administer exceedingly important; there unquestionably also exists a genuine problem of justice in connection with the deliberate design of political institutions, the problem to which Professor John Rawls has recently devoted an important book (*A Theory of Justice*). The fact which I regret and regard as confusing is MERELY that in this connection he employs the term 'social justice'. But I have no basic quarrel with an author who, before he proceeds to that problem, acknowledges that the task of selecting specific systems or distributions of desired things as just must be 'abandoned as mistaken in principle, and it is , in any case, not capable of definite answer. Rather, the principles of justice define the crucial constraints which institutions and joint activities must satisfy if persons engaging in them are to have no

---

[136] Freeman (ed.), *John Rawls: Collected Papers*, pp. x, 47. The original position is introduced in 1964 and the veil of ignorance is first applied to it in 1967.

[137] Freeman (ed.), *John Rawls: Collected Papers*, pp. 131–2.

[138] Freeman (ed.), *John Rawls: Lectures on the History of Political Philosophy*, p. 184; Hume, *Treatise of Human Nature*; Hume, *Enquiry*; Habermas, *The Inclusion of the Other*.

[139] Brittan, *Capitalism and the Permissive Society*, pp. 91, 96–7; Hayek, *Law, Legislation and Liberty*, Vol. 2, p. 153.

complaints against them. If these constraints are satisfied, the resulting distribution , whatever it is, may be accepted as just (or at least not unjust).' This is more or less what I have been trying to argue in this chapter.[140]

Incentives

The interaction between the systems of taxation and social security became of increasing political concern from the mid-1970s against a background of high unemployment and tightening public finances. The difficulties were most evident in low-income households in which moving out of unemployment and/or earning more income potentially left the household worse off in terms of its net income. If the unemployed took work, they could risk falling into the 'unemployment trap' in which their household net income fell as a result both of losing benefits and of undertaking (taxed) paid employment. Most starkly perhaps, the 'poverty trap' penalized those who were employed but who also saw most or all of any increase in income wiped away by a conse-quential increase in taxation and a reduction in benefits. In the 1980s this pernicious interaction of the tax and benefit systems particularly affected families receiving Family Income Supplement, a means-tested benefit for working people with children which was introduced in 1970. Similarly affected, though to a slightly lesser extent, were recipients of Housing Benefit paying income tax and National Insurance contributions.[141] As an extreme example of what could happen, a working family with children who paid income tax and National Insurance, and received Family Income Supplement (FIS) and Housing Benefit, could be made worse off by earning an extra £1. That extra £1 could lead to a 30p increase in income tax, a 9p increase in National Insurance contributions, a 50p reduction in entitlement to Family Income Supplement, and a 21p reduction in entitlement to Housing Benefit—a total of £1.10.[142] In 1983–1984, just over 1% of heads of working households faced marginal rates in excess of 100%, and 6.7% experienced rates greater

---

[140] F. A. Hayek, *Law, Legislation and Liberty, Vol. 2*, p. 100. And Hayek continues, referencing John Rawls, 'Constitutional Liberty and the Concept of Justice', *Nomos IV, Justice* (New York, 1963), p. 102, where the passage quoted is preceded by the statement that 'It is the system of institutions which has to be judged and judged from a general point of view.' I am not aware that Professor Rawls' later more widely read work A Theory of Justice (Harvard 1971) contains a comparatively clear statement of the main point , which may explain why this work seems often, but as it appears to me wrongly, to have been interpreted as lending support to socialist demands, e.g. by Daniel Bell, "On Meritocracy and Equality", Public Interest, Autumn 1972, p. 72, who describes Rawls's theory as 'the most comprehensive effort in modern philosophy to justify a socialistic ethic'.

[141] Dilnot and Stark, 'The poverty trap', p. 3.   [142] Dilnot and Stark, 'The poverty trap', p. 1.

than 60%.[143] In general, in 1984 slightly more than 500,000 people could face marginal tax rates in excess of 60% as a result of the combination of taxation and social security.[144] Although the severity of these poverty traps was systematically reduced from the late 1980s, many low-income individuals and families continued to face high marginal rates such that they could not raise their income.[145] Official figures in the mid-1990s showed that, if the pre-tax wages of a family rose from £50 to £200 per week, weekly spendable income increased by less than £10. Such tax rates could also bring about a strong substitution effect against work effort, and were therefore a major labour-supply disincentive.

Interacting Tax and Benefit Systems

Devising tax and benefit systems which minimize undesirable interactions between the tax and benefits systems is always complex, not least as the implicit tax rates facing any particular family will depend both on its size and com-position, and on the precise mix of benefits it receives.[146] In the later 1970s and 1980s such interaction between the tax and benefit systems became of increasing concern to politicians, not just in itself but for how it focused attention on the issue of incentives. As unemployment rose, so concern with incentives grew. This concern with incentives focused on both ends of the income scale and the substitution effects (substituting leisure for work) of marginal rates of taxation. This reflected wider concerns that the tax system in general was stifling incentives in the economy, and that greater priority should be given to improving tax and other incentives likely to promote economic growth, over and above concern with issues such as inequality. While the prime function of the tax system was to raise finance to cover public expenditure over the cycle, for almost one hundred years it had also been based on redistributive principles. Questions were increasingly asked as to the extent to which such principles conflicted with creating adequate incentives for economic growth. From the mid-1970s, taxation, its level, rates, and structure became an important topic of political debate, and from 1979 a move between direct and indirect taxation was begun. As economic growth improved and the tax system changed, so too did the inequality of wealth and income begin to widen, reversing the post-World War II trend of narrowing.

[143] Kay, 'The effects of increasing tax thresholds'.
[144] Dilnot and Stark, 'The poverty trap', p. 4.
[145] Johnson, 'The welfare state', p. 222.
[146] Barr, *The Economics of the Welfare State*, p. 225.

As the cumulative effects of this rising inequality became apparent, so too did the issue of inequality itself become of increasing political and public interest, notably in the twenty-first century.

Taxation

The widening of income inequality occurred at a time when the philosophical and economic bases of taxation were being questioned, with the theoretical and practical use of utilitarianism providing a focus for debate. Politically, taxation had become a central issue, and it coalesced well with talk of incentives, whatever the actual income effects of tax changes. Over the post-war period, the tax net had steadily widened, largely because the tax threshold effectively fell. In 1950 the tax threshold for a married man was 60% of average manual earnings and he did not begin paying standard rate until 175% of average earnings. By 1980, this figure had fallen to 35% of average earnings.[147] The political imperative to make tax cuts early in the government's life was recognized by Margaret Thatcher. As she recalled:

> Income tax cuts were vital, even if they had to be paid for by raising Value Added Tax (VAT) in this large leap. The decisive argument was that such a controversial increase in indirect taxes could only be made at the beginning of a parliament, when our mandate was fresh.[148]

Margaret Thatcher was clear that 'lower income tax combined with a shift from taxation on earnings to taxation on spending, would increase incentives', although logically, shifting the point of taxation, if it made no difference to total consumption, ought not to have affected work effort.[149]

Margaret Thatcher's embracing of the vocabulary of incentives and fiscal neutrality implicitly reflected contemporary concerns with utilitarianism as the basis of taxation. The utilitarian approach derived much of its strength from the diminishing marginal utility of income. That an additional one pound provides less additional utility to a rich man than it does to a poor man, because of the diminishing marginal utility of consumption. Taking the pound from the rich man and giving it to the poor man ought therefore to

---

[147] Atkinson, 'On the switch to indirect taxation', p. 5.

[148] Thatcher, *The Downing Street Years*, p. 43. Quoted by Riddell, 'The political economy of taxation', p. 1283.

[149] Thatcher, *The Downing Street Years*, 1993, p. 42. Quoted by Riddell, 'The political economy of taxation', p. 1283.

increase total social welfare.[150] The question of whether it was credible to discuss comparative marginal utilities in this fashion was raised by the economist Lionel Robbins in the 1930s and questions were asked of utilitarianism again in the 1970s.[151] One instance of this was a conference of economists and philosophers at University College London in February 1977 whose contributors included the philosopher Bernard Williams and the economists James Mirrlees and Amartya Sen.[152] Mirrlees in particular highlighted concern with how at the margin, a utilitarian approach to taxation might weaken incentives to work, and thereby reduce total output.[153] Given the concerns with incentives, unemployment, and economic growth in the later 1970s, Mirrlees' emphasis on the elasticity of work effort in relation to the marginal rate of taxation had political resonance at both ends of the income scale. A marginal rate of taxation could have a substitution effect as individuals substituted leisure for further work, whereas an increase in the average rate of taxation would have an income effect and require more work to be done to make up the taxed-away income. What the research of Mirrlees and others indicated was that an optimal tax structure was approximately linear, i.e. a constant marginal tax rate, with an exemption level below which negative tax supplements were payable, and that marginal tax rates should be low at both ends of the income scale and therefore fall rather than rise with income. The results of Mirrlees work surprised even himself: 'I had expected the rigorous analysis of income taxation in the utilitarian manner to provide an argument for high tax rates.'[154] It pointed up a need to reform the existing U shape of marginal rates of taxation in which effective rates were highest at the two ends of the income scale.

It was in this context of a lively debate amongst and between philosophers and economists concerning the aims and principles of redistribution that the Meade Committee was appointed in 1975.[155] This committee was not established by government, but by the privately funded Institute for Fiscal Studies

---

[150] Edgeworth in Phelps (ed.), *Economic Justice*, Introduction, p. 377.

[151] Not least in part because of Bergson's 1938 invention of the (Bergson) social welfare function (SWF); Robbins, *An Essay*; Robbins, 'Interpersonal comparisons of utility: A comment'.

[152] The conference papers and proceedings were subsequently published as *Utilitarianism and Beyond*, edited by Amartya Sen and Bernard Williams. The other contributors to the volume included the philosophers R. M. Hare, T. M. Scanlon, and John Rawls and the economists Partha Dasgupta and John Harsanyi.

[153] Mirrlees, 'The economic uses of utilitarianism', p. 65; Mirrlees, 'Notes on welfare economics, information and uncertainty'; Mirrlees, 'The theory of optimal taxation'; Y-K. Ng, 'Bentham or Bergson?'.

[154] Atkinson, 'How progressive should income tax be?', pp. 389, 390, 393–4; Fair, 'The optimal distribution of income'; Mirrlees, 'An exploration'.

[155] Chick, 'Incentives, inequality and taxation'.

which had been established in 1969. It was the Meade Report which 'put (the) IFS on the map' as Dick Taverne, the first Director of the IFS recalled.[156] The committee's chair, James Meade, was Emeritus Professor of Political Economy at the University of Cambridge, and in 1977 he and Bertil Ohlin were to be awarded the Nobel Laureate in Economics for their work on international trade and international capital movements.[157] In addition to Meade, the committee included some of the brightest academic economists of a younger generation such as John Kay, Mervyn King, and Tony Atkinson, initially in 1975 as research secretaries but from 1976 as full members of the committee. The Report had been 'commissioned by the Institute of Fiscal Studies after ministers rejected calls by the Sandilands Committee and others for a Royal Commission on the whole of the taxation system, on the grounds that it was too large an undertaking'.[158] Appropriately in 1975, when the annual rate of inflation was running at above 25%, part of the committee's remit was to review the system of direct taxation, just one of whose difficulties was its struggle to accommodate the effects of the inflation of the 1970s. As Meade explained in a letter to Geoffrey Howe, the Shadow Chancellor of the Exchequer, the intention of the Committee's proposed tax reforms was to 'provide the most favourable tax background for the development of private business enterprises and in particular for small business'; to stop the capital market being the 'hideous mess which it is at the moment due to the interplay of the present income tax, corporation tax and capital gains tax'; to provide a check in the shift from income to expenditure taxation on a government's ability to use inflation to increase its revenue; and to end at both ends of the income scale marginal tax rates at their 'present absurd levels'.[159] More widely, Meade wanted the committee to address the productivity problems of a stagnant economy, while also being concerned to prevent poverty and to remove unacceptable inequalities of opportunity, wealth, and privilege. While there might be some conflict between the two objectives of 'efficiency' and 'equality', that clash could 'be minimized by an appropriate choice of social, political and economic policies and institutions', with the structure of the tax system as one important element in the outcome.[160] Throughout its two-year life, in which remarkably it produced a report of 519 pages (including thirty-seven appendices) the Meade Committee was tracked by the Conservative

[156] https://www.ifs.org.uk/bundles/ifsabout/files/ifs_directors_reflections.pdf
[157] Offer and Söderberg, *The Nobel Factor*.
[158] TNA T364/149 (1977b), paras. 23, 24, 29, 32.
[159] Meade 6/2 (1977a).   [160] Meade, *The Structure and Reform*, p. xv.

Party Taxation Committee (CPTC), chaired by David Howell.[161] The Treasury and the Inland Revenue also kept a keen eye on the committee's activities, and equally throughout its proceedings the IFS was keen to keep the Treasury and Inland Revenue briefed.[162]

The Meade Committee, the CPTC, and the Treasury were all agreed that the highest marginal rate of taxation of 98% (83% marginal rate of income tax added to an investment income surcharge of 15%) was too high. For the CPTC the tax rate of 83% alone caused difficulties in recruiting senior industrial management when 'at 83%, our top rate on earned income leaves a take-home on marginal earnings of only about a third that of an American executive (top rate 50%) or a German executive (top rate 53%).'[163] The Treasury was well aware of industry and CBI claims about the disincentive and recruitment effects of high marginal tax rates, but it found such claims difficult to demonstrate.[164] While the marginal rate of taxation affected incentives, the average tax rate was the greater influence on the redistributive content of the tax system. Concern with high marginal rates of taxation could coexist with a falling tax burden. In 1969/70 the tax burden at 44% of GDP had been higher than it was in 1976 (forecast at 41%) and it was not especially high by international standards, although the UK did place more reliance than did other countries on income rather than on expenditure taxes to finance total expenditure.[165] The Treasury's estimate of those being taxed at a marginal rate of 83% in 1978–1979 was about 40,000, and of those 30,000 were also liable for the investment income surcharge at 15%, making for a marginal rate of 98% on investment income. This was higher than any other developed industrial country (the nearest was Japan at 93% including local income tax). Still unsure of to what extent the fact of very high marginal rates affected work incentives, the Treasury, like the Meade Committee, did think that there was a good case for aiming to reduce the 'top rate to at least 75% and possibly to 70% (or even 65%)'. However, in February 1979 its view was that 'the case for going further than this does not seem strong.'[166] While the CPTC asserted a negative effect of high marginal tax rates on recruitment, it was, at least in 1975, more cautious in discussing any impact of marginal tax rates on work effort. The CPTC confessed to being circumspect in adopting

[161] THCR 2/6/1/36, LCC (77)166, (1977), 'More Wealth for All'; THCR 2/6/1/27, (1975) letter from Keith Joseph.
[162] TNA T366/4, (1975), 'Visit', para 2; TNA T366/205 (1976a), Letter, Meade to Todd, 4 October 1976; Todd, *The Relative Efficiency*.
[163] THCR 2/6/1/35, (1975) 'The tax dilemma'.
[164] TNA T366/383 (1979), note, 'Research on taxation'.
[165] TNA T171/1426 (1977), paper. 'Short-term', paras. 5, 6, 15.
[166] TNA T171/1450, 'Income tax', (1979) paras. 5, 6, 7a, 9.

the vocabulary of 'incentives', this 'standby of past Conservative Governments', since 'we are aware that it is difficult to make a cast-iron academic case for it, and that many people find it unacceptable (though perhaps as many accept it).' In December 1975 the Conservative Research Department thought that it would be difficult for any 'future Conservative Chancellor, however much a man of steel, to argue, say for massive cuts on social services and wage restraint while at the same time awarding a "payrise" to many executives just to make them work harder'.[167]

An Expenditure Tax

In addition to recommending a reduction in the highest marginal rate of taxation, the Meade Committee also favoured a shift away from income tax and towards an expenditure tax. This approach ran back through Irving Fisher, Pigou, Marshall, J.S. Mill to Hobbes and had been most recently developed by Kaldor in his book *An Expenditure Tax* (1955).[168] When Meade sent Kaldor a draft copy of the committee's report, Kaldor wrote thanking him and admitting that while he had not yet had time to 'study it in any detail I found it very gratifying that you advocate an Expenditure Tax on much the same lines as I did when I wrote my book 23 years ago!'[169] Expenditure taxation rested on the philosophy that taxation should be on the basis of what an individual took from the economy rather than what he/she contributed to it. In its *Report* published on 26 January 1978, the committee recommended the adoption of a lifetime expenditure tax.[170] This both comprised an indirect tax on consumption, such as VAT, and also a tax on changes in the wealth held by individuals. Individuals wishing to save would be offered tax-free accounts. The committee had a specific proposal for reforming the taxation of inherited wealth: The Progressive Annual Wealth and Accessions Tax (PAWAT). This tax was to be a cumulative tax on all gifts and inheritances received by the donee at a progressive rate depending on the accumulated value of gifts already received. The existing taxation on inheritance was held to be clumsy, capable of being largely avoided, and unduly reliant on the frequency of death for its rate of incidence over a period of time, at which point it could present the less well-advised with lumpy bills. As two of the

[167] THCR 2/6/1/35, (1975), 'The tax dilemma'.
[168] Thirlwall, 'Expenditure tax'; Kaldor, *An Expenditure Tax*.
[169] Meade 6/11 (1977) Kaldor to Meade.
[170] TNA T364/149, paper, 'The Meade Report', A.H. Lovell, December 1977.

Meade Committee members, John Kay and Mervyn King, later noted in 1990, the inheritance tax favoured 'the healthy, wealthy and well advised'. Under the proposed PAWAT, the rate of tax would also depend on the age of the donee as a proxy for reflecting the length of time the wealth would be held. With an initial tax-free allowance, but then with bands of rising tax rates, encouragement was given to spread the estate. To reduce the incentive to skip generations (say, from grandparent to grandchild thereby skipping taxation on the death of the middle generation), the donee's inheritance was taxed at point of receipt as if the donee would live to be eighty-five. If the donee died before reaching the age of eighty-five, or transferred their inheritance, then tax refunds would be made. By taxing the donee and not the donor, the PAWAT left earned wealth alone but taxed the inheritance of unearned wealth. When recommended in 1978, the PAWAT idea came after a decade marked by unsuccessful attempts to reinvigorate the taxation of wealth and inheritance, and at a time when the Conservative Party had highlighted capital taxation as a key target.

For Meade, as for Tawney and as for Crosland, the unequal distribution of wealth was of much greater concern that that of income. To quote the Crosland of 1956, 'the largest inequalities stem not from the redistribution of earned incomes, but from the ownership of inherited capital.'[171] Tawney's *Equality* (1931) distinguished clearly between inequalities of income and wealth, and drew attention to the danger of allowing concentrations of wealth and power, as well as the corrosive social effects of the dominance of a class of great wealth largely acquired by inheritance.[172] Wealth allowed 'access' and for Tawney what was 'repulsive' was not income inequality but that 'some classes should be excluded from the heritage of civilization which others enjoy'.[173]

Of the three main tax proposals made by the Meade Committee (the reduction of top marginal income rates, a shift towards an expenditure tax, and a reform of inheritance so as to tax the recipients of unearned sums), the first two were adopted by later governments and the third (on inheritance tax) was not. In its very first Budget in June 1979 the Conservative government reduced the basic rate of income tax from 33% to 30% and the top rate on earnings from 83% to 60%. In that same June 1979 Budget the Chancellor Geoffrey Howe overcame Margaret Thatcher's concern about its inflationary effects, and increased VAT from 12.5% to 15%. The basic rate of income tax

---

[171] Phelps Brown, *Egalitarianism*, p. 343.   [172] Phelps Brown, *Egalitarianism*, p. 343.
[173] Kymlicka, 'Left-Liberalism revisited', p. 13; Tawney, *Equality*, p. 113.

was cut again to 29% in 1986, 27% in 1987, and 25% in 1988. Another cut was made to the top rate of tax, from 60% to 40% in 1988. By then, the Conservative government had moved a long way from the concern of the Conservative Taxation Committee in 1975 about 'awarding a "payrise" to many executives just to make them work harder'.[174] The change in the highest marginal income tax rate was greater than that which the Meade Committee (70%) and the Treasury (65% at most) in 1979 had thought likely to have any necessary effect on work/leisure incentives.[175] As such, the reduction of the top tax rates widened the philosophical and economic debate on distribution beyond issues of efficiency and incentives and on to those of ownership, entitlement, and community. The reduction in the top rate of income tax from 60% to 40% in March 1988 drew fierce criticism from the philosopher Gerry Cohen for what was seen as its encouragement of the separation of individuals from the interests of the community.[176] The tax cuts also placed the government at odds with Hayek's view that the individual could not make any intrinsic complete claim on his/her earnings and that it was 'precisely because in the cosmos of the market we all constantly receive benefits which we have not deserved in any moral sense that we are under an obligation also to accept equally undeserved diminutions of our income'.[177] Yet, the shift between direct and indirect taxation was purposeful. Tellingly, when pressure on the PSBR in 1993 required tax increases in two Budgets in that year, the two Chancellors introduced a package of tax increases which, while in terms of revenue raised, reversed most of the tax reductions of the late 1980s, they did not fall on income but on VAT for which the standard rate was raised from 15% to 17.5% and extended to include domestic fuel.[178]

That a shift between direct and indirect taxation was a regressive act did not prevent the entire tax system from remaining progressive.[179] Although there is more to the tax system than income tax, the income tax data is of interest. While the total number of income taxpayers increased slowly, the number of higher rate taxpayers grew much more quickly from around 3% of taxpayers in 1978–79 to around 12% in 2008–09, and that 12% was expected to contribute 56% of total income tax revenue in 2008–2009. By 2007–2008 the top 10% of income taxpayers were liable for over half of all income tax paid, and the top 1% paid 23% of all that was paid. This was a substantial increase since 1978–1979, despite the reductions in the higher rates of income

---

[174]   THCR 2/6/1/35, (1975) 'The tax dilemma'.   [175]   Brown and Sandford, *Taxes and Incentives*.
[176]   Cohen, 'Incentives, inequality and community', p. 282.
[177]   Hayek, *The Constitution of Liberty*, pp. 82–3; Hayek, *Law, Legislation and Liberty*, Vol. 2, p. 94.
[178]   Giles and Johnson, 'Tax reform in the UK'.
[179]   Giles and Johnson, 'Tax reform in the UK', p. 86.

tax.[180] In a sense, thresholds were more important than rates, and a system with an initial tax-free threshold had a progressive base.

As part of the shift from taxing income to taxing expenditure, the government also addressed many of the inconsistencies and absurdities identified by the Meade Committee, which had arisen from the interaction of income and expenditure taxes within the existing ostensibly income-based system. The discriminatory tax treatment of savings was one obvious example.[181] Contributions to pensions, life insurance policies, investments in capital assets with 100% capital allowances were tax exempt but not contributions to building society savings accounts. Income from building societies was then taxed again (double taxation). Capital gains when taxed were done so at rates lower than the higher income tax rates. The differential taxation between forms of income from saving and capital explained in part the rise from 29% in the mid-1960s to 64% at the end of the 1980s in the proportion of personal wealth accounted for by houses, life insurance policies, and pension funds. Over the same period, the personal holdings of equities and other marketable securities fell, as a proportion of wealth, by almost three-quarters, described by Kay and King as 'a truly dramatic switch in household portfolios'.[182] Tax-advantaged owner-occupied housing, pensions, and life insurance accounted for 88.9% of personal saving in the UK in 1972–1976 compared with 56% in 1972 in the United States.[183]

During the Thatcher governments, the maximum tax rates on investment income were reduced from 98% to 40% and the equalization of the marginal taxation of income and capital gain removed the incentive to convert income into capital gain. In 1984 income tax relief on premiums payable for life assurance was abolished, and the Thatcher governments did steadily pick away at the politically sensitive tax relief on the payment of mortgage interest. The Personal Equity Plan (PEP) and the Tax-Exempt Special Savings Account (TESSA) were introduced in 1987, these being superseded in turn by the Individual Savings Account which was similar in most important respects. In 1988 personal pensions were introduced which enjoyed the same tax relief on contributions, fund income, and withdrawals as employer-based occupational pensions. As the Meade Report had envisaged, most life-cycle savings came to qualify for expenditure tax treatment.[184]

[180] Adams, Browne and Heady, 'Taxation in the UK', p. 15, Table 1.5.
[181] TNA T366/205 (1976b), meeting with the Institute for Fiscal Studies, 10 January 1976.
[182] Kay and King, *The British Tax System*, p. 105. In the UK, the contribution of investment income to the income of the top 1% of income recipients fell from 41% in 1949 to 13% in 2003. Atkinson, *Inequality: What Can Be Done?*, p. 107.
[183] Daunton, *Just Taxes*, p. 334.
[184] Adams, Browne and Heady, 'Taxation in the UK'; Banks and Diamond, 'The base for direct taxation'.

The bulk of the Thatcher governments' tax reforms concerned the flows of income and expenditure. They were comparatively quiet on the taxation of the stock of wealth and there was downright hostility to the Meade Committee's proposals for a PAWAT.[185] When Meade presented an exposition of the Report's main principles and recommendations to a group of Conservative MPs on 22 November 1977 prior to its official publication, he drew a belligerent response from his audience. Following the meeting Meade wrote to its organizer, Sir Geoffrey Howe, expressing his 'surprise at the unmitigated hostility shown by the majority of your group'.[186] Howe subsequently acknowledged that 'the meeting started off from the difficulty that none of us had seen your document and only two or three the first draft—and that some months ago.' Howe's main defence was that 'unmitigated hostility' was 'not the real spirit of our reaction' but rather a 'political abhorrence, born of many Finance Bill Standing Committees, of anything which involved complex replacement of familiar fiscal machinery when simplification and adaptation, of course, on a basis of principle, would do as well'.[187] By way of an olive branch Howe commended to Meade chapter 3 of the Conservative Party's recently published pamphlet *The Right Approach to the Economy*, as well as Howe's own recent talk to the Addington Society which was reprinted in that year's *British Tax Review*.[188]

Whatever Howe's emollient words, there was no disguising the Conservative Party's determined opposition to suggestions of further taxation of capital. This had been a consistent theme from at least the mid-1970s, when the CPTC had expressed its forthright determination to end the 'political' taxation of the rich, particularly through capital transfer tax.[189] It was not simply that the Conservative Party was opposed to the disturbance of fundamental reform, but rather that it fundamentally disagreed with Meade's views on the redistribution of wealth.[190] Yet it was well known that inequality of wealth was much greater than inequality of income, and that it was the transfer of wealth across generations which formed the core of the intergenerational transfer not just of wealth itself, but of opportunities. While encouraging the accumulation of wealth was one form of incentive for enterprise, the inheritance of unearned wealth offered few such justifying incentives. It was in wealth that the greatest scope for redistribution existed. As Crosland noted

---

[185] Chick, *Business History*.   [186] Meade 6/2, letter to Howe, 23 November 1977.
[187] Meade 6/2, letter to Howe, 25 November 1977.   [188] Howe, 'Reform'.
[189] THCR 2/6/1/35 (1975). THCR 2/6/1/36 (1977).
[190] In correspondence with Margaret Thatcher and Keith Joseph, Howe would refer to Meade as a 'socialist'. Meade, *Efficiency*.

in his 1956 book, *The Future of Socialism*, '(we) have now reached the point where further redistribution would make little difference to the standard of living of the masses; to make the rich less rich would not make the poor significantly less poor'[191] and that 'the largest inequalities stem not from the redistribution of earned incomes, but from the ownership of inherited capital.'[192]

Since the publication of the Meade Report there has been a steady reshaping of the structure of taxation, notably in the shift from income tax and towards taxes on expenditure, of which Value Added Tax is the prime example. In 1978, 36.6% of government current account revenue came from income tax and 9.6% from VAT.[193] By the time of the successor to the Meade Report, the Tax *By Design* (2011) Report of the IFS committee chaired by James Mirrlees, income tax was expected to contribute 28% of government tax receipts and VAT 17.8%. Notably in the 2011–12 tax year, the expected contribution to total tax receipts from the taxation of capital was small: Capital Gains Tax (0.6%); inheritance tax (0.5%); stamp duty on land (1.05%); and stamp duty on shares (0.6%). Without fanfare, the UK moved towards taxing expenditure, a move which was reinforced by the tax relief offered for saving (the postponement of expenditure) in the various ISAs and PEPs and occupational pension schemes.[194] As marginal tax rates fell, so the incremental attractions of saving in these tax-free instruments may have declined in theory, but the practical ability to build up a large tax-free capital sum over a lifetime remained attractive.

The main asset held by households remained their home, and as the proportion of the electorate owning their home grew, so too did the taxing of inheritance become more politically sensitive. Changes in the availability of credit and low real interest rates contributed to rising property prices, and to asset prices (equities for example) in general (see chapter 6). While income inequality fell by some ten percentage points from 1938 to the 1970s and then rose by some ten percentage points between 1977 and 1991, inequality of wealth always remained much greater than that of income.[195] The Gini coefficient for the distribution of wealth was far higher than that for net incomes.[196] Between 1979 and 1989 there was a stabilization in the share of wealth held by the top 10% of taxpayers.[197] In 1976 the Gini coefficient was 66% and 65% in

[191] Crosland, *The Future of Socialism*, pp. 123–4.
[192] Phelps Brown, *Egalitarianism*, p. 343; Crosland, *The Future of Socialism*, p. 239.
[193] Central Statistical Office (1979), Table 7:1.
[194] Hannah, *Inventing Retirement*.
[195] Atkinson and Brandolini, 'On data'.   [196] Hills, *Income Inequality*, p. 30.
[197] Johnson, 'The assessment', p. 8.

1995. However, by 1999 the top 1% had increased their share of marketable net wealth to 23% of the total, from 17% in 1991. To some extent, this rise in the inequality of wealth distribution may have reflected the effects of the earlier increased income inequality, to which were added the effects of the stock market boom in the late 1990s and the rise in house prices.[198] Yet, while inequality of wealth increased in the 1990s, so too did the number of voters who felt vulnerable to inheritance tax. Given the decision not to pursue a Meade-style PAWAT approach to the taxation of inheritance and capital transfers, such liabilities could be lumpy and were a concern to many who did not regard themselves as wealthy, and who were likely to invoke arguments of earned entitlement. The concentration of wealth in housing among those with modest estates alongside rapid house price increases was largely responsible for the increase in the number of Inheritance Tax (IHT)payers from 18,000 to 34,000 (from 3% to 6% of deaths) between 1998/99 and 2006/07.[199] While larger estates had larger investments in shares and other assets, many who newly fell into the IHT net were in illiquid homes, in which they remained as the value to them of the home exceeded that to others of the house. Yet while causing resentment to many, IHT raised little revenue. Even following a decade of rising housing wealth, when the proportion of death estates liable for inheritance tax more than doubled in a decade—increasing from 2.3% of the total in 1996–1997 to 5.9% in 2006–2007 the revenue raised was still small.[200] Inheritance tax was paid on only 3% of estates in 2009/10 and raised less than 0.5% of all tax revenue.[201] This mismatch between the political controversy which they excited and the amount of revenue which they raised did nothing to increase the political appeal of wealth taxes. Even when previously another Kaldor-inspired idea, the Capital Gains Tax, had been introduced in the 1965 Budget, it had raised a disappointing level of revenue.[202]

Arguments persist over the use of the tax system to create incentives for work and entrepreneurship, while also addressing the inequality which was of concern to Meade. In his 2015 book *Inequality: What Can Be Done?*, Tony Atkinson pushed again for a more progressive income tax structure and for a revisiting of ideas for greater taxation of wealth.[203] In his 2014 book, *Capital in the Twenty-First Century*, Piketty expressed concern at how 'when the rate of return on capital exceeds the rate of growth of output and income', it gives rise to 'arbitrary and unsustainable inequalities that radically undermine the

---

[198] Hills, *Income Inequality*, p. 32.   [199] IFS, *Tax By Design*, p. 360.

[200] Adams, Browne, and Heady, 'Taxation', p. 22.   [201] IFS, *Tax By Design*, p. 358.

[202] Daunton, *Just Taxes*, p. 290; Kay and King, *British Tax System*, p. 93 on problems in following Flemming and Little's proposals for a wealth tax.

[203] Atkinson, *Inequality: What Can Be Done?*, ch. 7.

meritocratic values on which democratic societies are based'.[204] Some regard the Brexit vote as an expression of dissatisfaction by groups who feel that they no longer benefit from economic growth, and that, to reprise Tawney, who feel 'excluded' from the benefits enjoyed by others. The concentration of wealth and the protection of capital from taxation contributed to the inter-generational transfer of wealth and opportunities. This transfer to the future of inequality in the present sits uneasily with talk of incentives. The concern of Beveridge was never with inequality but with the development of his social insurance fund. That idea proved to be unsustainable given the decision to target relative rather than absolute poverty, and the financing of social security moved towards a graduated tax-funded system essentially on an OLG basis. State-provided health and education were also financed on a similar basis (see chapter 5) with again dependence on taxpayers to maintain such funding. Political resistance to taxation was eased by the incremental shift from direct towards indirect taxation, and this important shift in the basis of taxation was largely unaccompanied by fanfares. As seen, in chapter 2, with the rise in the proportion of transfer payments in the public finances, the shift to an expenditure-based form of taxation was important. The task of shifting to a full expenditure tax, which includes wealth, remains to be completed. As matters stand, taxation falls overwhelmingly on labour rather than capital, the taxes on labour often being paid by those who experience relative poverty. Currently, while in 2017, two-thirds of total UK income is paid in wages while one-third goes to owners of capital, taxes on labour account for 61% of tax revenues, and taxes on capital for 8%.[205]

Bibliography

Aaron, H., 'The social insurance paradox', *Canadian Journal of Economic and Political Science*, vol. 32, 1966, pp. 371–4.

Abel-Smith, B., 'The Beveridge Report: Its origins and outcomes', in Hills, Ditch, and Glennerster (eds.), *Beveridge and Social Security*, 1994, Oxford: Oxford University Press, pp. 10–22.

Abel-Smith, B., and P. Townsend, *The Poor and the Poorest*, 1965, Occasional papers in social administration, 17, London: G. Bell.

---

[204] Piketty, *Capital in the Twenty-First Century*, p. 1.
[205] For a recent discussion of wealth taxation, see Roger Farmer, 'Tax reform: A proposal for the Chancellor', Roger.Farmer.com, 12 November 2017. His proposal is to replace taxes on dividends, capital gains and inheritance tax with a 1.2% tax on wealth on those with wealth greater than £700,000 (the 95th percentile).

Adams, S., J. Browne, and C. Heady, 'Taxation in the UK', in J. Mirrlees, S. Adam, T. Besley, R. Blundell, S. Bond, R. Chote, M. Gammie, P. Johnson, G. Myles, and J. Poterba (eds.), *Dimensions of Tax Design: The Mirrlees Review*, 2010, Oxford, Oxford University Press for Institute for Fiscal Studies, pp. 1–77.

Akerlof, G., 'The market for "lemons": quality uncertainty and the market mechanism', *The Quarterly Journal of Economics*, vol. 84, no. 3, August 1970, pp. 488–500.

Antolin, P., T.-T Dang, and H. Oxley, *Poverty Dynamics in Four OECD Countries*, April 1999, OECD Economics Department Working paper, 212.

Arrow, K., 'Uncertainty and the welfare economics of medical care', *The American Economic Review*, vol. 53, no. 5, December 1963, pp. 941–73.

Atkinson, A. B., *Poverty in Britain and the Reform of Social Security*, 1969, Cambridge: Cambridge University Press.

Atkinson, A. B., *Incomes and the Welfare State: Essays on Britain and Europe*, 1995, Cambridge: Cambridge University Press.

Atkinson, A. B., 'On the measurement of inequality', *Journal of Economic Theory*, vol. 2, 1970, pp. 244–63.

Atkinson, A. B., 'How progressive should income tax be?', in Edmund S. Phelps (ed.), *Economic Justice: Selected Readings*, 1973, Harmondsworth: Penguin Education, pp. 386–408.

Atkinson, A. B., *The Economic Consequences of Rolling Back the Welfare State*, 1999, Cambridge, Mass., and London: The MIT Press.

Atkinson, A., *Inequality: What Can Be Done?*, 2015, Cambridge, Mass.: Harvard University Press.

Atkinson, A. B., 'Bringing income distribution in from the cold', *The Economic Journal*, March 1997, vol. 107, issue 441, pp. 297–321.

Atkinson, A. B., *Top Incomes in the UK Over the Twentieth Century*, January 2002, Discussion Paper in Economic and Social History No. 43, Oxford: University of Oxford.

Atkinson, A. B., 'What is happening to the distribution of income in the UK?', *Proceedings of the British Academy*, 1993, vol. 82, pp. 317–51.

Atkinson, A. B., 'On the switch to indirect taxation', *Fiscal Studies*, vol. 2, issue 2, July 1981, pp. 1–8.

Atkinson, Anthony B., *Inequality: What Can Be Done?*, 2015, Cambridge, Mass. and London: Harvard University Press.

Atkinson, A. B., and A. Brandolini, 'On data: a case study of the evolution of income inequality across timer and across countries', *Cambridge Journal of Economics*, vol. 33, issue 3, May 2009, pp. 381–404.

Backhouse, R., *The Puzzle of Modern Economics*, 2010, Cambridge: Cambridge University Press.

Banks, J., and P. Diamond, 'The base for direct taxation', in J. Mirrlees, S. Adam, T. Besley, R. Blundell, S. Bond, R. Chote, M. Gammie, P. Johnson, G. Myles, and J. Poterba (eds.), *Dimensions of Tax Design: The Mirrlees Review*, 2010, Oxford, Oxford University Press for Institute for Fiscal Studies, pp. 548–648.

Barr, Nicholas, *The Economics of the Welfare State*, 4th edition, 2004, Oxford: Oxford University Press.

Beckerman, W., and S. Clark, *Poverty and Social Security in Britain since 1961*, 1982, Oxford: Oxford University Press.

Bozio, Antoine, Rowena Crawford, and Gemma Tetlow, *The History of State Pensions in the UK, 1948 to 2010*, 2010, London: IFS Briefing Note, BN 105.

Bowley, A.L., and A.R. Burnett-Hurst, *Livelihood and Poverty: A Study in the Economic Conditions of Working-Class Households in Northampton, Warrington, Stanley and Reading*, 1915, London: Bell and Sons.

Bowley, A.L., and A.R. Burnett-Hurst, *Economic Conditions of Working-Class Households in Bolton, 1914: A Supplementary Chapter to 'Livelihood and Poverty*, 1920, London: Bell and Sons.

Bowley, A.L., and M.H. Hogg, *Has Poverty Diminished? A Sequel to 'Livelihood and Poverty*, 1925, London: King.

Bregman, Rutger., *Utopia for Realists: The Case For A Universal Basic Income, Open Borders and a 15-Hour Workweek*, 2016, The Correspondent.com, printed by Amazon.

Brewer, Mike, Tom Clark and Matthew Wakefield, 'Social Security in the UK under New Labour: What did the Third Way mean for welfare reform?', *Fiscal Studies*, vol. 23, no. 4, December 2002, pp. 505–37.

Brittan, Samuel, *Against the Flow: Reflections of an Individualist*, 2005, London: Atlantic Books.

Brittan, Samuel, *Capitalism and the Permissive Society*, 1973, London: Macmillan.

Brown, C.V., and C.T. Sandford, *Taxes and Incentives: The Effects of the 1988 Cuts in the Higher Rates of Income Tax*, 1990, London: Institute for Public Policy Research.

Brown, J. and A. Finkelstein, 'The interaction of public and private insurance: Medicaid and the long-term care insurance market', *American Economic Review*, vol. 98, no. 3, 2008, pp. 1083–102.

Brown, J. and A. Finkelstein, 2011, 'Insuring long-term costs in the United States', *Journal of Economic Perspectives*, vol. 25, no. 4, Fall 2011, pp. 119–42.

Burtless, G. and T. Smeeding, 'US poverty in a cross-sectional context', in S. Danziger and R. Haveman (eds.), *Understanding Poverty*, 2001, New York: Russell Sage Foundation, pp. 162–91.

Chick, Martin, 'Incentives, inequality and taxation: The Meade Committee report on the structure and reform of direct taxation', *Business History*, 2018, forthcoming.

Cohen, G., 'Incentives, inequality and community', in G. Peterson (ed.), *The Tanner Lectures on Human Values*, vol. 13, 1992, Salt Lake City: University of Utah Press, pp. 261–329.

Crosland, C.A.R., *The Future of Socialism*, 1963, London: Jonathan Cape Paperback, abridged and revised paperback edition.

Daunton, M., *Just Taxes: The Politics of Taxation in Britain, 1914–1979*, 2002, Cambridge: Cambridge University Press.

Dilnot, A., J. Kay, and C. Morris, *The Reform of Social Security*, 1984, Oxford: Institute of Fiscal Studies, Oxford University Press.

Dilnot, Andrew and Steven Webb, 'Reforming national insurance contributions: A progress report', *Fiscal Studies*, vol. 10, issue 2, May 1989, pp. 38–47.

Dilnot, Andrew, and Paul Johnson, 'What pension should the state provide?', *Fiscal Studies*, vol. 13, issue 4, November 1992, pp. 1–20.

Dilnot, A.W., and G.K. Stark, 'The poverty trap, tax cuts , and the reform of social security', *Fiscal Studies*, vol. 7, no. 1, February 1986, pp. 1–10.

Drèze, Jacques H., Pierre Pestieau, and Erik Schokkaert, 'Arrow's theorem of the deductible and long-term care insurance', *Economics Letters*, vol. 148, November 2016, pp. 103–5.

Edgeworth, F.Y., 'The pure theory of progressive taxation', in E.S. Phelps (ed.), *Economic Justice*, 1973, Harmondsworth: Penguin, pp. 371–85.

Evans, M., 'Social security: Dismantling the pyramids', in H. Glennerster and J. Hills (eds.), *The State of Welfare: The Economics of Social Spending*, second edition, 1998, Oxford, Oxford University Press, pp. 257–307.

Fair, R., 'The optimal distribution of income', *Quarterly Journal of Economics*, vol. 85, no. 4, November 1971, pp. 551–79.

Fiegehen, G.C., P.S. Lansley, and A.B. Smith, *Poverty and Progress in Britain, 1953–73*, 1977, Cambridge: Cambridge University Press.

Field, F., 'A pressure group for the poor', in D. Bull (ed.), *Family Poverty*, 1972, London: Duckworth.

Flemming, J.S. and I. Little, *Why We Need a Wealth Tax*, 1974, London: Methuen.

Ford, P., *Work and Wealth in a Modern Port: A Social Survey of Southampton*, 1934, London: Allen and Unwin.

Freeman, Samuel (ed.), *John Rawls: Collected Papers*, 1999, Cambridge, Mass. and London: Harvard University Press

Freeman, Samuel (ed.), *John Rawls: Lectures on the History of Political Philosophy*, 2007, Cambridge, Mass. and London: Belknap Press.

Friedman, Milton., with the assistance of Rose. D. Friedman, *Capitalism and Freedom*, 1962, Chicago: University of Chicago Press.

Gazeley, Ian., 'Income and living standards, 1870–2010', in R. Floud, J. Humphries, and P. Johnson (eds.), *The Cambridge Economic History of Modern Britain:*

Vol. I. 1870 to the Present, 2014, Cambridge: Cambridge University Press, pp. 151–80.

Gazeley, Ian, Hector Gutierrez, Andrew Newall, Kevin Reynolds, and Rebecca Searle, *The Poor and the Poorest, Fifty Years On; Evidence from British Household Expenditure Surveys of the 1950s and 1960s*, February 2014, University of Sussex, Working Paper Series, No. 93-2016.

Gheera, Manjit, and Robert Long, 'Social care reform: funding care for the future', SN/SP/6391, 26 September 2013, House of Commons Library.

Giles, C., and P. Johnson, 'Tax reform in the UK and changes in the progressivity of the tax system, 1985–95', *Fiscal Studies*, vol. 15, no. 3, August 1994, pp. 64–86.

Giles, C., and S. Webb, 'A guide to poverty statistics', *Fiscal Studies*, May 1993, vol. 14, no. 2, pp. 74–97.

Gini, C., Variabilità e Mutabilità, 1912, Bologna: Tipografia di Paolo Cuppini.

Glennerster, H., 'Why so different? Why so bad a future?', in Pemberton, Thane, and Whiteside (eds.), *Britain's Pensions Crisis*, 2006, Oxford: Oxford University Press, pp. 64–73.

Glennerster, H., 'Poverty policy from 1900 to the 1970s', in H. Glennerster, J. Hills, D. Piachaud, and J. Webb, *One Hundred Years of Poverty and Policy*, 2004, York: Joseph Rowntree Foundation, pp. 63–91.

Glennerster, Howard, John Hills, David Piachaud, and Jo Webb, *One Hundred Years of Poverty and Policy*, 2004, York: Joseph Rowntree Foundation.

Glennerster, H., and M. Evans, 'Beveridge and his assumptive worlds: the incompatibilities of a flawed design', in Hills, Ditch, and Glennerster (eds.), *Beveridge and Social Security: An International Perspective*, pp. 56–72.

Goodman, A., P. Johnson and S. Webb, *Inequality in the UK*, 1997, Oxford: Oxford University Press.

Gregg, P., and J. Wadsworth, 'More work in fewer households', in J. Hills (ed.), *New Inequalities*, 1996, Cambridge: Cambridge University Press.

Gregg, P., and J. Wadsworth, 'Everything you ever wanted to ask about measuring worklessness and polarization at the household level but were afraid to ask', *Oxford Bulletin of Economics and Statistics*, vol. 63, issue s1, September 2001, pp. 777–806.

Habermas, Jürgen, *The Inclusion of the Other: Studies in Political Theory*, 1998, Cambridge, Mass.: MIT Press.

Hannah, L., *Inventing Retirement: The Development of Occupational Pensions in Britain*, 1986, Cambridge, Cambridge University Press.

Harkness, S., S. Machin, and J. Waldfogel, 'Women's pay and family incomes in Britain, 1979–1991', in J. Hills (ed.), *New Inequalities: The Changing Distribution of Income and Wealth in the UK*, 1996, Cambridge: Cambridge University Press, pp. 158–80.

Harris, J., 'The Roots of Public Pensions Provision: Social Insurance and the Beveridge Plan', in Hugh Pemberton, Pat Thane, and Noel Whiteside (eds.), *Britain's Pensions Crisis*, pp. 27–38.

Haskey, J. C., 'One parent families in Great Britain', *Population Trends*, no. 45, 1986, pp. 5–11.

Haskey, J. C., 'One parent families and their children in Great Britain: numbers and characteristics', *Population Trends*, no. 55, 1989, pp. 27–33.

Hayek, F. A., *The Constitution of Liberty*, First published Chicago, 1960. Pbk edition, 2006, Abingdon: Routledge.

Hayek, F. A., *Law, Legislation and Liberty, Vol. 2: The Mirage of Social Justice*, 1976, London and Henley: Routledge & Kegan Paul.

Hemming, R., and J. A. Kay, 'The costs of the State Earnings Related Pension Scheme', *The Economic Journal*, vol. 92, June 1982, pp. 300–19.

Hemming, R., and J. A. Kay, 'Contracting out of the State Earnings Related Pension Scheme', *Fiscal Studies*, vol. 2, no. 3, November 1981, pp. 20–8.

Hills, J., 'Policy challenges and dilemmas for the next 29 years', in Glennerster, Hills, Piachaud, and Webb, *One Hundred Years of Poverty and Policy*, pp. 135–60.

Hills, J., 'The last quarter century: From New Right to New Labour', in Glennerster, Hills, Piachaud, and Webb, *One Hundred Years of Poverty and Policy*, pp. 92–131.

Hills, J., *Income Inequality in the UK*, 2004, Oxford: Oxford University Press.

Hills, J., with K. Gardiner, *The Future of Welfare: A Guide to the Debate*, 1997, rev. edn, York: Joseph Rowntree Foundation.

Howe, G., 'Reform of Taxation Machinery', *British Tax Review*, 1977, pp. 97–104.

Hume, David, *A Treatise of Human Nature*, 1984, Harmondsworth: Penguin Books.

Hume, David (ed. Stephen Buckle), *An Enquiry Concerning Human Understanding and Other Writings*, 2007, Cambridge: Cambridge University Press.

Institute for Fiscal Studies *Fiscal Policy and Labour Supply*, 1977, Bath: IFS.

Institute for Fiscal Studies, *The Structure and Reform of Direct Taxation*, 1978, London: George Allen & Unwin.

Institute for Fiscal Studies, *Tax By Design: The Mirrlees Review*, 2011, Oxford: Oxford University Press

Jenkins, S., J. Ermisch, and R. Wright, '"Adverse selection" features of poverty amongst lone mothers', *Fiscal Studies*, vol. 11, no. 2, May 1990, pp. 76–90.

Johnson, Paul, 'The welfare state', in Roderick Floud and Paul Johnson (eds.), *The Cambridge Economic History of Modern Britain: Vol. III, Structural Change and Growth, 1939–2000*, 2004, Cambridge: Cambridge University Press, pp. 213–37.

Johnson, P., 'The assessment: inequality', *Oxford Review of Economic Policy*, 1996, vol. 12, no. 1, pp. 1–14.

Jones, D.C., *Social Survey of Merseyside*, 1934, Liverpool, University Press of Liverpool.

Kay, John., 'The effects of increasing tax thresholds on the poverty and unemployment traps', *Fiscal Studies*, vol. 5, no. 1, 1984, pp. 32–4.

Kay, J., and M. King, *The British Tax System*, Fifth edition, 1990, Oxford: Oxford University Press.

Johnson, Paul., 'The assessment: inequality', *Oxford Review of Economic Policy*, vol. 12, no. 1, 1996, pp. 1–14.

Kaldor, Nicholas, *An Expenditure Tax*, 1955, London: George Allen and Unwin.

King's Fund, *Securing Good Care For Older People*, 2006, London: King's Fund.

Kymlicka, W., 'Left-Liberalism revisited', in C. Sypnowich (ed.), *The Egalitarian Conscience: Essays in Honour of G.A. Cohen*, 2006, Oxford: Oxford University Press.

Labour Party, *National Superannuation: Labour's Policy for Security in Old Age*, 1958, London: Labour Party.

Little, I., *Ethics, Economics and Politics*, 2002, Oxford: Oxford University Press, p. 70.

Llewellyn-Smith, H., 'The new survey of London life and labour, 1930–35', *Journal of the Royal Statistical Society*, vol. 92, no. 4, 1929, pp. 530–58.

Lydall, H.F., 'The long-term trend in the size distribution of income', *Journal of the Royal Statistical Society*, Series A (general), vol. 122, no. 1, (1959), pp. 1–46.

Machin, S., 'The changing nature of labour demand in the new economy and skill-biased technology change', *Oxford Bulletin of Economics and Statistics*, 63 (special issue), 2001, pp. 753–76.

Maynard, A., in M. H. Cooper (ed.), *Social Policy: A Survey of Recent Developments*, 1974, Oxford: Blackwell.

Meade, J., *Efficiency, Equality and the Ownership of Property*, 1964, London: George Allen & Unwin.

Meade, James, Preface, *The Structure and Reform of Direct Taxation*, 1978, London: George Allen & Unwin.

Meade, James E., *The Intelligent Radical's Guide To Economic Policy: The Mixed Economy*, 1975, London: George Allen & Unwin.

Meade archive, British Library of Political and Economic Science, 6/2, letter, Meade to Howe, 23 November 1977.

Meade 6/2, letter, Howe to Meade, 25 November 1977.

Meade 6/11, Nicholas Kaldor to James Meade, letter, 14 March 1977.

Mirrlees, J., 'An exploration in the theory of optimum income taxation', *Review of Economic Studies*, vol. 38, no. 2, April 1971, pp. 175–208.

Mirrlees, J.A., 'Notes on welfare economics, information and uncertainty', in M.S. Balach, D. McFadden and S.Y. Wu, *Essays on Economic Behaviour under Uncertainty*, 1974, Amsterdam: North Holland.

Mirrlees, J.A., 'The theory of optimal taxation', in K. J. Arrow and M. Intriligator (eds.), *Handbook of Mathematical Economics*, 1981, Amsterdam: North Holland.

Mirrlees, J.A., 'The economic uses of utilitarianism', in A. Sen and B. Williams (eds.) *Utilitarianism and Beyond*, 1982, Cambridge: Cambridge University Press, pp. 63–84.

Newbery, D., 'A theorem on the measurement of inequality', *Journal of Economic Theory*, vol. 2, issue 3, September 1970, pp. 264–6.

Nicholson, R.J., 'The distribution of personal income', *Lloyds Bank Review*, no. 83, 1967, pp. 11–21. Reprinted in A.B. Atkinson, (ed.), *Wealth, Income and Inequality*, 1973, Harmondsworth: Penguin, pp. 99–110.

Nickell, Stephen, 'Poverty and Worklessness in Britain', *The Economic Journal*, vol. 114, Issue 494, March 2004, pp. C1-25.

Ng, Y-K., 'Bentham or Bergson? Finite sensibility, utility functions and social welfare functions', *Review of Economic Studies*, vol. 42, 1975, pp. 545–69.

Offer, Avner and Gabriel Söderberg, *The Nobel Factor: The Prize in Economics, Social Democracy, And The Market Turn*, 2016, Princeton and Oxford: Princeton University Press.

Ogus, A.I., 'Great Britain', in P. A. Kohler and H. F. Zacher (eds.), *The Evolution of Social Insurance*, 1982, London: Frances Pinter.

Owen, A.D.K., *A Survey of the Standard of Living in Sheffield*, 1933, Survey pamphlet 9, Sheffield: Social Survey Committee.

Pauly, M., 'Overinsurance and public provision of insurance: The roles of moral hazard and adverse selection', *Quarterly Journal of Economics*, vol. 88, issue 1, February 1974, pp. 44–62.

Pemberton, Hugh., 'The failure of "nationalisation by attraction": Britain's cross-class alliance against earnings-related pensions in the 1950s', *The Economic History Review*, vol. 65, no. 4, 2012, pp. 1428–49.

Pemberton, H., 'Politics and pensions in post-war Britain', in Pemberton, Thane, and Whiteside (eds.), *Britain's Pensions Crisis*, pp. 39–63.

Pemberton, H., 'Economic policy and practice', in M. Wadsworth and J. Bynner (eds.), *A Companion To Life Course Studies: The Social And Historical Context Of The British Birth Cohort Studies*, 2011, London Routledge, pp. 91–121.

Phelps Brown, H., *Egalitarianism and the Generation of Inequality*, 1988, Oxford: Clarendon Press.

Piachaud, D., and J. Webb, 'Changes in Poverty', in Glennerster, Hills, Piachaud, and Webb, *One Hundred Years of Poverty and Policy*, pp. 29–47.

Piketty, T., *Capital in the Twenty-First Century*, 2014, Cambridge, Mass.: The Belknap Press of Harvard University Press.

Plant, Raymond, 'Citizenship and social security', *Fiscal Studies*, vol. 24, no. 2, 2003, pp. 153–66.

Robbins, L., *An Essay on the Nature and Significance of Economic Science*, 1932, London: Allen and Unwin.

Robbins, L., 'Interpersonal comparisons of utility: A comment', *Economic Journal*, vol. 48, 1938, pp. 635–41.

Rothschild, M., and J. Stiglitz, 'Equilibrium in competitive insurance markets: an essay on the economics of imperfect information', *Quarterly Journal of Economics*, vol. 90, 1976, pp. 629–49.

Runciman, W.G., *Relative Deprivation and Social Justice: a Study of Attitudes to Social Inequality in Twentieth Century England*, 1966, London: Institute of Community Studies, Routledge & Kegan Paul.

Rowntree, B.S., and G.R. Lavers, *Poverty and the Welfare State: A Third Social Survey of York Dealing With Only Economic Questions*, 1951, London: Longmans.

Samuelson, P.A., 'An exact consumption-loans model with or without the social contrivance of money', *Journal of Political Economy*, vol. 66, 1958, pp. 467–82.

Sen, A., *On Economic Inequality*, 1997, Oxford: Clarendon Press.

Sheshinski, E., 'Relation between a social welfare function and the Gini index of inequality', *Journal of Economic Theory*, vol. 4., issue 1, 1972, pp. 98–100.

Taylor, R.M., *A Social Survey of Plymouth: Second Report*, 1938, London: P.S. King and Son.

Tawney, R.H., *Equality*, 4th edition, 1964, London: Allen and Unwin.

Thane, Pat, 'The debate on the declining birth-rate in Britain: The "menace" of an ageing population, 1920s–1950s', *Continuity and Change*, vol. 5, issue 2, 1990, pp. 283–305.

Thane, P., 'The "Scandal" of women's pensions in Britain: How did it come about?', in Pemberton, Thane, and Whiteside (eds.), *Britain's Pensions Crisis*, pp. 77–90.

Thane, Pat, and Ruth Davidson, *The Child Poverty Action Group, 1965 to 2015*, May 2016, London: Child Poverty Action Group.

Thirlwall, A.P., 'Expenditure tax', in *The New Palgrave Dictionary of Economics*, 1987, London and Basingstoke: The Macmillan Press, pp. 239–40.

M. Thatcher, *The Downing Street Years*, 1993, London: Harper Collins, p. 43. Quoted by P. Riddell, Commentary on James Alt, Ian Preston, and Luke Sibieta, 'The political economy of taxation', in J. Mirrlees, S. Adam, T. Besley, R. Blundell, S. Bond, R. Chote, M. Gammie, P. Johnson, G. Myles, and J. Poterba (eds.), *Dimensions of Tax Design: The Mirrlees Review*, 2010, Oxford: Oxford University Press, chapter 13, p. 1283.

THCR 2/6/1/27, (1975) Thatcher papers, letter from Keith Joseph, 29 May 1975.

THCR 2/6/1/35, PD/75/2, paper, 'The tax dilemma', Conservative Research Department, 3 December 1975.

THCR 2/6/1/36 (1977) THCR 2/6/1/36, LCC (77)166, (1977), 'More Wealth for All', A Conservative Green Paper on the taxation of capital, third draft, December.

TNA CAB 87/76: SIC(41), minutes of 4th meeting. Quoted in H. Glennerster and M. Evans, 'Beveridge and his assumptive worlds: the incompatibilities of a flawed design', in John Hills, John Ditch, and Howard Glennerster (eds.), *Beveridge and Social Security: An International Retrospective*, 1994, Oxford: Clarendon Press, pp. 56–72, p. 59.

TNA T 161/1164/5484971/2, Keynes, letter to Sir. R. Hopkins in Glennerster and Evans in Hills, Ditch, and Glennerster, *Beveridge and Social Security*, p. 60.

TNA T230/101:n of SIC(41)20 See, for example, his discussions with Keynes in September 1942, TNA T161/1164/S484971/2.

TNA T 171/360, notes on the budget, J.M. Keynes, 3 November 1941. Quoted in M. Daunton, *Just Taxes: The Politics of Taxation in Britain, 1914–1979*, 2002, Cambridge: Cambridge University Press.

TNA T171/1426 (1977), paper. 'Short-term and medium-term fiscal strategy: conflicts and general prospects', D Todd, January, paras. 5, 6, 15.

TNA T171/1450, note, 'Income tax; higher rates and bands', Inland Revenue, February 1979.

TNA T364/149, paper, 'Meade Committee Report', paper, Inland Revenue, December 1977.

TNA T364/149, paper, 'The Meade Report', A.H. Lovell, December 1977.

TNA T366/4 (1975), note, 'Visit to the Institute for Fiscal Studies', A.H. Lovell, 27 October 1975.

TNA T366/205 (1976a), letter, Meade to Todd, 4 October 1976.

TNA T366/205 (1976b), meeting with the Institute for Fiscal Studies, 10 January.

TNA T366/383 (1979) TNA T366/383 (1979), note, 'Research on taxation and incentives', D. Todd.

Todd, D., *The Relative Efficiency of Small and Large Firms*, 1971, London: HMSO.

Tout, H., *The Standard of Living in Bristol*, 1938, Bristol: Arrowsmith.

Veit-Wilson, J., 'Paradigms of poverty: A rehabilitation of B.S.Rowntree', *Journal of Social Policy*, vol. 15, no. 1, 1986, pp. 69–99.

Social Insurance and Allied Services, Report by Sir William Beveridge, Cmd. 6404, November 1942, HMSO, London.

Social Insurance Part I, Cmnd. 6550 and *Social Insurance, Part II*, Cmnd. 6551, London, HMSO (1944).

Department of Health, *Independence, Well-being and Choice*, Cm 6499, March 2005.

Department of Health, *Our Health: Our Care, Our Say: A New Direction for Community Services*, CM 6737, January 2006.

Better Pensions, Cmnd. 5713, 1974, London: HMSO.

National Superannuation and Social Insurance, Cmnd. 3883, 1969, London: HMSO.

Report of the Committee on One-Parent Families, Cmnd. 5629, 1974, London: HMSO.

DHSS, *Reform of Social Security: Background Papers*, vol. 3, Cmnd 9519, 1985, London: HMSO.

Strategy for Pensions, Cmnd. 4715, 1971, London: HMSO.

5

Health and Education

As seen in chapter 2, since 1951, expenditure on health and education has accounted for a rising share of UK GDP. Expenditure on education has fluctuated more and risen less than that on health, although in both cases, expenditure more than doubled as a share of GDP between 1950/51 and 2010/11 (Tables 5.1 and 5.2). In 2015–2016, health and education were respectively the first and second largest elements in public service spending in the UK.[1] In both education and health, the importance of the personal care offered in both health and education, and the large and proportionately large share that labour formed of total costs made both services vulnerable to Baumol's cost disease of the personal services.[2] In part because of this, their costs tended to rise faster than GDP, as technological progress in other sections of the economy pulled up wages in labour-intensive public services. That this was so, although not necessarily why, was understood within government.[3]

Demand, Supply, and Demography

Health services and, if to a lesser extent, educational services have been subject to increasing demand since 1951. In part, the increased demand for health services arose from increased technological and pharmacological capability, and also from an income effect. As the level of per capita GNP grew, so too did willingness to spend on medical and healthcare. There was also an increasing demographic effect, not simply in the incidence of treatment but also in the lengthening of recovery times. The structure of the population changed and its longevity rose (Tables 5.3 and 5.4). While the UK resident population rose roughly 20% from 50.3 million in 1950 to 60.2 million in 2005, the number of those aged sixty-five almost doubled from 5.7 million in

---

[1] Belfield, Crawford, and Sibieta, *Long-run Comparisons*, p. 9.

[2] The observation that it still takes four people to play a Beethoven quartet might be nuanced by the fact that once recorded it becomes a manufactured good rather than a service. If then listened to by thousands, the productivity of a quartet might be judged to have increased. Middleton, *The Growth of the Public Sector*, pp. 121, 605.

[3] TNA T227/3054, 'National Health Service', 1969, para. 2.

Table 5.1. NHS Expenditure in market prices, per capita and share of GDP (selected years)

| Year | GDP at market prices £ billion | GDP per capita | NHS Expenditure | | | Total NHS as % of GDP | Total NHS cost per head |
			Public* £m	Patients** £m	Total £m		
1950/51	13.54	269	474	8	482	3.56	10
1960/61	26.29	501	839	45	883	3.36	17
1970/71	53.07	953	1,983	64	2,064	3.86	37
1980/81	238.96	4,242	11,396	281	11,677	4.89	207
1990/91	576.8	10,068	27,980	1,198	29,178	5.06	509
2000/01	989.55	16,788	57,210	1,069	58,279	5.89	989
2010/11e	1,473.0	23,633	130,872	1,526	132,398	8.99	2,124

e=OHE estimates

* Excluding patient charges

** Figures relate to NHS charges paid by patients for prescription medicines etc.

Source: Office of Health Economics, health statistics website, Table 2.2.

Table 5.2. Total managed expenditure: Education as a percentage of GDP

1955–6	1960–1	1965–1	1970–1	1975–6	1980–1
2.9	3.6	4.5	5.0	6.1	5.5
1985–6	1990–1	1995–6	2000–1	2005–6	2010–11
4.8	4.8	4.9	5.4	5.4	6.1

Source: The Institute for Fiscal Studies, 'Spending By Function', www.ifs.org.uk/fiscalFacts/fiscalAggregates

1950 to 10.8 million in 2005. If only because of this increase in number, over sixty-fives were likely to consume more medical and health care. By the 1990s, about half of the total expenditure of the hospital and community services went on the care of those aged over sixty-five. That it was more expensive to treat the oldest increased the cost very considerably more. In the 1990s, it was twenty-three times more expensive to provide healthcare for those over eighty-five as for those aged between sixteen and forty-four.[4] On a per capita basis, there being more old people per se does not wholly explain the increased use of resources. It was not time spent living beyond sixty-five but

[4] Glennerster, *Paying for Welfare: The 1990s*, pp. 165–6.

Table 5.3. Life expectancy at birth and at age sixty-five, by gender, UK (selected years)

Life expectancy at birth (years): Males			
1981	1991	2001	2008
70.81	73.16	75.62	77.71

Life expectancy at age sixty-five (years): Males			
1981	1991	2001	2008
12.96	14.14	15.92	17.60

Life expectancy at birth (years): Females			
1981	1991	2001	2008
76.8	78.7	80.36	81.88

Life expectancy at age sixty-five (years): Females			
1981	1991	2001	2008
16.91	17.9	19.01	20.24

Source: Office of Health Economics, health statistics website, Table 1.8.

Table 5.4. UK resident population by age group, selected years (millions)

	Age group								
Year	<5	<15	15–29	30–44	45–64	65–74	=>75	=>85	All ages
1950	4.3	11.3	10.6	11.2	11.8	3.7	1.8	0.2	50.3
1955	3.9	11.7	9.9	10.9	12.7	3.8	2.0	0.3	50.9
1960	4.1	12.2	10.2	10.5	13.3	3.9	2.2	0.3	52.4
1965	4.7	12.7	11.2	10.4	13.4	4.2	2.4	0.4	54.4
1970	4.6	13.4	11.6	9.9	13.5	4.7	2.6	0.4	55.6
1975	4.0	13.1	12.2	9.9	13.1	5.1	2.8	0.5	56.2
1980	3.5	11.8	12.7	10.9	12.5	5.2	3.2	0.6	56.3
1985	3.6	10.9	13.3	11.3	12.4	5.0	3.6	0.7	56.6
1990	3.8	10.9	13.1	12.0	12.3	5.0	4.0	0.8	57.2
1995	3.8	11.3	11.9	12.4	13.2	5.1	4.1	1.0	58.0
2000	3.6	11.2	11.2	13.3	13.9	4.9	4.4	1.1	58.9
2005	3.4	10.8	11.6	13.4	14.7	5.0	4.6	1.2	60.2

Source: Office of Health Economics, health statistics website, Table 1.1.

rather time spent dying which provided an important explanation of the statistical observation. Much of this health cost came in the final year of life, which is when about one-quarter of overall (public and private) life time healthcare spending occurred.[5]

Education was also subject to changes in demographic structure, such that the population of school age increased at a faster rate than the working

---

[5] Breyer, Costa-Font, and Felder, 'Ageing , health and health care', pp. 675, 680.

population between 1938 and 1959. The baby boom of the mid-1940s led to an expansion of primary education in the early 1950s, and then in turn to an increase in secondary education provision in the late 1950s and in higher education in the early 1960s. The baby boom of the late 1950s caused the cycle to be repeated.[6] Demand for education was also increased by the political decision to raise the school-leaving age from fourteen to fifteen in 1947 and then from fifteen to sixteen in 1973, and to expand the number receiving further and higher education after leaving school. The HE participation rate rose from around one in twenty in 1960 to one in three by 2000.[7] There were two marked periods of expansion. The first in the 1960s was that loosely associated with the Robbins Report and the upgrading of certain university colleges (including Exeter, Sheffield, and Southampton) and the sanctioning of seven new universities (Sussex, East Anglia, York, Essex, Lancaster, Kent, and Warwick). The Robbins Committee on Higher Education was established in 1961 and reported in 1963 with a recommended increase in student numbers from 8% to 17% of the relevant age group. This recommendation was accepted by government and then substantially exceeded, although in place of the proposed unitary system with the majority of students taught in some sixty universities, a 'binary' system was established with the creation between 1969 and 1973 of thirty polytechnics under local government control.[8] The second major period of expansion in higher education occurred in the 1990s when the distinction between traditional universities and polytechnics was ended and all higher-education institutions were granted university status from 1992 and given post-secondary degree awarding powers. As a result, between 1975 and 1998 the proportion of men with a post-secondary degree rose from 5.8% to 16.3% and those with higher vocational qualification from 4.7% to 12.1%, while those with no qualifications fell from 50.2% to 18.9%. The impact on women was even greater. Between 1975 and 1998, the proportion of women with a post-secondary degree rose from 2.2% to 12.5%. A smaller proportion than their male counterparts gained higher vocational qualifications (2.7% of working women in 1998), but as with men, there was a sharp fall in those with no qualifications from 58.3% to 23.3%.[9]

The number and proportion of those continuing in education beyond the school-leaving age rose significantly. Of those between sixteen and eighteen years old, whereas under 50% continued in full or part-time education in the mid-1980s, by the end of 2015 this share was 75%. About 430,000 young

[6] Lowe, *The Welfare State*, p. 193.
[7] Machin and Stevens, 'The Assessment: Education', p. 168.
[8] Lowe, *The Welfare State in Britain since 1945*, pp. 206–7.
[9] Machin and Vignoles, *What's the Good of Education?*, pp. 9, 90.

people aged sixteen and eighteen in England attended a school sixth form in 2015 (accounting for 22% of the population aged sixteen to eighteen).[10] There was also a significant rise in those entering higher education. Whereas in the 1980s about 15% of those aged eighteen to twenty-one were in higher education, by 1997 this participation rate had risen to around 33% of people aged eighteen to twenty-one or about 39% of people aged between seventeen and thirty by 1999–2000.[11] By 2005–2006, the participation rate of people aged between seventeen and thirty had risen to about 40% by 2005–2006 and it increased further to 46% in 2019–2010.[12]

Equity and Efficiency

While the share of public expenditure accounted for by the mainly publicly provided and financed health and education services rose, the criteria on which these funds were allocated were to change over time and in their use of time. In both education and health there was a professed concern with the criterion of equality in the distribution of resources. However, in the distribution of resources in education alongside a professed concern with equality there was always an interest in the efficiency with which were resources were allocated.

In education, the post-war interest in improving equality of opportunity, of ending a system in which, in Orwell's words, it was 'a mere accident of birth that decides whether a gifted child shall or shall not get the education it deserves' prompted a concentration in the 1944 Education Act on education according to 'age, ability and aptitude' and an increased emphasis on perceived intellectual intelligence in selecting for grammar school.[13] This coexistence of one view of efficiency in the selection of children allied to a broader concern with the efficiency with which resources were used, resulted in selective grammar schools being better resourced than other schools. This reflected a view that by educating an intelligent elite, benefits would 'trickle down' to the rest of the population. Between 1947 and 1963 the number of maintained (fully funded by the state) grammar schools increased from 1,207 to 1,295

[10]   Belfield, Crawford, and Sibieta, *Long-run Comparisons*, p. 19.
[11]   Belfield, Crawford, and Sibieta, *Long-run Comparisons*, p. 22.
[12]   Belfield, Crawford, and Sibieta, *Long-run Comparisons*, p. 22.
[13]   Wooldridge, *Measuring the Mind*, p. 254. Mass Observation reported in 1942 and 1944 that 71% of respondents said that what they would most like to see was equality of opportunity. Thom, 'The 1944 Education Act', p. 107; Orwell, 'The Lion and the Unicorn'; Lowe, *The Welfare State*, p. 204.

while the proportion of the total secondary school population attending these schools fell from 32.9% to 23.6%. In the same period, the number of direct grant (partly funded by the state) schools rose from 166 to 179, while the proportion of secondary pupils attending them fell from 5.1% to 3.7%. Like grammar schools, direct grant schools were usually selective.

Perceived inequality of access to educational resources was not simply a function of the selection process, but also a result of the spatial distribution of schools. Grammar schools were not evenly distributed across regions nor within each region. In the West Riding in 1952 for instance there were grammar school places for 40% of the children in one district and for only 15% of the children in another.[14] Unsurprisingly, dissatisfaction existed and grew among the bulk of parents whose children were not able to go to the grammar school. Among academics there was also concern with the criteria and process of selection for grammar schools and with the subsequent treatment of the majority of children who 'failed' the 11+ exam. A series of publications such as the Gurney- Dixon Report *Early Leaving* (1954), Jean Floud, Tony Halsey, and F. M. Martin's *Social Class and Educational Opportunity* (1956), the 1959 Crowther Report on the education of young people between fifteen and eighteen, and the 1963 Newsom Report, *Half Our Future*, on the education of children of average or below average ability between the ages of thirteen and sixteen, pointed to talent not being spotted at the age of eleven and subsequently failing to be nurtured in an educational system disproportionately geared to the needs of an elite.[15] From 1953, Labour Party policy moved towards supporting comprehensive education with minimal academic streaming so as to ameliorate a secondary educational system which Tony Crosland branded in 1956 as 'divisive, unjust and wasteful'.[16] Four years after the Sharpeville massacre in South Africa on the first day of spring, 21 March 1960, the 1964 Labour Party general election manifesto deployed the language of segregation, stating that 'Labour will get rid of the segregation of children into separate schools caused by 11-plus selection: secondary education will be re-organised on comprehensive lines.' In January 1965, Prime Minister Harold Wilson appointed Crosland as Minister of Education and Science, and the new minister assured his wife, Susan: 'if it's the last thing I do, I'm going to destroy every fucking grammar school in England. And Wales. And Northern Ireland.'[17] On 12 July 1965 Crosland issued Circular

---

[14] Wooldridge, *Measuring the Mind*, p. 261.
[15] Lowe, *The Welfare State*, p. 206–7; The Gurney-Dixon Report, *Early Leaving*.
[16] Lowe, *The Welfare* State, pp. 206–7.
[17] Wooldridge, *Measuring the Mind*, p. 330; Crosland, *Tony Crosland*, p. 148.

10/65 describing schemes for secondary school reorganization which would be acceptable to the Ministry, and asking LEAs to submit their reorganization plans by July 1966.[18]

Allocating Resources in the National Health Service

In health, an early concern of the Beveridge Report and of the legislation establishing the NHS was that treatment should be comprehensively available and free at the point of use. In 1942, Beveridge argued for a medical service free at the point of consumption to all, the benefits being both public and private.[19] For in Beveridge's words: 'If there is any prospect whatever of a charge, the patient may delay applying. If the line is taken that the health of the individual is a national and not an individual interest, medical services should be provided as freely as the services of a policeman or soldier.'[20]

This ambition found expression in the legislation which brought the NHS into existence on the Appointed Day of 5 July 1948, and which sought to ensure 'that in the future every man, woman and child can rely on getting the best medical and other facilities available; that their getting them shall not depend on whether they can pay for them or any other factor irrelevant to real need'.[21] That there should be a collective provision of medical care free at the point of delivery to the entire population and that this should be 'In Place of Fear' that may previously have existed.[22]

That the NHS was comprehensive and free at the point of use did not of course mean that there was equal access to health services. The hope enshrined in the 1944 White Paper A National Health Service that everyone 'irrespective of means, age, sex or occupation shall have equal opportunity to benefit from the best and most up to date medical and allied services available' remained just that; a hope.[23] By the 1970s variations within regions were greater than

---

[18] Wooldridge, Measuring the Mind, p. 330. TNA T227/1604, J R Jameson, paper, 'Progress under Circular 10/65', paper, March 1966.

[19] Webster, The Health Services since the War, p. 35; Beveridge, 'Basic problems of social security with Heads of a Scheme', December 1941, quoted in Harris, William Beveridge, p. 390.

[20] TNA MH 80/31, Beveridge to Maude, February 1942; Webster, The Health Services since the War, pp. 35–6.

[21] Cookson and Claxton, The Humble Economist, p. 73; Doorslaer, Wagstaff, and Rutten, Equity in the Finance and Delivery of Health Care.

[22] Donaldson, Why A National Health Service? p. 1; Bevan, In Place of Fear.

[23] Emmerson, Frayne, and Goodman, Pressures in UK Healthcare, p. 8.

they had been in the 1940s, and variations between regions also persisted, both in the number of consultants and general practitioners per capita, and in expenditure on medical and surgical supplies.[24] In 1969, the Minister of Health, Richard Crossman, declared geographical inequalities to be 'the single most difficult problem' to be faced.[25]

The original intention of the 1946 Act was that the Regional Health Boards (RHBs) would decide on the allocation of resources, both within their region but also, working together, between regions. In practice the regions had enjoyed considerable autonomy and clear-cut, obtainable, national standards had never existed. As one NHS chief medical officer put it, planning had amounted to 'the use of last year's budget with a bit added here and a bit taken off there... We never ask ourselves the big questions.'[26] Issues concerning the allocation of resources between health regions were not addressed until the 1970s. Until 1971, no explicit effort was made to reallocate resources to RHBs on the basis of a need formula. As the Under-Secretary of State for Health, Michael Alison, admitted on 27 July 1972: 'We had not developed any acceptable system for measuring the relative needs of regions.'[27]

In 1974, the Resource Allocation Working Parties under different acronyms (RAWP in England, SCRAWE in Scotland and Wales, and PARR in Northern Ireland) were established and charge with agreeing a measure of need. The original intention was to establish local measures of ill health—morbidity—by age, sex, and marital status, but sufficiently reliable data proved difficult to find. The studies therefore fell back on a proxy for measures of ill health: standardized mortality ratios (SMRs) or death rates from different diseases standardized by age.[28] The inadequacies of the SMRs attracted criticism, as did their apparent failure to take account of wider living conditions which affected the demand for health, although the official review of the RAWP formula in 1989 accepted that there should be some weighting for social deprivation.

[24] Glennerster, *Paying for Welfare: The 1990s*, pp. 169–70; Buxton and Klein, 'Distribution of hospital provision', pp. 345–9; Buxton and Klein, *Allocating Health Services*.
[25] Richard Crossman, reported in *The Guardian*, 27 November 1969; Cooper, 'Economics of Need', pp. 94, 102.
[26] Brotherston, in W. Latham and A. Newberry (eds.), *Community Medicine and Teaching, Research and Health Care*.
Cooper, 'Economics of Need', p. 94.
[27] Richard Crossman, reported in *The Guardian*, 27 November 1969; Cooper, 'Economics of Need', pp. 94, 102.
[28] Glennerster, *Paying for Welfare: The 1990s*, pp. 169–71.

Public Expenditure: Health and Education

Tables 5.5 and 5.6 provide a few labour measures of the growth of the NHS since 1951. In Table 5.5, the trebling in total employment is indicated and also underestimated, as not all categories of employment are included. Table 5.6 indicates that not only has the number of GPs risen in total, but also in per capita terms of the population. At its creation the NHS was the third largest civil employer in Britain, behind the 900,000 employees at the British Transport Commission and the 800,000 at the National Coal Board.[29] Large at inception, between 1951 and 2009 the total number of full-time equivalent staff in the NHS trebled from 410,479 to 1,266,374 in 2009 (see Table 5.5). The number of GPs rose, both in aggregate and per 100,000 of the population. While there were just under 32,000 GPs in 1985 and almost 48,000 by 2009, measured per 100,000 of population the number of GPs rose from 57/100,000 in 1985 to 78/100,000 in 2009. Following the collapse of the Soviet Union, the NHS became the third largest employer of labour in the world, albeit well behind the Chinese Red Army and closer behind the Indian Railways.[30]

While the labour costs of the NHS rose, most lumpy of these NHS costs were those associated with hospitals. These bulked sufficiently large in the NHS for Rudolf Klein to remark of the NHS in 1948 in his book, *The Politics of the NHS*, that it was 'essentially a national hospital service'.[31] In the 1960s, hospital running costs accounted for just under 60% of the total health budget, with hospital capital costs fluctuating between 3.4 and 7.6%. By the 1990s, about two-thirds of the total health budget was paid to staff, and nearly half of that to nursing staff.[32]

Given their large and lumpy fixed capital investment characteristics and subsequent labour requirements, there was a reluctance to construct new hospitals. In the first decade in the life of the NHS, no new hospitals were built. Approving investigations of the efficiency and cost-effectiveness of the NHS by the economists Claude W. Guillebaud and Brian Abel-Smith emphasized the low capital expenditure of the NHS during its first decade of existence.[33] Net fixed assets as a share of gross fixed capital formation fell from 0.83% in 1949/50 to 0.53% in 1953/4.[34]

---

[29] Webster, *The Health Services since the War*, p. 121.
[30] Hills, 'The National Health Service', p. 173.
[31] Webster, *The Health Services since the War*, pp. 257, 259; Klein, *The Politics of the NHS*, p. 7.
[32] Glennerster, *Paying for Welfare: The 1990s*, p. 166.
[33] Webster, *The Health Services since the War*, p. 205.
[34] Webster, *The Health Services since the War*, p. 209.

Table 5.5. Number of full-time equivalent staff employed in NHS hospitals and community services by category. UK, selected years

Year	Medical and dental	Nursing and midwifery	Professional and technical	Admin and clerical	Domestic ancillary	Total*
1951	15,210	188,580	14,110	29,021	163,666	410,479
1960	20,651	242,164	24,002	38,450	202,968	528,235
1970	28,511	343,664	41,696	56,877	229,313	700,061
1980	41,760	467,500	74,558	126,124	258,368	968,310
1990	55,838	507,100	103,097	164,370	156,995	987,400
2000	76,593	436,539	136,355	206,483	123,541	979,511
2009	117,589	507,434	184,136	302,269	154,947	1,266,374

*As not all categories of employment were included, the totals underestimate the size of the entire NHS workforce.

Source: Office of Health Economics, health statistics website, Table 3.1.

Table 5.6. Number of general medical practitioners in general practice, and per 100,000 population, by country, UK, selected years

	Headcount of medical practitioners*				
Year	England	Wales	Scotland	Northern Ireland	UK
1985	25,793	1,699	3,539	933	31,964
1990	27,184	1,800	3,689	969	33,642
1995	28,869	1,845	3,872	1,033	35,619
2000	30,252	1,903	4.067	1,092	37,314
2005	35,302	1,952	4,355	1,124	42,733
2009	39,798	2,101	4,776	1,221	47,896

	Per 100,000 population				
	England	Wales	Scotland	Northern Ireland	UK
1985	55	61	69	60	57
1990	57	63	73	61	59
1995	60	64	76	63	61
2000	61	65	80	65	63
2005	70	66	85	65	71
2009	77	70	92	68	78

*Comprising all medical practitioners in general practice, including GP registrars (trainees) but excluding GP retainers.

Source: Office of Health Economics, health statistics website, Table 4.2.

As in the 1970s public finances tightened and the NHS share of public expenditure increased, so too did the Treasury increasingly apply economic analysis to proposed expenditure within the NHS. This was especially true of hospitals. In the 1960s, the Treasury developed approaches to the appraisal of proposed new investment in the nationalized industries which emphasized the 'opportunity costs' of such investments in terms of other potential uses of the expenditure. The projected returns on the proposed investment were also evaluated in the context of the difference which they made to the performance of the whole system, and future returns were converted into their present value by using a chosen discount rate. While this approach was refined theoretically in the Treasury during the 1960s, its practical application from the later 1960s was often muddied by political considerations. Nevertheless, it is clearly evident in Treasury approaches to the appraisal of proposed investment in the NHS, as too is the generally larger role played by economics and economists in decisions concerning resource allocation. As Rudolf Klein noted:

> Economists, who did not exist as far as the Ministry of Health was concerned in the 1950s, had by the 1970s established themselves in the department as the twentieth-century equivalents of the domestic chaplains- keepers of the faith of efficiency. The translation of this ideology into practice was slow, halting and incomplete, but the permeation of its concepts and vocabulary into the policy debate helped to shape both the way in which problems were defined and the solutions that were considered.[35]

In the economics vocabulary and approach which the Treasury increasingly visited on the Department of Health and Social Security (DHSS), the decision to build (close) a hospital represented a marginal addition to an entire existing system whose social discounted costs and benefits required appraisal.[36] This approach came as a shock to the DHSS in the 1970s which had never previously attempted any such systematic cost–benefit analysis of the social rate of return on large-scale capital projects.[37] The preferred Treasury social cost–benefit approach both applied a discount rate to the medical aspects of proposed projects, and also accommodated travelling time both for patients and visitors. For patients, travelling times could prove a matter of life and death. For the patients' visitors, travelling times affected the frequency and total length of their visits.[38] As the Treasury fought its case with the DHSS,

---

[35] Klein, *The Politics of the National Health Service*, p. 64.
[36] TNA T379/74, Spackman, note, 'The Investment appraisal of hospitals, February 1977, para. 2.
[37] TNA T379/74, 'Investment appraisal techniques for the Health Capital Programme', February 1977, para. 14.
[38] TNA T379/74, Spackman, note, 'The investment appraisal of hospitals, February 1977, paras. 3, 5.

the usual arguments about the type and level of discount rate to be used ensued. However, there was a pragmatic recognition that while the intricacies of test discount rates, social time preference rates, and other conceptual approaches to expressing the future in terms of the present might not always be followed closely by politicians and administrators, nonetheless the use of a discount-rate approach fed through into their decision-making through a process of political osmosis. The test discount rate (TDR) affected the numbers which were fed to senior officials and ministers over a period of months and sometimes years leading up to a decision, and 'these numbers do affect the climate of opinion and hence the preferences of the decisions makers, even though these preferences are perceived as essentially "political" or "gut" feelings.'[39]

Just as economic analysis was increasingly applied to which hospitals were built, where and of what size, so too did an economic approach increasingly influence what operations and procedures were performed, and on whom. While within the NHS, a financial charge could not subsequently be made, procedures for determining who did and who did not receive resources (operations, drugs etc.) were increasingly influenced by considerations of the cost-effectiveness and the rate of return on the treatment. In general, in both health and education, this incorporation of future benefits into resource allocation decisions reflected both public finance pressures and a continuing shift to thinking in terms of the present and future value of human capital.

QALYs

In addition to the social discounting approach to the investment appraisal of potential hospitals, there developed a Quality-Adjusted Life Year (QALY) approach to allocating health resources between patients. Some of the origins of this approach can be found in Kenneth Arrow's 1963 *American Economic Review* article on 'Uncertainty and the Welfare Economics of Medical Care' and in Martin Feldstein's 1966 book of his doctoral dissertation, *Economic Analysis for Health Service Efficiency*.[40] QALYs combined an assessment of the cost of an operation or procedure, with an assessment of the ability of an individual to benefit, with the duration of this weighted benefit being expressed in terms of added life-years.[41] Added life-years reflected both life-expectancy

---

[39] TNA T379/74, Smallwood, note, 'Investment appraisal techniques for the Health Capital programme', February 1977.

[40] Feldstein, *Economic Analysis*.

[41] Culyer, 'The normative economics', p. 52; Rosser, 'A history'.

(as a measure of the extra life-years that might be procured) and a quality adjustment (as weights indicating the healthiness of the expected life-years).[42] In theory QALYs enabled comparisons to be made between different technologies, this theory being that setting the marginal cost per QALY as near as possible to equality across all technologies was an important step towards maximizing health gains. Those technologies with a 'low' marginal cost per QALY were to be preferred to those with a 'high' marginal cost per QALY.[43] This marked a change from the existing practice whereby the medical profession based its decision on medical criteria. When, for example, the new and expensive life-extending technology of renal dialysis became available in the early 1960s, a series of conferences, chaired by Lord Rosenheim, the President of the Royal College of Physicians, was organized. The outcome was a decision to concentrate renal dialysis facilities in a limited number of centres. This reflected a medical decision to concentrate expertise. Special resources were set aside for the creation of these centres, but the commitment was limited with the result that renal dialysis treatment in Britain continues to be limited. Thus in 1975 the number of patients being treated by dialysis (or with a functioning transplant) was 62.0 per 1,000,000 population in Britain, as against 136.1 in Switzerland, 312.4 in Denmark, 102.2 in France, 87.7 in Germany, and 85.4 in Sweden.[44] What QALYs offered was a more transparent and economic approach to establishing comparative criteria for the allocation and rationing of resources. What was true of renal dialysis could be, and was, applied to operations such as coronary artery bypass grafting.[45]

An important figure in the development of QALYs in Britain was Alan Williams, an economist at the University of York, who in 1966 was on a two-year stint on secondment to the Treasury as Director of Economic Studies at the Centre for Administrative Studies in London (the precursor of the Civil Service College).[46] While on secondment, Williams met Archie Cochrane, a Scottish GP who became a Professor of Medicine at the Welsh School of Medicine.[47] It was Cochrane who encouraged Williams's interest in devising better measures and criteria for the allocation of health resources, other than simple output measures. Later, when sitting down with his co-author Bob Sugden to write *The Principles of Practical Cost-Benefit Analysis* Williams'

[42] Culyer, 'The welfarist and extra-welfarist economics', pp. 108–9.
[43] Culyer, 'Economics, economists and ethics', p. 122.
[44] Klein, *The Politics of the National Health Service*, p. 85; Office of Health Economics, *Renal Failure*.
[45] Williams, 'Economics of Coronary Artery Bypass Grafting'.
[46] Williams, 'Primeval health economics in Britain', S5.
[47] Cochrane, *Effectiveness and Efficiency*.

ideas began to crystallize.[48] In thinking about how to distinguish between and value (rank) ostensibly similar forms of treatment (in this case obstetrics), Williams realized that what was needed was a 'cost-per-QALY league table for obstetrics' reflecting 'outcome measures in health' which would allow an 'escape from the tyranny of "*more means better*"'.[49]

Such thinking came at a time when a greater sense of the economic returns on health provision was being sought. Work on the distribution of health resources had been commissioned in 1967 by the British Medical Association (BMA) on Health Care Financing.[50] One of the economic papers commissioned by the BMA was by Cooper and Culyer on the 'territorial justice' of the distribution of healthcare.[51] Tony Culyer was to play an important role in the development and application of health economics, founding with Joe Newhouse in 1981 the *Journal of Health Economics*, the world's first academic journal in the field and in 1999–2003 serving as founding vice-chair of the National Institute for Health and Clinical Excellence (NICE).[52] For economists like Culyer and Williams, the University of York, and specifically its Centre for Health Economics (CHE) where its Health Economists' Study Group (HESG) held its first meeting in 1972 provided a physical and intellectual focus for their thinking.[53] The HESG was jointly sponsored by the DHSS and the University of York and it drew together economists with an interest in the economics of medical care.[54] Meetings were sometimes attended by members of the Treasury.[55]

Unsurprisingly, QALYs proved contentious, often being the target of vigorous opposition from academics and practitioners. Politically, QALY measures could afford ministers an enhanced bargaining power with the Treasury in the Public Expenditure Survey round, as evidence for the expected pay-off of judiciously targeted additional public expenditure, but politicians were wary

---

[48] Sugden and Williams, *The Principles of Practical Cost-Benefit Analysis*.

[49] Williams, 'Primeval health economics', S6.

[50] Culyer, 'Equity of what in health care?', p. 177; Williams, 'Primeval health economics', S6; British Medical Association, *Health Services Financing*, 1970. In the UK the first study of the territorial distribution of resources occurred in 1970, twenty-two years after the inception of an NHS dedicated to the principles of egalitarianism; moreover, that study was sponsored by the British Medical Association and not an official one.

[51] Cooper and Culyer, 'An economic assessment'; TNA T227/3054, Widdup, note, 'Health Services Financing', June 1970, para. 6; Williams, 'Primeval health economics', S7.

[52] Culyer also served as chair of the Office of Health Economics (OHE) editorial board (since 1997) and policy board (since 2001). The OHE was established in 1962 by the Association of the British Pharmaceutical Industry(ABPI) to commission, undertake, and disseminate health economic research and data collection. Hutton and Maynard, 'A NICE challenge'; Johannesson, 'The relationship'.

[53] Williams, 'Primeval health economics'.

[54] The proceedings were subsequently published as Hauser, *The Economics of Medical Care*.

[55] Williams, 'Primeval health economics', S6.

of employing the language and values of QALYs. Just as with the Value of Prevented Fatality (VPF) approach to road improvements, there was a reluctance to draw public attention to the criteria being used for resource allocation. The QALY approach also encouraged greater distinctions to be made between 'need' as distinct from 'demand', and the allied measure of 'ability to benefit'. From the 1960s there had been much work from philosophers and others on what 'need' in terms of health might mean, while 'ability to benefit' drew on Sen's 1980 notion of 'basic capabilities'.[56] Need had proven to be a relative rather than an absolute concept without there being any practicable possibility of having sufficient resources to eliminate all healthcare needs. In this sense, the NHS was founded upon a misconception of the need for healthcare resources.

While the QALY approach focused on the individual, it differed from the VPF) approach which helped to shape decisions on other aspects of government public works programmes.[57] While the VPF approach had an explicit core of economic valuation, the QALY approach had an 'ability to benefit' approach which paid more attention to the well-being of the individual than their economic use to others. Both the VPF and QALY approaches were awkward in their treatment of the aged. While the VPF approach distinguished between the warm-blooded (pensions) and cold-blooded (economic value) components of estimating a VPF, the QALY approach drifted towards the 'fair-innings' argument.[58] Public opinion surveys also indicated that most people (including the old) thought that the young should have priority over the old. This fair innings argument was not accepted by many who argued that the correct ethical position was to accord equal social value to what remained of every individual's life, irrespective of whether it was expected to be long, prosperous, and healthy, or nasty, brutish, and short.[59] Yet, part of the point of QALY was to correct a bias towards treatment to extend life.

Such issues came to the fore in the early negotiations over the use of QALYs. Alan Maynard of the Centre for Health Economics, University of York in a correspondence with Professor Wing of the Institute of Psychiatry, sought to demonstrate how the use of a QALY measure could allow a comparison to be made between allocating resources between treating hypertension and renal failure, not least as measures of blood pressure for hypertension studies and length of survival for dialysis patients were routinely taken. The question was how to compare the cost–benefits of the two treatments, the reductions in

---

[56] Sen, 'Equality of what?'.   [57] Williams, 'Discovering the QALY', p. 3.
[58] Williams, 'Intergenerational equity'.   [59] Harris, *The Value of Life*, p. 93.

blood pressure against additional years of life being like 'chalk and cheese; what reduction in blood pressure is of equal value to an additional year of life?' It was insufficient to measure additional years since this would bias resource allocation in favour of life saving therapies (e.g. dialysis and transplants) and away from therapies producing quality of life improvements (e.g. hip replacements).[60]

Within a fixed budget constraint, the approach to the allocation of health resources began to resemble that used to appraise proposed fixed capital investment in the nationalized industries. Established in 1999, the National Institute for Health and Clinical Excellence (NICE) became the main body responsible for the appraisal of medical intervention on behalf of the NHS and its patients.[61] Since 1999, the NICE Technology Appraisal Programme has been charged with producing guidance for the NHS in England and Wales on the appropriate use of new and existing healthcare programmes. Guidance is based on a number of factors including cost-effectiveness.[62] The QALY is the main measure used by NICE and for much of its first decade NICE seemed to work in a threshold range of between £20,000 and £30,000.[63] The focus was on the expected incremental cost-effectiveness ratio (ICER) which was a measure of the additional cost per additional unit of health gain produced by one intervention compared with another.[64] If the threshold was £20,000 and the proposed technology cost the NHS an additional £12,000 and produced an additional 0.8 QALY, then the ICER of £15,000 per QALY would bring the additional technology in under the £20,000 threshold and would be likely to be approved. Ethical concerns apart, questions remained as to whether the health benefits measured in QALYs should be discounted at the same rate as the cost, it being acknowledged that the value of health benefits might increase over time.[65]

Expanding and Financing Education

Setting aside demographic factors and the economics of Baumol's cost disease of the personal services, it is possible to increase the cost of providing education both by spending more per capita at any one time and/or by spending for

---

[60] TNA FD9/4584, Maynard, letter, February 1988.
[61] Earnshaw and Lewis, 'NICE guide'.   [62] Miners, 'Estimating "costs"'.
[63] McCabe, Claxton and Culyer, 'The NICE cost-effectiveness threshold'.
[64] McCabe, Claxton and Culyer, 'The NICE cost-effectiveness threshold'.
[65] Cairns, 'Discounting in economic evaluation'; Gravelle, Brouwer, Niessen, Postma, and Rutten, 'Discounting in economic evaluations'.

Table 5.7. Number of pupils and teachers: pupil/teacher ratios by school types. Numbers in thousands, full-time or full-time equivalent

	1975	1985	1990	1995**	2000
All schools or departments* Pupils	10,501.8	9,544.3	9,010.0	9,479.1	9,828.3
Teachers	518.7	546.0	532.5	542.1	545.6
Public sector mainstream schools or departments Nursery: pupils	44.5	57.3	59.4	62.2	75.3
Teachers	2	2.6	2.7	2.9	3.1
Pupils per teacher	22.2	21.8	21.8	21.7	24.2
Primary: pupils	5,987.5	4,513.6	4,747.7	5,061.6	5,167.9
Teachers	247.8	205.0	219.0	231.2	228.0
Pupils per teacher	24.2	22.0	21.7	21.9	22.7
Secondary: Pupils	4,332.0	4,243.6	3,419.6	3,650.9	3,859.0
Teachers	254.1	267.7	236.6	229.8	232.9
Pupils per teacher	17.0	15.9	14.8	15.9	16.6
Special schools: Pupils	137.7	133.1	114.6	113.7	107.4
Teachers	14.7	19.7	19.6	18.8	17.0
Pupils per teacher	9.3	6.8	5.8	6.0	6.3

*From 1980 onwards includes non-maintained schools or departments, including independent schools in Scotland.
**Provisional

Sources:
1975, *Annual Abstract of Statistics, 1984.*
1985, 1990, 1995, *Annual Abstract of Statistics, 1997*, Table 5.3.
2000, *Annual Abstract of Statistics, 2003.*

longer per capita over time. In schools per capita spending rose as class sizes fell. Across maintained primary and secondary schools the FTE pupil per teacher ratio fell from 26.1 in 1958 to 23.1 in 1968, the fall in infant and junior ratios being from 30.3 pupils per teacher in 1958 to 27.8 in 1968, and in senior classes from 20.9 to 18.1.[66] These trends slowed but continued until the 1990s when ratios began to rise again (see Table 5.7).

Spending for longer per capita was achieved by raising the school-leaving age and by expanding the numbers entering further and higher education. In contrast to health procedures, the economic benefits from education can take years to become apparent. While there are broader reasons other than the economic for educating people, in the annual fight for resources the ability to make an economic case became increasingly important. Unlike health, spending on education was to fluctuate. Like health, public expenditure on education

[66] Central Statistical Office, *Annual Abstract of Statistics, 1970*, Table 90.

rose as a share of GDP in the 1950s, 1960s, and into the 1970s, but unlike health it then fell back both as a share of GDP from 1976 and in absolute volume terms from 1979/80 until the late 1980s.[67] As the PSBR and public expenditure became of growing political concern from the 1970s, so too, as with health, did an increasingly economic rule begin to be run over requests for additional public expenditure on education. Again, as with health and the nationalized industries, many of the arguments deployed by the Treasury had been developed from the 1960s.

As with health, the Treasury challenge was to the view that 'more is better'. One instance of this concerned proposals to raise the school-leaving age. While the school-leaving age had been raised from fourteen to fifteen in 1947, it was not until 1973 that it was raised again, to sixteen.[68] In part this hiatus reflected Treasury scepticism as to the public benefits of incurring such additional expenditure. In 1963 the economist Maurice Peston captured some of these (welfare) economic concerns in a paper written for HM Treasury's Committee on the Economics of Education. Noting that both political parties were committed to raising the school-leaving age to sixteen, that the 1944 Butler Education Act stated that the increase to sixteen should happen as soon as practicable and with the Crowther Report of 1959 having suggested a date between 1966 and 1969, Peston continued:

> The dominant opinion at the present time in most fields is that quantity and quality are closely connected in the sense either that they are positively correlated, or that increased quantity is a precondition of improvement in quality. This is somewhat surprising to the economist. Usually empirical investigation in economics tends to show a negative correlation between quantity and quality, and the need for careful control of quality when expanding quantity... In education there is not a great deal of evidence that quality and quantity are positively correlated.[69]

Thinking in terms of the costs and benefits of increasing school education for one year at the margin, the temporal aspects of education came to the fore. That there were wide positive externalities to teaching the 3Rs seemed clear. That there were also substantial benefits to the individual concerned was also apparent. Poor literacy and, especially, poor numeracy have a devastating

---

[67] Glennerster, *Paying for Welfare: The 1990s*, p. 203; Glennerster and Low, 'Education and the welfare state'.

[68] Machin and Vignoles(eds.), *What's the Good of Education?*, p. 14; TNA T230/500, 'Education expenditure as a proportion of GNP', April 1960, para. 3; Woodin, McCulloch and Cowan, *Secondary Education*.

[69] TNA T 227/1348, Peston, paper, 'The school leaving age', October 1963, paras. 2 and 3.

effect on people's chances of well-paid and stable employment.[70] Even today, the poorer early language skills of additional language pupils and those receiving free school meals are known and widen over time.[71] Thereafter it could be argued that educational expenditure was being subject to diminishing returns, with these returns moving from being mainly public to becoming mainly private the longer a person spent in education. In part, the argument concerned the rate of return on educational expenditure and the appropriation of returns, as well as the emerging question of how much of the financing of additional expenditure should come from the public purse. That there was a causal relationship running from increased expenditure on education to increased economic growth was also questioned. It might equally be that education, and especially higher education, was increasingly a consumption good which a rising GDP allowed to be enjoyed. Many of these questions came to a head over the proposals to expand higher education in the 1960s.

Curiously perhaps, Lionel Robbins, the recruiter of Hayek to the LSE, chaired a committee on the expansion of higher education. If fully implemented, the Robbins Report's proposals for the expansion of higher education (by which was meant universities, colleges of education, and advanced further education) were thought likely to increase spending on higher education from 0.8% of GNP in 1965 to 1.6% by 1980 on an assumption of 4% annual growth in GNP.[72] The Treasury regarded such an additional claim on resources as 'really very large indeed'.[73] Indeed, the Treasury Second Permanent Secretary Richard Clarke's characteristically robust view of the Robbins Report was that it was 'really an expression of goodwill rather like saying that everybody who is ill ought to have first-class hospital accommodation, or that one ought to be able to drive from London to Sheffield without getting into any traffic jams'.[74] As with health, distinctions were drawn between need and demand. Part of Clarke's concern was with the costs of supply of higher education in the UK. In 1963, Clarke pointed a Treasury finger at a Staff Student Ratio (SSR) of 8:1 in the UK, compared with 12:1 in the USA and 30:1 in France.[75] Yet of more fundamental concern to the Treasury was the size and nature of the returns available on additional investment, and especially in higher education. In response to requests for increased educational expenditure so as to promote

---

[70] Wolf, *Does Education Matter?*, p. 34.
[71] Machin and Vignoles (eds.), *What's the Good of Education?*, p. 6; Wolf, *Does Education Matter?*, p. 33.
[72] TNA T227/2854, paper, 'Higher education: Areas of Choice', March 1968, para. 1.
[73] TNA T227/1618, Clarke, note, 'Robbins Report', September 1963, para. 10i.
[74] TNA T227/1618, Clarke, note, 'Robbins Report', September 1963, para. 3.
[75] TNA T227/1618, Clarke, note, 'Robbins Report', September 1963, para. 10ii.

economic growth, Treasury officials asked for evidence not only of this contribution but also of how it compared with that which might come from public spending on roads, housing, and infrastructure.[76]

Again, time formed an important strand of the costs and benefits of additional expenditure on education. That there existed a relationship in the long-run was not disputed by the Treasury, although as the Treasury observed in a note on 'Education and economic growth' in September 1961:

> It is important to get one's time-scales clear. It is one thing for the historian, looking at the progress of a nation over half a century, to say: 'The progress of education between X and Y undoubtedly contributed powerfully to the splendid advance which the nation made in this period.' He may very well be right in this conclusion, more particularly over a period of this length. But this is something very different from saying that education and economic growth have any demonstrably close link over a period of, say, 10 or 20 years. It is on this aspect that I fear the emergence of the de luxe bosh.[77]

Such 'de luxe bosh' was associated with a view of the benefits of expenditure on education which was dubbed by the Treasury as the Bellagio Doctrine. This appellation was first used to summarize the general view of the participants at the conferences organized by the International Association of Universities which took place in Bellagio in July 1960.[78] For the Treasury, the Bellagio Doctrine comprised the view that: 'the advanced countries are at present in a phase of educational expansion and development so rapid as to constitute a revolution'; that this demand for education is driven by rising incomes and living standards; that increased expenditure on education was necessary for the exploitation of the opportunities for economic progress which the accumulation of technical knowledge and of capital have opened up; that much talent was going to waste; and that 'the speed of expansion of education should be determined not by consideration of what a country can "afford" but by the technical and organizational factors which set a maximum to the pace of advance.'[79]

As the Treasury considered what the marginal social and private benefits of additional expenditure on education might be, the Chicago-based economist Gary Becker's book on *Human Capital* was published in 1964. This was read

---

[76] TNA T 227/1618, Clarke, note, 'Claim on Resources: 1965–1980', September 1963, para. 2.

[77] TNA T298/277, Vinter, note, 'Education and Economic Growth', September 1961, para. 2.

[78] TNA T298/277, 'Economic growth and investment in education', Washington, 16–20 October, 1961, list of papers; Schmelzer, *The Hegemony of Growth*, p. 205.

[79] TNA T298/277, Hopkin, paper, 'Investment in Education: The Bellagio Doctrine', September 1961, paras. 1–4.

and reviewed for the Treasury by the economist Ralph Turvey, who was to play a central role in the design of new approaches to the appraisal of nation-alized industry investment. While Turvey had some misgivings about Becker's work, nonetheless like the economist Kenneth Arrow's work on health eco-nomics the year before, *Human Capital* was to provide the theoretical basis for the economics of education as a distinct research field, even as it was modified and amended over time.[80] That Becker's *Human Capital* was being discussed seriously in the Treasury reflected the Treasury's interest in ascer-taining the rate of return on additional educational expenditure and its main beneficiaries. Private rates of return on education were measured in terms of income subsequently earned, the premium on higher education being the calculation of an assumed higher level of lifetime earnings minus the tuition costs and income foregone while in higher education.[81] While evidence sug-gested that graduates did have higher lifetime earnings, quite why was less clear. Evidence from schools seemed to indicate that vocational school gradu-ates were frequently less employable than academic school graduates and that employers were at least as much interested in the behaviour (punctuality, persistence, concentration, compliance, ability to work with others) as in the cognitive quality of what school graduates actually knew.[82] Indeed work by Gintis in the United States suggested that few workers ever made specific use of the cognitive knowledge acquired in schools. Such considerations were equally relevant at higher education level, particularly with the expansion of

---

[80] Turvey thought that Becker had underrated the social rate of return as he tended to capture only the direct returns, all effects on the output of other people being excluded; Einstein's gifts to the world for example. He thought that Becker had a tendency to estimate the contribution of education embodied in human capital as the residual after the expansion of the labour force and the growth of the stock of physical capital (unreliably estimated in Turvey's view) had been made. Turvey thought that Becker's calculations, which focused mainly on college-educated urban males, did not provide an indication of what the rate of return was likely to be on additional educational expenditure. While an association could be observed between the average cost of education and average earnings at various ages for groups with 8, 9, 10...etc. years of education, it was much more difficult to get from this to estimates of the marginal social rate of return, not least because of a need to correct for ability, the non-educational portion of income, and allowance for the fact that the marginal return was below the average return. TNA T230/536, Turvey, comments, 'Washington Conference', September 1961, para. 6; TNA T298/277, Turvey, paper, 'Returns to investment in education', September 1961; Machin and Vignoles, *What's the Good of Education?*, p. 3.

[81] TNA T227/1618, Clarke, note, 'Robbins Report', September 1963, para. 3; Machin and Stevens, 'The assessment'. The most common technique for estimating returns to education is to use cross-sectional data on earnings and education, in a regression of the logarithm of earnings on individual characteristics—known as a Mincerian earnings function, after Jacob Mincer whose work initiated this line of research in the 1970s.

[82] Psacharopoulos, *Higher Education in Developing Countries*; Blaug, 'Where are we now ?', p. 18; Bowles and Gintis, *Schooling in Capitalist America*; Bowles and Gintis, 'Does schooling raise earn-ings?'. The screening hypothesis argues that education beyond a basic level does not increase individ-ual productivity and that firms seek high-ability workers but are unable, prior to employing them, to distinguish them from those with low ability. Individuals therefore have an incentive to make themselves distinctive by some sort of signal.

higher education in the 1960s and again in the 1990s, when the employability of higher education graduates was a central issue. Graduate higher lifetime earnings might be at least as much because of screening effects as from any cognitive benefits of higher education.

Aside from the issue of the returns on expenditure on education, there was also the question of how this expenditure should be financed. As a means of helping to finance the expansion of higher education, Lionel Robbins also favoured a student loan scheme and higher fees. While his eponymous report 'recommended that the level of fees should be raised so that in future they covered at least 20% of current institutional expenditure', Robbins thought that this proportion should be much greater[83] and he found the general arguments, 'both in regard to equity and incentive...ultimately very difficult to resist'.[84] That his committee held off from recommending an immediate change to the financing of higher education was for fear of deterring the 'still many families where there is no experience of higher education' from availing themselves of higher education.[85] In 1963, the Treasury favoured an increase in fees to 40% of university costs, such that the University Grants Committee (UGC, 1919–1989) grant would be reduced from 70% to about 50% of current expenditure.[86] Fees of 40% of university costs were reported as being close to the pre-war proportion and similar to the proportion in the large American universities. Grants would include fees (possibly abandoning the means test) and maintenance placed on a loan basis with some provision for grants of a genuine scholarship kind and with provision for repayment of loans to be related to earnings.[87] Thus the system would shift from one of grants to universities to one of grants to students and a system of loans to students.[88] The charging of tuition fees and of devising a loans system with income-contingent repayments related to subsequent earnings had a considerable intellectual provenance.[89] While, in the 1960s it was decided not to pursue such a system, at the end of 1971 there was discussion of introducing a graduate tax. On this occasion worries that the government did not have sufficiently reliable information about the lifetime earnings of graduates so as to be able accurately to forecast the yield of such a tax counted against the graduate tax scheme which continued to be considered inferior to a loan

---

[83] Robbins, 'Recent discussion', pp. 31–2.   [84] Robbins, 'Recent discussion', p. 30.
[85] Robbins, 'Recent discussion', p. 30.
[86] TNA T227/1624, Clarke, draft letter to Wolfenden, October 1963; TNA T227/1618, Clarke, note, 'Robbins Report', September 1963, para. 12.
[87] TNA T227/1618, Clarke, note, 'Robbins Report', September 1963, para. 11.
[88] TNA T227/1618, Clarke, note, 'Robbins Report', September 1963, para. 15.
[89] Barr, 'Higher education funding', p. 269; Friedman, 'The role of government in education'; Barr and Crawford, *Financing Higher Education*.

scheme.[90] In 1997 the Dearing Report into Higher Education continued to emphasise the extent to which the gains made from higher education went to the private individual. Despite the increase in those holding a post-secondary degree, the returns to being so qualified rose sharply over the 1980s and remained relatively constant over the 1990s.[91] In both the USA and the UK, as the graduate share of the labour force rose, so too did wage differentials between graduates and non-graduates widen. The ratio of wages for graduate and non-graduate full-time workers rose between 1980 and 2000 from 1.36 to 1.66 in the USA, and from 1.48 to 1.64 in the UK.[92] The continued earnings premium on higher education pointed to an outward shift in the relative demand curve with the demand for skills outstripping supply.[93]

In response to the Dearing Report, in 1998 a £1,000 up-front, means-tested, inflation-linked tuition fee was introduced which was levied irrespective of the institution attended, or the subject studied. Fees for lower-income students were either partly or wholly subsidized. These fees were intended to supplement existing per-student teaching grants.[94] In 1999 maintenance grants, whose real value had been steadily falling, were abolished. They were replaced by means-tested loans, repayable on an income-contingent basis after graduation. Up to 1998, the cost of higher education teaching was funded by grants from central government via the main funding body, the Higher Education Funding Council for England (HEFCE). These teaching grants averaged £17,700 per student in 1990–1991, but had fallen to £13,200 per student by 1997–1998. While the total real expenditure on teaching grants remained unchanged, the higher student number cut the per capita spend.[95]

In 2004 the passing of the Higher Education Act allowed for the introduction of variable fees from 2006/7. Those universities in England who satisfied the Office for Fair Access could charge fees up to £3,000. Government-backed fee loans were introduced to help students finance the cost and up-front fees were thereby effectively abolished.[96] Loans were repayable on an income-contingent basis.[97] As the number in higher education continued to rise, the government commissioned a further report, this time from Lord Browne of Madingley, a former chairman of British Petroleum. Following Browne's

---

[90]   TNA T227/3658, Levitt, note, 'PAR: Higher Education', December 1971, para. 2.
[91]   Machin and Vignoles, *What's the Good of Education?*, p. 91; Barr and Crawford, 'The Dearing Report'.
[92]   Machin and Vignoles, *What's the Good of Education?*, p. 10.
[93]   Machin and Vignoles, *What's the Good of Education?*, p. 12.
[94]   Belfield, Crawford, and Sibieta, *Long-run Comparisons*, p. 22.
[95]   Belfield, Crawford, and Sibieta, *Long-run Comparisons*, p. 23.
[96]   Belfield, Crawford, and Sibieta, *Long-run Comparisons*, p. 24.
[97]   Machin and Vignoles, *What's the Good of Education?*, p. 92; Barr, 'Higher education funding', p. 273.

report in 2010, the government sanctioned a system of fees and loans for students starting in 2012–2013 which allowed universities to charge fees of up to £9,000 fees per year. These were again covered by tuition fee loans, with those loans paid back at 9% of income once the graduate reached an income threshold of £21,000. These loans were subject to a real interest rate of 0–3% depending on the graduate's income, and were written off after thirty years.[98] Subsequently, in 2017/18 on raising fees to £9,000, government also cut teaching grants from £11,500 per student in 2011–2012 to £2,300 in 2012–2013, shifting the weighting within the teaching funding system from teaching grants to tuition fees. Whereas in 1990, higher education was entirely funded through publicly funded teaching grants, such grants accounted for only 9% of funding by 2017. The remaining 91% came from graduate contributions through repaid tuition fee loans (51%) and public subsidies to these loans (40%). Overall the government subsidy per student fell from £15,800 in 2011–12 to £9,700 in 2012–13. However, the level of resources available to universities increased by over £7,000 per student over the course of their studies, as the increase in the graduate contribution more than offset the reduction in the government subsidy.[99]

Although universities gained additional income, class sizes grew. In 1972, the university Student:Staff Ratio (SSR) was 8.16:1, but with a firm Treasury intention of raising this to at least 10.1 across higher education, allied to efforts to restrict universities to 375,000–400,000 of the 800,000 places likely to be available by 1981. The consequent expansion in non-university institutions where unit costs were lower would be accompanied by a reduction in the proportion of places for the higher cost science and technology courses in favour of the arts and humanities.[100] In the 1990s, the SSR rose sharply and public funding per student fell by 36% between 1989 and 1997.[101] The average SSR across the HE sector rose from 9:1 in 1980, to 13.1 in 1990 and 17:1 in 1999. If funding for research, which is included in the average unit of funding, was excluded, then the SSR for 1999 was even higher at 23:1. Average class sizes in universities doubled in twenty years, as lecture classes grew in size and small tutorial groups came under pressure in many universities. Over the twenty years, real funding per student at university almost halved.[102]

[98] In 2018 the government sought to sell the loan book to commercial lenders.
[99] Belfield, Crawford, and Sibieta, *Long-run Comparisons*, pp. 8, 22, 26.
[100] TNA T227/3655, Forsyth, paper, 'PAR 1971 Higher Education', April 1972, para. 3.
[101] Machin and Vignoles, *What's the Good of Education?*, p. 92.
[102] Barr, 'Higher education funding', pp. 265–6; Greenaway and Haynes, 'Funding higher education in the UK', pp. F153–4.

Around the same time as fees were introduced, there was also a change in the allocation of public resources across the entire educational sector. This reflected a continuing interest in the public/social rate of return, as well as dissatisfaction with the perceived educational standards.[103] This was reflected in Prime Minister Callaghan's Ruskin College Oxford speech on 18 October 1976 and in concern with the results of international maths tests. Attention was increasingly focused on efforts to address the problem of the performance of the lowest third of school children. In the Education Reform Act of 1988 a National Curriculum was introduced for pupils aged between seven and sixteen with the aim of ensuring that all students reached a minimum standard by the age of sixteen. From the mid-1990s, external monitoring of school performance became easier with the introduction of the assessment of children at the ages of seven, eleven, fourteen and sixteen (Key Stages 1, 2, 3 and 4) and the assembling of these results into league tables.[104] In 1998, literacy and numeracy hours were added to the primary school curriculum, with the content of these lessons tightly prescribed by central government.[105] Early start reading schemes were also introduced.[106]

The external monitoring of children's performance and the introduction of national maths projects were aimed at ensuring that the lowest performing one-third of school pupils acquired a basic and measured set of skills. For better or for worse, unflattering comparisons were made with German methods of post-secondary-school continuing education and training which were well regarded and viewed as a significant contributor to German manufacturing productivity. Increasingly, economists concerned with improving UK productivity looked less at plant economies of scale and more at the quality of the labour force (human capital). This was in keeping with wider changes in industrial policy (see chapter 3). While some early-post-World War II Anglo-American Productivity Teams had left Britain to inspect the standardized methods and long production runs of the United States, by the 1980s the attention of economists of industrial structure like Sig Prais of the National Institute of Economic and Social Research (NIESR) had moved away from these untypical large operations of over 1,000 employees to the medium- to smaller-size operations in industries like clothing (30–250 employees), engineering (50–500) and biscuits (which could have more than 1,000 employees). While noting that Britain looked set to overtake Germany and Switzerland in its stock of university graduates by the early 1990s, both

[103] Cunha, Heckman, and Schennach, 'Estimating the technology'.
[104] Machin and Vignoles, *What's the Good of Education?*, p. 6.
[105] Machin and Vignoles, *What's the Good of Education?*, p. 18.
[106] George, Stokes, and Wilkinson, 'Does early education influence Key Stage 1 attainment?'.

Germany and Switzerland had 50–60% more of their graduates in engineering and technology than did Britain.[107] In contrast to university degrees, intermediate post-secondary school vocational qualifications corresponding to equivalents of the BTEC (Business and Technology Education Council) and City & Guilds certificates were held by two-thirds of the total workforce in Germany, the Netherlands, and Switzerland, compared with one-quarter in the UK.[108]

The specific argument made was that a relative deficiency in such qualifications and training fed through into productivity. That routine preventative maintenance which was normal on the Continent and carried out by vocationally qualified staff, in Britain was undertaken by maintenance teams much of whose time was spent 'fire-fighting' with little time left for routine maintenance. The broader argument made was that manufacturing had moved from a process of 'mechanization', often identified with 'Fordism', in which skilled craftsmen were replaced by machines operated by unskilled labour whose earnings rose, to a phase of 'automation' in which automatic devices (for feeding, transferring, and activating tasks in manufacturing) replaced unskilled operators of machines, with a consequent fall in demand for unskilled, inexperienced, and technically unqualified young people. Prais and the NIESR urged policymakers to shift their attention to 'the scholarly attainments of average and below-average school leavers than simply with those top attainers who are to join the ranks of university graduates.'[109] The concern with the lowest third seemed to be confirmed by the results of international maths tests.[110] These had been conducted since 1963–1964, but they excited particular concern in Britain in the late 1980s and 1990s. In 1991, of those with a score of 5 or lower (of a maximum score of 70) as many as 24% of all pupils in England were in that category, compared with only 8–10% in Germany, the Netherlands, and Japan; and 14% in France. Roughly speaking there were two to three times as many low attainers in England as in its leading European industrial competitors.[111] The work of the NIESR was read in Whitehall and used by the CBI in its submissions to governments. That productivity growth slackened in the 1970s and 1980s as the growth in the educational stock reached new heights encouraged a search for more specific 'causal' relationships between education and growth.[112]

---

[107] Prais, *Economic Performance and Education*; Murphy, 'A degree of waste'.
[108] Prais, *Economic Performance and Education*, p. 10.
[109] Prais, *Economic Performance and Education*, pp. 13, 18.
[110] Husen (ed.), *International Study of Achievements in Mathematics*.
[111] Prais, *Economic Performance and Education*, p. 21.
[112] Wolf, *Does Education Matter?*, p. 41–2. Madison, *Phases of Capitalist Development*, p. 11; Lal, *Nationalised Universities*.

These changed priorities began to be reflected within public expenditure on education. In 1990–1991 higher education spending at £5,900 per student per year (in 2016–2017 prices) was nearly three times the level of primary school spending per pupil, and it all came directly from government spending.[113] Further education spending was £5,000 per student, which was nearly 2.5 times the level of primary school spending and nearly 1.5 times the level of secondary school spending per pupil. Secondary school spending was £3,500, about 1.5 times the level of primary school spending per pupil (£2,100). Early years spending was very low (less than £100m in total).[114]

By 2015–2016 these ratios had changed. Higher education resources per student continued to be higher than resources at all other stages, but the sources of finance had shifted from public finance to tuition fees. School spending was prioritized by successive governments, including spending on early years which was motivated by a concern with child development and an interest in increasing maternal employment. Even so, early years spending per pupil was still less than half that in primary schools.[115] The main loser in the shifts of expenditure was further education and sixth forms, which were subject to a series of reviews and reforms, such as the Wolf Review of Vocational Education in 2011.[116] Whereas in 1990–1991, spending per student was nearly 50% higher than spending per student in secondary schools, by 2015–2016 it was 10% lower, at around £5,600 per student.[117]

Markets and Market Mechanisms

Coexisting with publicly financed and provided health and education were privately provided health and education services available to qualifying individuals with the necessary finance. Within the NHS in particular, there were also arguments as to the extent to which markets and market mechanisms such as prices might be used to allocate resources.

Access to privately provided healthcare was usually financed by membership of a health insurance scheme. This pooled risks, but also excluded very high-risk groups. Theoretical critiques of health insurance emphasize the problems of asymmetries of information, including that of the patient not

---

[113] Belfield, Crawford, and Sibieta, *Long-run Comparisons*, p. 28.
[114] Belfield, Crawford, and Sibieta, *Long-run Comparisons*, p. 29.
[115] Belfield, Crawford, and Sibieta, *Long-run Comparisons*, p. 30.
[116] Wolf, *Review of Vocational Training*; Belfield, Crawford, and Sibieta, *Long-run Comparisons*, p. 19.
[117] Belfield, Crawford, and Sibieta, *Long-run Comparisons*, p. 7.

knowing that he or she is ill. That the NHS should be free at the point of consumption was designed in part to encourage people to come forward and discover how much medical care they might need and could use. Part of the higher US healthcare costs seem likely to have arisen from the third-party payment problem, whereby the insurer (the third party) has insufficient control over the costs incurred by the patient and the consultant, neither of whom has an incentive to limit cost. As a state-financed service, the NHS could use the system of budgetary funding to overcome the 'third-party payment' problem.[118]

As part of the increased economic scrutiny of the NHS in the 1960s, in 1961 the Institute of Economic Affairs published a Hobart paper by Dennis Lee called *Health Through Choice*, which argued for a greater role for consumer choice in what was seen as a health market.[119] In 1970 the IEA published *Choice in Welfare*[120] by Harris and Seldon (an adviser to BUPA). One immediate objection to the IEA approach concerned precisely what was meant by a market. In perfect competition, a market might be characterized by frequent transactions, low barriers to entry for new aspirant suppliers, full information on the part of buyers and sellers, and an equal ability on the part of buyers and sellers to verify the quality of what was being sold. Such perfect markets rarely exist, and the market for health was far from being perfect. The Treasury's response to the publication of *Choice in Welfare*[121] by Harris and Seldon was to dismiss it as '99% rubbish; however, we ought not as impartial critics to forget the 1%'.[122] The objections were not only that the usual groups would not be covered, but also that there was little sense of what private prices would be.[123] Theoretically there was scope for the NHS to use its quasi-monopsonist position to negotiate better deals with suppliers, and from the consultants, and to exploit any technological and administrative economies of scale. If the NHS could derive benefits from exploiting its monopsony position, it might guard against monopoly abuse by encouraging competition amongst its suppliers. This was the basis of the purchaser–provider split in which the NHS sought to exploit its excess demand.

---

[118] Donaldson, *Why A National Health Service?*, p. 3; Cooper, 'Economics of Need', p. 89.

[119] Williams, 'Primeval health economics', S3.

[120] TNA 227/3287, 'Many favour contracting out of state welfare', *The Times* report, 8 January 1971; Harris, *Choice in Welfare*.

[121] TNA 227/3287, 'Many favour contracting out of state welfare', *The Times* report 8th January 1971; Harris, *Choice in* Welfare.

[122] TNA T227/3288, Levitt, note, 'Working Party on NHS Finance-Report on *Choice in Welfare*', February 1971; TNA T227/3288, Bowman, note, 'Choice in Welfare 1970', 1971, paras. 1 and 2.

[123] TNA T227/3288, 'Working Party on NHS Finance-'Insurance', paper, has a standard but useful list of groups who would not be covered by an insurance scheme.

Proposals for a more specific use of the pricing mechanism in the NHS, whether for prescriptions and/or for private beds within NHS hospitals, also generated strong responses. The main proposals for the use of pricing in the NHS were both as a means of restricting demand and as a means of raising finance. Controversially, the NHS introduced prescription charges in January 1951. Aneurin Bevan, the Minister of Health, did not object in principle to charging for prescriptions. As he remarked in 1949: 'I shudder to think of the ceaseless cascade of medicine which is pouring down British throats at the present time'.[124] It was not the principle but the context (rearmament for the Korean War) of the Attlee government's decision to introduce prescription charges which provoked Bevan's resignation in January 1951. Over time prescription charges came and went. Although under the 1946 Act patients were initially exempt from charges for drugs, appliances, dentistry, spectacles, and optician's services, in 1949 the Attlee government amended the 1946 Act so that charges could be made for these items. Charges were then actually introduced by the Conservative government.[125] On the route back to government, the Labour Party's 1964 manifesto pledged to abolish prescription charges, as happened in 1965 once government had been attained. As part of the post-1967 devaluation measures to reduce public expenditure to release resources for export, prescription charges were reintroduced and charges for dental treatment increased.[126] And so on.

Details of NHS expenditure are shown in Table 5.8. Prescription costs did rise, and fluctuated as a share of NHS costs, but prescription charges only ever produced a small offsetting revenue. In the 1990s, over three-quarters of the prescriptions issued were free to exempt groups such as children, low-income groups, and pensioners.[127] Even when prescription charges were variously introduced and withdrawn, the effects were not completely straightforward. When prescription charges were abolished in 1965, there was a greater than anticipated increase in cost because of a sharp rise in the number of prescriptions. Yet after the subsequent reintroduction of prescription charges, while the revenue produced by the charge was much as expected, there was also a sharp increase in the net ingredient cost per prescription even as the quantity of drugs prescribed fell. In part this was explained by fewer prescriptions being written for low-cost drugs, a shift towards more expensive drugs being marked from 1968 and heightened by the effects of devaluation. However,

---

[124] Webster, *The Health Services since the War*, pp. 144–5; Bevan, address to Parliamentary Labour Party and at University College London, *The Times*, 26 October 1949 and 16 November 1949.
[125] Glennerster, *Paying for Welfare: The 1990s*, pp. 167–8.
[126] TNA T227/2860, Crossman, note, 1969, paras. 7–8.
[127] Glennerster, *Paying for Welfare: The 1990s*, pp. 167–8.

Table 5.8. Estimated total NHS expenditure on pharmaceuticals at manufacturers' prices, UK, selected years* £ million (cash)

Year	Pharmaceutical services	Dispensing doctors	Hospital	Total NHS medicines	NHS medicines cost:		
					Per capita £(2009 prices)	% of NHS cost	% of GDP
1970	124	6	29	159	33.22	8.0	0.31
1975	208	12	59	279	31.08	5.4	0.26
1980	613	35	178	826	45.87	7.3	0.35
1985	1,217	74	336	1,627	64.62	9.5	0.45
1990	1,918	121	495	2,533	74.25	8.9	0.44
1995	3,406	286	891	4,583	111.80	11.0	0.63
2000	5,264	337	1,390	6,991	149.42	12.3	0.72
2005	7,377	471	2,409	10,258	188.78	10.6	0.82
2009	7,969	472	3,835	12,277	198.68	9.7	0.88

*All figures exclude dressings and appliance.
GDP at market prices.
Source: Office of Health Economics, health statistics website, Table 4.8.

doctors also prescribed in noticeably larger quantities (about 7% more) per prescription and this increase in quantity per prescription occurred across the board, both in high- and low-cost categories and for exempt and non-exempt patients. While this was noted by the Treasury, it did not necessarily object since if the doctor was satisfied that long-term medication was required, it was to the Exchequer's advantage that a single prescription be written, thereby saving on repeated chemists' fees, which were higher than prescription charges.[128]

Another source of finance, for the use of NHS beds and treatments was also politically controversial, principally because it was seen as giving advantage to higher income groups able to afford earlier treatment and more comfortable accommodation. Such issues became particularly live in the 1970s, as general concern with health and other inequalities grew. Barbara Castle, as Secretary of State for Health and Social Services, was persistent in reminding the Chancellor of the Exchequer, Denis Healey, of the 1974 Labour Party manifesto pledge to 'phase out private practice from the hospital service'.[129] Renée Short MP was equally dogged in raising the issue of the use by private patients of NHS facilities. Such private use of facilities was accommodated in the

[128] TNA T227/3134, Langdon, paper, 'Prescriptions', August 1969, para. 4.
[129] Klein, *The Politics of the National Health Service*, p. 119.

legislation establishing the NHS, just as was, necessitously, the scope for consultants to undertake private work.

For all of the political arguments surrounding them, charges never made a significant contribution to NHS income. In 1969 charges imposed by the central government yielded about £55 million a year, or less than 4% of the total cost of the Health Service in Britain. About £12 million came from charges from pay and amenity beds, £18 million from prescription charges, and £25 million from dental treatment, denture, and spectacle charges. This £55 million derived from charges can be compared with the much more important sources of revenue, namely the £180 million derived from the NHS contribution and the £1,350 millionm from taxation (see Table 5.9).[130]

The NHS contribution (the Health Stamp) had its origins in the Lloyd George National Insurance Act of 1911 which introduced a compulsory system of contributory health insurance for a major section of the manual workforce.[131] Although it was anomalous to have both a tax and an insurance form of revenue in health, the health contribution had the merit of continuing to collect revenue at low cost with resigned acceptance by contributors. As a tax it was regressive and left the Treasury vulnerable to demands that its proceeds should be hypothecated. Richard Crossman, as Secretary of State for Social

Table 5.9. NHS sources of finance, selected years

Year	Taxation		NHS contribution from National Insurance		Patients' payments*		Total NHS income**	NHS income as a % of UK government receipts***
	£m	%NHS	£m	%NHS	£m	%NHS	£m	
1950	477	100.0	–	–	–	–	477	8.7
1960	671	77.5	118	13.6	43	5.0	866	9.8
1970	1,635	82.6	209	10.6	60	3.0	1,979	8.7
1980	9,951	88.4	1,042	9.3	264	2.3	11,257	11.5
1990	22,992	80.9	4,288	15.1	1,146	4.0	28,426	12.9
2000	49,103	86.0	6,905	12.1	1,058	1.9	57,067	15.2
2009	102,541	80.9	22,679	17.9	1,479	1.2	126,699	24.6

* Patient charges for 2009 are not comparable with earlier years, as reliable data for PDS in England and Wales are not available before 2004/05 and therefore data prior to 2004/05 are based on GDS patient charges alone.

** Prior to 1974 total NHS income includes services provided by former Local Health Authorities (LHAs). From 1974 onwards, services provide by LHAs were transferred to the NHS.

*** UK government receipts include taxes and National Insurance contributions.

130 TNA T227/2860, Crossman, note, 1969, para. 3.
131 Webster, *The Health Services since the War*, p. 10.

Services (1968–1970), was adept in presenting any increase in revenue (via the NHS Contribution) as a 'saving' in NHS expenditure which might be ignored for public expenditure purposes.[132] Other suggestions for raising revenue, possibly as a substitute for the NHS Stamp, included the hypothecation of the duties on tobacco, spirits, and beer. In 1969, the spirits duty raised £155 million, while beer produced a further £225 million and tobacco £830 million. (Other duties included purchase tax at £535 million and oil including petrol at £410 million.)[133]

In the UK, the private insurance market for health was smaller than that in the United States and Germany where there was greater use of compulsory social insurance. As NHS funding tightened in the 1970s so too did the private purchase of health services increase. The use of private facilities was not restricted to the insured. In 2000 about 20% of patients in the private sector paid for treatment themselves. Aggregate (direct and insured) private health spending fell as a percentage of total health spending from 18% in 1964 to 9% in 1975, before rising to over 15% in 1997. As with education, the proportionate decline in the 1960s and early 1970s was largely due to private expenditure remaining constant as public health spending increased as a share of GDP. After 1975, private spending (in constant prices) on health more than tripled.[134] As NHS waiting lists grew, so too did private insurance numbers as people paid for time and avoided NHS queues (Table 5.10). In February 2000, 1.1 million patients in England were on an NHS in-patient waiting list, which was over 2% of the population. In 1978, 2.4 million people were covered by private health insurance; in 2000 it was 7 million. Two-thirds of that private medical insurance was employer-provider.[135] Private healthcare grew in part because of its ability to piggy-back on the NHS, preferring to offer a restricted range of relatively uncomplicated surgery with about two dozen procedures accounting for 70% of its expenditure.[136]

In the USA and Germany where there was a greater use of private insurance, a larger share of national income was spent on health and medical care than in the UK (United States 14% of GDP; Germany 10.7%; UK 6.8%). In some cases such as life expectancy and infant mortality the UK achieved better outcomes than the US.[137] Unsurprisingly, in the United States a large

[132] TNA T227/3422, Widdup, note, 'History of the National Health stamp', February 1970, para. 5; Crossman, *Paying for the Social Services*.
[133] TNA T227/3054, 'National Health Services Finances', paper, July 1969, Appendix V, paras. 1–2.
[134] Emmerson, Frayne and Goodman, *Pressures in UK Healthcare*, p. 24.
[135] Emmerson, Frayne and Goodman, *Pressures in UK Healthcare*, p. 1.
[136] Glennerster, *Paying for Welfare: The 1990s*, p. 176.
[137] Emmerson, Frayne and Goodman, *Pressures in UK Healthcare*, p. 1.

Table 5.10. Number of private medical insurance subscribers, people covered and payments, UK, selected years

Year	Subscribers (thousands)	People insured (thousands)	Subscriptions paid £m	Benefits paid £m	People insured as % of UK population	Subscriptions paid as % of total private healthcare spending
1955	274	585	2	2	1.2	–
1965	680	1,445	9	8	2.7	–
1975	1,087	2,315	55	46	4.1	41
1984	2,010	4,367	413	341	7.8	66
Laing and Buisson survey estimates for all insurers						
1985	2,380	5,057	520	456	8.9	70
1995	3,430	6,673	1,718	1,388	11.5	68
2005	3,511	6,359	3,106	2,401	10.6	35
2008	3,648	6,366	3,639	2,799	10.4	36

Source: Office of Health Economics, health statistics website, Table 2.13.

literature on health economics emerged, a seminal article being Kenneth Arrow's study of the welfare economics of medical care which appeared in the *American Economic Review* in 1963.[138] In the UK, private health insurance was strongly related to income, 40% of people in the richest 10% of the population being privately insured, compared with less than 5% in the bottom 40%. Prior to the July 1997 Budget, individuals aged over sixty did receive basic rate tax relief on the purchase of private medical insurance, regardless of whether they were taxpayers or not. Had the subsidy not been abolished in July 1997, it would have cost £135 million in 1999–2000.[139] However, the issue of inequality of access to healthcare services goes way beyond arguments about public or private payment, as was evidenced in the *Independent Inquiry into Inequalities in Health (1998)*[140] in England chaired by Sir Donald Acheson which underlined the close association between income inequality and health.[141]

In education, at school level, a large public sector had long coexisted with a smaller but politically important private sector. In 1951/2, about one-fifth of total private and state school expenditure was spent on private schools. As expenditure on the state sector rose in the 1950s and 1960s, so expenditure

---

[138] Arrow, 'Uncertainty and the welfare economics of medical care'.
[139] Emmerson, Frayne and Goodman, *Pressures in UK Healthcare*, pp. 27, 31; H.M. Treasury, 1997.
[140] Acheson, *Independent Inquiry*; Williams, 'Commentary on the Acheson Report'.
[141] Tudor Edwards, 'Paradigms and research programmes', p. 641.

on private schools fell to 10% of total expenditure.[142] While direct grant schools were abolished in 1975, public schools survived, albeit with fewer tax privileges.[143] As expenditure on state schools stagnated in the 1980s, so spending on private schools rose.[144] Although the proportion of private school pupils (about 7%) remained constant between the 1970s and 2000, private expenditure on education rose fivefold in that period. In England in 2000 the pupil:teacher ratio in private schools was 9.9:1 compared with 23:1 in state primary schools and 17:1 in state secondary schools. While 60% of pupils schooled through the private system in the 1980s and 1990s attained post-secondary degrees, only 16% of state schools pupils did so.[145]

In fact, contrary to many people's prior expectations, the expansion of the higher education sector was to benefit disproportionately those from higher-income groups. The educational inequality gap, measured as the gap in the degree proportion between the richest and the poorest 20% of the family income distribution, widened between 1981 and 1999 from 14 to 37%.[146] In 2002, 81% of children from professional backgrounds went to university; the comparable figure for children from manual backgrounds was 15%.[147] In 2005 Machin and Vignoles reported that in the UK 48% of young people from professional, managerial, and skilled non-manual background entered university, whilst only 18% from a skilled manual or unskilled background did so.[148] More generally, economists pointed to the greater use made of the welfare state by middle- rather than lower-income groups. In 1982, Le Grand's research indicated that educational expenditure on a child of a family in socio-economic group 1 (rich) was about 50% higher than that on a poor child.[149] The better-informed, more confident and expectant middle-class proved to be more effective in obtaining services from fellow middle-class providers in the welfare state than lower-income groups. One policy response was to shift more state activity to cash benefits which could be targeted on the poor.[150]

---

[142] Glennerster, *Paying for Welfare: The 1990s*, p. 211.

[143] Lowe, *The Welfare State*, 1993, p. 220.

[144] Glennerster, *Paying for Welfare: The 1990s*, p. 211. (Glennerster and Low 'Education and the welfare state'). Private education expenditure rose at more or less the same rate as incomes—an income elasticity of one—over the same period, and slightly faster in the 1980s.

[145] Machin and Vignoles, *What's the Good of Education?*, p. 19; Green, 'The problem of British education policy as economic policy'.

[146] Machin and Stevens, 'The assessment', pp. 168–9; Blanden and Machin, 2004.

[147] Barr, 'Higher education funding', p. 266.

[148] Machin and Vignoles, *What's the Good of Education?*, p. 16.

[149] Le Grand, *The Strategy of Equality*, Table 4.1; Barr, *The Economics of the Welfare State*, p. 313.

[150] Glennerster, *Paying for Welfare: The 1990s*.

From 1951 both the allocation of resources to and within health and education changed. Education and health's share of GDP rose, and notably from the 1970s resource allocation emphasized the private benefits over time to individuals rather than the more traditional concern with public benefits. In as much as the public benefit approach incorporated social benefits which were difficult to price in a market, then so too did such an approach favour the public provision of health and education. Once private benefits were emphasized, so it became easier to talk of the market in health and education. Both health and education had always had their private and public sectors, but the combination of the steadily rising share of GDP accounted for by health and education, and the increasing concern with public finances from the mid-1970s, created an environment in which cost–benefit analyses of expenditure in health and education attracted a wider political and administrative audience. In the absence of a significant specific increase in the financing of the NHS, as for example through hypothecated taxation, then the allocation and ranking of healthcare and procedures on a rate of return basis became increasingly likely. In education, new sources of finance for students in the form of fees could be tapped, but as with health, the private nature of the benefits over time were emphasized. At points in the healthcare system, the impact of this rate of return approach was clear, as in the decisions made by NICE. Elsewhere it was cloudier, as in the variation in the rate of referral among GPs and with evidence for income, gender, age, race, and geographical circumstances affecting access to hospital treatment, as in 1995 in the North East Thames Region for cataract, tonsil operations, and varicose vein operations.[151] In 2005, research by Propper et al., indicated that while the probability of receiving NHS treatment for arthritis was determined by the severity of arthritis and not by any other factors, the amount of NHS care received by an individual was positively associated not only with the severity but also by the education of the individual and, weakly, the interest in arthritis of the family doctor.[152] In education, access to universities remains strongly correlated to family income, whether through access to private schooling or by being able to afford to live in the catchment area of the more desired local schools.[153] Chapter 4 examined the changes in poverty and inequality since 1951. Chapter 6 examines the shifts in the ownership and value of assets. As with education and health, the concern is with the shift away from the provision of publicly financed and

---

[151] Scott and Gilmore, 'The Edinburgh Hospitals', p. 97.

[152] Chaturvedi and Ben-Shlomo, 'From the surgery to the surgeon'; Goddard and Smith, 'Equity of access'; Propper, Eachus, Chan, Pearson, and Davey Smith, 'Access to health care resources in the UK', p. 400.

[153] Jerrin, *Family Background*.

provided output and towards a marketable asset in which asset prices reflected both expectations of future returns and easier access to low-cost finance outside of the public sector.

Bibliography

Acheson, D., *Independent Inquiry into Inequalities on Health(Report)*, 1998, London: The Stationery Office.

Arrow, Kenneth, 'Uncertainty and the welfare economics of medical care', *American Economic Review*, vol. 53, issue 5, 1963, pp. 941–73.

Barr, N., 'Higher education funding', *Oxford Review of Economic Policy*, vol. 20, no. 2, 2004, pp. 264–83.

Barr, Nicholas, *The Economics of the Welfare State*, fourth edition, 2004, Oxford: Oxford University Press.

Barr, N., and I. Crawford, 'The Dearing Report and the government's response: A critique', *The Political Quarterly*, vol. 69, no. 1, 1998, pp. 72–84.

Barr, Nicholas, and Iain Crawford, *Financing Higher Education: Answers from the UK*, 2005, Abingdon: Routledge.

Belfield, Chris, Claire Crawford, and Luke Sibieta, *Long-run Comparisons of Spending Per Pupil Across Different Stages of Education*, 2017, London: Institute for Fiscal Studies.

Bevan, Aneurin, *In Place of Fear*, 1952, London: Heinemann.

Bevan, Aneurin, address to Parliamentary Labour Party and at University College London, *The Times*, 26 October 1949 and 16 November 1949.

Blanden, Jo and S. Machin, 'Educational inequality and the expansion of UK higher education', *Scottish Journal of Political Economy*, vol 51, no. 2, 2004, pp. 230–249.

Blaug, Marc, 'Where are we now in the economics of education?', *Economics of Education Review*, vol. 4, no. 1, 1985, pp. 17–28.

Bowles, S., and H. Gintis, *Schooling in Capitalist America*, 1976. London: Routledge and Kegan Paul.

Bowles, S., and H. Gintis, 'Does schooling raise earnings by making people smarter?', in Kenneth Arrow, Samuel Bowles, and Steven Durlauf (eds.), *Meritocracy and Economic Inequality*, 2000, Princeton: Princeton University Press, pp. 118–36.

Breyer, Friedrich, Joan Costa-Font, and Stefan Felder, 'Ageing , health and health care', *Oxford Review of Economic Policy*, vol. 26, no. 4, 2010, pp. 674–90.

British Medical Association, *Health Services Financing*, 1970, London: British Medical Association.

Brotherston, J.H.F., in W. Latham and A. Newberry (eds.), *Community Medicine and Teaching, Research and Health Care*, 1970, London: Butterworths.

Buxton, M.J., and R. Klein, 'Distribution of hospital provision: policy themes', *British Medical Journal*, 1975, 1:suppl, pp. 345–49.

Buxton, M.J., and R. Klein, *Allocating Health Services: A commentary on the report of the Resource Allocation Working Party*, Royal Commission on the National Health Service, Research paper no. 3, 1978, London: HMSO.

Cairns, J., 'Discounting in economic evaluation', in M.F. Drummond and A. McGuire (eds.), *Economic Evaluation in Health Care: Merging Theory with Practice*, 2001, New York: Oxford University Press.

Central Statistical Office, *Annual Abstract of Statistics, 1970*, 1970, No. 107, London: HMSO.

Chaturvedi, N., and B. Ben-Shlomo, 'From the surgery to the surgeon: does deprivation influence consultation and operation rates?', *British Journal of General Practice*, vol. 45, 1995, pp. 127–31.

Cochrane, A.L., *Effectiveness and Efficiency: Random Reflections on Health Services*, 1972, London: Nuffield Provincial Hospitals Trust.

Cook, D.R., 'The reorganisation of the N.H.S.: Viewpoint of the G.P.', *Journal of the Royal Society of Health*, vol. XCII, no. 1, 1972.

Cookson, R., and K. Claxton, *The Humble Economist: Tony Culyer on Health, Health Care and Social Decision Making*, 2012, York: University of York and Office of Health Economics.

Cooper, Michael, 'Economics of need: The experience of the British health service', in Mark Perlman (ed.), *The Economics of Health and Medical Care*, 1974, London and Basingstoke: The International Economic Association, Macmillan, pp. 89–107.

Cooper, M.H., and A.J. Culyer, 'An economic assessment of some aspects of the organisation of the National Health Service, Appendix A of the BMA Report', *Health Services Financing*, 1970, London: British Medical Association, pp. 187–250.

Crosland, Susan, *Tony Crosland*, 1982, London: Jonathan Cape.

Crossman, Richard, reported in *The Guardian*, 27 November 1969.

Crossman, Richard, *Paying for the Social Services*, 1969, London: Fabian Society.

Culyer, A.J., 'The normative economics of health care finance and provision', *Oxford Review of Economic Policy*, vol. 5, no. 1, spring 1989, pp. 34–58.

Culyer, Tony, 'Economics, economists and ethics in health care', in Richard Cookson and Karl Claxton (eds.), *The Humble Economist: Tony Culyer on Health, Health Care and Social Decision Making*, 2012, York: University of York and Office of Health Economics, pp. 119–32.

Culyer, Tony, 'Equity of what in health care? Bad slogans; good slogans', in Richard Cookson and Karl Claxton (eds.), *The Humble Economist: Tony Culyer on*

Health, Health Care and Social Decision Making, 2012, York: University of York and Office of Health Economics, pp. 171–84.

Culyer, Tony, 'The welfarist and extra-welfarist economics of health care finance and provision', in Richard Cookson and Karl Claxton (eds.), *The Humble Economist: Tony Culyer on Health, Health Care and Social Decision Making*, 2012, York: University of York and Office of Health Economics, pp. 79–115.

Culyer, Tony, 'The internal market and demand-side socialism: an acceptable means to a desirable end', in Richard Cookson and Karl Claxton (eds.), *The Humble Economist: Tony Culyer on Health, Health Care and Social Decision Making*, 2012, York: University of York and Office of Health Economics, pp. 213–30.

Cunha, F., J.J. Heckman, and S. Schennach, 'Estimating the technology of cognitive and noncognitive skill formation', *Econometrica*, vol. 78, 2010, pp. 883–931.

Donaldson, Cam, *Why A National Health Service?: The Economic Rationale*, 1998, London: Institute for Public Policy Research.

Doorslaer, E. van, A. Wagstaff, and F. Rutten (eds.), *Equity in the Finance and Delivery of Health Care: An International Perspective*, 1993, Oxford: Oxford University Press.

Earnshaw, Julia, and Gavin Lewis, 'NICE guide to the methods of technology appraisal', *Pharmaeconomics*, vol. 26, no. 9, 2008, pp. 725–27.

Emmerson, Carl, Christine Frayne, and Alissa Goodman, *Pressures in UK Healthcare; Challenges for the NHS*, 2000, London: The Institute for Fiscal Studies.

Feldstein, M.S., *Economic Analysis for Health Service Efficiency*, 1966, Amsterdam: North Holland.

Friedman, M., 'The role of government in education' in Robert A. Solo (ed.), *Economics and the Public Interest*, 1955, New Brunswick, N.J.: Rutgers University Press.

George, Anitha, Lucy Stokes and David Wilkinson, 'Does early education influence Key Stage 1 attainment? Evidence for England from the Millennium Cohort Study', *National Institute Economic Review*, vol. 222, no. 1, November 2012, pp. R67–80.

Glennerster, H., *Paying for Welfare: The 1990s*, 1992, New York: Harvester Wheatsheaf.

Glennerster, H., and W. Low, 'Education and the welfare state: does it add up?' in J. Hills (ed.), *The State of Welfare*, 1990, Oxford: Clarendon Press.

Goddard, M., and P. Smith, 'Equity of access to health care services', *Social Science and Medicine*, vol. 53, no. 9, 2001, pp. 1149–62.

Gravelle, Hugh, Werner Brouwer, Louis Niessen, Maarten Postma, and Frans Rutten, 'Discounting in economic evaluations: Stepping forward towards optimal decision rules', *Health Economics*, vol. 16, issue 3, March 2007, pp. 307–17.

Green, F., 'The problem of British education policy as economic policy', in D. Coffey and C. Thornley, *Industrial and Labour Market Policy and Performance*, 2003, London: Routledge.

Greenaway, David, and Michelle Haynes, 'Funding higher education in the UK: The role of fees and loans', *The Economic Journal*, vol. 113, Feb. 2003, F150–F166, pp. F153–4.

The Gurney-Dixon Report, *Early Leaving, A Report of the Central Advisory Council for Education (England)*, 1954, London: HMSO.

Harris, John, *The Value of Life: Introduction to Medical Ethics*, 1985, Routledge & Kegan Paul.

Harris, José, *William Beveridge: A Biography*, 1977, Oxford: Clarendon Press.

Harris, Ralph, *Choice in Welfare*, 1971, London: Institute of Economic Affairs.

Hauser, M.M. (ed.), *The Economics of Medical Care*, 1972, London: George Allen and Unwin.

Hills, John, 'The National Health Service: A systematic experience in appreciative frustration', *Australian and New Zealand Journal of Family Therapy*, vol. 27, no. 3, 2007.

Hutton, J., and A. Maynard, 'A NICE challenge for health economics', *Health Economics*, vol. 9, issue 2, 2000, pp. 89–93.

Jerrin, John, *Family Background and Access to 'High Status' Universities*, 2004, London: The Sutton Trust.

Johannesson, M., 'The relationship between cost-effectiveness analysis and cost-benefit analysis', *Social Science and Medicine*, vol. 41, no. 4, 1995, pp. 483–9.

Klein, Rudolf, *The Politics of the National Health Service*, second edition 1989, first published 1983, Longman: London and New York.

Lal, D., *Nationalised Universities: Paradox of the Privatisation Age*, 1989, London: Centre for Policy Studies.

Le Grand, Julian, *The Strategy of Equality*, 1982, London: George Allen & Unwin.

Lowe, Rodney, *The Welfare State in Britain since 1945*, 1993, Basingstoke: Macmillan, Houndmills.

Machin, S., and M. Stevens, 'The Assessment: Education', *Oxford Review of Economic Policy*, vol. 20, no. 2, June 2004, pp. 157–72.

Machin, Stephen, and Anna Vignoles (eds.), *What's the Good of Education?*, 2005, Princeton: Princeton University Press.

Madison, A., *Phases of Capitalist Development*, 1982, Oxford: Oxford University Press.

McCabe, Christopher, Karl Claxton, and Anthony J. Culyer, 'The NICE cost-effectiveness threshold', *Pharmaeconomics* 2008, vol. 26, no. 9, pp. 733–44.

Middleton, Roger, *The Growth of the Public Sector, Economic Management and British Economic Performance, c. 1890–1979*, 1996, Cheltenham: Edward Elgar.

Miners, Alec, 'Estimating "costs" for cost-effectiveness analysis', *Pharmaeconomics*, vol. 26, no. 9, 2008, pp. 745–51.

Murphy, James, 'A degree of waste: the economic benefits of educational expansion', *Oxford Review of Education*, vol. 19, no. 1, 1993, pp. 9–31.

Office of Health Economics, *Renal Failure*, 1978, London: Office of Health Economics.

Orwell, George, 'The Lion and the Unicorn' 19 February 1941, in George Orwell, *The Lion and the Unicorn, etc.*, 1962, London: Secker and Warburg.

Prais, S.J., *Economic Performance and Education: The Nature of Britain's Deficiencies*, National Institute of Economic and Social Research, 1993, Discussion paper no. 52, London: NIESR. Text of a paper read to the British Academy on 28 October 1993, pp. 5–8.

Propper, Carol, Jenny Eachus, Philip Chan, Nicky Pearson, and George Davey Smith, 'Access to health care resources in the UK: the case of care for arthritis', *Health Economics*, vol. 14, 2005, pp. 391–406.

Psacharopoulos, G., *Higher Education in Developing Countries: a Cost-Benefit Analysis*, 1980, Washington, DC: World Bank.

Robbins, Lionel, 'Recent discussion of the problems of higher education in Great Britain', in Lionel Robbins, *The University in the Modern World*, 1966, London: Macmillan, pp. 17–39.

Rosser, R.M., 'A history of the development of health indices', in G. Teeling Smith, (ed), *Measuring the Social Benefits of Medicine*, 1984, London: Office of Health Economics.

Sen, Amartya, 'Equality of what?' in S. McMurrin (ed.), *Tanner Lectures on Human Values*, vol. 1, 1980, Cambridge: University of Utah Press, Cambridge University Press, pp. 261–329.

Schmelzer, Matthias, *The Hegemony of Growth: The OECD and the Making of the Economic Growth Paradigm*, 2016, Cambridge: Cambridge University Press.

Scott, R., and M. Gilmore, 'The Edinburgh Hospitals', in G. McLauchlan(ed.), *Problems and Progress in Medical Care*, 1966, London: Oxford University Press.

Sugden, R., and A. Williams, *The Principles of Practical Cost-Benefit Analysis*, 1978, Oxford: Oxford University Press.

TNA CAB 87/76, SIC(41)20, Beveridge, 'Basic problems of social security with Heads of a Scheme', 11 December 1941.

TNA FD9/4584, Letter from Professor Alan Maynard, Centre for Health Economics, University of York to Professor John Wing, Institute of Psychiatry, Denmark Hill, London, 24 February 1988.

TNA MH 80/31 Beveridge to Maude, 22 February 1942.

TNA T227/1348, C.E.E.(63)6, paper, M.H. Peston, 'The school leaving age', H.M.Treasury committee on the economics of education, 4 October 1963, paras. 2 and 3.

TNA T227/1604, 'Reorganisation of secondary education: Future of the grammar schools', paper, November 1964.

TNA T227/1604, 'Progress under Circular 10/65', paper, J R Jameson, Department of Education and Science, 2 March 1966.

TNA T227/1618, 'Claim on Resources: 1965–1980', note, R.W.B. Clarke, 12 September 1963.

TNA T227/1618, 'Robbins Report', note by R.W.B. Clarke, 13 September 1963.

TNA T227/1624, R W B Clarke, draft letter to Sir John Wolfenden, 14 October 1963.

TNA T227/2854, paper, 'Higher education: areas of choice', Treasury draft paper, 12 March 1968.

TNA T227/2860 (10 July CC(69)32 concs, item 1), note, R.H.S. Crossman.

TNA T227/3054, Note, 'Health Services Financing', M. Widdup to Mr Jordan-Moss, 11 June 1970.

TNA T227/3054, 'National Health Services Finances', paper, July 1969.

TNA T227/3054, National Health Service', 1969.

TNA T227/3134, 'Prescriptions', paper by A.J. Langdon, 22 August 1969.

TNA T227/3287, 'Many favour contracting out of state welfare', The Times report 8 January 1971.

TNA T227/3288, 'Working Party on NHS Finance-Report on Choice in Welfare', note by M. S. Levitt, 17 February 1971.

TNA T227/3288, 'Choice in Welfare 1970', note by J. Bowman 1971.

TNA T227/3288, 'Working Party on NHS Finance-'Insurance', paper.

TNA T227/3422, 'History of the National Health stamp', note to Mr Stuart by M Widdup, SS Division, 2 February 1970.

TNA T227/3655, 'PAR 1971 Higher Education', paper, JMF 25 April 1972.

TNA T227/3658, 'PAR: Higher Education', Note, M. S. Levitt to Miss Forsyth, 13 December 1971.

TNA T230/500, 'Education expenditure as a proportion of GNP', April 1960.

TNA T230/536, 'Washington Conference: Economic growth and Investment in Education', comments by R Turvey to Mr Hopkin, September 1961.

TNA T298/277, R. Turvey, 'Returns to investment in education', September 1961.

TNA T298/277, 'Education and Economic Growth', note, F.R.P.Vinter to Mr Carswell, 14 September 1961.

TNA T298/277, 'Investment in Education: The Bellagio Doctrine', paper, W.A.B. Hopkin, September 1961.

TNA T298/277, 'Economic growth and investment in education', Washington, 16–20 October, 1961, list of papers.

TNA T379/74, Note, 'The investment appraisal of hospitals, M J Spackman to Mr Smallwood, 11 February 1977.

TNA T379/74, 'Investment appraisal techniques for the health capital programme', note by Mr Smallwood, 28 February 1977.

Thom, D., 'The 1944 Education Act: The Art of the Possible?', in Harold L. Smith (ed.), *War and Social Change: British Society in the Second World War*, 1986, Manchester.

Tudor Edwards, Rhiannon, 'Paradigms and research programmes', *Health Economics*, 10, 2001, pp.635–49.

Webster, Charles, *The Health Services since the War: Vol. 1, Problems of Health Care: The National Health Service Before 1957*, 1988, London: HMSO.

Williams, Alan, 'Economics of Coronary Artery Bypass Grafting', *British Medical Journal (Clin Res Ed)*, 3 August 1985, pp. 291–326.

Williams, Alan, 'Discovering the QALY; Or how Rachel Rosser changed my life', p. 3. www.york.ac.uk>che>documents

Williams, Alan, 'Intergenerational equity: An exploration of the "fair innings" argument', *Health Economics*, vol. 6, issue 2, March 1997, pp. 117–32.

Williams, Alan, 'Primeval health economics in Britain: A personal retrospect of the pre-HESG period', *Health Economics*, vol. 7, Issue Supplement S1, August 1998, pp. S3–S6, p. S6.

Williams, A., 'Commentary on the Acheson Report', *Health Econ*, vol. 8, no. 4, 2000, pp. 297–9.

Wolf, Alison, *Does Education Matter? Myths About Education and Economic Growth*, 2002, London: Penguin.

Wolf, Alison, *Review of Vocational Training: The Wolf Report*, 2011, London: Department for Education and Department for Business, Innovation and Skills.

Woodin, Tom, Gary McCulloch, and Steven Cowan, *Secondary Education and the Raising of the School-Leaving Age: Coming of Age?*, 2013, Basingstoke: Palgrave Macmillan.

Wooldridge, Adrian, *Measuring the Mind: Education and Psychology in England, c. 1860–1990*, 1994, Cambridge: Cambridge University Press.

6

Transferring Assets

Public Housing and Nationalized Industries

The rise and fall of public investment was discussed in chapter 2. There it was noted that while public expenditure as a share of national income remained broadly of a similar proportion from 1951, the composition of that expenditure changed. From the 1970s, expenditure on the health and social security programmes squeezed out expenditure on public fixed capital investment. Part of that fall in public investment arose from the decision to sell part of the existing stock of fixed capital investment. Industries and housing which were no longer publicly owned did not require further flows of public investment. Public housing and nationalized industry assets were sold in what was initially referred to in the case of the nationalized industries as denationalization, but which became more popularly known and promoted as a programme of privatization. This chapter examines the origins, processes, and effects of the privatization programme in public housing and the nationalized industries. As with the previous chapters, it draws attention to the temporal features of the privatization programme, and traces the increasing role of economics and economists in shaping how investment in and the sale of those public assets came to be viewed.

Privatization

While most privatization of public housing and nationalized industries occurred during the Thatcher governments (1979–1990), sales of similar public assets had preceded these governments. What marked out the Thatcher governments' approach was its extent and enthusiasm. While local authorities had previously sold off what they considered to be surplus housing stock, in the 'Right To Buy' programme as enacted in the Housing Act of October 1980, tenants were able to ask that their abode be sold to them at a discount as sitting tenants. Between 1979 and 1995, around 1.5 million council dwellings in England were sold under Right To Buy and other policies. These 1.5 million former council dwellings represented 9% of the stock and had accounted for 46% of the growth of the tenure between 1981 and 1991. In some localities the impact was striking. In New Towns, such as Harlow, Corby, and Stevenage, the owner-occupied sector was largely created through council house sales. In Harlow, where owner-occupation rose from 23% to 48% of households between 1981 and 1991, 97% of that growth was accounted for by sales of council/New Town properties. In Manchester, Birmingham, Nottingham, and Bristol, the sale of council housing also contributed strongly to the increase in owner-occupation. In Manchester, 90% of the growth in owner-occupation in the intercensal period was through council house sales.[1] Between 1980 and 1985 the share of owner-occupied dwellings rose from 56% to 67% of total housing, peaking at 69.3% in 2002 before falling back to 63.1% by early 2014. The rise in home ownership rates was principally due to the shrinking of the social rented sector, in particular due to RTB, with in England around 1.6 million social housing units being sold between 1980 and 2002.[2] Only one-fifth of the proceeds from the sale of council houses could be spent by local councils; the remaining four-fifths had to go towards paying off debts.[3] Some council houses were sold to non-governmental 'social landlords' who aimed to provide affordable housing. While in 1972 social landlords had only produced 9,750 new dwellings, this had increased to 39,328 by 1995.[4] However, this did not offset the fall in new local authority housing. Government-financed housing investment which had fluctuated around a rate of 2% of GDP and at around 5.5% of General Government Expenditure(GGE) in the two decades after 1956, effectively came to a halt between 1976 and 1982 and it was not to exceed significantly 1% thereafter. In 2000 it stood at –0.1%. From a peak of 151,824 new dwellings completed in 1976, the number fell to 39,960 in 1982 and to 1,058 by 1998, less than 1% of the 1976 level.[5] Publicly financed house-building was cut back and private and housing association-financed building failed to make good the shortfall. This fall in local authority house-building coincided with an increase in the total number of households, from 18.6 million in 1971 to 24.1 million in 2001. Housing costs rose through the 1980s promoting greater inequality.[6] In general, as stock was sold, so too did the asset valuation of the public sector fall. Estimates of the public sector net worth fell from 77.1% of GDP in 1980–1981 to 15.6% by 1999–2000.[7]

---

[1] Forrest, Gordon, and Murie, 'The position of former council homes', p. 127.

[2] Oxford Economics, *Forecasting UK House Prices*, pp. 4, 8.

[3] Florio, *The Great Divestiture*, p. 276.

[4] Clark, Elsby, and Love, 'Twenty-five years of falling investment?', p. 12.

[5] Clark, Elsby, and Love, 'Trends in British public investment', pp. 319, 322; Clark and Dilnot, *Long-term trends*, p. 15.

[6] Goodman and Webb, *For Richer, For Poorer*.   [7] Florio, *Great Divestiture*, p. 279.

Similarly, while the 'denationalization' of nationalized industries had long been spoken of, the 'privatization' programme added an extra bite and aggression to this sale of industrial assets. Denationalizing by selling shares in companies like British Airways, Amersham International (1982, £63 million), British Aerospace, oil companies, and other industries exposed to local and international competition was not of central contention. Privatizing network-containing industries like telecommunications, gas, and electricity which supplied the essentials of life was much more so. The sums raised were considerable, although in selling assets in profitable nationalized industries, future streams of earnings were foregone. In 1984 52% of British Telecom was sold for £3,916 million, with the further sale of 26% in 1991 and 21% in 1993 raising additional gross proceeds of £5,241 million and £5,202 million respectively. One hundred percent of British Gas was sold in 1986 for £5,434 million, while the complex privatization of the electricity industry saw 60% of nationalized industry generation (National Power and PowerGen) sold in 1991 for £2,100 million and a further 40% in 1995 for £3,590 million. The regional electricity companies (including the National Grid Company) were sold in their entirety for £5,100 million with the sales of the Scottish companies raising £2,900 million in 1991. Complications in the privatization of nuclear power generators caused only part of the industry to be privatized later as British Energy in 1996. Although not a network-containing utility, the privatization of the nationalized coal industry, eventually as the British Coal Corporation in 1994 for gross proceeds of £700 million, was contentious, continuing the politically charged history of coal-mining in Britain. In total, between 1979 and 1992, some thirty-nine UK companies were privatized by share sales and between 1985 and 1989, of the 23.6 billion raised by listed share sales, £16.6 billion or 70% were privatizations. Over the period 1979 to 1992 the government raised more than £40 billion by share sales. In July 1992 the top hundred quoted UK companies included seventeen privatized companies with a share valuation of £80 billion.[8]

In privatizing nationalized industries, the UK not only exchanged a flow of profits for an upfront capital payment, but it also reduced the flow of public fixed capital investment in the economy. This was especially true of the network utilities such as gas, electricity, water, rail, and fixed link telephony. Between 1850 and 1960 network utilities accounted for between 18 and 30% of the total net fixed assets in the UK, always larger than the share of

[8] Newbery, *Privatization, Restructuring and Regulation*, pp. 13, 16, 24–5.

manufacturing industry.[9] Privatizing industries with a high ratio of sunk (irrecoverable):marginal (variable) costs into a competitive market structure would also mark a break with much of their previous history. Given the concern to recover the initial capital costs of laying pipelines, cables, and building generating stations, utilities had previously usually been offered a protected period free of competition in which to recover these sunk costs. This was achieved either in concessions or as an outcome of their being restructured into a monopoly on their nationalization. How sunk capital costs would be recovered in a competitive market characterized by low marginal costs was unclear, assuming that new capital investment was forthcoming at all.

The sale of public housing also marked a break with the past, both in the decision to reduce the public financing and provision of new housing as well as in the decision to sell off some of the existing stock. The early post-war decades had seen a substantial programme of public housing construction. While Aneurin Bevan, the Labour Minister of Health, Housing and Local Government (1945–1951), pursued a construction target of 200,000 new houses, 90% of which was for public housing, his incoming Conservative successor, Harold Macmillan, at Housing and Local Government (1951–1954) raised the target to 300,000. During the first post-war Conservative government, 939,000 houses were completed for the public sector in 1952–1956, more than in any quinquennium before or since.[10] Between 1945 and 1965, local authorities built 60% of all new houses and half of all the local authority houses ever built in Britain were constructed in this period.[11] Whereas promises of building homes 'fit for heroes' were held not to have been met after World War I, in the immediate aftermath of World War II, twice as many houses (just over 1 million) were built compared with under half a million (475,000) between 1919/20 to 1924/5. By the end of 1953, new building for local authorities had almost doubled the size of the housing stock compared with its size on the eve of war. New building for private owners in this period was only 0.25 million, compared with almost 1.25 million for public authorities. Of the newly built accommodation the early emphasis was on houses, mostly of brick, but some 116,000 were 'pre-fabs' made from factory-made parts with an expected life of fifteen or twenty years.[12] While between 1951 and 1981 there was a slow rise in the size (4.05 million) and growth rate (12.9%) of the adult population, both the size (4.5 million) and growth (31.6%) of

[9] Newbery, *Privatization*, p. 27; Foreman-Peck and Millward, *Public and Private Ownership*, p. 3.
[10] Holmans, *Housing Policy in Britain*, p. 113.
[11] Malpass and Cairncross, *Building on the Past*, p. 4; Merrett, *State Housing in Britain*, pp. 320–1.
[12] Holmans, *Housing Policy in Britain*, pp. 113–14.

households was rapid. More and earlier marriage and a rising divorce rate all created new households. More widows and widowers continued to live independently, and an increasing proportion of never-married men and women headed households. Rising real incomes may also have helped the rise in household formation. As the number of households rose, their average size fell. Very large households became increasingly rare and interwar concerns with overcrowding were slowly to give way to post-war remarks on under-occupation.[13]

Similarly, privatization represented an unwinding of the decisions by the Attlee governments (1945–1951) to nationalize such industries as gas, electricity, coal mining, railways, inland waterways, road haulage transport, airlines, and iron and steel. In so doing, industries accounting for almost 20% of total gross domestic fixed capital investment were taken into public ownership. With the exception of the iron and steel industry which was denationalized in 1953, the incoming Churchill government (1951–1955) left the industries in their nationalized form and they largely remained so until privatized.[14]

While a history of troubled industrial relations as well as its close union affiliations to the Labour Party motivated the nationalization of coal mining in 1946, in electricity, telecommunications, and other network industries, there were concerns that essential output was not sufficiently available, either physically or in terms of price to lower-income groups and/or those living in rural areas.[15] In electricity a major aim of nationalization was to invest in extending the network and, as in all nationalized industries, to charge prices that were sufficient to cover the industry's costs. While some might object to private providers making profits from supplying water, gas, and electricity which were considered as essentials of life, equally, there was little support for a state-created monopoly doing other than cover its total costs. An important concern of the nationalization programme and that of the public construction of housing was with quality and availability. In nationalized industries, this found expression in its service ethic, as well as investment in extending networks. In housing the ambition was to clear slums and to provide housing on new socially mixed council estates and in New Towns. In Britain in 1951, 80% of households lived in accommodation that was considered to be either unfit, substandard, overcrowded, or shared with other families.[16] Between 1955 and 1975, 1.3 million dwellings were demolished under slum clearance powers.

---

[13] Holmans, *Housing Policy*, pp. 103–4, 108.   [14] Burk, *The First Privatisation.*
[15] Legislation passed in 1946 specified a 'vesting day' of 1 January 1947.
[16] Malpass and Cairncross, *Building on the Past*, p. 3; Department of the Environment, *Housing Policy, Technical Volume I*, p. 10. In West Germany, matters were much worse with only 10 million dwellings for 16 million households. Harloe, *The People's Home?* p. 256.

Bevan was particularly keen that new public housing should not be of a low quality, although this concern with quality faded under Macmillan as he pushed to increase the total supply of new units. Of the 1.25 million houses (including pre-fabs) built in the first post-war decade, three-quarters had three bedrooms (85% in 1946–1950), although a wish to build more accommodation partly motivated a shift to two-bedroomed houses and flats in the 1950s. Flats slowly became more popular with builders and by the mid-1960s there were as many flats as houses being built. Nearly half of the flats had only one bedroom, being intended mainly for older people.[17] The quality of housing itself changed with indoor toilets, bathrooms, hot water systems, and even central heating being standard in over 90% of British households by the turn of the twenty-first century, in contrast to their common absence from immediate post-war housing.[18]

Pricing and Demand

In both public housing and the nationalized industries, it was initially decided that rents and prices should do no more than reflect and cover average costs. These costs were both the initial construction costs and the annual operating costs. One of the advantages claimed for public ownership and finance was its ability to borrow at a lower cost than the private sector. Such lower-cost finance was thought to be particularly suitable for durable, long-lived projects, whether council housing or hydro-electricity projects in the north of Scotland. In both public housing and nationalized industries, costs were commonly pooled, with prices being based on these cross-subsidizing average costs. This average cost approach was contested by economists in the run-up to the nationalization of major utilities, but their objections were overridden by the 'common-sense' approach of politicians.[19]

Financing Public Housing

In the early post-war period, local authorities borrowed from the Public Works Loans Board (PWLB), although with the ending of early post-war 'Cheap

---

[17] Holmans, *Housing Policy in Britain*, p. 115.
[18] Malpass and Cairncross, *Building on the Past*, p. 3; Department of the Environment, *Housing Policy, Technical Volume I*; Wilcox, *UK Housing Review 2003/2004*, p. 104.
[19] Chick, *Industrial Policy*, ch. 5.

Money', the key PWLB rate for long-term local authorities' housing finance rose from 3% to 4.5% in March 1952.[20] As interest rates rose, so the Treasury sought to increase rents so as to reduce its subsidies to local authorities. From 1953, the Treasury also encouraged local authorities to borrow from the capital market rather than the Public Works Loans Board (PWLB), but most local authorities preferred to continue borrowing from the Board. However, from October 1955, local authorities could only borrow from the PWLB if they could demonstrate that they were unable to raise the money on the capital market. As loans were renewed, so too were the rising interest rates applied to existing debt as well as new capital expenditure. Loan charges per dwelling on housing revenue accounts rose and more of the outstanding debt became short-term. In 1955, 5.8% of the outstanding loan debt of local authorities in Britain had under one year to maturity; five years later the proportion had risen to 17.5%; in 1964 the proportion was 27.8% and in 1968 28.5%.[21]

Opportunity Costs and Returns on Capital

As well as concerns with the financial cost of capital, there was also concern with whether so much fixed capital investment was necessary. Among the nationalized industries, the Treasury was particularly concerned with the electricity industry which at 8% of total annual fixed capital investment, formed the single largest *bloc* of fixed capital investment in the economy. Charging average prices, the industry lacked an effective means to reduce demand at peak hours of the day, and yet given the inability to store electricity, this peak demand determined the total generating investment required by the industry. There was also concern at the extent of investment being undertaken by the North of Scotland Hydro-Electric Board, which accounted for 9% of the electricity industry's total fixed capital investment but was unlikely to contribute more than 2.5% of output.[22] Both of these concerns, the size of daily peak-load demand compared with average demand, and the extent of investment in hydro-electricity compared with thermal (oil- and coal-burning) generation both involved issues of time and its implications for the use of capital investment resources. Unable to persuade the electricity industry to introduce peak-hour tariffs, the Treasury focosed on the returns on capital being earned by the electricity (and thereafter all other nationalized) industry. Learning

[20] Holmans, *Housing Policy*, p. 324.   [21] A. E. Holmans, *Housing Policy*, pp. 324, 329–30.
[22] Chick, *Electricity and Energy* Policy, p. 93.

from developments in the French nationalized electricity industry (EDF), where around half of all French electricity output came from hydro-electric works compared with barely 2% in the UK, the Treasury began to emphasize not the financial cost of fixed capital investment, but rather the opportunity costs of using capital in one way rather than another.[23] In France as in the UK, hydro-electricity had justified its initial high upfront fixed capital investment by pointing to its long payback period. The French electricity industry turned this approach to investment on its head, emphasizing the longevity of the project as a source of risk, not least through technological obsolescence. To capture this relationship between current upfront costs and projected future returns on capital investment, the French applied test discount rates to proposed projects. The difficulty of the test depended on the level of discount rate chosen and the length of time over which future earnings were promised. In EDF, the test discount rate was applied on a systems basis, the discounted value of the marginal addition to the system being considered, and not just that of the plant itself. It was also *ex ante* in that tests were applied before plant was built, if it was at all. Having itself successfully applied this to the NSHEB so as effectively to stop future investment in hydro-electricity, the Treasury also applied this approach across all of the nationalized industries. This built on the earlier 1961 White Paper which had required nationalized industries to earn something like an *ex post* opportunity cost Required Rate of Return of 8% on existing assets.[24] In the 1967 White Paper, an *ex ante* Test Discount Rate of 8% was applied to all nationalized industries allied to pricing at long-run marginal cost.[25] This opportunity cost–based, discounted marginal system–based approach to investment appraisal was a long way from the initial, cost-covering, payback approach of the early days of the nationalized industries.[26]

Housing and Returns on Capital

As with nationalized industries, so too with public housing. As concern grew with the opportunity costs of fixed capital investment in housing, so it also

[23] M. Allais, 'Étude théorique des conditions générales', 5; M. Allais, 'Étude théorique des conditions générales', p. 8; Hutter, 'La théorie économique'; Boiteux, 'Sur la gestion des monopoles publics'; Chick, *Electricity*, chs. 4 and 5.
[24] Cmnd. 1337, (1961), *The Financial and Economic Obligations*.
[25] Cmnd. 3437, (1967), *Nationalised Industries*; Colvin, *Economic Ideal*, p. 47.
[26] I have skipped through the complexity of issues affecting pricing and investment in nationalized industries, and especially in electricity, as I have written about these in obsessive detail elsewhere Chick, 'Marginal cost pricing'; Chick, *Industrial Policy in Britain*; Chick, *Electricity and Energy Policy*.

became apparent that new investment was raising the average cost of public housing and thereby raising rents in line with average costs. To rising borrowing costs was added increased construction costs. This was partially obscured between 1951 and 1958 as smaller, lower quality units of accommodation were built, and the average costs of new local authority houses fell by about 25% in real terms. However, construction costs then rose by 60% per dwelling between 1958 and 1968. In house construction, relative price effects increased wages faster than industry productivity and the cost of obtaining land also rose. Between 1938 and 1947, building costs rose in real terms by about 35%, and unlike in 1913–20, this increase was never fully reversed. Although by the early 1960s building costs had fallen in real terms by 10% compared with 1947–1948, they remained some 20% higher than before the war. In the post-war period, building land prices were also increased by the effects of the Green-Belt protection and Town and Country Planning legislation which deliberately restricted the availability of land for building. The Town and Country Planning Act 1947 gave local authorities far-reaching powers to control land developments, including refusal of permission for change of use. The 1947 and 1968 Town and Country Planning Acts reflected concern with perceived suburban sprawl.[27] One response was to build up rather than out, and high-rise building rose to a peak in 1966. Yet, such construction was already in decline, before the gas explosion in the Ronan Point tower block in Newham, London in May 1968 which killed six people.[28] In part the construction of tower blocks reflected the resistance of locals to having housing slum clearance residents settled near them. The residents of Outer London objected to proposals to re-house near them those cleared from the slums of inner London. The residents of Warwickshire and Worcestershire were no more welcoming to their brethren from Birmingham, nor were the good folk of Cheshire any more favourably disposed to the former slum residents of Manchester. General local resistance to urban sprawl allied to rising building land prices provided incentives to build up rather than out and supplementary subsidies for high-rise building were provided by the Housing Subsidies Act 1956. Old people who featured highly in slum clearance found themselves living in new flats in the air.

As the cost of building new public housing rose, so too was pressure placed on rents whose average level was lifted by the new additions to the housing

[27]   TNA T414/50, Carr, note, 'General housing subsidies', October 1975; Holmans, *Housing Policy*, pp. 141, 144–6, 329.

[28]   For full details of the Ronan Point explosion, see Ministry of Housing and Local Government, *Report of the Inquiry into the Collapse of Flats at Ronan Point*. On high-rise flats see: Cooney, 'High flats'; Peter Scott, 'Friends in high places'; Dunleavy, *The Politics of Mass Housing*.

stock. By 1976, whilst the average capital cost of an existing dwelling was £2,700, the cost of adding to the stock was some £10,000. New stock also brought with it additional maintenance charges.[29] Public housing effectively had a rising long-run marginal cost. Increasing rents to cover this rising cost was politically difficult. Until the mid-1950s, differing rents were charged on pre- and post-war dwellings, reflecting their actual cost of construction, but from the mid-1950s until the early 1970s there was an increasing tendency towards pooling the costs of all housing, pre-or post-war, and charging an average rent on that basis. On the one hand, newer houses came with higher construction costs; on the other, inflation helped to reduce the real value of the loan charges on older houses. To an extent this was also true of national-ized industries, although by the 1970s the public finances imposed a tighten-ing constraint on the amount of modernizing investment which could be undertaken. Politicians in the 1970s lost their appetite for constructing new housing, as it both raised average rents and enlarged a stock of public housing which was not fully used. In nationalized industries, as public finance con-straints chafed in industries like telecommunications which needed to invest in new technology, such technological challenges also opened a wider discus-sion not just of the virtues or otherwise of public ownership, but also of the merits of these industries continuing in monopoly form.

In housing, as in its approach to industrial, health, and education policy, increasingly the Treasury discussed the programme in terms of its expected rate of return on capital. Indeed, by April 1979 some in the Treasury were speculating that the election of a Conservative government might bring them nearer to introducing a 'deemed rate of return' approach to housing invest-ment to replace the housing cost yardstick.[30] In thinking in terms of rates of return, attention was paid not simply to flows of additions to the existing stock but also to the use of that stock itself. One question raised was how the form of ownership/tenure affected the use of the stock.

One approach to improving returns on capital on public housing was to raise rents. Yet doing so potentially affected the very low-income groups for whom public housing had been built to help. Subsidies might be used to help such groups and following the lead of Conservative local authorities, and especially the Greater London Council, the Heath government (1970–1974) attempted to increase rents while focusing assistance on those most in need.[31]

---

[29] TNA T379/23, Carr, paper, 'Calculation of unsubsidised rents', May 1976, para. 2; TNA T379/23, Allen, paper, 'Unsubsidised rents', June 1976; Grey, Hepworth, and Odling-Smee *Housing Rents*.
[30] TNA T414/50, Bell, note, 'Deemed rate of return on housing investment', April 1979, paras. 1–2.
[31] Harris and Sewill, *British Economic Policy*, p. 30.

'Fair rents' were to be charged, although given that rent controls were prevalent in a small private rented sector, knowing what constituted a 'fair rent' was problematic. When the Heath government in the Housing Finance Act 1972 aligned 'fair rents' with those registered under the Rent Act 1965 for unfurnished private rented accommodation, the rents were around twice as high as the general run of local authority rents. Local authorities protested at the removal of the ability to set their own rents which they had enjoyed since 1923. As with the 1971 Industrial Relations Act, there was active resistance to the legislation and for refusing to implement the Act, Clay Cross UDC had its housing affairs transferred to a commissioner appointed by the government. The opposition to the Industrial Relations Act and the resistance of the councillors at Clay Cross were later cited by Margaret Thatcher in 1976 as examples of how the rule of law was 'at hazard in Britain'.[32] The rent increases consequent on the 1972 Housing Finance Act also sat uneasily alongside the 1972 and 1973 statutory incomes and prices policy. Interest rates rose sharply in 1973 and the boom in land prices and construction costs further increased the loan charges falling on housing revenue accounts. In terms of constant (1970/1) prices, total costs per dwelling rose by just about £49 (27%) between 1970/71 and 1974/5. There was also a perplexing rise in expenditure on the repair and supervision of the public housing stock from 1970. Total management and maintenance costs increased from 35% of unrebated rent revenue to 69% between 1970–1971 and 1978. Increases at this pace in expenditure on upkeep and management were novel.[33]

Given the costs of marginal additions to the existing stock and the political sensitivity of increasing rents, one potential response was simply to stop building public housing. The Treasury calculated that if from 1976 new building was halted for ten years and rents increased by an average of £1.5% to 2.5% p.a. in real terms, then subsidies could be phased out in ten years. If rents were to rise at no more than 3% in real terms (i.e. keep pace with expected earnings), it was thought possible to cover costs by 1986 if the house-building programme was reduced to between 5,000 and 40,000 dwellings per year.[34] In such a context, reducing the amount of new house building was of greater financial benefit than selling council houses.

As with the nationalized industries, not only was the financial cost of public housing emphasized, but so too was the opportunity cost of additional

[32] Saunders, '"Crisis? What crisis?' in Jackson and Saunders, *Making Thatcher's Britain*, p. 35; Mitchell, 'Clay Cross'.
[33] Foreman-Peck, 'The appraisal of sales', p. 80; Holmans, *Housing Policy*, pp. 327, 348–9, 354–5.
[34] TNA T379/23, Allen, paper, 'Unsubsidised rents', June 1976.

investment. Such an approach was not new to housing finance in the 1970s. Were there better uses which could be made of the money? In contrast to the greenfield building of post-war council estates, might the renovating of existing stock offer a better rate of return? The application of a marginal rate of return approach to the replacement of old stock with new in such areas as Halliwell in Bolton highlighted the benefits of renovating rather than replacing nineteenth-century housing stock. Such an approach helped to slow the rate of slum clearance and relieved some pressure from local authority waiting lists. Work by Needleman and other economists using 8% discount rates to appraise proposed projects also favoured the renovation of an existing house to extend its life by thirty years, instead of its demolition and replacement with a new house with an expected life of sixty years. Partly as a result of such findings, the maximum amount of discretionary improvement grants was raised from one-half of the £800 approved cost to one-half of £2000.[35]

Tenure: Owning, Renting, Taxing, and Selling

In 1945 Britain was still largely a nation of renters, with most households renting from private landlords, a tenth renting from local authorities, and fewer than a third owner-occupiers. By 2005, 70% were owner-occupiers, 10% were private tenants and the rest were in the social rented sector.[36] Owning a home was not always a British national preoccupation. In 1960, 21% of owner-occupiers with mortgages said that they would have preferred to rent rather than buy, being effectively forced to do so by the rapid transfer of accommodation out of the private rented sector. Indeed, it was this transfer of houses from the private-rented sector, not new building for private owners, which made owner-occupation the largest of the tenures by the end of the 1950s. In just under two decades after 1961, the number of owner-occupiers in England and Wales rose by some 4.25 million; tenancies of local authorities and housing associations (the 'social sector') by about 2.2 million; whereas the number of tenants renting from private landlords fell by about 2.8 million. In the 1970s, survey questions on tenure preferences gave very different results from those in 1960. It was not that the characteristics of owner-occupiers had materially changed, but rather that more households came to share those characteristics

---

[35] TNA HLG 118/3595, Brindley, 'A note on the impact of council house sales', September 1980, p. 9; Needleman, *The Economics of Housing*; Cmd. 3602, *Old Houses into New Homes*, paras. 9 and 23; Holmans, *Housing Policy in Britain*, p. 130.

[36] Malpass and Cairncross, *Building on the Past*, pp. 3–4; Forrest, Murie, and Williams, *Home Ownership*; Saunders, *A Nation of Home Owners*.

of reasonably stable and sufficient incomes. The growth of owner-occupation was heavily concentrated in the younger age groups. The Building Society Mortgage Survey consistently showed the proportion of first-time purchasers with building society mortgages who were aged forty-five and upwards to be under 10%. The proportion was 9.0% in 1970, 7.5% in 1973, and 7.8% in 1977. It also became easier to find mortgages as banks began to disrupt the traditional rationed supply of mortgages by building societies, and to a lesser extent local authorities and insurance companies. The Bank of England's 'consultative document' *Competition and Credit Control* published on 14 May 1971 and, then in the 1980s, continuing supportive statements from the Building Societies Association's Committee for Mortgage Finance, all marked a shift away from an administrative allocation of bank loans to one in which the rate of interest became a more important allocative mechanism.[37]

The Tax Advantages of Owner-Occupation

There were also increased tax advantages to owner-occupation. Until 1963 owner-occupiers were taxed under Schedule A on their imputed rental income. Put simply, had two-owner-occupiers swapped houses and rented to one another, then each would have been liable for taxation on their rental income. When they move back to their own house, they must effectively be receiving a rental income which, for tax purposes, was imputed to them.[38] The ending of this Schedule A taxation of imputed income from owner-occupation in 1963 in part reflected the shift of political interest away from the renting of public and private accommodation and towards the promotion of owner-occupation. In repealing Schedule A in 1963, the Conservative government, notwithstanding the contrary opinion of the Radcliffe Royal Commission, asserted that the notional or imputed income from owner-occupation was not a proper subject for taxation. In this, the Conservative government was supported by the Labour and Liberal Parties, with a consequential narrowing of the tax base and the loss of an annual Schedule A extraction of £50 million from owner-occupiers, so some 1.8% of an annual total tax yield of £2.8 billion. The tax relied on 1935/6 property valuations, and when these were revalued in

[37] Goodhart, 'Competition and credit control', p. 1. Appendix A to this paper is John Fforde's Christmas Eve 1970 impassioned plea from inside the Bank of England to end the ceiling controls on bank and finance house lending which had existed since the end of World War II. Holmans, *Housing Policy*, pp. 188–90, 209, 215, 236.

[38] TNA T414/50, Carr, note, 'General Housing Subsidies', October 1975.

1963, their use for raising tax was thought likely to prove highly unpopular. Obtaining evidence of rental valuations was problematic anyway, not least because of the operation of rent controls and its effect in reducing the supply of privately rented accommodation.[39]

The tax advantages of owner-occupiers were extended further in 1965, when the Labour government exempted owner-occupied houses from its new Capital Gains Tax. That Labour government also provided the option mortgage subsidy to complement tax relief in 1967, and retained tax relief on mortgage interest when most other reliefs on interest were withdrawn from individual taxpayers in 1969.[40] Although in 1974, tax relief on mortgages on second dwellings was ended and a limit of £25,000 imposed, the cost of tax relief grew in the 1970s. The distribution of tax relief between income groups drew criticism as attracting increasing amounts of capital simply to churn the existing stock of second-hand housing rather than adding to it.[41] Given that tax relief was withdrawn on personal loans and no longer given on interest payments generally, the tax relief on mortgage interest did look anomalous if the property was not treated as an asset but as a form of consumption. If it was an asset, then its income and capital gain were taxable but its costs (including that of the annual cost of borrowing) were deductible.[42]

Allowing owner-occupiers to escape imputed income taxation and capital gains tax while claiming mortgage interest tax relief, and at the same time subsiding local authority tenants through housing subsidies and rent rebates, while offering no equivalent financial treatment to private landlords, made efforts to obtain a more efficient allocation of housing resources extremely difficult.[43] In the Treasury in 1977, Ian Byatt (Head of the Public Sector Economic Unit) was very keen to reintroduce Schedule A, but Peter Shore, the Secretary of State for the Environment (1976–1979), was opposed to the taxation of imputed income.[44] Shore was keen to use the removal of higher rate tax relief on mortgage payments as a quid pro quo for reducing subsidies and consequently raising council house rents. Although the tax relief offered to owner-occupiers cost less than subsidies to local authority tenants, for some in the Treasury like Douglas Wass (Permanent Secretary to HM Treasury) it

[39] TNA T379/23, Houghton, draft note, 'Tax on the imputed income', May 1976, para. 14; TNA T414/50, Carr, note, 'General Housing Subsidies', October 1975; TNA T414/50, Carr, note, 'Review of Housing Finance', October 1975, para. 3.
[40] TNA T230/765, Kaldor, note, 'Comparison of the cost', November 1966; Holmans, *Housing Policy in Britain*, p. 155.
[41] Clark, 'Too much housing'; Grey, Hepworth and Odling Smee, *Housing Rents, Costs and Subsidies*.
[42] TNA T379/23, Houghton, draft note, 'Tax on the imputed income', May 1976, para. 11.
[43] TNA T414/50, Trench, paper, 'General Housing subsidies', October 1975, paras. 1–2.
[44] TNA T364/102, Downey, note, 'Housing Policy Review', April 1977, p. 4.

was thought that the scrapping of higher rate mortgage tax relief would remove an important incentive to managers who had no inherited capital. As he put it:

> It deals a pretty severe blow at the man who is on higher rate *and who has no capital*. It hits in fact the manager to whom the Chancellor has been trying to bring some relief. Higher-rate relief gives, in an unobtrusive way, some respite from our excessive marginal rate of tax on middle and higher income earners. It would seem to me to be foolish to take this away, at any rate until we can do something substantial on the rates themselves.[45]

Wass was not a lone voice. Others were concerned that even if mortgage interest tax relief was withdrawn gradually over a six-year period starting from April 1978, it would still introduce uncertainty into the lives of precisely that section of the young professional middle class who were viewed as important to economic recovery and that it would 'remove one of the incentives now open to a young executive to accept promotion and move from one locality to another'.[46] Higher rate relief mortgagors totalled nearly 1 million taxpayers with about 150,000 mortgagors above the 50% rate. In terms of yield, it was negligible. At current income the 50% restriction would yield £20 million, but not for six years.[47] The sensitivity over its restriction reflected the increasing concern with the marginal incentives being offered to what were hoped were the more entrepreneurial sections of the economy. Following the election of the first Thatcher government, on 13 July 1980 at a Sunday dinner at Chequers with other academic economists, Professor Robin Matthews raised the question of the reintroduction of Schedule A taxation or at least the removal of tax relief on mortgages, but was informed by the prime minister 'that neither of these were a starter'.[48]

Selling Housing Stock

As well as pressing for the scrapping of higher-rate mortgage tax relief, Peter Shore was also interested in increasing the rate of sale of council housing to its tenants. Powers to sell council housing had existed since the interwar years and powers to sell housing on special terms, as distinct from being subject to

---

[45] TNA T364/102, Wass, note, 'Housing Policy Review', April 1977, para. 5ii.
[46] TNA T364/102, Wass, note, 'Housing Policy Review', April 1977, para. 4.
[47] TNA T364/102, Lovell, paper, 'Housing Policy Review', April 1977, paras. 7, 10–11.
[48] TNA PREM 19/197, meeting with academic economists, July 1980, p. 5.

the ordinary duty on public authorities to get the best price for property sold, dated from 1952. Formally, the power to dispose of council housing lay in Section 104 of the Housing Act 1957, subject in the great majority of cases, to Ministerial consent.[49] In 1970 the Conservative government issued a general consent in a Departmental circular allowing local authorities to sell council housing, either at current market value with vacant possession or at a price reduced by up to 20% where certain restrictions of resale were imposed. Specific consents were also issued allowing particular authorities to offer reductions of up to 30% on current market value. In the Labour government's Circular No. 70 of 1974 issued to local authorities, the view taken was that the sale of council houses was neither good nor bad in itself, and that the main considerations were housing need and supply which must be assessed locally.[50] Within the Parliamentary Labour Party there was less widespread opposition than in the past to the principle of selling council houses, although the Labour Party manifesto committed the party to opposing the sale of council housing in areas of serious housing need.[51] The practice of discounting the sale price to sitting tenants was introduced by the Labour government in 1967, the aim being to place local authority tenants who lacked formal security of tenure on the same footing as sitting tenants when purchasing their houses from a landlord, and thereby obtain a lower, sitting-tenant, price.

At a meeting in Chequers in the summer of 1975 there was virtually unanimous acceptance of the selling of council houses. There was a widespread feeling that many council tenants wanted to buy their homes and that this ambition ought to be recognized. Following this meeting, the No. 10 Policy Unit put forward a number of specific schemes making provision for what amounted to long-term occupation of council houses but which allowed local authorities to retain control of the long-term future of the house concerned.[52] In 1975, the Chancellor of the Exchequer Denis Healey wrote to the Prime Minister, Harold Wilson, to give his immediate reactions to the paper by the 'Policy Unit setting out alternative schemes for encouraging the sale of council houses', and he remarked that he was 'interested in any scheme which promises to reduce public expenditure'.[53] In August 1976 Peter Shore wrote to Denis Healey arguing that the Labour government should give 'strong encouragement for home ownership. The gains from this would be enormous—not only

[49]   TNA T354/54, 'Draft Cabinet paper: Sale of Council Houses', June 1976, para. 2.
[50]   TNA T354/54, 'Draft Cabinet paper: Sale of Council Houses', June 1976, paras. 2–3.
[51]   TNA HLG 118/3497, Memorandum calling for Secretary of State, August 1979, para. 2.
[52]   TNA T354/54, 'Draft Cabinet paper: Sale of Council Houses', June 1976, paras. 4, 13.
[53]   TNA T386/77, Healey, draft letter, 1975.

is it what most people want but they are prepared to pay more for it out of their own pockets.'[54]

Quite what the net benefits to public expenditure would be from the sale of local authority accommodation were uncertain. In 1975 Denis Healey thought it 'essential for the achievement of early public expenditure savings that the sales should be financed from the private sector', which in practice meant 'the building societies since it is most unlikely that the banks would be able to provide funds for the purposes envisaged and there would in any case be no monetary benefit in their doing so'.[55] Hitherto the practice had been that when local authorities sold accommodation they almost always provided the finance for the purchaser, thereby giving them a different but continuing interest in the stock. In some local authorities, such as Birmingham and the GLC, local authorities had engaged in half-and-half purchase arrangements so as to assist those who could not otherwise have bought for the first time.[56]

In the mid-1970s, important ventures into increased sales of local authority stock were made in Leeds and Nottingham. In May 1976 the Conservative Party won control of Nottingham City Council from Labour and from June 1976 until March 1979 combined council house sales with a substantial reduction in local authority building and acquisitions. By 1978/9, capital expenditure had fallen to £20 million and council housing starts were down from 2,103 in 1975/6 to 272. Whereas under the previous Labour administration, 134 council houses were sold in 1975/6, the Conservative City Council had sold nearly 5,500 dwellings by March 1979. Sales were initially confined to sitting tenants and to properties acquired from private builders under Circular 70/74. However, early in 1977 the scope of the policy was extended to include the sale of re-lets and new completions. While priority was given to housing the homeless and those displaced from clearance areas, thereafter in Nottingham, sales took priority over almost all other demands. Most flats and all elderly persons' dwellings were excluded. When re-lets and new properties became available they were offered for sale for a period of three weeks; if a prospective purchaser was not found within that period they were returned to the stock for letting. With the exception of a few dwellings, only council tenants, nominees to housing associations, clearance area residents, and waiting list applicants were eligible to buy a council house. However, the waiting list was open, so it was possible to qualify simply by joining the list. Over the whole period 1976–1979, existing council tenants made up nearly two-thirds

[54] TNA T354/54, Shore, letter, August 1976.
[55] TNA T386/77, Healey, draft letter, 1975.
[56] TNA T354/54, 'Draft Cabinet paper: Sale of Council Houses', June 1976, para. 12.

of all purchasers, waiting list applicants almost one-third, and clearance area residents most of the remainder. Only 2% of buyers were not in these categories.[57] Of the sales made between 1976 and 1979, vacant properties, particularly re-lets, sold much better than tenanted properties. The average re-let was of the order of 3%, other sources of re-lets being the death or infirmity of existing tenants. Since those who were most likely to buy their houses tend to be middle-aged or younger tenants who wished to remain in their existing house, the sale of the property to them did not affect the rate of re-let significantly in the short- to medium-term. Generally, it was houses that tenants wanted to buy, not flats, and on the whole local authorities preferred to sell houses. In city areas, where flats were more common, proportionately fewer dwellings were sold.[58] New builds were less popular than older stock, both because of their higher price and because they were often on peripheral estates.[59] In Whitehall, it was not thought that the sale of houses would unduly affect the availability of accommodation. In 1976, while it was accepted that selling stock necessarily reduced in the short-term the possible rate of re-let, even in 1972 which was to date the peak year for selling as council house rents rose, the Department of the Environment noted that the 45,000 houses sold in England represented only about 1% of the housing stock of English local authorities.[60]

Time and the Social Cost–Benefits of Selling Public Housing

The social cost–benefits of selling council houses became a matter of fierce dispute during and after the 1979 general election campaign. The data from Leeds and Nottingham was at the centre of the arguments. In his 12 June 1979 Budget speech, the Chancellor of the Exchequer, Geoffrey Howe, claimed that £20 million of public expenditure would be saved by council house sales with a variation of between –£4,480 and +£9,220 per house sold depending on the assumptions adopted. In contrast, a study of sales in Nottingham, *Where Have All the Assets Gone?*, claimed a loss of £14,000 on each sale and the housing charity, Shelter, estimated a loss of £3,000 per sale.[61] On 21 August

---

[57] TNA HLG 118/3595, Brindley, 'A note on the impact of council house sales', September 1980, pp. 1–3, 5, 7.

[58] TNA T354/54, 'Draft Cabinet paper: Sale of Council Houses', June 1976, para. 7.

[59] TNA HLG 118/3595, Brindley, 'A note on the impact of council house sales', September 1980, p. 4.

[60] TNA T354/54, 'Draft Cabinet paper: Sale of Council Houses', June 1976, para. 6.

[61] Foreman-Peck, 'The appraisal of sales'; Cant, *Where Have All The Assets Gone?*; Schifferes, *Facts on Council House Sales*.

1979 Jack Straw (newly elected successor to Barbara Castle as Labour MP for Blackburn) wrote to Michael Heseltine (Conservative Secretary of State for the Environment) requesting clarity amidst the 'wildly differing claims about the financial consequences of sales' of council houses and calling on him immediately to establish an independent technical inquiry into the financial consequences of the sale of council houses.[62] Straw reminded Heseltine that during the general election campaign on 19 April 1979, he, Heseltine, had claimed that 'Selling council houses saves public money', adducing as evidence that 'since 1976 Nottingham's Conservative Council have sold £40 millions worth of council houses and made a profit of £18 million over the cost of building them. Leeds is saving £300 on average per cost of house sold'. Continuing, Heseltine had claimed that selling council houses would produce 'a substantial surplus to the community' with, on certain assumptions, each sale on average making 'a surplus of £290 a year for the community'.[63] Again, such claims were disputed. In contrast to Heseltine's claim that 'selling council houses saves public money', Shelter, the Labour Party, and *The Economist* all argued that in time the taxpayer and ratepayer would lose substantially from the sales programme.[64] Not only would future rental income be foregone, but mortgage interest relief was also a cost which *The Economist* in a leader dated 19 May 1979 reckoned in the previous year 'amounted to a subsidy per home-owner almost as great as the subsidy to council tenants'. Such calculations were time dependent. Using Heseltine's figures but including mortgage interest relief to which *The Economist* had drawn attention, Shelter concluded that in the first year the gain to the public sector from the 'average' sale was £141 rather than Heseltine's £290, but that over forty years the sale of this 'average' house resulted in a loss of £2,957 to the community.[65]

In Leeds, Bernard Kilroy, a housing expert from the Housing Centre Trust, estimated that rather than the net gains claimed by Leeds City Council for sales of a typical pre-war, post-war, and modern house capitalized at constant values of £2,028, £2,927, and £1,225 respectively, a reworking of the figures showed a net loss of £217, £3,285, and £9,405 respectively. In addition, Kilroy thought that there would be a net extra cost to the Exchequer, arising from the excess of mortgage interest relief over housing subsidy saved, of £104,

[62] TNA HLG 118/3497, Straw, letter, August 1979.
[63] TNA HLG 118/3497, 'Memorandum calling for Secretary of State', August 1979, para. 4.
[64] TNA HLG 118/3497, Straw, letter, August 1979.
[65] TNA HLG 118/3497, 'Memorandum calling for Secretary of State', August 1979, paras. 5–6; TNA HLG 118/3497, Straw, letter, Jack Straw, August 1979; Cmnd. 6851, *Housing Policy: A Consultative Document*, p. 107; *Housing: The Chartered Surveyors Report*, p. 27; Gleave and Palmer, 'Mobility of labour?'; Shelter, *Facts on Council House Sales*.

£132, and £32 respectively in the first year.[66] Where the local authority might gain, as in Leeds where about 90% of purchasers obtained their mortgage from the council, was that because mortgage repayments exceeded rents and the council was also no longer liable for the maintenance of the property, the council benefited from exchanging its role as landlord for that of money lender.[67] This did not however address Healey's concern that mortgages be financed by private building societies. Again, the time perspective affected the evaluation of this altered role. Would the receipts from the sale be higher than the income and costs of keeping the property over, say, the next ten years? While the receipts from selling (the interest received on the mortgage that financed the sale, and/or the interest saved as a consequence of capital receipts) were fixed in money terms, irrespective of what happened subsequently to the general price level, the rent and labour-intensive management and maintenance costs would rise in money terms.[68] Assumptions about future inflation rates and rent increases were uncertain but crucial to estimating the future social costs and benefits of the sale of local authority housing.[69] After six to seven years, councils could be getting a lower income from the sale than if they had continued to rent out the accommodation.[70]

A further concern raised by Straw was that some accommodation was being sold for a price below its original construction cost. This seemed to offend a long established principle that sales of dwellings at a discount should not take place below cost. Straw's instances of sales at below historic cost included a loss of £12,800 per dwelling in Thamesmead (Bexley) and a loss of £14,000 per dwelling in Campbell Road (Tower Hamlets) with debt still being owed on the property.[71] Yet concern with the recovery of construction costs was essentially a backwards-looking attempt to recover sunk costs. It was not the past costs but the future income (net of savings on maintenance and management) foregone which was the more salient issue. As with nationalized industries, the welfare economics maxim of letting byegones be byegones applied to any evaluation of the opportunity cost of selling council accommodation. This was true even if it was necessary to build a new house to replace the one sold, since the cost of the new building would be what it would be,

[66] TNA HLG 118/3497, 'Memorandum calling for Secretary of State', August 1979, para. 7.
[67] TNA HLG 118/3497, cutting from *The Economist*, August 1979, pp. 17–18.
[68] TNA HLG 118/3497, Holmans, note, 'Dr. Foreman Peck', paras. 3 and 4.
[69] TNA HLG 118/3497, 'Memorandum calling for Secretary of State', August 1979, para. 9.
[70] TNA HLG 118/3497, Cutting from *The Economist*, 25 August 1979, pp. 17–18.
[71] TNA HLG 118/3497, 'Memorandum calling for Secretary of State', August 1979, paras. 23–4.
The new general consent (DoE, 18 May 1979) reflected this by stating that where a discount was offered, the price on sale should in no case be less than the cost incurred by the authority in providing the house. GLC Council Minutes, 26.6.79, Question to Mr G. Tremlett.

irrespective of the cost of constructing the original building. The relevant calculation remained the extent to which the disposal price exceeded the present value of the rents foregone minus the savings in costs of upkeep and maintenance plus the present value of tax relief or option mortgage subsidy.[72] In developing and refining such a perspective, the Treasury, and notably Alan Holmans, received advice from James Foreman-Peck, a lecturer in economics at Newcastle University. From such a perspective, and paradoxically perhaps, because the level and annual rate of increases of rent were higher in Conservative-controlled than in Labour-controlled authorities, the opportunity costs of encouraging the sale of stock were greater in Conservative authorities encouraging sales than in the Labour authorities prohibiting sales. For example, within Greater London, the average weekly rent for a modern three-bedroomed house in 1978 varied from £13.22 in Hammersmith (Conservative and Liberal) to £6.69 in Tower Hamlets (Labour). The rate of rent increase between 1977 and 1978 was 12.8% in Hammersmith and 8.3% in Tower Hamlets. If Tower Hamlets had sold local authority accommodation, its opportunity cost would have been lower than that of Hammersmith.[73]

What the sale of local authority housing did constitute was a redistribution of wealth. Once a property was sold at below market price (because it was without vacant possession), by definition the opportunity was lost of selling it in the future when it would have become vacant. At that point a market price, and potential capital gain, could be realized. At the time of the sale to the sitting tenant, that future potential gain passed into private hands. One approach might have been to have included in the original sale price provision for replacement with suitable adjustment for depreciation. As James Foreman-Peck pointed out in 1982: 'To do otherwise is to dispose of public assets in a fashion arguably not in the best interests of the tax-payer who originally financed them; or alternatively to redistribute wealth from the State to the council house-buyer.'[74] On the basis of the losses in terms of opportunity cost, the policy might then be regarded as a redistributive one with wealth being redistributed from the state to the council house buyer in a form which had a particular value and was politically difficult to revoke.[75]

With the introduction of the Right to Buy (RTB), local authority control over what housing stock was sold was reduced. No longer was it the mid-1970s

---

[72] TNA HLG 118/3497, Holmans, note, 'Dr. Foreman Peck', August 1979, paras. 6–8.
[73] Foreman-Peck, 'The appraisal of sales', p. 80.
[74] Foreman-Peck, 'The appraisal of sales', p. 80.
[75] Foreman-Peck, 'The appraisal of sales', p. 79.

Table 6.1. Dwellings by tenure in Great Britain (%)

	Owner-occupied	Private rented	Housing associations	Total Public	(Thousands)
1980	56	11	2	31	20,937
1988	64	9	3	24	22,516
1995	67	10	4	19	23,832

Sources: Department of Environment, *Housing and Construction Statistics*, (various issues); Whitehead, 'The provision of finance', p. 658.

concern to sell surplus stock; now tenants had a right to buy. Discounts ranged from a minimum of 32% after two years' tenancy of a house to a maximum of 60% after thirty years. Flat dwellers qualified for a 44% discount after two years and the full 70% after fifteen years. Public sector tenants also had a statutory right to loan finance from the local authority.[76] Under RTB, a higher percentage of houses than flats were sold and three-bedroomed, semi-detached houses were heavily over-represented. This changed the nature of the remaining public stock. In England the proportion of public sector tenants living in flats increased by 5% between 1981 and 1993, and the increase was much greater among urban authorities that had large numbers of flats. As a consequence, households seeking council housing were much more likely than previously to be offered a flat. The contrast between dwelling types in owner-occupation and in local authority rented housing became more pronounced.[77] By the end of 1991, 14% of properties bought under RTB in England were estimated to have been sold. Of these 151,000 properties, 139,000 were in owner-occupation and 12,000 were in the private rental market.[78] The broad changes in housing tenure between 1980 and 1995 are shown in Table 6.1.

Nationalized Industries

Not only did the privatization of public housing and nationalized industries involve a transfer of a stock of assets from public to private ownership but it also proceeded from, and gave rise to, similar economic issues. Essentially, the problem which emerged in public housing was that the cost of new

---

[76] Forrest, Gordon and Murie, 'The position of former council homes', p. 125.
[77] Murie, 'Moving with the times', p. 23.
[78] Forrest, Gordon, and Murie, 'The position of former council homes', pp. 125–6.

investment became higher than the existing average cost of public housing, this average cost being the basis for public housing rents. Pricing also emerged as a central issue in the nationalized industries, especially in those industries with a high sunk:marginal cost ratio in which pricing at low marginal cost would not always cover the capital and average costs of the industry. In that sense, the political instruction that prices should cover average rather than marginal costs made some sense. However, it meant that the relative price structure between increasing-returns and decreasing-returns industries (electricity and coal mining respectively) became obscured, as prices failed to fully reflect the relative change in marginal costs. The slow adoption of marginal cost pricing also meant that time-of-day efforts sufficient to meet peak demand imposed additional requirements on these industries but without sufficient effort being made to price away some of this peak demand by raising prices to reflect long-run costs (the need to build additional capacity). The absence of road pricing is a recent instance of a similar neglect of peak-hour pricing mechanisms. Steadily the Treasury circumvented the 'arm's-length' public corporation model framing nationalized industry–government relations, which effectively prevented government directing these industries to change their pricing structure, by emphasizing the inefficient use of capital which mispricing encouraged.

The political motivations for eventually privatizing the nationalized industries were complex. Some of the most effective technical critiques of the financial practices and performance of nationalized industries were written in the late 1970s by Nicholas Ridley for the Nationalised Industries Policy Group, an internal committee of the Conservative Party.[79] Ridley's analysis displayed a firm technical grasp of the economic aspects of the pricing and total factor productivity issues affecting the nationalized industries. Both Ridley and Keith Joseph also had a strong interest in widening share ownership, not least by giving and selling shares (on preferential terms) to the employees of the industry.[80] Milton Friedman also suggested that rather than sell shares in privatized industries, that instead they should be distributed freely to all citizens. Similar ideas were advanced by Samuel Brittan in the *Financial Times* (26 July 1979), one such being that all adult citizens be given a share in the form of North Sea stock in the revenue from North Sea oil which they could sell (or buy). Such shares would pay dividends and be tradeable on the stock market. Similarly, Brittan suggested that the same principle be extended to all

[79] TNA T370/1434, Ridley, paper, 'Nationalised Industries Policy Group', May 1978.
[80] TNA T370/1434, meeting, 'Nationalised Industries', May 1978, para. 1.

nationalized industries and major private companies, although this would not help the PSBR. Similarly, Brittan thought that a similar use be made of the capital receipts from the sale of mobile telephone licences rather than, as happened, using them towards repaying the national debt.[81] As with the arguments over the taxation of the owner-occupation of housing, there was a keen interest in improving access to the capital stock, both in itself and as a means of encouraging capital accumulation as an important economic incentive in addition to that of earning income. In the 2002 Budget, Gordon Brown established the Child Trust Fund which provided each newborn infant with a small capital sum (£500 for the poorest third of families, falling to £250 for the rest) which would be invested in the financial markets and free to draw down from the age of eighteen.[82] Brittan's concern with the Brown scheme was that it was financed entirely from revenue, whereas if such ideas were to contribute to a wider distribution of wealth, some other source of funds, preferably of a capital nature, needed to be found.[83]

As well as criticizing the productivity performance of the nationalized industries and harbouring hopes for a spreading of capital ownership, the financial performance of these industries was also a popular political target. The early legislative break-even constraint placed on the industries tended to be overlooked in such attacks, as did their later subjection to price controls and the requirement that they continue particular loss-making operations, such as rural rail lines, because of their wider social benefits. As with housing, the interest in selling public assets was strongly influenced by the short-term benefits to the public finances. As to the benefits which a change of ownership from public to private would make, there was little evidence on the comparative performance of public and private ownership. In search of some, the Treasury contacted Robert Millward, Professor of Economics at the University of Salford, who had published in this area.[84] The evidence suggested that there was little difference in efficiency between state-owned network utilities and vertically integrated private network utilities subject to cost-of-service regulation. Subsequent evidence on the post-privatization productivity performance of privatized industries such as BT seemed to confirm that private ownership had had little impact.[85]

[81] Brittan, *Against the Flow*, p. 103.   [82] Brittan, *Against the Flow*, pp. 100–1.
[83] Brittan, *Against the Flow*, p. 102.
[84] TNA T502/3, Castree, letter, October 1983; Millward, 'Comparative performance'; Millward, 'Comparative performance' in Roll *The Mixed Economy*.
[85] Lynk, 'Privatisation'; Foreman-Peck, 'Ownership, competition and productivity growth'; Molyneux and Thompson, 'Nationalised industry performance'.

Competition

Where greater scope seemed to exist for improving the performance of these industries was in separating out their monopoly structure into its natural monopoly (usually the grid) and contestable sections. Evidence of the benefits from the deregulation and liberalization of other industries was cited in support of the introduction of competition in nationalized industries.[86] In the US, President Jimmy Carter and the economist Alfred Kahn of Cornell University had done much, as in the 1978 Airline Deregulation Act, to encourage competition in the airline industry, an industry in which, as Kahn remarked, planes were essentially marginal costs with wings. In the UK, disruption to the price cartels, whether the setting of international air fares by the International Air Transport Association (IATA) from 1945 or the domestic duopoly of the British Overseas Airways Corporation (BOAC) and British European Airways (BEA) on scheduled services, came gradually. In 1965 the government approved forty-six new licences for independent airlines and abolished the duopoly of BOAC and BEA on scheduled services. In the 1970s new schedule services, such as Laker's Sky Train (low fares, no frills) were introduced, triggering transatlantic price wars. The introduction of the Advanced Booking Charter in 1971 for groups and of Advanced Purchase Excursion Fares (APEX) fares for individuals from 1975 allowed a fuller utilization of scheduled services.

Competition could be introduced into network industries either by vertical separation in which the network could be separately regulated or by liberalizing across the network which required more complex regulation to prevent the network owner from exploiting the incumbency advantage. Not all network utilities lent themselves to liberalization and competition. The cost of moving water any significant distance through pipes was so high compared to its value that there was unlikely to be much competition in water supply. Competition between different train-operating companies using the same rail track was theoretically possible, but constrained by timetabling problems.[87] Here, competition might be for the field, rather than in the field. The early intention was to introduce competition into the privatized network utilities and this was encouraged initially by the advice that the financial markets could not digest the privatization of a network utility as a single entity. The first of the network utilities scheduled for privatization was telecommunications and the advice from Warburgs was that financial indigestion meant that

[86] Millward, *Private and Public Enterprise in Europe*, p. 240–1.
[87] Newbery, *Privatization*, pp. 3–4.

there was no possibility of floating off BT as a whole. On that basis plans were made to break the industry into ten or twelve regional bodies.[88] However, a subsequent report by Hambros suggested that just such a single entity sale would be possible.[89] The proposition was to establish a company with a market capitalization of about £3 billion. Of this £1.5 billion would be in the form of equity which would be created by converting its existing debt to the National Loans Fund into equity. The Government would then sell off 51% of this equity, thus surrendering control. This was held to be necessary so as to qualify the sale to contribute to reducing the PSBR, as was its sale for cash, the PSBR being a cash concept.[90] It was this importance attached to the PSBR which annoyed some like Keith Joseph who argued that some of the spirit of his and Ridley's work in the 1970s to encourage the distribution of capital assets to all citizens was being sacrificed to the concern with the PSBR. In government, Joseph reportedly expressed frustration that such ideas of his and Ridley, as well as the thrust of their thinking on nationalized industries, was being 'subverted' by the Treasury.[91] That assets could be sold to improve a cash indicator also suggested that the public sector balance sheet was not telling a full story. A public sector balance sheet which recorded the assets of the public sector as well as its liabilities might tell a very different story if public debt was reduced by privatization.[92]

The Hambros's scheme opened up the possibly of privatizing telecommunications more quickly than the minimum of five years envisioned for the regionalization of BT. It was recognized that opting for the quicker route would make regionalization 'more difficult to achieve in the long run' but the view taken was that 'the prize to be gained of early privatization seemed so great as to make it worth running this risk.'[93] Blunter perhaps was the opinion of the Treasury civil servant T. U. Burgner who thought that now 'the privatisation would be of an ideological rather than of a practical kind' and that because of the 'continuation of monopoly the industry would not be put into the market in any real sense, and because of the absence of competition privatisation would do little or nothing to promote efficiency.'[94] In fact, telecommunications was not privatized as a monopoly, but formally as a duopoly, although

---

[88] TNA T428/12, Ryrie, note, 'Privatisation', June 1981, paras. 1 and 5; TNA AN18/831, Redwood, note, January 1984.

[89] TNA T428/12, Ryrie, note, 'Privatisation ', June 1981, para. 1.

[90] TNA T370/2058, note, 'Privatisation and the PSBR', para. 2.

[91] TNA T370/2058, Howe, note, G Howe, March 1980, para. 1.

[92] Newbery, *Privatization*, p. 15.

[93] TNA T428/12, Ryrie, note, 'Privatisation of British Telecommunications', June 1981, para. 5.

[94] TNA T428/12, Burgner, paper, July 1981, para. 5.

with effectively little difference in terms of competition.[95] Mercury, formed in 1981 as a subsidiary of Cable & Wireless, was licensed as a national network operator in competition with BT in 1982, and the government announced its 'duopoly policy' in 1983 under which Mercury would be the *only* other fixed nationwide network to be licensed until 1990. Mercury launched its main services in 1986, and although it was successful in gaining market share for directly connected users in a few business sectors (such as the City of London), Mercury was less able to make inroads into the local network market. Duopoly policy also operated in the mobile sector, where two operators, Cellnet (in which BT had a controlling interest) and Vodafone, were licensed in 1985. When this mobile duopoly policy came to an end in 1991, two further operators were licensed: Mercury One-2-One (MOTO) and Orange.[96]

Considerations of political time also influenced the next major privatization of a network utility, that of gas, and again with consequences for the (un-) competitive structure of the privatized industry. Considerations of parliamentary time intruded. As Peter Walker, the Secretary of State for Energy, informed Margaret Thatcher in December 1983, even if it was assumed that the current Parliament would last for five years, because of the election 'shadow', it would probably still be necessary to have competed the major sales of shares by mid-1987, thereby requiring legislation to this end to be introduced in the '1984/85 Session with a view to beginning sale in, say, the early part of 1986'. Given the constraints of the parliamentary timetable, Walker feared that 'if his timetable is right, it may limit our scope for radical restructuring of the gas industry.'[97]

Electricity

Prioritizing timely political benefits, British Gas was privatized as a vertically integrated monopoly in 1986 with complete control of the distribution and transmission system needed to supply other customers. Although British Gas was required to allow other suppliers to use its network, and thereby encourage 'gas to gas' competition, these aspirant competitors had to negotiate with British Gas the terms on which gas could be transported across its network.[98] In addition, there were strong suspicions that British Gas would compete

---

[95] Telecommunications were taken out of the Ministry of Posts and Telecommunications in 1969 and became part of a new public corporation, the Post Office. In 1981, the telecom section became a public corporation in its own right as British Telecom.

[96] Armstrong, 'Competition in telecommunications', pp. 69, 72.

[97] TNA EG4/5081, Walker, letter, December 1983.

[98] Newbery, *Privatization, Restructuring*, p. 4.

aggressively in price in areas where it feared competitors might enter. Such entry deterrent behaviour is effective and difficult to track. Most new entrants concentrated on selling gas to the new power station market, where they achieved a market share of around 75% by March 1991, but they were conspicuous by their comparative absence in other gas markets. British Gas spent much of its first decade of existence preparing for or being investigated by the Monopolies and Mergers Commission.[99]

After the privatizations of telecommunications and gas, the next major network utility scheduled for privatization was the electricity supply industry. In between the privatization of gas and that of electricity came the stock market crash of 19 October 1987. Perhaps stung by criticisms of the failure to achieve sufficient competition in the previous privatizations of network utilities, and with a little less rush to privatize into a stock market which had lost some of its lustre with the electorate, a determined effort was made to introduce competition into the generating section of the electricity supply industry. Transmission was separated from generation, and the twelve Area Boards responsible for distribution and retail in England and Wales were left intact and privatized as regional electricity companies (REC) with joint ownership of the newly-created National Grid Company (NGC). The NGC had a statutory duty to facilitate competition and the focus fell on generation. Restructuring of generation was to precede privatization not least because previous attempts to liberalize the fuel and power industries and to introduce competition in the gas industry after privatization had not been successful.[100] In the Oil and Gas (Enterprise) Act of 1982, while British Gas's statutory monopoly on the pipeline system had been removed, it had been left free thereby to deter and exclude entrants by setting uneconomic access charges. Similarly, in the 1983 Energy Act, the CEGB had been left able to restructure tariffs so as to deter entry into potentially competitive markets.[101] Cecil Parkinson, who was appointed Secretary of State for Energy in 1987, subsequently stated that while he 'had no firm idea about the privatization of electricity, (he) was determined that we would not follow the pattern set by British Gas and British Telecom and take it to the market as a highly regulated monopoly'.[102]

Again, the political timetable intervened. An early proposal for restructuring the CEGB such that generation was divided between five fossil fuel companies who would jointly own a nuclear company fell foul of government concerns

[99] Green and Newbery, 'The regulation of the gas industry: lessons from electricity', pp. 38–9.
[100] Littlechild, 'Competition and regulation', p. 22.
[101] Chick, *Electricity and Energy Policy*.
[102] Henney, *A Study of the Privatisation*, p. 50; Parkinson, *Right at the Centre*.

with being able to complete any such break-up of the Central Electricity Generating Board (CEGB) before the summer of 1991, the likely date of the next general election. The government was also resistant to a substantial break-up of the CEGB since it wished to privatize the nuclear stations and to complete four pressurized water reactors (PWRs). It therefore decided to group the twelve nuclear stations with a large fossil generator, National Power. However, prospective shareholders were concerned about the future, unknown costs of decommissioning and fuel reprocessing, as well as the apportioning of risks in the construction of Sizewell B and three further PWRs. To finance the construction of the nuclear stations, very long contracts would need to be negotiated between National Power and the regional electricity companies (RECs) and both the cost and allocation of risk were uncertain. Unable to sell a pig in a poke, the government was forced to withdraw the nuclear power component from the privatization issue. Given time constraints, the concentrated structure of the industry designed to accommodate the now withdrawn nuclear component was left unchanged. In 1989, first the Magnox stations and then the advanced gas-cooled reactors and the Sizewell B pressurized-water reactor were withdrawn from the privatization issue. In the Electricity Act of 1989, National Power accounted for 60% and PowerGen for 40% of conventional generation capacity in the newly privatized industry. The high-tension grid was transferred to the National Grid Company (NGC) which in turn was transferred to the joint ownership of the RECs and these in turn were sold to the public in December 1990. Sixty per cent of National Power and Power Gen was subsequently sold to the public in March 1991, with its balance sold in March 1995.[103] At privatization all twelve nuclear stations were placed in Nuclear Electric. Subsequently in 1996 the five newer advanced gas-cooled reactors were privatized as British Energy. The seven old Magnox reactors were moved to the publicly owned British Nuclear Fuels plc, the fuel reprocessing company. The government had used public ownership to absorb the nuclear reactors which the market would not accept.[104]

At the time of privatization, the two largest generators, National Power and PowerGen together accounted for nearly 80% of total output in England and Wales—and when combined with Nuclear Electric, they accounted for nearly 95% of the market.[105] The presence of such large incumbents made it more difficult to develop competition, although the industry's first regulator, Stephen Littlechild, made ingenious efforts to do so. In the Electricity Pool designed

[103] Newbery, *Privatisation*, pp. 202–3.   [104] Chick, *Electricity and Energy Policy*, p. 115.
[105] Littlechild, 'Competition and regulation', p. 22.

by Littlechild, each supplier of electricity was invited to submit sealed bids for each half hour of the next day which it wished to supply. These bids when opened would form a supply curve and at the point at which this was crossed by the expected demand curve, the System Marginal Price would be set. However, with initially only two privatized competitors in electricity generation, opportunities arose for 'gaming' the system, with plant being withdrawn so as to edge up the system marginal price as more expensive plant was used to satisfy the final marginal units of demand. During the first three years of privatization, generation prices in the Pool increased rather than decreased. By early 1994 new entrants accounted for just 6% of the market. In an effort to increase competition in February 1994, National Power and PowerGen agreed to divest 6,000 Megawatts of their plant rather than be referred to the Monopolies and Mergers Commission (MMC). New entry gathered pace. However, in 1995, the government sold its 'golden shares' in the regional companies, some of which were bought by foreign companies and for some of which National Power and PowerGen also made takeover bids. These bids were blocked by the Secretary of State in the first instance but subsequently allowed, against the advice of the regulator, once the major generators had divested plant.[106] In October 1997, in response to complaints from large customers and competitors of the electricity supply industry, the government and the regulator began a review of the electricity trading arrangements in England & Wales. Under the resulting New Electricity Trading Arrangements (NETA), the monopoly of the pool was ended, and market participants could negotiate contracts bilaterally, on whatever terms best suited them and for however long ahead they choose. The financial bids in the Pool gave way to the physical bilateral contracting of the NETA.

Coal Mining

The privatization of electricity generation also spelt the end to a source of protection for the domestic coalmining industry since, as Peter Walker informed Margaret Thatcher in December 1983, a privatized electricity generating industry could not be expected to continue to provide 'a captive market for British coal'[107] As a nationalized industry, the National Coal Board (NCB) enjoyed a statutory monopoly of UK coal exploration and production. Imports

[106] Littlechild, 'Competition and regulation', pp. 23–4.
[107] TNA EG4/5081, Walker, letter, December 1983.

were allowed in principle which constrained NCB prices, but 70% of coal was for the CEGB and the South of Scotland Electricity Board (SSEB) who were informally banned from importing. Nonetheless, against a fluctuating international coal price, electricity coal prices had been generally competitive with imports. The main use which the NCB had made of its monopoly was to keep uneconomic pits open, using cross subsidies from profitable pits and discriminatory pricing to sell surplus production at low export prices. It was anticipated that in the long-run free competition at the pit level would close uneconomic pits and hold prices around import level.[108]

In March 1984 nearly 150,000 members of the National Union of Mineworkers went on strike in protest at NCB's plans to reduce capacity by some 4 million tons, implying the closure of around 20 collieries, and the loss of about 20,000 jobs.[109] If pits were to be closed, then one useful distinction to be made was between short- and long-run costs. At the time of the 1984/5 miners' strike, the overall operating 'loss-making' of the NCB in 1983/4 was put at £358 million and its receipt of government subsidies at £1.34 billion. In flourishing such figures, there was a reluctance to distinguish between the fixed (pensions, subsidence compensation, subsidies paid to cover the social costs of closure) and variable costs, the latter by definition changing as did production.[110] Valuing the coal which was dug was also complex. Coal that was dug, but unsold, was stored. This itself had costs which needed to be offset against any price realized in the future for the coal, that future price in turn being discounted back to its present value. However, to this needed to be added the consideration that if the coal had not been dug out, but the pit closed and allowed to flood, then that coal was probably economically irrecoverable. Any future demand for domestic coal would require resources to be spent digging other coal elsewhere. Continuing to operate the pit in the short-term at least, i.e. without making additional major long-term capital investment, meant that coal was produced, existing social capital (schools, housing) continued to be used, and unemployment benefit was not paid. Conversely if labour moved to a new area, it could create additional demands for social capital. The social capital needs of labour tended to be underestimated by those extolling the virtues of labour mobility. Such considerations in periods of unemployment were often the basis of arguments for selective (regional) employment subsidies.[111] Many of the arguments hinged on

[108] TNA T502/3, paper, 'Privatisation', October 1983, para. 10.3; Parker, *Thatcherism and the Fall of Coal*, ch. 4.

[109] Glyn, 'Economy and the UK Miners' Strike'; Glyn, 'The economic case against pit closures'.

[110] Cooper and Hopper, 'Introduction', p. 5.

[111] O'Donnell, 'Brought to accounting', p. 110.

assumptions of opportunity cost. The opportunity cost of using resources in one enterprise is the value of production which is foregone by society by those resources being so used. Closing pits to release labour became questionable if the labour did not find alternative employment.[112] Just as the economics of agglomeration could benefit clusters of new industries, so too could it make the revitalization of old industries much more difficult when they lay dispersed in remote areas as was often the case in the coal-mining industry. Renewal of older industries was more likely when they were within existing urban centres, whose facilities and buildings could be converted reasonably easily to new uses. For industries, like coal mining and fishing this was often less practicable. The optimistic view of opportunity cost was that if the miners could find employment, and the reduction of payments to the coal-mining industry actually created additional jobs, then there was an opportunity cost to their continued employment in coal mining. This approach did however also need to consider whether there were other programmes which were making even greater use of government funding which, if stopped or reduced, would have higher 'opportunity cost' benefits than those available from pit closures. In general, the most practical approach was to continue to run existing pits on a short-run cost basis, and steadily move to a gradual closure programme with provision for retraining built in.[113]

Regulation

That on privatization, competition was so limited in network utilities meant that regulation was required. Regulating industries with little or no competition was likely to be difficult, not least in terms of obtaining information on how much more efficient the industry could become. What was formally discussed as the economic problem of overcoming asymmetries of information within the principal-agent model was more informally expressed by William Ryrie (Second Permanent Secretary, Treasury) in the run-up to the privatization of BT:

> But the most obvious and difficult questions are about the monopoly position of the company and the proposed regulatory body. What do we gain by transferring a monopoly from the public to the private sector apart from freedom for BT to borrow? And how effective would a regulatory body be?

[112] *The Guardian*, 28 May 1984.
[113] Cooper and Hopper, 'Introduction', pp. 10–11; Davies and Metcalfe, 'Pit closures', p. 29.

It is one thing to have a regulatory body supervising 10 or 12 regional bodies and quite another to have a single regulatory body supervising a single powerful national monopoly.[114]

The familiar form of regulation in the United States was rate-of-return regulation, but this was eschewed in the United Kingdom. Part of this distaste arose from academic concerns regarding overcapitalization, that overly capital-intensive forms of production would be chosen when the regulated rate of return on capital exceeded the cost of capital.[115] Capital-based regulation was also thought to provide insufficient incentives to reduce costs, and to run the risk of regulatory capture as the technical expertise and information required to set an appropriate rate of return might incline regulators to be appointed who were overly familiar with, and sympathetic to, the industry. The favoured British approach of regulating prices rather than rate of return on capital ostensibly avoided such problems. The formula adopted for most privatized industries was RPI-X, with X being a number thought up in the regulator's office. As in the case of BT, the RPI-X price control was initially recommended for British Telecom as an interim measure, to 'hold the fort' until competition arrived. Where, as in water, a series of local monopolies existed and regulation was likely to be permanent in this rising cost industry in which investment was required, then a variation of the RPI-X formula was applied.[116] This was RPI+K, with the K (for fixed capital investment) varying across companies and time but being specifically designed to allow firms to upgrade capacity and meet quality standards.[117]

What was less discussed at the time of privatization was how, if competition did increase in markets, the consequent increase in risk and uncertainty would impact on the ability to attract new sunk investment. Rather than under-investment, it was concern with over-investment which was of most concern to those devising new regulatory incentive structures.[118] The mainly RPI-X regulatory periods were kept short to around five years, not least because their extension to ten or fifteen years was feared likely to allow sufficient time for a gap to emerge between operating costs and prices during which time costs savings would not be passed on to consumers. However, a five-year regulatory period was more likely to encourage operators to maximize their use of existing assets ('sweating assets') than to consider making substantial new

[114] TNA T428/12, Ryrie, note, 'Privatisation', June 1981, para. 9.
[115] Newbery, *Privatization*, pp. 38, 44; Averch and Johnson, 'The behaviour'; Baumol and Klevorick, 'Input choices'; Joskow, 'Pricing decisions'.
[116] Littlechild, 'Economic regulation'.
[117] Hunt and Lynk, 'Privatisation and efficiency', p. 374.
[118] Helm and Yarrow, 'The assessment', p. xxi.

investment in lumpy sunk assets. It was to provide some protection against this general uncertainty that electricity companies sought to integrate vertically. What was perhaps underappreciated at the time of privatization was the historical novelty of trying to induce large sunk investment from utilities operating in competitive markets. Both in the Victorian and Edwardian system of concessions, then as municipal enterprises and subsequently as nationalized monopolies, assurances on probable returns on fixed capital investment in utilities were given and were frequently accompanied and secured by a period free from competition. The 1870 Tramways Act inaugurated the system of providing limited period franchises which were initially usually for twenty-one years but were subsequently extended to forty-two years in 1888.[119] Nationalization represented an extension of this process in which (often national) monopolistic conditions were established as the norm, public ownership being preferred to regulation as a means of extracting for consumers the benefits of improvements in productivity. Thus, where privatization was eventually successful in not only transferring ownership but also in introducing competition into sections of each industry, then it reintroduced risk and uncertainty into markets from which it had been absent for decades. Potential investors in new nuclear generating capacity knew that their low marginal cost would give them a considerable share of base load. What they did not know was what the price of electricity would be (reflecting the costs of non-nuclear suppliers as well) and therefore at what rate they might recover their capital costs and earn a return on capital.

Incentives for New Investment

Some of these difficulties became evident in the negotiations over investment in the new Hinkley Point C nuclear power station in Somerset. Eventually what was agreed in 2016 between the UK government, on the one side, and EDF and its Chinese partners on the other, was that there would be a guaranteed 'strike price' of £92.50 per megawatt hour (MWh) in 2012 prices, indexed for thirty-five years. Given the low marginal cost of renewables which will account for a growing proportion of electricity generation, this locked-in price looked expensive, but without effectively offering assurance on the likely returns on sunk capital, it was difficult to see why anyone would invest in nuclear power. In general, an outcome of privatization was to reduce the incentives for making large additions to the existing stock of sunk investment.

---

[119] Byatt, *The British Electrical Industry*, p. 8.

Given the large reduction in government-fixed capital investment activity (see chapter 2) this incentive structure compounded the difficulties of accommodating future risks into current decisions on investment. In addition, for the privatized companies, raising new capital would involve a greater recourse to equity finance, which was likely to have a higher cost, because of higher expected rates of return, than the inherited debt or debt finance.[120] One suggested approach to encouraging greater investment, especially on long-term infrastructure projects, was to return to some form of RAB (Regulated Asset Base) approach. The equity risk in the RAB for the company was suggested as being zero, since the customers were compelled to pay for the RAB. Once a RAB was guaranteed, it could be financed by debt, rather than equity, making it cheaper to finance.[121]

Adding to the Housing Stock

In housing, similar concerns to those in privatized industries arose around the rate of addition to the existing stock. In housing, the impact of a flow of new investment was likely to be limited because of the proportionate low flow:stock ratio.[122] Of more pertinence was the efficiency of use of the stock, but the tax advantages of owner-occupation militated against this. To the tax advantages of owner-occupation which discouraged a more efficient use of the housing stock, were added changes in the availability of finance for the private purchase of housing which contributed to the price of housing as an asset rising faster than incomes.[123] For most of the post-war period, mortgage rationing usually as a multiple of income had been the norm, but from the early 1980s, building societies (the largest mortgage lenders in the UK) moved to using interest rates as a rationing mechanism.[124] Between 1992 and 2016 the multiple of average advances to average income of borrowers rose from two to three (see Table 6.2). One consequence was that price:earnings ratios for housing rose. In the first decade of the twenty-first century, this house-price boom occurred in the UK and many other economies, although notably not in Japan and Germany (Table 6.3).[125] In 2007, Robert Shiller was among those arguing

[120]   Helm, 'Infrastructure investment', p. 314.
[121]   Helm, Wardlaw, and Caldecott, *Delivering a 21st Century Infrastructure for Britain.*
[122]   Whitehead, 'Housing demand', p. 75; Meen, *Modelling Spatial Housing Markets;* Meen et al., *Affordability targets.*
[123]   Muellbauer and Murphy, 'Housing markets', p. 22; Mishkin, 'Housing and the monetary transmission mechanism'.
[124]   Meen, 'The removal of mortgage market constraints', p. 1.
[125]   Miles and Pillonca, 'Financial innovation'.

Table 6.2. Simple average house prices, average advances, and recorded incomes of borrowers for all dwellings in the UK (£), First quarter, 1992–2016

	Average dwelling price	Average advance	Average recorded income of borrowers
1992	62,000	44,000	21,000
1993	60,000	43,000	21,000
1994	62,000	45,000	22,000
1995	62,000	46,000	22,000
1996	66,000	49,000	23,000
1997	73,000	53,000	25,000
1998	78,000	56,000	26,000
1999	84,000	60,000	28,000
2000	97,000	68,000	30,000
2001	107,000	74,000	32,000
2002	113,000	78,000	34,000
2003	142,000	92,000	38,000
2004	169,000	104,000	40,000
2005	185,000	112,000	40,000
2006	193,000	132,000	49,000
2007	217,000	147,000	54,000
2008	227,000	150,000	54,000
2009	217,000	132,000	53,000
2010	253,000	151,000	58,000
2011	244,000	152,000	57,000
2012	239,000	153,000	55,000
2013	243,000	157,000	58,000
2014	260,000	171,000	59,000
2015	270,000	179,000	61,000
2016	293,000	195,000	65,000

Source: ONS, *House Price Index (HPI)*, Table 15, accessed 31 August 2016.

Table 6.3. Housing, all dwellings, UK, Annual price change (first quarter) Q1 2002=100

1970	1971	1972	1973	1974	1975	1976	1977	1978	1979	1980	1981
3.9	4.2	5.1	7.7	8.8	9.1	9.9	10.8	11.7	14.8	19.1	20.7
1982	1983	1984	1985	1986	1987	1988	1989	1990	1991	1992	1993
20.7	23.1	25.3	27.5	30.7	35.5	43.0	56.0	57.6	56.4	55.9	52.9
1994	1995	1996	1997	1998	1999	2000	2001	2002	2003	2004	2005
54.0	54.8	55.9	60.0	65.5	72.1	83.6	92.1	100.0	123.4	134.6	149.5
2006	2007	2008	2009	2010	2011	2012	2013	2014	2015	2016	
154.8	172.1	183.3	160.5	172.8	172.9	173.7	177.5	191.6	207.8	225.0	

Source: ONS, *House Price Index*, Table 10, accessed 31 August 2016.

that psychological factors had driven US and other house prices to greatly overvalued levels, with falls of as much as 50% in prospect.[126]

As seen in chapter 2, from the mid-1970s, the state reduced its involvement in the provision of social housing. The stock of the social rented sector peaked at about 5.5 million dwellings at the end of the 1970s and fell to 4.1 million by 2003. Building rates fell after the 1970s. In part demand fell as households, in particular couple households and those in the forty-five to sixty-four age range, took advantage of the RTB. By 2001, 2 million RTB sales affected both the size and composition of the social rented sector (particularly its age profile). Within the social rented sector there was a decline of multiple earner households, a growth in households with no earners, a continuing growth in one-person households (from 22% in 1977, to 35% in 1987, 41% in 1998/9, and 43% in 2003), and a decline in large adult households (18% in 1977, 14% in 1987, and 8% in 2003). The age structure of the social rented sector became more elderly, with the portion of tenants aged sixty-five or over increasing from 30% in 1977 to 40% in 1987, before falling back to 35% by 1999 and 34% in 2003.[127]

The decline in the social rented sector reduced its capacity to continue to house the lowest-income groups.[128] Rents also rose, reflecting a shift from subsidizing the supply of housing to subsidizing the demand for housing. This shift in subsidizing capital construction (supply) to subsidizing rent (demand) was anticipated by Nicholas Ridley, Secretary of State for the Environment in a House of Commons debate on 30 November 1987, when he stated that 'in the private sector, rents will move towards market levels' and that any future 'government support will focus on tenants, rather than on property'.[129]

The shift is also evidenced in Table 6.4. One assumption made was that middle-income households ineligible for housing benefit and adversely affected by rising rents would move on to become owner-occupiers.[130] However, the rise in price:income ratios of housing assets made it increasingly difficult for these households to make that transition and left them exposed to a private rented sector which was expensive in terms of household income but not especially so in terms of the rate of return on the value of the rented asset.[131] A widening gap emerged between the market for rented accommodation and that for the purchase of housing assets. While real rents rose by around 25% from 1992 to a high point before the financial crisis, they rose much less than real house prices.[132] Rising house prices did attract new construction activity,

---

[126] Muellbauer and Murphy, 'Housing markets', p. 4.
[127] Murie, 'Moving with the times', p. 29.   [128] Murie, 'Moving with the times', p. 29.
[129] Webb, *Bricks or benefits*, p. 10.   [130] Webb, *Bricks or benefits*, p. 10.
[131] Hughes, *Held-back Households*.   [132] Oxford Economics, *Forecasting UK House Prices*.

Table 6.4. Housing subsidy, 1975–1976 to 2003–2004 (£ billion, 2003–2004 prices)

	1975–1976	1980–1981	1985–1986	1992–1993	1999–2000	2000–2001	2001–2002	2002–2003	2003–2004
Capital	10.7	6.3	5.2	5.8	3.0	3.9	4.2	5.0	5.2
LA Revenue	3.3	4.3	1.8	0.6	–1.0	–1.2	0.4	0.3	0.2
TOTAL SUPPLY	14.0	10.6	7.0	6.4	2.0	2.7	4.6	5.3	5.4
Rent rebate	0.6	0.7	4.4	5.0	4.7	4.5	4.4	4.4	4.1
Rent allowance	0.1	0.1	1.7	4.0	5.5	5.6	5.8	6.4	6.3
Mortgage interest relief	2.4	4.6	7.8	6.1	1.9	0	0	0	0
Income support for mortgage interest	n/a	n/a	n/a	1.5	0.6	0.5	0.3	0.3	0.3
TOTAL DEMAND	3.1	5.4	13.9	16.6	12.7	10.6	10.5	11.1	10.7
TOTAL	17.1	15.9	20.9	23.0	14.7	13.3	15.1	16.4	16.1

Source: Stephens, Whitehead, and Munro, *Lessons from the Past*; Hills, *Ends and Means*, p. 56, Table 6.1.

Table 6.5. Household formation, 2001, 2011 (thousands, and percentage change)

	2001 Census total (thousands)	2011 Census total (thousands)	Percentage change 2001–2011
Households, all types:	21,660	23,366	7.9
One-person households	6,503	7,067	8.7
One-family only households	13,716	14,449	5.3
Other households	1,442	1,850	28.3
Total usually resident population	52,042	56,076	7.8
Persons in communal establishments	858	1,005	17.1
All persons in households	51,108	55,071	7.8
Adults in households	39,442	42,993	9.0
Dependent children in households	11,665	12,078	3.5

Source: 2001 and 2011 Census, Office for National Statistics.

such that between 1996 and 2006 the dwelling stock rose by 1.98 million units, outstripping the rise in household formation of 1.83 million.[133] Household formation rose in aggregate by 7.9% between 2001 and 2011 (see Table 6.5) although there was considerable variation among the differing component households and it was unclear as to the extent to which the rate of household formation was suppressed by the rental:income ratio. Aggregate data on what were essentially regional markets was of limited use, although the density factor did indicate the extent to which London differed from all other regions (Table 6.6). The data on household formation broke with the longer-term trend, with net additional household formation in England between 2001 and 2011 being some 20% lower, with almost 1 million fewer one-person households than had been projected.[134] Building more homes might itself encourage an increase in household formation.[135]

However, none of the concern for building new housing should distract attention from the tax and cost advantages of owning houses and essentially encouraging over-consumption of the existing stock. In addition to the absence of the taxation of imputed income from owner-occupation and of capital gains tax on the principal residence at time of sale, at time of death not only is capital gains tax rolled up into inheritance tax but considerable thresholds are

---

[133] Oxford Economics, *Forecasting UK House Prices*, p. 7.   [134] Holmans, *New Estimates*, p. 3.
[135] Meen, 'Ten new propositions'; Oxford Economics, *Forecasting UK House Prices*.

Table 6.6. Population density in England and Wales (people per square kilometre in government office regions)

	1981	1991	2001	2010
North East	307	302	296	304
North West	492	485	480	492
Yorkshire and the Humber	319	320	323	344
East Midlands	247	257	268	287
West Midlands	399	402	406	420
East	254	268	283	305
London	4,329	4,344	4,658	4,978
South East	380	400	421	447
South West	184	197	207	221
Wales	136	139	140	145

Source: Office for National Statistics, Population density in England and Wales, population estimates mid-1981 to 2010.

extended to owner-occupiers. While inheritance tax has become a largely ineffectual irritant, there is no compensation in the form of a more realistic local tax on property. This may be deemed to be too politically sensitive, but it may explain why in 2017, one in ten adults own a second property in addition to their own home.[136]

The transfer and addition of industrial and housing assets to and then from public ownership marked a movement in the stock of investment which was broadly in line with changes in the flow of public fixed capital investment. In both cases the timing of the privatization of the assets was affected by considerations of public finance and in the case of nationalized industries, privatization freed them from the financial capital constraints of the state. The early sale of shares in the former nationalized gas and telecommunications industries had also proved popular with sections of the electorate. Against that the costs of the sales were considerable (3–5% of receipts, which was about average for smaller new issues) and at 25% the degree of under-pricing was substantial, resulting in a loss of sales revenue of £2.5 billion relative to a normal under-pricing on new shares of 10%. This encouraged a wide initial public subscription and the experience of past under-pricing doubtless encouraged bids for later sales, though many small shareholders sold out; 4.4 million bought British Gas shares initially, but fewer than 2 million held them before 1994.[137]

---

[136] Johnson, 'If you're serious'.
[137] Newbery, *Privatization*, p. 13; Bishop and Green, *Privatisation and Recession*; Jenkinson and Mayer, 'The costs of privatisation in the UK and France'; Jenkinson, 'When debt turned to equity', *The Utilities Journal*.

Again, as with housing, the calculation of receipts of sale set against future costs and revenues foregone discounted back to present value needs to be made.

The shift to reliance on market and social security mechanisms to provide sufficient additions to the housing stock represented a sharp contrast with the public, provisionist programmes of governments for most of the first three post-war decades. Like the move from nationalized to privatized industries, it also marked a shift in the means of influencing the accessibility of basic necessities. In the early post-war period, the nationalized industries' early practice of pricing at average cost offered cross-subsidized prices to all income groups. By the 1980s, there was little appetite among policymakers for approaches towards tackling fuel poverty which involved a return to the past practices of interfering with the level or structure of prices. However, the lower-income groups were most vulnerable to the concern of privatized utilities to (re-)cover capital costs, not least through increases in standing charges. These formed a higher proportion of the total bill for low users of output, and were likely to rise faster than marginal unit consumption charges. The combined effect of increased standing and unit charges for electricity fell particularly on older (low usage) and poorer (low income and restricted usage) households. Lower-income groups spend a higher proportion of their household budget on energy than do higher-income households.[138] Income issues aside, in the mid-1980s the 30% of households living in council accommodation and the further 8% living in privately rented accommodation also had little, if any, choice over the type of heating in their households.[139] Being less likely to have gas central heating, the poorest also missed out on the slower increase in gas than in electricity charges.[140] As with social security in general, the cold-weather payments made from 1985–1986 to address the added cost of heating in the winter were paid to the old, rather than specifically to lower-income groups. While pensioners spent proportionately more on fuel than non-pensioner households, by no means were all pensioners in fuel poverty.[141] That issues of fuel poverty and of high rents as a share of household income were alive as issues in the twenty-first century was perhaps surprising given the additions to the stock of housing and utility capital which had been made since 1945. Whereas the nationalization of industries and the construction of public housing from the immediate post-war period had deliberately been concerned with making houses and utility output available and as affordable to as many

---

[138]   Burns, Crawford, and Dilnot, 'Regulation and Redistribution', p. 10.
[139]   Dilnot and Helm, 'Energy policy, merit goods and social security', pp. 34, 36, 38, 45.
[140]   Burns, Crawford, and Dilnot, 'Regulation and Redistribution', p. 13.
[141]   Burns, Crawford, and Dilnot, 'Regulation and Redistribution', p. 10.

who required them, those ambitions faded with the drift towards making greater use of market mechanisms in the pricing of utility output and housing. Accompanied by a very significant reduction in government public fixed capital investment activity, not only did it prove difficult to solicit new utility investment in more competitive markets, but problems also emerged in ensuring that there was sufficient housing available for lower-income households. The housing market itself bifurcated more clearly than before between the market in purchasing assets and that for renting. Given these conditions it was puzzling why in the wake of the financial crisis governments did not borrow at low real interest rates to build social housing for which rents exceeding the rate of interest could be charged, thereby contributing to a reduction in the structural deficit. Having transferred assets from public to private ownership, the state appeared very reluctant to engage once again with investing in asset provision, while at the same time the market in both housing and utility investment offered insufficient incentives either to make more efficient use of the existing housing stock or to encourage utility operators to engage in substantial programmes of fixed capital investment.

Bibliography

Allais, M., 'Étude théorique des conditions générales de l'aménagement économiquement optimum de la production, de la distribution et de l'utilisation des combustibles solides', *Annales des Mines*, vol. 5, 1952, pp. 3–45.

Allais, M., 'Étude théorique des conditions générales de l'aménagement économiquement optimum de la production, de la distribution et de l'utilisation des combustibles solides', *Annales des Mines*, vol. 8, 1952, pp. 3–75.

Armstrong, Mark, 'Competition in telecommunications', *Oxford Review of Economic Policy*, vol. 13, issue 1, March 1997, pp. 64–82.

Atkinson, A. B., and M. A. King, 'Housing policy, taxation and reform', *Midland Bank Review*, Spring 1980, pp. 7–15.

Averch, H., and L. Johnson, 'The behaviour of the firm under regulatory constraint', *American Economic Review*, vol. 52, December 1962, pp. 1052–69.

Baumol, William, and Alvin K. Klevorick, 'Input choices and rate-of-return regulation: An overview of the discussion', *Bell Journal of Economics*, vol. 1, issue 2, 1970, pp. 162–90.

Bishop, M., and M. Green, *Privatisation and Recession: The Miracle Tested*, 1995, Bath: Centre for the Study of Regulated Industries, Discussion paper 10.

Boiteux, M., 'Sur la gestion des monopoles publics astreints à l'équilibre budgétaire', *Econometrica*, vol. 24, no. 1, 1956, pp. 22–40.

Brittan, Samuel., *Against the Flow: Reflections of an Individualist*, 2005, London: Atlantic Books.

Burk, Kathleen, *The First Privatisation: The City and the Denationalisation of Steel*, 1988, London: The Historians' Press.

Burns, Philip, Ian Crawford and Andrew Dilnot, 'Regulation and redistribution in utilities', *Fiscal Studies*, vol. 16, issue 4, November 1995, pp. 1–22.

Byatt, I., *The British Electrical Industry, 1875–1914*, 1979, Oxford: Clarendon Press.

Cant, Alistair, *Where Have All The Assets Gone?*, 1979, Nottingham: Nottingham Alternative Publications.

Chick, Martin, 'Marginal cost pricing and the peak-hour demand for electricity', in Martin Chick (ed.), *Governments. Industries and Markets: Aspects of Government-Industry Relations in the UK, Japan, West Germany and the USA since 1945*, 1990, Aldershot: Edward Elgar, pp. 110–26.

Chick, Martin, *Industrial Policy in Britain 1945–1951: Economic Planning, Nationalisation and the Labour Governments*, 1998, Cambridge: Cambridge University Press.

Chick, Martin, *Electricity and Energy Policy in Britain, France and the United States since 1945*, 2007, Cheltenham: Edward Elgar.

Clark, M, 'Too much housing', *Lloyds Bank Review*, October 1977.

Coase, R. H., 'The nature of the firm', *Economica*, n.s. November 1937, vol. 4, no. 16, pp. 386–405.

Colvin, Phyllis, *The Economic Ideal In British Government: Calculating Costs and Benefits In The 1970s*, 1985, Manchester: Manchester University Press.

Cooney, E. W., 'High flats in local authority housing in England and Wales since 1945', in A. Sutcliffe (ed.), *Multi-Storey Living: The British Working-Class Experience*, 1974, London: Croom Helm.

Cooper, D. J., and T. M. Hopper, 'Introduction: Financial calculation in industrial and political debate', in David Cooper and Trevor Hopper (eds.), *Debating Coal Closures: Economic Calculation in the Coal Dispute, 1984–5*, 1988, Cambridge: Cambridge University Press, pp. 1–22.

Davies, G., and D. Metcalfe, 'Pit closures: some economics', in Cooper and Hopper (eds.), *Debating Coal Closures*, pp. 25–45.

Dilnot, Andrew, and Dieter Helm, 'Energy policy, merit goods and social security', *Fiscal Studies*, vol. 8, no. 3, 1987, pp. 29–48.

Dunleavy, P., *The Politics of Mass Housing in Britain, 1945–1975*, 1981, Oxford: Oxford University Press.

Florio, Massimo, *The Great Divestiture*, 2004, Cambridge, Mass.: The MIT Press, p. 276.

Foreman-Peck, J. S., 'The appraisal of sales of Local Authority rented accommodation: a comment', *Urban Studies*, vol. 19, 1982, pp. 79–82. Offprint in TNA HLG 118/3498.

Foreman-Peck, J., 'Ownership, competition and productivity growth, the impact of liberalisation and privatisation upon British Telecom', mimeo, 1989, University of Hull.

Foreman-Peck, James, and Robert Millward, *Public and Private Ownership of British Industry, 1820-1990*, 1994, Oxford: Oxford University Press.

Forrest, R., A. Murie and P. Williams, *Home Ownership: Differentiation and Fragmentation*, 1990, London: Unwin Hyman.

Forrest, Ray, David Gordon and Alan Murie, 'The position of former council homes in the housing market', *Urban Studies*, vol. 33, no. 1, 1996, pp. 125–36.

GLC Council Minutes, 26.6.79, Question to Mr G. Tremlett, Leader of the Housing Policy Committee). Report 2.7.79 to GLC Housing Policy Committee.

Gleave, D., and D. Palmer, 'Mobility of labour: Are council tenants really handicapped?' *CES Review*, May 1978.

Glyn, Andrew, 'Economy and the UK Miners' Strike', *Social Scientist*, vol. 13, no. 1, January 1985, pp. 23–31.

Glyn, Andrew., 'The economic case against pit closures', 1984, National Union of Mineworkers.

Goodhart, C. A. E., 'Competition and credit control', March 2014, LSE Financial Markets Group, Special Paper 229.

Green, Richard, and David Newbery, 'The Regulation of the gas industry: lessons from electricity', *Fiscal Studies*, vol. 14, no. 2, 1993, pp. 37–52.

Grey, A., N. P. Hepworth, and J. Odling-Smee *Housing Rents, Costs and Subsidies: A Discussion Document*, 1981, London: Chartered Institute of Public Finance and Accounting.

Harloe, M., *The People's Home? Social rented housing in Europe and America*, 1995, Oxford: Blackwell.

Harris, Ralph, and Brendan Sewill, *British Economic Policy 1970–4: Two Views*, 1975, London: Institute of Economic Affairs, London.

Helm, Dieter, 'Infrastructure investment, the cost of capital, and regulation: an assessment', *Oxford Review of Economic Policy*, vol. 25, no. 3, 2009, pp. 307–26.

Helm, Dieter, James Wardlaw, and Ben Caldecott, *Delivering a 21st Century Infrastructure for Britain*, 2009, London: Policy Exchange.

Helm, Dieter, and George Yarrow, 'The assessment: The regulation of utilities', *Oxford Review of Economic Policy*, vol. 4, no. 2., July 1988.

Henney, Alex, *A Study of the Privatisation of the Electricity Supply Industry in England and Wales*, 1994, London: EEE.

Hills, John, *Ends and Means: The Future Roles of Social Housing in England*, ESRC Research centre for Analysis of Social Exclusion, February 2007, Case Report 34, ISSN 1465–3001.

Holmans, A. E., *Housing Policy in Britain*, 1987, London: Croom Helm.

Holmans, Alan, *New Estimates Of Housing Demand And Need In England, 2011 to 2031*, 2013, Town and Country Planning, Tomorrow Series paper 16.

Hughes, N., *Held-back Households: How the Housing System Squeezes People on Low-Middle Incomes*, 2012, London: Shelter.

Hunt, Lester C., and Edward L. Lynk, 'Privatisation and efficiency in the UK water industry: An empirical analysis', *Oxford Bulletin of Economics and Statistics*, vol. 57, issue 3, August 1995, pp. 371–88.

Hutter, R., 'La théorie économique et la gestion commerciale des chemins de fer: le problème tarifaire', *Revue Générale des Chemins de Fer*, July 1950, pp. 318–32.

Jenkinson, T. J., and C. M. Mayer, 'The costs of privatisation in the UK and France', in Matthew Bishop, John Kay, and Colin Mayer (eds.), *Privatisation and Economic Performance*, 1994, Oxford: Oxford University Press, pp. 290–8.

Jenkinson, T., 'When debt turned to equity', *The Utilities Journal*, March 2001.

Johnson, Paul, 'If you're serious about helping young buyers, hard choices lie ahead', *The Times*, 27 November 2017. Also on IFS website.

Joskow, Paul L., 'Pricing decisions of regulated firms: A behavioural approach', *Bell Journal of Economics*, The RAND Corporation, vol. 4, no. 1, Spring 1973, pp. 118–40.

Little, I. M. D. *The Price of Fuel*, 1953, Oxford: Clarendon.

Littlechild, Stephen, 'Economic regulation of privatised water authorities and some further reflections', *Oxford Review of Economic Policy*, vol. 4, no. 2, 1988, pp. 40–68.

Littlechild, Stephen C., 'Competition and regulation in the U.K. electricity industry', *Journal of Applied Corporate Finance*, vol. 13, no. 4, Winter 2001, pp. 21–38.

Lynk, E. L., 'Privatisation, joint production and the comparative efficiencies of private and public ownership: The UK water industry case', *Fiscal Studies*, vol. 14, no. 2, 1993, pp. 98–116.

Malpass, Peter, and Liz Cairncross, *Building on the Past: Visions of Housing Futures*, 2006, Bristol: The Policy Press.

Meen, Geoffrey P., 'The removal of mortgage market constraints and the implications for econometric modelling of UK house prices', *Oxford Bulletin of Economics and Statistics*, vol. 52, no. 1, 1990, pp. 1–23.

Meen, G., *Modelling Spatial Housing Markets*, 2001, Dordrecht: Kluwer Academic Publishers

Meen, G, et al., *Affordability Targets: Implications for Housing Supply*, 2005, London: Office of Deputy Prime Minister.

Meen, G., 'Ten new propositions in UK housing macroeconomics: an overview of the first years of the century', *Urban Studies*, vol. 45, no. 13, 2008, pp. 2759–81.

Merrett, S., *State Housing in Britain*, 1979, London: Routledge and Kegan Paul.

Miles, David, and Vladimir Pillonca, 'Financial innovation and European housing and mortgage markets', *Oxford Review of Economic Policy*, vol. 24, no. 1, 2008, pp. 145–75.

Millward, R., 'Comparative performance of public and private ownership' in. E.Roll (ed.), *The Mixed Economy*, 1982, London: Palgrave Macmillan, pp. 59–93.

Millward, R., 'Comparative performance of public and private ownership', *Salford Papers in Economics*, pp. 80–4.

Millward, Robert, 'Price restraint, anti-inflation policy and public and private industry in the UK', *Economic Journal*, vol. 86, no. 342, 1976, pp. 226–42.

Millward, Robert, *Private and Public Enterprise in Europe: Energy, Telecommunications and Transport, 1830–1990*, 2005, Cambridge: Cambridge University Press.

Mitchell, A., 'Clay Cross', *Political Quarterly*, vol. 45, 1974, pp. 165–78.

Mishkin, Frederick S., 'Housing and the monetary transmission mechanism', 2007, NBER Working Paper, No. 13518.

Molyneux, Richard, and David Thompson, 'Nationalised industry performance: still third rate?', *Fiscal Studies*, vol. 8, no. 1, February 1987, pp. 48–82.

Monk, Sarah, Alan Holmans, Michael Jones, Diane Lister, Christina Short, Christine Whitehead, *The Demand For Social Rented Housing- A Review of Data sources and Supporting Case Study Analysis*, March 2006, Cambridge Centre for Housing and Planning Research, University of Cambridge.

Muellbauer, John, and Anthony Murphy, 'Housing markets and the economy: the assessment', *Oxford Review of Economic Policy*, vol. 24, no. 1, 2008, pp. 1–33.

Murie, Alan, 'Moving with the times: changing frameworks for housing research and policy', in Peter Malpass and Liz Cairncross (eds.), *Building on the Past: Visions of Housing Futures*, 2006, Bristol: The Policy Press, pp. 15–49.

Newbery, David, *Privatization, Restructuring and Regulation of Network Utilities*, 1999, Cambridge, Mass.: The MIT Press.

Newbery, David, *Privatization, Restructuring and Regulation of Network Utilities*, 1999, Cambridge, Mass.: The MIT Press.

Needleman, L., *The Economics of Housing*, 1965, London: Staples Press.

O'Donnell, K., 'Brought to accounting: The NCB and the case for coal', *Capital and Class*, vol. 26, 1985, pp. 105–23.

Oxford Economics, *Forecasting UK House Prices And Home Ownership: A Report For The Redfern Review Into The Decline Of Home Ownership*, November 2016, Oxford.

Parker, M. J., *Thatcherism and the Fall of Coal*, 2000, Oxford: Oxford University Press.

Parkinson, Cecil, *Right at the Centre*, 1992, London: Weidenfeld & Nicolson.

Poterba, J. M., 'Tax subsidies to owner-occupied housing: An asset market approach', *Quarterly Journal of Economics*, vol. 99, no. 4, November 1984, pp. 9–21.

Saunders, P., *A Nation of Home Owners*, 1990, London: Routledge.

Saunders, Robert, " 'Crisis? What crisis?" Thatcherism and the "seventies" ', in Ben Jackson and Robert Saunders, *Making Thatcher's Britain*, 2012, Cambridge: Cambridge University Press, pp. 25–42.

Schifferes, Steve, *Facts on Council House Sales*, 1979, London: Shelter.

Scott, Peter, 'Friends in high places: Government-industry relations in public sector house-building during Britain's tower block era', *Business History*, online, 2 April 2018.

Shelter, *Facts on Council House Sales*, Shelter.

Stephens, M., C. Whitehead, and M. Munro, *Lessons from the Past, Challenges for the Future of Housing Policy*, 2003, London: Office of Deputy Prime Minister.

Sutcliffe, A., (ed.), *Multi-Storey Living: The British Working-Class Experience*, Croom Helm, London 1974.

TNA AN18/831, Note, John Redwood to Prime Minister, Policy Unit, 20 January 1984.

TNA AN18/831, C. D. Foster, 'The economics of rail privatisation', lecture at the University of Leeds, 10 March 1994. Copy sent to Bob Reid, Chairman, British Railways Board.

TNA EG4/5081, Letter, Peter Walker, Secretary of State for Energy to Margaret Thatcher, 20 December 1983.

TNA HLG 118/3497, Memorandum calling for Secretary of State to establish an independent technical enquiry into the financial consequences of the sale of council houses, by Jack Straw, MP to the Secretary of State for the Environment, August 1979.

TNA HLG 118/3497, Letter, Jack Straw MP to Michael Heseltine, Secretary of State for the Environment, 21 August 1979.

TNA HLG 118/3497, Cutting from *The Economist*, 25 August 1979, pp. 17–18.

TNA HLG 118/3497, 'Dr. Foreman Peck', note by A E Holmans, 31 August 1979.

TNA HLG 118/3595, 'A note on the impact of council house sales; the experience of Nottingham, 1976–79', by T S Brindley, Building Research Establishment, Department of the Environment, September 1980, PD 116/80.

TNA PREM 19/197, meeting with academic economists at Chequers on Sunday 13 July 1980.

TNA T230/765, 'Comparison of the cost to the public sector of private and public authority housing', Note by N. Kaldor to Mr Holmans, 7 November 1966.

TNA T230/765, 'Local Authority mortgage lending', note, R.F. Bretherton 25 November 1966.

TNA T354/54, 'Draft Cabinet paper: Sale of Council Houses', Department of the Environment, June 1976.

TNA T354/54, letter, Peter Shore (Department of the Environment) to Denis Healey, 2 August 1976.

TNA T364/102, 'Housing Policy Review', note, Douglas Wass, 25 April 1977.

TNA T364/102, 'Housing Policy Review', note, G S Downey to Sir Douglas Wass, 21 April 1977.

TNA T370/1434, 'Nationalised Industries Policy Group', Discussion paper by the Chairman on policy for the future of the industries, PG/18/76, Nicholas Ridley, May 1978.

TNA T370/1434, 'Nationalised Industries', minutes of a meeting held on 10th May 1978 in the Leader's Room at the House of Commons.

TNA T370/2058, note, G Howe to F Jones, 7 March 1980.

TNA T370/2058, 'Privatisation and the PSBR', Note by Treasury Officials.

TNA T379/23, 'Calculation of unsubsidised rents', paper by J L Carr, 10 May 1976.

TNA T379/23, 'Tax on the imputed income from owner-occupation', Draft note by B T Houghton, 27 May 1976.

TNA T379/23, 'Unsubsidised rents', paper by D. R. Allen, 9 June 1976.

TNA T386/77, Draft letter, Denis Healey to Prime Minister, 1975.

TNA T414/50, 'Deemed rate of return on housing investment', note by M J V Bell, 25 April 1979.

TNA T414/50, Review of Housing Finance Steering Group, paper by Peter Trench, 'General Housing subsidies', no author, Department of the Environment, 23 October 1975.

TNA T414/50, General Housing Subsidies, note J L Carr to Ian Byatt, 27 October 1975.

TNA T414/50, Review of Housing Finance: Schedule A tax and tax relief on mortgage interest, note, J L Carr to Mr Byatt, 27 October 1975.

TNA T414/50, General Housing Subsidies, note J L Carr to Ian Byatt, 27 October 1975.

TNA T428/12, 'Privatisation of British Telecommunications', Note from W S Ryrie to Mr Burgner, 29th June 1981.

TNA T428/12, paper, T U Burgner, 3 July 1981.

TNA T502/3, Treasury, 'Privatisation: Structure and Competition, paper, PEAU, October 1983.

TNA T502/3, letter, J R Castree, Treasury to R Millward, Department of Economics, University of Salford, 13 October 1983.

Webb, Kate, *Bricks or Benefits: Replacing Housing Investment*, May 2012, Shelter Report.

Whitehead, Christine M. E., 'The provision of finance for social housing: The UK experience', *Urban Studies*, vol. 36. no. 4, 1999, pp. 657–72.

Whitehead, Christine M. E., 'Housing demand, supply and the geography of inequality', in Peter Malpass and Liz Cairncross (eds.), *Building on the Past: Visions of Housing Futures*, 2006, Bristol: The Policy Press.

Wilcox, S., *UK Housing Review 2003/2004*, 2004, Coventry/London: Chartered Institute of Housing/COML.

Cmnd. 1337, (1961), *The Financial and Economic Obligations of the Nationalised Industries*, London: HMSO.

Cmnd. 3437, (1967), *Nationalised Industries: A Review of Economic and Financial Objectives*, London: HMSO.

Department of the Environment, 1977, *Housing Policy, Technical Volume I*, London: HMSO.

Housing Policy: A Consultative Document, Department of Environment, Cmnd. 6851, HMSO, 1971.

Housing: The Chartered Surveyors Report, RICS, 1976.

Old Houses into New Homes, Cmd. 3602, 1968.

Ministry of Housing and Local Government, *Report of the Inquiry into the Collapse of Flats at Ronan Point*, Canning Town, 1968, London: HMSO.

The Guardian, 28 May 1984.

7

Environment, Time, and Space

Between 5 and 8 December 1952 London was hit by smog, in which at least 4,000 people in the Greater London area were thought to have died. These additional deaths were mainly attributed to circulatory and/or respiratory difficulties.[1] Smog was a physical and linguistic mix of smoke and fog, with the smoke resulting from the incomplete combustion of coal and heavy oil so as to result in the emission of sulphur dioxide and impurities. Smog reduced visibility and exacerbated bronchitis and breathing difficulties. Reduced visibility caused a performance of La Traviata at Sadler's Wells on 6 December 1952 to be stopped after the first act as the theatre filled with fog.[2] Bronchitis was a common and potentially serious condition after World War II. In Britain in 1951, the death rates from bronchitis for men and women were 107.9 and 62.7 per 100,000 in England and Wales compared with 2.2 and 1.9 in Denmark, and 5.0 and 4.0 in Sweden.[3] The difference was attributed largely to the effects of smoke and sulphur dioxide pollution in a more urban country with low chimneys and bituminous coal being burnt in open grates.[4]

Smogs were essentially local urban events. During the post-war period both the spatial and temporal dimensions of pollution and debate about environmental issues widened and lengthened. The problem of pollution moved from being a local issue of smog and smoke, through the cross-country problem of acid rain, to ultimately becoming the global problem of greenhouse gases (GHGs) and global warming. As the spatial extent of pollution widened, so too did temporal concerns for its effects lengthen, notably in the case of global warming raising the question of what a current generation should do to mitigate the effects of pollution on future, as yet unborn, generations. This valuation of the future in terms of the present brought the social discount rate to the centre of discussions among economists with arguments as to what this rate should be. Disagreements also persisted as to the appropriate mechanisms for addressing environmental issues. The political and industrial approach

---

[1] Sheail, *Environmental History of Twentieth-Century Britain*, p. 248.
[2] *The Times*, 9 December, 1952, p. 8, col. D.   [3] Gloag, 'Air pollutants', p. 723.
[4] Scarrow, 'The impact of British domestic air pollution', p. 261.

favoured quantifying the amount of permitted pollution and then distributing and/or selling the right to pollute. The economists' preferred approach was to reflect the social cost of the pollution commonly by imposing a tax, which could rise over time as the additional flow of pollution added to the existing stock of pollutants and thereby increased the damage caused (damage being a function of the size of the stock). Ultimately, in the response to GHGs, it proved politically difficult to introduce a carbon tax, and the quantitative approach of issuing permits to pollute was preferred. This was unsurprising, indeed almost familiar. The economic theory of the use of taxation to reflect the social costs of negative externalities had been set out by the Cambridge economist A.C. Pigou in the 1920s.[5] In the year, 1953, following the London Smog, the Oxford economist, Ian Little, had devoted an entire book, *The Price of Fuel*, as to how coal should be priced so as to reflect its resource costs, rather than being subject to price controls such that the rationing of domestic coal persisted until 1958 in the United Kingdom.[6] Yet the response to the London Smog of 1952 was legislative and administrative, an eschewing of the economic approach which was to be very recognizable some fifty years later when considering approaches to reducing the emissions of carbon dioxide and other GHGs.

Space, Smog, and Legislation

Following the smog of December 1952, the Beaver Committee on Air Pollution was (eventually) appointed in July 1953.[7] It confirmed the domestic fire as the worst offender, with about half of atmospheric smoke emanating from this source (the remainder being from industry and railways). The committee confirmed the local nature of the problem, a map created by the Beaver Committee providing the basis for an informal designation of 325 local authorities in England and Wales as 'black areas' of exceptionally heavy pollution. These were mostly the large conurbations although with the conspicuous exception of London, virtually all of the black areas containing nearly 40% of the population of England were located in the northern parts of the country.[8]

In turn, the local nature of the problem was reflected in the response of the national central government. Having taken seven months after December

[5] Pigou, *The Economics of Welfare*.   [6] Little, *The Price of Fuel*.
[7] Ashby and Anderson, 'Studies in the politics of environmental protection'.
[8] TNA CAB 134/3350, 'Background information', para. 6.40. Scarrow, 'The impact of British domestic air pollution', p. 263.

1952 smog to appoint the Beaver committee, following the publication of the committee's report in November 1954 it was only an initiative by the MP Gerald Nabarro to introduce a Private Member's Clean Air Bill that prompted government to write its own Clean Air Bill. Even then, government was originally only willing to provide half the cost of adapting fireplaces to burn smokeless fuels from public funds, 37.5% from the Exchequer and 12.5% from the local authority. Consideration was also given to making any new regulation applicable only to new projects, such that while all benefited from cleaner air only a few new marginal polluters would pay. Eventually the Treasury agreed to meet 40% of the costs of adapting domestic fireplaces, with not less than 30% of the cost being met by the relevant local authority.[9]

Similarly, power and responsibility for the implementation of the legislation lay at the local level. The 1956 Clean Air Act gave local authorities powers to control dark smoke emissions and to declare areas to be 'smokeless', although often its emphasis on action by, and at the discretion of, local authorities only confirmed what was already happening. In 1946, Manchester had obtained through a private act powers to establish smokeless areas, and by 1956, nineteen additional local authorities had obtained similar powers by private act. By the same token, many local authorities had not taken much, if any, action. In all, while the Beaver Committee estimated that the domestic smoke control programme would take no more than ten to fifteen years to complete, by 1970 only twelve local authorities had completed their programmes, and the median estimated completion date for the remainder was 1975. By far the greatest progress was made in Greater London, where by 1970 nearly three-quarters of its acreage and premises were covered with control orders. In contrast, the local authorities in the Northern Region and the Midlands had accomplished only about one-third or less of their targets.[10] Annual progress was best described as steady(Table 7.1). In one of its few reports and only after prompting by the new Department of the Environment, in 1972 the Clean Air Council investigated why some local authorities in North East England had still not declared nineteen of the Beaver Report's 'black' areas as smoke control zones. A mixture of greater concern with local unemployment, the local importance of coal mining in Northumberland and Durham as well as miners' receipt of free coal all played a role.[11] There may also have been a mixture of concerns with free-riding and externalities. Of sixty-six authorities which had attained progress of 50% or more, sixty were contiguous to another in the

[9] Sheail, *Environmental History*, p. 249.
[10] Scarrow, 'The impact of British domestic air pollution', pp. 262, 265.
[11] Giussani, 'The UK Clean Air Act'.

Table 7.1. Progress of smoke control in England, 1964–1970

	Central plus local government grant (£m)	Number of premises covered in Black Areas (thousands)	Percentage of total premises in Black Areas converted (%)
1 April 1964	5.4*	–	–
1 April 1965	2.4	2,277**	27.8
1 April 1966	2.7	335	4.0
1 April 1967	3.8	463	7.8
1 April 1968	4.8	418	5.4
1 April 1969	4.5	353	4.5
1 April 1970	4.5	331	4.2
TOTAL	28.1	4,177	53.7

*From start of Clean Air Act to 1 April 1964.
**From start of Clean Air Act to 1 April 1965.
Source: TNA AB15/7734, Programmes Analysis Unit, P.A.U. M. 20, 'An economic and technical appraisal of air pollution in the United Kingdom', 1972, Didcot, Berks: HMSO,Table II.5.

group; and of the forty-seven authorities which had reached less than 10% of their goal, forty-one were contiguous.[12] Reducing your emissions benefited your neighbour who might then continue to pollute your shared atmosphere. The smaller the authority, then the more likely this was to be so.

Nevertheless, smoke emissions did diminish. Between 1956 and 1966 smoke emissions from domestic sources declined by 38%, with Greater London leading the way with a reduction of 76% from the Midlands at 30%, and the remainder of the North at 21%.[13] Total smoke produced in factories in Britain fell from 2.3 million tonnes in 1953 to 0.9 million tonnes in 1968. Although urban population and industrial output increased during the 1960s, the average smoke concentration in urban areas in Britain fell by 60% and sulphur oxide concentrations fell by 30%.[14] In general, annual average urban concentrations of smoke fell by over 80% between the mid-60s and mid-80s while average ground-level concentrations of sulphur dioxide had fallen by more than 70% since 1960.[15]

Smoke emissions reduced even when local authorities did little. In York, the local authorities did not start to implement smoke control zoning until 1970 and this was not completed until 1990, but York experienced its greatest decline in concentrations between 1960 and 1970.[16] Within smokeless areas, householders had often already converted to smokeless appliances by the time their area was scheduled to become smokeless and therefore did not apply for

[12] Scarrow, 'The impact of British domestic air pollution', p. 265.
[13] Scarrow, 'The impact of British domestic air pollution', p. 271.
[14] Beckerman, *Small Is Stupid*, p. 6.   [15] Weidner, *Clean Air Policy in Great Britain*.
[16] Giussani, 'The UK Clean Air Act'; Brimblecombe and Bowler, 'The history of air pollution in York England'.

the conversion grant. In 1960 in London the number of conversions required was only 24%, 76% of the householders having already converted or for other reasons failed to claim the grant due to them. Another survey of the London area conducted in 1963 put the figure of voluntary conversions at 60%.[17] The increasing use of gas and electricity for domestic heating allied to the virtual disappearance of domestic servants to clear grates, changes in household occupation as women went to work, and increased efficiency of fuel burn and dispersion from industrial and commercial sources all contributed to the fall in smoke emissions (Table 7.2).[18]

Smogs continued to occur, but less often and with less serious consequences. Between 3 and 7 December 1962, smog in London was associated with an estimated 340 deaths.[19] While the sulphur dioxide concentrations in

Table 7.2. Consumption of fuels in Great Britain, 1952–1967 (million tonnes)

	1952	1954	1956	1958	1960	1962	1964	1966*	1967*
Coal									
– Domestic use	37.3	38.7	37.9	36.6	34.6	32.9	28.0	25.5	23.0
– Electricity works	35.5	39.6	45.6	46.1	51.1	60.4	67.4	67.9	66.6
– Railways	14.1	13.6	12.8	11.3	9.5	6.7	4.2	1.7	0.8
– Industry	63.3	64.6	60.4	52.1	47.2	42.0	38.5	36.0	30.9
– Coke ovens	25.1	26.6	29.3	27.8	28.5	23.5	25.5	24.3	23.1
– Gas works	27.7	27.3	27.8	24.8	22.3	22.1	20.2	16.7	14.4
Coke									
– Domestic use**	3.0	3.8	4.2	4.1	4.8	5.4	6.0	6.4	6.3
– Blast furnaces	11.3	11.9	13.1	11.4	13.0	10.6	11.8	10.6	9.9
– Industry	18.1	18.1	17.4	16.2	15.3	15.0	12.9	11.7	11.5
Oil									
– Motor spirit	5.3	5.8	6.2	6.5	7.4	8.3	9.8	11.5	12.3
– Kerosene	1.4	1.3	1.4	1.5	1.5	1.6	1.6	1.8	1.9
Gas diesel oil									
– derv oil	1.2	1.4	1.8	2.0	2.5	3.0	3.6	4.0	4.3
– other users	1.6	1.9	2.4	3.0	3.5	4.5	5.9	7.5	8.0
Fuel oil									
– electricity works	0.1	0.2	0.3	2.5	5.3	5.5	5.3	6.8	7.3
– other users	3.4	4.2	6.1	8.0	11.7	15.4	18.8	22.8	24.5
Refinery fuel	1.2	1.9	2.2	2.5	3.3	3.7	4.0	4.6	4.7

*Estimates.

**Including other manufactured solid smokeless fuels.

Source: TNA AB15/7734, Programmes Analysis Unit, P.A.U. M. 20, 'An economic and technical appraisal of air pollution in the United Kingdom', 1972, Didcot, Berks: HMSO, Table II.1.

---

[17] Scarrow, 'Impact', p. 278.   [18] Giussani, 'The UK Clean Air Act'.
[19] Newbery, 'Acid rain', p. 310; Park, *Acid Rain*, p. 127; Pearce and Markandya, *Environmental Policy Benefits*.

December 1962 were similar to those of 1952, there was now less smoke (Tables 7.3 and 7.4). That this time an estimated 340 died suggested that the earlier episode was so deadly because of synergistic interactions between smoke particles and SO_2. As the 'smoke blanket' reduced, so could sunlight get through to warm the air near the ground, so breaking up the temperature inversions that caused gases as well as particles to become trapped at a low level. As smoke reduced, so visibility improved. It became possible to see right across London most of the winter as the average hours of winter sunshine in London doubled during the 1960s, and average winter visibility improved

Table 7.3. Emissions of sulphur dioxide in Great Britain, 1952–1965 (million tonnes)

	1952	1954	1956	1958	1960	1962	1964	1966	1967
Coal – domestic use	0.9	0.93	0.91	0.94	0.89	0.84	0.72	0.65	0.59
– electricity works	0.95	1.06	1.22	1.32	1.46	1.73	1.93	2.02	1.88
– railways	0.38	0.37	0.35	0.33	0.27	0.19	0.12	0.05	0.02
– industry	1.72	1.75	1.63	1.50	1.36	1.21	1.11	1.04	0.97
– coke ovens	0.1	0.11	0.12	0.11	0.11	0.09	0.10	0.09	0.08
– gas works	0.2	0.2	0.2	0.18	0.16	0.16	0.15	0.12	0.1
Coke – domestic use	0.07	0.08	0.09	0.09	0.1	0.11	0.12	0.14	0.14
– industry	0.42	0.43	0.41	0.38	0.35	0.35	0.3	0.15	0.14
Oil – motor spirit & kerosene	0.01	0.01	0.01	0.02	0.02	0.02	0.02	0.02	0.02
– gas diesel oil	0.04	0.05	0.06	0.08	0.07	0.09	0.11	0.13	0.15
– fuel oil, electricity works	0.01	0.01	0.01	0.14	0.41	0.43	0.4	0.49	0.47
– fuel oil, other users	0.22	0.29	0.40	0.51	0.74	0.94	1.13	1.35	1.46
TOTAL	5.02	5.29	5.41	5.60	5.94	6.16	6.21	6.25	6.02

Source: TNA AB15/7734, Programmes Analysis Unit, P.A.U. M. 20, 'An economic and technical appraisal of air pollution in the United Kingdom', 1972, Didcot, Berks: HMSO, Table II.3.

Table 7.4. Emissions of smoke in Great Britain, 1952–1965 (million tonnes)

	1952	1954	1956	1958	1960	1962	1964	1966	1967
Coal – domestic use	1.26	1.31	1.27	1.23	1.16	1.10	0.92	0.83	0.75
– railways	0.28	0.27	0.26	0.23	0.19	0.13	0.08	0.03	0.02
– industry	0.76	0.78	0.73	0.50	0.35	0.21	0.19	0.11	0.10
TOTAL	2.30	2.36	2.26	1.96	1.70	1.44	1.19	0.97	0.87

Source: TNA AB15/7734, Programmes Analysis Unit, P.A.U. M. 20, 'An economic and technical appraisal of air pollution in the United Kingdom', 1972, Didcot, Berks: HMSO, Table II.4.

from being one mile in 1958 to averaging four by the early 1970s.[20] In general, pollution improved sufficiently in London for magpies to return to nesting in Hyde Park for the first time in living ornithological memory.

The fall in sulphur dioxide emissions lagged that of smoke. The total quantity of sulphur oxides emitted into the air began to decline from around 1962 and the concentration of sulphur dioxide in urban centres fell by about one-third during the 1960s.[21] Sulphur was pushed higher into the air by taller chimneys although most of the sulphur emitted reached the ground within 100 km of the point of emission.[22] Lichens, which are sensitive to sulphur dioxide levels, began to return, including some not seen since 1800. When a two-day fog, the worst since 1962, enveloped London in December 1975 the consequences for health were less serious than previously. Hourly readings for sulphur dioxide of over 500g/m^3 and daily mean sulphur dioxide concentrations of over 1000 tg/m^3 (five or six times the winter average) at many sites were under one-sixth of the 1962 values (and in 1952, forty-eight-hour averages of 3700ug/m^3 were recorded).[23]

Acid Rain

Ironically, one effect of emitting from taller chimneys was to push a greater proportion of sulphur emissions overseas where they contributed to an increase in acid rain (more properly acidic deposition) downwind from the source. Some of the sulphur emitted, whether from high-level or low-level sources, travelled long distances (in some cases 1,000 km or more) and as sulphur dioxide along with nitrogen oxides and chlorides it precipitated over the mountains of Southern Scandinavia to fall as an acid rain mix of sulphuric acid, nitric acid, and hydrochloric acid. In time the effects of acid rain became apparent as trees died, lakes became acidified, and fish were killed. The UK was a net exporter of airborne sulphur and the largest single contributor to the acid rain falling on southern Norway.[24] Acid rain refers to the deposition of the acidic combustion products sulphur dioxide, SO_2, various nitrogen oxides, NOx, and chloride, Cl-, either as dry gases or particles, or as wet deposits

[20] Beckerman, *Small Is Stupid*, p. 6.   [21] Beckerman, *Small Is Stupid*, p. 6.
[22] TNA CAB 134/4024, Official Committee on Environmental Protection, Working Group, 'Sulphur Pollution', 23 November 1976, para. 1.4.
[23] Gloag, 'Air pollutants', pp. 723–4.
[24] TNA CAB 134/4024, Official Committee on Environmental Protection, Working Group, 'Sulphur Pollution', 23 November 1976, para. 3.9; Sheail, *Environmental History*, p. 252; OECD, *The OECD Programme on Long Range Transport of Air Pollutants*.

in rain, snow, sleet, hail, mist, or fog. Acid rain can have indirect effects by releasing toxic heavy metals and aluminium into water supplies. Most SO_2 came from large combustion plants. In 1987, 85% came from such combustion plants, and 73% from power stations. Of UK emissions from fossil fuel combustion, 79% came from coal combustion and 12% from fuel oil. Only part of total SO_2 emissions come from man-made sources; other important sources include volcanoes, biological decay, and forest fires. These natural sources might account for 80–290 million tonnes per annum worldwide, compared to total man-made emissions of 75–100 million tonnes.[25]

Acid rain was one of the foremost examples of regional air pollution and received worldwide attention because acidification damages were often the result of the atmospheric transport of sulphur and nitrogen emissions across state and/or national boundaries. In Europe, acidic deposition crossed national boundaries, with Scandinavian countries (principally) concerned with acidification damage resulting from emissions coming from the United Kingdom and the central and eastern European countries[26] Scandinavian concern with acid rain grew from the 1960s[27] and attracted increased attention in the US in the 1970s following the discovery of acidic lakes and the possible loss of native brook trout in the Adirondack Mountain region of New York.[28] North-eastern states were concerned about emissions transported primarily from states in the Midwest and, to a lesser extent, from south-eastern Canada. Concern with nitrogen oxide emissions also grew in the 1970s, with the issue first being raised by the US Department of Transportation in 1971 in relation to nitrogen oxide emissions from supersonic aircraft.[29] While in both Europe and the United States, the primary motivating factor for regulations to control SO_2 emissions before the 1970s was concern for local public health, damage to natural ecosystems received little or no attention.[30] This was to change, not least because of Scandinavian concerns with the effects of acid rain. In 1969, the Scandinavians began to push for an international conference to discuss acid rain, and this formed an important part of the background to the decision of the UN General Assembly in 1969 to convene in Stockholm in 1972 the United Nations Conference on the Human Environment.[31]

---

[25] Newbery, 'Acid Rain', pp. 301, 305.   [26] Menz and Seip, 'Acid rain', p. 253.

[27] Oden, 'The Acidification of Air Precipitation'. W.C. Brøgger first established the occurrence of long-range transport of pollutants from the United Kingdom to Norway. Brøgger, 'Note on a contaminated snowfall', cited in Menz and Seip, 'Acid rain in Europe and the United States'.

[28] Oden, 'The Acidification of Air Precipitation'; Schofield, 'Acid precipitation'.

[29] Sandler, Global Collective Action, p. 226.

[30] Menz and Seip, 'Acid rain in Europe and the United States', p. 254; Newbery, 'Acid Rain', p. 310.

[31] TNA CAB 134/3350, 'Background information on Environmental Protection', 11 September 1970, para. 11.11.

The 1972 United Nations Conference on the Human Environment was the first major international conference on environmental issues and it signalled an important and growing role for the UN itself in investigating and seeking to resolve global environmental problems. Importantly, research was initiated to track the diffusion and depositing of sulphur. The Air Management Group of the Organisation for Economic Co-Operation and Development (OECD) launched a cooperative study of the movement of sulphur compounds within north-west Europe.[32] In 1977, the Co-operative Programme for Monitoring and Evaluation of the Long-Range Transmission of Air Pollutants in Europe (EMEP) was initiated to measure the transport, emission, and deposition of sulphur and NOx.[33] Its findings were important in demonstrating how, for large countries in particular, much of their pollution fell on to their own land. Conversely, the smaller a country was, the more the country was sinned against than sinning. Britain stood out as the greatest sinner, and the Scandinavian countries as those most sinned against.[34] Seeing the EMEP matrix measurement results, countries began to understand that they had much to gain from limiting their own emissions, particularly in the case of sulphur.[35] On 13 November 1979, the Long-Range Transboundary Air Pollution Convention (LRTAP) was adopted at a high-level meeting of the UN Economic Commission for Europe on the Protection of the Environment. The Convention was ratified on 16 March 1983 and virtually all of Europe signed up. On 8 July 1985, the Helsinki Protocol to the LRTAP was adopted and committed ratifiers to reduce sulphur emissions by 30% based on 1980 levels, as soon as possible or by 1993. The Protocol entered into force on 2 September 1987.

The information provided by EMEP increased the incentives for larger countries in particular to reduce their sulphur emissions, since much of it fell in their own country. As with the later concern to reduce CO_2 emissions, there was a tension between a political and administrative instinct to reduce emissions in general and the economist's instinct to compare the marginal costs and benefits of reducing particular emissions.[36] Although acid rain was not a pure public good in that a tonne of sulphur deposited in one place did not land elsewhere, there was only limited scope for adopting the bargaining approach developed by Ronald Coase in which the polluter compensated

[32] TNA CAB 134/4024, Official Committee on Environmental Protection, Working Group, 'Sulphur Pollution', 23 November 1976.
[33] Sandler, *Global Collective Action*, p. 227; Eliassen and Saltbones, 'Modelling of Long-Range Transport of Sulphur over Europe'.
[34] Newbery, 'Acid rain', p. 305.   [35] Sandler, *Global Collective Action*, p. 228.
[36] Newbery, 'Acid rain', pp. 336.

the polluted for the damage caused.[37] Acid rain fell over a number of countries and varied day-to-day in the value of the damage caused in each country according to what was damaged and its local value. The same quantity of pollution from the same power station might therefore have a differing social cost from one day-to-another. Equally the value of the electricity generated varied according to time of day. One means of reducing sulphur dioxide emissions was to fit Flue Gas Desulphurization (FGD) equipment to power stations. This in turn would also vary in terms of cost per tonne SO_2 depending on whether an integrated FGD system could be installed at the time of construction of a new station, or whether it had to be retrofitted. If it was retrofitted, the cost would depend on the number of gigawatt (GW) hours the plant would produce over the remainder of its life. For a base load plant with a long expected life, the cost would be low, but for a plant near the end of its life, or one which was primarily used for peaking, the cost would be high.[38]

As well as the EMEP data emphasizing the incentives for large countries to limit their sulphur emissions for their own national benefit, acid rain also provided an occasion for the use of licences to pollute. Initially easier to negotiate than taxes at an international level and agreeable to current pollutants if the free distribution of licences reflected current polluting activity, licences transferred the cost of abatement to consumers.

Significantly, progress in reducing nitrous oxide emissions was slower. NOx emissions were lighter than sulphur, stayed in the air longer and travelled further. While a higher proportion of SO_2 was deposited within 100 km of the source, and a larger fraction of SO_2 came from stationary sources, predominantly power stations, nitrogen oxides were produced both by large stationary sources and by numerous small mobile sources such as road vehicles. The cost of reducing automobile emissions was high, the health gains small, and the ecological benefits uncertain. Against that, it was probably cheap to reduce NOx emissions from stationary sources, using better burner designs and chemical additives.[39] In the case of NOX emissions, protocols were much slower and less stringent. On 31 October, the Sofia Protocol was signed, requiring reductions in NOX to return emissions to 1987 levels by 31 December 1994. The Protocol did not enter into force until 14 February 1991.[40]

The convening of the first UN Conference on the Human Environment in Stockholm in 1972 also reflected a more general growing interest in environmental issues. As the historian Keith Thomas noted, as late as 1967

[37] Coase, 'The problem of social cost'.   [38] Newbery, 'Acid rain', pp. 320–1.
[39] Newbery, 'Acid rain', pp. 320, 336.   [40] Sandler, *Global Collective Action*, p. 229.

the *Encyclopedia of Philosophy* had no entry for 'environment' but proceeded straight from 'entropy' to 'Epictetus'.[41] Between 1967 and 1973, three books were published which were not only to become staples of reading lists on environmental issues, but which were also bought by the general public. These books were Edward Mishan's 1967 *The Costs of Economic Growth*, the Club of Rome *Report* of 1972 with its Malthusian warnings of population growth outstretching the natural resources of the planet, and in 1973 there was E. F. Schumacher's *Small is Beautiful*.[42] All three publications were written by economists. In 1967 Mishan was Reader in Economics at the London School of Economics. Schumacher had served as Economic Advisor with the British Control Commission in Germany (1946–1950) before becoming Economic Adviser (1950–1970) at the National Coal Board. The Club of Rome was a collection of thirty individuals including economists and scientists from ten counties who gathered first in April 1968 in the Accademia dei Lincei in Rome at the instigation of Dr Aurelio Peccei, an Italian industrialist.[43] What was new by the 1970s was the level of public interest in what economists had to say on such matters. This reflected an increased public awareness and concern at perceived environmental depredation, such that Professor George Steiner thought it 'very likely the most important revolution of feeling since the Second World War'.[44] Reflecting such concern, the UK government established the Royal Commission on Environmental Pollution in 1970 as well as the world's first Department of the Environment.[45] Yet while books by economists reflected and captured this heightened public interest, economists themselves were by no means in agreement as to the nature of, and response to, perceived environmental problems. Particular scepticism, at times bordering on scorn, was reserved for *The Club of Rome Report* with some branding the Club of Rome model as 'worthless'.[46] Some economists shifted from eco-sympathy to eco-scepticism. The Oxford economist Wilfred Beckerman was initially happy to review Mishan's book favourably and to urge the importance of environmental issues so strongly on his friend Anthony Crosland that he, Beckerman, found himself appointed to the Royal Commission on Environmental Pollution which Crosland established in 1970. It was only then that, as Beckerman recalled, 'within a few weeks of taking up my appointment

---

[41] K. Thomas, introduction, p. 3, Taylor, *Ethics and the Environment*.
[42] Mishan, *Costs of Economic Growth*; Meadows, Meadows, Randers, and Behrens, *The Limits to Growth*; Schumacher, *Small is Beautiful*.
[43] Meadows, Meadows, Randers, and Behrens, *The Limits to Growth*, p. 9.
[44] Thomas, introduction, p. 3; Steiner, *The Listener*, 537.
[45] Grove-White, 'The rise of the environmental movement', p. 45.
[46] Kay and Mirrlees, 'The desirability of natural resource depletion'.

and studying the evidence, I discovered, somewhat to my embarrassment, that the impression I had gained from the media, and from much environmentalist literature about pollution trends of the exhaustion of finite resources, was quite false.'[47] Later, amidst concern about global warming, Beckerman was to express his politically incorrect scepticism in a book entitled with a taunting nod towards Schumacher, *Small Is Stupid: Blowing the Whistle on the Greens*. He and other economists were also to disagree strongly with the main recommendations of the 2006 Stern Review of *The Economics of Climate Change* on the timing, cost, and benefits of action to mitigate climate change.[48]

Why environmental issues became of increased concern towards the end of the 1960s is not entirely clear. It is common to read references to the publication of Rachel Carson's book *Silent Spring* in 1962 as having triggered heightened environmental concerns, but there is a problem of cause and effect here.[49] After all, the London smog which was thought to have caused the death of 800 people between 27 November and the beginning of December 1948, and claimed a further 4,000 lives four years later between 5 and 8 December 1952 was not followed by an increased general concern for environmental issues. While shocking, the television pictures of seabirds struggling to fly with wings covered in oil after the wreck of the Liberian-registered oil tanker the Torrey Canyon between the Islands of Scilly and Land's End on 18 March 1967 does not of itself explain the heightened interest in environmental issues from the later 1960s. As bombs were dropped on the oil slick in an effort to ignite it, and 40,000 tonnes of the tanker's 117,000 tonnes of Kuwait crude oil was washed on to Cornish beaches, the disaster provided one of the more dramatic televisual reminders of the cost of energy.[50] But then so too had the Aberfan disaster of 21 October 1966 when a coal slag heap had slid down onto the village below, killing 144 people, 116 of them children. Yet paradoxically, visible, tangible, physical evidence of environmental problems was not what the environmental movement thrived on. Slag heaps, smog, oil spills could all potentially be stopped or at least reduced. It was when environmental problems were less visible, because they were at a distance in space and/or in time, that they seemed to acquire a heightened fearful grip. What was striking about many of the environmental issues which caught people's attention from the 1970s was their lengthening spatial and temporal distance.

[47] Beckerman, *Small Is Stupid*, p. 6.   [48] Stern, *The Economics of Climate Change*.
[49] Carson, *Silent Spring*.   [50] Sheail, *An Environmental History*, p. 221.

CFCs and the Ozone Hole

The problem of chloroflurocarbons (CFCs) and their impact on the ozone layer provided an interesting comparison with both the case of acid rain and the later concerns with GHGs. While the theory of how chlorine from CFCs might break down ozone was developed by Mario Molina and Frank Sherwood Rowland in 1974, it was only the chance discovery in 1983 of the extent of depletion of ozone levels over the Antarctic by Joe Farman, Brian Gardiner, and Jonathan Shanklin of the British Antarctic Survey which gave worrying empirical evidence to support the theorizing.[51] When a paper reporting the results was submitted to *Nature* in 1985, one of the referees commented: 'This is impossible. However, if it is true, it is important'.[52] In the light of the British Antarctic Survey evidence in 1985 that there was an alarming 40% decline (from 1964 levels) in the springtime atmospheric concentration of ozone over Halley Bay, Antarctica, serious attention was paid to the problem of curbing the international release of ozone-depleting substances.[53] Important among these were chlorofluorocarbons (CFCs) which by the early 1970s were widely used in aerosol sprays, refrigerators, air conditioning units, and in plastic foam. While CFCs emitted from, say, refrigerators were safe in the lower atmosphere, once they had risen slowly into the stratosphere, 10–14 kilometres above the earth, they were broken down by the sun's ultraviolet radiation and chlorine released. Over the Antarctic the strong winter winds (the polar vortex) isolated the Antarctic atmosphere and delayed the bonding and stabilization of chlorine with other atoms, such that chlorine began to accumulate in great volume. When the spring sun shone on Antarctica, the ultraviolet rays released the chlorine with depletion effects on the ozone layer. The ability of the ozone layer to prevent harmful ultraviolet radiation from reaching the Earth's surface was thereby reduced, the increased exposure to ultraviolet radiation not only retarding plant growth, harming plankton, and damaging polymers, but also causing cataracts, immune suppression, and skin cancers including melanomas.[54] Here was not a transboundary problem, but a global one.

---

[51] They published their findings in *Nature* 28 June 1974. In 1995 the Nobel Prize in Chemistry was awarded jointly to Mario Molina, Frank Sherwood Rowland (and Paul Crutzen) for their work in atmospheric chemistry particularly concerning the formation and decomposition of ozone. Aisling Irwin, 'An environmental fairy tale', The Molina-Rowland chemical equations and the CFC problem', in Farmelo (ed.), *It Must Be Beautiful*.

[52] Farman, Gardiner, and Shanklin, 'Large losses of total ozone'; Farman, 'First Person feature'.

[53] Sandler, *Global Collective Action*, p. 214. Previous restrictive measures had been taken in the United States.

[54] Barrett, *Why Cooperate?*, pp. 75–6.

Ostensibly the restriction of CFCs required a global agreement for all to stop using CFCs and to switch to alternatives. Theoretically, efforts to reach international agreement and to take effective action would be bedevilled by the problem of free-riding. In practice, however, because the United States was so directly affected by the depletion of the ozone layer it was prepared to carry free-riders. This motivation was greatly bolstered by two Environmental Protection Agency reports in 1987 which estimated that a 50% cut in CFC emissions from 1986 levels could save the United States $64 trillion by 2075 in reduced costs associated with skin cancers. In the long-run the costs from cutting CFC use were estimated at anywhere between $20 and $40 billion during the 1989–2075 period, given the projected CFC use growth rates.[55] So, unlike acid rain which was rival (what landed in one place did not land elsewhere), the depletion of the ozone layer was a global good (or bad) but whose consequences significantly affected the developed economies, notably the United States. The willingness of the United States to finance moves towards the use of available substitutes and to carry free-riders was crucial to the success of the Montreal Protocol on Substances that Deplete the Ozone Layer of 1987 (hereafter Montreal Protocol). Almost symbolically, in August a month before the Montreal Protocol was adopted, President Ronald Reagan had a skin cancer removed from the tip of his nose. Cost–benefit calculations by Scott Barrett indicated that for the United States the benefit which it would receive by implementing Montreal, assuming that other countries did nothing, exceeded the cost by 65 to 1. Such calculations rested in part on estimates of the opportunity cost of saving a statistical life, i.e. what would it cost to reduce the number of deaths each year by some other means such as improving road safety. While not enjoying such a high benefit:cost ratio as the United States, many developed countries with white-skinned people who were vulnerable to skin cancer were also willing to finance the implementation of the Montreal Protocol. Belgium, Canada, Norway, and Sweden all banned the use of CFCs in aerosols at the same time as the US. In the first renegotiation of the Montreal Protocol, held in London in 1990, the industrialized country parties agreed to pay for the 'incremental costs' of implementation by developing countries. This meant that developing countries could not be made worse off by acceding to the agreement; they could only gain.[56]

In sharp contrast, in the case of GHGs, the United States was the largest producer of carbon dioxide and the worst effects of climate change would not be visited on it but on the less developed economies. In 1996 of the world's

---

[55] Sandler, *Global Collective Action*, p. 214.   [56] Barrett, *Why Cooperate?*, pp. 26, 76, 79–81.

total emissions of carbon dioxide, the USA accounted for 22.2%; China 14.1%; Russian Federation 6.6%; Japan 4.9%; India 4.2%; Germany 3.6%; UK 2.3%.[57] In contrast to the effects of the CFCs, the main effects of a rise in global warming were likely to fall on the tropical and subtropical low-income regions of the world. These poorer countries were the least able to mitigate climate change. The incentives to carry free-riders were seriously reduced and made notions of basing Kyoto on the 1987 Montreal Protocol inappropriate. In the case of GHGs, the incentives to inaction were significant. The marginal cost of abatement rose as the marginal benefit fell, essentially as the easiest and cheapest means of making reductions were tried first and completed. Investment to reduce emissions had opportunity costs not least in terms of investment in adapting to, rather than resisting, climate change. In part it was the difficulty of solving public goods problems once they went beyond national boundaries. While free-riding will occur within a nation, it may be more tolerable and might even be compensated for or offset through redistributive mechanisms.

Property Rights, the Tragedy of the Commons, and Fishing

One response to the problem of GHGs was to issue licences to pollute. This ability to issue licences proceeds from the establishment of property rights over the natural resource of the atmosphere. Essentially the argument made was that in the absence of property rights a resource would be over-consumed (above a judged rate of sustainability), pollution being viewed as the consumption of the global good that is the atmosphere. Often cited in this context is an article by Garrett Hardin titled 'The Tragedy of the Commons' and published in the journal *Science* in 1968.[58] Hardin's main themes were subsequently developed by economists and political scientists, including Elinor Ostrom who in 2009 was awarded a Nobel Prize in economics for her work in this area.[59] Although 'The Tragedy of the Commons' is sometimes referred to as concerning an absence of property rights, 'commons' in that sense is misleading since common ownership, and therefore the ability to restrict entry, could exist. In local commons, assets are owned by small communities who know each other. Actions are observable, reputation matters and community

---

[57] Sandler, *Global Collective Action*, p. 222.   [58] Hardin, 'The Tragedy of the Commons'.
[59] Ostrom, *Governing the Commons*.

pressure is potentially powerful.[60] Little of this is true of the global commons, and crucially, unlike the village community or even the national government, there is no global government able to ensure compliance or to offset taxes in one area by benefits elsewhere.[61] As a global good the incentives to reduce pollution of the atmosphere were reduced by the problem of free-riding which arose when no one could be excluded from benefiting even if they did not contribute.[62] This differed from the small group prisoners' dilemma in game theory which is a problem of the availability and distribution of information. If both prisoners were interviewed together in the same room and were able to look and speak to each other, it was much more likely that even if they continued to distrust each other that they would say nothing and walk free. With global atmospheric pollution, everyone could sit in the same room informed to the hilt and still have individual incentives to contribute little or nothing.[63] While with the prisoners the actions of the individual have a causal effect on the outcome, they do not in the large group problem. While Prisoners' Dilemmas can give rise to collective action failures, not all collective action failures are Prisoners' Dilemmas.[64]

In general, it is probably better to think of the 'Tragedy of the Commons' as a problem of open access, which in turn might well arise from an absence of property rights.[65] Where, as with the atmosphere, no one owns the resource and therefore no one can charge for its use, then this is an open-access resource. Issues of open access are particularly relevant when a balance has to be struck between the flow and stock of a resource. Pollution is a flow of pollutants being added to an existing stock. Fishing causes a flow of fish away from the existing stock. The impact of changes in the rate of flow of pollution depends in part on the longevity of the stock of pollutants. So, in addition to free-riding issues, that the stock of CFCs in the atmosphere has a shorter life than carbon dioxide causes reductions in the flow to have a higher proportionate impact on solving the problem of the ozone hole problem than on that of global warming. Similarly, the stock of fish depends in part on the speed of reproduction and the minimum size of a sustainable stock. The costs of flow depend in part on the characteristics of the stock. Into such considerations, then intrude differences between private and social/public perspectives. One

---

[60] For evidence of local fishing communities' ability to restrict catches voluntarily, see Berkes, 'Fishermen and the "Tragedy of the Commons"'; Berkes (ed.), *Common Property Resources*; McCay and Acheson, *The Question of the Commons*; Woodhatch and Crean, 'The gentleman's agreements'.
[61] Seabright, 'Managing Local Commons', p. 114.   [62] Sandler, *Global Collective Action*, p. 47.
[63] Tuck, *Free Riding*, p. 19; Buchanan, 'Ethical rules'.
[64] Sandler, *Global Collective Action*, p. 25.
[65] Turner, Pearce, and Bateman, *Environmental Economics*, p. 80.

individual taking one more boat into a fishery sees his/her private costs. Theoretically he/she will maximize current profit until marginal revenue falls below marginal cost. So long as profits remain available, boats will continue to enter the fishery. As each boat enters, so it increases the fishing costs of other boats as they now have to travel further and fish for longer to make their catch. This effect is an externality, a cost arising from one person's activity for which a charge cannot be made. Such negative externalities are likely to be common in an open-access resource and in fishing they include stock externalities, which arise if the cost of catching fish increases as the fish population falls; gear externalities, which result if the type of fishing gear used affects the rate of growth of the population; crowding externalities, resulting from congestion of vessels on grounds where the stock is concentrated in a small area; and 'fish-stock' externalities, which result from the fact that in many cases, predation by man is a disturbance in the trophic chain, or food cycle, of a complex ecological system.[66] Because of these externalities, the industry's long-run average cost curve is rising throughout, and is backward-sloping for effort beyond sustainable maximum yield because of the shape of the yield curve.[67] Many of these issues affecting fisheries were set out clearly by Scott and Gordon some fifteen years before Hardin's article.[68]

The question of who owned the sea around a nation's coast became of increasing interest after World War II, largely because of concern with over-fishing and because of increasing interest in off-shore oil extraction. Negotiations over access to coastal waters literally involved negotiations at different levels. On the surface of the sea, the main issue was one of territorial waters and historically concerned questions of national security. Eventually, twelve miles was agreed via the International Court of Justice at The Hague as the extent of territorial limits. Under the sea, there was the question of who had the right to drill into the continental shelf seabed which ran outwards from the coast. The negotiation of the 1958 Geneva Continental Shelf Convention extended the sovereign rights of the littoral states to include the exploration and exploitation of the natural resources of the seabed on the continental shelf to a depth of 200 metres or 'to where the depth of the super adjacent waters admits of the exploitation of natural resources'. The extent of each state's rights depended upon its reaching agreement with other

[66] Butlin, 'Optimal depletion', pp. 97–8; Cheung, 'The structure of a contract'; Scott, 'The fishery'.
[67] Copes, 'The backward-bending supply curve'.
[68] Levhari and Mirman, 'The Great Fish War', p. 323; Scott, 'The Fishery'; Smith, 'Economics of Production'; Gordon, 'The economic theory'; Turvey, 'Optimisation, and sub-optimisation in fisheries regulation'.

bordering countries, and given mutual agreement, the boundary line could be determined by any set of principles. However, failing such agreement Article 6 of the Convention established the principle of equidistance to guide countries that were partners to the Treaty. Between two coastal states, such as the UK and Norway, the boundary line was the median line between them and indeed the line demarcating the UK sector of the North Sea was the result of five separate agreements, each of which was consistent with this principle of equidistance. The principle of equidistance favoured countries like Norway with a long coastline (and a small population).

The question of who was allowed to harvest the resources of the sea in Exclusive Economic Zones (EEZs) was negotiated at the UN Law of the Sea Conferences. The UN convened the first two conferences in Geneva in 1958 and 1960 and the Third Conference began in New York in 1973 and then dragged on moving between meetings in Caracas (20 June to 29 August 1974), Geneva (17 March to 9 May 1975), and New York (15 March to 7 May 1976)[69] until 1982. There were also three UN Food and Agriculture Organization conferences on fishing (1957, 1962, and 1973). As EEZs were discussed, some countries took matters into their own hands. When the 1958 Law of the Sea Conference ended and no agreement had been reached on the width of fishery limits, Iceland, 85–95% of whose export earnings came from fish and fish products, extended its own fishery limits from four to twelve miles in September 1958. The First Cod War ensued between the UK and Iceland and lasted until February 1961, when a three year agreement was struck allowing British boats into certain areas within the twelve mile zone and with any future disputes over fishing limits being referred to the International Court of Justice. In July, 1971, a newly elected coalition government of Iceland declared its intention to establish fifty-mile fishing limits, rejecting the 1961 agreement with the UK government and refusing to accept a role for the International Court of Justice in resolving fishery limit disputes. The Althing (Icelandic Parliament) approved the fifty-mile fishery limit on 15 February 1972. In the second cod war which followed, Royal Navy frigates were used to protect trawlers from the warp-cutting ambitions of Icelandic coastguards, and on 26 May 1973 an Icelandic vessel shelled and hit a British trawler. Iceland used the threat of shutting the Keflavic airbase to NATO planes to bring pressure to bear on the UK and US governments. On 15 October after a meeting between Prime Minister Edward Heath and his Icelandic counterpart, Olafur Johannesson, in London, a two-year agreement was announced. The number and size of British trawlers fishing in Icelandic waters were to be reduced, and

---

[69] TNA 193/129, 'Problems for the Community fishing industry', 22 December 1975.

the catch was to be restricted to an annual harvest 70,000 metric tonnes below the average British catch between 1960 and 1969. Three areas, designated for 'conservation' purposes, were to be closed at specified times to improve spawning, other areas were to be set aside for the exclusive use of the Icelandic small-boat fleet, and the remaining waters between twelve and fifty miles from the Icelandic coast were to be divided into six zones open to British trawlers on a rotating basis.[70] When this agreement expired in November 1975, the third 'Cod War' (November 1975–June 1976) began, with Iceland declaring an extension of its fishing limits to 200 miles (370 km) and again threatening to close the NATO base at Keflavík. This time, UK Prime Minister Harold Wilson and Icelandic PM Mr Geir Hallgrimsson met at Chequers on Saturday 24 January 1976.[71] Ultimately, the UK government agreed that from 1 December 1976 British vessels would not fish within the 200-mile limit, a decision which fell hard on the fishing towns of Grimsby, Hull, and Fleetwood.

In Britain, the approach to the Law of the Sea Conferences and the negotiation of territorial limits, EEZs and the limits of the continental shelf was increasingly complicated by the growing importance of off-shore oil. Initially, the concern was with the differing interests of the inshore and distant-water fishing fleets. Inshore, pelagic fish like herring and mackerel were caught near the surface of the sea. Demersal fish like cod, haddock, and plaice were trawled from the bottom of the sea. Demersal fish formed about 75% of the British catch by volume and about 90% by value.[72] Half of the UK demersal catch was caught in third-country waters, with as much as 70% of the total cod catch being so. The UK distant-water fleet fished to depths of 1200 feet off Newfoundland, Labrador, Greenland, Iceland, the Norway Coast, Bear Island, and grounds in the Barents Sea. Almost without exception these grounds would fall within the UN-projected 200 mile EEZs of other states.[73] This would impact on an industry which, in the run-up to the Third Law of the Sea Conference, was hit by a fourfold rise in fuel prices in 1973–1974.[74] Any phasing out of the distant-water fleet would place 2,000 to 3,000 sea-going employees out of work with many of the areas affected like Humberside and Fleetwood already assisted under regional development policy.[75] In the event, the number of distant-water vessels did decline from 535 in 1969 to 126 at the end of March

---

[70] Mitchell, 'Politics, Fish, and International Resource Management', pp. 128–30.
[71] TNA PREM 16/871, 'Note of a meeting between the Prime Minister and the Prime Minister of Iceland at Chequers on Saturday, 24 January 1976'.
[72] TNA CAB 193/130, 'The Fishing Industry', February 1976.
[73] TNA CAB 164/1353, 'Policy for the fishing industry', June 1976, para. 13.
[74] TNA CAB 164/1353, 'Policy for the fishing industry', June 1976, para. 27.
[75] TNA CAB 164/1353, 'Policy for the fishing industry', June 1976, para. 73.

1976, although the number of larger inshore vessels increased from 1,400 in 1965 to 2,140 in 1975.[76] However, the inshore fishing industry also faced considerable difficulties. The unemployment rate was generally high in Cornwall and about 70% of the working population at Newlyn was directly or indirectly dependent upon fishing. There was also growing concern at the impact of Common Market policies on fishing boxes off the Cornish coast.[77] While the extension of coastal property rights and EEZs restricted the activities of the deep-water boats, the communal approach of the Common Market fishing policy was about to widen access to what would have been UK EEZs.

A particular twist to the stance of UK governments towards the international negotiation of the extent of off-shore fisheries and the continental shelf was provided by the differing interests of England and Scotland. Having originally in UN LOSC negotiations favoured narrow EEZs so as to protect the interests of the distant-water fishing fleets, with the discovery of North Sea oil and gas reserves, UK negotiators switched to arguing for wider EEZs. Although legally different, since drilling rights to oil and gas arose from continental shelf legislation, negotiators became concerned at disparities between the areas covered in EEZ and continental shelf agreements and laws. In Scotland, most of the fisheries were inshore and increasingly, as the interest in oil began to overtake that in gas, the offshore oil and gas industry also moved into the Scottish section of the North Sea. At first, companies had been mainly interested in the natural gas reserves in the relatively shallow waters in the southern part of the British North Sea. In October 1965 British Petroleum made the first gas strike in the West Sole field which was about forty miles from the Humber estuary and in 1966 three more large gas fields (Hewett, Leman Bank, and Indefatigable) were discovered off the Norfolk coast.[78] With further finds and the fact that natural gas had a calorific value more than twice that of manufactured gas, Britain underwent a conversion to natural gas which was virtually complete by late 1976.

North Sea Oil

The discovery of oil in the North Sea came in the Danish sector in 1966, although this proved to be a small non-commercial find. However, in November/December 1969 there was the major discovery by the Phillips

---

[76] TNA CAB 164/1353, 'Policy for the fishing industry', June 1976, para. 4.
[77] TNA CAB 164/1353, 'Policy for the fishing industry', June 1976, Appendix VI, para. 2.
[78] MacKay and Mackay, *The Political Economy of North Sea Oil*, p. 58.

group in Norwegian waters of the large Ekofisk oil field which triggered feverish activity in the northern North Sea.[79] During the next six years there were numerous oil discoveries (Forties, Brent) mainly in the British sector, though another large field (Statfjord) was found on the Norwegian side of the median line. The first substantial quantities of North Sea oil began to flow in mid-1975; deliveries by tanker from the relatively small Argyll field started in summer 1975 followed by pipeline deliveries to Britain from the Norwegian Ekofisk field and from BP's Forties fields in the British sector.[80]

The right to allocate licences to explore and drill for off-shore oil derived from the 1958 Geneva Continental Shelf Convention which was implemented in the UK in the 1964 Continental Shelf Act. For the purposes of licensing, the North Sea was divided into equal blocks of approximately 100 square miles. While the first licensing round in 1964 concentrated heavily on the southern North Sea (the English sector), the subsequent three rounds (1965, 1970, and 1971–1972) all concentrated on the northern (Scottish) sector. The fourth round was the largest, covering 24,000 square miles. In the first three rounds, licences to explore and drill were allocated by means of discretionary licensing, whereby the UK government essentially chose who should receive licences.[81] However, with the Ekofisk and Forties discoveries, it was clear that the balance between the perceived risks and rewards of oil exploration had changed. By the spring of 1971 the Northern basin was looking attractive to the oil companies who had done extensive seismic work there and this encouraged the UK government to experiment with a limited auction of some licences. This experiment with auctioning was a precursor to the later auction of other natural resources such as the 3G licences.[82]

Time

As the spatial dimensions of environmental issues changed over time running from the local to global, then so too did their temporal characteristics stretch out both backwards and forwards in time. The best example of looking forwards to consider as yet unborn generations was that of the Stern Review. Stretching back might be viewed in a number of ways. One was a hankering

---

[79] MacKay and Mackay, *The Political Economy of the North Sea*, p. 59.

[80] Hashem Pesaran, 'An Econometric Analysis', p. 376.

[81] TNA POWE 63/954, 'The Fourth Round Terms', 27 February 1973, para. 1.

[82] TNA POWE 63/350, 'The pricing of North Sea gas', Derek Eagers, 18 June 1970; Dam, 'The pricing of North Sea gas in Britain'; Coase, 'The auction system and North Sea gas'; Dam, 'Oil and Gas Licensing and the North Sea'; Binmore and Klemperer, 'The biggest auction ever'.

for past times when life was held to have been better. Another was simply stopping and reversing a trend of decline and disappearance of an inherited environment. Conservation and protection were watchwords of such an approach as reflected in the Nature Conservancy Council, Wildlife Conservation, and the Royal Society for the Protection of Birds. As part of the increased concern with environmental issues in the 1970s, the RSPB membership grew rapidly.[83] The decline in the number of particular birds such as the peregrine, sparrowhawk, and kestrel underlined the ecological interaction at the centre of the working of the environment. Work by the Nature Conservancy's Monks Wood, the Royal Society for the Protection of Birds (RSPB), the British Trust for Ornithology (BTO), and the Game Conservancy at the start of the 1960s indicated that the seed-eating birds were dying because they ate corn dressed with the very toxic persistent organochlorine insecticides aldrin, dieldrin, and heptachlor. Birds of prey, foxes, and badgers were dying from eating the seed-eating birds, which had built up considerable residues of these chemicals or their metabolites in their fat. Sub-lethal doses of the much less toxic DDT were affecting the eggshell thickness of birds of prey. Evidence from the US suggested that the persistence of pesticides was probably more important than their toxicity. As a result of such concern, the use of aldrin, dieldrin, and heptachlor as a cereal seed dressing at spring sowing was phased out quite quickly. While it took several years before the other uses of these chemicals were withdrawn, eventually they were, and the populations of peregrine, sparrowhawk, and kestrel recovered as the persistent organochlorines disappeared from the environment.[84] Persistent organochlorine insecticide residues discovered in the bodies of seabirds and their eggs and in the bodies of Antarctic birds pointed to environmental contamination as a global problem.

Embedded in the language of conservation and preservation was an implicit concern for the future. As Norman Moore of the Nature Conservancy Council commented in the opening sentence of his book *The Bird of Time* 'Conservation is about the future.'[85] Given the increasing evidence of and concern with the health of species and their habitat, part of the conservationists' concern was simply to palliate the worst effects of the industrialization of agriculture and to mark off areas of land which were protected from aggressive economic development. Following the war, the National Parks Act 1949, the Town and Country Planning Act 1947, and the Agriculture Act 1947

---

[83]   Alexander, *The English Love Affair With Nature*, ch. 3.10.
[84]   Moore, 'Toxic chemicals and wildlife', pp. 26–7.   [85]   Moore, *The Bird of Time*, p. xvii.

sought to protect rural landscape and amenity and in 1968 the Countryside Act enabled local authorities to make provision for countryside recreation.[86] Concern with the industrialization of the countryside seemed to gather pace from the end of the 1950s and by 1970, reflecting the more combative tone to environmentalists' approach, Marion Shoard of the Council for the Protection of Rural England (CPRE) was to write of *The Theft of the Countryside*.[87] The wartime 'Dig for Victory' campaign and the early post-war emphasis on the maximization of agricultural output in conditions of full employment had encouraged the mechanization of agriculture. There was both a widening and a deepening of investment. Fields were enlarged to suit machinery and hedgerows grubbed up. The length of hedgerows declined from 495,000 miles in 1947 to 386,000 miles in 1985. Agriculture became more specialized. The eastern counties increasingly concentrated on arable cropping in general and on cereals in particular. The west of the country specialized in grazing livestock. Pig and poultry production which were once common on practically all farms became concentrated in specialist production units.[88] Wildlife habitat was lost. In the forty years following the Second World War, about 95% of lowland meadow was lost, 80% of chalk downland, 60% of lowland bogs, 50% of lowland marsh, and 40% of lowland heath. Nor was concern with the industrialization of the countryside confined to agriculture. Objections were raised to monoculture in trees and the factory forests of the Forestry Commission. Efforts were made to conserve the original woodlands in areas like Rothiemurchus in Scotland and by July 1969, interest in marine conservation was being voiced in Parliament.

By the start of the 1970s the ecological limits to further economic growth were being emphasized and more youthful environmental groups were adopting a more campaigning approach in the pursuit of often quite specific ends. As well as talk of preservation and conservation, the more dramatic language of 'survival' was heard more. Over lunchtime meetings of hunks of cheese, loaves of bread, and an early form of Fairtrade coffee (unpleasant coffee dust from Tanzania) students would flick through new magazines such as *The Ecologist*, *Your Environment*, and *The Vole* as well as planning the monthly collection of newspaper and glass for recycling. Those wishing to join national groups could sign up to Friends of the Earth or Transport 2000, and there was considerable cross-membership of environmental and international development groups,

---

[86] Warren, 'The legalities and perceptions of marine conservation', p. 106. Dower, 'New pressure on the land', p. 37.

[87] Grove-White, 'The rise of the environmental movement', p. 46; Moore, 'Toxic chemicals and wildlife', p. 25.

[88] Dwyer and Hodge, 'The challenge of change', pp. 117–18.

such as Third World First. International campaigns often targeted particular animals, be it the whale or Siberian Tiger, or specific concerns such as acid rain or nuclear waste. The emphasis was on action now to safeguard the future, which marked a shift of emphasis from the earlier focus on conservation. In truth many of the concerns were the same, if now more international, but the attraction of younger people to the environmental movement allowed expressions of concern for the future to emerge naturally.

A familiar bridge from the present to concern about the future was provided by population growth and the strain which it placed on resources. While Malthus's fears proved largely unfounded in the short term, and were subject to fierce criticism by, among others, Marx and Engels, Malthusian concerns periodically recurred.[89] In 1968 Paul Ehrlich's book *The Population Bomb*[90] excited much attention, and in 1972 he became President of the Conservation Society (ConSoc) in which capacity he made his Presidential Address at Central Hall, Westminster to a full house of 2,600, with several hundred more turned away at the door. ConSoc had been established in 1966 by Dr Douglas MacEwan as a result of his reading an article on over-population by Sir Julian Huxley in *Playboy* magazine. Interest in the Society reached its peak of 8,700 in November 1973 but ConSoc then slowly and steadily lost ground to new groups like Friends of the Earth (founded in late 1970) whose members (termed 'supporters') grew from 1,000 by the end of 1971 to 5,000 in 1976 and 16,000 by 1979.[91] While concern with over-population died down, Huxley's concern with pressure on the resources had also formed an important theme of Hardin's 1968 article on 'The Tragedy of the Commons'. Hardin's concern was with a particular type of pressure on the Commons, namely with population density in relation to local environmental resources, rather than with population size in aggregate. For Hardin not only was 'the pollution problem...a consequence of population...as population became denser, the natural chemical and biological recycling processes became overloaded, calling for a redefinition of property rights' but also that 'analysis of the pollution problem as a function of population density uncovers a not generally recognized principle of morality, namely: *the morality of an act is a function of the state of the system at the time it is performed.*'[92] While ConSoc might promote the greater availability of birth control, some of the Hardin's conclusions bordered on the extreme. In the section of his article sub-headed 'Freedom to Breed is Intolerable' Hardin wrote:

[89]   Meek (ed.), *Marx and Engels on Malthus*.   [90]   Ehrlich, *The Population Bomb*.
[91]   Herring, 'The Conservation Society', p. 386.
[92]   Hardin, 'The Tragedy of the Commons'. Hardin references Fletcher, *Situation Ethics*.

If each human family were dependent only on its own resources; if the children of improvident parents starved to death; *if*, thus, over-breeding brought its own 'punishment' to the germ line—*then* there would be no public interest in controlling the breeding of families. But our society is deeply committed to the welfare state, and hence is confronted with another aspect of the tragedy of the commons... To couple the concept of freedom to breed with the belief that everyone born has an equal right to the commons is to lock the world into a tragic course of action.[93]

Global Warming

Issues of time formed the core of arguments as to when and how to respond to the challenge of climate change. This change itself resulted from the accumulation of carbon dioxide and other GHGs so as to trap infrared radiation (heat radiation) in the atmosphere causing 'the greenhouse effect'.[94] Since industrialization, the concentration of gases had increased by about one-third. In the twentieth century human activity was thought to have caused most of the 0.6°C rise in mean global temperature, which was expected to continue to rise throughout and beyond the twenty-first century. The main consequences of global warming lay in the future and the possible nature and severity depended on the rate of temperature increase. A gradual rate of change allowing time for learning and adaptation might not be very disruptive, although it would have distributive effects as agricultural productivity changed between regions. A rate of climate change which outpaced the expected lifetime of installed capital and natural ecosystems would be serious. A fundamental change, even over a long period of time, such as would be caused by the melting of Greenland ice or the disintegration of the West Antarctic Ice Sheet, would have many unpredictable but costly effects.[95]

The distinction between those consequences of global warming which were thought capable of being estimated and those which were fundamentally unpredictable was often expressed in terms of probability and uncertainty, risk applying when some assessment of probabilities was possible and uncertainty existing when an assessment of probabilities was not possible.[96] In the face of uncertainty a 'precautionary principle' was often invoked to justify some action, but such action was by definition not contingent on the event

---

[93] Hardin, 'The Tragedy of the Commons', p. 1246.
[94] Stern, *The Economics of Climate Change*, p. 5.   [95] Barrett, *Why Cooperate?*, p. 86.
[96] Stern, *The Economics of Climate Change*, p. 38.

occurring. In the main, discussions concentrated on the extent to which action should be taken now in the present, so as to reduce the current rate of CO_2 emissions and thereby slow the rate of addition to the existing stock of CO_2. Since CO_2 persists in the atmosphere for about one hundred years and since the main economic and social effects of climate change lay in the future, the question asked was how action to combat global warming should be distributed between the present and the future. One simultaneously neat and complex way of thinking about this concerned the choice of social discount rate. It was the rate used in the Stern Review which emerged as a central point of contention.

In July 2005 the UK government appointed a team led by the economist Nicholas Stern to examine the economics of climate change, or more formally to assess 'the economics of moving to a low-carbon global economy, focussing on the medium to long-term perspective, and drawing implications for the timescales for action, and the choice of policies and institutions'.[97] Reporting in the autumn of 2006, the leading headline conclusion of the review was that: 'There is still time to avoid the worst impacts of climate change, if we take strong action now'.[98] In the absence of any action, the Stern Report estimated the overall costs and risks of climate change as equivalent to losing 5% of global GDP each year 'now and forever'. If the range of risks and impacts was widened, then the potential estimated damage could rise to 20% of GDP or more. In contrast, Stern estimated that the cost of taking action to reduce GHG emissions and avoiding the worst impact of climate change could be limited to 1% of global GDP each year.[99] Central to the estimation of both the loss of income likely to be caused by climate change and to the cost and timing of action to reduce GHG emissions was the social discount rate used in the Stern Report. At 1.4% this social discount rate was controversially very low, and given that it only reflected the possibility of extinction (being hit by an asteroid or whatever) then effectively the Report's social discount rate could be regarded as being near zero.[100]

As noted in the introduction to this book, seven of the thirty-seven bibliographical references in chapter 2 of the Stern Review on 'Economics, ethics and climate change' were published between 1921 and 1931. This was in part a return in the twenty-first century to the concerns of Pigou and Ramsey. The ethical objections of Ramsey and Pigou to discounting on the basis of pure

[97] Stern, *The Economics of Climate Change*, p. ix.
[98] Stern, *The Economics of Climate Change*, p. xv.
[99] Stern, *The Economics of Climate Change*, p. xv.
[100] Nordhaus, 'A review of the Stern Review'; Weitzman, 'A review of the Stern Review'.

time preference (impatience) remained and were effectively zero since in climate change economics the benefits were so distant as to render impatience irrelevant.[101] Indeed, given the length of time between investment in the present to mitigate some effects of climate change and the distant beneficiaries of such change, the common approach to discounting was awkward. This was neither a calculation of discounted returns within a single generation nor across overlapping generations, but an attempt to compare the costs of action now with benefits in a very distant future. The principal component of the discount rate remained the expectation that future generations would be wealthier than the present, and that therefore one more unit of consumption was more useful now than in the future, the presumption being of declining marginal utility of consumption across time. Formally, putting the impatience of pure time preference to one side, the resulting discount rate reflected the elasticity of marginal utility multiplied by the growth rate of per capita income. Yet, given the length of the time period under consideration, even a low social discount rate had a very significant effect on calculations of the present value of proposed projects. Indeed it could be socially efficient to use a hyperbolic discount rate, that being a higher rate in the short run and a lower one in the longer term.[102] In addition, in climate change economics, the discount rate was prescriptive rather than descriptive (reflecting current opportunity costs of capital), and it was also distributive across space. Most of the investment made in the present would be made by developed economies at least as much, if not more, for the benefit of future distant less developed countries.[103]

The impact of a positive discount rate over the length of time concerned in climate change economics formed one of the main economic concerns of the Stern Report, such that 'the only sound ethical basis for placing less value on the utility (as opposed to consumption) of future generations was the uncertainty over whether or not the world will exist, or whether those generations will be present' (i.e. the extinction possibility).[104] As Stern later argued in a defence of the Report's choice of discount rate:

If a pure-time discount rate of 2% is selected, then a life that starts in 2010 would be assigned approximately twice the social value of a life that starts in 2045. If we were to have applied these values consistently over time, a life that started in 1970 would have been, and would continue to be, assigned

[101] Gollier, *Pricing the Planet's Future*, p. 29; Broome, *Counting the Cost of Global Warming*.
[102] Gollier, *Pricing the Planet's Future*, p. 8. On the use of declining and constant discount rates, see Arrow et al., 'Determining benefits and costs for future generations'.
[103] Schelling, 'Intergenerational discounting'.
[104] Beckerman and Hepburn, 'Ethics of the discount rate in the Stern Review', p. 198.

twice the value of one starting in 2005. In other words, someone born later counts for less. In effect, this is discrimination by date of birth. Surely many would find this very difficult to justify.[105]

The view of Stern was at odds with those of his fellow economists like William Nordhaus who viewed a real discount rate of 5% as socially efficient.[106] Estimating the net present value of the future damages generated by one more tonne of CO_2 emitted at $8, if applied this suggested that much of the expenditure on carbon sequestration, wind generation, solar power, or bio-fuel technologies was not socially desirable, and that funds would be better spent on research and development as part of a slowly rising ramped response as technology costs fell and demand rose. Stern's use of a smaller real discount rate of 1.4% produced a present value calculation of around 85 dollars per tonne of CO_2.[107]

The difficulty of discounting over long periods of time also affected calculations of the costs in the future of current decisions, for example, to produce and store radioactive waste with a long half-life. One suspicion was that quite apart from arguments as to what should be the chosen discount rate, that chosen rate undervalued future lives. This applied both to individuals and to individuals in clusters. The cost of a nuclear accident which kills the population of a town is greater than the sum of the individual lives because those individuals worked together as a clustered networked group whose value was greater than the sum of its parts. Conventional discounting largely expresses future benefits in a present value. How well it expresses future costs or damage in present terms is less clear.[108] A little of this tension was present in evaluations of QALYs, as in the question of whether costs and future benefits should be discounted at the same rate. The changed treatment of the future was also evident in the VPF treatment of human life. If the VPF approach was employed, then the value of the human lives lost in a nuclear accident rose considerably.[109] It is an issue which concerned the philosopher Derek Parfit, who was critical of the discounted approach in which:

> we shall not be troubled by the fact that some nuclear waste will be radioactive for thousands of years. At a discount rate of five per cent, one death

[105] Stern, *A Blueprint for a Safer Planet*, p. 83.
[106] Nordhaus, *A Question of Balance*; Nordhaus, 'The Stern Review', p. 3.
[107] Gollier, *Pricing the Planet's Future*, p. 6.
[108] Schulze, Brookshire, and Sandler, 'The social rate of discount'.
[109] NERA Economic Consulting, *Human Costs of a Nuclear Accident*.

next year counts for more than a billion deaths in 500 years. On this view, catastrophes in the further future can now be regarded as morally trivial.[110]

Parfit also regarded 'remoteness in time' as having 'no more significance than remoteness in space':

> Suppose that I shoot some arrow into a distant wood, where it wounds some person, I am guilty of gross negligence. Because this person is far away, I cannot identify the person whom I harm. But this is no excuse. Nor is it any excuse that this person is far away. We should make the same claims about the effects on people who are temporally remote.[111]

Yet the expectation of economic growth does, as reflected in the use of a positive discount rate, distinguish between people in the present and in the future. Once this spatial dimension is admitted, then the concern must be at least as much with those living in the present who we do not know, as with the yet unborn. As the economist Robert Solow remarked about sustainability,

> once you think about sustainability, you are almost forced logically to think about equity, not between periods of time but equity right now...(If you think that)...some people are likely to be short-changed, namely in the future, (t)hen I think you are obligated to ask whether anybody is being short-changed right now.[112]

The concern with intergenerational (between generations) and intragenerational (in a lifetime) developed slowly.[113] In his 1971 *A Theory of Justice*, Rawls's chapter on 'Distributive Shares' did contain a section on 'The Problem of Justice Between Generations', in which Rawls struggled to analyse what the obligations of the present to future generations could or should be. However, Rawls was unusual at the time for giving sustained consideration to the issue and his lead was taken up by Sikora and Barry (eds.), *Obligations to Future Generations* and by Daniels, *Am I My Parents' Keeper?*. In Parfit's *Reasons and Persons* the whole fourth and final part of the book was titled 'Future Generations'. Whatever our sympathy with Ramsey's distaste for treating people differently according to when they are born, the view of Laslett and

---

[110] Parfit, *Reasons and Persons*, p. 357.   [111] Parfit, *Reasons and Persons*, p. 357.
[112] Solow, 'Sustainability: an economist's perspective'.
[113] Hellweg, Hofstetter, and Hungerbuhler, 'Discounting and the environment'.

Fishkin that our sense of identity for each generation fades as they become ever more distant from us seems to reflect a human preference.[114]

In efforts to reduce CO_2 emissions, the mix of administrative and market mechanisms was again an area of elbow wrestling. Theoretically, the application of a (carbon) tax reflecting the marginal social cost of CO_2 emissions was desirable. Not only would the tax reflect the social cost of CO_2 emissions in the prices paid by consumers, but as the social cost of emissions rose as they added to the stock of CO_2, then so too could the tax be increased. The trend of a rising carbon tax would also be reasonably predictable and would provide clear signals to those investing in new capital equipment, that they should favour plant which was as emissions-efficient as possible. In practice, it proved difficult to introduce such a tax. Internationally, developing economies raised objections to being penalized for adding to a stock of CO_2 which was largely not of their making. A political preference for equity over efficiency favoured the allocation of permits for pollution, both spatially across the global economy, as well as temporally in not penalizing those who were saddled with older plant bought in the past (the grandfathering principle). At a more pecuniary level, there was also more money for the private sector in developing and operating carbon trading, than in allowing the public collection of a carbon tax. Yet while a tax sets a price and allows quantity to adjust, permits set a quantity for which price adjustments are made through trading.[115] Fixing a predetermined quantity before trading occurred is rigid and potentially out-of-kilter with subsequent economic development. In the EU Emissions Trading System (ETS) the limits were determined before the 2008 financial crash, such that there was a surplus of emissions rights which was unlikely to be removed before mid-2020. Subsequent rounds of decisions on the size of per-mitted emissions and the arrangements for trading will be subject to lobbying by interested groups, and the outcomes are unpredictable. This provides less guidance for those making fixed capital investment decisions than does a carbon tax. While some forms of carbon taxation, such as the UK Climate Change Levy (2001–) have been introduced, and particular states and coun-tries have had more success than others, the global nature of the CO_2 problem means that the resistance to carbon taxation on a cross-international level is of concern. At a local level, where price increases are targeted on particular groups, then resistance can be fierce. The protests of road haulage drivers in the UK in 2000 and in France in 2018 are examples of this. More likely to

---

[114] Laslett and Fishkin (eds.), 'Introduction' to *Justice between Age Groups and Generations*, p. 1.
[115] Sorrell and Sijm, 'Carbon trading'.

succeed is a carbon tax levied at borders on non-carbon taxed imports with the proceeds earmarked for clear public purposes. One such idea is for countries to form a Carbon Club in which members accept that the social cost of carbon is at least $36 (2018, $ per tonne of CO_2) and that members would invest as if the target carbon price was $50 per tonne CO_2. At present carbon taxes are around $3, so 10% of the estimated social cost of carbon at a time when the annual growth of CO_2 emissions is around 1.8% p.a. (1970–2017). Those who did not join the Club would be subject to a tariff of 3%.[116] The function of the Club approach is to address the issue of free-riding which is itself a function of the spatial widening of problems of pollution. In the past, as with the smogs in Britain, the amelioration has come through techno-logical progress (the shift from coal to electricity), with economic theory sug-gesting that price signals are at least as important as legislative approaches. Legislation and taxation also assume the presence of a sovereign govern-ment for the area affected. What might work for single countries when tack-ling local issues is more difficult to translate into effective policies of global pollution abatement given free-riding behaviour and the absence of global institutions able and willing to impose taxes on the use of carbon. This tension between global and local issues and the role of global institutions also con-cerns our next chapter, on international trade.

Bibliography

Alexander, Ian, *The English Love Affair With Nature*, 2015, Oxford and Shrewsbury: Youcaxton Publications.

Arrow, K., M. Cropper, C. Gollier, B. Groom, G. Heal, R. Newell, W. Nordhaus, R. Pindyck, W. Pizer, P. Portney, T. Sterner, R.S.J. Tol, and M. Weitzman, 'Determining benefits and costs for future generations', *Science*, vol. 341, issue 6144, 26 July 2013, pp. 349–50.

Ashby, E, and M. Anderson, 'Studies in the politics of environmental protec-tion: the historical roots of the British Clean Air Act, 1956. II. The ripening of public opinion, 1898–1952', *Interdisciplinary Science Review*, 2, 1977, pp. 190–206.

Barrett, Scott, *Why Cooperate? The Incentive to Supply Public Goods*, 2007, Oxford, Oxford University Press.

Beckerman, W., *Small Is Stupid: Blowing the Whistle on the Greens*, 1995, London, Duckworth.

[116] Nordhaus, 'Climate clubs'.

Beckerman, Wilfred and Cameron Hepburn, 'Ethics of the discount rate in the Stern Review on the Economics of Climate Change', *World Economics*, Jan–Mar 2007, vol. 8, no. 1, pp. 187–210.

Berkes, F., 'Fishermen and the "Tragedy of the Commons"', *Environmental Conservation*, vol. 12, no. 3, 1985, pp. 199–206.

Berkes, F. (ed.), *Common Property Resources—Ecology and Community-based Sustainable Development*, 1989, London: Belhaven Press.

Bernes, C. (ed.), *Acidification and Liming of Swedish Freshwaters*, 1991, Stockholm: Swedish Environmental Protection Agency.

Binmore, Ken., and Paul Klemperer, 'The biggest auction ever: The sale of the British 3G Telecom licences', *The Economic Journal*, vol. 112, no. 478, Conference papers (Mar. 2002), pp. C74–C96.

Brimblecombe, P., and C. Bowler, 'The history of air pollution in York England', *Journal of Air Waste Management Association*, vol. 42, 1992, pp. 1562–6.

Broome, J., *Counting the Cost of Global Warming*, 1992, Cambridge: White Horse Press.

Brøgger, W.C., 'Note on a contaminated snowfall under the heading 'Mindre meddelelser' (Short communication), *Naturen*, vol. 5, 1881, p. 47.

Buchanan, James, 'Ethical rules, expected values and large numbers', *Ethics*, vol. 76, no. 1, October 1965, pp. 1–13.

Butlin, J., 'Optimal depletion of a replenish-able resource: An evaluation of recent contributions to fisheries economics', in D. Pearce (ed.), *The Economics of Natural Resource Depletion*, 1975, London: Macmillan, pp. 85–114.

Carson, Rachel, *Silent Spring*, 1962, Cambridge, Mass.: The Riverside Press.

Cheung, S.N.S., 'The structure of a contract and the theory of a non-exclusive resource', *Journal of Land Economics*, vol. 13, no. 1, 1970, pp. 49–70.

Coase, R., 'The problem of social cost', *Journal of Law and Economics*, vol. 3, October 1960, pp. 1–44.

Coase, R.H., 'The auction system and North Sea gas: A comment', *The Journal of Law and Economics*, vol. 13, no. 1, April 1970, pp. 45–7.

Copes, P., 'The backward-bending supply curve of the fishing industry', *Scottish Journal of Political Economy*, vol. 17, no. 1, February 1970, pp. 69–77.

Dam, K.W., 'Oil and Gas Licensing and the North Sea', *The Journal of Law and Economics*, vol. 8, October 1965, pp. 51–75.

Dam, Kenneth W., 'The pricing of North Sea gas in Britain', *The Journal of Law and Economics*, vol. 13, no. 1, April 1970, pp. 11–44.

Daniels, Norman, *Am I My Parents' Keeper: An Essay on Justice Between the Young and the Old*, 1988, New York and Oxford: Oxford University Press.

Dasgupta, P.S., and G. Heal, 'The optimal depletion of exhaustible resources', *The Review of Economic Studies*, vol. 41, 1974, pp. 3–28.

Dasgupta, Partha, Karl-Göran Mäler, and Scott Barrett, 'Intergenerational Equity, Social Discount Rates and Global Warming', April 2000. This is a revised version of a paper with the same title, which appeared in Paul Portney and John Weyant (eds.), *Discounting and Intergenerational Equity*, 1999, Washington, D.C.: Resources for the Future.

Dower, Michael, 'New pressure on the land; recreation', in T. C. Smout (ed.), *Nature, Landscape and People Since the Second World War*, 2001, East Lothian: Tuckwell Press, pp. 32–43.

Dwyer, Janet, and Ian Hodge, 'The challenge of change: demands and expectations for farmed land', in T. C. Smout (ed.), *Nature, Landscape and People Since the Second World War*, 2001, East Lothian: Tuckwell Press, pp. 117–34.

Ehrlich, Paul, *The Population Bomb*, 1968, New York: Ballantine.

Eliassen, Anton, and Jørgen Saltbones, 'Modelling of Long-Range Transport of Sulphur over Europe: A Two-Year Model Run and Some Model Experiments', *Atmospheric Environment*, vol. 17, no. 8, 1983, pp. 1457–73.

Farman, J., B.G. Gardiner, and J.D. Shanklin, 'Large losses of total ozone in Antarctica reveal seasonal ClOx/NOx interaction', *Nature*, vol. 315, 1985, pp. 207–10.

Farman, Joe, 'First Person feature', *FT.Com Magazine*, Pearson, London, 30/31 October 2010.

Favero, Carlo A., 'Taxation and the Optimization of Oil Exploration and Production: The UK Continental Shelf', *Oxford Economic Papers*, New Series, vol. 44, no. 2, April 1992, pp. 187–208.

Fletcher, Joseph F., *Situation Ethics: The New Morality*, 1966, Philadelphia: Westminster Press.

Gimingham, Charles H., and Michael B. Usher, 'Applying ecology to wildlife conservation: Have attitudes changed?', in T. C. Smout (ed.), *Nature, Landscape and People Since the Second World War*, 2001, Tuckwell Press, East Lothian, pp. 79–96, p. 89.

Giussani, Vanessa, 'The UK Clean Air Act: An empirical investigation', Centre for Social and Economic Research on the Global Environment, University College London and University of East Anglia.

Gloag, Daphne, 'Air pollutants: the "classical" pollutants', *British Medical Journal*, vol. 282, 28 February 1981, pp. 723–5.

Gollier, Christian, *Pricing the Planet's Future: The Economics of Discounting in an Uncertain World*, 2013, Princeton and Oxford: Princeton University Press.

Grove-White, Robin, 'The rise of the environmental movement, 1970–1990', in T. C. Smout (ed.), *Nature, Landscape and People Since the Second World War*, 2001, East Lothian: Tuckwell Press, pp. 44–51.

Hardin, Garrett, 'The Tragedy of the Commons', *Science*, vol. 162, issue 3859, 13 December 1968, pp. 1243–8.

Hashem Pesaran, M., 'An Econometric Analysis of Exploration and Extraction of Oil in the U.K. Continental Shelf', *The Economic Journal*, vol. 100, no. 401, June 1990, pp. 367–90.

Hellweg, Stefanie., Thomas B. Hofstetter, and Konrad Hungerbuhler, 'Discounting and the environment. Should current impacts be weighted differently than impacts harming future generations?', *The International Journal of Life Cycle Assessment*, vol. 8, no. 1, January 2003, 8–18.

Herring, Horace, 'The Conservation Society: Harbinger of the 1970s environment movement in the UK, *Environment and History*, vol. 7, 2001, pp. 381–401.

Hotelling, H., 'The economics of exhaustible resources', *The Journal of Political Economy*, vol. 39, issue 2, April 1931, pp. 137–75.

Irwin, Aisling, 'An environmental fairy tale; The Molina-Rowland chemical equations and the CFC problem', in Graham Farmelo (ed.), *It Must Be Beautiful: Great Expectations of Modern Science*, 2002, London and New York: Granta Books, pp. 87–109.

Kay, John A., and James A. Mirrlees, 'The desirability of natural resource depletion', in D. W. Pearce (ed.), *The Economics of Natural Resource Depletion*, 1975, London: Macmillan, pp. 140–76.

Kerry Turner, R., D. Pearce, and I. Bateman, *Environmental Economics*, 1994, Hemel Hempstead: Harvester Wheatsheaf.

Koopmans, T.C., 'Some observations on an "optimal" economic growth and exhaustible resources', in H.C. Bos, H. Linnemann and P. de Woolf (eds.), *Economic Structure and Development: Essays in Honour of Jan Tinbergen*, 1973, Amsterdam: North-Holland, pp. 239–55.

Laslett, Peter, and James S. Fishkin (eds.) 'Introduction' to *Justice between Age Groups and Generations*, 1992, New Haven and London: Yale University Press.

Levhari, David, and Leonard J. Mirman, 'The Great Fish War: An Example Using a Dynamic Cournot-Nash Solution', *The Bell Journal of Economics*, vol. 11, no. 1, Spring 1980, pp. 322–34.

Little, I.M.D., *The Price of Fuel*, 1953, Oxford: Clarendon Press.

McCay, B.J., and J.M. Acheson, *The Question of the Commons: the Culture and Ecology of Communal Resources*, 1987, Tuscon: University of Arizona Press.

MacKay, D.I., and G.A. Mackay, *The Political Economy of North Sea Oil*, 1975, London: Martin Robertson.

Meadows, Donella H., Dennis L. Meadows, Jørgen Randers, William W. Behrens III, *The Limits to Growth: A Report for the Club of Rome's Project on the Predicament of Mankind*, 1972, London: A Potomac Associates Book, Earth Island Limited.

Meek, R.L. (ed.), *Marx and Engels on Malthus*, 1953, London: Lawrence & Wishart.

Menz, Frederic C., and Hans M. Seip, 'Acid rain in Europe and the United States: an update', *Environmental Science & Policy*, vol. 7, 2004, pp. 253–65.

Mishan, E.J., *The Costs of Economic Growth*, 1967, London: Staples Press.

Mitchell, Bruce, 'Politics, Fish, and International Resource Management: The British-Icelandic Cod War', *Geographical Review*, vol. 66, no. 2, April 1976, pp. 127–38.

Moore, N.W., *The Bird of Time: The Science and Politics of Nature Conservation*, 1987, Cambridge, Cambridge University Press.

Moore, Norman W., 'Toxic chemicals and wildlife: raising awareness and reducing damage', in T. C. Smout (ed.), *Nature, Landscape and People Since the Second World War*, 2001, East Lothian: Tuckwell Press, pp. 25–31.

NERA Economic Consulting, *Human Costs of a Nuclear Accident: Final Report*, 3 July 2007.

Newbery, David M., 'Acid Rain', *Economic Policy*, vol. 5, no. 11, Oct. 1990, pp. 297–346

Nordhaus, W.D., *A Question of Balance: Weighing the Options on Global Warming Policies*, 2008, New Haven, CT: Yale University Press.

Nordhaus, William D., 'A review of the Stern Review on the Economics of Climate Change', *Journal of Economic Literature*, vol. XLV, Sept. 2007, pp. 686–702.

Nordhaus, William, 'The Stern Review on the Economics of Climate Change', paper, 17 November, 2006.

Nordhaus, William., 'Climate clubs: Overcoming free-rising in international climate policy', *American Economic Review*, vol. 105, no. 4, April 2015, pp. 1339–70.

Oden, S., 1968, 'The Acidification of Air Precipitation and its Consequences in Natural Environment, Ecology Committee, Bulletin No. 1, Swedish Sciences Research Council. Stockholm.

OECD, *The OECD Programme on Long Range Transport of Air Pollutants*, 1977, Paris: OECD.

Ostrom, Elinor, *Governing the Commons: The Evolution of Institutions for Collective Action*, 1990, Cambridge: Cambridge University Press.

Parfit, Derek, *Reasons and Persons*, Clarendon Press, Oxford. First published 1984, reprinted paperback with corrections 1987.

Park, C.P., *Acid Rain: Rhetoric and Reality*, 1987, London: Methuen.

Pearce, D., and A. Markandya, *Environmental Policy Benefits: Monetary Valuation*, 1989, Paris: OECD.

Pigou, A.C., *The Economics of Welfare*, 1920, London: Macmillan.

Pogge, T. (ed.), *Freedom from Poverty as a Human Right*, 2007, Oxford: Oxford University Press.

Ramsey, F., 'A mathematical theory of saving', *Economic Journal*, vol. 38, no. 4, 1928, pp. 543–59.

Rawls, John, *A Theory of Justice*, 1971, Cambridge, Mass.: Belknap Press.

Sandler, Todd., *Global Collective Action*, 2004: Cambridge: Cambridge University Press.

Scarrow, Howard A., 'The impact of British domestic air pollution', *British Journal of Political Science*, vol. 2, no. 3, July 1972, pp. 261–82.

Thomas C. Schelling, 'Intergenerational discounting', in Paul R. Portney and John P. Weyant, *Discounting and Intergenerational Equity*, 1999, Washington, D.C.: Resources for the Future, pp. 99–109.

C.L. Schofield, 'Acid precipitation: effects on fish', *Ambio*, vol. 5, 1976, 228–30.

Schulze, William D., David S. Brookshire, and Todd Sandler, 'The social rate of discount for nuclear waste storage: Economics or ethics', *Natural Resources Journal*, vol. 21, issue 4, 1981, pp. 811–32.

Schumacher, E.F., *Small is Beautiful: A Study of Economics As If People Mattered*, 1973, London: Blond & Briggs.

Scott, A. 'The Fishery: The Objectives of Sole Ownership', *Journal of Political Economy*, vol. 63, no. 2, 1955, pp. 116–24.

Scott Gordon, H., 'The economic theory of a common-property resource: The Fishery', *Journal of Political Economy*, vol. 62, no. 2, April 1954, pp. 124–42.

Seabright, Paul, 'Managing Local Commons: Theoretical Issues in Incentive Design', *The Journal of Economic Perspectives*, vol. 7, no. 4, Autumn 1993, pp. 113–34.

Sheail, John, *An Environmental History of Twentieth-Century Britain*, 2002, Houndmills: Palgrave.

Sikora, R.I., and Brian Barry, *Obligations to Future Generations*, 1978, Philadelphia, Pa.: Temple University Press.

Smith, V.L., 'Economics of Production from Natural Resources', *American Economic Review*, vol. 58, issue 3, Part 1, June 1968, pp. 409–31.

Solow, R.M., 'Sustainability: an economist's perspective', *National Geographic Research and Exploration*, vol. 8, no. 1, 1992, pp. 10–21.

Sorrell, Steven and Jos Sijm, 'Carbon trading in the policy mix', *Oxford Review of Economic policy*, 2003, vol. 19, no. 3, pp. 420–37.

Steiner, G., *The Listener*, vol. 97, 1977, London: BBC, p. 537.

Stern, Nicholas, *The Economics of Climate Change: The Stern Review*, 2007, Cambridge: Cambridge University Press.

Stern, N., *A Blueprint for a Safer Planet*, 2009, London: The Bodley Head.

Stiglitz, Joseph, 'Growth with exhaustible natural resources: efficient and optimal growth paths', *The Review of Economic Studies*, vol. 41, 1974, pp. 123–37.

The Times, 9 December, 1952, p. 8, col. D.

Thomas, Keith, 'Introduction', in C.C. W. Taylor (ed.), *Ethics and the Environment*, 1992, Oxford: Corpus Christi College.

Tickell, Crispin, *The Times*, London: The Astor Family, 27 August 1991, p. 8.

TNA CAB 134/3350, 'Background information on Environmental Protection', 11 September 1970.

TNA CAB 134/4024, EV(W)(76)11, Cabinet, Official Committee on Environmental Protection, Working Group, 'Sulphur Pollution', 23 November 1976.

TNA CAB 164/1353, 'Policy for the fishing industry', June 1976.

TNA CAB 193/129, SEC(75)4503 final, 'Problems for the Community fishing industry raised by the establishment of the 200-mile economic zones: Commission working paper', Brussels, 22 December 1975.

TNA CAB 193/130, 'The Fishing Industry: A Background Note', February 1976

TNA POWE 63/208, Draft paper, 'A National Hydrocarbons Corporation', Petroleum Division, 5 July 1968.

TNA POWE 63/208, Note of Meeting between Ministry officials and the Labour Party's North Sea Study Group, 19 June 1968.

TNA POWE 63/208, Draft paper, 'A National Hydrocarbons Corporation', Petroleum Division, 5 July 1968.

TNA POWE 63/350, 'The pricing of North Sea gas', Derek Eagers, 18 June 1970.

TNA POWE 63/954, 'The Fourth Round Terms', paper, Petroleum Division, 27 February 1973.

TNA POWE 63/1027, DTI, 'North Sea Oil Depletion Policy', 8 October 1973.

TNA PREM 16/871, 'Note of a meeting between the Prime Minister and the Prime Minister of Iceland at Chequers on Saturday, 24 January 1976.

Tuck, Richard, *Free Riding*, 2008, Cambridge, Mass.: Harvard University Press.

Turvey, R., 'Optimisation and sub-optimisation in fisheries regulation', *American Economic Review*, vol. 54, no. 2, Part 1, March 1964, pp. 64–76.

Warren, Lynda M., 'The legalities and perceptions of marine conservation', in T. C. Smout (ed.), *Nature, Landscape and People Since the Second World War*, 2001, East Lothian: Tuckwell Press, pp. 106–16.

Weidner, H., *Clean Air Policy in Great Britain*, 1987, Berlin: Edition Sigma.

Weitzman, Martin L., 'A review of the Stern Review on the Economics of Climate Change', *Journal of Economic Literature*, vol. XLV, Sept. 2007, pp. 703–24.

Woodhatch, Libby, and Kevin Crean, 'The gentleman's agreements: a fisheries management case study from the Southwest of England' *Marine Policy*, vol. 23, no. 1, 1999, pp. 23–35.

8

Trading Spaces

During the second half of the twentieth century there was a rapid expansion in international trade. Between 1948 and 1990 the volume of world trade grew at an annual average rate of 7%.[1] The spurt of growth in trade in the early post-war period surprised many economists and government planners who were expecting more subdued activity. In fact, between 1948 and 1960 the volume of world exports rose at an annual compound rate of above 6%, manufactures by over 8% per annum, and primary products other than fuels by more than 4%.[2] This was the fastest rate of growth for over one hundred years. This growth during the Golden Age (1945–1973) occurred within a framework of rules and restrictions negotiated at international meetings towards the end of World War II. The best known of these was held in July 1944 involving 730 delegates from forty-four countries at the Mount Washington Hotel, Bretton Woods, New Hampshire in the United States. The main agreement reached at Bretton Woods was that there should be a fixed but adjustable international system of fixed exchange rates linked to gold through the dollar at $35 per ounce. All countries pegged to the dollar and thereby to each other. Ideally all currencies would be convertible one with another, although practically convertibility for dollars was the most sought, not least as the United States was the leading source of the capital goods required for post-war recovery. Importantly, the movement of private financial capital was restricted as exchange controls were agreed. As Keynes noted of the Bretton Woods agreement, every government had the 'explicit right to control all capital movements' on a permanent basis, and that 'what used to be heresy is now endorsed as orthodoxy'.[3] One lesson drawn from the interwar experience was that if the perceived benefits of a stable pegged exchange rate system were to be squared with allowing national governments' sovereignty over their economic policy, then capital flows would need to be restricted. At Bretton Woods Keynes envisaged that capital controls would operate as a permanent feature of the international

---

[1] Rodrik, *Globalisation Paradox*, p. 71.
[2] Kaldor, 'The problem of international liquidity', in *Further Essays*, p. 28.
[3] Quoted in Dani Rodrik, *The Globalisation Paradox*, p. 95.

monetary system although he agreed that convertibility of currencies should exist on current account once international conditions permitted.

There was also concern that international trade be subject to agreed rules and that steps be taken to ease the balancing of trade accounts. Work by the economist James Meade on a free trade organization which eventually emerged as the International Trade Organization (ITO) was regarded as complementary to Keynes's negotiations for an international clearing union.[4] Keynes's idea was that an International Clearing Union would provide an automatic system by which bilateral surpluses and deficits between countries could be balanced. The surpluses and deficits would be accounted for on the books of the ICU and denominated in a new international unit of account, the Bancor. This idea eventually proved too ambitious for American politicians to accept.[5] So as to ensure adequate liquidity in the post-war world, the International Monetary Fund (IMF) was also established at Bretton Woods, as too was the International Bank for Reconstruction and Development (IBRD). In the short run, the role of the IBRD was overtaken by the announcement of Marshall Aid by the United States Secretary of State General George Marshall in June 1948. Marshall Aid was equivalent to about 5–10% of the 1949 GNP of recipients, and about 2% of that of the USA.[6] In the longer run, the IBRD and its lending arm the International Development Association were to become collectively the World Bank.

Just as the interwar experience of the Gold Standard, competitive currency depreciations, and the disruptive movement of private capital cast a long shadow over the negotiations on exchange rates and capital movements, so too did concerns with tariffs and autarchy hang over discussions of the creation of the ITO and General Agreement on Tariffs and Trade (GATT). The negotiations to establish an ITO were less immediately successful than those at Bretton Woods. At a series of meetings in London in 1945, Geneva in 1947, and Havana in 1948, agreement also proved to be elusive as arguments between the USA and UK over such issues as non-discrimination and Imperial Preference, and disagreements on trade rules between richer and poorer countries, prevented plans for an ITO being realized. Instead, a summary interim charter drawn up the Americans and signed by delegates in Geneva in 1947 was formalized as the GATT. It was from these unprepossessing beginnings that GATT gave rise to 'rounds' of international trade

---

[4] Atkinson and Weale, 'James Edward Meade, 1907–1995', p. 481.
[5] Schenk, *International Economic Relations*, p. 24.
[6] Schenk, *International Economic Relations*, p. 33.

negotiations.[7] The focus of negotiations during the 1950s and 1960s was the liberalization of markets in manufactures, but not in all sectors of the economy. Agriculture was often subsidized and/or protected, and capital flows remained controlled.[8]

The UK shared in the post-1945 growth in international trade, although its share of international trade fell over the period. As a share of UK GDP, trade was never to regain its proportionate weight of the 1870–1913 period when it formed around 60% of GDP on average. In the post–World War II period, UK trade as a proportion of GDP climbed above its interwar share of 31% in 1933 and its nadir of 20% in 1943 to reach 55% in 1955, before rising again in 1973, after the first Organization of the Petroleum Exporting Countries (OPEC) oil price hike, and again from the end of the 1980s, albeit with intervening meanderings.[9] As with UK public expenditure, the greater changes were not in the aggregate size of trade, but in its composition. The proportionate importance of exports of manufactured goods fell, although manufactures remained the most valuable group of exports (see Tables 8.1 and 8.2). Services grew in importance relative to goods, this change in relative importance being greater in exports. By 2011, 39% of exports were of services (see Table 8.3). In part this reflected change in the structure of the economy itself. In 1950, measured by sectoral employment, the share of agriculture was 5.3%, industry 48.8%, and services 45.9%. In 1974, the shares were agriculture (2.8%), industry (42.0%), and services (55.2%), and in 2004 agriculture (1.3%), industry (22.3%), and services (76.4%).[10]

Within UK trade, there was also a shift away from primary goods and towards manufactured goods to the disadvantage of Commonwealth countries. Natural products began to be replaced by synthetic substitutes and cotton, jute, wool, hides, skins, and natural rubber all faced increasing competition from oil and fat-based synthetics. Between 1955 and 1973, while the production of pullovers, jumpers, and cardigans rose from 75 million to 150 million, those made of wool declined from 61 million to 30 million. In yarn weaving, the share of cotton fell from 71% in 1955 to 47%, while the share of natural rubber in total UK rubber consumption fell from 82% to 36%. Although the move to synthetics was slow in the footwear industry, by 1973, only 60% of shoes made in the UK had leather uppers. Imports of crude timber

---

[7] These rounds were: Geneva 1947; Annecy 1949; Torquay, 1950–1951; Geneva, 1955–1956; Dillon, 1960–1962; Kennedy 1964–1967; Tokyo 1973–1979; and Uruguay 1986–1993.

[8] Schenk, *International Economic Relations*, p. 77.

[9] O'Rourke, 'From Empire to Europe', pp. 61–2.

[10] Crafts and Toniolo, 'Aggregate growth 1950–2005', pp. 316–17, Table 12:11.

Table 8.1. Value of UK exports of goods, by commodity 1956, 1960, 1970, 1980, 1990, 2000, 2010 (total exports in £m and as percentage of total exports)

	1956	1960	1970	1980	1990	2000	2010
Total (£m)	3,143.3	3,647.6	8,169.9	47,357.1	103,691	187,936	266,079
Food and live animals	3.3%	3.0%	3.0%	4.3%	4.2%	3.1%	3.8%
Beverages and tobacco	2.5	2.6	3.2	2.5	2.7	2.2	2.3
Crude materials, inedible	3.4	3.3	3.0	2.9	2.1	1.3	2.6
Mineral fuels, lubricants etc.	5.1	3.6	2.6	13.6	7.6	9.1	13.6
Animal and vegetable oils and fats	0.3	0.2	0.1	0.1	0.1	0.1	0.2
Chemicals	7.8	8.8	9.5	11.2	12.7	13.3	19.1
Manufactured goods	28.5	27.1	24.7	18.5	15.3	12.1	11.0
Machinery and transport equipment	39.1	42.0	41.8	34.4	40.4	46.7	34.9
Miscellaneous manufactured articles	5.9	6.0	8.7	9.5	12.8	11.3	11.8
Other unclassified commodities and transactions	4.1	3.5	3.4	3.0	2.2	0.9	0.8

Note: Percentages may not sum to 100% due to rounding.

Sources:
1956: Central Statistical Office, *Annual Abstract of Statistics*, 1965, No. 102, London: HMSO, Table 267.
1960: Central Statistical Office, *Annual Abstract of Statistics*, 1969, No. 106, London: HMSO, Table 269.
1970: Central Statistical Office, *Annual Abstract of Statistics*, 1980, London: HMSO, Table 12.5.
1980: Central Statistical Office, *Annual Abstract of Statistics*, 1988, London: HMSO, Table 12.3.
1990: Office for National Statistics, *Annual Abstract of Statistics*, 1997, London: The Stationery Office, Table 12.3.
2000 and 2010: Office for National Statistics, *Annual Abstract of Statistics*, 2011, London: Dandy Booksellers, Table 6.3.

and wood pulp rose during the 1950s and 1960s but fell thereafter, as steel pit props were preferred to their wooden forerunners, in an industry in which pits were closing. The fall in new housebuilding in the mid-1970s decreased demand for sawn softwood imports, while hardwood imports fell as plastic-faced particle board and other substitutes were used instead.[11]

---

[11] Rowthorn and Wells, *De-industrialisation and Foreign Trade*, pp. 112–3, 180.

Table 8.2. Value of UK imports of goods by commodity 1956, 1960, 1970, 1980, 1990, 2000, 2010 (total imports in £m and as percentage of total imports)

	1956	1960	1970	1980	1990	2000	2010
Total	£3,861.5m	£4,655.3	£9,163.3	£49,772.9	£126,087	£220,912	£363,278
Food and live animals	34.3%	29.9%	20.3%	11.0%	8.3%	6.0%	7.4%
Beverages and tobacco	2.9	3.1	2.1	1.4	1.5	2.0	1.8
Crude materials, inedible	27.1	22.0	13.8	7.6	4.5	2.6	2.5
Mineral fuels, lubricants etc.	10.7	10.3	10.4	13.8	6.2	4.5	12.5
Animal and vegetable oils and fats	1.3	1.2	1.1	0.5	0.3	0.2	0.3
Chemicals	2.6	3.8	5.8	6.3	8.6	9.3	12.3
Manufactured goods	14.5	17.8	21.4	20.8	17.4	13.2	12.0
Machinery and transport equipment	4.2	7.4	17.5	25.2	37.4	46.4	35.4
Miscellaneous manufactured articles	1.8	3.6	6.3	10.3	14.4	14.8	15.0
Other unclassified commodities and transactions	0.3	0.7	1.4	3.0	1.4	0.8	0.8

Note: Percentages may not sum to 100% due to rounding.

Sources:

1956: Central Statistical Office, *Annual Abstract of Statistics*, 1965, London: HMSO, Table 266.
1960: Central Statistical Office, *Annual Abstract of Statistics*, 1969, No. 106, London: HMSO, Table 268.
1970: Central Statistical Office, *Annual Abstract of Statistics*, 1980, London: HMSO, Table 12.6.
1980: Central Statistical Office, *Annual Abstract of Statistics*, 1988, London: HMSO, Table 12.4.
1990: Office for National Statistics, *Annual Abstract of Statistics*, 1997, London: The Stationery Office, Table 12.4.
2000 and 2010: Office for National Statistics, *Annual Abstract of Statistics*, 2011, London: Dandy Booksellers, Table 6.4.

Table 8.3. UK trade in goods and services

	As % of total imports		As % of total exports	
	Goods	Services	Goods	Services
1951	81	19	76	24
1961	75	25	74	26
1971	74	26	71	29
1981	79	21	75	25
1991	80	20	73	27
2001	76	24	68	32
2011	77	23	61	39

Note: Based on ONS database series: KTMW, KTMX, and KTMY.

Source: House of Commons Library, Grahame Allen, *UK Trade Statistics*, SNEP 6211, 8 October 2012, Table 3.

As UK trade grew, so too did it spatially contract. This might seem counter-intuitive, especially as from the 1980s talk of internationalization gave way to that of globalization, as decreasing transportation and communications costs made trade and the management of international operations cheaper and easier.[12] Yet at the same time that UK trade grew in volume, so too over time did it spatially contract (Tables 8.4, 8.5, 8.6, and 8.7). The share of UK exports to the EEC/EU market rose from 29.4% in 1970 to 53.5% in 2010. Even allowing for the increased number of member countries of what was now the European Union, this was still a significant shift of exports towards Europe. Imports followed a similar pattern. In 1913, Western Europe had been the UK's principal trading partner, but this trade had declined significantly across the interwar period and two world wars. However, by 1983, Western Europe was more important as a trading partner for Britain than it had been in 1913. By the mid-1970s, imported manufactures had returned to the levels prevailing before World War I. In general, UK trade shifted away from the lower-income Commonwealth and Sterling Area markets to the higher-income markets of Europe and the United States.[13] A gravity trade model in which, in Newtonian fashion, economies traded proportionately with those largest and closest to them, was coexisting with globalization which exemplified Adam Smith's division of labour.

---

[12] Schenk, *International Economic Relations*, pp. 44, 77. Between 1950 and 1970 passenger air travel costs halved and the average price of a three-minute call from New York to London fell by 40%.

[13] Rowthorn and Wells, *De-industrialisation and Foreign Trade*, pp. 168, 184.

Table 8.4. UK exports by destination, 1955, 1960, 1965, 1970 (% of total exports, by value)

	1955	1960	1965	1970
Sterling area	48.0%	39.2%	33.6%	27.2
Non-sterling area:	52.0	60.1	66.4	72.4
North America	11.3	15.7	14.9	15.3
Western Europe	27.4	29.5	37.4	41.1
Rest of the World	13.3	15.7	8.4	9.3
Commonwealth	42.0	36.3	–	–
Latin America	3.9	4.7	3.3	3.5
European Economic Community*	13.0	15.4	20.0	21.7
European Free Trade Association	11.9	11.9	14.0	15.8
Middle East	5.5	5.7	–	–
Soviet Union and Eastern Europe	1.3	2.1	2.4	3.2
South Africa	5.8	4.4	5.4	4.1
India	4.5	4.1	2.4	0.9
Australia	9.9	7.1	5.8	4.3
New Zealand	4.8	3.3	2.6	1.6
Canada	4.9	5.9	4.2	3.6
Irish Republic	3.8	3.1	3.8	4.7
United States of America	6.4	9.7	10.6	11.7

*The EEC comprises the Six: West Germany; Netherlands; Belgium; Luxembourg; France; and Italy.

Note: Percentages may not sum to 100% because of rounding. Lacunae in data reflect changes in categorization in the *Annual Abstract of Statistics*.

Sources:
1955: Central Statistical Office, *Annual Abstract of Statistics*, 1963, No. 100, London: HMSO, Table 264.
1960: Central Statistical Office, *Annual Abstract of Statistics*, 1969, No. 106, London: HMSO, Table 271.
1965 and 1970: Central Statistical Office, *Annual Abstract of Statistics*, 1972, London: HMSO, Table 286.

Europe

The shift in UK trade towards Europe preceded its accession to the European Economic Community (EEC) on 1 January 1973. The question of whether the UK should seek membership of the EEC had arisen intermittently during the Golden Age. Contrary to what is often stated, the origins of what became the EEC did not lie in an overriding concern for peace in Europe, but in the more prosaic question of who got access to coal reserves. To ease its coal shortages, France had initially negotiated for a share of the West German coal reserves.[14] When that had been stopped by the United States government, France then negotiated for German coal and steel resources to be shared in what became the European Coal and Steel Community (ECSC). Given that Britain was the largest coal producer in Western Europe, it was invited on

[14] Perron, *Le Marché du Charbon*.

Table 8.5. UK imports by source, 1955, 1960, 1965, 1970 (% of total imports, by value)

	1955	1960	1965	1970
Sterling area	39.2	33.8	30.1	25.3
Non-sterling area:	60.8	66.2	69.9	74.4
North America	19.8	20.4	19.7	20.5
Western Europe	25.9	28.7	33.0	37.7
Rest of the World	15.1	17.1	17.3	16.2
Commonwealth	43.0	32.3	–	–
Latin America	6.2	6.7	4.9	3.6
European Economic Community*	12.6	14.4	17.3	20.2
European Free Trade Association	11.6	12.1	13.6	15.5
Middle East	6.4	7.4	–	–
Soviet Union and Eastern Europe	2.7	3.0	3.8	3.9
South Africa	2.1	3.0	3.1	2.9
India	4.1	3.2	2.2	1.2
Australia	6.8	4.2	3.8	2.9
New Zealand	4.7	3.9	3.6	2.2
Canada	8.9	8.1	8.0	7.5
Irish Republic	2.5	2.7	3.0	3.8
United States of America	10.9	12.3	11.7	13.0

*The EEC comprises the Six: West Germany; Netherlands; Belgium; Luxembourg; France; and Italy.

Note: Percentages may not sum to 100% because of rounding. Lacunae in data reflect changes in categorization in the *Annual Abstract of Statistics*.

Sources:
1955: Central Statistical Office, *Annual Abstract of Statistics*, 1963, No. 100, London: HMSO, Table 263.
1960: Central Statistical Office, *Annual Abstract of Statistics*, 1969, No. 106, London: HMSO, Table 270.
1965 and 1970: Central Statistical Office, *Annual Abstract of Statistics*, 1972, London: HMSO, Table 285.

several occasions to join what became the ECSC. In 1952, the ECSC and UK hard coal industries were approximately the same size, with Britain's coal output being twice that of West Germany, and three times that of France and Belgium combined.[15] The UK's decision not to join the ECSC reflected the hostility of the National Coal Board to membership and a political preference for maintaining a global outlook rather than being drawn into a European club, most of whose members, with the exception of West Germany, were regarded as economic laggards. Approached by Dean Acheson, the US Secretary of State to take a lead in Europe, the UK Foreign Secretary Ernie Bevin informed Acheson that the UK could not 'accept obligations to Western Europe which would prevent or restrict the implementation of our responsibilities elsewhere'.[16] Five days after receiving Bevin's message, Acheson made a direct appeal to

[15] In 1952, West Germany's output of hard coal was 123.3 million metric tonnes, and 85 million metric tonnes of brown coal. The comparative comments in the text apply only to hard coal. Mitchell, *European Historical Statistics, 1750–1970*, Table E2.
[16] Milward, *The Reconstruction of Western Europe*, p. 44.

Table 8.6. UK exports of goods by destination, 1970, 1980, 1990, 2000, 2010 (% of total trade by value)

	1970	1980	1990	2000	2010
European Economic Community*	29.4	43.4	56.9	59.8	53.5
Rest of Western Europe**	16.8	14.3	4.4%	3.8	4.5
Canada	3.6	1.6	1.8	1.9	1.6
United States***	11.6	9.6	12.5	13.6	14.4
South Africa	4.1	2.1	1.1	0.8	1.1
Japan	1.8	1.3	2.5	2.0	1.6
Australia	4.2	1.7	1.6	1.4	1.7
New Zealand	1.6	0.5	0.4	0.2	0.2
Oil-exporting countries	5.8	10.1	5.4	3.2	4.7
Other developing countries	16.8	12.3			
Hong Kong			1.2	1.4	1.7
Singapore			1.0	0.9	1.3
China			0.5	0.8	2.9
India			1.2	1.1	1.5
Centrally planned economies	3.8	2.8			
Eastern Europe			1.4		
Russia				0.4	1.4

*In *Annual Abstract of Statistics 1980*, EEC comprises: France; Belgium; Luxembourg; Netherlands; Federal Republic of Germany; Italy; Irish Republic; and Denmark.
**In 1990 the Rest of Western Europe category comprised Norway, Switzerland, Turkey, and Iceland. In 2000, the EEC is categorized as European Union, and additional members are Cyprus (0.2%), Malta (0.1), Slovakia (0.1), Slovenia (0.1), Bulgaria (0.05), Czech Republic (0.5), Estonia (0.05), Hungary (0.3), Latvia (0.04), Lithuania (0.07), Poland (0.7), and Romania (0.2).
***In 2000 and 2010, the United States data include Puerto Rica.

Sources:
1970: Central Statistical Office, *Annual Abstract of Statistics*, 1980, London: HMSO, Table 12.7.
1980: Central Statistical Office, *Annual Abstract of Statistics*, 1988, London: HMSO, Table 12.5.
1990: Office for National Statistics, *Annual Abstract of Statistics*, 1997, London: The Stationery Office, Table 12.5.
2000 and 2010: Office for National Statistics, *Annual Abstract of Statistics*, 2011, London: Dandy Booksellers, Table 6.5. Includes Greece (0.7%), Portugal (1.0%), Spain (3.6%), Sweden (2.6%), Finland (1.0%), and Austria (0.7%) which move (9.6% in total) out of the Rest of Western Europe category.

Robert Schuman, the Foreign Minister of France. The consequent Schuman Plan formed the basis of the Treaty of Paris and the ECSC, which began its life in 1952 following the signing of the Treaty of Paris in 1951. Almost immediately imports of steel products into France and the Saar soared from 27.2 thousand tonnes in 1952 to 117.6 thousand in 1953.[17] Between 1953 and 1957 intra-ECSC trade in treaty products increased by 171%, while production increased by only 43%. This importance of intra-Western European trade and the higher growth rate of trade over output or GDP presaged the future characteristics of EEC development.

[17] Neal, *The Economics of Europe*, p. 37.

Table 8.7. UK imports of goods by source, 1970, 1980, 1990, 2000, 2010 (% of total trade by value)

	1970	1980	1990	2000	2010
European Economic Community*	27.1	41.3	57.7	53.3	50.8
Rest of Western Europe**	14.4	14.6	7.4	5.9	9.4
Canada	7.5	2.8	1.8	1.8	1.6
United States***	12.9	12.1	11.4	13.1	7.6
South Africa	2.9	1.5	0.9	1.2	1.2
Japan	1.5	3.4	5.4	4.6	2.2
Australia	2.8	1.0	0.8	0.7	0.6
New Zealand	2.2	0.8	0.4	0.2	0.2
Oil-exporting countries	9.1	8.5	2.4	1.9	3.1
Other developing countries	15.0	11.4			
Hong Kong			1.6	2.7	2.2
Singapore			0.8	1.1	1.1
China			0.5	2.2	8.4
India			0.6	0.7	1.6
Centrally planned economies	4.2	2.1			
Eastern Europe			1.4		
Russia				0.7	1.4

*In AAS 1980 EEC comprises: France; Belgium; Luxembourg; Netherlands; Federal Republic of Germany; Italy; Irish Republic; and Denmark.
**In 1990 the Rest of Western Europe category comprised Norway, Switzerland, Turkey and Iceland. In 2000, the EEC is categorized as European Union, and additional members are Cyprus, Malta, Slovakia, Slovenia, Bulgaria, Czech Republic, Estonia, Hungary, Latvia, Lithuania, Poland, and Romania.
***In 2000 and 2010, the United States data include Puerto Rica.

Sources:
1970: Central Statistical Office, *Annual Abstract of Statistics*, 1980, London: HMSO, Table 12.8.
1980: Central Statistical Office, *Annual Abstract of Statistics*, 1988, London: HMSO, Table 12.6.
1990: Office for National Statistics, *Annual Abstract of Statistics*, 1997, London: The Stationery Office, Table 12.6.
2000 and 2010: Office for National Statistics, *Annual Abstract of Statistics*, 2011, London: Dandy Booksellers, Table 6.6. Includes Greece, Portugal, Spain, Sweden, Finland, and Austria, which move out of the Rest of Western Europe category.

Encouraged by the success of the ECSC, in 1955 the foreign ministers of the ECSC met in the Spaak Committee (1955–1956) to discuss how a common market and a European Atomic Energy Community might be established. Its report published in April 1956 was to form the basis for the establishment of the EEC and EURATOM. The UK, and its representative Russell Bretherton, who had been invited onto the Spaak Committee by the ECSC member states, decided to leave the committee in 1955. The UK was opposed to a customs union and wary of sharing its atomic secrets with Western Europe, and thereby potentially weakening its special 'atomic' relationship with the United States. While opposed to a customs union, the UK did go on in the Stockholm Convention of 4 January 1960 to form a European Free Trade Area (EFTA) with Norway, Sweden, Denmark, Austria, and Switzerland.[18] While in both a customs union and a free trade area, there is free trade between members, in a customs union a Common External Tariff is set on trade with non-members. In a free trade area, any tariffs set for non-members are a matter for each individual member country. EFTA had a marginal impact on total UK imports; by 1965 UK exports were about 2% higher than they might have been.

In 1957, the six ECSC Western European economies (France, West Germany, Italy, Belgium, the Netherlands, and Luxembourg) signed the Treaty of Rome which established the EEC (also known as the Common Market) which began its life on 1 January 1958. That the UK was not a founding member of the EEC was in considerable part because it chose not to be a founding member of the European Coal and Steel Community (ECSC). That the National Coal Board (NCB) did not wish to join the ECSC reflected its interests as a nationalized public monopoly extracting a rationed price-controlled fuel. Its primary concern was to increase supply so as to attempt to meet the excess demand for price-controlled coal in the UK. It had little interest in exporting, even though the world price for coal was £1.00 per tonne higher than in the UK. As a nationalized industry required to cover costs, the profits foregone were of less interest to the NCB than investing so as to increase supply. Had the NCB joined the ECSC, it would have come under strong pressure both to increase exports to the ECSC and to end the practice of applying price controls to domestic sales of coal. These price controls were criticized as constituting 'dual pricing' and were at odds with the Schuman Plan's concern to secure 'fairness' of managed competition. In declining an invitation to join what became the ECSC, the NCB was happy to associate itself with the sentiments of the steel trades unions, the Engineering Advisory Council, and the Iron and Steel Board whose opposition to ECSC membership was couched in terms of their preference for their relations with the Community being allowed to develop out of normal commercial negotiations.[19]

The EEC

Theoretically, the EEC offended the spirit of GATT. While the EEC sought to eliminate all tariffs between its members, as a customs union it did set a Common External Tariff (CET) for those not in the customs union. Despite

---

[18] Foreman-Peck, 'Trade and the balance of payments', p. 160.
[19] Chick, *Electricity and Energy Policy*, p. 44.

GATT intentions, this customs union was tolerated by the US, being viewed as contributing to economic and political stability in Western Europe at a time of concern at the potential expansion of the Eastern European *bloc*. In fact, the CET set by the EEC was low and the tariff cuts agreed in the Treaty of Rome were extended to all Organization for European Economic Co-Operation (OEEC) and GATT members. In addition, in the 1962 Trade Expansion Act, the US Congress gave President Kennedy greater discretion in negotiating GATT tariffs, and the 1962 Kennedy Round saw tariff cuts of 50%.[20] As intra-European trade grew and as the annual growth rates of its members exceeded that of the UK (Table 8.8), so did the UK become more interested in joining the EEC.[21] The UK applied twice, in 1961 and 1967, and on both occasions its applications were vetoed by General de Gaulle who had returned to be president of France in 1959 following the disintegration of the Fourth Republic in the midst of the Algerian crisis. The hoped for benefit for the UK of joining centred on the potential export-led growth for UK manufacturing. Worryingly though, the leading advocate of the case for export-led growth, and adviser to the Wilson governments, Nicholas Kaldor, was sceptical that UK manufacturing was sufficiently efficient to exploit the potential benefits of being inside the customs union. If anything, by joining it would expose itself to greater competition from more efficient EEC exporters.[22]

Alongside Kaldor's concerns about manufacturing were long-standing worries from economists like James Meade as to the impact of accession to the EEC on the UK's relationship with the Commonwealth. Meade's concern in 1962 following the UK's first application to join was that while 'association with the EEC instead of the Commonwealth means *perhaps* association with

Table 8.8. Growth of GDP per man year in the UK compared with six other industrial countries, 1937–1973

	UK	USA	Sweden	France	Germany	Italy	Japan
1937–1951	1.0	2.3	2.6	1.7	1.0	1.4	−1.3
1951–1964	2.3	2.5	3.3	4.3	5.1	5.6	7.6
1964–1973	2.6	1.6	2.7	4.6	4.4	5.0	8.4

Source: Matthews, Feinstein, and Odling-Smee, *British Economic Growth, 1856–1973*, p. 31, Table 2.5.

[20] Foreman-Peck, 'Trade and the balance of payments', p. 161.
[21] Eichengreen, *The European* Economy, p. 179, Table 6.1.
[22] Neal, *The Economics of Europe*, pp. 41–2. Export-led growth models could also overlap with the capital stock Harrod-Domar growth model. See Matthews, Feinstein, and Odling-Smee, *British Economic Growth*, pp. 131–9. Lamfalussy, *The United Kingdom and the Six*.

a more rapidly growing market; it means *certainly* association with what is at present a much smaller market'.[23] In 1962 the UK sold 50% of its exports to the Commonwealth countries and about 15% of its exports to the EEC. The Commonwealth was a valuable source of low-cost imports of food and raw materials which membership of the EEC would disrupt.[24] From 1962, being a member of the EEC would also mean being a member of the Common Agricultural Policy (CAP) which was viewed with considerable justification as an autarchic, inefficient price-floor system. The UK subsidized its agricultural sector but then exposed it to Commonwealth and international competition. This subsidized approach to modernization through increased investment and improved techniques saw UK agricultural productivity improve while acreage and employment declined. Between 1948 and 1984 agricultural production rose by 160%. Milk yield rose by 24% between 1965 and 1980 and wheat production by 2% p.a. from 1946.[25] Much of this increase was achieved by the use of artificial fertilizers, weedkillers, and pesticides, but some was also due to new varieties of plant and livestock. In contrast to the UK approach of offering subsidies for modernization alongside exposure to international competition, the CAP through its European Agricultural Guidance and Guarantee Fund (EAGGF) offered guaranteed prices above world market prices in a closed system. Initially, all agricultural products were included and the level of coverage was 87% in 1970 and 91% in 1986 following the accession of more agricultural economies. Between 1968 and 1972, the EAGGF accounted for nearly 90% of the EU's budget and it made the EEC more than a customs union since, in the CAP, it had an instrument of redistribution.[26]

To an extent, just as the composition of UK trade had moved away from primary products, so too were there changes in the composition of its trade with the Commonwealth and in its imports of food. While total UK food imports fell by 12.6% between 1963 and 1980, imports of mutton and lamb fell by 45%, butter by 51%, sugar by 29%, wheat imports by 44%, and cheese by 27%. Even before the UK joined the EEC, primary product imports from the Community were increasing and this trend continued after accession in 1973. Between 1951 and 1983, UK primary product imports from the EEC increased, both absolutely and as a share of the total (from 14.2% to 33.8%). In part, this reflected an increasing UK predilection for wine and cheese. As incomes rose, so wine consumption increased. Between the early fifties and

[23] Meade, *UK, Commonwealth and Common Market*, p. 12.
[24] Meade, *UK, Commonwealth and Common Market*, pp. 12, 17.
[25] Rowthorn and Wells, *De-industrialisation and Foreign Trade*, pp. 102, 104.
[26] Neal, *The Economics of Europe*, p. 69.

early seventies, imports of alcoholic beverages increased fivefold in volume terms, much of which was wine. Nonetheless, when the UK did join the EEC, the combined share of Canada, Australia, New Zealand, and South Africa in UK food imports, having been stationary for about ten years, declined, between 1972 and 1982 from 30.0% to 16.2% whilst, over the same period, the EEC's share rose from 32.7% to 52.0%.[27]

The Collapse of Bretton Woods

The major gains from the UK's accession to the EEC were to come in the 1980s and were to flow mainly to the financial and business services industries, not least after the negotiation of the Single European Act in 1986. Ironically, the financial services industry benefited from the collapse of the Bretton Woods system of fixed, but adjustable, exchange rates. That the Bretton Woods system did collapse itself reflected not simply rigidities in the structure of the system, but also changing patterns of international growth and trade. At the core of the Bretton Woods system lay the fixed, if adjustable, linking of all currencies effectively to the United States dollar (and therefore to every other currency), and the fixed value of the dollar to gold. While in 1925, in *The Economic Consequences of Mr Churchill*, Keynes was to criticize Winston Churchill's decision as Chancellor of the Exchequer to return to gold, Keynes's objection was not to a gold standard per se, but to the chosen price of gold and the political willingness to place the burden of adjusting to an over-valued exchange rate on labour costs in export industries such as coal mining. Quite what the dollar price of gold should be, and at what rate currencies should fix to the dollar remained central questions, both during the early post-war 'dollar shortage' and in the mid-1960s when a surplus of dollars became of concern.

For the UK, the initial post-war $:£ exchange rate of $4.03:£1 looked high. Over the course of the two world wars, the UK had lost international assets and gained international debt. In World War II, in contrast to the period before 1914, there was no cushion in the form of an initial favourable current balance, so that the wartime deterioration caused adverse current balances of enormous size throughout the war. In World War II disinvestment was financed by making military-related purchases in India, Egypt, and other countries and not paying the bills; by selling some $1.1 billion in foreign investments (mainly those in the United States); and by running down

---

[27] Rowthorn and Wells, *De-industrialisation and Foreign Trade*, pp. 169, 179–81.

Table 8.9. Overseas assets and liabilities, 1913–1973 (£ billion at current prices values at end of year)

	Assets	Liabilities	Net Assets	Ratio of net assets to GDP
1913	4.6	0.4	4.2	1.8
1924	6.8	1.6	5.2	1.3
1937	5.3	1.3	4.0	0.9
1951	6.9	7.6	−0.7	−0.05
1964	14.8	13.0	1.8	0.06
1973	67.8	60.4	7.4	0.12

Source: R.C.O. Matthews, Feinstein, and Odling-Smee, *British Economic Growth, 1856–1973*, p. 128, Table 5.2.

short-term dollar assets. The switch from being a net creditor before World War II to being a net debtor afterwards was mainly the result of incurring very large liabilities. One response to this loss of investment income was the post-war export drive and by 1951 the UK's export surplus in manufactures was equal to 11% of GDP—more than three times its pre-war level.[28]

As in World War I, the ratio of net overseas assets to GDP fell because of the failure of gross overseas assets to appreciate sufficiently, as well as because of the needs of war finance. World wars were costly for the UK capital account (Table 8.9). The reduction in the real value of overseas assets is estimated to have wiped out over 15% of Britain's total net assets during World War I and nearly 28% during World War II. The effects of the two world wars on UK assets was so large that from the start of World War I to the ending of World War II, the total real wealth of the UK scarcely increased at all.[29] With the unexpectedly early ending of the war with Japan in August 1945 the UK had to negotiate the Anglo-American Loan Agreement of July 1946, in which the USA made a loan to the UK of $3.7 billion to finance the UK's balance of payments requirements for three years, but as part of which Keynes negotiating for the UK was forced, against his better judgement, to agree that currencies in the Bretton Woods exchange system would become convertible. The date set for convertibility was 15 July 1947.[30] Keynes died on 21 April 1946 before the Loan Agreement was signed, but he proved to be dead right. Reserve losses in the single month of convertibility exceeded $1 billion. Convertibility was suspended on 20 August 1947.[31] Full convertibility on current account

---

[28] Rowthorn and Wells, *De-industrialisation and Foreign Trade*, p. 97.

[29] Matthews, Feinstein and Odling-Smee, *British Economic Growth*, pp. 129–30.

[30] Eichengreen, *Reconstructing Europe's Trade and Payments*, p. 70.

[31] Obstfeld and Taylor, *Global Capital Markets*, p. 154; Newton, 'The Sterling crisis of 1947'.

was not restored until 1 January 1959 in Western Europe and later in Japan. Controls on capital account remained. In the absence of full convertibility and concerns as to how trade imbalances could be cleared, the European Payments Union (EPU) was established in July 1950. Within the EPU, participating economies agreed to accept the currency of any other member in payment for exports, and with temporary trade deficits being covered by credits. Again, as more narrowly with the ECSC, there was a striking increase in intra-European trade, this rising in value from $10 billion in 1950 to $23 billion in 1959.[32]

The suspension of convertibility exacerbated the shortage of dollars in Europe at a time when Europe was running a current account deficit with the United States of $5.6 billion in 1947, $3.4 billion in 1948, and $3.2 billion in 1949.[33] To ease the dollar shortage, Marshall Aid was announced in June 1947. To ease the pressure on the pound, its fixed exchange rate to the dollar was changed when in 1949 sterling was devalued by 30.5% from $4.03:£1 to $2.80:£1. It was to be devalued again in 1967 by 14% from a par value of $2.80 to $2.40 in 1967. One aim of the 1949 devaluation was to increase the incentives for exporters to sell to dollar rather than sterling markets. The 1967 devaluation was a more general effort to increase exports. Whether in general the pound would have been better simply to have floated against the dollar was a question raised specifically in 1952 by the Chancellor of the Exchequer, R.A.B. Butler and three leading civil servants, and more generally by economists as politically different as James Meade and Milton Friedman, both of whom made the general case for flexible exchange rates.[34] Meade favoured a system in which exchange rates varied with movements in foreign exchange reserves, rather than in relation to the current account of the balance of payments. However, since in the early post-war period Meade envisaged a world in which private capital movement would be controlled, his system effectively became one in which exchange rates changed in response to current account imbalances.[35]

As the dollar shortage eased, and as dollars became arguably too available in the 1960s, so too did the difficulties of operating a fixed exchange rate system with the dollar, linked to gold, as its central pillar become increasingly evident. These problems were essentially those of asymmetry and inelasticity. The asymmetry related to a system fixed to the dollar, in which countries were

---

[32] Eichengreen, *Reconstructing Europe's Trade and Payments*, p. 27.
[33] Eichengreen, *Reconstructing Europe's Trade and Payments*, p. 11.
[34] Meade, 'Financial policy'; Friedman, 'The case for flexible exchange rates'.
[35] Atkinson and Weale, 'Meade', p. 481.

happier, if not happy, to devalue against the dollar rather than to revalue. If domestic costs and resource use could be contained following devaluation, then exports, economies of scale, and employment might all rise. Revaluation offered the counter-prospect of more import substitution of domestic production and lower quantities (if not value) of exports. Even as trade surpluses emerged in West Germany and Japan, and inflation rates widened between these economies and the United States where inflation reached 4.3% by 1968, West Germany, and Japan showed little inclination to revalue their exchange rates against the dollar.[36] Following *les evenements* principally in France in May 1968, France did devalue the franc by 11% in August 1969 and, reluctantly, the Deutsche Mark (DM) was revalued by 10% in October 1969. But in general, movements upwards against the dollar were infrequent.

The reluctance of countries to revalue their exchange rates against the dollar reflected both concerns with domestic employment and plant capacity utilization, and also a willingness to hold gold-backed dollars as a store of wealth. For as long as this continued, the US enjoyed what de Gaulle dubbed its 'exorbitant privilege' of being able to print the world's reserve currency and thereby if it wished, to engage in deficit financing as it did in the 1960s in funding the Great Society project and the Vietnam War. Dollars flowed out of the US, not least in financing US multinational expansion overseas, and some, because of Regulation Q restrictions which limited interest payments on demand deposit accounts, became trapped outside the US forming the basis of a Eurodollar market in London at the end of the 1950s. The (Triffin) dilemma was that countries gained gold-backed dollars as the US ran a deficit with them, and as that deficit was caused by printing dollars, then so too was the credibility of a gold-backed dollar weakened.[37] There was always a tension between an elastic supply of dollars and an inelastic supply of gold but in the early post-war period the US held 70% of global gold reserves, lending a tangible credibility to the idea of a gold-backed dollar.

By the 1960s this credibility was fading.[38] At the end of 1959, foreign-held external dollar liabilities were higher than the US money gold stock. Between 1945 and 1969, while total monetary gold stocks grew by about 200 million ounces ($7 billion at the official price of $35 an ounce), the US sold over 250 million ounces during the same period. The principal source of monetary gold to most countries was neither new gold production nor Soviet gold sales,

[36] Buiter, Corsetti, and Pesenti, *Financial Markets*, p. 21.

[37] Cooper, 'The Gold Standard', pp. 21–2.

[38] The US's share of global gold reserves had doubled from 35% to 70% between the mid-1930s to the mid-1940s as the US took gold in compensation for its contribution to the war effort.

but a redistribution of gold from the US.[39] As part of efforts to defend the price of gold, in 1961 the (London) Gold Pool was established which sought to share the cost of maintaining the London price of gold at $35 an ounce rather than deplete American gold reserves. However, following the November 1967 devaluation of sterling by 14.3%, there was a run on the Gold Pool and in March 1968 the Pool collapsed. In its place a two-tier gold market was created, with a gold price determined freely on the private market and the rate of $35 per ounce being retained for transactions between central banks. In 1967 Special Drawing Rights (SDRs) were devised which were to act as a reserve asset for use by the IMF as a supplement to the US$.[40] The SDRs formed part of a long-standing series of proposals for the establishment of an international commodity reserve currency issued by the IMF in the form of certificates fully backed by stocks of all the main commodities entering into international trade.[41]

By the later 1960s, the stresses on the Bretton Woods system were beginning to tell. In addition to the efforts to establish a reserve asset in addition to the dollar, adjustments in the fixed exchange rate structure were occurring. In 1967 the pound was devalued from $2.80 to $2.40, the French franc was devalued in August 1969, and the German DM was revalued in October 1969. In response to its own deteriorating balance of trade and inflation, US interest rates were increased from 4% in October 1967, to 6% in mid-1968, and to 9.2% in October 1969 before falling again as monetary policy reacted to fears of a recession. These shifts in interest rates caused capital to flow into and then out of New York, exacerbating the already accumulating difficulties of managing a pegged rate system based on a fixed gold value of the US dollar. On 5 August 1971 President Nixon closed the official gold window, effectively bringing the exchange rate arrangements of the Bretton Woods regime to an end. In August 1971 the pound floated. On Sunday 15 August 1971 in the 'Nixon measures', the convertibility of gold for dollars was ended, a 10% surcharge was introduced, and overseas aid was cut. The result of subsequent international meetings was the Smithsonian Agreement in which other countries agreed to adjust their exchange rates against the dollar and the gold value of the dollar was increased from $35 to $38 per ounce (although the US dollar was no longer convertible to gold). The 10% import surcharge was lifted. At the start of 1973 there was another speculative run on the US dollar and Japan

---

[39] Cooper, 'The Gold Standard', pp. 21–2.
[40] Eichengreen, *Global Imbalances*, pp. 11, 17, 43.
[41] Graham, *World Commodities and World Currency*; Kaldor, 'The problem of international liquidity'.

abandoned parity on 10 February 1973. At a subsequent G10 meeting there was agreement to devalue the dollar to $42.2/oz. Between the 1 and 19 March 1973 international currency markets in the US were shut, by which time most currencies were floating. Bretton Woods was dead, although its death was not formally pronounced by the IMF until 1976, when the IMF agreed to accept the legitimacy of permanently floating exchange rates regimes.[42]

European Monetary Union

Even before the collapse of the Bretton Woods system of exchange rates, the devaluation of the franc in August 1969, the revaluation of the DM in October 1969, as well as the faltering of the Bretton Woods system prompted EEC leaders to consider future European currency and trading arrangements. In France de Gaulle had been replaced as president by Georges Pompidou in January 1969 and at his suggestion a meeting of the Heads of State was held in The Hague on 1 and 2 December 1969. It was agreed both to open negotiations with Denmark, the UK, Ireland, and Norway on their possible accession to the Community, and to develop plans for deepening the political and economic unification of the Community. A committee chaired by Pierre Werner, prime minister of Luxembourg, was appointed and its report in 1970 called for monetary union within ten years in a three-stage process. Initial progress would be to limit exchange rate fluctuations and to begin coordinating governments' monetary and fiscal policies. Then, exchange rate variability and price divergences would be further reduced, and in the third stage, exchange rates would be irrevocably fixed, capital controls would be removed, and a Community system of central banks, modelled loosely on the US Federal Reserve, would assume control of the monetary policies of the member countries. The size of the Community budget would also be increased dramatically, and the Community would coordinate national tax and expenditure programmes. A single currency was preferred to fixed exchange rates, but they were left as alternatives.[43]

As the Bretton Woods system disintegrated, so the Six moved to make their own arrangements for the management of their exchange rates. In April 1972, in an arrangement which became known as the Snake, each member country committed to limit to 2.25% the fluctuation of its own currency around the

[42]   Schenk, *International Economic Relations*, p. 53.
[43]   Eichengreen, 'European monetary unification', p. 1,323.

dollar parity. Later the UK, Ireland, Denmark, and Norway would join this managed exchange rate system. In fixing itself broadly to the dollar and to each of the other Snake currencies, central banks would use European currencies to hold parities within the Snake, and dollars to maintain the position of the Snake to the dollar.[44] However, in keeping within the 2.25% range, it was the central bank of the currency at the bottom of the band which had to intervene to support it. This asymmetry of support weakened the appeal of the Snake for weaker currencies and, as with the dollar in the Bretton Woods system, tended in practice to mean that all countries aligned to a pole star currency, in this case the DM. The UK joined the Snake and then left after eight weeks. The lira left in February 1973. France also left and was then unsuccessful in trying to rejoin.

UK Exchange Rate Policy, North Sea Oil, and a Floating Pound

Having left the Snake, the pound initially floated downwards, but then received some support from OPEC petrodollars being recycled through London.[45] It then fell again to the sufficient alarm of politicians that the UK borrowed from the IMF. In return for IMF loans the UK government signed Letters of Intent in which the UK agreed to maintain a competitive exchange rate fixed in terms of export price competitiveness around its level in the fourth quarter of 1976. This would have implied an indicator of export competitiveness of around 92.5 and an exchange rate of about $1.67 in the early part of 1977. The more general aim was to keep in the range $1.60 to $1.72, although this rate was tweaked, usually downwards, in subsequent meetings with the IMF where the virtues of export-led growth were extolled. The concern to maintain the competitiveness of the UK exchange rate was highlighted by the knowledge that the benefits of North Sea oil would begin to flow. While these were expected to 'transform the balance of payments', it was also recognized that a high exchange rate could cause damage to the manufacturing sector which remained important for employment and exports.[46]

---

[44] Buiter, Corsetti, and Pesenti, *Financial Markets*, p. 23.
[45] Foreman-Peck, 'Trade and the balance of payments', p. 169.
[46] TNA T382/20, Hedley-Miller, paper, 'Management of the exchange rate', paper, January 1977, paras. 1–3, 5; TNA T382/25, Andrew Britton, paper, 'The exchange rate and economic strategy', October 1977, para. 1.

Lurking in the background were fears of the UK contracting a case of the 'Dutch Disease'. Following the discovery and subsequent extraction of natural gas in Holland in 1959 the increase in income benefited non-tradeable goods and services (restaurants, hairdressers) whose prices could rise but damaged tradeable goods whose prices were determined on the world market but whose internal costs rose as its domestic labour and other costs rose. Internally, resources switched into the 'boom' sector and exported manufacturing output and employment fell.[47] While the Dutch Disease had occurred in a fixed exchange rate system, whereas the pound was now floating, it seemed likely, as the Treasury noted, that 'because of the effect of North Sea oil there is the possibility of continuing upward pressure on the exchange rate of a sort we have not experienced in modern times.'[48]

In theory, one possible means of mitigating the effects of oil sales on the exchange rate was simply to drill less oil and slow the rate of depletion. In theoretical terms, decisions on the optimal rate of depletion of exhaustible reserves were strongly influenced by expectations of future prices. Accounting for only 5% of world oil consumption in 1984, the UK was an oil price-taker.[49] It was recognized that to extract and sell oil as quickly as possible might be to forego higher income from sufficiently higher oil prices in the future. The economic theory of depletion was well developed thanks to the work of economists like Gray, Hotelling, and Solow.[50] In Solow's asset equilibrium approach, the rate of return expressed as a capital gain from holding the asset under the sea was compared with the opportunity cost of the depleted oil invested in alternative (and more diversified) assets. Central to both approaches was the comparison of future net earnings discounted back to present value with the opportunity cost returns foregone as expressed in the interest/discount rate used. Even if owners chose to deplete, speculators could still buy and hold oil if they held a sufficiently more optimistic view of future price than did the original owners.[51]

The issue of the rate of depletion was considered by an interdepartmental Working Group on Depletion Policy which first reported in January 1976.[52] Particularly in the wake of the OPEC1 price hike, there was speculation that

[47] Bean, 'Sterling misalignment and British Trade performance'; Corden, 'Booming sector'; TNA T381/70, Bottrill, paper, 'Economic aspects of North Sea oil', 1978, para. 18.

[48] TNA T382/25, note, 'Exchange rate policy in the medium term', October 1977.

[49] Weyman-Jones, *The Economics of Energy Policy*, p. 184.

[50] Solow, 'The economics of resources'; Gray, 'Rent under the assumptions of exhaustibility'; Hotelling, 'The economics of exhaustible resources'.

[51] TNA T381/70, Bottrill, paper, 'Economic aspects of North Sea Oil', 1978, paras. 10–13.

[52] Kemp, *The Official History of North Sea Oil and Gas: Volume 1*, p. 535.

oil prices could double or even treble in real terms by the end of the century.[53] On that basis, oil conserved in the 1980s for use in the 1990s and beyond would have an increased value. Indeed, as was remarked in the second review of depletion policy, the UK government's much-vaunted aim of becoming self-sufficient in oil probably came at a high economic cost, a better strategy being to import oil at the current world price and extract the reserves at a later higher price.[54]

Suggestions that the rate of depletion be reduced were not received well by the owners of the rigs, who had borne the risk of exploration, development, and now production. Worried about political interference in their activities, they had obtained assurances (the Varley Assurances) that no restriction would be imposed on North Sea oil finds made before the end of 1975, and that if they were imposed on later discoveries, the oil companies would be allowed to recover at least 150% of their capital investment in the field.[55] In the short-term, the respecting of the Varley Assurances meant that the UK government had almost no control over the rate of depletion. However, since oil fields discovered after 1975 were not protected by the Varley Assurances, then discussion of future depletion policy remained very pertinent.

An alternative longer-term approach to slowing the rate of depletion was to have smaller licensing rounds. Again, had the British National Oil Corporation (BNOC), established by the UK government in 1976, participated in the early risk stages of exploration and development, then it might have exercised more influence over development and extraction rates.[56] Instead BNOC was 'carried' (i.e. it did not contribute) in the exploration stage, and did not operate on a pay-as-you-go basis. This was the subject of sharp disagreement between the Department of Energy under Tony Benn and the Treasury with Denis Healey as Chancellor. For the Fifth Round of licensing in 1976, Mr Benn proposed that participation be at 51% in every licence and that licences be issued only after the conclusion of a satisfactory Operating Agreement between BNOC and its partners. The Cabinet supported Benn's proposal although the Treasury was less keen on 'putting up Government money to finance North Sea development when the alternative is for the oil companies—some of whom may have a better credit rating than HMG on overseas markets—to do it for us'.[57] However, with the election of the Conservative government in May 1979, BNOC's days were numbered. Had it not been for the heightened

---

[53] Cmnd. 7101, *Green Paper on Energy Policy*; Cmnd. 7143, *The Challenge of North Sea Oil*.
[54] TNA POWE 63/1586, 'Depletion Policy', October 1978, p. 20, para 27.
[55] Kemp, *Official History: Volume 1*, pp. 351, 545.   [56] Chick, 'Property rights'.
[57] TNA POWE 63/1528, Barnett, letter, September 1976.

concern with the security of oil supply following the revolution in Iran in 1979, then BNOC might well have been privatized in that year.[58] As it was, BNOC only had to wait until August 1982 to see its production assets, but not its trading assets, transferred to a new company called Britoil.[59]

The election of the first Thatcher government in 1979 also marked a change in depletion policy. While in 1977 the Department of Energy was discussing how, while respecting the Varley Assurances, cuts could be made to production, from 1979 these mainly microeconomic assessments of the socially optimal rate of depletion intruded more into political macroeconomic considerations. The Chancellor of the Exchequer, Geoffrey Howe, became concerned at the effect on tax revenues of any cuts in oil production. Cuts of 5 million tonnes in 1982 and 10 million in 1983 were estimated to increase the Public Sector Borrowing Requirement by £600 million in 1982/3 and £1.7 billion in 1983/4. Further, any receipts from the privatization of BNOC's and BGC's oil interests would be depressed and further investment in the North Sea could be discouraged. Howe was supported by Nigel Lawson at the Department of Energy who questioned the assumption that oil prices would be higher in the future. A similar view had also been expressed by Alan Walters, the Special Adviser to the prime minister. Lawson wrote a note to the prime minister arguing that it was no part of the Government's philosophy to engage in commodity speculation, such as was entailed by storing oil in the ground. The Central Policy Review Staff, a government think tank, expressed its reservations, but the prime minister agreed with Nigel Lawson. Events proved the Lawson and Walters perspective to be correct, whatever their multiplicity of reasons for holding such views. The oil price fell sharply in 1986, and in real terms had not recovered to the levels seen in 1980 and 1981 by 2007 (see Table 8.10). Broadly speaking, extra oil in the ground would not have proved a good investment in that period.

The election of the first Thatcher government also coincided with, if not entirely caused, a shift of emphasis regarding the accommodation of North Sea oil income in exchange rate policy. As seen, in the wake of the discussions with the IMF, there had been concern with the competitiveness of the exchange rate. However an alternative view was that it was by letting the exchange rise that the economic benefits of North Sea oil would be realized. From 1977 especially, some of the broad lines of this approach were increasingly set out mainly by monetarist economists, often in the national newspapers or in stockbrokers' papers. In *The Sunday Times*, the London Business School

---

[58] Kemp, *Official History: Volume 1*, pp. 542–3.   [59] Chick, 'Property rights', pp. 159–60.

Table 8.10. Crude oil prices, 1950–2004

	Current prices $	2012 prices $
1950	1.71	16.30
1955	1.93	16.54
1960	1.90	14.71
1965	1.80	13.08
1970	1.80	10.64
1971	2.24	12.68
1972	2.48	13.61
1973	3.29	17.00
1974	11.58	53.94
1975	11.53	49.21
1976	12.80	51.63
1977	13.92	52.70
1978	14.02	49.37
1979	31.61	99.97
1980	36.83	102.62
1981	35.93	90.75
1982	32.97	78.44
1983	29.55	68.12
1984	28.78	63.60
1985	27.56	58.61
1986	14.43	30.23
1987	18.44	37.26
1988	14.92	28.96
1989	18.23	33.75
1990	23.73	41.68
1991	20.00	33.72
1992	19.32	31.62
1993	16.97	26.97
1994	15.82	24.50
1995	17.02	25.64
1996	20.67	30.24
1997	19.09	27.31
1998	12.72	17.91
1999	17.97	24.76
2000	28.50	37.99
2001	25.44	31.69
2002	25.02	31.94
2003	28.83	35.97
2004	38.27	46.51
2005	54.52	64.09
2006	65.14	74.19
2007	72.39	80.16
2008	97.26	103.71
2009	61.67	66.00
2010	79.50	83.70
2011	111.26	113.56
2012	111.67	111.67

Note: 1950, 1955, 1960, 1965, 1970–1983 Arabian Light posted at Ras Tanura. 1984–2012 Brent dated.

Source: BP Statistical Review of World Energy, June 2013.

economists Terry Burns and Alan Budd argued for allowing the exchange rate to rise, thereby causing interest rates and inflation to fall, both directly through lower import prices and indirectly through reduced wage settlements.[60] The fall in nominal interest rates would stimulate investment and consumption, as lower inflation reduced the need to force consumers to save in order to maintain the real value of their financial balances. Broadly similar views were expressed, again in 1977, in various newspaper articles and stockbrokers' papers by Samuel Brittan, Peter Jay, Gordon Pepper (Greenwells), Tim Congdon (Messels), and Patrick Minford of Liverpool University. Their favoured response was to keep monetary policy tight and allow the exchange rate to drift upwards, thereby taking the benefit of North Sea oil in the form of lower inflation and improved terms of trade. It was recognized that a rise in the exchange rate would reduce the price competitiveness of UK exports, but as Patrick Minford remarked in the December 1977 issue of *The Banker*, just as past depreciations had not improved competitiveness, so future appreciations would not worsen it.[61] It was doubted that long-term improvements in competitiveness were achieved by means of short-term manipulation of the exchange rate. Historically, devaluation was viewed as leading to higher wage claims as workers sought compensation for higher food and other import prices. As firms used higher profits arising from devaluation to meet these wage claims, so competitiveness would revert to its long-term level. If there was little to be done about competitiveness in this way, then why not concentrate on reducing inflation? In similar vein, the ability of incomes policy to contain wage demands and limit the rise in real wages was viewed with scepticism. Better to reduce money wages by creating expectations of a lower rate of inflation by having a tight monetary policy and an appreciating exchange rate.[62] There was also a view that as the foreign exchange market would know well in advance that the North Sea oil wells were running dry, then it was probable that market forces would restore competitiveness to the industrial sector of the economy gradually over a period of years, i.e. in sufficient time to permit new investment and the transfer of resources back from other sectors of the economy.[63] Mention was also made of Fama's efficient market hypothesis (EMH) such that capital markets would operate in such a way as

[60] TNA T378/56, Britton, note, '1977: How to survive it', January 1977, paras. 1–2.

[61] TNA 378/56, Middleton, paper, 'Exchange Rate Policy', May 1977, paras. 7, 8f; TNA T381/70, Bottrill, paper, 'Economic aspects of North Sea oil', 1978, paras. 16, 18; TNA T378/56, Britton, note, '1977: How to survive it', January 1977, para. 3.

[62] TNA 378/56, Middleton, paper, 'Exchange rate policy', May 1977, paras. 8c, 8.e; TNA T382/18, Britton, paper, 'Positioning paper on economic strategy', November 1975, para. 4.

[63] TNA T382/25, note, 'Exchange rate policy in the medium term', October 1977.

to achieve the maximum possible social benefit. This took a rather benign view of the outlook of foreign-exchange dealers who might well recognize the long-term prospects for sterling, but preferred to take their profits in shorter-term speculative activity.[64] It also conflated all activities in the economy into a similar time period. While financial capital might well move easily and quickly between different currencies viewed as assets, the impact on fixed capital investment in exporting industries of an appreciating exchange rate was likely to be of much slower and longer duration, and, if plant closed, less easily remedied. Assumptions that as oil prices and exchange rates fell then manufacturing would return not only ignored the general process of deindustrialization occurring in the developing world, but also ignored the possibility of a hysteresis effect occurring in the traded goods market, similar to that seen in the labour market.[65]

The movements in the nominal US$:£ exchange rate are shown in Table 8.11. The fluctuations in the exchange rate from $1.75 in 1977 to $2.33 by 1980, and then from $2.33 in 1980 to £1.3 by 1985 were considerable. Expressed as a real exchange rate, the relative unit costs often considered to be the best measure of the real exchange rate, rose by over 55% from 1977 to 1981, an unparalleled increase.[66] While the oil price hike of 1979–1981 and the rise in US interest rates in 1980 may explain some of the appreciation of the real exchange rate, so too did a monetary squeeze and a reduction in official action to reduce the exchange rate rise.[67] When in 1977 the exchange rate rose, the UK government added £9.6 billion to the official reserves (including the UK's reserve position in the IMF). In 1979 and 1980 combined, the increase in official reserves was only £1.3 billion. In 1979, there was an unexpected fall in money supply, interest rates rose as money became scarcer, and the government's Medium Term Financial Strategy was announced in March 1980. On one estimate, every 1% reduction in the rate of monetary growth at first raised

Table 8.11. Sterling: US dollar exchange rate 1975–1986

1975	1976	1977	1978	1979	1980	1981	1982	1983	1984	1985	1986
2.22	1.80	1.75	1.92	2.12	2.33	2.03	1.75	1.52	1.34	1.3	1.47

Source: Central Statistical Office, *Economic Trends: Annual Supplement, 1996* edition, 1995, London: CSO, Table 5:1, p. 223.

[64] Fama, 'Efficient capital markets'; TNA T378/57, Allen, paper, 'Some recent evidence on short-run exchange rate behaviour'. September 1977.

[65] Bean, 'Sterling misalignment', p. 42; Blanchard and Summers, 'Hysteresis'; Lindbeck and Snower, 'Wage setting'.

[66] Backhouse, *Applied UK Macroeconomics*, p. 249.   [67] Bean, 'Sterling misalignment'.

Table 8.12. GDP at factor cost, UK, 1971–1990 (1990=100)

1971	1972	1973	1974	1975	1976	1977	1978	1979	1980
65.3	67.1	72.2	71.1	70.6	72.5	74.4	76.4	78.5	76.9
1981	1982	1983	1984	1985	1986	1987	1988	1989	1990
76.0	77.4	80.3	81.9	85.2	88.6	92.7	97.3	99.4	100.0

Source: Central Statistical Office, *Economic Trends: Annual Supplement*, 1996, No. 21, London: HMSO, Table 1.1.

the exchange rate by 2.3%.[68] Added to this was the spending effect of North Sea oil, and this may have hastened the shift from manufacturing to services. Manufacturing's share of GDP fell from 31.7% of GDP in 1973 to 24.2% in 1988. The rate of fall from 29.3% in 1978 to 25.0% in 1981, a fall of more than 4% in three years, was particularly striking.[69] More generally, economic activity slowed from 1979 and GDP did not exceed its level of 1979 until 1983 (see Table 8.12). The mixture of the rise in the exchange rate, the reduction in income tax rates, and the addition to national income represented by North Sea oil income encouraged consumption and imports. This import substitution, while common in many economies, was already becoming a particular problem in the UK before the advent of North Sea oil revenues. Between 1974 and 1985 manufactured consumer goods imports more than doubled. Import penetration, measured by the ratio of import value to apparent consumption, rose from 19% to 36%. The increase was particularly rapid between 1979 and 1982.[70]

Apart from manufacturing export industries, some traded goods service sectors also went into what proved to be irreversible decline. Tourism, which had previously been a large net earner of foreign exchange for the UK, swung into deficit for most of the 1980s. Tourist trips and holidays overseas were given a fillip by rising exchange rates, cheaper airfares, and the increased number and range of destinations offered by package tour companies to sun-starved Brits. In the midst of rapid deindustrialization, there was also in the 1980s a slump in the deep-sea transport account as it moved into deficit. In 1968, UK registered ships carried 59% by weight of all British exports to America, Asia, and other distant continents. By 1980, this share had fallen to 22%. Between 1977 and 1983, the total tonnage of ships (including oil tankers, bulk carriers, and container ships) registered under the UK flag fell

[68] Foreman-Peck, 'Trade and the balance of payments', pp. 170, 177; Buiter and Miller, 'The Thatcher experiment'.

[69] Backhouse, *Applied UK Macroeconomics*, p. 191.

[70] Foreman-Peck, 'Trade and the balance of payments', p. 150.

by nearly 50%, from 30 million gross tonnes to 16 million gross tonnes. Such a decline in capacity, with almost half the fleet gone, made a recovery of market share extremely unlikely.[71]

Changing Times after Bretton Woods

The Bretton Woods system of fixed, if adjustable, exchange rates was accompanied by restrictions on the movement of capital in and out of economies. Restrictions on the convertibility of currencies had been lifted from 1 January 1959, but this applied only to the current account of the balance of payments. The restrictions on movements out of capital account remained. In general, at the Bretton Woods negotiations there had been a distrust of private capital movements and of the ability of the international movement of 'hot money' to disrupt efforts to achieve free trade based on fixed exchange rates.[72] In the 1940s and 1950s, there had been concern that easing capital controls would undermine efforts to support the international role of sterling as a reserve currency. By the 1960s, the dollar had clearly supplanted sterling as the world's principal reserve currency, and sterling's role in financing world trade had fallen from around 50% after 1945 through 35% in 1960 to 20% by 1970.[73] In similar fashion, while sterling had comprised 87% of the official reserves of overseas sterling countries, this had fallen to 65% by 1967.[74] Yet while the concern to support the international role of sterling may have lessened, there was still concern about short-term capital movements in response to interest rate differentials in a fixed exchange rate system which did not clear the imbalance between surplus economies like Germany and deficit economies like the United States and the UK. While the UK government did not impose controls on capital inflows coming from the growing Eurodollar market, it retained controls on capital outflows.[75]

Capital controls were abolished in October 1979. The collapse of Bretton Woods and the floating of the pound made this step possible and both the greater movement of capital and floating exchange rates brought benefits to the City of London. The City of London had already benefited from the flow of US Foreign Direct Investment (FDI) into Western Europe and the development of the Eurobond market from the end of the 1950s. In the 1950s, FDI in

---

[71] Rowthorn and Wells, *De-industrialisation and Foreign Trade*, p. 127, 129–31.
[72] Krugman and Obstfeld, *International Economics*, p. 549.
[73] Schenk, 'The new City', p. 326.   [74] Schenk, 'The new City', p. 327.
[75] Schenk, 'The new City', p. 334.

the UK rose from $542 million to $1.6 billion, and 81% of the 230 new foreign company subsidiaries opening in Britain were American. By 1963 it was estimated that foreign companies accounted for about 10% of the net output of British manufacturing.[76] In contrast to restrictions in the United States, the more relaxed regulatory regime in the City of London attracted foreign banks to open branches in London, especially in the second half of the 1960s. Between 1965 and 1971, sixty-nine foreign banks opened branches in London, and 40% of these were US banks. In the 1950s, only two US banks had opened branches in London.[77] Whereas in the 1950s, the world of financial investment was largely the preserve of rich individuals with fewer than 10% of the stocks on the New York Stock Exchange being held by institutions, by 2008, institutions held 63% of stocks.[78]

The loosening of the rule-based Bretton Woods system and the ending of the restrictions on the movement of capital encouraged greater arbitraging operations between financial markets. With greater financial mobility and fluctuating exchange rates and oil and other commodity prices, there was increased interest in the development of futures markets both in themselves and as one means of hedging future risks of price movements.[79] The Chicago Mercantile Exchange was established in 1972 to allow future exchange rates to be fixed for future transactions, and in so doing it also allowed speculation against future movements in exchange rates.[80] As oil price volatility grew, so futures trading picked up in 1978 ahead of the 1979 oil price rise and then again in 1986 as the oil price fall encouraged the search for futures contracts.[81] What might be termed as the financialization of finance occurred. With exchange rates fluctuating and no longer linked to a gold standard, money-making opportunities arose.[82] The ability to move capital more freely also encouraged the development of the 'carry trade' in which money was borrowed in currencies with low interest rates and lent in currencies with higher interest rates.

While investors and companies sought to hedge against future price movements, the international banking system was itself subject to shocks. Oil dollars flowing into Western banks were lent to what were then termed as Less

---

[76] Schenk, *The Decline of Sterling*, p. 18; Schenk, *International Economic Relations*, p. 44. The stock of inward FDI in the United Kingdom amounted to about 6.5% of GDP in 1960 and it was to rise to 27% by the end of 1999. In the 1970s, about 10% of this US outward FDI was in banking and insurance.

[77] Schenk, 'The new City', p. 325.   [78] Authers, *The Fearful Rise of Markets*, p. 10.

[79] Schenk, 'The oil market and global finance in the 1980s', p. 63; Favero and Faloppa, 'Price regimes, price series and price trends', pp. 15–34, p. 27.

[80] Authers, *The Fearful Rise of Markets*, pp. 65, 67.

[81] Schenk, 'The oil market and global finance in the 1980s', pp.64–5.

[82] Authers, *The Fearful Rise of Markets*, p. 32.

Developed Countries, the capital and interest on whose loans required repayment in hard currencies such as the US dollar. These loans became very sensitive to rises in interest rates such as those attributed to Paul Volcker at the Federal Reserve in 1980 in his efforts to reduce the domestic rate of inflation. To the interest rate movements could be added unfavourable movements in exchange rates, not least because of rising interest rates and tightening monetary policy, such that borrowers struggled to make repayments. In August 1982, Mexico announced that it was unable to make further payments on its debt followed by Venezuela, Chile, Peru, the Philippines, and a few African countries. Latin American debts of $51 billion, stood at nearly twice the value of the nine largest US banks. In time the situation was gradually defused by the US Secretaries of the Treasury James Baker (1985–1988) and Nicholas Brady (1988–1993) using such devices as debt reduction and debt-equity swaps.[83] In the meantime, concerned that governments would refuse to meet their debt obligations, investors began to pool their risks and their lending. In place of bank lending to Lesser Developed Countries there was a move to an Emerging Markets approach in which the developing fund management industry started to pool investments in exotic exchanges.[84] As fund management grew, so too did banks look for new business. In the UK, seeing developments in the US where the Reagan administration allowed banks to package mortgage loans into bonds and sell them to investors, banks began to engage in mortgage lending alongside the traditional building societies. In turn, the building societies often sought to demutualize to become traded share-owned banks.[85] Among investment banks, partnerships began to unwind themselves, so as to be able to float on the market. The assets accumulated in the past were sold to the present, and the newly owned investment banks with less of their own skin in the game began to lend and trade with more of the money of others.[86] In London, many of the older investment banks and brokers were absorbed into larger public banks. Change was given a further boost by the effects of Big Bang, which removed the old distinctions between stockbrokers and market makers.[87] All of these changes occurred at the same time as the volume of financial trading rose. In global foreign exchange trading, the daily average value of trading was over $500 billion per day in April 1989 of which $187 billion was traded daily in London, $129 billion in the US, and $115 billion in Tokyo. Only nine years later, in April 1998, the daily global value of foreign exchange trading had jumped to around $1.7 trillion,

---

[83] Cooper, 'The Gold Standard'; Obstfeld, 'The global capital market', pp. 9–30.
[84] Authers, *The Fearful Rise of Markets*, p. 40.   [85] Authers, *The Fearful Rise of Markets*, p. 49.
[86] Taleb, *Skin in the Game*.   [87] Authers, *The Fearful Rise of Markets*, p. 79.

of which $637 billion was traded daily in London, $351 billion in New York, and $149 billion in Tokyo.[88] In general, the world capital markets grew on a scale not seen since 1914.[89] As the financial world became more sophisticated, so it seemed also to become more unstable. Even before the development of some of the more abstruse financial instruments, national governments in a post–Bretton Woods world sought assurance in the management of current and future exchange rates.

The Euro

While the UK was worrying about accommodating North Sea oil revenues into its exchange rate policy, the European Commission had been moving towards establishing the European Monetary Union (EMU). In 1977, encouraged by Roy Jenkins, the former Labour government Chancellor of the Exchequer and Home Secretary, and now President of the European Commission, discussions and negotiation of a EMU culminated in the adoption of a European Monetary System (EMS) by the European Council on 5 and 6 December 1978 in Brussels. Specifically designed so as not to require an amendment of the Treaty of Rome, the EMS came into operation on 13 March 1979. The UK pound was not a member, but all other member currencies were. The EMS was a more modest version of the EMU, although those grander ambitions remained alive. The EMS comprised three main elements. The first of these was the European Currency Unit (ECU), which was valued as a weighted basket of participating currencies of which the DM formed about one-third, and the pound, even though the UK was not in the EMS, about 13%. Members would peg their exchange rates to the ECU (with margins of +/- 2.25%) and so anchor to an exchange rate mechanism, which was the second main element of the EMS. The third was the European Monetary Cooperation Fund.[90] In its early years the EMS combined limited ambition with a welcome dullness. With a strong and rising dollar, a low-inflation West Germany at its centre, capital controls retained, and with the possibility of realignments by higher inflation economies following mutual agreement between participating Member States and the Commission, the ERM enjoyed a period of quiet stability for the first years of the EMS.[91]

---

[88] Krugman and Obstfeld, *International Economics*, p. 335.
[89] 'Symposium', pp. 3–84.   [90] Backhouse, *Applied UK Macroeconomics*, p. 253.
[91] Buiter, Corsetti, and Pesenti, *Financial Markets and European Monetary Co-operation*, pp. 24–5.

Encouraged by the convergent stability which began to appear in the EMS, in 1984 Jacques Delors, France's Minister of Finance and future President of the European Commission (1985–1995), issued a White Paper on the development of an internal market. This became the basis of the Single European Act (SEA) adopted by the Commission in 1986, which was the first revision of the Community's founding Treaty of Rome. While tariffs had already been eliminated within the EEC, the SEA sought to remove all other institutional and regulatory barriers to trade. The aim was to move the EEC from a customs union to a single market in goods and services, labour, and capital within six years.[92] The removal of capital controls increased the risk of speculative attacks on currencies, but no realignment of ERM currencies occurred between January 1987 and September 1992, and this may have encouraged thoughts of a single market operating with a single currency. In 1988 the European Council appointed a committee chaired by Jacques Delors to study the feasibility of supplementing the single market with a monetary union. The recommendations of the Committee for the Study of Economic and Monetary Union (1989), published as the Delors Report, were endorsed as the official blueprint for monetary unification in Europe by the European Council at the Madrid Summit in June 1989.[93] The Delors Report provided the framework for intergovernmental negotiations in 1991 and the Maastricht Treaty.[94] In contrast to the Werner Report which had recommended removing capital controls at the end of a process of harmonization, the Delors Report preferred their removal at the beginning. On 7 February 1992 the Maastricht Treaty (The Treaty on European Union) was signed, which formally established the European Union in 1993, essentially as a fiscal and monetary union with common economic policies and more centralized administration. With the formation of the European Union in 1993, the EEC was incorporated and renamed the European Community (EC). In 2009, the EC's institutions were absorbed into the EU's wider framework and the Community ceased to exist.

The ERM and the Euro

Since the demise of Bretton Woods, the UK had tended to eschew managed exchange rate systems. It had joined the Snake in the tunnel very briefly (May to June 1972) as a token gesture of its commitment to membership of

---

[92] Schenk, *International Economic Relations*, p. 94.
[93] Buiter, Corsetti, and Pesenti, *Financial Markets and European Monetary Co-operation*, p. 29.
[94] Eichengreen, 'European monetary unification', p. 1,324.

the EEC. In part its attitude may have been coloured by the fact that unlike the rest of the EEC it was going to be an oil exporter and the price of oil was set in US dollars by OPEC.[95] However, in the mid-1980s the question of joining the ERM resurfaced. UK monetary policy had changed with the targeting of broad money (M3) being abandoned in 1985 in favour of the narrower M0 measure, the oil price falling (see Table 8.10) and the exchange rate falling to a new low as US interest rates rose. There was a stock market crash in October 1987, in response to which a shot of fiscal stimulus was injected into the economy. This, together with the rise in broad money from 1985/1986 contributed to a boom. The current account deficit stood at 4% by the beginning of 1989, but reluctant to use a falling exchange rate to raise import prices, the Chancellor Nigel Lawson preferred to raise interest rates to reduce demand and the trade deficit.[96]

When the UK did join the ERM in 1990, almost immediately and perversely the ERM began to lose its stability. The failure of Danish voters to approve the Maastricht Treaty in a referendum in June 1992 and uncertainty about the outcome of the next scheduled referendum on the Maastricht Treaty in France on 20 September 1992 raised doubts about the political viability of the Maastricht Treaty's wider ambitions. As the Bundesbank in the aftermath of German reunification in 1990 ran with high interest rates, speculators wondered for how long the Italian and UK governments would remain in the ERM, not least as a weakening US dollar put pressure on European trade balances. Ultimately, after Finland had unpegged the Markka from the DM in early September 1992, the Swedish krona resorted to interest rates of 75%, and for a time, 500% to defend itself from speculative attack. The Italian lira was allowed to devalue by 7% against the rest of the currencies. On Monday, 14 September 1992, speculators turned their attention to the pound. On Black Wednesday 16 September 1992 the pound sterling was withdrawn from the ERM, the Italian lira was allowed to float, and the Spanish peseta was devalued by 5% against all the remaining EMS currencies. Both Spain and Portugal devalued their currencies further against the ECU in November and again in May 1993. In February 1993, the Irish pound devalued by 10% against the ECU. While French voters very narrowly approved (51% of the votes) the Maastricht Treaty, the ERM was effectively ended. Forced out of the ERM, the pound depreciated 25% against ERM currencies like the French franc, German mark, and Dutch guilder in the five months following exit from the ERM.

[95] Neal, *The Economics of Europe*, p. 99.
[96] Foreman-Peck, 'Trade and the balance of payments', p. 171.

UK exports were boosted and the UK seemed to secure an inflation-free recovery from recession while a DM-linked French economy suffered slow growth and rising unemployment.[97]

Perhaps surprisingly, the collapse of the ERM renewed interest in the adoption of a single currency within the European Union. Given the unhelpful reduction in relative wage flexibility caused by moving to a single currency so early in the process of German reunification, it was not as if there was no recent experience of the inflexibility introduced by a single currency.[98] While the ERM did break down, it had enjoyed early years of convergent stability. The appeal of a single currency lay in terms, obviously, of eliminating exchange rates and their swings together with the apparent contribution which a single currency made to the completion of the single market project. There were further potential administrative benefits, not least in managing the CAP. When France and West Germany had realigned their currencies in 1969, the CAP had moved to set agricultural prices in a green currency which did not match changes in members' nominal exchange rates but moved in equal proportion to them. However, this in itself created new incentives within the CAP, such as that for farmers in strongly devaluing countries to export their output to other EEC members rather than sell it domestically. To prevent this happening when the French franc was devalued in 1969, the EEC placed a tax on French exports to the rest of the EEC and a subsidy on French imports from the EEC. These taxes and subsidies were referred to as *monetary compensation amounts*, or MCAs.[99] Yet all of these potential benefits needed to be set against the increased difficulties of clearing trade imbalances within the EU and of allowing national economies to adjust to economic shocks.

Whatever the misgivings of economists, on 1 January 1999 the Euro was introduced as an accounting currency and it replaced the ECU. The EMU came into being on 1 January 1999, with an initial complement of eleven out of the fifteen EU countries. On 1 January 2002 Euro notes and coins came into circulation. Eligibility for participation in the EMU depended on satisfying a set of criteria set out in the Treaty on European Union (the Treaty of Maastricht). These criteria were that: the national central bank of the country concerned should be independent; that its currency should have participated without stress in the ERM for at least two years; that the country's inflation rate should not have been 1.5 percentage points above the unweighted average of the three benchmark EU member states with the lowest inflation rate;

[97] Krugman and Obstfeld, *International Economics*, p. 437; Neal, *The Economics of Europe*, pp. 104–5.
[98] Goodhart, 'European monetary integration', p. 1,086; Bofinger, 'The German monetary unification'.
[99] Buiter, Corsetti, and Pesenti, *Financial Markets and European Monetary Co-operation*, p. 20.

that its long-term interest rate should have been within 2 percentage points of that of the three best inflation performers; that the ratio of the budget deficit to GDP should not exceed 3%; and that its debt-to-GDP ratio should not exceed 60%. In the event, the criteria relating to the ratio of government debt to GDP was effectively ignored and neither Finland nor Italy fulfilled the letter of the criterion pertaining to exchange rate performance. Greece failed to meet the criteria, whilst the UK and Denmark exercised the opt-outs negotiated in the Maastricht Treaty.[100]

In its turn, HM Treasury produced its own list of five tests which were to be applied to consideration of whether or not the UK should join the Euro. These tests were vague, probably deliberately so. They were: that there should be sustainable convergence between the UK and the economies of a single currency; that there should remain sufficient flexibility to cope with subsequent economic change; and that the effects on investment, the financial services, and employment should all be considered.[101] This vagueness left the decision ultimately as a political one. This was entirely appropriate as the Euro project always had a strong political element to it. Tellingly, the Delors Report insisted on the early introduction of a single currency to ensure 'the irreversibility of the move to monetary union', although at the same time Delors had proposed that national budgetary policies should not be transferred to the Community, but that countries should be subject to budget deficit rules.[102] This reflected the political reality of a mismatch between a federal currency and national budget sovereignty. In adopting the Euro, national control over monetary policy was surrendered, and this became centralized in the ECB which enjoyed considerable political independence and whose main remit was to maintain price stability within the European Union.[103]

This mix of centralized monetary powers and decentralized political and fiscal power spanning a collection of sovereign states with little clear interest in federal centralization looked awkward.[104] The removal of national exchange rates removed the ability of national economies to adjust to economic shocks through their exchange rate. Removing national currencies made it no longer possible to reflect changes in regional competitiveness in balance of payments data, this now finding expression in falling output and employment. Without centralized political and fiscal authority, it became difficult to distribute funds to struggling regions. As the economist Robert Mundell had recognized in his 1961 article on optimal currency areas:

---

[100] Artis, 'Should the UK join EMU?'.   [101] Artis, 'Should the UK join EMU?'.
[102] Eichengreen, 'European monetary unification', p. 1,325.
[103] Neal, *The Economics of Europe*, p. 9.
[104] Goodhart, 'European monetary integration', p. 1,084.

A system of flexible exchange rates was originally propounded as an alternative to the gold-standard mechanism that many economists blamed for the worldwide spread of depression after 1929. But if the arguments against the gold standard were correct, then why should a similar argument not apply against a common currency system in a multi-regional country?...Today, if the case for flexible exchange rates is a strong one, it is, in logic, a case for flexible exchange rates based on *regional* currencies, not on national currencies. The optimum currency area is the region.[105]

Mundell recognized that while the region was an economic unit, the currency area was a larger expression of national sovereignty.[106] Where there was no over-arching federal sovereignty, then it was less clear why regions or EU countries would surrender their national currency and with it the possibility of running a flexible exchange rate policy. The core of the Mundell analysis had always been that countries or regions constituted an optimum currency area when the real benefits for their economies of fixing irreversibly their exchange rates (or in practice adopting a single currency) exceeded the real costs.[107] The conflating idea that a widening single European trade area could be overlaid with a single currency area was at odds with the theoretical work on what constituted an optimal currency area.

The idea of an optimum currency area(s) came to Mundell in the academic year 1955–1956 when he was writing a dissertation under James Meade for the Massachusetts Institute for Technology (MIT) at the LSE. As Mundell recalled, at the time flexible and fixed exchange rates was 'a hot subject at the LSE'. In the following academic year, 1956–1957, Mundell was a postdoctoral fellow in political economy at the University of Chicago, where Milton Friedman, like Meade, championed flexible exchange rates, but for very different reasons. Meade, the liberal socialist, saw flexible rates as a device for achieving external balance while freeing policy tools for the implementation of national planning objectives. Friedman, the libertarian conservative, saw flexible exchange rates as a way of getting rid of exchange and trade controls. Both economists saw flexible rates as a means of altering real wages when money wage rigidities would otherwise cause unemployment.[108]

---

[105] Mundell, 'A theory of optimum currency areas'.
[106] Mundell, 'A theory of optimum currency areas'.
[107] Blejer, Frenkel, Leiderman, Razion with Cheney, *Optimum Currency Area*, p. 8; Kenen, *Economic and Monetary Union in Europe*, p. 81.
[108] Mundell, 'Updating the agenda for monetary union', pp. 29–30.

At the time that Mundell was developing his ideas, there was little immediate prospect that 'national currencies would ever be abandoned in favour of any other arrangement'.[109] However, that did not mean that with the creation of the EEC, the subject of a common currency for the six countries was not discussed. In the 1950s, James Meade's view was that the conditions for a common currency in Western Europe did not exist, and that, especially because of the lack of labour mobility, a system of flexible exchange rates would be more effective in promoting balance of payments equilibrium and internal stability.[110] This view was broadly opposed by the Tibor Scitovsky, a Hungarian economist based at Stanford, who favoured a common currency believing that it would induce a greater degree of capital mobility, although accepting that steps should be taken to make labour more mobile and to facilitate supranational employment policies. What was common to both approaches was the view that an essential ingredient of a common currency, or a single currency area, was a high degree of factor mobility.[111]

As in the wake of Bretton Woods there was an increase in the mobility of private capital, so national economies and national governments became more vulnerable to the movements of funds across foreign exchanges. Specifically, the mobility of financial capital limited the scope for setting national interest rates, or even for conducting monetary and fiscal policies best geared to their own national requirements. Whatever the problems of a fixed exchange rate, in combination with capital controls it had permitted more national economic policies to be devised. With flexible exchange rates and capital mobility, the Mundell-Fleming trilemma broadly applied, that of only ever being allowed two out of three from free capital movement, a fixed exchange rate, and an independent monetary policy. Once the genie had been released from the lamp of capital controls, then international capital mobility effectively meant that economies could choose between running their own exchange rate policy or their own independent monetary policy, but could not have both. In the presence of mobile financial capital, Eurozone members effectively chose a stable exchange rate. Yet the implications of the Mundell-Fleming trilemma did not simply apply to large economic areas like the Eurozone. They also were highly relevant to smaller economies, such as that of Scotland.

---

[109] Mundell, 'A theory of optimum currency areas'.
[110] Meade, 'The balance of payments problems'; Meade, 'The case for variable exchange rates'.
[111] Mundell, 'A theory of optimum currency areas'; Scitovsky, *Economic Theory and Western European Integration*, ch. 2; McKinnon, 'Optimum Currency Areas'.

Scotland

In the UK, the question of what constituted an optimum currency area arose as the fortunes of the Scottish National Party (SNP) improved. To the questions of whether an independent Scotland should have its own currency and whether an open trade border would exist with England, its largest trading partner, was added the complication of accommodating the large increase (approximately 50%) which North Sea oil could add to the GNP of an independent Scotland. The discovery of oil in what would be an independent Scotland's section of the North Sea boosted the political fortunes of the SNP although the rising popularity of the SNP pre-dated the discovery of North Sea oil. In October 1968, the Labour MPs for Aberdeen South (Donald Dewar) and Caithness and Sutherland (Robert Maclennan) warned the Labour Party of the political threat of nationalism which 'Labour must recognise or run the risk of disastrous results in Scotland at the next election'.[112] The discovery of oil poured fuel on the fire of the SNP. The SNP registered 21.9% of the vote in the February 1974 general election when seven MPs were elected, and increased this to 30.4% of the vote with the election of eleven MPs in the October 1974 election. In January 1975, in a note written for the Treasury, Tam Dalyell, Chairman of the Scottish Labour Group of MPs in January 1975, argued that the success of the SNP in October 1974 had

> far less to do with an Assembly and forms of Government in general, than with the disposal of the Oil Revenues; the SNP car stickers did not say, 'Give us 142 Assemblymen in Edinburgh, paid for out of our taxes', but 'It's oor (sic) Oil'...The SNP got across to many people that somehow Scotland was being done, by the wicked English, out of a dripping roast in the North Sea, which was the Scottish Heritage.[113]

On 3 March 1979 there was a Scottish Referendum on Devolution, which was a vote for or against devolution and the establishment of a Scottish Assembly. The 'Yes' vote won the referendum narrowly by 51.6% to 48.4% but to no avail as an amendment to the 1978 Scotland Bill by a backbench Labour MP required that the Yes vote be 40% of all registered voters. The 'Yes' vote was 32.8% of registered voters. On 18 September 2014, a referendum was held on the question of Scottish independence. This time there was no requirement as

---

[112] TNA CAB 151/46, Memorandum on devolution in Scotland, 25 October 1968.
[113] TNA T319/2929, Note written for the Treasury by Tam Dalyell, January 1975, para. 9.

to what share of the total registered electorate should vote, one way or the other. The turnout was 84.6% of the total electorate. Of those voters, 44.65% voted in favour of independence, 55.25% voted against, with 0.1% of voting papers being rejected.

As an independent sovereign state, the government of Scotland would be able to tax the exploitation of the oil reserves of its continental shelf. In the 1970s, accepted international conventions for drawing the median lines separating the continental shelf between sovereign states indicated that all of the oil finds and most of the geologically promising areas were on the Scottish side of this line.[114] North Sea oil extraction grew rapidly from 1975–1976, as did the tax revenues. Oil production was negligible before 1975 but by 1980 it had risen to 603 million barrels per annum, 2.6% of world production. By 1985, partly because of a continued rise in UK production to 953 million barrels a year, and partly because OPEC virtually halved its production in an attempt to keep the price of oil high, UK production accounted for 4.6% of world production.[115]

A government of an independent Scotland would very likely have sought to slow the rate of depletion, even if only to ease pressure on what may have been its independent exchange rate.[116] On the basis of the contribution of oil taxes to UK GDP (see Table 8.13) over this same period, had all of that tax revenue gone to an independent Scotland, then the GDP of Scotland would have increased by about one-third in the mid-1980s. North Sea oil tax revenue as a percentage of GDP peaked in 1984–1985 at 3.6%.[117]

It was recognized that the potential revenues from North Sea oil would dramatically transform the finances and balance of payments of an independent Scotland and that, whether or not it chose to slow the rate of oil depletion, it might also follow the Norwegian example and create an offshore sovereign wealth fund. Clearly none of this was in the interest of the rest of the UK and the UK government was keen to use both the oil itself and the oil taxes to improve its balance of payments and public finances. As Peter Mountfield in the Treasury observed in February 1974, 'Scottish oil is going to become a major political issue whether we like it or not', and that 'much of the balance of payments advantages of North Sea oil will be lost unless the profits are taxed in the UK'. His concern was that while:

[114]   TNA T341/919, Leslie T Minchin, 'Whose oil, whose gas?', *The Spectator*, 7 December 1974, p. 729.
[115]   Backhouse, *Applied UK Macroeconomics*, p. 187.
[116]   TNA T319/2828, 'Kilbrandon Report: Possible devolution', para. 2.
[117]   Institute for Fiscal Studies.

Table 8.13. North Sea oil tax revenue
as a percentage of GDP, 1973–1992

1973–1974	0.0
1974–1975	0.0
1975–1976	0.0
1976–1977	0.1
1977–1978	0.2
1978–1979	0.3
1979–1980	1.1
1980–1981	1.5
1981–1982	2.5
1982–1983	2.7
1983–1984	2.8
1984–1985	3.6
1985–1986	3.1
1986–1987	1.2
1987–1988	1.0
1988–1989	0.7
1989–1990	0.4
1990–1991	0.4
1991–1992	0.2

Source: Institute for Fiscal Studies.

it does not matter, from a balance of payments point of view, whether those taxes accrue to a regional Government or to the federal or national Government; what does matter is that a regional Government might decide that it had more oil revenue than it needed, and might therefore slow down the exploitation of Scottish oil, exchanging revenue now for revenue in the future, as some of the Arabs may decide to do.[118]

Paradoxically, it was the size of the oil revenues which created the largest problems for the Treasury and which made it almost impossible to uncouple the allocation of the oil revenues from the political status of Scotland. As the Treasury economist C J Carey noted, almost from the start of the discussions of devolution, 'to an Englishman' the case against devolving licensing or exploitation funds seemed 'overwhelming' since:

(T)his is basically a political issue, and objective arguments about possible economic damage to the United Kingdom as a whole may not cut much ice with the proponents of devolution... It boils down, I think, to the point that

---

[118] T3219/2928, 'North Sea oil and Kilbrandon', 15 February 1974. In the run-up to the 2014 referendum on Scottish independence, similar ideas for swapping future oil tax revenues for a reduction in Scotland's share of UK debt were advanced by the National Institute of Economic and Social Research in 2013. Armstrong and Ebell, *Scotland's Currency Options*, p. 37; H.M. Government, *Scotland Analysis*.

because of the magnitudes involved on the tax side there is little sense in talk of devolution in this field unless one is prepared to contemplate (the) break-up of the existing economic and monetary union between Scotland and the rest of the United Kingdom.[119]

The size of the oil revenues not only 'completely overturned the traditional economic case against Scottish nationalism' as the Scottish Office economist, Gavin McCrone recognized in an internal paper on 'The Economics of Nationalism Re-Examined' circulated on 5 April 1974, but as such it also meant that 'for the first time since the Act of Union was passed, it can now be credibly argued that Scotland's *economic* advantage lies in its repeal'.[120] Another issue pointed to by McCrone was the danger of the 'Dutch Disease'. If an independent, oil-rich Scotland opted for its own currency, then without careful management of the Scottish exchange rate which McCrone thought could rise to '£1 Scots to 120p sterling within two years of independence', then an increase in GDP might also be accompanied by accelerated deindustrialization.[121] Concerns that if Scotland gained independence then England might impose 'an import surcharge, a quantitative control or even a tariff on goods coming from Scotland' were allayed by the recent accession of the UK to the EEC in 1973. Membership of the EEC would require both England and Scotland to respect EEC rules. Were England to leave the EEC then it was expected in the 1970s that Scottish access to the other countries 'could in time largely compensate for any restrictions that might arise on English trade'.[122]

It was in the wake of the financial disaster of the Darien Scheme in the late-1690s that representatives of Scotland had agreed to the Act of Union in 1707. In the twenty-first century, a financial crisis with an unwanted leading role for Scottish banks, the Halifax Bank of Scotland, and notably the Royal Bank of Scotland, formed part of the background to the 2014 referendum on independence. Perhaps scarred by the 1970s discussion of the potential 'Dutch Disease' effects of an independent currency, in 2014 the SNP campaigned on the basis of continuing to use the pound sterling as the currency of an independent Scotland as part of a formal monetary union with the rest of the United Kingdom. Whether a monetary union would have been negotiated after a Yes vote will not now be known. Yet, as Mervyn King, who was governor of the Bank of England at the time of referendum, subsequently pointed out after resigning as Governor, the 'sterlingization' option, whereby Scotland

---

[119] TNA T319/2928, 'Kilbrandon: Devolution of North Sea Oil Functions', paras. 2 and 3.
[120] TNA CAB 198/100, McCrone, 'Economics of Nationalism'.
[121] TNA CAB 198/100, McCrone, 'Economics of Nationalism'.
[122] TNA CAB 198/100, McCrone, 'Economics of Nationalism'.

simply continued to use sterling, was perfectly viable.[123] It might not sit well with SNP notions of being independent, since it would offer the least monetary, exchange rate, and possibly fiscal flexibility, but it was a practicable option. With the UK as a whole, but not Scotland itself, voting for 'Brexit', then the currency question became potentially more complicated. If in another referendum, Scotland was to vote for independence, it would then seek (or would have already negotiated, subject to being independent) membership of the European Union. It might be expected to join the Euro, but given the fact that two-thirds of its trade is with England, this would clearly fall foul of the criteria for an optimal currency area.[124]

Brexit

By the second decade of the twenty-first century the UK was facing a serious possibility of Scotland becoming independent, while the UK, or Rest of the UK depending on the fact, timing and outcome of any second Scottish Independence Referendum, sought to avoid a 'hard Brexit' following the referendum on the UK's EU membership. The Prime Minister, David Cameron, had agreed to hold a referendum if the Conservative party was elected into government in the 2015 General Election. The referendum was held on Thursday 23 June 2016, and of those who voted, 51.9% (17, 410,742) voted to leave the EU and 48.1% (16,141,241) to remain—a margin of 1,269,501, or 3.9% of those who voted, and 2.7% of the electorate. The turnout was 72.2%, higher than in either of the two previous UK-wide referendums, on the EEC in 1975 (63.9% turnout) and on the alternative vote system in 2011 (42.0%).[125] Immigration formed a theme of the 'Leave' campaign, the most recent background to this being the accession of (relatively poor) eastern European countries in 2004 and 2007. The stock of EEA immigrants in the UK rose from 0.9 million to 2.8 million between 1995 and 2011 of whom 0.4 million were employed in 1995 and 1.5 million in 2011.[126] Between 1995 and 2015, the number of EU nationals living in the UK tripled, mainly after the accession of Poland and other former communist countries in 2004. Contrary to populist notions, EEA immigrants made a net fiscal contribution estimated at

---

[123] King, *The End of Alchemy*, p. 244.
[124] Mundell, 'A theory of optimum currency areas'; Blejer, Frenkel, Leiderman, Razion with Cheney, *Optimum Currency Areas*, p. 8; Kenen, *Economic and Monetary Union in Europe*, p. 81.
[125] Menon and Fowler, 'Hard or soft? The politics of Brexit', R4.
[126] Dustmann and Frattini, 'The fiscal effects of immigration to the UK'.

£28.7 billion (at 2011 prices) between 2001 and 2011.[127] However, in the referendum, the Leave vote was highest, not so much in areas of high immigration, but in areas where it had increased most rapidly from low levels. Of the twenty areas in the UK with the lowest levels of EU migration, fifteen voted 'Leave', whereas of the twenty with the highest, eighteen voted 'Remain'. There also appeared to be some correlation between voting behaviour and level of education. The 'Leave' vote share was highest in local authority areas where average levels of schooling were low, whereas all twenty of the 'most educated' areas in the UK voted 'Remain'. In national geographical terms, England (53.4%) and Wales (52.5%) voted to leave, while Northern Ireland (55.8%) and Scotland (62.0%) voted to remain. Every English region voted to leave except London. By local authority area, everyone in Scotland voted to remain, while 241 of 293 (82%) in England outside London voted to leave.[128]

On 29 March 2017 the UK government notified the European Council of the UK's intention to leave the European Union in accordance with Article 50 of the Treaty on European Union. Once this notification had been given, then under Article 50 of the Lisbon Treaty, the EU institutions and the departing member state moved to negotiate an agreement setting out the arrangements for its withdrawal, taking account of the framework for its future relationship with the European Union. The broad categories of possible outcomes were topped and tailed by 'hard' and 'soft' Brexits with varying degrees of rigidity in-between.[129] In comparison to the UK's accession to the EEC in 1973, the Brexit negotiations occurred in strikingly different circumstances. In the 1970s, the UK was essentially negotiating to join a customs union with a subsequent phased-in membership of the CAP. The 1970s were characterized by high inflation, rising unemployment, a tightening monetary policy, and an exchange rate driven by a mix of real interest rates and the prospect of North Sea oil revenue. In 2017 inflation was low, real interest rates were close to zero, monetary policy was loose, attempts to wind up Quantitative Easing (QE) were tepid, the prospects of North Sea oil subdued, and unemployment politically acceptable. By 2017 the EU had become the UK's major export market (Table 8.14). In 2016, UK exports to the EU were £241 billion (44% of all UK exports) while UK imports from the EU were £321 billion (53% of all UK imports).[130] However, the composition of UK trade with the EU had changed since the 1970s. In 2017, as the UK negotiated its exit from a customs union,

---

[127] Dustmann and Frattini, 'The fiscal effects of immigration to the UK'.
[128] Menon and Fowler, 'Hard or soft? The politics of Brexit', R7.
[129] Van Reenan, 'Brexit's long-run effects on the UK economy', p. 371; House of Commons Library, 'Leaving the EU'.
[130] Ward, *Statistics on UK-EU Trade*, p. 3.

Table 8.14. UK trade in goods and services with its main trading partners in 2011

Partner	Exports ($bn)	Export share %	Imports ($bn)	Import share %
EU28	347.1	47.0	389.4	49.9
USA	109.4	14.8	88.5	11.4
China	26.2	3.5	58.4	7.5
India	19.0	2.6	24.8	3.2
Canada	18.4	2.5	13.3	1.7
Australia	16.7	2.3	7.7	1.0
Japan	16.4	2.2	17.1	2.2
Russia	15.1	2.0	14.1	1.8
Switzerland	13.7	1.9	8.7	1.1
Norway	10.5	1.4	46.1	5.9
Rest of world	146.2	19.8	111.8	14.3
Total	738.7	100.0	779.9	100.0

Source: Holmes, Rollo, and Winters, 'Negotiating the UK's post-Brexit trade arrangements', pp. R22–R30, Table 1.

the proportionate importance of exports of goods was lower than in the 1970s, and the height of tariff walls had continued to diminish. Over the course of the UK's membership of the EU, UK (EU) tariffs on manufactures fell from around 10% (8%) on average on the eve of the UK's entry into the EU to an average common external tariff of 4% in 2017.[131] Under WTO Most-Favoured Nation status, the UK would be subject to an average tariff of 9%.[132]

More important than the export of goods was the exports of services. In 2015, services formed 44.3% of UK exports and 25.2% of UK imports.[133] Of services, financial and other business services were particularly important.[134] The EU (39%) was the largest export destination for UK services, with the United States (23%) and Germany (6.5%) being respectively the first and second largest destination countries for UK export services at the start of 2018.[135] Services benefited from access to the single market, the implied barriers to trade being two to three times higher for services than for goods. While the often physical transport barriers to trade in goods had continued to fall, services were more vulnerable to changes in non-tariff barriers such as regulatory constraints, which were especially important for high-value-added business services such as financial services, legal services, or accountancy.[136]

---

[131] Crafts, 'The growth effects of EU membership for the UK', p. 12.
[132] Ebell and Warren, 'The long-term economic impact of leaving the EU', p. 125.
[133] Kirby, with Carreras, Meaning, Piggott, and Warren, 'Prospects for the UK economy', Table C3.
[134] Ward, *Statistics on UK-EU Trade*, p. 3.
[135] Office for National Statistics, *International Trade in Services*, Q1 2018, 16 July 2018.
[136] Ebell, 'Assessing the impact of trade agreements on trade', R31; Miroudot, Sauvage, and Shepherd, 'Measuring the costs of international trade in services'.

While there were over fifteen financial hubs in the UK, there was a concentration in London and the South East.[137]

An immediate and persistent effect of the Brexit vote was a fall in the value of the pound, such that three weeks after the Brexit referendum the exchange rate was still lower by 9% on a trade-weighted basis and by 8, 10, and 10% against the euro, dollar, and yen respectively.[138] This followed a rise in the UK's real effective exchange rate of 15% over the period 2013–2015.[139] By November 2016, sterling had depreciated by around 15% on a trade-weighted basis since the referendum, encouraging hopes that it would contribute to close the widening current account deficit which had reached a record 7% of GDP in the final quarter of 2015.[140] As a fall in the exchange rate tends to affect the price of imports before exports, an immediate effect of the fall in the exchange rates was to depress real wages. Quite apart from any effects of Brexit on future GDP, it seemed reasonable to assume that real wages would fall more sharply than GDP and that the greatest pain would be felt by households. Whether exports subsequently improved in response to the fall in the exchange rate remained to be seen. One estimate was that by 2030, exports would increase by only about 0.1% for every 1% decline in the effective exchange rate.[141] Balance of payments difficulties were also likely to intensify as uncertainty surrounding the nature of any new relationship with the EU caused foreign direct investment to be postponed or diverted to other economies.[142] The UK was the largest recipient of FDI inflows in the EU, receiving some 20% of all inflows since 1993. Of this inward FDI to the EU, 85% was related to services and nearly 80% of that to financial services.[143]

If the service sector bears the brunt of the effects of Brexit, and a lower exchange rate persists, then there might be some regional and industrial restructuring in the UK. It is unlikely that large-scale manufacturing will return, but small and medium size businesses might do better than is commonly presumed. There is a possibility that company earnings in some areas will suffer less than GDP and household budgets. Any regional and sector adjustments are also like to be affected by the UK withdrawal from EU policies

---

[137] Bernick, Davies, and Valero, *Industry in Britain-An Atlas*, p. 10.
[138] Kirby, with Carreras, Meaning, Piggott, and Warren, 'Prospects for the UK economy', August, F46.
[139] Kirby, with Carreras, Meaning, Piggott, and Warren, 'Prospects for the UK economy', May 2017, F41, Table A1.
[140] Kirby, with Carreras, Meaning, Piggott, and Warren, 'Prospects for the UK economy', November 2016, F66.
[141] Ebell and Warren, 'The long-term economic impact of leaving the EU', p. 133.
[142] Ebell and Warren, 'The long-term economic impact of leaving the EU', p. 136.
[143] Kirby, with Carreras, Meaning, Piggott, and Warren, 'Prospects for the UK economy', August 2016, F61.

such as the CAP. The CAP accounted for a substantial proportion of the UK net contribution to the EU, although overall the size of the UK's net contribution (£8.6 billion) to the EU was only 0.5% of UK GDP.[144] Outside of the EU, the UK would face EU tariffs which while generally low, could be high on agricultural products such as animal products (15.0%) and dairy products (33.5%).[145] Departure from the CAP will affect British farms which receive around £3 billion in subsidies, mainly as a payment per hectare for land ownership through the Single Farm payment. Given that farming output is £9 billion, these subsidies are considerable and questionable.[146] The withdrawal from the Common Fisheries Policy will also produce complex arguments over property rights, quotas, and sustainability. Depending on the formal terms of Brexit, higher education, which accounts for about 10% of UK's total exports of services, will be adversely affected, with the Scottish university sector, London University, and smaller universities being particularly vulnerable.[147] The loss of EU Structural Funding (from the European Regional Development Fund (ERDF) and the European Social Fund (ESF) will also be felt in Scotland and other parts of the UK.

The ability of the UK government to mitigate such effects of Brexit by reinvigorating its industrial policy is greatest in the case of a hard Brexit when, under WTO rules, it would have more scope to develop an industrial policy. If the UK remains in the European Economic Area (EEA), then the existing restrictions on state aid apply.[148] Whatever the outcome of Brexit negotiations, it seems likely that the UK economy will endure about ten years of disruption which commonly follows such a structural break. Given that ten years after the financial crisis, growth, real wages, productivity, and the trade deficit remain of concern, then a further ten years of disruption will add to concerns about intergenerational equity and inequalities of wealth, income, and opportunity.

[144] Ebell and Warren, 'The long-term economic impact of leaving the EU', p. 127.
[145] Ward, *Statistics on UK-EU Trade*, pp. 3, 8.   [146] Helm, 'Agriculture after Brexit', p. S125.
[147] Mayhew, 'UK higher education and Brexit', p. S156.
[148] Crafts, 'Brexit and state aid'. By a 'soft' Brexit was usually meant continued membership of the single market by means of membership of the European Economic Area (EEA). This, the Norway option, still required acceptance of the four freedoms (of goods, services, labour, and capital) and a commitment to accept current and future single market law and judgments by the European Court of Justice. EEA members contributed financially to the EU's redistributive support for less developed EU state and regions, and on this basis, Norway's financial per capita contribution to the European Union was about 83% of the UK per capita payment. Under a 'hard' Brexit, the UK would have no preferential relationship with the single market and would rely on World Trade Organization rules. In between the hard and soft bookends existed various potential arrangements which might or might not resemble the EU–Canada Economic and Trade Agreement (CETA) or the EU–US Transatlantic Trade and Investment Partnership (TTIP).

For all of the complexities of the Brexit negotiations, it is worth pondering quite how Brexit would have been managed had the UK previously signed up to the Euro. In losing the UK, the EU will lose a vocal critic of the Euro. Many of the criticisms made of the Euro today simply echo concerns set out fifty years ago by the economist James Meade. It was recognized by Meade that a European currency system would require:

> an increasing measure of intervention in each other's domestic and monetary policies…Suppose that in the EEC one member (the UK, for example) were in deficit and others (including, for example, Germany) were in surplus. If direct controls on trade and payments are ruled out and if exchange rates are fixed, then Germany can if she wishes do nothing. The only result for her will be an accumulation of perhaps unwanted foreign exchange reserves. But if Germany does nothing, the UK must severely deflate her internal monetary demand for goods and services (by a dear money policy and by higher rates of taxation)…The system can work only if the surplus members inflate at least as much as the deficit countries deflate.[149]

This is pretty much what happened in the EMU. For the first ten years after 1999, German costs fell relative to those in the rest of Europe, causing the German real exchange rate and competitiveness to improve steadily relative to other counties in the union. By contrast, the countries of the European periphery, Greece, Italy, Ireland, Portugal, and Spain, experienced excessive growth in domestic demand and inflation over the first ten years of the EMU, with steadily worsening competitive positions. Divergence rather than convergence characterized the economic performance of the EMU member states with substantial and enduring differences between countries in terms of inflation of prices and labour costs. Contrary to what might have been hoped, prices and wages did not smoothly adjust across products, sectors, and regions, thereby embedding the accumulated losses of competitiveness. In addition, while in theory the surplus on the German current account should have triggered increased German government expenditure and rising relative inflation, this did not happen. Germany retained her competitive advantage and her current account surplus kept increasing. Wages in higher inflation economies proved to be 'sticky' downwards and the early existence of the same interest rates across the Eurozone meant that in relatively higher inflation economies, the real rate of interest was relatively lower. Capital moved from the centre to the periphery, while relatively higher real interest rates in Germany

---

[149] Meade, *UK, Commonwealth and Common Market*, p. 45.

helped to constrain expenditure. This was pretty much what Alan Walters had warned of in his critique of the European Monetary System in the 1980s.[150] It was also reminiscent of Keynes's interwar concerns about the workings of the gold standard. The surrender of national exchange rates and the adoption of a single currency with interest rates set by a European Central Bank placed unnecessary pressure on national economies and national governments to achieve improvements in relative competitiveness by pressing down on wages. This pressure was intensified when surplus economies did not feel an equal pressure to increase domestic prices, and there existed a fundamental asymmetry between economies sharing the same currency but each of which had a national, rather than a European federal, government to which it mainly took its grievances.

Protection

Such grievances are exacerbated by 'globalization'. The Eurozone provided a heightened example of the political dilemma facing national governments of being electorally accountable for the performance of a national economy over which they had reduced independent powers than previously. To the Mundell-Fleming economic trilemma of choosing two of three of free capital movement, a fixed exchange rate, or an independent monetary policy, can be added Dani Rodrik's political trilemma of two from three of restricting *democracy* in the interests of minimizing international transaction costs, *limiting globalization* in the hope of building democratic legitimacy at home, and globalizing *democracy* at the cost of national sovereignty.[151] That national governments might wish to contain the effects of free trade on their population was recognized by Keynes. Speaking in Dublin on 19 April 1933 and thinking that there was 'no prospect for the next generation of a uniformity of economic system throughout the world, such as existed, broadly speaking, during the nineteenth century', Keynes inveighed against the existing 'decadent international but individualistic capitalism', which was neither a success nor intelligent, beautiful, just, or virtuous.[152] Emphasizing that 'advisable domestic policies might often be easier to compass, if the phenomenon known as the "'flight of capital'" could be ruled out', Keynes argued that in these conditions the traditional respect for Free Trade as not only 'an economic doctrine...but almost a part

---

[150] Temin and Vines, *The Leaderless Economy*, pp. 184, 185, 187, 190.
[151] Rodrik, *The Globalisation Paradox*, p. 200.
[152] Keynes, 'National Self-Sufficiency', *The Yale Review*.

of the moral law', needed rethinking. Indeed, Keynes admitted 'the orientation of my mind is changed', and he began to argue that 'national self-sufficiency' is something which 'we can afford'.[153] In fact, the Bretton Woods system, the GATT arrangements, and the controls over capital all provided a post-war world more to Keynes's liking. Behind fixed exchange rates, protection could be used so as better to manage industrial restructuring. The UK employed such 'voluntary export restraints' for cotton textiles in 1959 and in 1962 had committed itself to the Long Term Arrangement on the Cotton Textile Trade in which, along with other industrial countries, it agreed to eliminate import restrictions in return for a period of time in which imports would be held below market levels while domestic producers adjusted. This industrial adjustment took longer than anticipated and the original agreement was extended until 1974. Between 1950 and 1970 cotton textile employment fell from over a quarter of a million to 76,000.[154] The UK then signed up as a member of the EEC to the Multi-Fibre Arrangement (MFA).[155]

The postponement of convertibility until 1 January 1959 was a further source of protection and in general Bretton Woods offered protecting over-valued exchange rates designed to improve the real wages of citizens. Not that politicians were keen to incur a reputation for weakening the pound, and again to avoid this they could resort to specific protectionist measures. It was in an effort to avoid devaluation that on 26 October 1964 the Labour government announced a 15% surcharge on imports of manufactures and semi-manufactures. The effect, following the small (around 7% for most industrial countries) reduction in the Dillon Round of tariff cuts of 1961 allied to the subsequent devaluation of 1967 and the imposition of import deposits in 1968, was to raise protection of the UK domestic market to an extent exceeding the first instalment of the Kennedy Round Tariffs introduced in 1968.[156] It was on joining the EEC in 1973, that the UK joined a customs union with an albeit low Common External Tariff, and exposed itself to greater competition from within the EEC. Paradoxically in joining the EEC, the UK also joined the CAP which was itself a protective system designed to guarantee prices and to compel all EEC members to buy from it in the first instance.

That the ending of Bretton Woods permitted capital controls to be lifted raised the Mundell-Fleming trilemma. Yet given the speed with which financial

---

[153] Keynes, 'National Self-Sufficiency', *The Yale Review*.

[154] Rowthorn and Wells, *De-industrialisation and Foreign Trade*, p. 183; Foreman-Peck, 'Trade and the balance of payments', p. 162.

[155] Rodrik, *The Globalisation Paradox*, p. 73.

[156] Brittan, *Capitalism and the Permissive Society*, p. 298; Foreman-Peck, 'Trade and the balance of payments', pp. 161, 168.

contagion can spread, it may in fact be more a dilemma than a trilemma. If increased financial capital mobility both increased asset prices and contributed to financial instability, then the choice may be binary, between the 'irreconcilable duo' of independent monetary policy and free capital mobility.[157] Excessive credit growth proved one of the better predictors of crisis and in as much as the absence of capital controls encouraged rising asset prices, deceptively strong bank balance sheets and increased lending then the case began to be heard for more controls on the flow of capital.[158] James Tobin's view in 1978 of the need 'to throw some sand in the wheels of our excessively efficient international money markets' by taxing short-term foreign exchange transactions did not appeal to policymakers at the time, but may find a better hearing now.[159] That this might be achieved through a convening of a second Bretton Woods seems unlikely. While there are calls for coordinated action by large systemic central banks through, for example, the Committee on the Global Financial System of the Bank for International Settlements (BIS) to discuss the implications of their policies for global liquidity, leverage, and exposures, it is difficult to be optimistic as to what will be achieved.[160] For all their international meetings at the G7 summits of 1986 (Tokyo) and 1987 (Venice) and onwards, the effects on monetary policies were not apparent.[161] As with climate change, global solutions seem difficult to find. In that sense, what was achieved at Bretton Woods was remarkable, but also possible because the circumstances were remarkable. At Bretton Woods the concerns of Keynes and others were with establishing rules, with clearing imbalances, and with restricting flows of private capital. Thanks to technology, capital now flows ever faster in a world economy which is increasingly interconnected. Against that background, we now turn to the most recent and most serious of the increasingly frequent financial crises that have occurred since the late 1970s.

Bibliography

Green Paper on Energy Policy, Cmnd. 7101.

White Paper, *'The Challenge of North Sea Oil'*, Cmnd. 7143.

H.M. Government, *Scotland Analysis: Assessment of a Sterling Currency Union*, February 2014, Cm. 8815.

---

[157] Roy, 'Dilemma, not trilemma'.
[158] Rodrik, *The Globalisation Paradox*; Roy, 'Dilemma, not trilemma'.
[159] Tobin, 'A proposal for monetary reform'; Rodrik, *The Globalisation Paradox*, pp. 107–8.
[160] Roy, 'Dilemma, not trilemma'.   [161] Roy, 'Dilemma, not trilemma'.

Armstrong, Angus, and Monique Ebell, *Scotland's Currency Options*, National Institute of Economic and Social Research Discussion paper, 8 October 2013, no. 415.

Artis, Michael, 'Should the UK join EMU?', *National Institute Economic Review*, no. 171, January 2000, pp. 70–81.

Atkinson, A.B., and Martin Weale, 'James Edward Meade, 1907–1995', *Proceedings of the British Academy*, vol. 105, 2000, pp. 473–500, p. 481.

Authers, John, *The Fearful Rise of Markets: Global Bubbles, Synchonised Meltdowns, and How To Prevent Them in the Future*, 2010, New Jersey: FT Press.

Backhouse, Roger, *Applied UK Macroeconomics*, 1991, Oxford: Basil Blackwell.

Bhagwati, Jagdish, 'The capital myth: The difference between trade in widgets and dollars', *Foreign Affairs*, vol. 77, no. 3, May–June 1998, pp. 7–12.

Bean, Charles R., 'Sterling misalignment and British trade performance', in Richard C. Marston (ed.), *Misalignment of Exchange Rates: Effects on Trade and Industry*, 1988, Chicago: University of Chicago Press, pp. 39–76.

Bernick, Sandra, Richard Davies, and Anna Valero, *Industry in Britain-An Atlas*, Centre for Economic Performance, Special paper No. 34, September 2017.

Blanchard, Oliver J., and Lawrence H. Summers, 'Hysteresis and the European unemployment problem', *NBER Macroeconomics Annual*, vol. 1, 1986, pp. 15–90.

Blejer, Mario I., Jacob A. Frenkel, Leonardo Leiderman, Assaf Razion, with David M. Cheney, *Optimum Currency Areas: New Analytical and Policy Developments*, 1997, Washington: International Monetary Fund.

Bofinger, Peter, 'The German monetary unification (Gmu): Converting Marks to D-Marks', *Federal Reserve Bank of St. Louis Review*, vol. 72, no. 4, 1 July 1990.

Buiter, Willem H., Giancarlo Corsetti, and Paolo A. Pesenti, *Financial Markets and European Monetary Co-operation: The Lessons of the 1992–93 Exchange Rate Mechanism Crisis*, 1998, Cambridge: Cambridge University Press.

Buiter, Willem, and Marcus Miller, 'The Thatcher experiment: The first two years', *Brookings Papers*, vol. 2, 1981, pp. 315–97.

Chick, Martin, *Electricity and Energy Policy in Britain, France and the United States since 1945*, 2007, Cheltenham: Edward Elgar.

Chick, Martin, 'Property rights, economic rents, BNOC and North Sea oil', in Franco Amatori, Robert Millward, and Pierangelo Toninelli (eds.), *Reappraising State-Owned Enterprise: A Comparison of the UK and Italy*, 2011, Abingdon: Routledge, pp. 145–63.

Chiswick, B., and T. Hatton, 'International migration and the integration of labour markets', in M. Bordo, A. Taylor, and J. Williamson (eds.), *Globalisation in Historical* Perspective, 2003, Chicago: University of Chicago Press, pp. 65–120.

Cooper, Richard N., 'The Gold Standard: Historical facts and future prospects', *Brookings Papers on Economic Activity*, vol. 1, 1982, pp. 1–56, pp. 21–2.

Corden, W.M., 'Booming sector and Dutch Disease economics: Survey and consolidation', *Oxford Economic Papers*, vol. 36, no. 3, 1984, pp. 359–80.

Crafts, Nicholas, 'The growth effects of EU membership for the UK: Review of the evidence', SMF/CAGE, Global Perspectives Series, paper 7, April 2016.

Crafts, Nicholas, 'Brexit and state aid', *Oxford Review of Economic Policy*, vol. 33, Issue suppl. 1, March 2017, pp. S105–12.

Crafts, Nicholas, and Gianni Toniolo, 'Aggregate growth 1950–2005', in Stephen Broadberry and Kevin H. O'Rourke (eds.), *The Cambridge Economic History of Europe, vol. 2, 1870 to the Present*, 2010, Cambridge: Cambridge University Press, pp. 296–332.

Dustmann, C., and T. Frattini (2014), 'The fiscal effects of immigration to the UK', *Economic Journal*, vol. 124, F593–643.

Ebell, Monique, 'Assessing the impact of trade agreements on trade', *National Institute Economic Review*, no. 238, November 2016, R31–R42.

Ebell, Monique, and James Warren, 'The long-term economic impact of leaving the EU', National Institute Economic Review, no. 236, May 2016, pp. 121–38.

Eichengreen, Barry, 'European monetary unification', *Journal of Economic Literature*, vol. 31, September 1993, pp. 1321–57.

Eichengreen, Barry, *Reconstructing Europe's Trade and Payments*, 1993, Manchester: Manchester University Press.

Eichengreen, Barry, *Global Imbalances and the Lessons of Bretton Woods*, 2007, Cambridge, Mass.: The MIT Press.

Eichengreen, Barry, *The European Economy since 1945*, 2007, Princeton and Oxford: Princeton University Press.

Fama, Eugene F., 'Efficient capital markets: a review of theory and empirical work', *The Journal of Finance*, vol. 25, no. 2, May 1970, pp. 383–417.

Favero, Giovanni,and Angela Faloppa, 'Price regimes, price series and price trends: oil shocks and cunter-shocks in historical perspective', in Duccio Basosi, Giuliano Garavini, and Massimiliano Trentin (eds.), *Counter-Shock: The Oil Counter-Revolution of the 1980s*, 2018, London and New York: I.B. Tauris, pp. 15–34.

Foreman-Peck, James, 'Trade and the balance of payments', in N.F.R. Crafts and N. W.C. Woodward (eds.), *The British Economy since 1945*, 1991, Oxford: Clarendon Press, pp. 141–79.

Friedman, Milton, 'The case for flexible exchange rates ' in *Essays in Positive Economics*, 1953, Chicago: The University of Chicago Press, pp. 157–203.

Glyn, Andrew, *Capitalism Unleashed*, 2006, Oxford: Oxford University Press.

Goodhart, Charles, 'European monetary integration', *European Economic Review*, vol. 40, issues 3–5, April 1996, pp. 1083–90.

Gordon, Robert J., *The Rise and Fall of American Growth: The U.S. Standard of Living since the Civil War*, 2016, Princeton and Oxford: Princeton University Press.

Graham, Benjamin, *World Commodities and World Currency*, 1944, New York: McGraw-Hill.

Gray, Lynn, 'Rent under the assumptions of exhaustibility', *Quarterly Journal of Economics*, vol. 28, 1914, pp. 466–89.

Helm, Dieter, 'Agriculture after Brexit', *Oxford Review of Economic Policy*, vol. 33, issue suppl. 1, March 2017, pp. S124–33.

Holmes, Peter, Jim Rollo, and L. Alan Winters, 'Negotiating the UK's post-Brexit trade arrangements', *National Institute Economic Review*, no. 238, November 2016, pp. R22–R30, Table 1.

Hotelling, Harold, 'The economics of exhaustible resources', *Journal of Political Economy*, vol. 39, 1931, pp. 135–75.

House of Commons Library, 'Leaving the EU', Research paper no. 13/14, 2013, London.

Kaldor, Nicholas, 'The problem of international liquidity', in *Further Essays on Applied Economics*, 1978, New York: Holmes & Meier Publishers Inc, pp. 28–46.

Kemp, Alex, *The Official History of North Sea Oil and Gas: Volume 1: The Growing Dominance of the State*, 2012, Abingdon: Routledge.

Kenen, P.B., *Economic and Monetary Union in Europe: Moving Beyond Maastricht*, 1995, Cambridge: Cambridge University Press.

Keynes, J.M., 'The Economic Consequences of Mr. Churchill', 1925, in John Maynard Keynes, *Essays in Persuasion*, first published 1931. Published in the Norton Library, 1963, New York: W.W.Norton, pp. 244–270.

Keynes, J.M., *The Economic Consequences of the Peace*, 1919, *The Collected Writings of John Maynard Keynes*, vol. II, published for The Royal Economics Society by Cambridge University Press, Cambridge University Press, 1971, p. 7.

Keynes, J.M., 'National Self-Sufficiency', *The Yale Review*, vol. 22, no. 4, June 1933, pp. 755–69.

King, Mervyn, *The End of Alchemy: Money, Banking and the Future of the Global Economy*, 2016, London: Little, Brown.

Kirby, Simon, with Oriol Carreras, Jack Meaning, Rebecca Piggott, and James Warren, 'Prospects for the UK economy', *National Institute Economic Review*, no. 237, August 2016, F42–F68.

Kirby, Simon, with Oriol Carreras, Jack Meaning, Rebecca Piggott, and James Warren, 'Prospects for the UK economy', *National Institute Economic Review*, no. 240, May 2017, F14–F49.

Kirby, Simon, with Oriol Carreras, Jack Meaning, Rebecca Piggott, and James Warren, 'Prospects for the UK economy', *National Institute Economic Review*, no. 238, November 2016, F46–78.

Krugman, Paul R., and Maurice Obstfeld, *International Economics: Theory and Policy*, Fifth edition, 2000, Reading, Mass.: Addison-Wesley.

Krugman, Paul, 'Trade and wages, reconsidered', *Brookings Papers on Economic Activity*, vol. 39, issue 1, Spring 2008, pp. 103–54.

Lamfalussy, Alexandre, *The United Kingdom and the Six: An Essay on Economic Growth in Western Europe*, 1963, London: Macmillan.

Lindbeck, Assar, and Dennis J. Snower, 'Wage setting, unemployment, and insider-outsider relations', *American Economic Review*, vol. 76, issue 2, May 1986, pp. 235–9.

Matthews, R.C.O., C.H. Feinstein, and J.C. Odling-Smee, *British Economic Growth, 1856–1973*, 1982, Oxford: Clarendon Press.

Mayhew, Ken, 'UK higher education and Brexit', *Oxford Review of Economic Policy*, vol. 33, issue suppl. 1, March 2017, pp. S155–61.

McKinnon, Ronald, 'Optimum currency areas', *American Economic* Review, vol. 53, no. 4, 1963, pp. 717–25.

Meade, J.E., 'Financial policy and the balance of payments', *Economica*, n.s., vol. 15, no. 58, May, 1948, pp. 101–15.

Meade, J.E., 'The case for variable exchange rates ', *Three Banks Review*, No. 27, September 1955, pp. 3–27.

Meade, J.E., 'The balance of payments problems of a European free trade area', *Economic Journal*, vol. 67, no. 267, September 1957, pp. 379–96.

Meade, James, *UK, Commonwealth and Common Market*, 1962, London: Institute of Economic Affairs.

Menon, Anan, and Brigid Fowler, 'Hard or soft? The politics of Brexit', *National Institute Economic Review*, no. 238, November 2016, R4–21.

Milward, Alan, *The Reconstruction of Western* Europe, 2002, London: Routledge.

Miroudot, S., J. Sauvage, and J. Shepherd, 'Measuring the costs of international trade in services'. *World Trade Review*, vol. 12, no. 4, January 2013.

Mitchell, B.R., *European Historical Statistics, 1750–1970*, 1975, New York Press: Columbia University Press.

Mundell, Robert A, 'A theory of optimum currency areas', *American Economic Review*, vol. 51, no. 4, September 1961, pp. 657–65.

Mundell, Robert A., 'Updating the agenda for monetary union', in Mario I. Blejer, Jacob A. Frenkel, Leonardo Leiderman, Assaf Razion, with David M. Cheney, *Optimum Currency Areas: New Analytical and Policy Developments*, 1999, Washington, D.C.: International Monetary Fund, pp. 29–48.

Neal, Larry, *The Economics of Europe and the European Union*, 2007, Cambridge: Cambridge University Press.

Newton, C.C.S., 'The Sterling crisis of 1947 and the British response to the Marshall Plan', *The Economic History Review*, 2nd series, vol. 37, no. 3, August 1984, pp. 391–408.

Obstfeld, Maurice, 'The global capital market', Journal of Economic Perspectives, vol. 12, no. 4, Fall 1998, pp. 9–30.

Obstfeld, Maurice, and Alan Taylor, *Global Capital Markets: Integration, Crisis and Growth*, 2005, Cambridge: Cambridge University Press.

O'Rourke, K.H., 'From Empire to Europe: Britain in the World Economy', Roderick Floud, Jane Humphries and Paul Johnson (eds.), *The Cambridge Economic History of Modern Britain, Vol II*, 2014, Cambridge: Cambridge University Press, pp. 60–94.

Perron, Régine, *Le Marché du Charbon: Un Enjeu Entre l'Europe et les Etats-Unis de 1945 à 1958*, 1996, Paris: Publications de la Sorbonne.

Rodrik, Dani, *The Globalisation Paradox: Why Global Markets, States and Democracy Can't Exist*, 2011, Oxford: Oxford University Press.

Rollings, Neil, *British Business in the Formative Years of European Integration, 1945–1973*, 2007, Cambridge: Cambridge University Press.

Rowthorn, R.E., and J.R. Wells, *De-industrialisation and Foreign Trade*, 1987, Cambridge: Cambridge University Press.

Roy, Hélène, 'Dilemma, not trilemma: The global financal cycle and monetary policy independence', paper, August 2013.

Schenk, 'The oil market and global finance in the 1980s', in Duccio Basosi, Giuliano Garavini, and Massimiliano Trentin (eds.), *Counter-Shock: The Oil Counter-Revolution of the 1980s*, 2018, London and New York: I.B. Tauris, pp. 55–75.

Schenk, Catherine, *The Decline of Sterling: Managing the Retreat of an International Currency, 1945–1992*, 2010, Cambridge: Cambridge University Press.

Schenk, Catherine R., *International Economic Relations since 1945*, 2011, Abingdon: Routledge.

Schenk, Catherine, 'The new City and the state in the 1960s', in Ranald Michie and Philip Williamson (eds.), *The British Government and the City of London in the Twentieth Century*, 2004, Cambridge: Cambridge University Press, pp. 322–39.

Scitovsky, Tibor, *Economic Theory and Western European Integration*, 1958, London: Geo. Allen and Unwin.

Solow, Robert, 'The economics of resources, and the resources of economics', *American Economic Review*, vol. 64, issue 2, 1974, pp. 1–14.

'Symposium: Global financial instability', *Journal of Economic Perspectives*, v. 13, No. 4, Fall 1999, pp. 3–84.

Taleb, Nassim Nicholas, *Skin in the Game: Hidden Asymmetries in Daily Life*, 2018, London: Allen Lane.

Temin, Peter, and David Vines, *The Leaderless Economy: Why the World Economic System Fell Apart and How to Fix It*, 2013, Princeton and Oxford: Princeton University Press.

TNA CAB 151/46, Memorandum on devolution in Scotland, by Robert Maclennan MP and Donald Dewar MP, 25 October 1968.

TNA CAB 198/100, Gavin McCrone, 'The Economics of Nationalism Re-Examined', paper circulated on 5 April 1974.

TNA POWE 63/1528, Joel Barnett, Treasury, to Anthony Wedgwood Benn, letter, Fifth Licensing Round: BNOC contribution to costs, Secretary of State, Department of Energy, 13 September 1976.

TNA POWE 63/1586, Department of Energy, Working Group on Depletion Policy, 'Depletion Policy', 12 October 1978.

TNA T319/2828, 'Kilbrandon Report: Possible devolution of functions involving offshore oil', memorandum by the Department of Energy, 12 February 1974.

TNA T319/2928, 'Kilbrandon: Devolution of North Sea Oil Functions, C J Carey to P. Mountfield, 15 February 1974.

TNA T319/2929, Note written for the Treasury by Tam Dalyell, Chairman of the Scottish Labour Group of MPs, January 1975.

TNA T341/919, Leslie T Minchin, 'Whose oil, whose gas?', *The Spectator*, 7 December 1974.

TNA T378/56, '1977: How to survive it', note, AJ.C. Britton to Sir Bryan Hopkin, 20 January 1977.

TNA 378/56, 'Exchange Rate Policy', paper by Peter Middleton, 6 May 1977.

TNA T378/57, 'Some recent evidence on short-run exchange rate behaviour', paper, W.A. Allen and C.A. Enoch, September 1977.

TNA T381/70, paper, 'Economic aspects of North Sea oil', A Bottrill, 1978.

TNA T382/20, 'Management of the exchange rate', paper, M E Hedley-Miller, 11 January 1977.

TNA T382/25, 'The exchange rate and economic strategy', paper, A J C Britton, 18 October 1977.

TNA T382/25, 'Exchange rate policy in the medium term', EFQ(77), note by the Treasury, October 1977.

TNA T3219/2928, 'North Sea oil and Kilbrandon', note, P. Mountfield to Mr Harrop, 15 February 1974.

Tobin, James, 'A proposal for monetary reform', *Eastern Economic Journal*, vol. 4, nos. 3–4, July-October 1978, pp. 153–9.

Van Reenan, John, 'Brexit's long-run effects on the UK economy', *Brookings Papers on Economic Activity*, Fall 2016, pp. 367–83.

Ward, Matthew, *Statistics on UK-EU Trade*, House of Commons Library, Briefing Paper, Number 7851, 4 July 2017.

Weyman-Jones, Thomas, *The Economics of Energy Policy*, 1986, Aldershot: Gower.

9

Banking, Crises, and Conclusions

We are suffering just now from a bad attack of economic pessimism.

John Maynard Keynes, *Economic Possibilities for Our Grandchildren*, 1930, opening sentence[1]

When a small boy, heavy with parental warnings, approaches a pond on which people are skating, his knowledge of the risks which he incurs by joining them is small. The rational judgement that the greater their numbers the greater will be his risk, is likely to be submerged by the mere contagion of confidence which persuades him that the greater their numbers the more safely he himself may venture. Indeed the confidence of each skater in his own safety is likely to be reinforced rather than diminished by the presence of numbers of his fellows. And when, in the order of nature, the sound of a crack is heard and confidence is transformed into apprehension, that apprehension, whose influence on a solitary skater might be small, being reflected from one to another, reinforces itself rapidly and cumulatively, and may, if its natural vent in action be impeded, rise to a panic in the general effort to escape.

F. Lavington, *The Trade Cycle*, pp. 32–3

Banks make money out of time. What is perhaps surprising is that banking is not an especially profitable activity.[2] The central activity of banking is with changing temporality, the 'alchemy' of converting safe, liquid, short-term deposits into riskier, much less liquid, long-term loans.[3] This process involves risk, not simply in appraising the risk of the loan being made, but also in assessing the value of the collateral supporting the loan. The value of collateral is itself a function of time and space. Assets, such as houses, sold in forced fire sales at the same time and in the same place fetch prices lower than their presumed collateral value. The perception of the future riskiness of other banks also affects the availability of liquidity, the oil of the banking system. Time-related risk is also apparent in the length of the loans made, their

---

[1] Keynes, 'Economic possibilities', p. 358.
[2] Kay, *Other People's Money*.   [3] King, *The End of Alchemy*.

maturity transformation. Attitudes to risk are also affected by whose money is being risked. Subsequent post-crisis analysis suggested that banks might have been more cautious had more of their own equity been at stake, rather than externally borrowed funds as reflected in increasing levels of leverage. Aspects of liquidity, risk, collateral, and leverage all characterized the 2007–2008 banking crisis in Britain, and in the United States. This closing chapter begins by outlining the bald chronology of the banking crisis in both economies, before discussing its causes and effects, and closing with some general comments on the development of the political economy of Britain since 1951.

Great Britain

The bare bones of the crisis in Britain were that on 13 September 2007 queues of worried savers wishing to withdraw money formed outside branches of the Northern Rock bank (formerly the Northern Rock Building Society, which became a bank in 1997). There was concern that contagion might spread to other one-time building societies and new banks such as the Bradford & Bingley bank (demutualized in 2000) and the Cheltenham & Gloucester (demutualized in 1995 after a takeover approach from Lloyds TSB). To douse any such contagion, on 17 September 2007, the UK government announced a full guarantee of Northern Rock's retail deposits. On 1 October 2007 the UK authorities strengthened the deposit guarantee scheme by eliminating a provision whereby deposits between £2,000 and £35,000 were only 90% guaranteed.[4] Even so, matters deteriorated sufficiently that on 17 February 2008, Northern Rock was nationalized. In September 2008, rather than receiving a substantial injection of capital from the government, the Alliance and Leicester Bank was taken over by Santander, a Spanish bank which already owned Abbey National.[5] Santander also bought the branches of the Bradford & Bingley from the government, after the Bradford & Bingley had been nationalized on 29 September 2008. Twelve days before that, on 17 September 2008 the government supported the £12.2 billion takeover of Halifax Bank of Scotland (HBOS) by Lloyds TSB. Ultimately, the problems of HBOS proved too large for Lloyds TSB to manage unaided. On 8 October 2010 the UK government announced a £500 billion rescue programme for UK banks: up to £50 billion for purchase of equity; an increase in the Bank of England's

---

[4] Goodhart, 'Is a less pro-cyclical financial system an achievable goal?', R21; Valdez and Molyneux, *An Introduction*, p. 286; King, *End of Alchemy*, p. 107.
[5] Turner, *Banking in Crisis*, p. 96.

'special liquidity scheme' from £100 billion to £200 billion; and £250 billion in credit guarantees. Ultimately, the equity went only to Lloyds HBOS and to the Royal Bank of Scotland (RBS). Having become briefly the biggest bank in the world by assets partly through a series of takeovers, RBS began its steep decline, brought down in part by some of those acquisitions such as ABN-AMRO.[6] Most of ABN-AMRO was bought in a debt-financed deal which left RBS with limited equity at the end of 2007: 4% of risk-weighted assets (RWA) (1.2% of assets). RBS then incurred large losses on proprietary trading, structured credit, derivatives, and write-downs of goodwill from recent acquisitions. The £12 billion of new equity which RBS raised from existing shareholders in 2008 was insufficient to cover its position, and the government decided to provide another £45 billion of equity and to insure some assets against extreme losses.[7] The UK government ended up owning 82% of the equity of RBS, and 43% of Lloyds HBOS. The RBS, HBOS, and Lloyds-TSB, which had been ranked second, third, and fifth, respectively, in the UK in terms of 2006 assets, owed their survival to major injections of capital by the UK government. This use of public money to save private banks was large and vital. Six of the nine major UK banks were effectively insolvent in 2008. In terms of total assets, 51.8% of the British banking system required a government bailout. In addition very considerable central bank intervention and support was required to safeguard the survival of the banking system in general.[8]

The United States

In the United States, on 7 September 2008, the US government took the two government-sponsored enterprises, Fannie Mae and Freddie Mac, which then guaranteed three-quarters of US mortgages, into 'conservatorship'. On 15 September 2008 the investment bank Lehman Brothers sought Chapter 11 protection in the largest bankruptcy ever filed. Only eight months previously Lehman Brothers had reported record revenues of nearly $60 billion and record earnings of over $4 billion for its fiscal year ending 30 November 2007.[9] On Sunday 14 September 2008 it was announced that Merrill Lynch had been sold to Bank of America for $50 billion, or $29 a share, a big premium above its share price of $17, but a reduction of 61% on its share price of

---

[6] Wolf, *The Shifts and the Shocks*, p. 22; King, *End of Alchemy*, p. 37.
[7] Independent Commission on Banking, *Final Report*; Shin, 'Reflections on Northern Rock'.
[8] Wolf, *The Shifts and the Shocks*, p. 26; Turner, *Banking in Crisis*, p. 96.
[9] Wolf, *The Shifts and the Shocks*, p. 21; McDonald, *Lehman Brothers*, p. 1.

$75 a year before and 70% from its pre-crisis peak. In all, in the United States between March and September 2008, eight major US financial institutions failed—Bear Stearns, IndyMac, Fannie Mae, Freddie Mac, Lehman Brothers, AIG, Washington Mutual, and Wachovia—six of them in September alone.[10] On 9 October 2008, Wells Fargo, the country's fifth largest commercial bank, agreed to a takeover of Wachovia, the country's fourth largest.[11]

Central Banks to the Rescue

Similar stories can be told across Europe. Between July 2007 and February 2009, more than twenty Europeans banks across ten countries required to be financially rescued, either by their national governments or by other banks. The Belgian and Dutch governments shared responsibility for the Fortis bank, with the bank being broken up on national lines; the Spanish government rescued the Caja (savings) banks; and the German government rescued Hypo Bank. In some cases, the government action came at a very high cost. The decision by the Irish government on 30 September 2008 to guarantee all the money in Irish banks proved very costly for Irish taxpayers and the Irish economy. The fiscal cost of injecting capital in the Anglo-Irish bank in Ireland in 2009 amounted to 35% of Ireland's GDP. Bank rescues in Spain in 2011 similarly contributed to the debt crisis in that country.[12]

Of much that was striking about the crisis, the enormity and asymmetry of risk was eye-catching and often eye-watering. On the way up, private banks grew into major global operations. On the way down, banks turned to national governments for help. As Mervyn King, Governor of the Bank of England (2003–2013) quipped: banks were 'international in life, but national in death'. In 1970, the fifty largest banks in the world had total assets relative to world GDP of 15%; by 2015 their assets had increased to 83% of world GDP. In comparison, the ratio of total assets of the fifty biggest US banks relative to US GDP increased to 83% in the second quarter of 2015 from only 25% in 1970. Not only were banks much larger relative to world GDP, they had also become more concentrated. The largest twenty-five banks accounted for about half of the total assets of all banks worldwide. The assets of the same banks are almost two-thirds of world GDP. Among the twenty biggest banks in the world, the ratio of the assets of the largest to the smallest was little more

[10] Paulson, *On the Brink*, pp. 435–6. Quoted in Wolf, *The Shifts and the Shocks*, p. 17.
[11] Wolf, *The Shifts and the Shocks*, p. 22.
[12] Blinder, *After the Music Stopped*, p. 170; Barth and Wihlborg, 'Too big to fail', R28.

than two to one. Taken together, however, these twenty banks accounted for assets of $42 trillion in 2014, compared with world GDP of around $80 trillion, and for almost 40% of total worldwide banking assets.[13] Global banks had become enormous relative to some national GNPs.

House Prices

What then were the causes of the 2007–2008 financial crises? In the United States, a high proportion of loans were made for the purchase of property, which contributed to the sub-prime crisis. In Britain, property prices had risen and loans had increased both in size and as a proportion of asset value and income (see Table 9.1), but there was no equivalent sub-prime crisis. British house prices and mortgages were sensitive to hikes in interest rates, as had been seen when the UK bank base rate doubled from 7.5% to 15% from 1987 to 1990. This rate rise was partly induced by the higher rates stemming from German reunification in 1990, and with inflation high and the UK in the Exchange Rate Mechanism, it proved difficult to bring rates down quickly. When the UK left the ERM in September 1992, unemployment rose sharply, and house prices fell. At its worst, in the 1990s around 20% of mortgages were in negative equity and the payment arrears (delinquencies) rate for three month defaults probably peaked at over 5%. Cumulatively, 3% of mortgage borrowers suffered mortgage repossessions (foreclosures) in the 1990s.[14] Unpopular and stressful as the experience of negative equity was, it did not result in a banking crisis.

In the 2000s, household debt was higher than it had been in the 1980s. This was especially so in those countries that experienced booms in both periods, where the rise in the later period was 59% compared to 47% in the earlier boom.[15] In the UK there had been a property boom which had ended in 2008, but left households with overstretched budgets and over-extended debts relative to their assets. However, at its peak in early 2009, the UK repossessions rate reached only about half that of the 1990s repossessions peak. A deeper UK repossessions crisis was avoided mainly through dramatic monetary policy interventions, lenders' forbearance policy, and increased government income support for those with payment difficulties. A key difference from

---

[13] Wolf, *The Shifts and the Shocks*, p. 22; Barth and Wihlborg. ' Too big to fail', R30; King, *End of Alchemy*, p. 92.

[14] Aron and Muellbauer, 'Modelling and forecasting mortgage delinquency'.

[15] Armstrong and Davis, 'Comparing housing booms', R5.

Table 9.1. Changes in house prices, income and debt during booms, 1985–2006

Percentage change	Real house prices		Real personal disposable income		Real household debt		Nominal house prices		Real gross financial wealth	
	1985–1989	2002–2006	1985–1989	2002–2006	1985–1989	2002–2006	1985–1989	2002–2006	1985–1989	2002–2006
U.K.	71	49	23	10	74	50	112	65	61	17
USA	12	29	17	14	40	48	31	44	31	33
Germany	1	-2	18	5	18	-3	6	4	37	9
France	28	64	14	11	51	42	49	78	65	26
Spain	110	62	27	17	23	83	190	90	95	41
Japan	27	-17	22	4	59	0	33	-20	80	16

Source: BIS and OECD. Adapted from Armstrong and Davis, 'Comparing housing booms and mortgage supply in the major OECD countries', R3–R15, R4, Table 1.

1990–1992 was that there was low inflation and a flexible exchange rate, and the Bank of England's policy interest rate (base rate) could be brought down quickly to half a percentage point. This rapidly lowered mortgage rates, and hence the debt service ratio for borrowers, given the predominance of adjustable rate mortgages in the UK. House prices were supported, preventing major rises in the proportion of households with negative equity. This played a key role in stabilizing mortgage markets and the wider economy.[16]

Caught Short

That mortgage lenders like Northern Rock ran into difficulties, was not primarily to do with the housing market but rather to their borrowing practices. When making loans, it drew proportionately less on its own deposits and more on its own external borrowing in the wholesale market. Its leverage rose, such that by 2007 it lay somewhere between 60:1 and 80:1, which was very high. It did overlend, sometimes up to 125% of the value of a property, but its Achilles heel was that 60% of its lending came to be financed by short-term borrowing. In June 2007 only 23% of its funding was from retail deposits, with most of that being wholesale funding (e.g. securitizations, covered bonds).[17] In addition, many of Northern Rock's mortgage loans were not held on its own balance sheets, but had been sold on to other investors. The market for such transactions closed in the late summer of 2007, leaving Northern Rock struggling to find funds with which to finance its assets. Northern Rock initially ran into difficulties, not in the first instance because of problems with the value of its mortgages, but simply because it held very low liquid assets on its balance sheet. When short-term lenders refused to continue lending and/ or depositors wanted to withdraw their savings, it lacked the funds to pay.[18]

Northern Rock was an extreme, but by no means isolated, example of the bank practice of short-term borrowing from the wholesale market being used to finance the purchase of long-term assets. It was a matter of both the size of leverage and its term-structure. The median leverage in the UK banking system doubled and it grew in size from about 300% of GDP in 2000 to about 500% in 2007. As well as Northern Rock, the Bradford & Bingley, Alliance and Leicester, RBS, and HBOS all became increasingly dependent on the 'permanent availability of a large-scale interbank funding and/or their

---

[16] Aron and Muellbauer, 'Modelling and forecasting mortgage delinquency'.
[17] Independent Commission on Banking, *Final Report*, p. 32; Wolf, *The Shifts and the Shocks*, p. 19.
[18] King, *End of Alchemy*, p. 139.

continuous ability to securitise and sell down rapidly accumulating credit assets, particularly in the mortgage market.[19] At the end of 2007, 56% of HBOS's funding was wholesale and more than half of that was short term.[20] In general, during the thirty years preceding the 2007/8 crisis, the average maturity—the length of life of a loan—of wholesale funding issued by banks declined by two-thirds in the UK and by around three-quarters in the US. In fewer than fifty years, the share of highly liquid assets held by UK banks declined from around one-third of their assets to less than 2%. In the US the share had fallen to below 1% just before the crisis.[21] At Lehman's, most of its balance sheet was financed in the short-term repo market to the tune of over $200 million per day in 2008. It relied on short-term secured financing to conduct its daily operations.[22] It was over thirty times leveraged,[23] while its assets stood at around $700 billion together with corresponding liabilities on capital of about $25 billion. Lehman borrowed heavily to meet its cash needs, creating a high debt-to-equity ratio. This high risk to high leverage model was not unique to Lehman's. It was commonly employed by major investment banks at the time. Again, as with Northern Rock, the initial problem was not its holdings of illiquid assets, but its reliance on short-term funding from lenders who eventually lost confidence, causing problems of liquidity.[24]

It was in this context that when losses on property were incurred, they hit lenders hard. Bradford & Bingley was heavily exposed to the risky buy-to-let and self-certified mortgage markets, with 60% of its mortgage portfolio in the former and 20% in the latter. Bradford & Bingley accounted for about 20% of the UK buy-to-let market. Northern Rock had also made loans to riskier parts of the mortgage market and on loan-to-value ratios close to or more than 100%. The bank, which allowed individuals to borrow up to 125% of the value of their home, attracted sub-prime borrowers and resulted in high levels of arrears in the subsequent downturn. Of the big banks, the corporate division of HBOS was estimated to have lost £6.793 billion in 2008 alone, mainly on commercial property loans. That division's losses occurred because the commercial property market collapsed even further than the residential property market in the eighteen months after June 2007, retail property falling to 2002 levels and the office market to 1998 levels. The RBS was also heavily exposed to the commercial property sector. Of its cumulative impairment loss on

[19] Turner, *Banking in Crisis*, p. 98. Quoting from *The Turner Review*, p. 35.
[20] Independent Commission on Banking, *Final Report*, p. 32.
[21] King, *End of Alchemy*, p. 97.   [22] McDonald, *Lehman Brothers*, p. 90.
[23] Independent Commission on Banking, *Final Report*, p. 32.
[24] McDonald, *Lehman Brothers*, pp. 89–90.

loans and advances of £30.396 billion in the period 2008–2010, 8% of these losses came directly from residential mortgages and 34% came directly from commercial property lending.[25]

Fire Sales: Same Time, Same Space

That losses were incurred points to fire sales of assets having occurred. Fire sales occur when external obligations to other lenders are urgently pressing and/or if there is a serious shortage of liquidity. In such conditions asset values can reduce quickly. As McDonald noted of the Lehman bankruptcy proceedings, they 'raised the question of how and why value can disappear, and then return after a few years, at least when measured in terms of price'.[26] As asset sales were forced, so assets revealed their chimeric side. Their present value may represent the discounted flow of future earnings, but their immediate sale value depends on the interaction of supply and demand at the present time. As asset prices fall then the test of loans shifts from the value of the collateral itself to the ability or willingness of individuals to continue to pay the mortgage, especially when its size exceeds that of the now perceived value of the house.

As losses on property to highly leveraged banks occurred, so liquidity dried up. Liquidity is a fair-weather friend, seldom around when really needed, or only showing up grudgingly at a high cost to you. There had been previous occasions when liquidity had absented itself, notably on 19 October 1987 ('Black Monday') when the Dow Jones Industrial Average fell 23%. From mid-2007, dollar funding began to dry up, making it extremely difficult to finance long maturity dollar assets with short-term dollar borrowing. Matters worsened considerably following the bankruptcy of Lehman Brothers in September 2008. Not only was funding more difficult to find but dollar assets on banks' balance sheets became difficult to sell into illiquid markets without realizing major losses. In terms of time, the effective holding period of assets became longer just as the maturity of available funding got shorter.[27] The more wary banks became of lending to each other, the more liquidity dried up. The more liquidity dried up, the greater the risk that banks would fail, therefore increasing the unwillingness of banks to lend to each other. And so on.[28] The LIBOR (London Inter-Bank Offer Rate) swung wildly while transactions

---

[25] Turner, *Banking in Crisis*, pp. 98–9.   [26] McDonald, *Lehman Brothers*, p. 159.
[27] Cecchetti, Domanski, and von Peter, 'New regulation', R31.
[28] De Nicolò, 'Liquidity regulation', R18; Brunnermeier, 'Deciphering the liquidity'.

fell. As this market became thinner, so pricing in interest rates became more difficult.[29] What business was done was of shortening maturity and against the highest-quality collateral.[30] It became increasingly difficult to distinguish between a liquidity crisis and one of insolvency.[31] Although technically a firm is insolvent when the value of its liabilities exceed those of its assets, and illiquid when it is short of cash but has net value, for financial companies whose business is moving cash and whose leverage is high, a shortage of liquidity which forces a sale of assets can result in insolvency. Illiquidity became insolvency for Bear Stearns and Lehman Bros.[32]

Securitizing the Future

It was in this context of high leverage and shortening maturity of loans that the mysterious, almost fantastical, world of securitization and derivatives provided so much bemused interest to the public. Books such as *The Big Short* as well as the film of the book sold well.[33] An alphabet soup of acronyms such as MBS, CDO, and CDS was tossed across dinner tables. Derivative traders became targets of scorn, yet derivatives can and do perform a useful economic function. Again they have a strong temporal aspect. Derivatives are essentially claims on the future income from other assets. They play a useful role, allowing airline companies for example to hedge their future fuel costs and often also their future exchange rates. Forward and futures contracts relating to the purchase of a commodity to be delivered at a future date; options on the right to buy or sell at a given price in the future; and swaps, where two parties exchange a stream of cash flows in different currencies or in different profiles of interest payments, are all types of derivatives. Being time-based, derivatives can also provide an instrument for speculation about the future movement of prices. Typically, derivatives require little up-front payment but form a contract between two parties to exchange a flow of returns or commodities in the future. Yet, while derivatives can reduce risk, they cannot correct for mispricing of the original asset and their very complexity and

---

[29] Even well after the crisis, in 2011, there was little borrowing between banks at maturities of four months and above in sterling and above six months in dollars.

[30] Cecchetti, Domanski, and von Peter, 'New regulation', R31. Interbank lending dried up first followed by problems in repo and FX swap markets. Reflecting the rise of credit and liquidity premia, spreads on Libor and FX swaps widened. Michaud and Upper, 'What drives interbank rates?'; Hordahl and King, 'Developments in repo markets'; Gorton, 'Information, liquidity, and the (ongoing) panic of 2007'.

[31] King, *End of Alchemy*, p. 110.

[32] Blinder, *After the Music Stopped*, p. 104.   [33] Michael Lewis, *The Big Short*.

opacity may obscure the degree of risk. Also, unlike conventional loans, there are no obvious limits to the size of transactions in derivative financial instruments, and most buying and selling of derivatives is carried out by large banks and hedge funds. The sheer size of this business was again eye-watering. Lower than in their heyday but still at over $20 trillion at the end of 2014, the gross market value of derivatives accounted for around one-half of the assets of the largest twenty banks in the world (and of the same magnitude as total lending to households and businesses).[34] As the investor Warren Buffet observed long before the financial crisis, derivatives had the potential to be financial weapons of mass destruction.

An example of how derivatives could magnify a problem was evident in the losses made on real estate by Lehman, Bear Stearns, IndyMac, and Washington Mutual. It was not simply a matter of the losses themselves, but also the fact of the securitization of the mortgages into Mortgage-Backed Securities (MBS).[35] The MBS was essentially a claim on future mortgage payments. They were a derivative, in that their value derived from an underlying asset. One effect of securitization was to increase the dependence of those risk assessments on the quality of the risk assessment made of the original loan and asset. In the case of the MBS, the asset was usually the house, which provided the collateral for the mortgage. The risk was two-fold. That the mortgagee would cease to make the payments and that once the keys were handed back, the asset would be worth less than the loan. Judgements on the risk of lending and on the mortgage to house value were supposed to be made responsibly on a case-by-case basis by the lender. In fact, banks operating in a low-interest environment began to earn more money in fees by rearranging mortgages. Initial low-interest-rate 'teaser' mortgages were offered in the hope of earning fee income each time that the mortgage was subsequently renegotiated. Mortgages with teaser rates and balloon payments were particularly advantageous to the lenders as they entailed repeated refinancing.[36] In addition, a MBS represented a bundle of mortgages, making it almost impossible to know what the riskiness of the case-by-case assessment of borrowers and assets by lenders had been. In general, guided by history, purchasers of MBSs tended to assume that they were a low-risk security on which money could be made. Unlike in the US, before 2000 securitized credit played a small role in the UK mortgage market, although by 2007, 18% of UK mortgage credit was funded through securitization.[37]

---

[34] King, *End of Alchemy*, pp. 98, 141–2.   [35] Barth and Wihlborg, 'Too big to fail', R34–5.
[36] Stiglitz, *Freefall*, p. 85.
[37] *The Turner Review*, pp. 32–5; Wolf, *The Shifts and the Shocks*, p. 126.

In addition to MBSs, other derivative products included a credit default swap (CDS) in which insurance was sold against the collapse of other banks and firms. Once one financial institution had taken out insurance against another going bankrupt, it had an incentive to see that happen.[38] The American insurance corporation AIG was hit hard by credit default swaps. Another securitized product, although not always a derivative, was the collateralized debt obligation (CDO) which again made a claim on future cash flows from other bonds and assets which were divided into tranches, with the lower tranche absorbing losses first and the highest tranche going last. Investors could choose in which tranches to invest. With all these complex bundles of securitized products, assessing risk was difficult and for help potential pur- chasers looked to credit rating agencies. Yet, credit rating agencies were paid by the issuers of the security and since rating such securitized products as CDOs was a lucrative activity, the credit ratings agencies competed against one another for business.[39] Even so, any risk assessment was unable by definition to be able to offer a basis for insurance against uncertainty.[40] In retrospect, where risk assessments were sanguine was in understating the possible size of correlation between ostensibly different risks. As popularly depicted in *The Big Short* film and Michael Lewis book, in a CDO the risks of each tranche were not separated completely from each other, but correlated. What was important was to know the strength of that correlation. One approach to measuring the strength of correlation within the CDO was to employ the Gaussian Copula Model, invented by David X Li in 1999.[41] The model's aim was to provide one number which gave the probability of all the defaults in a pool of securities or mortgages taking place at once. As with the CDO Evaluator used by Standard & Poor from November 2001, such models had the appeal of speed, which was important as so many CDOs based on mort- gages were being issued. One headline number had the appeal of simplicity and clarity, and the model was widely applied by rating agencies not only to CDOs, but also often separately to MBSs. However, the assets underlying CDOs were often also mortgages rather than pools of corporate debt, whereas the Copula Model was primarily designed to measure the correlations between bonds in the CDOs. In historic terms, bonds had been very stable before 2007 and the model was more sensitive to this past performance than it was to future potential changes in house prices or mortgage loan

[38] Stiglitz, *Freefall*, pp. 169–71.   [39] McDonald, *Lehman Brothers*, p. 169.
[40] King, *Alchemy*, p. 145.
[41] McDonald, *Lehman Brothers*, p. 166. The model was developed by David X Li in two papers: 'The Valuation of Basket Credit Derivatives' and 'On Default Correlation'; Mackenzie, 'The credit crisis'.

performance. Losses on CDOs based on mortgages were to cost Citigroup $34 billion, Merrill Lynch $26 billion, UBS $22 billion, and AIG $33 billion.[42]

Risking Others' Money

The financial crisis of 2007–2008, although the largest, was one of an increasingly frequent number of financial and banking crises. Why should this be, and why crises should be more common, is of interest. In part, finance had been freer of restrictions. Capital controls were ended in many economies. Social norms had changed.[43] Until the later 1950s/60s, mortgages were allocated as a multiple of income. That changed to replace a system of administrative allocation with one giving preference to interest rates. In September 1971 the Competition and Credit Control policy ended quantitative lending restrictions as well as the required 8% cash and 28% liquidity ratios. Bankers themselves used to be subject to an informal but nonetheless effective supervisory system which encouraged caution on the size and nature of lending and could require banks to hold significant quantities of low-risk government debt. In the 1960s, these controls loosened. The Big Five Banks (Barclays, Lloyds, Midland, National Provincial, and Westminster) were subject to increasing competition from building societies and trustee savings banks, consumer credit institutions, such as hire purchase companies, and foreign banks. While the London Clearing banks had less than 50% of the UK market in deposits in 1962, by 1970 that share had fallen to just over one-third as building societies increased their market share. Banking activity was also beginning to outgrow the administrative capabilities of the Bank of England to supervise it. In 1973, there were 323 full banks, but a staff of only twelve in the Bank of England's Discount Office.[44]

As a result of such changes and in the wake of the September 1971 Competition and Credit Control policy lending rose quickly. Between October 1971 and December 1973, sterling advances to UK resident borrowers by the clearing banks grew from £5,367 million to £11,379 million, while secondary bank advances rose from £395 million to £3,366 million over the same period. Secondary banks were non-clearing banks and they reflected the growth of the money market with the development of the interbank market and the market for certificates of deposit (CDs). By the end of 1973 these

---

[42] McDonald, *Lehman Brothers*, pp. 168–71.   [43] Stearns, *Electronic Value Exchange*.
[44] Turner, *Banking in Crisis*, pp. 7, 187, 189, 190.

secondary banks had become larger lenders than the clearing houses for property development and house prices rose sharply from the last quarter of 1971 until the last quarter of 1973. When house prices then fell significantly in real terms in 1974, secondary banks found themselves over-exposed in a property sector in which they typically had loan-to-value ratios ranging from 90 to 100% and in which they sometimes held equity stakes in the properties themselves.[45]

Given the possibility of further financial and banking crises, a pressing concern was how best to protect the essential fabric of the banking system. In June 2010 the incoming coalition government established the Independent Commission on Banking under the chairmanship of Sir John Vickers, former Director General of the Office of Fair Trading. In September 2011 the Commission recommended that 'a high ring-fence be placed around vital retail banking activities in the UK' and that riskier activities such as trading and investment banking be placed outside the firewall.[46] Recommendations made in the Liikanen report produced by the European Commission offered almost a mirror image of the Vickers Report. While the Liikanen Commission favoured ring-fencing trading from the rest of the business, the Vickers Commission recommended ring-fencing retail banking from the rest of the business instead.[47] Of itself, building a firewall between the essential retail activities of banks and their riskier activities was insufficient, without accompanying measures to address other sources of risk to the system such as leverage and the extent of equity involvement of the banks.

In the US, discussion of whether to separate out a core retail banking business focused on economic history and the Glass-Steagall Act of 1933. This Act, which concerned bank affiliates more than the banks themselves, had allowed banks to deal in or underwrite 'safe' US government securities, the securities of Fannie Mae and Freddie Mac, and the general obligation bonds of states and municipalities. They were allowed to buy and sell securities based on assets, such as mortgages, but they could not deal in or underwrite mortgage-backed securities (MBSs), a restriction which remained in place even after the Glass-Steagall Act's repeal by the Gramm-Leach-Bliley Act(GLBA) of 1999. They could now be affiliated with firms engaged in underwriting or dealing in securities, including MBSs.[48] After the financial crisis, the introduction of the Volcker rule prohibited banks and their

[45] Turner, *Banking in Crisis*, pp. 91–3; Reid, *The Secondary Banking Crisis*.
[46] Independent Commission on Banking, *Final Report*, p. 29, para. 2.27.
[47] Wolf, *The Shifts and the Shocks*, pp. 230–1.   [48] McDonald, *Lehman Brothers*, p. 81.

affiliates from engaging in 'proprietary trading', and investments in hedge funds and private equity firms were restricted. Yet as in the UK, such changes were likely to be most effective as part of a defence system which also incorporated changes to leverage and its causes, and raised the amount of equity invested by the banks themselves.[49]

Leverage refers to the use of borrowed funds to purchase assets. The converse of too much leverage was too little capital. Just as leverage is the ratio of assets to capital, so low capital and high leverage means the same thing. Leverage was certainly embedded in derivatives where, in the financial sector itself, leverage could be extremely high. Freed from administrative multiples of income limits to the size of mortgages, individuals increased their leverage, as house buyers borrowed more relative to the presumed value of houses. One approach to reining in borrowing was to return to some set of rules governing leverage ratios. Leverage ratios measuring capital relative to total (unweighted) assets might be set. A Bank of England study of 116 large global banks during the crisis (of which seventy-four survived and forty-two failed) found that the simple but robust leverage ratio was better at predicting which banks would fail than the more sophisticated risk-weighted measures of capital. One difficulty with prioritizing the assessment of risk, and then setting capital requirements accordingly, was that such a risk-weighted-asset approach might simply be both unreliable and inadequate.[50] Northern Rock had the highest ratio of capital to risk-weighted assets, because mortgages were judged to be safe. What it also had was an extremely high leverage ratio. In general, the ratio of risk-weighted assets to unweighted assets for the four largest UK banks (among the largest banks in the world) fell from close to 55% to close to 35% between 2004 and 2008.[51]

The risk-weighted-asset approach to regulation was favoured by the Basel Committee on Banking Supervision, an international committee of banking supervisors, which set the international regulatory rules for banking. Basel I, II, and III all gave priority to risk-weighted assets (RWA). In 1988, in Basel I, assets were assigned a level of capital (risk-weight) ranging from zero (safest) to 100% (riskiest) depending on the nature of the asset.[52] Sovereign debt was treated as risk free and could be funded without equity. This created problems in the Eurozone where formally German and Greek debt was of equivalent

---

[49] Independent Commission on Banking, *Final Report*, p. 45, para. 3.25; Shin, 'Reflections on Northern Rock'; Barth and Wihlborg, 'Too big to fail', R34; Blinder, *After the Music Stopped*, p. 267; Admati and Hellwig, *The Bankers' New Clothes*.
[50] King, *End of Alchemy*, p. 139.   [51] Wolf, *The Shifts and the Shocks*, p. 132.
[52] Le Leslé and Avramova, 'Revisiting Risk-Weight Assets', p. 37.

risk. In fact, from 2007, the spreads on different governments' bonds began to widen, such that by late January 2009, spreads on Greek government bonds over German bunds had hit 280 basis points (2.8 percentage points). Two years before, they had been less than a tenth of that level.[53] Some adjustments to calculating RWAs were introduced in Basel II between 2004 and 2009 and then under Basel III the capital requirements were raised.[54] Even so, the Basel II and III equity levels remained low and capital requirements remained low relative to risk-weighted assets (RWA) with continuing doubts as to how those assessments were made.[55] Banks were still able to operate with a very small proportion of equity capital and very high levels of debt to finance risky and difficult to assess portfolios.[56] In phasing in the Basel III capital requirement between 2013 to 2019, the aim was that the leverage ratio would be 3% in 2019 and the risk-based capital requirement as high as 13% for some banks.[57] There was also a move through Basel I, II, and III to shift from simple capital requirements to risk assessments which were themselves related to market conditions.[58] The risk of the RWA approach was that risk was poorly assessed, that risk weights actually fell as risk was rising, and that too much store was set in the risk-weightings.[59] A belief in the permanent stability of risk weightings was itself a source of risk.[60] As Mervyn King emphasized, in a crisis, risk can give way to 'radical uncertainty, not risk, despite the words used by regulators.'[61]

Irrespective of the risk assessments made, the incentive to take risks was affected by the amount of the bank or financial institution's equity capital which was at risk. As the financial historian John Turner commented:

> Banking is an intrinsically risky business, and the reason is simple: bankers lend other people's money, not their own. This creates an incentive problem because bankers get most of the benefit if the risky loans they make do well, whereas depositors, not bankers, incur most of the costs if loans go bad. Unless it is addressed, this incentive problem eventually results in unstable banking.[62]

[53] Wolf, *The Shifts and the Shocks*, pp. 47, 139.
[54] Le Leslé and Avramova, 'Revisiting Risk-Weight Assets', p. 37.
[55] Admati, 'The missed opportunity', R7.
[56] Miles, 'Regulatory failure', R15.
[57] Barth and Wihlborg, 'Too big to fail', R 35.
[58] Goodhart, 'Is a less pro-cyclical financial system an achievable goal?'
[59] Independent Commission on Banking, *Final Report*, p. 8.
[60] Goodhart, 'Is a less pro-cyclical financial system an achievable goal?', R20; Minsky, 'A theory of systemic fragility'; Minsky, 'Can "It" Happen Again?'
[61] King, *End of Alchemy*, p. 138.   [62] Turner, *Banking in Crisis*, p. 6.

If CEO salaries were linked to the size of their banks and their business, then a low-equity, leveraged approach was likely to encourage more leveraged, riskier strategies.[63] While there were limits on the ratio of capital to 'risk-weighted' assets, there was no restriction on leverage. In the run-up to the crisis, leverage ratios of assets to equity capital had risen to around forty times, twice their historically normal level. Requiring banks to invest more equity would redistribute risk towards them. This equity would be shareholders equity (or other forms of 'loss absorbing capital'). An established shareholder liability had existed in British banking until the 1950s when it was removed. In 1900 the average ratio of what shareholders were potentially liable to pay in the event of failure to total deposits was around 33%, but only about 3% by 1950.[64] Over the same 1900–1950 period the ratio of capital to deposits had also fallen from 18% in 1900 to 4% in 1950. Wartime inflation (in both world wars) had contributed substantially to increasing the size of deposits without any commensurate increase in extended liability or banks' capital resources. Thus, by the 1940s, shareholders stood to lose relatively little should the bank fail.

Banking Costs

The economic costs of banking and financial crises were considerable. One IMF estimate of the cost of banking crises alone, rather than major currency crises and sovereign debt crises, was that the average cost in terms of lost output relative to trend in advanced economies was a staggering 33%, with on average the public debt to GDP ratio increased by 21.4 percentage points.[65] By mid to late 2009, central bank and government support of the financial system in capital injections, asset purchase, guarantees, and insurance was estimated by Piergiogio Alessandri and Andrew Haldane of the Bank of England at 18% of Eurozone GDP, 73% of US GDP, 74% of UK GDP, and, taken together, 25% of world GDP.[66]

Banks were bailed out because they were considered to be 'too big to fail'(TBTF). These global banks were bailed out by their national governments

---

[63] Barrell, Fic, Fitz Gerald, Orazgani, and Whitworth, 'The banking sector', R41; Goodhart, 'Is a less pro-cyclical financial system and achievable goal?', R20.
[64] Turner, *Banking in Crisis*, pp. 9–10.
[65] Laeven and Valencia, *Systematic Banking Crisis Database*, p. 3.
[66] Wolf, *The Shifts and the Shocks*, p. 28.

for fear of the effects of their defaulting on the banking system and economy.[67] In part national economies had benefited from the growth of banking and financial services. Not only did the City and the banks generate large invisible earnings for the UK economy, but it also grew at a faster rate than the rest of the economy. Between 1997 and 2007, while average UK GDP annual growth was 3%, that of the financial sector was 6%. The share of nominal GDP accounted for by financial services was slightly less than 6% in 1997; by 2007, it was contributing almost 9%.[68] As a result of this growth, banking sector assets grew from almost 300% of GDP in 1997 to approximately 500% in 2007. The ratio of financial intermediation to UK output, having been broadly stable since the start of the twentieth century, increased by about 60% between the 1980s and the crisis. In part the success was also the problem. The success made the banks and the City a powerful lobby group. But if financial crises were to occur more regularly and at a very large cost, then the costs-benefits of the financial and banking sector became less clear. Even the Basel Committee on Banking Supervision (BCBS) gave a range of estimates of 19–163% of annual GDP for the net present value cost to output from financial crises, with a median estimate of 63%. The same study estimated that financial crises occurred approximately every twenty to twenty-five years (4–5% of years). On that basis, the cost was about 3% p.a. of GDP.[69]

Following the banking crisis of 2008, world output fell by more than 1% in 2009, and OECD output by around 3.5%. The effects on output were more pronounced in the Euro Area and the UK than in the US or Canada. The effect on banks was greater in the US, the UK, the Euro Area, and the rest of Europe than in Canada, Australia, and Japan.[70] Between the third quarter of 2008 and the first quarter of 2009, the annualized rate of decline in GDP in the six largest high-income countries ranged from 6.4% in France, 7% in the UK, and 7.1% in the US, to 10.2% in Italy, 11.7% in Germany, and 13.8% in Japan.[71] Though relatively mild when compared to the US and to Germany, the UK recession of 1929–1931 saw real GDP fall by 5.6% between 1929 and 1931. In other words, the Great Depression contraction in the UK was similar in magnitude to the recession of 2008–2009.[72]

---

[67] De Nicolò, 'Liquidity regulation', R18.   [68] Turner, *Banking in Crisis*, p. 217.
[69] Independent Commission on Banking, *Final Report*, p. 124, para. 5.8.
[70] Ray Barrell, 'Policy responses', R1.   [71] Wolf, *The Shifts and the Shocks*, p. 32.
[72] Crafts and Fearon, 'Depression and Recovery', p. 18.

The Recovery Position?

Recovery rates were noticeably slow, not least in comparison with previous periods of economic recovery.[73] Surprisingly, the impact on unemployment in the UK was less than might have been expected, although the usual groups suffered. Employment fell by 580,000 between the beginning of 2008 and early 2010. This was a smaller decline than in the 1980s recession, when it fell by 1.6 million between November 1980 and May 1983, and in the recession of the early 1990s, when employment fell by 1.7 million between May 1990 and February 1993. This decline in employment was concentrated among men, male employment falling by 3% and female by 0.7%. In accounting for 84% of the overall fall in employment, falling male employment was not dissimilar to its accounting for 78% of employment losses in the recession of the early 1980s, and 81% of job reductions in the early 1990s recession. The young were also disproportionately affected by unemployment. Comprising only 19.5% of the UK working age population, 74% of the decline in employment has been among those aged sixteen to twenty-four. Males accounted for 44% of the decline and females for 30%. By contrast, employment increased by 173,000 among men and women over pension age. Youth unemployment rates in the UK were especially high, particularly in relation to overall rates, with a ratio of youth to adult rates of 2.53. This was higher than the vast majority of countries, with the major exceptions being Belgium (2.77), Greece (2.68), Italy (3.36), and Sweden (2.94).[74]

The initial government response, in addition to trying to keep the banking system afloat, included a mix of QE and some fiscal stimulus. In June 2010 that changed, when the UK switched fiscal policy from supporting demand in a Keynesian fashion to focusing on deficit reduction mainly through cuts in current expenditure and reductions in transfers to individuals. Unlike the interwar period, governments had run structural deficits even before the crisis. In the 1929–1938 period, Germany, the UK, and the US mainly ran structural budget surpluses.[75] The UK budgetary structural deficit was –4% of GDP in 2007, which then increased unsurprisingly to –6.5% in 2008 and –9.0% in 2009, before falling a little to –7.8% in 2010 and a –6.3% deficit in 2011. In 2007, structural deficits also existed in the Euro Area (–2.3%) and in

---

[73] Vaitilingam, *Recovery Britain*, ch. 2; Crafts, 'Return to growth in the U.K.', Vox CEPR Policy Portal, 25 October 2012.

[74] Bell and Blanchflower, 'UK unemployment', R4.

[75] Crafts and Fearon, 'Depression and Recovery', p. 17, Table 1.4.

the US (−2.8%), which peaked in the Euro Area in 2009 at a deficit of −6.4% of GDP and in the US in 2010 at −7.8% of GDP. Suspecting that governments were subject to 'deficit bias', there were moves to place important decision-making centres beyond the political reach of government. The granting of independence to the Bank of England and the establishment of the Monetary Policy Committee and the Office for Budget Responsibility were examples of such moves as part of a wider rules vs. discretion debate.[76] Proposals were also advanced for an independent fiscal policy committee.[77]

The move in 2010 to focus on deficit reduction occurred in the US and the UK, although in the US it was the result of a political stand-off between the two parties, while in the UK it was a deliberate policy.[78] The June 2010 'Emergency' Budget outlined significant real cuts of 2.7% p.a. between 2011/12 and 2014/15, although some of these were reined in a little by the Comprehensive Sending Review (CSR) in October 2010. The health and school education programmes were ring-fenced, but cuts fell heavily on the welfare budget and on capital expenditure. Real government consumption was planned to fall by 1.5% in 2011 and by a further 2% in 2012, a striking strategy at a time when national GDP had fallen by almost 5% as a consequence of the financial crisis.

In justification of this move to deficit reduction and austerity, concern with debt was adduced.[79] In the period from the mid-1970s to the mid-1990s, OECD debt did rise from around 40% of GDP to around 75% of GDP. Yet, the level of debt in 2008 was not high by historic standards. As posters, mugs, and T-shirts appeared exhorting everyone to 'Keep Calm and Carry On', the conjuring up of wartime and immediate post-war memories of austerity was unduly selective. The postwar Attlee government inherited a large national debt of 237.7% of GDP[80] (Table 9.2). The Attlee government also initiated a large programme of fixed capital investment, while holding personal consumption down. Rationing persisted after the war, and in the case of bread and potatoes was introduced after the war had ended. Personal consumption rose by only 1% per annum, leading some like the economist Roy Harrod to question if these hardships were really necessary. In a longer historical perspective, the national debt/GDP ratio had been much higher after the Napoleonic Wars and two world wars. The economists Reinhart and Rogoff suggested that once public debt exceeded 90% of GDP then growth came

---

[76] Wyplos, 'Fiscal policy', p. 73.   [77] Wren-Lewis, 'Lessons from failure', R34.
[78] Wolf, *The Shifts and Shocks*, p. 268; Wolf, 'How Austerity has failed'.
[79] Slater, *National Debt*, ch. 12; Tomlinson, *Managing The Economy*, ch. 5; Wren-Lewis, *The Lies*, chs. 1 and 3.
[80] Turner, *Banking in Crisis*, p. 181.

Table 9.2. Key public finance data (% of GDP)

	Total receipts	Total spending	Public sector net borrowing	Public sector net debt
1945–1946	38.9	53.7	−14.8	240.2
1950–1951	41.2	37.7	3.4	194.8
1955–1956	36.5	36.3	0.2	138.7
1960–1961	34.1	36.6	−2.5	108.8
1965–1966	38.0	39.5	−1.5	87.3
1970–1971	41.4	40.8	0.6	64.7
1975–1976	42.3	48.9	−6.7	52.2
1980–1981	41.3	46.0	−4.6	43.4
1985–1986	41.5	43.9	−2.3	40.3
1990–1991	36.6	37.6	−1.0	23.6
1995–1996	35.7	40.1	−4.4	39.1
2000–2001	37.7	36.1	1.6	29.9
2005–2006	37.0	40.1	−3.1	35.4
2010–2011	36.7	45.3	−8.7	71.7
2014–2015	35.7	40.8	−5.0	83.7

Source: Office for Budget Responsibility, Key public finances since 1920: Outturns and forecasts as of March 2016 Economic and Fiscal Outlook.

close to zero, but this was more guilt by association than any demonstration of causation. It also raised the question of how the previous post-war debt:GDP positions had been reduced.[81] Comparisons made between Greek national debt, denominated in Euros under the care of the ECB, and UK debt, denominated in sterling under the Bank of England outside of the Eurozone, were curious. There was almost no possibility of the UK defaulting on its debt, and confidence that this was so was reflected in the cost and composition of the debt. Interest payments on debts issued in the 1980s but still held in the mid-1990s carried high interest rates, but interest rates since then had generally fallen, pushed down both by a surplus of savings and perhaps, by 1%, by quantitative easing.[82] By 2010, interest rates on UK government borrowing with ten years to maturity were just over 3 percentage points, compared with 5 percentage points in the second quarter of 2007, just before the financial crisis struck. Rates of return on medium length (fifteen-year) index-linked government borrowing fell to around 1%. In 2009 some 22% of UK government debt (18% of GDP) was held by non-residents, which was well below the average in the rest of Europe.[83] As a share of GDP, public sector debt interest payments were half those of the mid-1980s (Table 9.3).

[81] Wolf, *The Shifts and Shocks*, p. 269. [82] Wren-Lewis, 'The macroeconomic record', R8, 15.
[83] Barrell and Kirby, 'Fiscal policy', F61–2.

Table 9.3. Public sector debt interest payments, 1949/50–2009/10 (£ billion, 2012–2013 prices) and as percentage of national income

	Public sector net debt interest payments £ billion	% GDP	PS Gross debt interest payments	% GDP	GDP £ billion	TME less social security less gross debt	% GDP
1949–1950	9.3	2.9	15.8	4.9	322.2	87.5	27.2
1954–1955	8.9	2.4	16.5	4.5	369.7	104.5	28.3
1959–1960	15.8	3.8	18.6	4.4	419.2	110.4	26.3
1964–1965	17.7	3.5	22.0	4.3	506.9	139.9	27.6
1969–1970	21.2	3.6	26.8	4.6	582.1	175.1	30.1
1974–1975	25.1	3.7	32.6	4.8	675.3	240.5	35.6
1979–1980	30.0	4.0	37.9	5.0	751.1	222.8	29.7
1984–1985	33.0	4.1	41.3	5.2	795.2	238.0	29.9
1989–1990	25.9	2.6	38.1	3.9	982.1	243.0	24.7
1994–1995	29.2	2.7	35.4	3.3	1070.4	267.9	25.0
1999–2000	28.2	2.2	34.1	2.7	1267.0	282.6	2.3
2004–2005	22.9	1.6	30.3	2.1	1474.1	401.4	27.2
2009–2010	29.9	2.0	33.5	2.2	1530.8	487.4	31.8

Source: Institute for Fiscal Studies.

Arguably what was of more concern than national debt was household debt. In the US and UK over the Great Moderation, household debt (calculated as housing credit plus consumer debt to facilitate comparability) rose by over 30% of GDP. The increases in household debt were lower (just over 10%) in France, Canada, and Italy, while in Germany and Japan, household debt grew at broadly the same rate as GDP. In Japan, the property market was only recovering slowly from the 1990s crash, and in Germany the ready availability of rental accommodation made real estate purchase less attractive than elsewhere. While households' vulnerability to default could be mitigated by a rise in financial assets, exceptionally in the UK during the Great Moderation net financial wealth declined by over 40% of GDP between 1997 and 2006. All other countries, with the exception of Canada, saw a rise in net financial assets during the period of tranquil economic developments.[84] In 2002–2006, the debt/income ratio for households rose by around 25 percentage points compared to only 8–9% in 1985–1989.

In short, the size of debt was not that high in historic terms, and the costs of servicing the debt were historically low. Given this, the debt-based arguments for 'austerity' looked suspect at best, and counterproductive at worst if 'austerity' proved to be 'self-defeating', i.e. that it contributed to increasing

[84]   Davis, 'The evolution of financial structure', R13.

rather than decreasing the debt:GDP ratio.[85] This concerned the UK, but also EU countries where spillover effects could cause reduced growth in one country to also reduce growth in other countries, through trade linkages.[86] With interest rates close to zero, the scope for further use of monetary policy was limited and in this context the impact of fiscal policy in terms of its multiplier effects on output was uncertain.[87] Multipliers are time and state dependent and there was some evidence that fiscal multipliers were larger in a depressed economy than in a strong one. On that basis, the government cuts of 40% in public investment in 2010–2011 and 2011–2012 were likely to have had multiplier effects larger than those allowed for in the OBR estimate that 2% of GDP was lost due to austerity policies (1% in 2010–2011 and 2011–2012).[88] Given the limited ability of monetary policy to mitigate any larger than expected effects of a fiscal squeeze, the concern was that capacity would be lost, potential output reduced, and costs incurred as long-term hysteresis effects occurred.[89]

What tended also to be conspicuous by its bashfulness was public investment. In general, gross fixed capital formation fell by 13.4% between 2008 and 2009 and to maintain the level of public capital to GDP at a growth-maximizing level, public investment of about 2.7% of GDP per year was needed. In the UK it fell from 2.4 to 1.9% of GDP between 2010 and 2014.[90] There was also a sharp contrast between those investment schemes which governments did support after the 2008 crisis, and those favoured by Keynes in his discussion of the role of government in emerging from an economic slump. In a series of articles written for *The Times* in March 1933 and therefore preceding the publication of *The General Theory* in 1936, Keynes had argued that, while as a first step to recovery bank credit should be cheap and abundant, and that, as a second step, the long-term rate of interest should be low for all reasonably sound borrowers, that these were necessary but not sufficient conditions for economic recovery.[91] The reluctance of business to expand until *after* profits begin to recover, and the fact that increased working capital would not be required until *after* output began increasing, meant, in Keynes' view, that an important role fell to those public and semi-public bodies who undertook 'a very large proportion of our *normal* programmes of loan-expenditure'. In contrast to the 'comparatively small' new loan-expenditure required in a year

---

[85] Holland and Portes, 'Self-defeating austerity?', F4.   [86] Tooze, *Crashed.*
[87] Wren Lewis, 'The macroeconomic record'; Alesina and Ardegna, 'Large changes in fiscal policy'; Holland and Portes, 'Self-defeating austerity?', F4.
[88] van Reenen, 'Austerity in the U.K.'.   [89] De Long and Summers, 'Fiscal policy'.
[90] Crafts' 'UK economic growth', R23.   [91] Keynes, *The Means To Prosperity.*

by trade and industry, Keynes emphasized how 'building, transport and public utilities are responsible at all times for a very large proportion of current loan expenditure', and the proportionately important areas of investment in durable assets such as dwellings, public utilities, roads and railways where there was usually little risk, the annual rate of depreciation was low and the rate of interest was an important influence.[92]

Keynes' proposal was not one of bald deficit financing, but that contributions to the Sinking Fund, the money which government collected to pay off existing debt, might be suspended. Keynes argued throughout World War II that the ordinary, as opposed to the capital, budget should be kept in balance. In the event, in the 1944 *White Paper on Employment Policy*, the capital budget was folded into the ordinary budget.[93] In 2008 the possibility existed of increasing debt so as to fund a social house-building programme, whose subsequent rents would exceed the costs of borrowing and thereby in turn contribute to a reduction in the structural deficit. That this was not done was a pity for at least two reasons. Firstly, there is a perversity to the British housing market. As David Laidler observed when otherwise reflecting on the monetarist experiment, the great challenge was to end the peculiarity of the British housing market and the consequent reduction of labour mobility caused by reliance on owner occupation and local authority rentals which provide housing for close to 90% of the population.[94] Secondly, and mainly, the paucity of efforts to intervene directly in the house-building programme reflected a continuing refusal to accept a central message of *The General Theory*, namely that in conditions of slump, government has a crucial role to play in affecting and influencing expectations of (Marginal Efficiency of Investment)MEI. Keynes wrote specifically about the expected MEI available on projects, and some of this specificity was lost in the translation to the IS/LM model. For the Golden Age it was not a serious loss. Private fixed capital investment responding to both optimistic and subsidized expected profits was higher than had been expected, the state itself was a formidable presence in fixed capital investment, and the system was underpinned by buoyant public finances. In the aftermath of the 2008 financial crisis, a government approach to encourage investment in long-lived assets such as housing, utilities, and roads would have regionally dispersed multiplier effects with, as in the case of social housing, rents exceeding borrowing costs.

---

[92] Keynes, *The Means to Prosperity*, ch. 3, pp. 21–2; Kahn, *Making*, p. 149.
[93] Bateman, 'Keynes and Keynesianism', pp. 275–7.
[94] Laidler, 'Monetary policy', p. 41.

Private investment did not make up the gap, which given liquidity shortages, increased risk premia in investment decisions, and a consequent fall in the equilibrium capital:output ratio was not surprising. Curiously perhaps, those capital investment schemes which were favoured, such as the £3 billion to be spent on HS2 up to 2021, offered distant and spatially highly specific improvements to travel times, compared with a range of smaller and geographically scattered dispersed improvements which offered high benefit:cost ratios. As seen in chapter 6, difficulties persisted in providing sufficient incentives to utility companies to invest in capacity and infrastructure. This echoed concerns in the wake of privatization that gains were arising from sweating assets rather than replacing them. It was certainly some way from Keynes's presumptions as to how government should encourage investment. As QE and falling real interest rates were used to bring consumption forward in time, while government was nervous of offering assurance of marginal rates of return on fixed capital investment, echoes of the debates in the 1930s between Keynes and Hayek were easy to hear.

That despite falling public fixed capital investment, government expenditure remained high as a percentage of GDP reflected the shift in the composition in public expenditure away from fixed capital investment and towards transfer payments (chapters 2 and 5). These had an intergenerational aspect which demographic pressures were only likely to intensify. As the baby boomers born just after the end of World War II turned sixty-five, so over the decade 2012 and 2022 was the share of the population aged sixty-five and over expected to accelerate to 22%, while the growth in the overall population dropped back slightly to 6%. By 2022, 20% of the population would be aged sixty-five or over. In 2012, that share was 17%.[95] The likely rise in life expectancy would place greater pressure on pensions (and health spending).[96] The costs of making private provision for old age rose as the real rate of interest and the rate of return on government bonds fell. This weakening of the power of compound interest was potentially significant, especially if accompanied by persistent low rates of economic growth. Opinion varied as to whether the global economy was suffering a savings glut or whether it had entered a period of secular decline with a long-run diminishing of the rate of return on capital. One view was that the economy was in a 'debt supercycle' in which the excessive expansion in credit that led to the global financial crisis was followed by a deleveraging which was a persistent drag on growth. As this

---

[95] Emmerson, Heald and Hood, *The Changing Face of Retirement*, p. 6.
[96] DeLong, 'On the proper size', p. 201.

process worked itself out, so growth would return. This carried echoes of the Hayek of the 1930s (chapter 2). Alternatively, there was the secular stagnation hypothesis first developed by Lawrence H. Summers at an IMF conference in 2013. On this view, there was a chronic excess of savings over investment—as evidenced in lower yields, sluggish growth, and below target inflation—such that economies were likely to continue with low or even negative real interest rates for the foreseeable future. Aggregate demand management would remain difficult as central banks were constrained by the zero lower bound. The low or negative equilibrium real interest rates would lead to a greater and riskier search for yield, resulting in bubbles and increasing the risks of finan-cial instability.[97]

The power of compound interest formed a central strand of Keynes's 'Economic Possibilities' paper, the first version of which was read to a student society at Winchester School at the beginning of 1928. The final version of the essay was included in 1930 in Keynes's *Essays in Persuasion*.[98] In 1928 the *Economic Journal,* which Keynes edited, published Frank Ramsey's article 'A Theory of Saving' and both this article and Keynes's 'Economic possibilities' shared an interest in how each generation saved and how capital, often show-ing up in technology, accumulated and contributed to growth.[99] The power of compound growth was evident, although the outcomes of economic growth were not as Keynes expected. While accepting that it would not come to pass for one hundred years, Keynes thought that the biggest problem in the future would be what to do with leisure time since 'for many ages to come the old Adam will be so strong in us that everybody will need to do *some* work if he is to be contented.' In Keynes's opinion 'Three-hour shifts or a fifteen-hour week may put off the problem for a great while...For three hours a day is quite enough to satisfy the old Adam in most of us!'[100] By 2000 individuals spent a lower proportion of their lifetime in paid employment than they had in 1930, not least because by 2000 life expectancy in Great Britain was about twenty years longer than it had been in 1930 (seventeen in the United States) while retirement age fell.[101] The standard working week was about forty-four hours in the vast majority of manufacturing industries in 1946–1948, and about forty hours in 1969.[102] Rising per capita GDP did not lead to a commensurate proportionate increase in leisure time. In the first decade of the twenty-first century, while per capita GDP in the United States was 30–40% higher than

---

[97] Blanchard and Portillo, 'A road map', p. 2; Koo, *The Other Half*, pp. 259–61.
[98] Pecchi and Piga, *Revisiting Keynes*, p. 2.   [99] Solow, 'Whose grandchildren?', p. 87.
[100] Keynes, 'Economic possibilities', pp. 368–9.
[101] Zilibotti, 'Economic Possibilities', p. 32.   [102] Gazeley, 'Manual work and pay', p. 62.

in France and Germany, employed Americans worked 30% more hours over the year than their counterparts in France and Germany; 'the workaholic rich replaced the idle rich.'[103] In part, the nature and interest of work had changed for some, while additional income allowed a growing range of consumer durables to be bought, and rising asset prices (notably property) to be financed.

In his original essay on 'Economic possibilities' Keynes did not discuss how increased income and accumulated wealth might be distributed.[104] For much of the period from the mid-1970s, increasing GDP per capita and widening income and wealth inequality co-existed (chapter 4). In the wake of the 2008 crisis, the intergenerational aspects of the inequalities of income and wealth attracted particular attention.[105] Post-crisis pensioner household income did rise faster than non-pensioner household income, but pensioner household incomes remained considerably lower than non-pensioner household incomes. In general, while there was concern that intergenerational inequality existed between baby boomers and the younger generation, intragenerational inequality remained greater than intergenerational inequality. Income inequality, which had increased between 1975–1995, did experience a slowing of this rate of increase in the twenty-first century as wage growth, while favouring higher earners, was much more evenly spread, and redistributive tax and benefit policies, especially in the early 2000s, had some restraining effect on income inequality. Yet, as in the United States, in the UK median wages grew significantly less than per capita GDP as an increasing proportion of the increase in average (mean) incomes went to those at the top of the income distribution. Between 1999/2000 and 2013/14 about a quarter of the growth in real pre-tax incomes accrued to the top 1% of (income) taxpayers; almost as much as went to the bottom 50%. Younger people on low and middle incomes suffered in particular. Again, wealth inequality easily exceeded income inequality. Over two-thirds of property wealth belonged to the wealthiest third of the population, and as such the inheritance of the high-priced property of the older generation would go to a restricted portion of the younger generation.[106]

While the costs of higher education continued to be subsidized, an increasing proportion of the younger generation did enter the labour market carrying debt from university tuition fees, the financial return from which would depend on future earnings.[107] Those graduating in the wake of the 2008 crisis were likely to suffer a lifelong loss of earnings. This was also generally true of

---

[103] Pecchi and Piga, *Revisiting Keynes*, p. 6.   [104] Pecchi and Piga, *Revisiting Keynes*, p. 5.
[105] Willetts, *The Pinch*.
[106] Portes, 'Commentary', F10.   [107] Metcalf, 'Paying for university', p. 106.

school leavers. The lifetime earnings of school leavers who find their first job in a recession is 10–15% lower than the lifetime earnings of those who enter the labour market in a boom.[108] The labour market in which the younger generation sought employment was significantly different from that which had faced their parents when they first entered the labour market. Collective organizations such as trade unions declined, placing more responsibility on individuals to negotiate their way through employment contracts and conditions. Union membership peaked in the 1970s with union density—the proportion of workers who are members of trade unions—at a little over 50%. By 2007 union density in Great Britain had fallen to 25%. In 2007 the union density rate for private sector employees was 15.9%. Union membership rates among the young in the UK were especially low. The union density rate for sixteen- to nineteen-year-olds in 2004 was 4.3%, and 9.8% for sixteen- to twenty-four-year-olds in 2007 (chapter 3).[109]

Discussion of such changes in the position of individuals, and the emphasis placed on their individual decisions and responsibilities, was sometimes 'justified' by references to Adam Smith's invisible hand.[110] While before Smith, it was Mirabeau who had noted in 1763 that 'the whole magic of well-ordered society is that each man works for others, while believing that he is working only for himself', it was Smith's observation in 1776 that 'it is not from the benevolence of the butcher, the brewer, or the baker, that we expect our dinner, but from their regard to their own interest' that found political popularity in the last quarter of the twentieth century.[111] That Smith's two-hundred-year-old observation should become so popular reflected a political interest in using economics to provide a vocabulary of apparent political liberty. As with the selective use of Hayek, the use of Smith to assert that the pursuit of self-interest also unintentionally provided for the collective good ignored Smith's work in *The Theory of Moral Sentiments* and did not, of itself, preclude a role for government. What it also glossed over was the question of what a market was and how it came to exist. Hayek was very clear on the element of luck in the distribution of rewards in a labour market, and he and Keynes had both been very aware of the importance of the variety of times which existed within a market. It was not simply a question of consumption and investment

---

[108] Farmer, *Prosperity for All*, p. 98; Oreopoulos, Von-Wachter, and Heisz, 'The short- and long-term career effects'.

[109] Bell and Blanchflower, 'UK unemployment', R11.

[110] Korsgaard, *Self-Constitution*.
For a nuanced view of Smith, see Medema, *The Hesitant Hand*; Fischer and Ravizza, *Responsibility and Control*, ch. 7.

[111] Milgate and Stimson, *After Adam Smith*, p. 82; Smith, *The Wealth of Nations*, p. 119.

decisions partly reflecting expectations of the future, but also that the supply-side resulted from past investment decisions. The variety of times co-existing in a 'market' remained a particular concern among Austrian economists such as Israel Kirzner.[112]

If there was only limited political concern with the complexity of what constituted a market, this was not true of the increasingly popular field of behavioural economics. In 2008 the UK government had even established what became known as the Nudge unit.[113] Behavioural economics had grown in popularity from the mid-1990s and it built on work by the likes of Kahneman and Tversky who in 1979 had published their now famous article on 'Prospect theory: An analysis of decision under risk' in *Econometrica*.[114] In one sense, the approach marked a return to the concern with what constituted utility, such as had concerned Lionel Robbins some fifty years earlier. Robbins had recognized that such decisions involved psychological factors and in analysing people's perception and valuation of expected utility, behavioural economics added psychology to the more usual probability in its study of human decision-making under uncertainty.[115] Individual decision-making in time and between (inter-temporal) times provided for a fertile interaction of behavioural economics and discounting, especially in a context in which current behaviour (smoking, over-eating) was known to run a risk of future damage.[116] As the opening line of George Ainslie's *Piconomics* declared: 'This book examines an elementary human paradox—perhaps *the* elementary human paradox—that we are endangered by our own wishes.'[117] Behavioural economics also provided a basis for the development of behavioural finance which offered a challenge to the efficient market hypothesis (EMH).[118] The EMH was associated principally with Chicago economists such as Eugene Fama, who was to be awarded the Nobel Prize in 2013.[119] The EMH was sanguine that markets were always efficient, rational, and self-adjusting, with market prices providing accurate information which was correctly and immediately processed by market participants. A market was 'informationally efficient' if prices at each moment incorporated all available information about

[112] Kirzner, *Economic Point*.   [113] Thaler, *Misbehaving*, p. 330.

[114] Kahneman and Tversky, 'An analysis of decision under risk'.

[115] Heukelom, *Behavioural Economics*, p. 119; Camerer, Loewenstein and Rabin, *Advances in Behavioural Economics*.

[116] Loewenstein and Elster, *Choice Over Time*; Mazzocchi, Bruce Traill, and Shogren, *Fat Economics*; Frederick, Loewenstein, and O'Donoghue, 'Time discounting and time preference'; Heukelom, *Behavioural Economics*, p. 1.

[117] Ainslie, *Picoeconomics*, p. xi; Offer, *The Challenge of Affluence*.

[118] Samuelson and Barnett, *Inside the Economist's Mind*, p. 61.

[119] Fama, 'Efficient capital markets'; Heukelom, *Behavioural Economics*, p. 143; Farmer, *Prosperity for All*, p. 10.

future values.[120] Quite apart from scepticism about the ability of financial markets to overcome uncertainty, any efficiency sat alongside increased volatility. Using the cyclically *adjusted price earnings ratio* (CAPE) developed by William Sharpe (Nobel winner in 1990), rather than this measure being constant it had been as low as 5 in 1919 and as high as 44 in 1998. And, as Nassim Nicholas Taleb pointed out, the market movements that followed the Lehman Brothers crash in September 2008 were, if conventional theory was to be believed, a seven-standard deviation event.[121]

Politically, not only was the volatility of financial markets problematic, but financial economics tended in the public sphere at least to encourage assumptions as to the efficiency of markets. Yet while the EMH might fit data on widely traded stocks, not all factors of production move as quickly or as easily as stock. [122] This was not simply an issue of how the sub-division of production brought global benefits in aggregate but potentially at a cost to national labour forces who held their national governments responsible. It also marked a further contrast with the incorporation of time into post-war economic thinking when publicly financed and/or publicly provided fixed capital investment formed a higher share of total public expenditure. The concern with fixed capital investment prompted concern with the trade cycle, risk, and uncertainty, not least because of the irreversibility of any fixed capital investment decision. In this situation Keynes clearly saw a role for government, although not the role which the Attlee and succeeding governments came to assume with nationalization etc. The incentives to invest, to overcome time risks on such investments, still form a concern, but one which need not be addressed by a return to public ownership. The significance of the Golden Age lay as much in the mechanisms governments employed as in the macroeconomic aims they pursued. Public ownership, the financing and provision of fixed capital investment, and a concern to cover the past costs of that investment gave way in time to an approach which gave a greater role to private ownership, which was less sceptical of the ability of markets to allocate resources efficiently in and across time, and which looked forward to the future value of benefits which it then expressed in terms of the present time.

Accompanying this shift in time perspective within governments' allocation of resources, there was also an extension in the application of the term 'capital'. The temporal postponement of current consumption in the

---

[120] Stiglitz, *Freefall*, p. 258.
[121] Farmer, *Prosperity for All*, pp. 10, 112; Taleb, *The Black Swan*.
[122] Blinder, *After the Music Stopped*, p. 65.

expectation of future higher returns was seen as characterizing education, in which human capital was developed and larger future, mainly private, gains were made. Access to capital assets, such as housing and shares, had been viewed as an important incentive to increased effort and entrepreneurship from the mid-1970s. Financial capital was also released from controls from the late 1970s, both with the removing of exchange controls and in the loosening of formal and informal controls over the financial and banking markets. Ironically, combined later with falling real interest rates, the increasing availability of financial capital helped to increase the price of capital assets like houses and shares. That process was compounded by QE. The tax treatment of financial assets, be it owner-occupied housing or the making of tax-free capital gains within large Investment Savings Accounts, further encouraged asset holding. As asset price increases outstripped real wages, then assets ceased to have the same incentive effect for the increasing number of households for whom they became unaffordable. Some of this disquiet over inequality of opportunity was reflected in the popularity of Piketty's tome *Capital in the Twenty-First Century*. While public comment focused mainly on income, it was wealth, that store of time, where inequality was far greater. Wealth is the past acting on the future through the present. Incentives to accumulate wealth, to acquire choice, are important in market economies, but government does need to ensure that incentives, such an access to assets, remain widely available. Such a capital-sharing political economy was what was urged by James Meade, by Keith Joseph, and Samuel Brittan in the 1970s and 1980s. It recognizes the role of incentives and of the compounding property of wealth. It also implicitly recognizes the role of time, and in so doing it raises the central question of how temporal and spatial considerations should shape what government does, and does not, do in an economy. Long-run research and development is a familiar area for government involvement, as too are negative externalities such a pollution. In pollution, what was familiarly termed as market failure is probably more accurately seen as a missing market, but one in which the assertion of proxy ownership rights has enhanced the potential for allowing economic mechanisms to address the problems. The failure to introduce adequate carbon taxes indicates that spatial considerations and free-riding, as well as the reluctance of the present to pay for the future, offer serious obstacles to the implementation of theoretical solutions. Neither rules nor economic mechanisms are applied adequately to pollution, but instead an unnecessary market in quantity permits is created. Rules provide some assurance about the future. Rules were and are applied to labour. They are applied less to capital, and where uncertainty exists, as in the provision of utility output in increasing returns industries, there is a reluctance to reduce uncertainty by offering regulated rates of return on capital investment. In carbon trading, administrative approaches are preferred. In exchange rates, the Eurozone operates another administrative mechanism, the Euro, at the cost of a loss of flexibility. Vested interests crowd round administrative arrangements and defend them, even when they are clearly not achieving the objectives sought. To return to the economist David Ricardo's concern which was quoted in the first chapter of this book, it was not so much the rate of economic growth which is of concern, but the nature of that growth and the distribution of its benefits. The market is one distributive mechanism and source of incentives; the government is another. In thinking about the apportionment of roles and responsibilities between the two, it is useful to think in terms of time and space. What were the temporal challenges which are most suited to markets, or government, or a mix of both? Equally, what are the spatial considerations which should affect our thinking on this division of roles and responsibilities, and our choice of mechanisms? Considerations of time and space affect all of the major issues of concern today (housing, utility output, global warming, infrastructure, educational opportunities, access to healthcare, trade, the internet, and so on) just as they often did in the past. Time and space are long-standing concerns in economics, and should also figure more prominently in considerations of policy.

Bibliography

Admati, Anat, and Martin Hellwig, *The Bankers' New Clothes*, 2013, Princeton and Oxford: Princeton University Press.

Admati, Anat R., 'The missed opportunity and challenge of capital regulation', *National Institute Economic Review*, no. 235, February 2016, R4–14.

Ainslie, George, *Picoeconomics: The Strategic Interaction of Successive Motivational States within the Person*, 1992, Cambridge: Cambridge University Press.

Alesina, Alberto, and Silvia Ardegna, 'Large changes in fiscal policy: Taxes versus spending', NBER Working paper, No. 15438, October 2009.

Armstrong, Angus, and E. Philip Davis, 'Comparing housing booms and mortgage supply in the major OECD countries', *National Institute Economic Review*, no. 230, November 2014, R3–R15.

Aron, Janine, and John Muellbauer, 'Modelling and forecasting mortgage delinquency and foreclosure in the UK', VOX CEPR's Policy Portal, 31 August 2016.

Also Department of Economics, University of Oxford Discussion Paper, April 2016, Ref. 793.

Barrell, Ray, 'Policy responses to the collapse of the financial sector: Introduction', *National Institute Economic Review*, no. 211, January 2010, R1–R2.

Barrell, Ray, and Simon Kirby, 'Fiscal policy and government spending', *National Institute Economic Review*, no. 214, October 2010, F61–F66.

Barrell, Ray, Tatiana Fic, John Fitz Gerald, Ali Orazgani, and Rachel Whitworth, 'The banking sector and recovery in the EU economy', *National Institute Economic Review*, no. 216, April 2011, R41–52.

Barth, James R., and Clas Wihlborg, 'Too big to fail and too big to save: Dilemmas for banking reform', *National Institute Economic* Review, vol. 235, no. 1, February 2016, R27–R39.

Bell, David N.F., and David G. Blanchflower, 'UK unemployment in the great recession', *National Institute Economic Review*, no. 214, October 2010, R3–R25.

Blanchard, Olivier, and Rafael Portillo, 'A road map to "progress and confusion"', in Olivier Blanchard, Raghuram Rajan, Kenneth Rogoff, and Lawrence H. Summers (eds.), *Progress and Confusion: The State of Macroeconomic Policy*, 2016, Cambridge, Mass.: The MIT Press, pp. 1–15.

Blinder, Alan, *After the Music Stopped: The Financial Crisis, the Response, and the Work Ahead*, 2013, New York: The Penguin Press.

Brunnermeier, M.K., 'Deciphering the liquidity and credit crunch of 2007–2008', *Journal of Economic Perspectives*, 2009, vol. 23, pp. 77–100.

Camerer, Colin F., George Loewenstein, and Matthew Rabin, *Advances in Behavioural Economics*, 2004, New York: Russell Sage Foundation.

Cecchetti, Stephen G., Dietrich Domanski, and Goetz von Peter, 'New regulation and the new world of global banking', *National Institute Economic Review*, no. 216, April 2011, R29–40.

Crafts, Nicholas and Peter Fearon, 'Depression and Recovery in the 1930s: An overview', in Nicholas Crafts and Peter Fearon, *The Great Depression of the 1930s: Lessons for Today*, 2013, Oxford: Oxford University Press, pp. 1–44.

Crafts, Nicholas., 'Return to growth in the U.K.: Policy lessons from history', Vox CEPR Policy Portal, 25 October 2012.

Crafts, Nicholas, 'UK economic growth since 2010: Is it as bad as it seems?', *National Institute Economic Review*, no. 231, February 2015, R17–R29.

Davis, E. Philip, 'The evolution of financial structure in the G-7 over 1997–2010', *National Institute Economic* Review, no. 221, July 2012, R11–22.

DeLong, J. Bradford, 'On the proper size of the public sector and the level of debt in the twenty-first century', in Olivier Blanchard, Raghuram Rajan, Kenneth Rogoff, and Lawrence H. Summers (eds.), *Progress and Confusion: The State of Macroeconomic Policy*, 2016, Cambridge, Mass.: The MIT Press, pp. 197–209.

De Long, J.B., and L.H. Summers, 'Fiscal policy in a depressed economy', *Brookings Papers on Economic Activity*, Spring 2012, pp. 233–97.

De Nicolò, Gianni, 'Liquidity regulation: Rationales, benefits and costs', *National Institute Economic Review*, no. 235, February 2016, R18–26.

Emmerson, Carl, Katherine Heald, and Andrew Hood, *The Changing Face of Retirement: Future Patterns of Work, Health, Care and Income among the Older Population*, IFS Report, R95, 2014, London: Institute for Fiscal Studies.

Fama, Eugene F., 'Efficient capital markets: A review of theory and empirical work', *The Journal of Finance*, vol. 25, no. 2, May 1970, pp. 383–417.

Farmer, Roger E.A., *Prosperity for All*, 2017, Oxford: Oxford University Press.

Fischer, John Martin, and Mark Ravizza, *Responsibility and Control: A Theory of Moral Responsibility*, 1998, Cambridge: Cambridge University Press.

Frederick, S., G. Loewenstein, and T. O'Donoghue, 'Time discounting and time preference: A critical review', *Journal of Economic Literature*, vol. 40, no. 2, June 2002, pp. 351–401.

Gazeley, Ian, 'Manual work and pay, 1900–70', in Nicholas Crafts, Ian Gazeley, and Andrew Newall, *Work and Pay in Twentieth Century Britain*, 2007, Oxford: Oxford University Press, pp. 55–79.

Goodhart, Charles, 'Is a less pro-cyclical financial system an achievable goal?', *National Institute Economic Review*, no. 211, January 2010, R17–26.

Gorton, G., 'Information, liquidity, and the (ongoing) panic of 2007', *American Economic Review: Papers and Proceedings*, vol. 99, no. 2, May 2009, pp. 567–72.

Heukelom, Floris, *Behavioural Economics: A History*, 2014, Cambridge: Cambridge University Press.

Holland, Dawn, and Jonathan Portes, 'Self-defeating austerity?', *National Institute Economic Review*, no. 222, October 2012, F4–10.

Hordahl, P., and M. King, 'Developments in repo markets during the financial turmoil', *BIS Quarterly Review*, December 2008.

Independent Commission on Banking, *Final Report* Recommendations, September 2011, London: Stationery Office.

Kahneman, Daniel, and Amos Tversky, 'An analysis of decision under risk', *Econometrica*, vol. 47, no. 2, March 1979, pp. 263–91.

Kay, John, *Other People's Money: The Real Business of Finance*, 2015, New York: Public Affairs.

Keynes, John Maynard, 'Economic possibilities for our grandchildren', 1930, in John Maynard Keynes, *Essays in Persuasion*, First published: 1931, London: Macmillan. First published in the Norton Library, 1963, New York: W.W.Norton & Company, pp. 358–73.

King, Mervyn, *The End of Alchemy: Money, Banking and the Future of the Global Economy*, 2016, London, Little, Brown.

Kirzner, Israel M., *The Economic Point of View: An Essay in the History of Economic Thought*, 2009, Indiana: Liberty Fund.

Koo, Richard C., *The Other Half of Macroeconomics and the Fate of Globalization*, 2018, Chichester: John Wiley & Sons.

Korsgaard, Christine M. *Self-Constitution: Agency, Identity, and Integrity*, 2009, Oxford: Oxford University Press.

Laeven, Luc, and Fabián Valencia, *Systematic Banking Crisis Database: An Update*, IMF Working Paper, WP/12/163, June 2012.

Lavington, F., *The Trade Cycle: An Account of the Causes Producing Rhythmical Changes in the Activity of Business*, 1928, London: P.S.King & Son.

Leslé, Vanessa Le, and Sofiya Avramova, 'Revisiting Risk-Weight Assets: Why do RWAs differ across countries and what can be done about it?', IMF Working Paper, March 2012.

Lewis, Michael, *The Big Short: Inside the Doomsday Machine*, 2010, London: Allen Lane.

Li, David X, 'The Valuation of Basket Credit Derivatives', *Credit Metrics Monitor*, April 1999, pp. 34–50.

Li, David X, 'On Default Correlation: A Copula Function Approach', *Journal of Fixed Income*, 2000, vol. 9, no. 4, pp. 43–54.

Loewenstein, George, and John Elster, *Choice Over Time*, 1992, New York: Russell Sage Foundation.

Mackenzie, Donald, 'The credit crisis as a problem in the sociology of knowledge', *American Journal of Sociology*, vol. 116, no. 6, May 2011, pp. 1778–841.

McDonald, Oonagh, *Lehman Brothers: A Crisis of Value*, 2016, Manchester: Manchester University Press.

Mazzocchi, Mario, W. Bruce Traill, and Jason F. Shogren, *Fat Economics Nutrition, Health and Economic Policy*, 2009, Oxford: Oxford University Press.

Medema, Steven G., *The Hesitant Hand: Taming Self-Interest in the History of Economic Ideas*, 2009, Princeton: Princeton University Press.

Metcalf, Hilary, 'Paying for university: The impact of increasing costs on student employment, debt and satisfaction', *National Institute Economic Review*, vol. 191, issue 1, January 2005, pp. 106–17.

Michaud, F.-L., and C. Upper, 'What drives interbank rates? Evidence from the Libor panel', *BIS Quarterly Review*, March 2008.

Miles, David, 'Regulatory failure and regulatory change in the banking sector', *National Institute Economic Review*, no. 235, February 2016, R15–R17.

Milgate, Murray, and Shannon C. Stimson, *After Adam Smith: A Century of Transformation in Politics and Political* Economy, 2009, Princeton and Oxford: Princeton University Press.

Minsky, H.P., 'A theory of systemic fragility', in E.I.Altman and A.W. Sametz (eds.), *Financial Crises*, 1977, New York: Wiley.

Minsky, H.P., 'Can "It" Happen Again?': *Essays on Instability and Finance*, 1982, New York: M.E. Sharpe, Inc.

Nicolò, Gianni De, 'Liquidity regulation: Rationales, benefits and costs', *National Institute Economic Review*, no. 235, February 2016, R18–26.

Offer, Avner, *The Challenge of Affluence: Self-Control and Well-Being in the United States and Britain since 1950*, 2006, Oxford: Oxford University Press.

Oreopoulos, P., T. Von-Wachter, and A. Heisz, 'The short- and long-term career effects of graduating in a recession: Hysteresis and heterogeneity in the market for college graduates', *American Economic Journal: Applied Economics*, vol. 4, no. 1, January 2012, pp. 1–29.

Paulson, Hank, *On the Brink: Inside the Race to Stop the Collapse of the Global Financial System*, 2010, New York and London: Business Plus and Headline.

Pecchi, Lorenzo, and Gustavo Piga, *Revisiting Keynes: Economic Possibilities for our Grandchildren* (eds.), 2008, Cambridge, Mass.: The MIT Press.

Piketty, Thomas (translated by Arthur Goldhammer), *Capital in the Twenty-First Century*, 2014, Cambridge, Mass.: Belknap Press.

Portes, Jonathan, 'Commentary: Intergenerational and intragenerational equity', *National Institute Economic Review*, no. 227, February 2014, F4–F11.

Reid, Margaret, *The Secondary Banking Crisis, 1973–75: Causes and Course*, 1982, London: Palgrave Macmillan.

Reenen, John van., 'Austerity in the U.K.: past, present and future', British Politics and Policy blog, LSE, 11 March 2015.

Samuelson, Paul A., and William A. Barnett, *Inside the Economist's Mind: Conversations with Eminent Economists*, 2007, Oxford: Blackwell.

Shin, H.S., 'Reflections on Northern Rock: The bank run that heralded the global financial crisis, *Journal of Economic Perspectives*, vol. 23, no. 1, 2009, pp. 101–19.

Slater, Martin, *The National Debt: A Short History*, 2018, New York: Oxford University Press.

Smith, Adam, *The Wealth of Nations* (originally, *An Inquiry into the Nature and Causes of the Wealth of Nations*, 1776), 1999, London: Penguin English Library.

Solow, Robert, 'Whose grandchildren?', in Lorenzo Pecchi and Gustavo Piga (eds.), *Revisiting Keynes: Economic Possibilities for our Grandchildren*, 2008, Cambridge, Mass.: The MIT Press, pp. 87–93.

Stearns, Dave, *Electronic Value Exchange: Origins of the VISA Electronic Payment System*, 2011, London: Springer.

Stiglitz, Joseph, *Freefall; Free Markets and the Sinking of the Global* Economy, 2010, Allen Lane: London.

Taleb, Nassim, *The Black Swan: The Impact of the Highly Improbable*, 2008, London: Penguin.

Thaler, Richard, *Misbehaving: The Making of Behavioural Economics*, 2015, London: Allen Lane.

Turner, Adair, *The Turner Review: A Regulatory Response to the Global Banking Crisis*, 2009, London: Financial Services Authority.

Tomlinson, Jim, *Managing The Economy, Managing The People: Narratives of Economic Life in Britain from Beveridge to Brexit*, 2017, Oxford: Oxford University Press.

Tooze, Adam., *Crashed: How A Decade of Financial Crisis Changed The World*, 2018, London: Allen Lane.

Turner, John D., *Banking in Crisis: The Rise and Fall of British Banking Stability, 1800 to the Present*, 2014, Cambridge: Cambridge University Press.

Vaitilingam, Romesh, *Recovery Britain: Research Evidence to Underpin a Productive, Fair and Sustainable Return to Growth*, 2009, Swindon: Economic and Social Research Council.

Valdez, Stephen, and Philip Molyneux, *An Introduction to Global Financial Markets*, 2010, Houndmills: Palgrave Macmillan.

Willetts, David, *The Pinch: How the Baby Boomers Stole Their Children's Future And How They Can Give It Back*, 2010, London: Atlantic Books.

Wolf, Martin, 'How Austerity has failed', *New York Review of Books*, vol. LX, no. 12, 11 July–4 August 2013.

Wolf, Martin, *The Shifts and the Shocks: What We've Learned-And Have Still To Learn-From The Financial Crisis*, 2014, London: Allen Lane.

Wren-Lewis, Simon, 'Lessons from failure: Fiscal policy, indulgence and ideology', *National Institute Economic Review*, no. 217, July 2011, R31–46.

Wren-Lewis, Simon, 'The macroeconomic record of the coalition government', *National Institute Economic Review*, no. 231, February 2015, R5–R16.

Wren-Lewis, Simon, *The Lies We Were Told*, 2018, Bristol: Bristol University Press.

Wyplos, Charles, 'Fiscal policy: Institutions versus rules', *National Institute Economic Review*, no. 191, January 2005, pp. 64–78.

Zilibotti, Fabrizio, 'Economic Possibilities for our Grandchildren 75 Years After: A Global Perspective', in Lorenzo Pecchi and Gustavo Piga (eds.), *Revisiting Keynes: Economic Possibilities for our Grandchildren*, 2008, Cambridge, Mass.: The MIT Press, pp. 27–39.

Statistical Appendix

Table 1.1. GDP annual growth rates: France, Germany, Japan, U.K., and U.S.A., 1980–2016 (%)

	France	Germany	Japan	U.K.	U.S.A.
1980	1.6	1.4	2.8	−2.0	−0.2
1981	1.1	0.5	4.2	−0.8	2.6
1982	2.5	−0.4	3.4	2.0	−1.9
1983	1.3	1.6	3.1	4.2	4.6
1984	1.5	2.8	4.5	2.3	7.3
1985	1.6	2.3	6.3	4.2	4.2
1986	2.4	2.3	2.8	3.1	3.5
1987	2.6	1.4	4.1	5.3	3.5
1988	4.7	3.7	7.1	5.7	4.2
1989	4.4	3.9	5.4	2.6	3.7
1990	2.9	5.2	5.6	0.7	1.9
1991	1.0	5.1	3.3	0.7	−0.1
1992	1.6	1.9	0.8	0.4	3.6
1993	−0.6	−1.0	0.2	2.5	2.7
1994	2.3	2.5	0.9	3.9	4.0
1995	2.1	1.7	2.7	2.5	2.7
1996	1.4	0.8	3.1	2.5	3.8
1997	2.3	1.8	1.1	4.0	4.5
1998	3.6	2.0	−1.1	3.1	4.4
1999	3.4	2.0	−0.3	3.2	4.7
2000	3.9	3.0	2.8	3.7	4.1
2001	2.0	1.7	0.4	2.5	1.0
2002	1.1	0.0	0.1	2.5	1.8
2003	0.8	−0.7	1.5	3.3	2.8
2004	2.8	1.2	2.2	2.4	3.8
2005	1.6	0.7	1.7	3.1	3.3
2006	2.4	3.7	1.4	2.5	2.7
2007	2.4	3.3	1.7	2.4	1.8
2008	0.2	1.1	−1.1	−0.5	−0.3
2009	−2.9	−5.6	−5.4	−4.2	−2.8
2010	2.0	4.1	4.2	1.7	2.5
2011	2.1	3.7	−0.1	1.5	1.6
2012	0.2	0.5	1.5	1.5	2.2
2013	0.6	0.5	2.0	2.1	1.7
2014	0.9	1.9	0.3	3.1	2.6
2015	1.1	1.7	1.1	2.3	2.9
2016	1.2	1.9	1.0	1.8	1.5

Source: OECD. Stat., *National Account Statistics*.

Table 1.2. National GDP per capita (1990, US $), selected economies

	France	Germany	U.K.	U.S.A.	Japan	China	India
1951	5,461	4,206	7,123	10,116	2,126	596	623
1961	7,718	7,952	8,857	11,402	4,426	548	758
1971	11,845	11,077	10,941	15,304	10,040	907	856
1981	14,840	14,149	12,747	18,856	13,754	1,231	977
1991	17,724	16,606	16,196	22,876	19,358	1,935	1,305
2001	20,931	18,985	20,702	28,782	20,998	3,528	1,957
2011	22,303	21,380	22,375	31,163	22,228	8,039	3,583
2016	22,567	22,122	23,887	33,259	23,808	9,885	4,602

Source: Maddison Project.

Table 1.3. Parliamentary general election results since 1945

	England and Wales — Number of votes cast as % of electorate	Scotland — Number of votes cast as % of electorate	Number of U.K. Members of Parliament elected						
			Conservative	Labour	Liberal/Liberal Democrat*	Social Democratic Party	Scottish National Party	Plaid Cymru	Others**
5 July 1945	75.5	75.1	212	393	12	–	–	–	23
23 Feb 1950	84.4	80.9	297	315	9	–	–	–	4
25 Oct 1951	82.8	81.2	320	295	6	–	–	–	4
26 May 1955	77.0	75.1	344	277	6	–	–	–	3
8 Oct 1959	79.1	78.1	364	258	6	–	–	–	2
15 Oct 1964	77.1	77.6	303	317	9	–	–	–	1
31 March 1966	76.1	76.0	253	363	12	–	–	–	2
18 June 1970	71.2	73.5	330	287	6	–	1	–	6
28 Feb 1974	78.1	77.9	296	301	14	–	7	2	15
10 Oct 1974	72.5	74.5	276	319	13	–	11	3	13
3 May 1979	75.2	76.0	339	268	11	–	2	2	13
9 June 1983	71.8	71.8	396	209	17	6	2	2	18
11 June 1987	74.8	74.3	375	229	17	5	3	3	18
9 April 1992	77.5	74.2	336	271	20		3	4	17
1 May 1997	71.5	71.3	165	418	46		6	4	20
7 June 2001	59.3	58.1	166	412	52		5	4	20

5 May 2005	61.4	60.8	198	355	62	6	3	22
6 May 2010	65.4	63.8	306	258	57	6	3	20
7 May 2015	66.0(E) 65.7(W)	71.0	331	232	8	56	3	20
8 June 2017	69.1(E) 68.6(W)	66.4	317	262	12	35	4	20

* Liberals before 1992

** Others includes the Speaker

Source: The number of M.P.s elected to the House of Commons was: 640 (1945); 625 (1950, 1951); 630 (1955, 1959, 1964, 1966, 1970, 1974, 1979); 650 (1983, 1987); 651 (1992); 659 (1997, 2001); 646 (2005); 650 (2010, 2015, 2017).

The Representation of the Peoples Act 1969 lowered the minimum voting age from twenty-one to eighteen years with effect from 16 February 1970.

Sources: 1945–2010: Annual Abstract of Statistics, various.

2015: The Electoral Commission, *U.K. General Election Results*, electoralcommission.org.uk

2017: House of Commons, *General Election, 2017: Results and Analysis*, second edition, Briefing Paper Number CBP7979, updated 3 April 2018.

Table 2.1. Components of public sector expenditure (economic categories) % of GDP

	Total managed expenditure	Current spending	Public sector net investment	Depreciation
1949–1950	38.4	33.2	1.7	3.6
1954–1955	38.5	30.9	4.1	3.5
1959–1960	36.7	29.8	3.4	3.4
1964–1965	38.0	28.8	5.5	3.7
1969–1970	41.4	31.3	6.2	3.9
1974–1975	47.0	36.6	5.8	4.6
1979–1980	43.7	36.5	2.9	4.6
1984–1985	46.3	40.0	2.1	4.2
1989–1990	37.5	33.0	1.5	2.9
1994–1995	40.5	36.8	1.6	2.1
1999–2000	36.0	33.3	0.7	2.0
2004–2005	40.1	36.4	1.8	1.9
2009–2010	45.7	40.4	3.3	2.0
2014–2015	40.6	37.0	1.7	2.0

Source: Institute for Fiscal Studies, LR Gov Spending Data. Accessed 18 May 2017.

Table 2.2. Gross capital formation as percentage of GDP

1950	12.0
1955	17.1
1960	19.0
1965	20.3
1970	20.2
1975	19.4
1980	17.6
1985	18.4
1990	20.1
1995	17.0
2000	17.5
2005	17.1
2010	15.6
2015	16.9

Note: Gross Capital Formation comprises Gross Fixed Capital Formation, changes in inventories and acquisitions less disposal of valuables.

(2010–2015) ONS website, *UK National Accounts: The Blue Book*, release date 29 July 2016

Sources: (1950–2005) National Statistics, *Economic Trends Annual Supplement*, 2006 edition, Palgrave Macmillan, Table 2.1A.

Table 2.3. Gross domestic fixed capital formation, by sector and by dwellings

	Analysed by sector as percentage of total GDFCF			Dwellings as percentage of total GDFCF		
	Private sector	General government	Public corporations	Private	Public	Total
1950	52.3	30.9	16.6	3.4	16.3	19.7
1955	54.4	25.9	19.6	10.1	12.8	22.9
1960	61.1	20.3	18.6	11.6	6.4	18.0
1965	58.0	22.5	19.5	12.5	8.4	20.1
1970	57.7	25.1	17.2	11.0	8.2	19.2
1975	57.6	23.7	18.6	13.0	9.3	22.3
1980	70.0	13.6	16.4	14.7	6.2	20.9
1985	78.9	11.3	9.8	15.9	4.2	20.1
1990	83.6	11.8	4.6	16.0	3.9	19.9
1994	82.6	12.6	4.8	18.2	2.7	20.9

Source: Economic Trends, Annual Supplement 1996, Table 1.8.

Table 2.4. Housing completions (Great Britain, thousands)

	Private enterprise	Housing associations	Local authorities, new towns and government departments	Total
1950	27.4	1.6	169.2	198.2
1955	113.5	4.6	199.4	317.5
1960	168.6	1.8	127.4	297.8
1965	213.8	4.0	164.5	382.3
1970	170.3	8.5	171.6	350.4
1975	150.8	14.7	147.6	313.1
1980	128.4	21.1	86.0	235.5
1985	156.5	13.1	27.2	196.8
1990	160.7	17.0	16.6	194.3
1994	146.0	34.3	1.9	182.2

Source: Economic Trends, 1996, p. 191.

Table 2.5. Gross domestic product and retail prices, 1971–1990

	GDP at factor cost (£M, 1990 prices)*	GDP at factor cost** (volume 1990 prices, 1990=100)	Index of retail prices*** (all items, 1985=100)
1971	312,855	65.3	21.4
1972	321,555	67.1	23.0
1973	345,816	72.2	25.1
1974	340,683	71.1	29.1
1975	338,138	70.6	36.1
1976	347,129	72.5	42.1
1977	356,101	74.4	48.8
1978	365,920	76.4	52.8
1979	375,974	78.5	59.9
1980	368,216	76.9	70.7
1981	364,055	76.0	79.1
1982	370,493	77.4	85.9
1983	384,351	80.3	89.8
1984	392,067	81.9	94.3
1985	407,844	85.2	100.0
1986	424,214	88.6	103.4
1987	443,817	92.7	107.7
1988	465,746	97.3	113.0
1989	476,228	99.4	121.8
1990	478,886	100.0	133.3

* *Source*: *Economic Trends, Annual Supplement* 1996, p. 12, Table 1.2.
** *Source*: *Economic Trends, Annual Supplement* 1996, p. 8, Table 8.
*** *Source*: *Economic Trends, Annual Supplement*, 1996, Table 2.1, p. 149.

Table 2.6. Public sector net borrowing, 1970/1–1988/9 % of GDP

1970/1	1971/2	1972/3	1973/4	1974/5	1975/6	1976/7	1977/8	1978/9	1979/80
–0.6	1.0	2.6	4.1	5.7	6.4	5.0	3.9	4.5	3.7

1980/1	1981/2	1982/3	1983/4	1984/5	1985/6	1986/7	1987/8	1988/9
4.3	2.0	2.6	3.3	3.3	2.1	1.9	0.9	–1.1

Office for National Statistics and Office for Budget Responsibility.

Source: House of Commons Library, 'Government borrowing, debt and debt interest: historical statistics and forecasts', Briefing paper, Number 05745, 2 May 2017.

Table 2.7. The PSBR and the growth of £M3

	PSBR £BN	% of GDP at market prices	Growth of £M3(%)*
1972–73	2.5	3.8	25.2
1973–74	4.4	6.1	24.0
1974–75	7.9	9.1	8.4
1975–76	10.6	9.8	6.9
1976–77	8.5	6.8	8.4
1977–78	5.5	3.8	14.5

*Growth of seasonally adjusted stock between the ends of successive first quarters

TNA ES140/01, 'Monetary targets and the PSBR' by P E Middleton, C.J. Mowl, J.C. Odling-Smee, and C.J. Riley, 27 April 1979, para. 10.

Source: Financial Statistics, Table 7.1 and 7.3, *Economic Trends*

Table 2.8. Components of public sector expenditure(main programmes) % of GDP

	Social security	Health	Education	Defence	Public order and safety	Transport
1949–1950	4.1	3.6	–	–	–	–
1954–1955	4.0	2.9	2.8	8.4	–	–
1959–1960	4.9	3.1	3.5	6.1	–	–
1964–1965	5.2	3.3	4.2	5.6	–	–
1969–1970	6.5	3.5	4.7	4.5	–	–
1974–1975	7.3	4.3	5.5	4.5	–	–
1979–1980	8.5	4.2	5.0	4.4	1.5	1.5
1984–1985	10.5	4.6	4.8	5.0	1.8	1.7
1989–1990	8.5	4.2	4.5	3.6	1.8	1.3
1994–1995	11.1	5.2	4.8	3.1	2.1	1.5
1999–2000	10.1	5.0	4.3	–	2.6	1.9
2004–2005	10.7	6.5	5.1	–	2.3	2.2
2009–2010	12.5	7.8	5.9	–	2.5	2.3
2014–2015	11.8	7.4	4.7	–	2.0	1.65

Source: Institute for Fiscal Studies, LR Gov Spending Data. Accessed 18 May 2017.

Table 3.1. Shares of value-added in manufacturing, 1951–1973 (percent)

	1951	1964	1973
Food, drink, tobacco	9.5%	11.0%	10.8%
Chemicals	7.2	8.8	7.6
Iron and steel	7.5	6.6	5.0
Electrical engineering	7.4	9.2	10.0
Mechanical engineering and shipbuilding	15.4	15.8	16.9
Vehicles	8.7	10.8	10.7
Other metal industries	7.6	7.9	8.7
Textiles	12.6	7.2	5.9
Clothing	4.9	3.8	3.5
Bricks, pottery, glass, cement	4.2	4.3	4.4
Timber, furniture	3.4	2.9	3.7
Paper, printing, publishing	7.8	7.8	8.5
Leather and other manufacturing	3.8	4.0	4.3
Total manufacturing	100.0	100.0	100.0

Source: Matthews, Feinstein, and Odling-Smee, *British Economic Growth, 1856–1973*, p. 239, Table 2.6.

Table 3.2. Value added by industry as share of GDP (%) Selected industries, *1970 and 2000*

Industry	1970	2010
Agriculture	2.85	1.08
Oil and gas	0.07	2.78
Coal and other mining	1.04	0.3
Chemicals and pharmaceuticals	2.06	1.9
Basic metals and metal goods	3.65	1.99
Mechanical engineering	7.79	1.51
Electrical engineering and electronics	2.52	2.68
Vehicles	3.89	1.91
Food, drink, and tobacco	3.07	2.51
Textiles, clothing, and leather	3.64	0.81
Paper, printing, and publishing	1.89	2.53
Other manufacturing	2.31	2.01
Construction	6.02	5.38
Wholesale, vehicle sales, and repairs	7.8	7.04
Retailing	4.03	5.53
Hotels and catering	2.12	3.45
Communications	2.37	3.2
Finance	5.78	4.99
Business services (excluding housing services)	5.76	17.00
Public administration and defence	6.26	5.01
Education	4.18	6.06
Health and social work	3.31	6.91
Others	17.59	13.42
Whole economy	100.0	100.0

Source: Nicholas Oulton and Sylaja Srinivasan, 'Productivity growth in UK industries, 1970–2000: structural change and the role of ICT', *Bank of England Working Paper*, no. 259, 2005.

Table 3.3. Number unemployed in Great Britain, selected industries at June in each year

	1977	1978	1979	1980	1981	1982
Total, all industries and services (1)	1,285,716	1,324,866	1,238,468	1,441,389	2,456,883	2,856,465
Total manufacturing industries	330,576	333,668	314,036	399,714	754,928	811,401
Agriculture, forestry, fishing	23,738	24,087	21,845	22,722	37,844	43,359
Mining and quarrying	16,595	22,125	23,321	24,835	31,648	37,604
Food, drink and tobacco	40,408	43,971	40,340	47,259	72,504	86,622
Coke and petroleum products	2,274	2,057	2,049	2,259	3,647	5,073
Chemicals and allied industries	16,408	16,457	15,490	19,003	33,602	38,388
Metal manufacture	23,622	27,542	25,433	35,741	72,929	72,741
Mechanical engineering	38,063	36,915	34,877	45,169	97,108	100,916
Electrical engineering	26,830	26,798	25,227	30,762	60,503	65,439
Shipbuilding and marine engineering	9,038	8,970	9,987	13,316	16,170	16,093
Vehicles	20,818	19,577	19,660	23,540	61,258	75,920
Metal goods, not elsewhere specified	33,426	33,364	31,728	38,893	86,064	88,683
Textiles	26,547	27,572	24,991	34,985	59,018	57,953
Paper, printing, and publishing	18,621	17,295	16,264	18,754	38,141	42,135
Construction	204,108	186,480	160,012	189,554	356,862	366,354
Gas, electricity, and water	9,213	8,617	7,687	7,589	10,199	13,451
Transport and communication	59,667	58,419	54,334	63,415	105,733	121,784
Distributive trades	131,740	132,680	122,787	146,723	238,046	285,690
Insurance, banking, finance, and business services	28,828	28,126	27,657	34,252	55,408	64,997
Professional and scientific services	48,313	54,082	53,713	61,074	90,268	110,610
Public administration and defence	68,686	76,181	72,323	77,023	105,475	130,731

Sources: CSO, *Annual Abstract of Statistics, 1981* edition, London: HMSO, 1981, no. 117, Table 6.7.
1981 data from CSO, *Annual Abstract of Statistics, 1982*, London: HMSO, 1982, no. 118, Table 6.7.
1982 data from CSO, *Annual Abstract of Statistics, 1983*, London: HMSO, 1983, no. 119, Table 6.7.

Table 3.4. Stock changes £ million, current prices

	Mining and quarrying	Manufacturing	Electricity, gas, and water supply	Wholesale distribution	Retail distribution	Other industries	All industries
1965	-2	322	35	47	23	36	461
1970	-48	314	-18	111	-6	29	382
1971	29	-162	38	154	8	47	114
1972	-10	-169	1	114	18	71	25
1973	-10	718	-22	312	264	267	1,529
1974	-39	1,086	-6	323	-152	-167	1,045
1975	193	-1,063	98	-247	-91	-244	-1,354
1976	-24	396	73	182	271	3	901
1977	26	807	-88	544	51	484	1,824
1978	112	255	10	560	456	411	1,804
1979	-87	359	-73	1,061	481	421	2,162
1980	302	-2,546	135	-392	-429	358	-2,572
1981	-26	-2,115	130	-260	190	-687	-2,768
1982	108	-1,855	441	-68	1	185	-1,188
1983	-101	-3	432	169	-35	1,003	1,465
1984	-41	836	-445	12	465	470	1,296
1985	-314	-493	373	-85	267	1,073	821
1986	-115	-555	-28	237	720	423	682
1987	-34	-335	-93	587	755	348	1,228
1988	24	873	37	971	791	1,637	4,333
1989	214	164	113	775	346	1,065	2,677
1990	-103	-1,913	-129	-552	181	716	-1,800
1991	172	-3,769	177	-648	-401	-458	-4,927
1992	74	-1,544	-136	96	230	-657	-1,937
1993	-71	-1,544	-253	843	411	912	329
1994	-210	1,231	-533	511	953	1,352	3,303

Source: Central Statistical Office, *Economic Trends: Annual Supplement, 1996 edition*, London: HMSO, 1995, Table 4.7.

Table 3.5. Working days lost each year through all stoppages in progress, 1970–1982 United Kingdom (thousands)

	1970	1971	1972	1973	1974	1975	1976	1977	1978	1979	1980	1981	1982
All industries and services	10,980	13,551	23,909	7,197	14,750	6,012	3,284	10,142	9,405	29,474	11,964	4,266	5,313
Mining & quarrying	1,092	65	10,800	91	5,628	56	78	97	201	128	166	237	374
Metals, engineering shipbuilding, and vehicles	4,540	6,035	6,636	4,800	5,837	3,932	1,977	6,133	5,985	20,390	10,155	1,731	1,457
Textiles	192	58	236	140	236	257	39	208	131	72	36	20	45
Clothing and footwear	192	13	38	53	19	93	26	56	47	38	8	19	21
Construction	242	255	4,188	176	252	247	570	297	416	834	281	86	44
Transport and communications	1,313	6,539	876	331	705	422	132	301	360	1,420	253	359	1,675
All other industries and services	3,409	586	1,135	1,608	2,072	1,006	461	3,050	2,264	6,594	1,065	1,814	1,697

Notes: This data shows the total working days lost within each year as a result of stoppages in progress in that year whether beginning in that or an earlier year. Figures are based on the Standard Industrial Classification 1968.

Sources: 1970–1979, Central Statistical Office, *Annual Abstract of Statistics, 1981 edition*, London: HMSO, 1981, Table 6.15; 1980–1982, Central Statistical Office, *Annual Abstract of Statistics, 1984 edition*, London: HMSO, 1984, Table 6.14.

Table 3.6. Average weeks of work lost per year though holidays, sickness, and industrial disputes, 1913–1973

	Holidays	Sickness	Industrial Disputes	Total
1913	1.4	1.7	0.07	3.2
1924	2.1	2.2	0.08	4.4
1937	2.3	2.1	0.03	4.5
1951	3.1	2.5	0.01	5.6
1955	3.5	2.3	0.02	5.8
1960	3.6	2.3	0.02	5.9
1964	3.5	2.4	0.01	5.9
1968	3.8	2.3	0.03	6.2
1973	4.7	2.3	0.06	7.0

Source: R.C.O. Matthews, C.H. Feinstein, and J.C. Odling-Smee, *British Economic Growth, 1856–1973*, p. 76, Table 3.16.

Table 3.7. Working days lost each year through all stoppages in progress, 1983–1994 United Kingdom (thousands)

	1983	1984	1985	1986	1987	1988	1989	1990	1991	1992	1993	1994
All industries and services	3,753	27,135	6,399	1,923	3,545	3,702	4,128	1,903	761	528	649	278
Coal extraction	484	22,483	4,142	143	217	222	50	59	29	8	27	–
Other energy and water	888	36	57	6	9	16	20	39	4	26	–	–
Metals, minerals, and chemicals	229	185	167	192	60	70	42	42	27	14	6	8
Engineering and vehicles	1,242	1,965	481	744	422	1,409	617	922	160	63	91	36
Other manufacturing industries	302	510	261	135	115	151	91	106	35	16	13	15
Construction	68	334	50	33	22	17	128	14	14	10	1	5
Transport and communication	295	666	197	190	1,705	1,491	624	177	60	13	160	87
Public admin, sanitary services, and education	115	764	957	449	939	254	2,237	175	362	328	339	92
Medical and health services	6	22	33	11	6	36	151	345	1	1	2	1
All other industries and services	124	170	54	20	53	30	167	20	69	50	9	35

Notes: Stoppages have been classified using Standard Industrial Classification 1980.

Sources: 1983–1987, Central Statistical Office, *Annual Abstract of Statistics, 1989 Edition*, London: HMSO, 1989, Table 6.11; 1988–1991, Central Statistical Office, *Annual Abstract of Statistics, 1993*, London: HMSO, 1993, Table 6.11; 1992–1994, Central Statistical Office, *Annual Abstract of Statistics, 1997*, London: HMSO, 1997, Table 6.10.

Table 3.8. Unemployment rate (16+), UK regions and countries, 2007–2016

	2007	2008	2009	2010	2011	2012	2013	2014	2015	2016
North East	6.1	7.4	9.5	9.7	10.4	10.6	9.9	8.5	7.7	6.6
North West	5.6	6.3	8.5	8.0	8.4	8.5	7.9	7.1	5.3	5.2
Yorks and Humber	5.4	6.2	8.5	8.7	9.4	9.3	9.0	7.4	6.0	5.2
East Midlands	5.0	5.8	7.3	7.4	8.1	7.9	7.4	5.6	4.7	4.3
West Midlands	5.9	6.9	9.4	8.8	9.3	8.7	8.5	6.8	5.8	5.5
East	4.3	4.9	6.3	6.6	6.7	6.6	6.1	5.2	4.0	3.8
London	6.9	7.0	9.2	8.9	9.5	9.2	8.7	7.0	6.1	5.7
South East	4.2	4.4	5.9	6.0	5.9	6.0	5.7	4.8	4.2	4.0
South West	3.9	4.1	6.2	5.9	6.0	5.8	5.8	5.1	3.9	4.1
Wales	5.5	6.3	8.2	8.3	8.3	8.3	7.9	6.8	5.9	4.6
Scotland	4.7	4.9	6.9	7.7	8.2	8.0	7.7	6.2	5.8	4.8
Northern Ireland	4.1	3.9	6.6	7.0	7.2	7.3	7.3	6.4	6.0	6.1
UK	5.2	5.7	7.6	7.6	8.0	7.9	7.5	6.2	5.3	4.9

Source: Office for National Statistics, Regional labour market statistics.

Table 3.9. Median weekly earnings, UK regions and countries, 2006–2016 (even numbered years) Percentage variation from UK median weekly earnings

	2006	2008	2010	2012	2014	2016
North East	88.2	88.1	88.9	90.0	91.9	91.2
North West	94.6	94.2	94.4	93.4	93.6	93.1
Yorks and Humber	93.0	92.8	92.9	92.0	92.3	92.0
East Midlands	95.4	94.0	94.3	94.0	93.3	93.1
West Midlands	93.75	94.0	94.1	92.8	92.9	94.2
East	105.0	104.2	105.0	105.1	104.0	105.6
London	121.1	121.5	121.6	121.2	119.1	117.3
South East	109.6	109.6	110.0	109.9	109.4	108.0
South West	94.8	94.4	94.0	94.3	95.6	95.2
Wales	91.1	88.8	91.4	90.0	92.5	92.4
Scotland	96.4	96.7	97.6	98.4	100.0	99.6
Northern Ireland	96.4	87.2	87.9	90.5	88.6	91.8
UK	100.0	100.0	100.0	100.0	100.0	100.0

Note: Calculated from earnings data in Office for National Statistics, *Annual Survey of Hours and Earnings*.

Table 3.10. Geographical distribution of the population (thousands)

	1951	%	1971	%	1991	%	2001	%	2010	%
Population of Great Britain	48,854	100	54,388	100	55,831	100	57,424	100	60,463	100
England, standard regions:	41,159	84.2	46,412	85.3	47,875	85.7	49,450	86.1	52,234	86.4
North	3,009	6.2	3,152	5.8	3,073	5.5	3,028	5.3	3,101	5.1
Yorkshire & Humberside	4,567	9.3	4,902	9.0	4,936	8.8	4,977	8.7	5,301	8.8
East Midlands	3,118	6.4	3,652	6.7	4,011	7.2	4,190	7.3	4,481	7.4
East Anglia	1,381	2.8	1,688	3.1	2,068	3.7	2,181	3.8	2,372	3.9
South East	14,877	30.5	17,125	31.5	17,511	31.4	18,566	32.3	19,809	32.8
South West	3,479	7.1	4,112	7.6	4,688	8.4	4,943	8.6	5,274	8.7
West Midlands	4,423	9.1	5,146	9.5	5,230	9.4	5,281	9.2	5,455	9.0
North West	6,305	12.9	6,634	12.2	6,357	11.4	6,285	10.9	6,441	10.7
Wales	2,599	5.3	2,740	5.0	2,873	5.1	2,910	5.1	3,006	5.0
Scotland	5,096	10.4	5,236	9.6	5,083	9.1	5,064	8.8	5,222	8.6

Note: Population as enumerated in Census.

Source: Annual Abstract of Statistics, 2011, edition, No. 147, Office for National Statistics, 2012, Table 15.5, pp. 259–60.

Table 3.11. Distribution of the population between cities, principal metropolitan, and non-metropolitan areas (thousands)

	1951	%	1971	%	1991	%	2001	%	2010	%
Population of Great Britain	48,854	100	54,388	100	55,831	100	57,424	100	60,463	100
Greater London	8,197	16.8	7,529	13.9	6,829	12.2	7,322	12.8	7,825	12.9
Inner London	3,679	7.5	3,060	5.6	2,599	4.7	2,859	5.0	3,083	5.1
Outer London	4,518	9.2	4,470	8.2	4,230	7.6	4,463	7.8	4,742	7.8
Metropolitan areas of England & Wales	11,365	23.3	11,862	21.8	11,085	19.9	10,888	19.0	14,135	23.4
Tyne and Wear	1,201	2.5	1,218	2.2	1,124	2.0	1,087	1.9	1,120	1.9
West Yorkshire	1,985	4.1	2,090	3.8	2,062	3.7	2,083	3.6	2,250	3.7
South Yorkshire	1,253	2.6	1,331	2.4	1,289	2.3	1,266	2.2	1,328	2.2
West Midlands	2,547	5.2	2,811	5.2	2,619	4.7	2,568	4.5	2,629	4.3
Greater Manchester	2,716	5.6	2,750	5.1	2,554	4.6	2,516	4.4		
Merseyside	1,663	3.4	1,662	3.1	1,438	2.6	1,368	2.4	1,353	2.2
Principal metropolitan cities and non-metropolitan districts of England & Wales										
Newcastle	292	0.6	312	0.6	275	0.5	266	0.5	292	0.5
Leeds	505	1.0	749	1.4	707	1.3	716	1.2	799	1.3
Sheffield	513	1.1	579	1.1	520	0.9	513	0.9	556	0.9
Birmingham	1,113	2.3	1,107	2.0	1,005	1.8	985	1.7	1,037	1.7
Manchester	703	1.4	554	1.0	433	0.8	423	0.7	499	0.8
Liverpool	789	1.6	610	1.1	476	0.9	442	0.8	445	0.7
Leicester	285	0.6	285	0.5	281	0.5	283	0.5	307	0.5
Nottingham	308	0.6	302	0.6	279	0.5	269	0.5	307	0.5
Bristol	443	0.9	433	0.8	392	0.7	390	0.7	441	0.7
Plymouth	225	0.5	249	0.5	251	0.4	241	0.4	259	0.4
Cardiff	244	0.5	291	0.5	297	0.5	310	0.5	341	0.6
City of Edinburgh local government district	467	1.0	478	0.9	436	0.8	449	0.8	486	0.8
City of Glasgow local government district	1,090	2.2	983	1.8	629	1.1	579	1.0	593	1.0

Note: Population as enumerated in Census.

Source: Annual Abstract of Statistics, 2011, edition, No. 147, Office for National Statistics, 2012, Table 15.5, pp. 259–60.

Table 5.1. NHS Expenditure in market prices, per capita and share of GDP (selected years)

| Year | GDP at market prices £ billion | GDP per capita | NHS Expenditure | | | Total NHS as % of GDP | Total NHS cost per head |
			Public* £m	Patients** £m	Total £m		
1950/51	13.54	269	474	8	482	3.56	10
1960/61	26.29	501	839	45	883	3.36	17
1970/71	53.07	953	1,983	64	2,064	3.86	37
1980/81	238.96	4,242	11,396	281	11,677	4.89	207
1990/91	576.8	10,068	27,980	1,198	29,178	5.06	509
2000/01	989.55	16,788	57,210	1,069	58,279	5.89	989
2010/11e	1,473.0	23,633	130,872	1,526	132,398	8.99	2,124

e=OHE estimates

* Excluding patient charges

** Figures relate to NHS charges paid by patients for prescription medicines etc.

Source: Office of Health Economics, health statistics website, Table 2.2.

Table 5.2. Total managed expenditure: Education as a percentage of GDP

1955–6	1960–1	1965–1	1970–1	1975–6	1980–1
2.9	3.6	4.5	5.0	6.1	5.5
1985–6	1990–1	1995–6	2000–1	2005–6	2010–11
4.8	4.8	4.9	5.4	5.4	6.1

Source: The Institute for Fiscal Studies, 'Spending By Function', www.ifs.org.
uk/fiscalFacts/fiscalAggregates

Table 5.3. Life expectancy at birth and at age sixty-five, by gender, UK (selected years)

Life expectancy at birth (years): Males

1981	1991	2001	2008
70.81	73.16	75.62	77.71

Life expectancy at age sixty-five (years): Males

1981	1991	2001	2008
12.96	14.14	15.92	17.60

Life expectancy at birth (years): Females

1981	1991	2001	2008
76.8	78.7	80.36	81.88

Life expectancy at age sixty-five (years): Females

1981	1991	2001	2008
16.91	17.9	19.01	20.24

Source: Office of Health Economics, health statistics website, Table 1.8.

Table 5.4. UK resident population by age group, selected years (millions)

Year	<5	<15	15–29	30–44	45–64	65–74	=>75	=>85	All ages
1950	4.3	11.3	10.6	11.2	11.8	3.7	1.8	0.2	50.3
1955	3.9	11.7	9.9	10.9	12.7	3.8	2.0	0.3	50.9
1960	4.1	12.2	10.2	10.5	13.3	3.9	2.2	0.3	52.4
1965	4.7	12.7	11.2	10.4	13.4	4.2	2.4	0.4	54.4
1970	4.6	13.4	11.6	9.9	13.5	4.7	2.6	0.4	55.6
1975	4.0	13.1	12.2	9.9	13.1	5.1	2.8	0.5	56.2
1980	3.5	11.8	12.7	10.9	12.5	5.2	3.2	0.6	56.3
1985	3.6	10.9	13.3	11.3	12.4	5.0	3.6	0.7	56.6
1990	3.8	10.9	13.1	12.0	12.3	5.0	4.0	0.8	57.2
1995	3.8	11.3	11.9	12.4	13.2	5.1	4.1	1.0	58.0
2000	3.6	11.2	11.2	13.3	13.9	4.9	4.4	1.1	58.9
2005	3.4	10.8	11.6	13.4	14.7	5.0	4.6	1.2	60.2

Source: Office of Health Economics, health statistics website, Table 1.1.

Table 5.5. Number of full-time equivalent staff employed in NHS hospitals and community services by category. UK, selected years

Year	Medical and dental	Nursing and midwifery	Professional and technical	Admin and clerical	Domestic ancillary	Total*
1951	15,210	188,580	14,110	29,021	163,666	410,479
1960	20,651	242,164	24,002	38,450	202,968	528,235
1970	28,511	343,664	41,696	56,877	229,313	700,061
1980	41,760	467,500	74,558	126,124	258,368	968,310
1990	55,838	507,100	103,097	164,370	156,995	987,400
2000	76,593	436,539	136,355	206,483	123,541	979,511
2009	117,589	507,434	184,136	302,269	154,947	1,266,374

*As not all categories of employment were included, the totals underestimate the size of the entire NHS workforce.

Source: Office of Health Economics, health statistics website, Table 3.1.

Table 5.6. Number of general medical practitioners in general practice, and per 100,000 population, by country, UK, selected years

| Year | Headcount of medical practitioners* | | | | |
	England	Wales	Scotland	Northern Ireland	UK
1985	25,793	1,699	3,539	933	31,964
1990	27,184	1,800	3,689	969	33,642
1995	28,869	1,845	3,872	1,033	35,619
2000	30,252	1,903	4.067	1,092	37,314
2005	35,302	1,952	4,355	1,124	42,733
2009	39,798	2,101	4,776	1,221	47,896

| | Per 100,000 population | | | | |
	England	Wales	Scotland	Northern Ireland	UK
1985	55	61	69	60	57
1990	57	63	73	61	59
1995	60	64	76	63	61
2000	61	65	80	65	63
2005	70	66	85	65	71
2009	77	70	92	68	78

*Comprising all medical practitioners in general practice, including GP registrars (trainees) but excluding GP retainers.

Source: Office of Health Economics, health statistics website, Table 4.2.

Table 5.7. Number of pupils and teachers: pupil/teacher ratios by school types. Numbers in thousands, full-time or full-time equivalent

	1975	1985	1990	1995**	2000
All schools or departments* Pupils	10,501.8	9,544.3	9,010.0	9,479.1	9,828.3
Teachers	518.7	546.0	532.5	542.1	545.6
Public sector mainstream schools or departments Nursery: pupils	44.5	57.3	59.4	62.2	75.3
Teachers	2	2.6	2.7	2.9	3.1
Pupils per teacher	22.2	21.8	21.8	21.7	24.2
Primary: pupils	5,987.5	4,513.6	4,747.7	5,061.6	5,167.9
Teachers	247.8	205.0	219.0	231.2	228.0
Pupils per teacher	24.2	22.0	21.7	21.9	22.7
Secondary: Pupils	4,332.0	4,243.6	3,419.6	3,650.9	3,859.0
Teachers	254.1	267.7	236.6	229.8	232.9
Pupils per teacher	17.0	15.9	14.8	15.9	16.6
Special schools: Pupils	137.7	133.1	114.6	113.7	107.4
Teachers	14.7	19.7	19.6	18.8	17.0
Pupils per teacher	9.3	6.8	5.8	6.0	6.3

*From 1980 onwards includes non-maintained schools or departments, including independent schools in Scotland.
**Provisional

Sources:
1975, *Annual Abstract of Statistics, 1984.*
1985, 1990, 1995, *Annual Abstract of Statistics, 1997,* Table 5.3.
2000, *Annual Abstract of Statistics, 2003.*

Table 5.8. Estimated total NHS expenditure on pharmaceuticals at manufacturers' prices, UK, selected years* £ million (cash)

Year	Pharmaceutical services	Dispensing doctors	Hospital	Total NHS medicines	NHS medicines cost:		
					Per capita £(2009 prices)	% of NHS cost	% of GDP
1970	124	6	29	159	33.22	8.0	0.31
1975	208	12	59	279	31.08	5.4	0.26
1980	613	35	178	826	45.87	7.3	0.35
1985	1,217	74	336	1,627	64.62	9.5	0.45
1990	1,918	121	495	2,533	74.25	8.9	0.44
1995	3,406	286	891	4,583	111.80	11.0	0.63
2000	5,264	337	1,390	6,991	149.42	12.3	0.72
2005	7,377	471	2,409	10,258	188.78	10.6	0.82
2009	7,969	472	3,835	12,277	198.68	9.7	0.88

*All figures exclude dressings and appliance.
GDP at market prices.

Source: Office of Health Economics, health statistics website, Table 4.8.

Table 5.9. NHS sources of finance, selected years

Year	Taxation		NHS contribution from National Insurance		Patients' payments*		Total NHS income**	NHS income as a % of UK government receipts***
	£m	%NHS	£m	%NHS	£m	%NHS	£m	
1950	477	100.0	–	–	–	–	477	8.7
1960	671	77.5	118	13.6	43	5.0	866	9.8
1970	1,635	82.6	209	10.6	60	3.0	1,979	8.7
1980	9,951	88.4	1,042	9.3	264	2.3	11,257	11.5
1990	22,992	80.9	4,288	15.1	1,146	4.0	28,426	12.9
2000	49,103	86.0	6,905	12.1	1,058	1.9	57,067	15.2
2009	102,541	80.9	22,679	17.9	1,479	1.2	126,699	24.6

* Patient charges for 2009 are not comparable with earlier years, as reliable data for PDS in England and Wales are not available before 2004/05 and therefore data prior to 2004/05 are based on GDS patient charges alone.

** Prior to 1974 total NHS income includes services provided by former Local Health Authorities (LHAs). From 1974 onwards, services provide by LHAs were transferred to the NHS.

*** UK government receipts include taxes and National Insurance contributions.

Table 5.10. Number of private medical insurance subscribers, people covered and payments, UK, selected years

Year	Subscribers (thousands)	People insured (thousands)	Subscriptions paid £m	Benefits paid £m	People insured as % of UK population	Subscriptions paid as % of total private healthcare spending
1955	274	585	2	2	1.2	–
1965	680	1,445	9	8	2.7	–
1975	1,087	2,315	55	46	4.1	41
1984	2,010	4,367	413	341	7.8	66
Laing and Buisson survey estimates for all insurers						
1985	2,380	5,057	520	456	8.9	70
1995	3,430	6,673	1,718	1,388	11.5	68
2005	3,511	6,359	3,106	2,401	10.6	35
2008	3,648	6,366	3,639	2,799	10.4	36

Source: Office of Health Economics, health statistics website, Table 2.13.

Table 6.1. Dwellings by tenure in Great Britain (%)

	Owner-occupied	Private rented	Housing associations	Total Public	(Thousands)
1980	56	11	2	31	20,937
1988	64	9	3	24	22,516
1995	67	10	4	19	23,832

Sources: Department of Environment, *Housing and Construction Statistics*, (various issues); Whitehead, 'The provision of finance', p. 658.

Table 6.2. Simple average house prices, average advances, and recorded incomes of borrowers for all dwellings in the UK (£), First quarter, 1992–2016

	Average dwelling price	Average advance	Average recorded income of borrowers
1992	62,000	44,000	21,000
1993	60,000	43,000	21,000
1994	62,000	45,000	22,000
1995	62,000	46,000	22,000
1996	66,000	49,000	23,000
1997	73,000	53,000	25,000
1998	78,000	56,000	26,000
1999	84,000	60,000	28,000
2000	97,000	68,000	30,000
2001	107,000	74,000	32,000
2002	113,000	78,000	34,000
2003	142,000	92,000	38,000
2004	169,000	104,000	40,000
2005	185,000	112,000	40,000
2006	193,000	132,000	49,000
2007	217,000	147,000	54,000
2008	227,000	150,000	54,000
2009	217,000	132,000	53,000
2010	253,000	151,000	58,000
2011	244,000	152,000	57,000
2012	239,000	153,000	55,000
2013	243,000	157,000	58,000
2014	260,000	171,000	59,000
2015	270,000	179,000	61,000
2016	293,000	195,000	65,000

Source: ONS, *House Price Index (HPI)*, Table 15, accessed 31 August 2016.

Table 6.3. Housing, all dwellings, UK, Annual price change (first quarter) Q1 2002=100

1970	1971	1972	1973	1974	1975	1976	1977	1978	1979	1980	1981
3.9	4.2	5.1	7.7	8.8	9.1	9.9	10.8	11.7	14.8	19.1	20.7
1982	1983	1984	1985	1986	1987	1988	1989	1990	1991	1992	1993
20.7	23.1	25.3	27.5	30.7	35.5	43.0	56.0	57.6	56.4	55.9	52.9
1994	1995	1996	1997	1998	1999	2000	2001	2002	2003	2004	2005
54.0	54.8	55.9	60.0	65.5	72.1	83.6	92.1	100.0	123.4	134.6	149.5
2006	2007	2008	2009	2010	2011	2012	2013	2014	2015	2016	
154.8	172.1	183.3	160.5	172.8	172.9	173.7	177.5	191.6	207.8	225.0	

Source: ONS, *House Price Index*, Table 10, accessed 31 August 2016.

Table 6.4. Housing subsidy, 1975–1976 to 2003–2004 (£ billion, 2003–2004 prices)

	1975–1976	1980–1981	1985–1986	1992–1993	1999–2000	2000–2001	2001–2002	2002–2003	2003–2004
Capital	10.7	6.3	5.2	5.8	3.0	3.9	4.2	5.0	5.2
LA Revenue	3.3	4.3	1.8	0.6	−1.0	−1.2	0.4	0.3	0.2
TOTAL SUPPLY	14.0	10.6	7.0	6.4	2.0	2.7	4.6	5.3	5.4
Rent rebate	0.6	0.7	4.4	5.0	4.7	4.5	4.4	4.4	4.1
Rent allowance	0.1	0.1	1.7	4.0	5.5	5.6	5.8	6.4	6.3
Mortgage interest relief	2.4	4.6	7.8	6.1	1.9	0	0	0	0
Income support for mortgage interest	n/a	n/a	n/a	1.5	0.6	0.5	0.3	0.3	0.3
TOTAL DEMAND	3.1	5.4	13.9	16.6	12.7	10.6	10.5	11.1	10.7
TOTAL	17.1	15.9	20.9	23.0	14.7	13.3	15.1	16.4	16.1

Source: Stephens, Whitehead, and Munro, Lessons from the Past; Hills, Ends and Means, p. 56, Table 6.1.

Table 6.5. Household formation, 2001, 2011 (thousands, and percentage change)

	2001 Census total (thousands)	2011 Census total (thousands)	Percentage change 2001–2011
Households, all types:	21,660	23,366	7.9
One-person households	6,503	7,067	8.7
One-family only households	13,716	14,449	5.3
Other households	1,442	1,850	28.3
Total usually resident population	52,042	56,076	7.8
Persons in communal establishments	858	1,005	17.1
All persons in households	51,108	55,071	7.8
Adults in households	39,442	42,993	9.0
Dependent children in households	11,665	12,078	3.5

Source: 2001 and 2011 Census, Office for National Statistics.

Table 6.6. Population density in England and Wales (people per square kilometre in government office regions)

	1981	1991	2001	2010
North East	307	302	296	304
North West	492	485	480	492
Yorkshire and the Humber	319	320	323	344
East Midlands	247	257	268	287
West Midlands	399	402	406	420
East	254	268	283	305
London	4,329	4,344	4,658	4,978
South East	380	400	421	447
South West	184	197	207	221
Wales	136	139	140	145

Source: Office for National Statistics, Population density in England and Wales, population estimates mid-1981 to 2010.

Table 7.1. Progress of smoke control in England, 1964–1970

	Central plus local government grant (£m)	Number of premises covered in Black Areas (thousands)	Percentage of total premises in Black Areas converted (%)
1 April 1964	5.4*	–	–
1 April 1965	2.4	2,277**	27.8
1 April 1966	2.7	335	4.0
1 April 1967	3.8	463	7.8
1 April 1968	4.8	418	5.4
1 April 1969	4.5	353	4.5
1 April 1970	4.5	331	4.2
TOTAL	28.1	4,177	53.7

*From start of Clean Air Act to 1 April 1964.

**From start of Clean Air Act to 1 April 1965.

Source: TNA AB15/7734, Programmes Analysis Unit, P.A.U. M. 20, 'An economic and technical appraisal of air pollution in the United Kingdom', 1972, Didcot, Berks: HMSO,Table II.5.

Table 7.2. Consumption of fuels in Great Britain, 1952–1967 (million tonnes)

	1952	1954	1956	1958	1960	1962	1964	1966*	1967*
Coal – Domestic use	37.3	38.7	37.9	36.6	34.6	32.9	28.0	25.5	23.0
– Electricity works	35.5	39.6	45.6	46.1	51.1	60.4	67.4	67.9	66.6
– Railways	14.1	13.6	12.8	11.3	9.5	6.7	4.2	1.7	0.8
– Industry	63.3	64.6	60.4	52.1	47.2	42.0	38.5	36.0	30.9
– Coke ovens	25.1	26.6	29.3	27.8	28.5	23.5	25.5	24.3	23.1
– Gas works	27.7	27.3	27.8	24.8	22.3	22.1	20.2	16.7	14.4
Coke – Domestic use**	3.0	3.8	4.2	4.1	4.8	5.4	6.0	6.4	6.3
– Blast furnaces	11.3	11.9	13.1	11.4	13.0	10.6	11.8	10.6	9.9
– Industry	18.1	18.1	17.4	16.2	15.3	15.0	12.9	11.7	11.5
Oil – Motor spirit	5.3	5.8	6.2	6.5	7.4	8.3	9.8	11.5	12.3
– Kerosene	1.4	1.3	1.4	1.5	1.5	1.6	1.6	1.8	1.9
Gas diesel oil – derv oil	1.2	1.4	1.8	2.0	2.5	3.0	3.6	4.0	4.3
– other users	1.6	1.9	2.4	3.0	3.5	4.5	5.9	7.5	8.0
Fuel oil – electricity works	0.1	0.2	0.3	2.5	5.3	5.5	5.3	6.8	7.3
– other users	3.4	4.2	6.1	8.0	11.7	15.4	18.8	22.8	24.5
Refinery fuel	1.2	1.9	2.2	2.5	3.3	3.7	4.0	4.6	4.7

*Estimates.

**Including other manufactured solid smokeless fuels.

Source: TNA AB15/7734, Programmes Analysis Unit, P.A.U. M. 20, 'An economic and technical appraisal of air pollution in the United Kingdom', 1972, Didcot, Berks: HMSO,Table II.1.

Table 7.3. Emissions of Sulphur Dioxide in Great Britain, 1952–1965 (million tonnes)

	1952	1954	1956	1958	1960	1962	1964	1966	1967
Coal	0.9	0.93	0.91	0.94	0.89	0.84	0.72	0.65	0.59
– domestic use									
– electricity works	0.95	1.06	1.22	1.32	1.46	1.73	1.93	2.02	1.88
– railways	0.38	0.37	0.35	0.33	0.27	0.19	0.12	0.05	0.02
– industry	1.72	1.75	1.63	1.50	1.36	1.21	1.11	1.04	0.97
– coke ovens	0.1	0.11	0.12	0.11	0.11	0.09	0.10	0.09	0.08
– gas works	0.2	0.2	0.2	0.18	0.16	0.16	0.15	0.12	0.1
Coke	0.07	0.08	0.09	0.09	0.1	0.11	0.12	0.14	0.14
– domestic use									
– industry	0.42	0.43	0.41	0.38	0.35	0.35	0.3	0.15	0.14
Oil	0.01	0.01	0.01	0.02	0.02	0.02	0.02	0.02	0.02
– motor spirit & kerosene									
– gas diesel oil	0.04	0.05	0.06	0.08	0.07	0.09	0.11	0.13	0.15
– fuel oil, electricity works	0.01	0.01	0.01	0.14	0.41	0.43	0.4	0.49	0.47
– fuel oil, other users	0.22	0.29	0.40	0.51	0.74	0.94	1.13	1.35	1.46
TOTAL	5.02	5.29	5.41	5.60	5.94	6.16	6.21	6.25	6.02

Source: TNA AB15/7734, Programmes Analysis Unit, P.A.U. M. 20, 'An economic and technical appraisal of air pollution in the United Kingdom', 1972, Didcot, Berks: HMSO, Table II.3.

Table 7.4. Emissions of smoke in Great Britain, 1952–1965 (million tonnes)

	1952	1954	1956	1958	1960	1962	1964	1966	1967
Coal	1.26	1.31	1.27	1.23	1.16	1.10	0.92	0.83	0.75
– domestic use									
– railways	0.28	0.27	0.26	0.23	0.19	0.13	0.08	0.03	0.02
– industry	0.76	0.78	0.73	0.50	0.35	0.21	0.19	0.11	0.10
TOTAL	2.30	2.36	2.26	1.96	1.70	1.44	1.19	0.97	0.87

Source: TNA AB15/7734, Programmes Analysis Unit, P.A.U. M. 20, 'An economic and technical appraisal of air pollution in the United Kingdom', 1972, Didcot, Berks: HMSO, Table II.4.

Table 8.1. Value of UK exports of goods, by commodity 1956, 1960, 1970, 1980, 1990, 2000, 2010 (total exports in £m and as percentage of total exports)

	1956	1960	1970	1980	1990	2000	2010
Total (£m)	3,143.3	3,647.6	8,169.9	47,357.1	103,691	187,936	266,079
Food and live animals	3.3%	3.0%	3.0%	4.3%	4.2%	3.1%	3.8%
Beverages and tobacco	2.5	2.6	3.2	2.5	2.7	2.2	2.3
Crude materials, inedible	3.4	3.3	3.0	2.9	2.1	1.3	2.6
Mineral fuels, lubricants etc.	5.1	3.6	2.6	13.6	7.6	9.1	13.6
Animal and vegetable oils and fats	0.3	0.2	0.1	0.1	0.1	0.1	0.2
Chemicals	7.8	8.8	9.5	11.2	12.7	13.3	19.1
Manufactured goods	28.5	27.1	24.7	18.5	15.3	12.1	11.0
Machinery and transport equipment	39.1	42.0	41.8	34.4	40.4	46.7	34.9
Miscellaneous manufactured articles	5.9	6.0	8.7	9.5	12.8	11.3	11.8
Other unclassified commodities and transactions	4.1	3.5	3.4	3.0	2.2	0.9	0.8

Note: Percentages may not sum to 100% due to rounding.

Sources:
1956: Central Statistical Office, *Annual Abstract of Statistics*, 1965, No. 102, London: HMSO, Table 267.
1960: Central Statistical Office, *Annual Abstract of Statistics*, 1969, No. 106, London: HMSO, Table 269.
1970: Central Statistical Office, *Annual Abstract of Statistics*, 1980, London: HMSO, Table 12.5.
1980: Central Statistical Office, *Annual Abstract of Statistics*, 1988, London: HMSO, Table 12.3.
1990: Office for National Statistics, *Annual Abstract of Statistics*, 1997, London: The Stationery Office, Table 12.3.
2000 and 2010: Office for National Statistics, *Annual Abstract of Statistics*, 2011, London: Dandy Booksellers, Table 6.3.

Table 8.2. Value of UK imports of goods by commodity 1956, 1960, 1970, 1980, 1990, 2000, 2010 (total imports in £m and as percentage of total imports)

	1956	1960	1970	1980	1990	2000	2010
Total	£3,861.5m	£4,655.3	£9,163.3	£49,772.9	£126,087	£220,912	£363,278
Food and live animals	34.3%	29.9%	20.3%	11.0%	8.3%	6.0%	7.4%
Beverages and tobacco	2.9	3.1	2.1	1.4	1.5	2.0	1.8
Crude materials, inedible	27.1	22.0	13.8	7.6	4.5	2.6	2.5
Mineral fuels, lubricants etc.	10.7	10.3	10.4	13.8	6.2	4.5	12.5
Animal and vegetable oils and fats	1.3	1.2	1.1	0.5	0.3	0.2	0.3
Chemicals	2.6	3.8	5.8	6.3	8.6	9.3	12.3
Manufactured goods	14.5	17.8	21.4	20.8	17.4	13.2	12.0
Machinery and transport equipment	4.2	7.4	17.5	25.2	37.4	46.4	35.4
Miscellaneous manufactured articles	1.8	3.6	6.3	10.3	14.4	14.8	15.0
Other unclassified commodities and transactions	0.3	0.7	1.4	3.0	1.4	0.8	0.8

Note: Percentages may not sum to 100% due to rounding.

Sources:
1956: Central Statistical Office, *Annual Abstract of Statistics*, 1965, London: HMSO, Table 266.
1960: Central Statistical Office, *Annual Abstract of Statistics*, 1969, No. 106, London: HMSO, Table 268.
1970: Central Statistical Office, *Annual Abstract of Statistics*, 1980, London: HMSO, Table 12.6.
1980: Central Statistical Office, *Annual Abstract of Statistics*, 1988, London: HMSO, Table 12.4.
1990: Office for National Statistics, *Annual Abstract of Statistics*, 1997, London: The Stationery Office, Table 12.4.
2000 and 2010: Office for National Statistics, *Annual Abstract of Statistics*, 2011, London: Dandy Booksellers, Table 6.4.

Table 8.3. UK trade in goods and services

	As % of total imports		As % of total exports	
	Goods	Services	Goods	Services
1951	81	19	76	24
1961	75	25	74	26
1971	74	26	71	29
1981	79	21	75	25
1991	80	20	73	27
2001	76	24	68	32
2011	77	23	61	39

Note: Based on ONS database series: KTMW, KTMX, and KTMY.

Source: House of Commons Library, Grahame Allen, *UK Trade Statistics*, SNEP 6211, 8 October 2012, Table 3.

Table 8.4. UK exports by destination, 1955, 1960, 1965, 1970 (% of total exports, by value)

	1955	1960	1965	1970
Sterling area	48.0%	39.2%	33.6%	27.2
Non-sterling area:	52.0	60.1	66.4	72.4
North America	11.3	15.7	14.9	15.3
Western Europe	27.4	29.5	37.4	41.1
Rest of the World	13.3	15.7	8.4	9.3
Commonwealth	42.0	36.3	–	–
Latin America	3.9	4.7	3.3	3.5
European Economic Community*	13.0	15.4	20.0	21.7
European Free Trade Association	11.9	11.9	14.0	15.8
Middle East	5.5	5.7	–	–
Soviet Union and Eastern Europe	1.3	2.1	2.4	3.2
South Africa	5.8	4.4	5.4	4.1
India	4.5	4.1	2.4	0.9
Australia	9.9	7.1	5.8	4.3
New Zealand	4.8	3.3	2.6	1.6
Canada	4.9	5.9	4.2	3.6
Irish Republic	3.8	3.1	3.8	4.7
United States of America	6.4	9.7	10.6	11.7

*The EEC comprises the Six: West Germany; Netherlands; Belgium; Luxembourg; France; and Italy.

Note: Percentages may not sum to 100% because of rounding. Lacunae in data reflect changes in categorization in the *Annual Abstract of Statistics*.

Sources:
1955: Central Statistical Office, *Annual Abstract of Statistics*, 1963, No. 100, London: HMSO, Table 264.
1960: Central Statistical Office, *Annual Abstract of Statistics*, 1969, No. 106, London: HMSO, Table 271.
1965 and 1970: Central Statistical Office, *Annual Abstract of Statistics*, 1972, London: HMSO, Table 286.

Table 8.5. UK imports by source, 1955, 1960, 1965, 1970 (% of total imports, by value)

	1955	1960	1965	1970
Sterling area	39.2	33.8	30.1	25.3
Non-sterling area:	60.8	66.2	69.9	74.4
North America	19.8	20.4	19.7	20.5
Western Europe	25.9	28.7	33.0	37.7
Rest of the World	15.1	17.1	17.3	16.2
Commonwealth	43.0	32.3	–	–
Latin America	6.2	6.7	4.9	3.6
European Economic Community*	12.6	14.4	17.3	20.2
European Free Trade Association	11.6	12.1	13.6	15.5
Middle East	6.4	7.4	–	–
Soviet Union and Eastern Europe	2.7	3.0	3.8	3.9
South Africa	2.1	3.0	3.1	2.9
India	4.1	3.2	2.2	1.2
Australia	6.8	4.2	3.8	2.9
New Zealand	4.7	3.9	3.6	2.2
Canada	8.9	8.1	8.0	7.5
Irish Republic	2.5	2.7	3.0	3.8
United States of America	10.9	12.3	11.7	13.0

*The EEC comprises the Six: West Germany; Netherlands; Belgium; Luxembourg; France; and Italy.

Note: Percentages may not sum to 100% because of rounding. Lacunae in data reflect changes in categorization in the *Annual Abstract of Statistics*.

Sources:
1955: Central Statistical Office, *Annual Abstract of Statistics*, 1963, No. 100, London: HMSO, Table 263.
1960: Central Statistical Office, *Annual Abstract of Statistics*, 1969, No. 106, London: HMSO, Table 270.
1965 and 1970: Central Statistical Office, *Annual Abstract of Statistics*, 1972, London: HMSO, Table 285.

Table 8.6. UK exports of goods by destination, 1970, 1980, 1990, 2000, 2010 (% of total trade by value)

	1970	1980	1990	2000	2010
European Economic Community*	29.4	43.4	56.9	59.8	53.5
Rest of Western Europe**	16.8	14.3	4.4%	3.8	4.5
Canada	3.6	1.6	1.8	1.9	1.6
United States***	11.6	9.6	12.5	13.6	14.4
South Africa	4.1	2.1	1.1	0.8	1.1
Japan	1.8	1.3	2.5	2.0	1.6
Australia	4.2	1.7	1.6	1.4	1.7
New Zealand	1.6	0.5	0.4	0.2	0.2
Oil-exporting countries	5.8	10.1	5.4	3.2	4.7
Other developing countries	16.8	12.3			
Hong Kong			1.2	1.4	1.7
Singapore			1.0	0.9	1.3
China			0.5	0.8	2.9
India			1.2	1.1	1.5
Centrally planned economies	3.8	2.8			
Eastern Europe			1.4		
Russia				0.4	1.4

*In *Annual Abstract of Statistics 1980*, EEC comprises: France; Belgium; Luxembourg; Netherlands; Federal Republic of Germany; Italy; Irish Republic; and Denmark.
**In 1990 the Rest of Western Europe category comprised Norway, Switzerland, Turkey, and Iceland. In 2000, the EEC is categorized as European Union, and additional members are Cyprus (0.2%), Malta (0.1), Slovakia (0.1), Slovenia (0.1), Bulgaria (0.05), Czech Republic (0.5), Estonia (0.05), Hungary (0.3), Latvia (0.04), Lithuania (0.07), Poland (0.7), and Romania (0.2).
***In 2000 and 2010, the United States data include Puerto Rica.

Sources:
1970: Central Statistical Office, *Annual Abstract of Statistics*, 1980, London: HMSO, Table 12.7.
1980: Central Statistical Office, *Annual Abstract of Statistics*, 1988, London: HMSO, Table 12.5.
1990: Office for National Statistics, *Annual Abstract of Statistics*, 1997, London: The Stationery Office, Table 12.5.
2000 and 2010: Office for National Statistics, *Annual Abstract of Statistics*, 2011, London: Dandy Booksellers, Table 6.5. Includes Greece (0.7%), Portugal (1.0%), Spain (3.6%), Sweden (2.6%), Finland (1.0%), and Austria (0.7%) which move (9.6% in total) out of the Rest of Western Europe category.

Table 8.7. UK imports of goods by source, 1970, 1980, 1990, 2000, 2010 (% of total trade by value)

	1970	1980	1990	2000	2010
European Economic Community*	27.1	41.3	57.7	53.3	50.8
Rest of Western Europe**	14.4	14.6	7.4	5.9	9.4
Canada	7.5	2.8	1.8	1.8	1.6
United States***	12.9	12.1	11.4	13.1	7.6
South Africa	2.9	1.5	0.9	1.2	1.2
Japan	1.5	3.4	5.4	4.6	2.2
Australia	2.8	1.0	0.8	0.7	0.6
New Zealand	2.2	0.8	0.4	0.2	0.2
Oil-exporting countries	9.1	8.5	2.4	1.9	3.1
Other developing countries	15.0	11.4			
Hong Kong			1.6	2.7	2.2
Singapore			0.8	1.1	1.1
China			0.5	2.2	8.4
India			0.6	0.7	1.6
Centrally planned economies	4.2	2.1			
Eastern Europe			1.4		
Russia				0.7	1.4

*In AAS 1980 EEC comprises: France; Belgium; Luxembourg; Netherlands; Federal Republic of Germany; Italy; Irish Republic; and Denmark.
**In 1990 the Rest of Western Europe category comprised Norway, Switzerland, Turkey and Iceland. In 2000, the EEC is categorized as European Union, and additional members are Cyprus, Malta, Slovakia, Slovenia, Bulgaria, Czech Republic, Estonia, Hungary, Latvia, Lithuania, Poland, and Romania.
***In 2000 and 2010, the United States data include Puerto Rica.

Sources:
1970: Central Statistical Office, *Annual Abstract of Statistics*, 1980, London: HMSO, Table 12.8.
1980: Central Statistical Office, *Annual Abstract of Statistics*, 1988, London: HMSO, Table 12.6.
1990: Office for National Statistics, *Annual Abstract of Statistics*, 1997, London: The Stationery Office, Table 12.6.
2000 and 2010: Office for National Statistics, *Annual Abstract of Statistics*, 2011, London: Dandy Booksellers, Table 6.6. Includes Greece, Portugal, Spain, Sweden, Finland, and Austria, which move out of the Rest of Western Europe category.

Table 8.8. Growth of GDP per man year in the UK compared with six other industrial countries, 1937–1973

	UK	USA	Sweden	France	Germany	Italy	Japan
1937–1951	1.0	2.3	2.6	1.7	1.0	1.4	−1.3
1951–1964	2.3	2.5	3.3	4.3	5.1	5.6	7.6
1964–1973	2.6	1.6	2.7	4.6	4.4	5.0	8.4

Source: Matthews, Feinstein, and Odling-Smee, *British Economic Growth, 1856–1973*, p. 31, Table 2.5.

Table 8.9. Overseas assets and liabilities, 1913–1973 (£ billion at current prices values at end of year)

	Assets	Liabilities	Net Assets	Ratio of net assets to GDP
1913	4.6	0.4	4.2	1.8
1924	6.8	1.6	5.2	1.3
1937	5.3	1.3	4.0	0.9
1951	6.9	7.6	−0.7	−0.05
1964	14.8	13.0	1.8	0.06
1973	67.8	60.4	7.4	0.12

Source: R.C.O. Matthews, Feinstein, and Odling-Smee, *British Economic Growth, 1856–1973*, p. 128, Table 5.2.

Table 8.10. Crude oil prices, 1950–2004

	Current prices $	2012 prices $
1950	1.71	16.30
1955	1.93	16.54
1960	1.90	14.71
1965	1.80	13.08
1970	1.80	10.64
1971	2.24	12.68
1972	2.48	13.61
1973	3.29	17.00
1974	11.58	53.94
1975	11.53	49.21
1976	12.80	51.63
1977	13.92	52.70
1978	14.02	49.37
1979	31.61	99.97
1980	36.83	102.62
1981	35.93	90.75
1982	32.97	78.44
1983	29.55	68.12
1984	28.78	63.60
1985	27.56	58.61
1986	14.43	30.23

1987	18.44	37.26
1988	14.92	28.96
1989	18.23	33.75
1990	23.73	41.68
1991	20.00	33.72
1992	19.32	31.62
1993	16.97	26.97
1994	15.82	24.50
1995	17.02	25.64
1996	20.67	30.24
1997	19.09	27.31
1998	12.72	17.91
1999	17.97	24.76
2000	28.50	37.99
2001	25.44	31.69
2002	25.02	31.94
2003	28.83	35.97
2004	38.27	46.51
2005	54.52	64.09
2006	65.14	74.19
2007	72.39	80.16
2008	97.26	103.71
2009	61.67	66.00
2010	79.50	83.70
2011	111.26	113.56
2012	111.67	111.67

Note: 1950, 1955, 1960, 1965, 1970–1983 Arabian Light posted at Ras Tanura. 1984–2012 Brent dated.

Source: BP Statistical Review of World Energy, June 2013.

Table 8.11. Sterling: US dollar exchange rate 1975–1986

1975	1976	1977	1978	1979	1980	1981	1982	1983	1984	1985	1986
2.22	1.80	1.75	1.92	2.12	2.33	2.03	1.75	1.52	1.34	1.3	1.47

Source: Central Statistical Office, *Economic Trends: Annual Supplement, 1996* edition, 1995, London: CSO, Table 5:1, p. 223.

Table 8.12. GDP at factor cost, UK, 1971–1990 (1990=100)

1971	1972	1973	1974	1975	1976	1977	1978	1979	1980
65.3	67.1	72.2	71.1	70.6	72.5	74.4	76.4	78.5	76.9
1981	1982	1983	1984	1985	1986	1987	1988	1989	1990
76.0	77.4	80.3	81.9	85.2	88.6	92.7	97.3	99.4	100.0

Source: Central Statistical Office, *Economic Trends: Annual Supplement*, 1996, No. 21, London: HMSO, Table 1.1.

Table 8.13. North Sea oil tax revenue as a
percentage of GDP, 1973–1992

1973–1974	0.0
1974–1975	0.0
1975–1976	0.0
1976–1977	0.1
1977–1978	0.2
1978–1979	0.3
1979–1980	1.1
1980–1981	1.5
1981–1982	2.5
1982–1983	2.7
1983–1984	2.8
1984–1985	3.6
1985–1986	3.1
1986–1987	1.2
1987–1988	1.0
1988–1989	0.7
1989–1990	0.4
1990–1991	0.4
1991–1992	0.2

Source: Institute for Fiscal Studies.

Table 8.14. UK trade in goods and services with its main trading partners in 2011

Partner	Exports ($bn)	Export share %	Imports ($bn)	Import share %
EU28	347.1	47.0	389.4	49.9
USA	109.4	14.8	88.5	11.4
China	26.2	3.5	58.4	7.5
India	19.0	2.6	24.8	3.2
Canada	18.4	2.5	13.3	1.7
Australia	16.7	2.3	7.7	1.0
Japan	16.4	2.2	17.1	2.2
Russia	15.1	2.0	14.1	1.8
Switzerland	13.7	1.9	8.7	1.1
Norway	10.5	1.4	46.1	5.9
Rest of world	146.2	19.8	111.8	14.3
Total	738.7	100.0	779.9	100.0

Source: Holmes, Rollo, and Winters, 'Negotiating the UK's post-Brexit trade arrangements', pp. R22–R30, Table 1.

Table 9.1. Changes in house prices, income and debt during booms, 1985–2006

Percentage change	Real house prices		Real personal disposable income		Real household debt		Nominal house prices		Real gross financial wealth	
	1985–1989	2002–2006	1985–1989	2002–2006	1985–1989	2002–2006	1985–1989	2002–2006	1985–1989	2002–2006
U.K.	71	49	23	10	74	50	112	65	61	17
USA	12	29	17	14	40	48	31	44	31	33
Germany	1	–2	18	5	18	–3	6	4	37	9
France	28	64	14	11	51	42	49	78	65	26
Spain	110	62	27	17	23	83	190	90	95	41
Japan	27	–17	22	4	59	0	33	–20	80	16

Source: BIS and OECD. Adapted from Armstrong and Davis, 'Comparing housing booms and mortgage supply in the major OECD countries', R3–R15, R4, Table 1.

Table 9.2. Key public finance data (% of GDP)

	Total receipts	Total spending	Public sector net borrowing	Public sector net debt
1945–1946	38.9	53.7	−14.8	240.2
1950–1951	41.2	37.7	3.4	194.8
1955–1956	36.5	36.3	0.2	138.7
1960–1961	34.1	36.6	−2.5	108.8
1965–1966	38.0	39.5	−1.5	87.3
1970–1971	41.4	40.8	0.6	64.7
1975–1976	42.3	48.9	−6.7	52.2
1980–1981	41.3	46.0	−4.6	43.4
1985–1986	41.5	43.9	−2.3	40.3
1990–1991	36.6	37.6	−1.0	23.6
1995–1996	35.7	40.1	−4.4	39.1
2000–2001	37.7	36.1	1.6	29.9
2005–2006	37.0	40.1	−3.1	35.4
2010–2011	36.7	45.3	−8.7	71.7
2014–2015	35.7	40.8	−5.0	83.7

Source: Office for Budget Responsibility, Key public finances since 1920: Outturns and forecasts as of March 2016 Economic and Fiscal Outlook.

Table 9.3. Public sector debt interest payments, 1949/50–2009/10 (£ billion, 2012–2013 prices) and as percentage of national income

	Public sector net debt interest payments £ billion	% GDP	PS Gross debt interest payments	% GDP	GDP £ billion	TME less social security less gross debt	% GDP
1949–1950	9.3	2.9	15.8	4.9	322.2	87.5	27.2
1954–1955	8.9	2.4	16.5	4.5	369.7	104.5	28.3
1959–1960	15.8	3.8	18.6	4.4	419.2	110.4	26.3
1964–1965	17.7	3.5	22.0	4.3	506.9	139.9	27.6
1969–1970	21.2	3.6	26.8	4.6	582.1	175.1	30.1
1974–1975	25.1	3.7	32.6	4.8	675.3	240.5	35.6
1979–1980	30.0	4.0	37.9	5.0	751.1	222.8	29.7
1984–1985	33.0	4.1	41.3	5.2	795.2	238.0	29.9
1989–1990	25.9	2.6	38.1	3.9	982.1	243.0	24.7
1994–1995	29.2	2.7	35.4	3.3	1070.4	267.9	25.0
1999–2000	28.2	2.2	34.1	2.7	1267.0	282.6	2.3
2004–2005	22.9	1.6	30.3	2.1	1474.1	401.4	27.2
2009–2010	29.9	2.0	33.5	2.2	1530.8	487.4	31.8

Source: Institute for Fiscal Studies.

Index